)USING CONSTRUCTION FINANCE DIRECTORY
anson and Anthony J. Mullen

)USING MARKETS: PROJECT PLANNING AND FEASIBILITY

echt

EAL ESTATE JOINT VENTURES

/IANAGING AND LEASING COMMERCIAL PROPERTIES
Shenkman

THE REAL ESTATE PR
REAL ESTATE DE
FROM WILEY LAW

CONSTRUCTION OWNER'S HANDBOOK OF PR
Robert F. Cushman and Peter J. King, I

DEVELOPING RETIREMENT FACILITIES (SEC
Paul A. Gordon

FOREIGN INVESTMENT IN UNITED STATES R
Jeremy D. Smith

INSTITUTIONAL AND PENSION FUND REAL E
Stephen P. Jarchow

MANAGING AND LEASING COMMERCIAL PR
Alan A. Alexander and Richard F. Mu

MANAGING AND LEASING COMMERCIAL PR
Alan A. Alexander and Richard F. Mu

MANAGING AND LEASING COMMERCIAL PR
Alan A. Alexander and Richard F. Mu

MANAGING AND LEASING RESIDENTIAL PR
Paul D. Lapides

MANAGING AND LEASING RESIDENTIAL PR
Paul D. Lapides and E. Robert Miller

MANAGING CORPORATE REAL ESTATE
Robert Kevin Brown, Alvin L. Arnold
Paul D. Lapides, Scott B. Blanchard a

PASSIVE ACTIVITY RULES: LAW AND TAX
Ronald D. Saake, Michael J. Novograd

REAL ESTATE DEVELOPMENT: STRATEGIES
Stuart M. Saft

REAL ESTATE INVESTMENT TRUSTS: TAX, S
Stephen P. Jarchow

REAL ESTATE LIMITED PARTNERSHIPS (TH
Theodore S. Lynn, Harry F. Goldberg

REAL ESTATE VALUATION: GUIDE TO INVE
Terry Vaughn Grissom and Julian Dia

REHABILITATING OLDER AND HISTORIC B
Stephen L. Kass, Judith M. LaBelle, a

RETIREME
David

RETIREME
ANALYSIS
Susan

STRUCTUR
Rober

TAX GUID
Marti

SUBSCRIPTION NOTICE

This Wiley product is updated on a periodic basis (e.g., annual supplements) to reflect important changes in the subject matter. If you purchased this product directly from John Wiley & Sons, we have already recorded your subscription for this update service.

If, however, you purchased this product from a bookstore and wish to receive any current update at no additional charge, and future updates, revised, or related volumes billed separately with a 30-day examination review, please send your name, company name (if applicable), address, and the title of the product to:

Supplement Department
John Wiley & Sons, Inc.
One Wiley Drive
Somerset, NJ 08875
1-800-225-5945

For customers outside the United States, please contact the Wiley office nearest you:

Professional and Reference Division
John Wiley & Sons Canada, Ltd.
22 Worcester Road
Rexdale, Ontario M9W 1L1
Canada
(416)675-3580
1-800-263-1590 in Canada

John Wiley & Sons, Ltd.
Baffins Lane
Chichester
West Sussex PO19 1UD
United Kingdom
(44)(243)779777

Professional, Reference and Trade Division
Jacaranda Wiley Ltd.
PO Box 174
Ryde, NSW 2113
Australia
(02)805-1100

Managing Corporate Real Estate

BOARD OF ADVISORS

Managing Corporate Real Estate

ROBERT KEVIN BROWN
ALVIN L. ARNOLD
JOSEPH S. RABIANSKI
NEIL G. CARN
PAUL D. LAPIDES
SCOTT B. BLANCHARD
EDMOND P. RONDEAU

JOHN WILEY & SONS, INC.
New York • Chichester • Brisbane • Toronto • Singapore

This text is printed on acid-free paper.

Library of Congress Cataloging in Publication Data:

Managing corporate real estate / Robert Kevin Brown . . . [et al.].
p. cm. — (Real estate practice library)
Includes index.
ISBN 0-471-55497-9 (cloth)
1. Real estate management—United States. 2. Office buildings—United States—Management. 3. Commercial buildings—United States—Management. 4. Industrial buildings—United States—Management. I. Brown, Robert Kevin. II. Series.
HD1394.M38 1993
658.2—dc20 92-47023

Printed in the United States of America

10 9 8 7 6 5 4 3 2 1

Foreword

Having spent over 20 years serving corporations both as an employee and an independent consultant, I have seen the importance of sound real estate practices. I have participated in some and benchmarked many on how they identify and employ those practices and services that are best for their respective organizations.

When I first entered the corporate real estate services field I was reminded that the business objective of any corporation is to provide its owners a competitive return on their invested capital. I discovered that many corporations represent portfolio investments in one or more businesses and that these corporations fund businesses, not projects. The essential issue of a corporate strategy thus was to manage the portfolio to provide a desired yield of both cash and growth and, in turn, deal with major allocations of critical resources—particularly capital.

After a few years of identifying, piloting, and employing new programs, I found that the surest way to identify strategies that could produce early results was to learn from those who have just such experience. One of those early resources who helped me consider alternatives and challenged me to think beyond the immediate problem and an equally immediate solution was Dr. Robert Kevin Brown, then the Director of Corporate Real Estate with Rockwell Corporation. He shared with me tested strategies and introduced me to his book, *Corporate Real Estate—Executive Strategies for Profit-Making.* From these early exchanges, I was able to craft many of the niche strategies I successfully employed while supporting corporate real estate initiatives for my clients. Many of the practices and techniques he shared with me have survived and remain appropriate for use today.

Corporations are recognizing the need for change and challenging the status quo at all levels. They are redefining strategic plans, processes, and activities to produce dramatic improvements in operating efficiencies. This condition has once again created a significant and immediate challenge to all those responsible for the services supporting the planning, acquisition, management, and redeployment of real property assets used by corporations. Well-managed corporations recognize the economics of real estate and the benefits of adopting sound real estate management strategies toward improving operating efficiencies.

Recent writings about the corporate real estate industry have typically been focused on either general instructions or personal inspiration and experience. Rarely has anyone been able to capture both, and yet, I can think of no one better qualified than these authors to do just that. Dr. Brown and his colleagues have created a truly unique book. *Managing Corporate Real Estate* explores the issues driving this industry today. I believe this book will be invaluable to anyone concerned with managing a company. For those experienced in the corporate real estate industry, each should find this book thought provoking and perhaps come away with ideas on how to improve their own business environment. Those with little or no direct knowledge or experience in dealing with the issues of corporate real estate should find this book to be of great importance and benefit.

I look forward to monitoring the impact this articulate and practical guide will have on the next generation of those leading the corporate real estate industry.

John J. Dues
Principal and Firmwide Director of
Corporate Real Estate Services
Arthur Andersen & Co.
Washington, D.C.

Preface

The real estate industry has changed philosophically, structurally, and dramatically. Regardless of your level of economic understanding and market smarts, everyone by now seems to know something bad has happened to the engine that drove the real estate industry through a solid decade and a half of unparalleled commercial growth.

We are left today with a projected ten-year excess of new and used vacant office space; tens of millions of square feet of idle vacant manufacturing square footage; and retail, distribution, hotel, and special-purpose facilities involved in company bankruptcies across the country. We are also custodians of a financial system still spinning downward from the collapse of the real estate credit industry via the savings and loan disaster and with the commercial banking and insurance industries still suspect. We have depressed residential and commercial real estate development sectors still scratching for new survival solutions.

The inescapable conclusion and the solution to this mess appear boldly before us. The already identified, long-term solutions, together with solutions yet to be discovered, must be tested and implemented. Real estate asset management professionals and associated professionals in related disciplines—legal, financial, accounting, human relations, and government at all levels—must lead the parade if we are going to be successful in rebuilding and recasting the real estate industry as a solid market-ready institution.

Happily, there is a bright side, not withstanding the challenges each of us must confront. The major industry trends are identifiable; usable solutions are readily available; and a large core of true corporate real estate professionals exist—as executives of American corporations and/or third-party service providers and counselors—to implement the solutions.

Managing Corporate Real Estate systematically and thoroughly examines the issues facing corporate and commercial real estate asset managers today. This book has been created specifically to help you meet and conquer the challenges that exist in the industry. Successful techniques and real-life applications appear in every chapter. Of utmost importance, though, is our commitment to discuss techniques and applications against a full discussion of *why* they work successfully and *how* they can work for you. We want to provide a full briefing on the background of every topic listed in the Contents.

The real estate industry does not need any more "quick fee" participants with little or no knowledge of how the national economic and monetary systems relate to the real estate market and, in a direct line, to the corporate real estate market. Also, corporations can no longer afford to pay only scant, passing attention to the effective management of their real estate assets, thereby missing a marvelous opportunity to increase their competitive edge in the marketplace. This is hard language, but it is the truth—and this book is based on the "tell it like it is" philosophy that you will need to perform successfully in the practical world of the corporate real estate marketplace.

In the beginning chapters of this book, we examine the formative period of the corporate real estate management industry and the present period of disarray and uncertainty. We spend most of our time in the remaining chapters on the bright future of the business—and the future is bright, indeed.

We find it particularly interesting that the book on which this volume is based in part, *Corporate Real Estate—Executive Strategies for Profit-Making* (Dow-Jones/Irwin, Homewood, IL), was published in 1979. This book was a landmark work, pointing as it did to trends, real estate asset management techniques, and asset/market relationships only now coming into widespread vogue. This material has been greatly enlarged and refined in the present volume—witness the expanded list of authors, their extensive and experienced professional backgrounds, and the broad scope of the contents. The truth of those earlier observations and predictions has been proven. The path we must take is now clear, undeniable, and forward looking.

Managing Corporate Real Estate is organized into groups of related topics. Chapters One through Four build a base of understanding about the real estate asset-management industry, both corporate and commercial. An understanding of technical materials treated subsequently in the book must be based on a familiarity with the economic, social, and political forces that shape, mold, and guide corporate real estate decisions.

The first group of chapters begins, then, with an organizational view of the real estate asset-management business, corporate and commercial, set against the macroanalysis of national economic factors and translated into the significant reasons the industry is undergoing such dramatic, permanent changes. We will show you how to adapt and take advantage of these changes in your own career.

Chapters Five through Twelve form the "transaction," or implementation, heart of our book. These chapters are loaded with practical techniques to help you get the job done with an eye always on the strategic business mission implications of your asset management, real estate discussions.

Chapter Five begins a detailed, idea-loaded examination of the most visible and performance-accountable activity in corporate real estate. The disposition of surplus owned and leased real estate is vitally important to the job tenure of the corporate real estate executive and the continued employment of any third-party marketing service providers. We take this challenge very seriously, particularly since it is so visible to corporate senior management and commercial ownership. We have presented the forms, the procedures, and the "nuts and bolts" of successful marketing, which, when coupled with the negotiating strategies described in Chapter Eleven, equip you to perform at your best.

Chapters Six, Seven, Eight, and Nine concern subjects we could label "important facility planning issues." These subjects—space planning, location strategies, facility development, and tenure/occupancy issues—have many individual characteristics, definitions, and applications that unite each to the other through the specific triggering function of the real estate action to the company bottom line.

Chapters Ten, Eleven, and Twelve discuss three very important "market active" subjects from the acquisition function (buying and leasing) and associated negotiating strategies to the implementation of cost-effective professional management programs.

The next group of chapters, encompassing Chapters Thirteen through Fifteen, builds on the "whys" and "hows" learned from previous chapters. We take this knowledge and turn our attention to an in-depth discussion of topics that give a strong hint of the emergence of profit opportunities never imagined or considered important to the corporate bottom line a generation ago.

One of the significant side effects of real estate industry reengineering, still continuing after six years or so, has been reflected in a return of property values to the marketplace. That is, the artificiality of "tax shelter" arithmetic and other value-defining gimmicks has been replaced by a sounder look at the demand-and-supply preference curves of buyers and sellers in a commodity market rather than a pure financial calculation.

This group of chapters introduces you to the new analytical foundations on which real values rest. Many of the procedures discussed depend on the widespread availability of computers (particularly personal computers) and sophisticated application software. Chapter

Fifteen summarizes this section by illustrating the importance that accuracy and speed can play in making sound corporate real estate business decisions. Possession of a comprehensive, quality database of real estate information and a responsive software system is an absolute must for any serious-mined asset manager, corporate or commercial. It will show you how to go about this important task effectively and profitably.

The last group of chapters—Sixteen through Eighteen—discusses important concepts that go beyond the traditional market-oriented subjects we have been discussing, into the larger issues of corporate citizenship, the world of environmental concerns and the bipartisan relationships that are created between the corporate real estate user and the community. Our corporate real estate world is changing and nowhere is this more evident than in the dramatic increase in corporate awareness of "quality of life" issues with its direct impact on competitiveness and, ultimately, earnings-per-share.

Managing Corporate Real Estate represents a collaborative effort to create a unique book, combining both a panoramic and a specific view of a major industry in transition. It also provides almost limitless ideas for you to use in capitalizing on all the bottom-line opportunities this type of industry restructuring provides for all of us.

If you discover errors in the book or have suggestions for topics you would like to have addressed or expanded in the supplements or the next edition, please contact the publisher: John Wiley & Sons, Inc., Real Estate Editor, 605 Third Avenue, New York, NY 10158.

ROBERT KEVIN BROWN
ALVIN L. ARNOLD
JOSEPH S. RABIANSKI
NEIL G. CARN
PAUL D. LAPIDES
SCOTT B. BLANCHARD
EDMOND P. RONDEAU

Atlanta, Georgia
New York, New York
March 1993

Acknowledgments

Corporate real estate industry professionals are only now able to visualize and experience the true scope, depth, and wide breadth of their business universe. We seem, finally, at a significant—almost magical—"meeting point" where all our past experiences and all the past and present professional players in the corporate real estate game have focused on where we have been and where we need to go.

The same point holds true, of course, for the authors of this watershed book. Much of what you will read and learn in this book, we have gathered over the years from a large array of professionals—known and unknown—who also sought a clearer path toward understanding. At the same time, our personal and professional lives have been influenced by family, friends, mentors, colleagues, and authors who have contributed so much to our trip through life in general and the world of corporate real estate in particular.

First, we have all profited a great deal from the writings of and conversations with many gifted pioneering professionals. Those we wish to thank all belong to one or more of the following organizations:

Industrial Development Research Council	(IDRC)
International Association of Corporate Real Estate Executives	(NACORE)
International Facility Management Association	(IFMA)
Urban Land Institute	(ULI)
American Real Estate Society	(ARES)
National Association of Industrial and Office Parks	(NAIOP)
Building and Owners Management Association	(BOMA)

National Association of Realtors, Its Local Boards, and National Affiliates (NAR)

- American Society of Real Estate Counselors (ASREC)
- Society of Office and Industrial Realtors (SOIR)
- Institute of Real Estate Management (IREM)

Second, this manuscript has benefited from the contributions of some very special people. Included in this select group are the members of our Board of Advisors, for their contributions to the industry as a whole, to the authors collectively, and to this book. Our thanks and recognition to:

- Ralph Rieves, Editor, Richard D. Irwin Company, Homewood, Illinois, for having the foresight, in 1979, to publish the original *Corporate Real Estate—Executive Strategies for Profit-Making*—the first book on the subject ever published anywhere.
- Paula S. Stephens, Editor/Associate Publisher, *National Real Estate Investor,* for helping to create a unique and worthwhile forum for the publication of corporate real estate ideas.
- Margaret A. Soens, Vice President, Asset Management, Minerva Real Estate Investments, Atlanta, Georgia, for valuable insights into the world of commercial real estate explored in Chapters Two and Three.
- Samuel P. Latone, a polished asset management professional in every respect, who touched the manuscript in many positive ways while a Graduate Research Assistant at Georgia State University; now an Asset Manager with Branch and Associates, Atlanta, Georgia.

Our thanks also to Peter Williams and Howard Lavitt, Williams, Lavitt & Company/BDO Seidman, New York, NY; Frank A. Robinson, Tandem Computers, Inc., Cupertino, CA; Kendl P. Philbrick, Lockheed Corp., Calabasas, CA; Jack L. Brophy, USG Properties—USG Corp., Chicago, IL; David Scribner, Jr., New York University, New York, NY; Richard A. Olson, Rockwell International Corporation, Chicago, IL; Betty L. Gabriel, Rockwell International Corporation, Pittsburgh, PA; John W. Frank, LiPera Frank, Inc., Summit, NJ; Thomas R. Long, Wilma Southeast, Atlanta, GA; Irving E. Cohen, Fuller Corporate Realty Partners, New York, NY; John F. Harris, J.F. Harris & Associates, Dunwoody, GA; Wayne L. Sterling, Director, Development Board, Columbia, SC; and Ann G. Summer, Nationsbank, Columbia, SC, for their insights, suggestions, and material for this book.

We thank them all while, at the same time, reserving unto ourselves the full responsibility for any errors in adaption or interpretations that may appear in the completed book.

The list of our collaborators, both cited and unsung, is extensive. It should be, given the broad scope of the field of corporate real estate. The dramatic expansion of important information about the subject has been explosive in the past six years. To all our friends and professional associates, many thanks for the valuable, shared insights, conversations, opinions, and experiences that helped with the creation of this book—whether you meant to or not, you did!

Third, the authors also wish to express their special gratitude to Daniel R. Sayre, Editor, and Assistant Editor, Janet Feeney, Professional Reference and Trade Group, John Wiley & Sons, New York, for encouragement, support, and editorial guidance throughout the project. We thank Debbie Keeran and Dianne Caudell for their editorial assistance and Sheila Bostic, Hal Prather, and Bill Anderson, staff members of the Department of Real Estate, Georgia State University, for their extraordinary assistance with the preparation of the manuscript. We are also grateful for the significant editorial and production help from Nancy Marcus Land and the staff at Publications Development Company.

Finally, and most importantly, we wish to express our united sense of love, deep appreciation, and respect to our parents, children, and spouses for their overall support, devotion, and encouragement. This book is dedicated lovingly to each of them.

About the Authors

ROBERT KEVIN BROWN is professor of real estate and chairman of the Department of Real Estate, College of Business Administration, Georgia State University. He served previously as corporate director of real estate, Rockwell International Corporation, and as vice president, Rockwell Graphics Systems Group and president, Narland Corporation and Standard Property Land Company, wholly owned Rockwell subsidiaries.

Dr Brown holds a B.S. degree from The Johns Hopkins University and M.A. and Ph.D. degrees from the University of Pittsburgh. A nationally-known lecturer and consultant on asset management strategies to many Fortune 500 companies, he is the co-developer of the first commercially available PC-based corporate real estate asset management system. He is the author of numerous articles and nine books on real estate, including *The Real Estate Primer, Essentials of Real Estate, Real Estate Economics* and *Corporate Real Estate—Executive Strategies for Profit Making.* Dr. Brown is the contributing editor of the Corporate Real Estate column in National Real Estate Investor magazine. He also serves as a member of the Asset Management Editorial Board of *National Real Estate Investor Magazine.*

Dr. Brown is a member of the American Society of Real Estate Counselors (CRE) and serves currently as a member of the Board of Governors. He holds memberships in the American Real Estate Society (ARES); American Institute of Certified Planners (AICP); Industrial Development Research Council (IDRC): and International Association of Corporate Real Estate Executives (NACORE) where he served on the Board of Directors. He is also a member of the International Facility Management Association (IFMA).

ALVIN L. ARNOLD is a managing consultant with BDO Seidman, an international accounting and consulting firm, where he specializes in originating, writing, and editing real estate, legal, and professional service publications. From 1969 to 1990, he was vice president for real estate publications at Warren, Gorham & Lamont.

Mr. Arnold originated and since 1968 has written the semimonthly newsletter, *The Mortgage and Real Estate Executives Report,* and originated and for many years was executive editor of *Real Estate Review.* He is the author of *Real Estate Transactions: Structure and Analysis, The Arnold Encyclopedia of Real Estate, Real Estate Investor's Deskbook, Modern Real Estate and Mortgage Forms, Modern Ownership and Investment Forms, Real Estate Syndication Manual,* and *Construction and Development Financing.*

A member of the New York bar, Mr. Arnold has taught real estate courses at the Real Estate Institute of New York University and the Graduate School of Business, Long Island University. He is a graduate of Cornell University and Harvard Law School.

JOSEPH S. RABIANSKI is a member of the faculty, Department of Real Estate, College of Business Administration, Georgia State University. He received a Ph.D. in economics from the University of Illinois-Champaign in 1970.

Dr. Rabianski teaches courses in real estate finance, investment, market analysis, and appraisal. In addition, he has taught courses in microeconomics and macroeconomics. His research interests are industrial and commercial location theory and market analysis techniques. He is an instructor for the American Institute.

Dr. Rabianski is the co-author of *Principles of Real Estate Decisions, Real Estate Market Analysis: Methods and Techniques,* and *Shopping Center Appraisal and Analysis.* In addition, he has published articles in *The Appraisal Journal, Appraisal Review Journal, Real Estate Review, Real Estate Appraiser and Analyst, Real Estate Issues, Real Estate Securities Journal, Real Estate Law Journal, Journal of the American Real Estate and Urban Economics Association, Growth and Change, AREUEA Journal, Journal of Human Resources, Journal of Regional Science, American Economist, National Real Estate Investor, Shopping Center World,* and *Industrial Development.*

Dr. Rabianski serves as a consultant and expert witness concerning office, retail and hotel/motel properties.

NEIL G. CARN is a member of the faculty, Department of Real Estate, College of Business Administration, Georgia State University. He holds a B.S. and M.S. from Florida State University and a M.B.A. and Ph.D. in Land Economics and Urban Affairs from Georgia State University.

Dr. Carn teaches graduate and undergraduate courses in appraisal, real estate finance, development regulations, market analysis, investment analysis, strategic planning and research design. Dr. Carn is a co-author of *Winning at Zoning* and *Real Estate Market Analysis: Applications and Techniques* and a chapter in *The Real Estate Handbook* and *Real Estate Market Analyses.* In addition, he has published articles in *Appraisal Journal, Appraisal Review Journal, Real Estate Review, Real Estate Issues, National Real Estate Investor* and several other industry publications. He has also co-authored and taught several professional education seminars for the Appraisal Institute and private businesses. Dr. Carn has served as a consultant and expert witness concerning office, retail, and hotel/motel properties as well as hospital site selection, zoning, and tax issues. Dr. Carn holds the American Institute of Certified Planners (AICP) designation of the American Planning Association.

PAUL D. LAPIDES is a managing consultant with BDO Seidman, an international accounting and consulting firm, where he specializes in the areas of asset management, marketing, and strategic planning. His real estate experience includes advising many of America's Fortune 500 companies, managing a diversified portfolio of $3 billion of real estate, raising more than $175 million in real estate equity, and providing litigation services.

Mr. Lapides is also an assistant professor of management at Life College in Marietta, Georgia, and an adjunct assistant professor of real estate at New York University. He is the author of numerous articles and books, including *Managing and Leasing Residential Properties,* co-author of *Real Estate Investment: Strategy, Analysis, Decisions,* and contributing author of *The Real Estate Workout Desk Book, Problem Real Estate,* and *Real Estate Syndication Manual.*

A CPA, Mr. Lapides is a member of the American Institute of Certified Public Accountants (AICPA), American Real Estate Society (ARES), Apartment Owners & Managers Association (AOMA), National Association of Corporate Directors (NACD), and the Urban Land Institute (ULI). He received a B.S. with honors in Economics from The Wharton School of the University of Pennsylvania and an M.B.A. from New York University.

SCOTT B. BLANCHARD is a partner with Libra Property Advisors, a consulting firm offering facility planning and asset management services, based in La Crosse, Wisconsin. Mr. Blanchard has held positions in financial and market analysis, brokerage and asset management. He has also served as planning director for the real estate subsidiary of The Jefferson Company where he coordinated the development and disposition of surplus property.

Mr. Blanchard devoted a substantial amount of time to academic matters, including work with the Industrial Development Research Foundation to develop research and educational materials in the field of corporate real estate. He has also authored technical materials on issues such as the effect of corporate accounting methods on real estate asset management strategies, and the consideration of evidence of development potential in the valuation of real estate for the purposes of just compensation. His current research is concerned with business ethics and the externalities of corporate facilities.

Mr. Blanchard is a graduate of the Carlson School of Management at the University of Minnesota, the Master of Science in Real Estate program at Georgia State University, and William Mitchell College of Law. He has taught real estate courses at Georgia State University and currently teaches a variety of topics in real estate seminars. Mr. Blanchard is a member of the Beta Gamma Sigma honor society, and has received a number of awards, including the Harwood Award from the Real Estate Educators Association.

EDMOND P. RONDEAU is a principal with Rondeau & Associates, a corporate facility and real estate consulting firm based in Atlanta, Georgia. He formerly served as the Manager of Corporate Real Estate for Contel Corporation where in addition to his real estate and facility management responsibilities, he managed the development and implementation of a computerized real estate management system to track Contel's 4000 plus owned and leased properties.

His corporate experience also includes serving as the vice president of property management for The National Bank of Georgia, as the vice president of design and construction and the director of real estate and construction for Arby's, Inc., and as a construction manager for The Coca-Cola Company.

Mr. Rondeau holds an M.B.A. in real estate from Georgia State University and a Bachelor of Architecture from Georgia Tech. He served as the 1988 president of the International Facility Management Association (IFMA), was the 1990 chairman of the IFMA Foundation, and was elected as a fellow of the IFMA in 1992.

In addition to addressing groups in the United States, he has made presentations in Australia, Canada, England, Japan, Germany, Mexico, and New Zealand. Mr. Rondeau is also the author of the *Principles of Corporate Real Estate* and is the co-author of the real estate management information system known as *LeaseKIT*.

Summary Contents

Detailed Contents

12 Property Management 409

One

An Overview of Corporate Real Estate Management

§ 1.1 INTRODUCTION

As the United States grapples with reindustrialization—undoubtedly one of the biggest corporate challenges in the final quarter of this century—the question arises how best to use industry's fixed assets: land, physical plant, and equipment. Fixed-asset management can be defined as activities and efforts instituted in an organized fashion to identify and sustain a balance between assets and liabilities. The results of the fixed-asset management effort are reflected on every firm's balance sheet. This information is readily available in the annual reports of publicly traded companies.

This book addresses effective corporate real estate asset management. A partial listing of topics to be explored includes:

- Exploring the myth of "We are not in the real estate business."
- Developing equity by corporate owners/users.
- Increasing shareholder wealth by treating corporate real estate as a profit center.
- Leasing versus buying within the framework of the tax reform.
- Negotiating leases.
- What corporations are looking for in a leased office space—from backroom to state-of-the-art.
- Intracorporate structures.
- Environmental issues and their impact on real estate assets marketability.

- The changing role of Wall Street financial houses.
- Creating and manipulating a fixed-asset database.
- Trends forcing companies to pay attention to their fixed assets: mergers, tax law, SEC reporting requirements.
- How corporations are selecting and purchasing architectural, engineering, and other related third-party services—or *outsourcing.*
- Opportunities for the corporate real estate executive in the 1990s.

This introduction defines what corporate real estate asset management is all about and sets the stage for the rest of the book. The terms refer to optimum use of all real estate assets utilized by a corporation in pursuit of its primary business mission.

(a) DEFINITIONS

Every trade, business, industry, profession has its own language and definitions. Corporate real estate asset management is no exception; the players and the rules of the game are readily identifiable to the experienced observer. Our main goal in writing this book is to equip you to be a successful player, or participant, in the business of corporate real estate. Let's begin with a definitional look at corporate real estate management and the key, pivotal professionals in the business.

The three primary participants with varying roles in the business are:

1. Corporate real estate manager.
2. Facilities manager.
3. Asset manager.

Exhibit 1.1 depicts the four major types of real estate organizations and the basic real estate utilization theories they employ. By reading the grid, you can see how the traditional corporate real estate organization funnels its strategies to various levels of players depending on the functions they perform. The real estate director or manager has the highest rank and the most authority/responsibility for the entire real estate department day-to-day operations. In this book, we will use the term *corporate real estate executive* for such individuals.

Additional definitions relating to types of companies engaged in real estate transactions and the manner in which they use their real estate assets include:

Terms to Describe Companies and Real Estate Holdings

- *Traditional Corporation.* A company whose primary corporate purpose involves producing goods and services, but that incidentally

EXHIBIT 1.1 Framework for Real Estate Asset Management

Functions \ Type of Entity	Traditional Real Estate Organization	Real Estate Equity Fund	Real Estate Lender/ Mortgage Fund	Traditional Corporation
Strategy	Developer/Owner/ Syndicator	Portfolio Manager	Portfolio Manager	Sr. Management/ CFO/Treasurer/ VP Finance [Corporate Real Estate Executive]
Management and Control	Asset Manager/ Supervisory Property Manager	Asset Manager/ Supervisory Property Manager	Asset Manager	Corporate Real Estate Director/ Manager/ Executive
Operations	Property Manager and On-Site Staff Services	Property Manager and On-Site Staff Services	Debtor	Facilities Manager/Property Administrator Staff

owns and/or leases and manages real estate to achieve corporate production and objectives.

- *Corporate Real Estate.* Real properties that house productive activities of a traditional corporation.
- *Investment Real Estate.* Real property owned by a traditional corporation normally held in a wholly owned subsidiary or structured as a joint venture to avoid possible "dealer" status by IRS definition for the principal purpose of obtaining income or other benefits of ownership and investment. Such properties may or may not be occupied by corporate business mission activities.
- *Traditional Real Estate Organization.* Those companies with a primary purpose of owning, developing, brokering, leasing, and/or managing real estate.

Terms to Describe Real Estate Management Activities

- *Real Estate Asset Management.* The general process of managing all aspects of real estate assets, including acquisition and disposition, devising management strategies, management of building/facility operations, financial management, and all aspects of accounting and reporting on real estate held. The corporate real estate executive will also be responsible for developing information, assisting or coordinating decisions regarding property or facility operations, devising procedures, and executing policies to achieve real estate objectives.
- *Property Management Administration.* The general description for overseeing and executing the day-to-day tasks required for real estate assets to function properly. These tasks may include administrative management (collections, record keeping, reporting), marketing management (marketing strategy, tenant selection, rent schedules), and physical management (maintenance, rehabilitation/renovation).
- *Facilities Planning.* The process of developing general and precise information about real estate assets for the purposes of assisting facility decision making, developing policies and procedures for facilities operations, construction planning, cost estimating and value engineering, and conducting other activities to provide efficient asset management.
- *Facilities Management.* The general function of coordinating the needs of people, equipment, and operational activities into the physical workplace. When performed by an in-house corporate organization, it usually refers to performing those activities dealing with the acquisition and disposition, physical upkeep, record keeping, and reporting tasks for corporate-owned real estate.

While the corporate real estate executive has historically *supported* the strategic planning effort in a very important advisory, proactive role, he or she is increasingly becoming an *essential* participant in the strategic planning process. The facilities manager, property administrator and related staff report to this executive.

(b) UNDERLYING ASSUMPTIONS

The real estate asset management system results in a significant contribution to the company's effective balancing of its asset/liability ratio through a professional, continuous management of the real estate inventory. The real estate system functions in concert with defined business mission strategies and rests on a series of underlying assumptions that are key elements in the process, including:

- The real estate decision is *always* subordinate to the operating decision.
- No real estate decision should occur in a vacuum—it should be linked to the operating decision.
- Every real estate action should be designed to promote the success of the business mission—to the ultimate bottom-line benefit of the shareholders through enhanced stock value and earnings per share.
- Real estate decisions are *long-term*—determined by economic and physical characteristics and the markets in which the property is traded. Management operating decisions tend to be *short-term,* in keeping with the risk/reward system of most corporations; hence, professional real estate asset management requires crisis or conflict management.

The corporate real estate executive who does not understand and subscribe to the simple truths of these assumptions has much to learn.

§ 1.2 THE STRUCTURE OF THE CORPORATE REAL ESTATE MARKET

Real estate asset management is ignored by many corporations, but this special function of the corporate machinery deserves an intensive investigation. Billions of dollars of fixed assets are involved and this function can bring about significant economic changes.

The "we-are-not-in-the-real-estate-business" attitude of many otherwise knowledgeable corporate executives is typical of a general ignorance about the corporate real estate business and about how intelligent management of corporate real property inventory can have a positive impact on businesses.

(a) THE PHILOSOPHY OF ACCOUNTABILITY

Examining real estate's rightful place in the corporation to provide a positive impact on corporate profit planning and maximization activities is crucial. Corporate real estate activities create profit—measured in dollars—that is earned from a related business decision.

A developer seeks to earn a return on invested real estate capital. But until recently, few industrial/manufacturing/financial corporations with real estate holdings have attempted to do the same. The developer seeks a return solely from real estate inventory, whereas most industrial corporations seek to profit only from their products or services rendered. That corporate attitude ignores limitless profit opportunities. This book indicates how profit opportunities arise in corporate real estate and, most importantly, how you can capitalize on those opportunities.

No mission of the corporate entity is better understood or more critically judged than profit performance. The real estate unit should also be judged on the basis of its contribution to profit performance, and it should be directly accountable to top management on the same basis as other operating units. When you finish this book, you will press for answers to questions such as these: What is our stake in the real estate business? How can we organize a real estate operation? What will the operation cost? How can I measure its effectiveness? What will its profit impact be? Why aren't we in the real estate business?

Successful business enterprises are able to make business forecasts and, on that basis, to program equity and debt investments, to employ assets effectively, and in general to pursue profit for the benefit of the stockholders. There is a direct relationship between corporate profit planning and the ways in which real estate profit planning can improve the utilization of corporate assets, increase return on assets (ROA), and favorably affect cash flow and earnings per share (EPS).

These positive outcomes must be measured; therefore, our mission in this chapter is fourfold:

1. We need to understand the basics of the general market environment within which the specific firm's real estate activity occurs.
2. We need to appreciate the logic of the term *strategy* and to understand how strategy relates to the measurement and control of business risk and uncertainty.
3. We need to relate real estate inventory planning to overall corporate planning and find ways to achieve this relationship externally in our daily activities and convey this relationship internally within top management.

4. We need to examine the interrelationships between the corporate real estate function and the corporate profit mission. This will enable the real estate department and other corporate departments to organize a program for implementing its distinctive opportunities to obtain profits.

(b) THE REAL ESTATE MARKET

Real estate market activity occurs within a complex framework. We define the real estate market as that place in which real estate transactions occur, and the participants in that market are those persons who buy, sell, lease, and mortgage real estate and otherwise participate in real estate transactions. Thus, the participants in the real estate market include a host of functionaries, such as bankers, attorneys, and insurers who aid in real property transactions. The task of the real estate specialist—the corporate real estate professional, in this case—is more difficult than that of specialists who trade in other commodities because the real estate specialist, like other specialists, must be knowledgeable about a particular commodity; but unlike other specialists, he or she must accumulate this knowledge without the benefits of a central market. There is no central place for all the information that the real estate specialist needs, nor is there any nationwide or regionwide pattern of market activity that is identifiable with the commodity as a nonsegmented, generic product. The market environment for the utilization of real estate is exceedingly complex and requires study and professional observation. It includes different types of properties, such as:

1. Industrial properties
   a. Manufacturing plants, including foundries and rock quarries
   b. Warehouses
   c. Railroad terminals and yards
   d. Docks and piers
   e. Distribution facilities
2. Commercial property
   a. Stores
   b. Office buildings
   c. Miscellaneous other properties
3. Natural resource property
   a. Coal
   b. Oil
   c. Other mineral and timber resources
4. Dwellings
   a. "Standard" new homes
   b. Older houses, that are not yet obsolete

    c. Obsolete houses
    d. Special types—"submarket houses"
    e. Multifamily residences
5. Vacant land, zoned for various potential uses
6. Farms

Many properties do not fall into any one classification, and such properties are sometimes incorrectly described as "transitional." This term should be applied only to properties that are moving from one category into another.

(c) THE IMPERFECTIONS OF THE REAL ESTATE MARKET

The general leveling achieved by supply and demand sets the real estate market pattern, but since the real estate market consists of only a few participants, the leveling process works imperfectly. Few buyers are able to comprehensively shop the real estate market, and no buyer or seller really can have the "full knowledge of the market" that is presumed in the definition of market value. This lack of full knowledge results in real estate sales at prices that depart from the average for the type of property in question. Most sales of real estate closely approximate the averages, but a continuous minority of transactions deviate considerably from the averages.

The imperfections of the real estate market result in part from the vast diversity of the available inventory. This diversity includes locational differences that sometimes produce hard-to-explain value discrepancies. Two communities may be only a few miles apart, and the same general contractors may work in both locations; yet, the difference in the real estate values of the two communities may exceed anything that can be explained in terms of land costs. In the central cities, although building codes, restrictive labor practices, and other factors raise costs considerably, buyers are still willing to pay for locational advantages.

The imperfections of the real estate market become very noticeable when fast sales are involved. An owner in a hurry can seldom get an average price. Conversely, an owner, especially one whose property is distinctive and who is willing to wait, can often get more than the average price simply by holding out for a buyer who likes the property for some special reason or has an immediate need to fulfill.

Atypical sales at the high and low limits of the market range are a continual plague to observers of the real estate market. For example, companies that contract to buy at a price above the average level of the market become annoyed when financial institutions fail to recognize the excessive prices that those companies, for their special reasons, have agreed to pay. Because of these circumstances, real estate professionals must be aware of the distinction between market value and investment value.

Investment value appropriately reflects the aforementioned imperfections, whereas market value does not.

The corporate real estate executive must be well acquainted with the real estate market to predict what the average buyer and the average seller will do in particular situations and to compensate automatically for market aberrations. The market is the collective result of individual acts that as a group determine the average.

The corporate real estate function occurs within this market framework, unstructured as it may appear to be, and it is within this framework that the application of philosophical and procedural concepts takes place. The quality of the real estate function is tested in a measurable way in a tough, real-world arena that provides abundant opportunities for smart corporations to save dollars and make real profits.

Our aim in this book is to show how you can wisely utilize and accurately evaluate the corporate investment in a real estate program.

First, we will explore how the corporate real estate function relates to the control of business risk and, concurrently, to corporate business planning strategy.

§ 1.3 THE PHILOSOPHY OF CORPORATE PLANNING

Corporate planning is a formal, systematic, managerial process, organized by responsibility, time, and information, to ensure that operational planning, project planning, and strategic planning are performed in such a way that top management can control the future of the enterprise. This generally accepted definition of the planning process within the corporate structure suggests that there is a substructure of three distinct types of planning:

1. Strategic planning.
2. Project planning.
3. Operational planning.

Exhibit 1.2 shows the critical differences among the three levels of planning. Note that each level relates to the primary thrust of the planning mission, namely, to reduce the element of uncertainty and to control the degree of risk inherent in a business decision.

(a) PLANNING

Strategic planning provides the overall corporate direction subject to the external environment, resources available, and resources obtainable. Strategic planning typically involves dealing with very complex and abstract issues, as the "ripple effects" of their implementation

EXHIBIT 1.2 Types of Corporate Planning

	Degree of Uncertainty	Degree of Complexity	Penalties for Errors
Strategic planning	Very high	Very high	Possible loss or bankruptcy
Project planning	Ranges from high to low, depending on project	High-medium	Loss of capital or opportunity
Operational planning	Low in the short-term, but increasing with time	Low	Short-term loss

through the organization are very difficult to anticipate. Strategic planning normally considers the broad approaches or the general plans that are needed to achieve certain long-term objectives.

Operational planning is involved primarily with the more detailed, specific aspects of implementing strategic plans or changing current operating activity.

Project planning is the generation and analysis of, the commitment to, and the working out of the detailed execution of an action outside the scope of present operations. Project planning is capable of separate analysis and control. Normally, the corporate real estate executive will be involved only in the project planning phase of the total corporate planning process. Unless the executive is a member of the planning team, he or she may not even be involved in that effort, but will be expected to implement an established plan. This type of organizational exclusion is an error both for the real estate department and for the corporation. The real estate professional can be an exceptionally valuable "ear in the marketplace," as well as a contributing ally when new or alternative facilities are required.

It is important to stress the word *strategic* does not always denote the planning activity under way is more important than any other level of planning activity. Frequently, operational planning decisions affecting the day-to-day existence of the business enterprise are more important than the development of long-run objectives. Thus, starting at the top of an imaginary pyramid and moving toward the bottom, is the strategic planning approach at the top, operational planning activities somewhere in the middle, and at the very bottom, where the greatest concentration of effort is required, project planning.

In strategic, long-range planning, the business decisions consist of a number of common sense factors and involve actions normally performed on a day-to-day basis. In Exhibit 1.3, the dotted lines indicate that feedback is essential to the strategic planning process. Input from the corporate real estate professional should be an important part of this feedback. How should the corporate real estate department relate to business planning? At what level of decision making is the department's input valuable?

Within your own internal strategic planning function, you may find a high degree of indifference and even resistance to the inclusion of real estate executives in efforts to chart the overall business mission of the corporation. This is an error. Although the input of the real estate department may normally be solicited only at the project planning stage, the corporation can profit from including its opinions and points of view at other levels of the planning process.

The traditional concept of strategic planning is becoming outmoded as the time horizon for investment planning shrinks and, thus, moves closer to the plateaus of operational and project planning—the real estate department's acknowledged sphere of experience. The corporate real estate staff is routinely involved in both new facility acquisition programs and surplus property marketing efforts. Decisions related to both new facility acquisitions and surplus property dispositions are based on the same kind of logic; that is, both types of decisions imply that an operating division (and this relates to the entire corporate mission) requires facilities in certain market areas and not in others. If properties are no longer required in certain locations, they will normally be replaced with facilities in other locations. Knowledge of long-term economic and social factors that make certain regions attractive is a significant weapon in the creation of a truly viable real estate/facilities inventory.

Let us sharpen our focus further by relating strategic planning to a facilities acquisition problem. Facilities searches and similar activities are often better accomplished in-house, because no one is as familiar with your internal operating posture as your own operating and staff personnel.

Exhibit 1.4 is an investment strategy chart showing a facilities search and the kind of feedback information that the facilities team develops as it goes back to the operating division with its recommendations.

If you turn back to Exhibit 1.3, you can readily perceive the similarities between the two exhibits and, more importantly, how "new facilities" information should be required input for both the environmental appraisal and the corporate appraisal that enter into strategic planning.

EXHIBIT 1.3 Strategic Planning: Key Steps

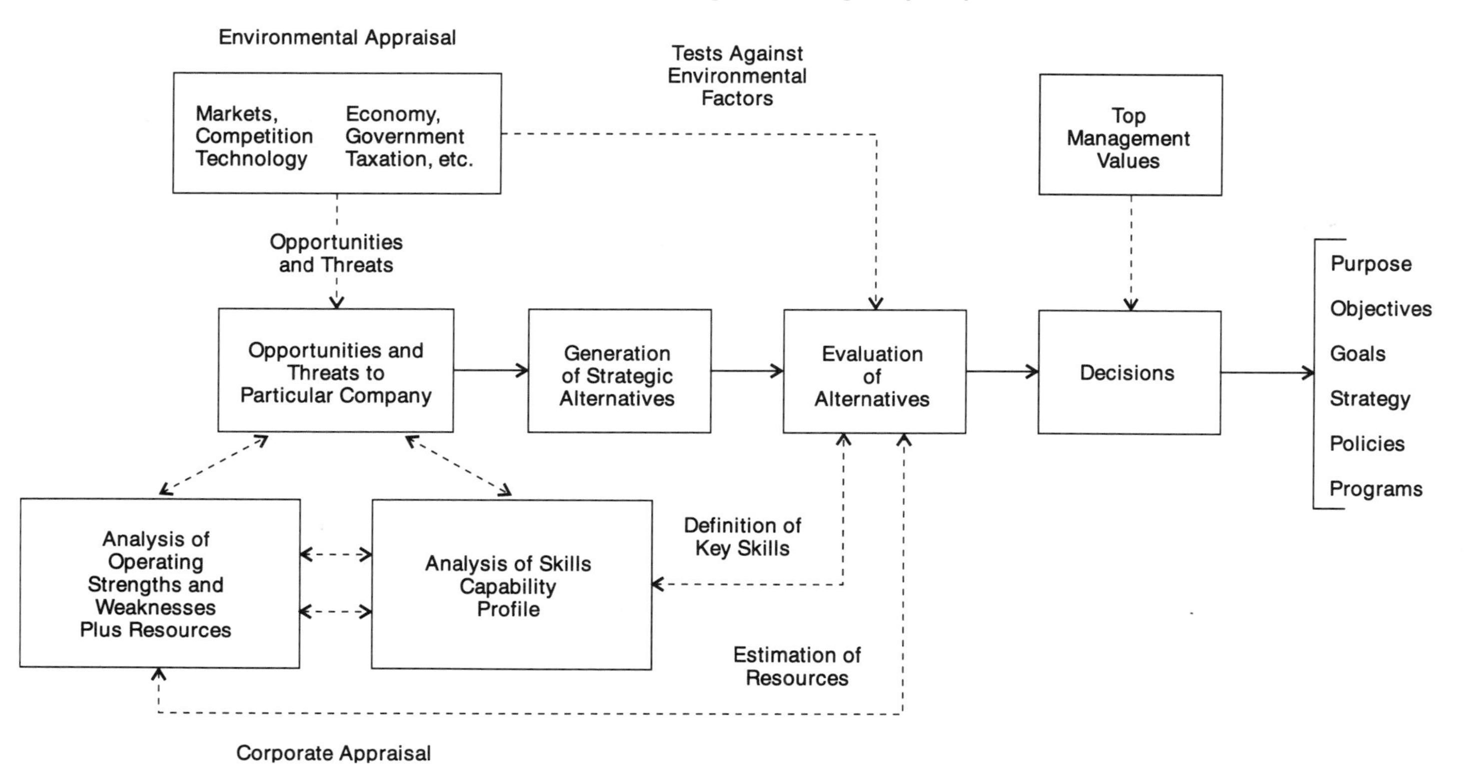

EXHIBIT 1.4 Investment/Marketing Concept Design

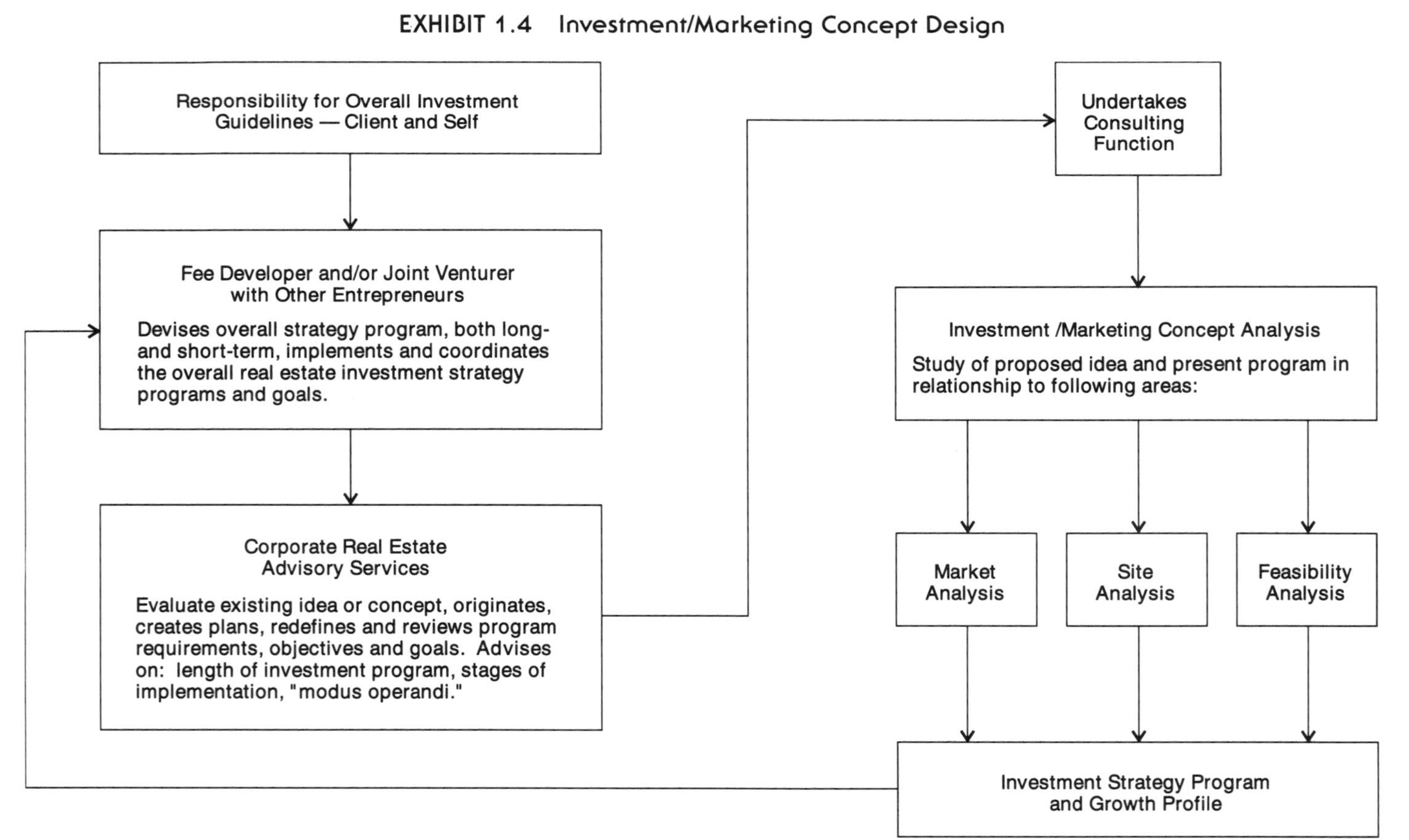

EXHIBIT 1.5 Real Estate Decision System

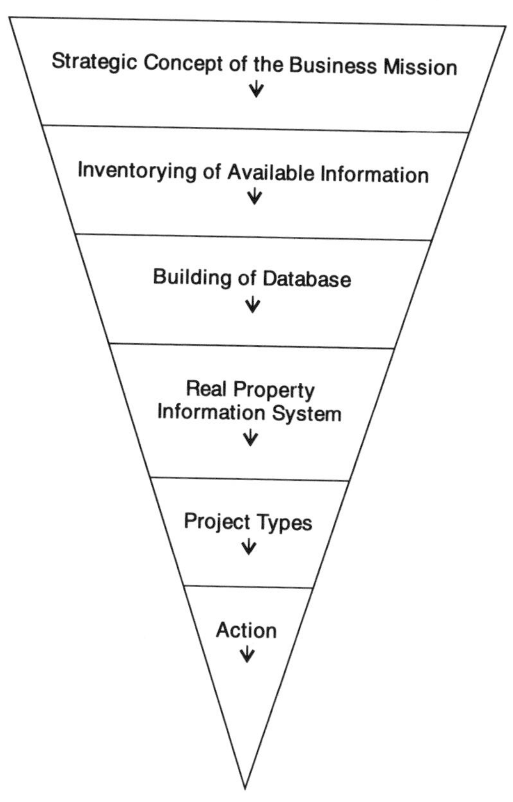

(b) ORGANIZATION OF THE CORPORATE REAL ESTATE DEPARTMENT

The real estate system's structure (Exhibit 1.5) resembles an inverted pyramid with movement from top to bottom. The initial issues addressed, therefore, are organizational, procedural, and interpretative with formalization usually occurring in a Policies and Procedure manual. The specific definition of real estate functions/actions emanates from these decisions. In § 1.4, we describe these functions.

§ 1.4 FUNCTIONS OF REAL ESTATE ASSET MANAGEMENT

Real estate asset management is the process of managing all aspects of real estate assets from acquisition to disposition. More specifically, we can list the functions of real estate asset management as:

1. Protection of the market values of the real estate inventory.
2. Assisting in capital accumulation.
3. Origination of strategic moves.
4. Information networking among divisions and operations that provides the basis for:
   - Annual Operating Plan (AOP)
   - Long-Range Business Plan (LRBP)
   - Strategic Business Plan (SBP)
   - Long-Range Facilities Plan (LRFP) as part of the manufacturing strategic plan.
5. Risk assessment and control.
6. Deal structuring:
   - Lease versus buy.
   - Specific project assignments including making hold versus sell decisions.
   - Acquisitions and divestitures.
   - Buy/sell.
   - Lease arbitrage.
   - Market studies.
   - Highest and best use analyses.
   - Strategic management reports on the inventory status and forecast.
   - Miscellaneous studies.

All of these functions represent profit opportunities for both the client/user and the real estate expert, with success depending on the skill with which the opportunities are exploited.

Our nation's quest for more competitive, efficient, leaner manufacturing postures will require better, more productive use of the real estate asset inventory. We know of no better method available than to begin to manage—professionally—the corporate real estate inventory.

Professional asset management, particularly of real estate and related fixed assets, is one key to total gross national product (GNP) growth. The reemphasis on and redirection of fixed-asset management, valuation, marketing, and investment are not revolutionary—just revealing—as U.S. industry, feeling the now inescapable pressure of world market competition, finally begins in earnest to reexamine its own entrepreneurial balance sheet.

Success in the future lies not in technological achievements alone, but in our ability to manage them—including the ability to effectively manage the real estate and related fixed assets so necessary to technological and business success.

§ 1.5 SYNCHRONIZING CORPORATE PLANNING AND CORPORATE REAL ESTATE

The strategic implications of fixed-asset facility support plans will receive increasing capital planning attention in this decade as businesses strive to maximize bottom-line performance. Realistic facilities delivery and construction schedules are required to develop accurate capital expenditure forecasts for calculating the many important financial ratios used in planning. Therefore, the preparation of the interdependent strategic business plan and the fixed-asset facilities support plan must be concurrent. Neither can be prepared in a vacuum. The moment of truth comes when strategic business plans are received at the corporate offices and the requirements for capital facilities investments are reviewed. Answers must be found for a host of questions: How much capital should the company be investing each year? How does the firm compare with its competition? Should the company spend more to improve productivity? Is it investing in facilities for products for which there is a declining market? Will the new facilities improve competitive posture? Have the new facilities been properly located? Are these capital programs affordable? Most questions are strategic rather than operational. This is why we have placed the corporate real estate executive at the strategic level of corporate planning.

The fixed-asset facilities support plan must be based on the operational plans of the operating division. Similarly, business plans must reflect the realities of existing capacities and operating costs as well as requirements for additional capital investment, real estate leases, and other facilities expenses. Acquisition or construction of new facilities also takes time. Consequently, facilities must be planned on a long-term basis, but with contingency plans that can accommodate short-term deviations in business projections.

Early on, the corporate real estate department should perform a facilities utilization audit to answer the following three groups of questions:

1. How much space is needed to generate a project at a given location for a given segment of a business? What useful standards can be developed to measure facility utilization, such as square feet of space per employee dollar of profit?
2. How does a business's productive capacity relate to the near-term and long-term marketing objective? How many manufacturing plants and distribution facilities does a business have? Do their locations relate efficiently to the business plan, to one another, to availability of raw materials, to cost-effective labor, and to designated markets and customers?

3. How much physical production capacity will be needed—and when—to meet growth objectives? Should the facility even be located on its present site, or are substantial incremental investments needed at existing locations just because they are there?

Corporate decisions to acquire or dispose of real estate are investment decisions. The competition for corporate dollars by operating divisions is conducted using traditional methods: Resources are allocated by capital budgeting techniques, particularly where the resources of the corporation are being committed to long-term fixed capital assets. Generally, fixed-asset values relate to manufacturing, distributing, and marketing corporate goods. On the other hand, the dominant measure of the profitability of an individual real estate investment decision is based on the concept of discounted cash flow, where the timed sequential return of investment dollars receives priority.

Evaluation motives clash as the traditional corporate financial executive thinks about ways to publicize the shareholder ownership value through EPS growth, dividend policy, and stock and bond prices (normally on a short-term basis), while the real estate investment analyst is looking at available depreciation that can be added to net income. Much more effort will be expended over the balance of the 1990s to resolve the bookkeeping and reporting paradox that now exists, with fixed-asset investments being looked at in ways that differ from accepted practice. The corporate real estate management executive will be asked increasingly to provide reasoned, factual advice on this important point.

How has the evolving investment climate affected the industrial corporation's need for specialized real estate services? The scope of required services has expanded dramatically, which means the real estate analyst or marketing specialist must be equipped with the expertise and insight necessary to take advantage of the new opportunities in real estate asset management, such as:

- Real estate portfolio review and analysis through the establishment of corporate real estate program/profit objectives, along with corporate real estate policy and procedures.
- The raising of corporate funds through the planning, packaging, and marketing of surplus corporate assets; the disposition and marketing of surplus corporate buildings and leaseholds; and corporate real estate financing.
- Analyses and implementation of corporate plans for growth and contraction through merger, acquisition, divestiture, and liquidation of assets.
- Marketing and management of fixed-asset projects.

§ 1.6 OPERATING ORGANIZATION OF A CORPORATE REAL ESTATE DEPARTMENT

The real estate department functions within a formal organizational structure. It must, therefore, be responsive to an organization's internal philosophy as well as to external market influences that affect the organization's ability to perform. We discuss methods for performance measurement in Chapter Three; but for the moment, we'll concentrate on organizational aspects.

How do formal structures vary? We can perceive variations in terms of:

- The number of interdependent units established within the total organization.
- The levels of formal authority designated in the hierarchy.
- The size of each formally designated unit within the organization.
- The kind of authority formally delegated to the various units.
- The work done by the formally designated units.
- The location of the work.
- The degree of autonomy granted to each unit.

Throughout this book, we are going to describe the specifics of real estate department organization with these points in mind. Exhibit 1.6 shows a hypothetical corporate office organization. We will use a large, multinational manufacturing conglomerate as our reference base, for three reasons. First, this type of company is complex operationally, with a full complement of line and staff departments, providing excellent organization perspectives. Second, we will assume the real estate department will be established as an operational entity from day one; therefore, it will inherit little in the way of nonproductive attitudes or personnel. Third, senior management has created the type of asset management atmosphere that will make the real estate program work. The organization of this department is designed to implement effectively our example corporation's fixed asset management program, which is both cost and operationally effective.

Designated interface personnel, carried on division and group budgets, will assist the real estate department in the fixed asset management function. The existence of the liaison group is a key ingredient in the program because it not only provides knowledgeable personnel, maintained at noncorporate expense, but also creates a responsive communications channel between the real estate department and the operating division. A second interface group consists of other corporate departments and corresponding division and staff groups that provide advice, counsel, and expert support in a wide variety of technical areas, without appearing on

EXHIBIT 1.6 Corporate Real Estate Department Organization Chart

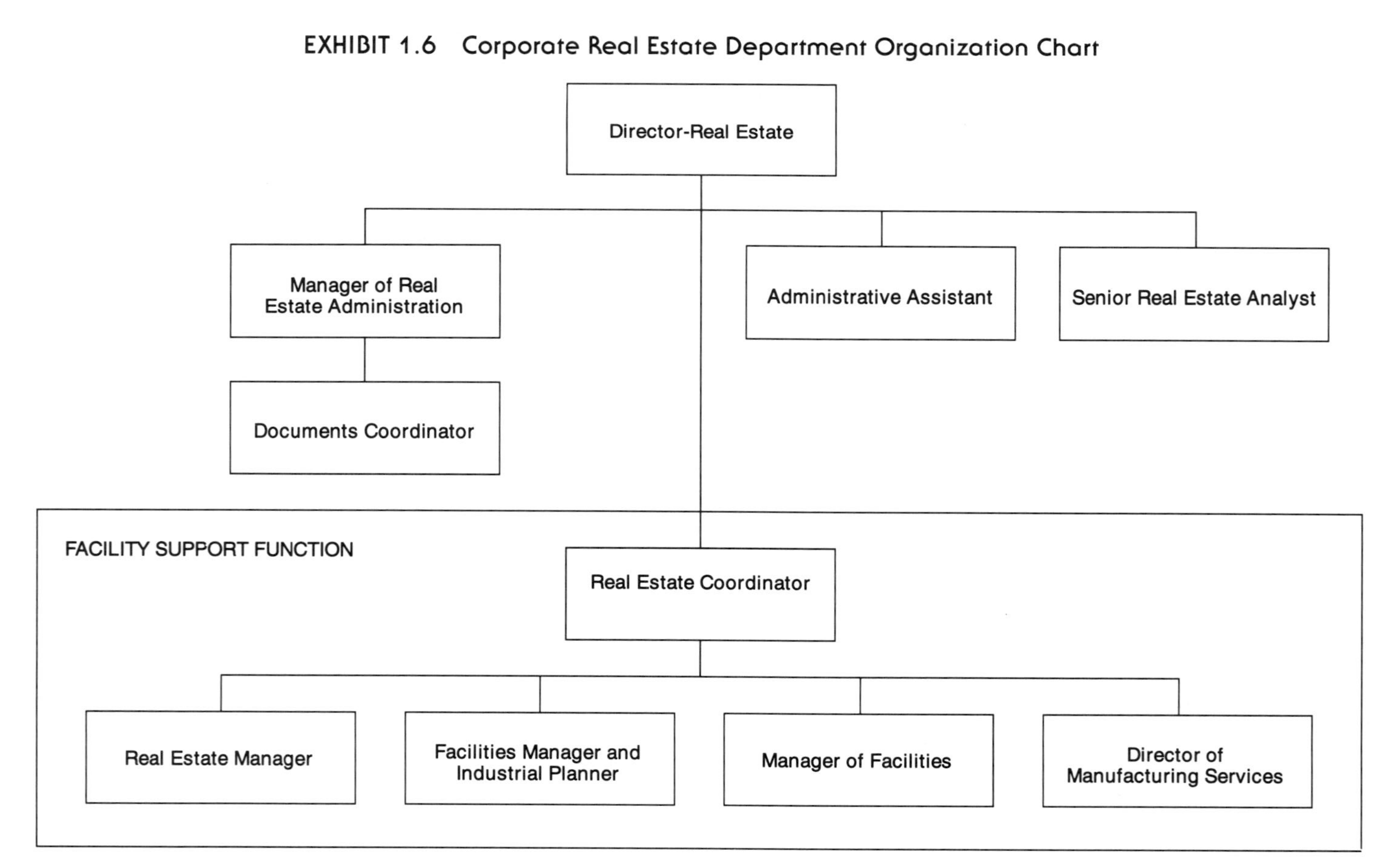

the departmental budget. Exhibit 1.7 is an example of one possible interface scenario.

Succeeding chapters explore more fully the specific functions and methods that fall within this organization's structure. The goal, is to be cost and operationally effective.

Extending the organization chart upward, the corporate real estate executive reports through the operations side of the corporate staff to the Senior Vice President—Operations. In some cases, the direct line reporting relationship will be different—the Chief Financial Officer, Treasurer, the Senior Vice President—Human Resources, the General Counsel and other prevalent choices. The corporate real estate executive also develops relations with division and group presidents and their respective line and staff personnel. (If this did not happen, the lack of two-way communication would probably signal serious faults in program effectiveness.)

(a) INTERFACE RELATIONSHIPS WITH OTHER CORPORATE STAFFS

Let's examine the functions of each of the other primary corporate staffs to see how the real estate department relates to and complements those staffs.

Exhibit 1.7 defines the many continuing interface relationships with other corporate office staffs. The level at which these relationships occur will depend on company size and on the relative position of the staffs on the hierarchical scale. We are going to make two assumptions: first, that the influence of the real estate department permeates all levels of corporate management; second, that our corporation is very large and divisionalized, with a full complement of staff departments. You can adjust this scenario to suit your specific situation.

(1) Chief Financial Officer (CFO)

The influence of the CFO permeates the highest levels of corporate decision making. Financial decisions are interwoven with operating and related decisions into composite decisions that set the tone and determine the posture and character of the corporate business mission.

There are four essential management requirements of any financial officer:

1. To make sure that corporate goals are attainable from a financial standpoint.
2. To contribute financial expertise and viewpoint to management decisions.
3. To serve as a communicator on financial aspects of the business to investors, employees, and the public.

EXHIBIT 1.7 Organization Chart Traditional Corporation

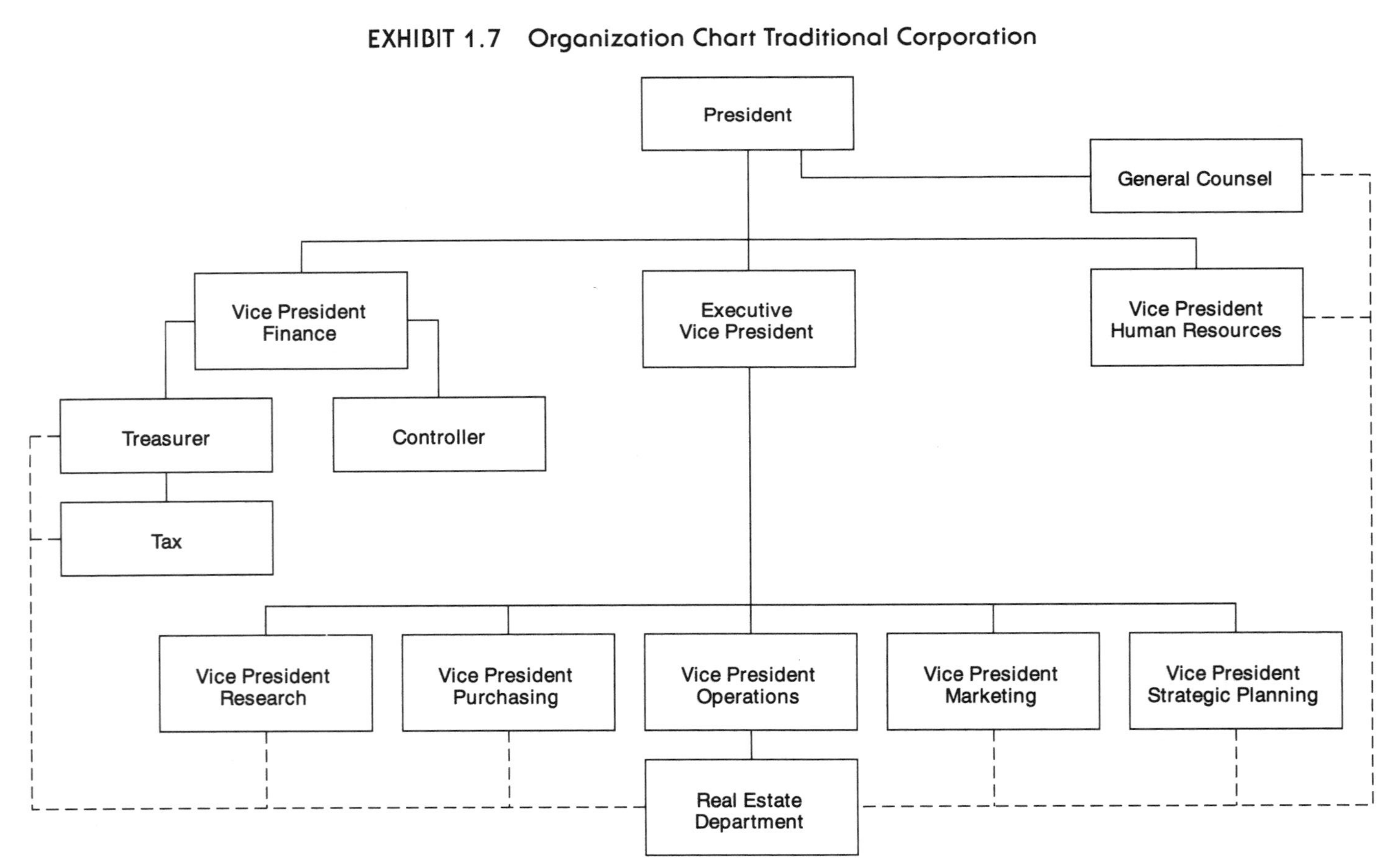

4. To insist on corporate conduct that adheres scrupulously to ethical practices in financial matters.[1]

These requirements are achieved on two levels—a philosophical impact on top-level strategy and the establishment and implementation of financial goals and controls.

The real estate department becomes an arm of financial policy through its understanding of corporate financial objectives and its implementation of corporate financial policy. Top management creates broad policies; the real estate department is cognizant of those policies; and the actual implementation with the resultant corporate staff interfacing, occurs at levels subordinate to the top management level.

(2) Treasurer

In a substantial, diversified, and divisionalized company, not only will the CFO be the financial policymaker, but subordinate finance functions may be split between the accounting-controller function and the finance-treasurer function. The treasurer reports to the vice president-finance and directs the conduct of corporate treasury activities, including:

- A continuing evaluation of the company's capital structure.
- The development of long-range plans for capital acquisition and utilization.
- The care and custody of funds and other financial assets.
- The supervision of banking—domestic and foreign.
- Corporate-level aspects of credit, insurance, and risk management.

These functions, translated in terms of treasury/real estate relationships, are reflected in the following treasurer planning responsibilities:

- Prepares long- and short-range plans and strategies for short-term debt and long-term debt.
- Reviews the foreign and domestic cash positions of the company on a daily basis; through cash and other financial forecasts, plans for the maintenance of adequate funds to meet outstanding and planned commitments.
- Reviews the implications of general economic, business, and financial developments, and forecasts their impact on the corporation's treasury operations, policies, and cash requirements.

[1] J. Fred Weston and Maurice B. Goudzwaard (eds.), *The Treasurer's Handbook* (Homewood, IL: Dow Jones-Irwin, 1976), p. 114.

Thus, the cash or credit conditions of surplus real estate sales and the lease versus buy considerations of facility acquisitions would fall within the treasurer's province as he or she exercises custodial responsibilities over cash and debt and their interplay in the corporate capital structure.

(3) Controller

The other side of the finance function—namely the budget, accounting, financial controls and systems, financial reporting, and internal auditing—is administered by the corporate controller. The vice president-controller reports to the vice president-finance. He or she directs the corporation's accounting, financial reporting, contracts and pricing, financial planning, and operations analysis, and government fiscal relations activities on a global basis. Main functions include:

- Directing the entire company's accounting, contracts and pricing, government fiscal relations, and financial planning and procedures.
- Executing arrangements with outside auditors.
- Directing the preparation of the company's official financial statements.
- Reviewing all major contracts and proposals and amendments and changes thereto, including proposed pricing strategy.
- Establishing corporate financial goals and preparing long-range and annual operating plans, forecasts, and associated operating and capital budgets.
- Analyzing the corporation's operating results and the operating results of its various elements, identifying and analyzing potential problem areas, and presenting the results and recommended corrective action plans to operations corporate senior management.
- Evaluating major investment opportunities.

The real estate department will routinely work with the controller's office when transmitting cash deposits on surplus sales and total remainder cash payments on prior sales upon the closing of the sale. Beyond this obvious relationship, though, the real estate department will be (or should be) deeply involved in financial planning and controls activities. This involvement will be heightened in companies that have a formal procedure for capital dollar requests (both for acquisitions and dispositions). This formal procedure, requiring the submission of a formal document or an appropriation request (AR), is examined in detail in Chapter Three. Appropriation requests require input from each participating corporate staff department as well as originating division and group documentation. The real estate department will be called on to analyze the real estate aspects of the appropriation request; hence, the department becomes part of the corporate financial control mechanism. Normally the department will have been intimately involved in the planning behind the proposed acquisition/disposition, so that it can act on the program ensuing from approval smoothly, knowledgeably, and enthusiastically.

(4) Tax Affairs Department

The tax consequences of acquisitions and dispositions permeate every real estate transaction. Accordingly, there should be a great deal of interaction between the tax and real estate departments. To illustrate the general responsibilities of the tax affairs department, a typical job description for a senior corporate tax person reads, "To handle all tax affairs of the corporation and its related entities with a view to ensuring compliance within the limits of all applicable laws in a multinational environment at the least cost to the overall organization. In addition, to handle all matters relating to the renegotiation of contracts with the U.S. government." The principal responsibilities of the tax affairs department are:

- Negotiating and/or reviewing and approving major transactions in their formative stages and proposing changes to achieve the best tax results.
- Studying existing corporate structures, policies, operations, procedures, and business practices and recommending changes that would reduce tax costs.
- Requesting rulings from and conducting negotiations with taxing authorities.
- Formulating policies for and administering compliance with tax laws. This includes preparing and filing returns, approving and scheduling tax payments, and negotiating with tax examiners.
- Advising senior management on the impact of new tax laws, decisions, regulations, and rulings and of proposed tax legislation on its strategic plans.
- Recommending, authorizing, and conducting or controlling tax litigation.
- Filing corporate renegotiation reports and handling the audits and administrative proceedings relating thereto.

The principal contracts between the tax affairs department and the real estate department will occur in the following areas:

- The administration and evaluation of property taxes.
- The analysis of the tax implications of sales (capital gains or losses).

- The analysis of the tax implications of acquisitions (industrial revenue bond financing, for example).
- The analysis of extended term sales (evaluation of the credit risk and gain or loss implications).

Much interaction should occur between tax and real estate, and the dollar aspects are very significant. One example to illustrate the point occurred several years ago when the real estate department of Company S, the seller, was given the assignment of developing and implementing strategies for divesting the company's real estate inventory of 1,540 acres of land—comprising approximately two-thirds of a southeastern town. The 1,540 acres contained 1,600,000 square feet of manufacturing space (not included in the disposal analysis), an airport, a nine-hole private golf course, the municipal sewage system, several dozen automobile garages, a railroad, a foundry, a 30,000-square-foot office building, a rod and gun club, and 1,100 acres of vacant land in various zoning classifications. The company-owned high-pressure steam heating system provided heat to several municipal buildings. It was, by any standards, a true "company town," with all the remnants of nineteenth-century feudalist industrialization. There were other complicating factors, but those mentioned will suffice for purposes of stage-setting.

As a first step, the real estate department elected to dispose of the unimproved property, as well as the airport and the golf course. Once these activities were completed, the department turned its attention to developing a plan for the sale of the improved facilities, including the possibility of a sale/leaseback for portions of the manufacturing space that the company still needed for manufacturing operations.

Concentrating on the manufacturing space, the department developed a list of alternatives and made detailed analyses of conversion and operating expenses, on the theory that these would be factors whether the corporation sold and leased back or decided to become the landlord and leased surplus space itself.

There were severe limitations whatever course of action was chosen. The property tax bill was $525,000. Further, the property taxes had just been increased to $765,000 despite the reduction through sale of approximately $1 million in the assessed value base. Something was clearly wrong. Immediate contact was made with the property tax section of the corporate tax affairs department, and an in-depth analysis of the situation began. The excessive tax bill would be a significant burden for any owner, and it severely hampered the company's ability to find a suitable buyer—let alone to continue operating a depressed business.

Conferences were scheduled and held with the community's officials, including its assessor. An official protest was filed. These efforts proved fruitless, so the company decided—reluctantly, because of the potential adverse publicity—to seek legal relief. Neither the town nor the company would profit from litigation, but some equitable remedy had to be achieved for the community to survive and the company to remain a viable employer.

Finally, with litigation a possibility, the officials of the community agreed to discuss a plan that had been submitted previously by the company. A compromise plan was accepted that yielded cash savings of approximately $1,800,000 over a five-year period. The tax reduction significantly enhanced the marketability of the property, improving the prospects for attracting new employers.

(5) Corporate General Counsel

The most obvious of the interface staff relationships is that between the real estate department and the office of the corporate general counsel, since all real estate transactions require the use of legal contracts and, hopefully, are negotiated with professional guidance from staff members of the office of the corporate general counsel. The office of the corporate general counsel performs these functions:

- Protects the company's interests through the drafting or review of effective legal documents.
- Offers opinions and recommendations, based on sound legal interpretations, concerning problems posed by corporate staffs and divisions.
- Participates in the preparation of cases in litigation.
- Collaborates with outside legal counsel in various legal matters.
- In the area of real estate, in addition to reviewing or drafting legal documents and all required forms, participates in contract negotiations and supervises the preparation of closing documents for real estate dispositions.

If a company has a large legal staff with a correspondingly large volume of real estate activity, one or more staff members may be assigned to the real estate department on a full-time or first-call basis. Frequently, a legal staff member will participate in real estate contract negotiations, particularly those involving complex, big-ticket deals, so the development of good working relationships between the two staffs can be highly beneficial.

(6) Other Corporate Staff Relationships

In addition to the staff relationships just discussed, the real estate department will have relationships with the insurance department, the facilities department, the purchasing department, the personnel department, and the public relations department. The primary elements of these interdepartmental contacts are discussed next.

(i) Insurance Department The insurance department will be notified of any changes in the real estate inventory—owned or leased, acquisitions, or dispositions—to avoid excesses or inadequacies in insurance coverage. If the corporation is contemplating the acquisition of an existing facility, the insurance department can arrange an independent inspection of the facility by an underwriter (such as IRI-Industrial Risk Insurers) to evaluate potential loss exposures and the costs of eliminating them. For example, one building that a company was negotiating to buy had about 430,000 square feet of space, including 20,000 square feet of office space. It was approximately 60 percent complete. Adverse business conditions had forced the owner to cease construction. Since the facility would be acquired on an "as is" basis, estimates of the costs to complete it were critical in formulating a negotiating position. A detailed inspection by an underwriter disclosed the need to spend an additional $400,000 for completion of the sprinkler system, auxiliary water supply, fire curtains, and two fire walls. These items were then successfully negotiated out of the purchase price.

(ii) Facilities Department The real estate and facilities functions are closely related and are frequently considered together for staff reporting purposes with facilities reporting to the corporate real estate executive. Their respective missions, however, should not be confused. The facilities department is primarily responsible for:

- Environmental control.
- Energy conservation.
- Facilities design.
- Construction engineering and project management.
- Requirements analysis (AR reviews).
- Equipment redeployment.
- Industrial planning.

The facilities department is concerned primarily with the effective utilization of existing facilities, including the internal location of equipment and work processes. Where the construction of new facilities is contemplated, the department will review the projected construction costs, facility specifications, and design, as well as the selection of architects and engineers.

The real estate department will usually be involved at the front end of new facilities projects via the selection of a site and purchase or lease negotiations. (See Chapters Seven and Ten for an elaboration of this aspect of real estate department operations.)

There will also be significant interplay between the two functions in facility redeployment programs (where facilities declared surplus by one corporate division are reassigned to another) and in the accumulation of real estate and facilities information for the data file. (See Chapter Five for a discussion of Marketing Corporate Facilities.)

Frequently, the lead position of the real estate department in acquisition/disposition activities will provide opportunities for advance notification to other departments. For example, the real estate department will or should know of a plant closure date well in advance, and it can tell the facilities function that an occasion may arise for equipment redeployment.

(iii) Purchasing Department The real estate department will work with the purchasing department primarily when seeking a site for new construction. Since purchasing will be involved in the negotiation of architectural and engineering contracts (because of the "purchased services" nature of such contracts), lead time notification from the real estate department will increase corporate operating efficiency.

Real estate–planning interaction may also be useful if the corporation "buys" month-to-month public warehouse space and services with purchase orders. The purchasing department will know about such space, but the real estate department may not, and as a result thousands of square feet of space may be leased with little or no centralized accounting. Although such arrangements are made to meet short-term storage needs, they often grow into long-term stays, and unless the real estate department is notified, effective control cannot be achieved. To maximize the opportunities for effective asset management, written lease agreements should be required for all leased premises, regardless of the duration of the lease.

(iv) Human Resources Department We will take up the relationship between the real estate department and the human resources department in some detail in Chapter Seven. The human resources or personnel department will also do studies on union matters in potential locations. These items weigh heavily in financial decisions on new facility locations.

Working relationships will also exist between the corporate real estate department and other group/division staff personnel, particularly finance, facilities, and manufacturing operations. The real estate director or vice president will also have many one-on-one relationships with senior group/division presidents, vice presidents, and so forth. To maximize real estate profit opportunities, the "peer group" pressures of corporate management will require strong support, then, from the corporate office.

(b) CORPORATE DIRECTIVES AND PROCEDURES

As a first step toward dollar effectiveness, written corporate directives and procedures that provide a realistic framework for achieving defined goals should be developed, approved by senior management, and implemented. Senior management commitment is vital to the success of any real estate asset management program. The primary corporate directive, signed by a corporate officer, should provide the "muscle" for the fixed asset management program. Its key operating words should state, ". . . authority for the negotiation and document preparation and/or execution for all acquisitions, disposals, and similar transactions that affect the rights of the corporation in real property is retained in the Corporate Offices."

A complete nondelegated function and, as a result, maximum control over the real estate inventory—both coming and going—is the requisite for a successful program. A series of supporting procedures, designed to instruct divisions on the proper ways of complying with the corporate directive, are titled:

1. Real Estate—General and Definitions.
2. Acquisition of Real Estate.
3. Disposition of Real Estate.
4. Reassignment of Real Estate.
5. Management of Company-Owned or -Leased Real Estate.
6. Improvement to Company-Leased Real Estate.
7. Site Selection Procedures.

Exhibit 1.8 (p. 32) reproduces the procedure on the acquisition of real estate (item 2) to provide an example of the language used to convey corporate office authority and direction.

The organizational structure we have just described is patterned to achieve both perceived and defined goals. This structure is only one solution to the intricate problems of effective real estate asset management. Your solution may be a variation on this one.

§ 1.7 OBTAINING THE BOTTOM LINE

Solutions to fixed-asset management/marketing/utilization issues must be comprehensive. A search for solutions must start with a restatement of philosophy, conditioned by experiences that have shaped academic and empirical professional development.

Fixed-asset management professionals of the industrial corporation, the pension fund, and the fiduciary entity must share a common, comprehensive problem-solving philosophy with the outside real estate experts they employ.

Toward this end, the professional education process must be addressed in a more balanced, comprehensive way than ever before. A credible curriculum for the fixed-asset management professional and adviser must be developed. The continuing challenge remains to create a unified body of knowledge and an identifiable professional group conversant in that discipline.

Professional asset management, particularly as applied to fixed assets, is the key to total gross national product growth. Reemphasizing and redirecting fixed-asset management valuation, marketing, and investment are not revolutionary ideas. But as U.S. industry feels the acute pressure of world market competition, including the need for fixed-asset utilization efficiencies, it must earnestly reexamine its own entrepreneurial balance sheet. The challenges of this task will have to be met and conquered by the corporate real estate executives who are the professional custodians of fixed, intangible and cash assets as well as by the outside professional marketing and management specialists that those executives employ in an advisory capacity.

Fixed-asset management is a universal business activity that is basic to the financial health of every company; therefore, doing it well is key to each company's effective competition in its industry.

The administration of a company's real estate resources is one task of asset management that is never completed. Despite its sometimes repetitive nature, it is not an easy job. The corporate real estate function used to be considered routine—companies bought, sold, leased, and so forth, on an "as needed" basis, giving little thought to whether that unpredictable creature known as the "real estate market" would accommodate such haphazard planning.

Today there is a strong, inescapable trend toward considering real estate as a working asset from which the corporation should get maximum profits. Far from being regarded as a symbol of success, excessive or idle real estate assets are being viewed increasingly as a sign of management inefficiency.

EXHIBIT 1.8 Acquisition of Real Estate—Form

I. General

A. Acquisition of real estate involves, but is not specifically limited to, the following actions: planning, forecasting, definition, and approval; negotiation, preparation, execution, and control of transaction documents; and inspection, acceptance, and identification of the property.

B. Authority to negotiate and execute transaction documents involving the acquisition of real estate is retained in the Corporate Offices. The staff Vice President—Production (Eastern Region) has negotiation and execution responsibility for all real estate transactions.

C. The requesting organization (Operations, Group, Division, or Corporate function) is responsible for:

1. The planning, forecasting, criteria development, and specific need determination.
2. The preparation and submittal of a Proposed Real Estate Lease Summary or a Proposed Real Estate Purchase Summary as appropriate, before submittal of the required Appropriation Request, to the Corporate Director of Real Estate.
3. The preparation and submittal of an Appropriation Request (AR) for real estate requirements to Corporate Financial Planning and Analysis in accordance with Finance Policy when the requirement exceeds the delegated authority of the concerned Operations/Group/Division President. If a proposed lease or lease extension is within the amount delegated to Operations or Group Presidents in total lease commitments, it must be approved in accordance with current delegated authority at the appropriate organization level. Evidence of such approval must be supplied to the Staff Vice President—Production (Eastern Region), to enable negotiation and execution of the lease.

   Such requirements will be coordinated through the office of the Staff Vice President—Production (Eastern Region), normally during preparation and review of Annual Operating (AOP) and Long Range (LRP) Plans. In short lead time circumstances, required coordination should be accomplished as early as possible in the AR process. Assistance will be provided to requesting functions by the office of the Staff Vice President—Production (Eastern Region), as requested.

D. Proposed site evaluation and selection and selection activities will be coordinated by the office of the Staff Vice President—Production (Eastern Region), in close conjunction with requesting personnel to maintain a discreet planning and prenegotiation position. Exception is made for small sales/service offices in direct daily contact with the public. For such offices, where annual lease cost is $15,000 or less, responsibility for site selection and preliminary negotiation (noncontractual) will rest with the requesting organization; however, lease documents will be transmitted to the Corporate Real Estate

Department, which will obtain legal review of the proposed contractual terms and conditions and arrange for execution, etc. (See II-B.)

E. The Director—Real Estate will, in coordination with the requestor, negotiate the acquisition of approved real estate, arrange for preparation of appropriate agreement(s), complete required coordination, and forward to the Staff Vice President—Production (Eastern Region) for signatures as required.

F. Foreign locations of the Corporate Offices and foreign subsidiaries, other than those in Canada and Mexico, are authorized to search for, select, and enter into preliminary (noncontractual) negotiations for the lease or purchase of real estate, after first obtaining the approval of the Operations or Group President of direct report. Following completion of preliminary negotiations outlining the salient features of the proposed transaction, will be sent to the Corporate Director of Real Estate for review. After such review, the requestor will be notified by letter as to changes that may be required and given a delegation of authority from the Staff Vice President—Production (Eastern Region) to conduct final negotiations, obtain review by local legal counsel, and execute the final transactions documents. If, during final negotiations, there are any significant changes to the terms of the agreement, the Director of Real Estate will be immediately notified for direction before final execution of the documents. (See II-C.)

II. Procedure

A. After approval of the project (in accordance with Corporate Finance Policy), the requesting organization should forward a formal request by IL to the Director—Real Estate for appropriate acquisition action. Such request must reference the approved AR (or other corporate approval) and include any specifications and data, other pertinent conditions, unusual requirements or limitations, etc., relating to the approved acquisition action.

B. The Director—Real Estate will:

1. Review project approval package, coordinate with the corporate Staff Vice President—Production (Eastern Region), and initiate required acquisition action.
2. Conduct all negotiations with seller or lessor and arrange for preparation of purchase, lease, or exchange agreement (including changes thereto); exercise purchase or lease options; and submit to the corporate Staff Vice President—Production (Eastern Region) for approval and signature as required.
3. Coordinate with the offices of the Vice President and General Counsel (or designed foreign legal counsel), Vice President—Finance, and other Corporate Staffs as appropriate. Transactions involving foreign locations will also be coordinated with the office of the Vice President—International.
4. Maintain contact and coordinate final acquisition action with the concerned requestor.
5. Issue formal acquisition notification and forward all original transaction documents to Records Management.

6. Coordinate activation requirements.
7. Establish and maintain a master file of owned and leased real estate and a data retrieval system, and provide follow-up contacts with lessor as required.
8. Provide timely lease expiration notices to the Groups/Divisions informing them that future action is necessary on particular documents.
9. Provide and maintain a lending system for transaction documents and project files.

C. Corporate Field Offices, Divisions, Groups, Operations, or Plant Personnel (Facilities Department or Equivalent) will:
1. Perform or monitor the inspection, acceptance, and identification of company-owned or company-leased real estate in coordination with division Financial (Property Administration, Taxes, and Insurance) and other concerned functions as appropriate.
2. Accomplish AR-approved activation and occupancy projects in coordination with the Director-Real Estate.
3. Complete up-to-date Floor Plan Drawing for each leased facility where our hypothetical company is required to maintain the real estate during the life of the lease. It is recommended that photographs be taken of newly leased premises as a record of condition at time of occupancy.
4. Maintain communications with the Director-Real Estate to assure adequate interchange of information regarding real estate acquisition activities and problems.

D. Foreign locations and foreign subsidiaries. Original real estate transaction documents involving foreign locations and subsidiaries will be maintained in the files of the affected location whenever local practice allows.

Two

An Overview of Commercial Real Estate Asset Management

§ 2.1 AN INDUSTRY IN TRANSITION

In this chapter, we are going to examine the "commercial" side of the asset management industry. Recall the definitions we discussed in Chapter One and the functional difference for the terms. The key difference between corporate and commercial asset management centers more on *intent and philosophy* than on individual functions. For example, the corporate real estate executive's goal is to improve the achievement of the overall corporate business mission through quality asset management decisions. Historically, his or her performance was tied to total company operational success, rather than the market performance of the specific real estate asset(s). The commercial real estate asset manager, on the other hand, is concerned with the performance of the real estate assets on behalf of a third party investor looking for specific investment income. Herein lies one of the pervasive factors contributing to the powerful structural and ongoing changes occurring in the real estate asset management industry. As the corporate real estate asset user accelerates its own restructuring, downsizing, and decentralization activities, it will turn increasingly toward third-party real estate functionaries who, by and large, represent the "commercial" rather than the "corporate" point of view. Many of the techniques for effective real estate asset management that will be applied to corporate real estate inventories will come from the commercial, third-party side of the business. There will be assimilation and merger over time of profit-driven commercial asset management attitudes and techniques and the internal-looking, business-mission corporate approach to real estate asset management. Countless profit-making opportunities will emerge as the real estate asset management industry, now in transition, takes on the characteristics of permanence, structure, and substance.

The purpose of this chapter is (a) to explain the interwoven macro- and microeconomic relationships that ultimately drive the real estate asset management industry; (b) to discuss the commercial real estate asset management industry and the role of the asset manager; (c) to provide an overview of profit-making techniques; and (d) to discuss how you, as a corporate real estate executive or as a third party, outsourcing service provider, can incorporate these techniques into your business.

§ 2.2 MACRO FACTORS OF CHANGE

The real estate asset management industry—corporate and commercial—is in transition. Many of the changes are taking place in response to factors of change in our national economy. You should understand the more important factors and their interrelationships to identify and understand real estate industry structural changes and the resulting profit opportunities that emerge.

Let's look first at a composite set of basic economic information to illustrate the relationship of national economic indicators to local real estate markets. We have used as starting points two events—(1) savings and loans (S&L) deregulation (10/15/82) and (2) the creation of the Resolution Trust Corporation (RTC) (8/9/89). Exhibit 2.1 shows what has happened to some key national economic indicators since these events.

(a) PRIME RATE

The base lending rate or *prime rate* is utilized for pricing larger floating rate corporate/commercial loans. In general, prime rate movements have

EXHIBIT 2.1 Economic Indicators

	S&L Deregulation (10/15/82)	RTC Establ. (8/9/89)	2nd Qtr. '91	1st Qtr. '92
Prime Rate	13.50%	11.00%	8.50%	6.5%
GDP-Nominal	3760.3	5340.4	5252.6	5809.3
GDP-Real (1987 $)	3149.6	4859.7	4840.7	4891.9
Unemployment	10.1%	5.2%	6.8%	7.1%
S&P 500	122.40	317.98	371.16	408.79
DJIA	896.20	244.10	2906.80	3223.39
Inf. Rate (prev. yr.)	10.3%	4.1%	6.1%	6.3%
Federal Debt	1149.2	2852.5	3562.9	3901.2

Source: Federal Reserve Bulletin, The Board of Governors of the Federal Reserve System.

an inverse effect on the demand for debt capital. A decrease in the prime rate will increase the demand for debt capital which will be leveraged through our economy by increasing the total amount of consumption and private investment spending. The reverse is also true.

Prime rate changes typically occur in response to changes in the policy of the Board of Governors of the Federal Reserve System (Fed) with respect to an expanding or contracting economy.

The primary tools that the Fed uses to implement policy changes are adjustments to the federal funds rate, open market operations with respect to the purchase and sale of U.S. securities in the open market, and the discount rate.

The federal funds rate is the rate of interest for short-term (usually overnight) borrowing between member banks. When one bank is short of reserves, it will borrow from another bank that has excess reserves, at the federal funds rate. Excess reserves add to the money supply and can be thought of as additional loanable funds. The more excess reserves there are in the banking system, the greater the availability of credit and, consequently, the lower the federal funds rate. Through open market operations, the Fed can increase or decrease the federal funds rate. By purchasing government securities in the open market, the Fed injects additional reserves into the banking system, thereby decreasing the probability of a member institution being short of reserves, which decreases demand for federal funds, which in turn decreases the federal funds rate.

The discount rate is the interest rate that the Federal Reserve Banks charge depository institutions when they borrow reserves. Recently, the discount rate has been more effective as a general signaling device rather than a policy implementation method because only a small minority of member banks utilize the Fed to shore up their reserves. Most member banks use federal funds instead to adjust reserve positions.

By injecting reserves into the banking system, the Fed increases the total bank reserves, which increases excess reserves (total reserves = required reserves + excess reserves) and, ultimately, the supply of loanable funds. The funds loaned are utilized by individuals to purchase goods and services, which increases demands at the business level. Companies must make new plant and equipment investments to increase capacity to meet the additional demand, but also the hurdle rate used in the capital budgeting process to make capital investment will have decreased, thereby making such investment more feasible. These increases in consumer spending and private investment directly affect Gross Domestic Product (GDP), the next economic variable in Exhibit 2.1.

The decreasing trend of the prime rate reflected in Exhibit 2.1 is consistent with the accumulation of our nation's debt during the indicated period. To "cool down" the economy, the Fed policy will proceed opposite to the previous discussion.

(b) GROSS DOMESTIC PRODUCT (GDP)

The gross domestic product (GDP) is the market value of all currently produced domestic goods and services, during the time period under study, that are sold, but not resold. The basic model for GDP can be expressed as follows:

$$Q = C + I + G + X$$

where:

Q = the GDP
C = the value of all goods and services sold at the consumer level
I = the value of private investment spending
G = the value of goods and services consumed by local, state and federal government
X = the value of net exports or exports less imports

Changes in the value of any of the model's variables will affect the value of GDP by more than a 1:1 ratio because of what economists call *the spending multiplier.* The spending multiplier represents the ripple effect of a change in the level of any of the components of GDP, as they filter from the aggregate to microlevels of the economy.

GDP is of primary importance to the Fed with respect to setting monetary policy, since it is a direct reflection of the level of health of the economy as well as a meaningful indicator of the level of implicit inflation within the economy, a primary decision-making variable for the current Board of Governors.

As implied, GDP has both a price and output component. This is seen by looking at Exhibit 2.1. The price component is observed by the difference between real and nominal GNP and the output component is observed by changes in the real GDP. Real GDP in the 2nd quarter of 1991 was less than on the date the RTC was established. This reflects a decline in real total output that was a response to the Fed's desire to counteract the jump in inflation over the same period. Given the Fed's goal, reserves were drained from the banking system in the spring of 1990 in an effort to "cool the economy" and reduce accelerating inflation.

Although the Fed's intent was to slow the rate of price increases, the multiplier effect described earlier was instrumental in sending the economy into a recession in the summer of 1990. The Fed's response has been to steadily decrease the federal funds rate in an effort to ignite consumption and investment, creating the cycle that was discussed in the prime rate section.

(c) UNEMPLOYMENT

The usual relationship between real GDP and unemployment is inverse, lagged, and highly correlated. This is evident by the data in Exhibit 2.1. The recession in 1990 created a vicious circle with respect to the GDP/unemployment relationship. The evidence of recession shown by decreasing real GDP created fear of increasing unemployment at the consumer level. As a result, consumer spending decreased. The slide in sales caused corporate margins to deteriorate, which in turn prompted corporations to trim their work forces to shore up profits by decreasing operating costs. Thus, the fear created the reality.

(d) S&P 500/DJIA

The S&P 500 is a composite index created by the Standard and Poor's Company, of the performance of 500 corporations with respect to share price. The Dow Jones Industrial Average (DJIA) is a composite of 30 industrial companies traded on the New York Stock Exchange. Both indexes tend to move in the same direction; however, the S&P 500 is generally more representative of broad market performance.

The values of the indexes are driven by stock prices that are driven, in turn, by corporate dividends and expectations with respect to future profitability. Increased sales, other things being equal, will increase profits, dividends, and stock prices. The reverse is true as well.

Stock prices are also driven by investors' perceptions with regard to inflation. Accelerating inflation tends to increase interest rates, which increases the corporate cost of capital, which increases expenses, thus decreasing corporate profitability. Again, the reverse is also true. The merit of these indexes is their signal about corporate profitability because that, in many respects, is a direct indicator of the economy's health.

(e) INFLATION

The current Fed has repeatedly indicated that monetary policy will be highly driven by a desire to eliminate inflation. Given this objective, the Fed's perception of the inflationary environment will be the starting point for the movement of most economic variables.

For instance, if the economy appears to be overheated, the Fed will drain reserves from the banking system, to raise interest rates and decrease the supply of money. This, in turn, decreases consumption and investment spending (GNP), which decreases corporate profitability and increases unemployment. Nothing in the statistics provides a solid basis for the economic concerns and pessimistic forecasts that currently abound. Instead, the present situation seems to reflect the normal cyclical adjustments to our economy. Even when we add in some banking statistics from Exhibit 2.2, no self-evident truth emerges to support all the doom and gloom, since the aggregate picture of mortgage debt outstanding shows that the considerable decrease in S&L holdings has virtually been offset by the increased holdings of mortgage pools and trusts (these are primarily mortgage-backed securities). We do seem to have a crisis of contradiction where facts do not support fiction. Our rationale for this observation is important: National macroeconomic statistics can reveal many truths if you look deep enough. When the structural changes we have been discussing are permanently in place and we are back to the basics of the real value marketplace, many opportunities for

EXHIBIT 2.2 Banking Statistics

	S&L Deregulation (10/15/82) (%)	RTC Establ. (8/9/89) (%)	Third Qtr. (9/30/91) (%)	Fourth Qtr. (12/31/91) (%)
S&L mortgage debt outstanding (% of total)	35	25	19	17
Banks mortgage debt outstanding (% of total)	18	21	22	22
Life companies mortgage debt outstanding (% of total)	8	7	7	7
Federal and related agencies mortgage debt outstanding (% of total)	8	7	7	7
Mortgage pools and trusts mortgage debt outstanding (% of total)	12	31	31	31
Individuals and other mortgage debt outstanding (% of total)	16	16	16	16

Source: Federal Reserve Bulletin, The Board of Governors of the Federal Reserve System.

professional success become vividly apparent. The statistics support optimism about the real estate asset management industry.

The operative words for us, therefore, must be less economic and short-term and more structural and long-term. Fundamental shifts in the economy and the real estate industry are creating changes that are accentuated by our current inability to identify and accept the profound and permanent alterations now visible in the real estate asset management industry.

§ 2.3 THE NATIONAL OPERATIVE WORDS

A number of words or terms that can be called "trigger points" most closely describe the relationship between the national economy and the real estate asset management industry. No one word or term says it all, but collectively, they provide a sound basis for determining basic directions for the real estate asset management industry. The following list includes operative words or terms, some of which are discussed below.

The National Scene: Operative Words

- *Capital*
  - (1) The Players
  - (2) Amount
  - (3) Circulation/Speed/Savings Rate
  - (4) Yields
  - (5) Tax and Fiscal Policy
  - (6) Productivity
- *The Fixed Asset Base*
  - (1) Total Value and Physical Inventory
  - (2) Inflation
  - (3) Supply, Demand, Consumption
  - (4) The Valuation Process
- *Consumer Confidence*
  - (1) Public Opinion
  - (2) Faith, Hope and Charity

Capital includes the amount of money in circulation, the speed with which it circulates, or is redistributed, throughout the economy, its price, and its availability. Fed policy has a significant effect on the price and availability of capital. Although the Fed has been more accommodating recently, their preoccupation with eliminating inflation will tend to restrict the growth of the money supply. Congressional mandates to boost bank capital standards as well as the increasingly conservative standards with respect to loan classification and valuation have increased bank reserve requirements, further restricting the availability of loanable funds.

As a result, as it relates to real estate, debt capital for investment is extremely scarce increasing the need for equity. The 1986 tax reforms decreased the availability and increased the price of equity by reducing tax shelter benefits. The combined disruptions to the debt and equity markets, which in effect have decreased the availability and increased the overall cost of capital for real estate, are the primary exogenous forces behind the significant devaluation of real estate assets in the past decade.

Tax and fiscal policy, as discussed earlier, have been significant factors behind the lack of capital and resulting devaluation of real estate assets. The Tax Reform Act of 1986 significantly reduced the tax shelter benefits associated with real estate investment: (a) By lengthening the number of years required to fully depreciate real property, annual depreciation deductions were severely curtailed; and (b) taxable losses associated with real property were redefined as passive losses. Therefore, unless the ownership entity is a C-corporation, or the owner is recognized by the IRS as a "dealer," losses will be suspended until such time as sufficient passive losses exist as an offsetting device. For most owners, this does not occur until the property is sold. Therefore, considering the time value of money, the present value of these losses is less.

With respect to fiscal policy, the budget deficits we have been experiencing are keeping long-term interest rates artificially high, due to excess government demand for borrowed funds. Since the deregulation of the S&L industry, the ratio of total federal debt with respect to nominal GDP has grown from 30.5 percent to 67.1 percent. The result is that debt constants are higher than they should be, increasing equity requirements due to reduced loan amounts.

The fixed asset base includes the finite value of the standing stock of property, plant and equipment. It increases and decreases with inflation and, with respect to market forces affecting real estate fixed assets, the relationship among supply, demand, and absorption rates (existing and forecasted or perceived). Most importantly, we must include the major assumption: the continuing existence of an all-forgiving, all-consuming, steadily growing markets for all the products being produced. The appraisal professionals who created most of the artificial value base must also be considered. *Something clearly went wrong* and in so doing told us we needed to return the real estate market back to basics.

Consumer confidence, public opinion, faith, hope, and charity—call it what you will—is a barometer of our national economic health. The American public is the real force behind the economy. The current low level of consumer confidence restrains business expansion, maintaining high levels of unemployment and resulting in slow rates of real estate space absorption and high vacancy rate, due to decreased demand in all real estate sectors including commercial, industrial, and residential.

§ 2.4 CORPORATE REAL ESTATE ASSET MANAGEMENT OPERATIVE WORDS

The national macrooperative words we have just discussed lead to the same thrust of logic in the real estate asset management world. Let's see how they are related:

The Real Estate Asset Management Scene: Operative Words

- The Players
- Downsizing
- Decentralization
- Entrepreneurship/Competition
- Outsourcing
- The Service Arena
- Compensation
- The Global Markets

All of the national macrooperative words weave their singular, but connected threads into an exceedingly complex environmental web within which the corporate real estate asset management moves are made. All of these factors combined to create a major U.S. economic restructuring and changed the rules of the corporate real estate game now and forever. What are these profound, permanent changes and what do they forecast for the future?

§ 2.5 REAL ESTATE AS A STRATEGIC CORPORATE ASSET

There are three well-accepted components of the strategic planning process:

1. The evaluation of strategic opportunities for the company and an assessment of its resources as a measure of potential risk. Real estate assets occupy a significant portion of a company's resources—somewhere between 30 percent and 45 percent of total assets for the vast majority of American companies.
2. The cyclical nature of the evaluative thought process involving the accumulation and evaluation of interrelated strategic information.

3. The combination of tangible data objectively evaluated and intangible data superimposed subjectively to form, ultimately, the basis and direction of business strategy.

Full-time corporate staff and the third-party professional—the commercial real estate manager—must coordinate their efforts to find effective solutions for corporate real estate utilization issues. Neither party will be as successful alone as they will be together.

John Sculley, chief executive officer of Apple Computer, Inc., is a successful business leader and an implementer of innovative changes in the evolving philosophy of corporate leadership. His book, *Odyssey,* identified inescapable shifts in the ways business is poising itself to increase productivity and, therefore, competitiveness for the balance of this century and beyond. Sculley emphasized the need for and trend toward workplace and thinking environments that are less rigid and less dependent on the status quo and certainty—less traditional and "corporate"—with an emphasis on creativity and entrepreneurship.[1]

Corporate downsizing and decentralization are being accompanied by senior management's encouragement of divisional independence and increased entrepreneurship. However, while trying to become more like the traditional third-party real estate commercial brokerage company, corporations are demanding the third-party brokerage company become more structured, more rigid, more business strategy oriented—"more corporate."

The third-party consulting world is responding effectively, particularly those new to the corporate real estate game—the accounting firms, the management consulting firms, the Wall Street firms—where being "corporate" has been a fact of life for decades. Their primary problem still remains, however: learning more about corporate real estate and recruiting staff members who are expert at solving political and financial problems associated with effective, productive corporate real estate programs. The large regional and national real estate firms also are moving toward the partnership, although grudgingly, as market rate commissions give way to prenegotiated fees, contingent commissions change into salaried and performance bonus compensation packages, and the isolated deal becomes a part of the larger corporate business strategy.

The trend is identifiable and inescapable. The changes are profound for the traditional real estate brokerage/development industry and, in particular, for the old corporate client, space user. These are major changes impacting the corporate client/user as they, too, become more entrepreneurial and a member in partnership with third-party outsourced commercial real estate asset management industry.

[1] John Sculley, with John A. Byrne, *Odyssey, Pepsi to Apple . . . A Journey of Adventure, Ideas, and the Future* (New York: Harper & Row, 1987).

On the other hand, if the corporation has been following industry trends by downsizing, restructuring, decentralizing, and outsourcing, the corporate real estate executive may face a completely different set of circumstances. He or she may be caught in a personal survival mode as the corporation seeks to reduce staff overhead costs. In that case, the concepts we are discussing still come into play because the transition of the real estate asset management industry from in-house staffs to third-party outsourced service providers will increase, not decrease, corporate dependency on the profit orientation techniques and attitude of the commercial real estate asset manager. To continue controlling the process internally, the corporate real estate executive must learn the techniques being utilized by leading third-party consultants.

Certain significant structural changes are already occurring in the traditional view of real estate assets held by corporate users. Once considered reactionary and custodial, the corporate real estate function is now acquiring new luster and prominence, albeit at the expense of large central staffs and to the benefit of the third-party service providers.

§ 2.6 THE ROLE OF THE COMMERCIAL ASSET MANAGER

The commercial real estate asset management industry, comprised of traditional real estate organizations, exists to make a profit. This is a fairly logical statement; but let's take it one step further: The commercial real estate asset management industry exists to make a profit *from corporate users who utilize the asset in exchange for economic payment.* Through this economic exchange, the savvy commercial asset manager can turn over handsome profits utilizing techniques that offer a competitive market advantage. Commercial asset managers have developed these sophisticated techniques to achieve profit because the survival of their business depends on it. If the corporate investment in real estate is substantial, then it is very likely to have greatly profited commercial real estate investors and professionals. If a corporation has provided favorable returns to third parties, why not learn these techniques and incorporate them into your asset management program? The efficient utilization of these techniques can produce a favorable cost/profit ratio within your company.

In commercial real estate, the performance of the asset is controlled by an asset manager although the title "asset manager" may not be used. This manager has the following objectives:

- Protects the market value of the real estate inventory.
- Assists in capital accumulation.
- Originates strategic moves.

All the preceding objectives are profit oriented. Because the pursuit of profit is their main objective, knowledgeable commercial asset managers have developed a system in which the management approach is a purely capitalistic enterprise focused toward profit enhancement. The corporation can adopt this profit-oriented philosophy to manage the real estate fixed-asset portion of its balance sheet.

To enhance your understanding of the structural environment of commercial asset managers, we will explore the evolution of their role and compare the key attributes of that role with the role corporate real estate executives, who theoretically serve in a comparable position within the corporate structure.

Exhibit 2.3 compares the key attributes governing the motives of the commercial asset manager and corporate real estate executive.

The key differences can be attributed to the inherent profit motives governing the respective positions. For the commercial real estate asset manager, profit is the key to survival. For the corporate real estate executive, the evolution and development of profit motives will be the key to future success. Each of the characteristics identified in Exhibit 2.3 is examined below.

(a) GOALS

In commercial real estate asset management, the goals of the owner play a key role in formulating the strategic plan of the asset manager. Commercial real estate asset management can be defined as the process of overseeing a commercial asset in a manner that will ensure the

EXHIBIT 2.3 Commercial Asset Manager versus Corporate Real Estate Executive

	Commercial Asset Manager	Corporate Real Estate Executive
Goals	Profit oriented	Expense minimization
Performance Measurement	Tangible	Intangible
Legal Structure	Complex	Simplistic
Authority	Asset management agreement	Bureaucracy
Liability	Highly sensitive	Minimal
Compensation	Performance-based	Salary-based
Longevity	Contingent	Ongoing concern
Communication	To Owner	In-house

goals of the owner are achieved. Thus, the goal of the owner is transmitted to the asset manager who has been hired as a third-party fiduciary responsible for obtaining these goals.

Generally, the goals of the owner are profit oriented. For example, the goal may be to operate the asset for a specific period of time and then liquidate at a profit.

Economic considerations are inherent in the vast majority of commercial real estate investments. However, in some cases, the goals of the owner may not be 100 percent profit oriented. In some instances, the owner may have acquired the asset because of its emotional or aesthetic value, or for its pleasurable amenities.

The role of the corporate real estate executive, on the other hand, is to facilitate the utilization of the asset in a manner that will achieve profit within some other department. Because the corporation holds real estate assets for indirect rather than direct profit motives (such as a facility used to manufacture items), specific profit-oriented goals are usually not established. In addition, long-term goals concerning the asset are not subject to common corporate staff operating policy procedures, thus limiting the corporate real estate executive's control over the long-term performance of the asset. Instead, the performance of the asset is usually tied to cost minimization or limits established during the operational budgeting process for other in-line profit endeavors.

Tangible economic goals govern the strategic planning environment for the commercial real estate asset manager. Through this strategic planning process, the asset manager can better control and influence the profitability of the asset. The lack of promoting goal policies within the corporate environment complicates the corporate real estate executive's ability to effectively manage the long-term performance of the asset. Without strategic planning, profit enhancement techniques are ineffective, thus impeding the profit potential of corporate real estate assets.

(b) PERFORMANCE MEASUREMENT

In the absence of specific economic goals, performance measurement is difficult, which brings us to a fundamental difference between the commercial real estate asset manager and corporate real estate executive. This fundamental difference is attributed to the motivation associated with compensation/reward. Commercial asset managers are generally rewarded or compensated on their achievement of profit-specific goals.

Because corporations usually do not have specific profit-oriented goals for their real estate holdings, tangible guidelines to measure performance are difficult to establish. Strategic planning is usually ineffective in the absence of specific goals, and thus the performance of the corporate real estate executive is tied to the overall performance of the corporation. (For a detailed discussion on performance measurement and specific techniques within the corporate environment, see Chapter Three.)

(c) LEGAL STRUCTURE OF OWNING ENTITY

In commercial real estate, the asset manager is usually exposed to numerous and complex legal structures of the owning entities. These complex structures usually mandate sophisticated prior experience by the asset manager. Examples of these structures include:

- Limited Partnerships
- General Partnerships
- Corporations
- Sole Proprietors
- Foreign Entities

The responsibilities of the asset manager are further complicated by the administrative duties associated with these various ownerships. For example, it is not uncommon to have a syndicated general partnership with more than 100 individual investors. Depending on the residence of these individual investors (i.e., domestic or foreign), further administrative work is required to handle tax returns and other responsibilities in an accurate and timely manner and within the regulations of numerous jurisdictions.

The corporate real estate executive generally does not have the authority to administer or manage these complex holding structures.

(d) AUTHORITY

Commercial asset managers derive authority from an asset management agreement, a partnership agreement, or power of attorney, which outlines the scope and responsibilities of their role.

Corporate real estate executives derive authority from the board of directors or chief operating officer. It is common for the corporate real estate executive to work under the supervision of an operational vice president who depending on his or her corporate rank, will authorize transactions.

Much like the corporate real estate executive, once a year (or on some other timetable as defined in the asset management agreement or determined by corporate policymakers), the asset manager will submit a detailed budget to the owner, outlining the expenditures anticipated for the upcoming year. The owner usually has a specified time period to approve or disapprove the proposed transactions. The approved budget authorizes approximately 95 percent of the transactions that occur during the year. The asset management agreement usually provides authority limits with the remaining 5 percent of the transactions. These transactions usually are nonrecurring and include new loans, large leases, decisions to purchase or sell all or a portion of the investment, large capital expenditures, and unanticipated emergency expenditures.

The authority limitations imposed on the corporate real estate executive and commercial asset manager are similar. When dealing with complicated corporate structures, the approval process can take up to two years. In the absence of profit motivation and specific performance measurements, the motivation by corporate executives to authorize transactions is passive. As a result, valuable employee-hours are wasted in prolonged approval processes.

(e) LIABILITY

Liability is another key difference in the position of the commercial real estate manager and corporate real estate executive. The liability associated with the third-party fiduciary role of the commercial asset manager is material and warrants careful attention to legal restrictions governing responsibilities. For example, the asset manager is responsible for the timely and orderly payment of the monthly mortgage. Failure of the asset manager to perform this duty could result in substantial legal and economic consequences to the owner.

Although it could be argued that the corporate real estate executive operates within a quagmire of restrictive operating procedures, the commercial asset manager is in a similar environment because of legal liability. Careful ongoing adherence to legal documents and operating procedures is necessary to minimize the liability exposure on behalf of the owner and asset manager.

(f) COMPENSATION

The central ongoing concern of the commercial real estate company is achieving a profit. The commercial asset manager is usually positioned as a profit center in which fiduciary management services are offered in exchange for a fee or some other compensation. The continuation of their position is directly correlated to performance. It is this direct profit/performance relationship that motivates the commercial asset manager to achieve optimum performance.

In the absence of direct performance measurements, the compensation for the corporate real estate executive is not tied to measurable events; rather, compensation is usually tied to the company's overall performance. (This subject is treated extensively in Chapter Three.)

(g) LONGEVITY

Employment of the commercial real estate asset managers is directly tied to their performance. For example, an inferior performance will usually jeopardize the continuation of their employment. This is true for the corporate real estate executive as well; if there are tangible performance measurements. The lack of tangible performance measurements means that the corporate real estate executive's duration of employment is tied to the company's overall performance.

(h) COMMUNICATION

The commercial real estate asset manager oversees transactions associated with the real estate asset and, based on some predefined schedule, reports these events to the owner. For the commercial asset manager, the owner is usually a readily identifiable tangible person. For the corporate real estate executive, the owner is the board of directors in their capacity as a representative of the corporate stockholders.

The major difference in the communication structure of the two positions can be attributed to the presence of liability and the need for asset profit performance. The presence of liability for the commercial asset manager mandates an effective communication policy. Open, efficient communication channels between the owner, asset manager, and professionals minimize misunderstandings. In addition, for critical situations, the combined expertise of collective brain power can better solve problems that threaten profitability.

§ 2.7 THE STRUCTURE OF THE COMMERCIAL REAL ESTATE ASSET MANAGEMENT FIRM

The structure of the commercial asset management firm has evolved to function within the circumstances of its environment. Major duties associated with asset management have been segmented and are delegated to professionals with specialized education and expertise in their specific profession. For example, the leasing function is usually delegated to a leasing company with expertise in the particular asset type and market. It would not make sense to hire a leasing company that specializes in industrial leasing in Texas to lease a shopping center located in Florida, with the anticipation that its performance might be comparable to that of professionals specializing in Florida shopping center leasing.

In the commercial asset management firm, this specialized division of responsibility accomplishes three objectives:

1. Liability is removed from the owner and assumed by a professional with expertise.
2. Profit potential is maximized by utilizing the expertise for the specific duty.
3. Managers who do not achieve their goals can be easily replaced.

The structure is closely allied with profit-oriented objectives. Liability control is technically considered profit oriented because liabilities greatly threaten the profitability of the asset in numerous ways. Large insurance premiums, valuable time expended in lawsuits, or the potentially enormous expense of litigation can seriously jeopardize the owner's profits.

Exhibit 2.4 gives an overview of the structure of the commercial asset management organization and the various disciplines of professionals associated with it. The top tier is occupied by the owner who is the final authority in the decision-making process and the profit beneficiary who has assumed the liability associated with owning the asset. The second tier is occupied by the asset (or portfolio) manager who is responsible for overseeing the operation of the asset and who is the main communication link between the various professionals and owner. Between the asset manager and the property, the multiple disciplines involved during the holding period are:

- Performing real estate analysis
- Preparing tax return
- Managing property
- Leasing
- Lending/borrowing
- Handling legal aspects
- Selling/appraising.

Within these specific areas, there is a further division of duties. The property management firm, for example, will delineate and delegate the functions associated with property management, such as:

- Accountant/Controller
- Property manager
- Lawyer
- Insurance agent

All of these individual professionals are motivated by the successful economic performance of the asset. No one of these disciplines has greater significance than the others, as the performance of all these

EXHIBIT 2.4 Structure of a Commercial Real Estate Asset Management Firm

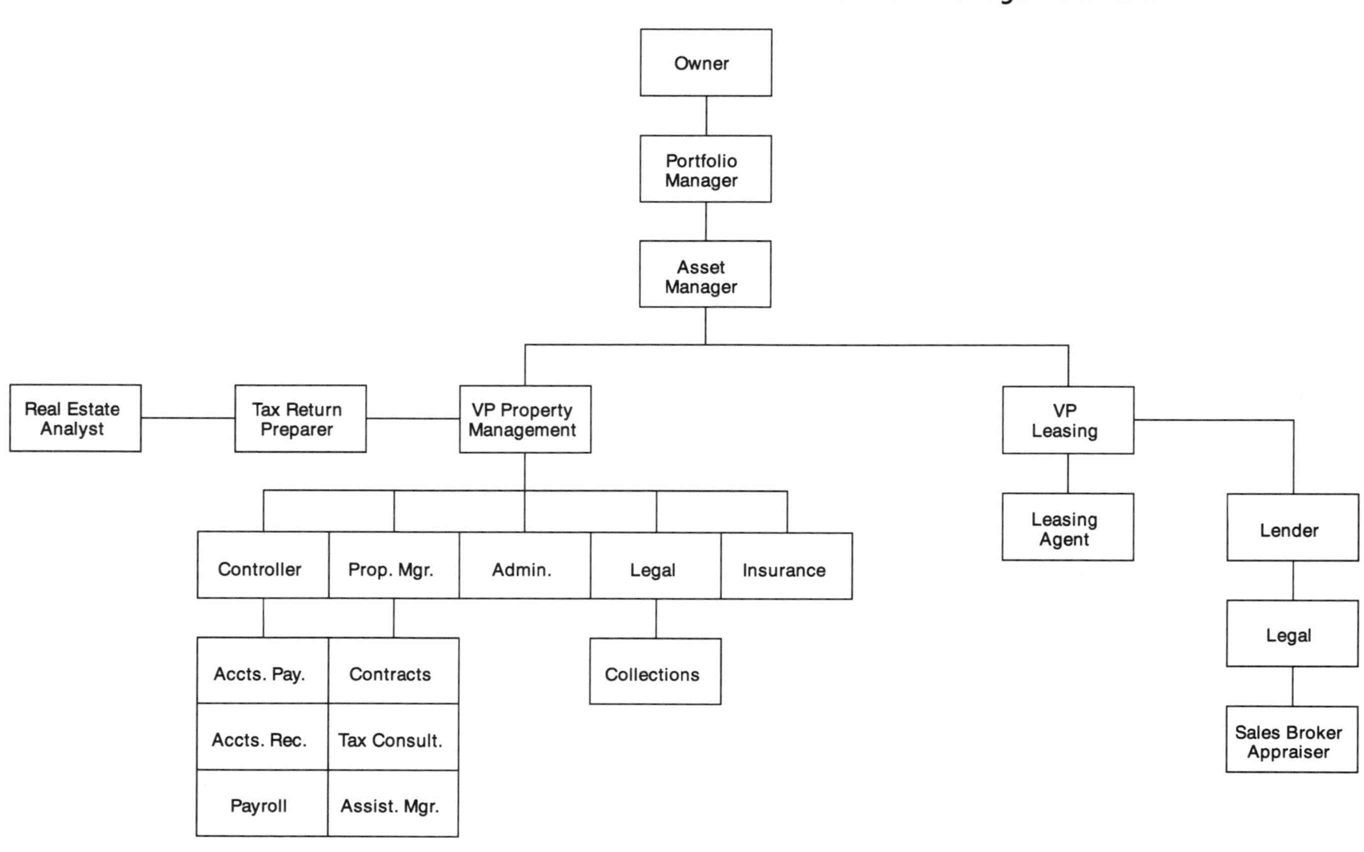

individuals is consequential to the overall performance of the asset. For example, a continuous high-quality performance by the leasing agent will provide the property with quality tenants thus simplifying the property manager's implementation of a tenant relations program. Likewise, the property manager who advocates a good tenant relations program by promptly and professionally handling tenant problems will improve the leasing agent's ability to renew tenants when their leases expire.

The asset manager coordinates the professionals' responsibilities and organizes an effective asset management system that channels the flow of information between the various professionals to promote a streamlined decision process. This asset management structure establishes a system of checks and balances to ensure that information necessary to maximize profitability reaches the appropriate decision-authority. Without an efficient asset management system, the decision-making process is ineffectual and hence opportunities to achieve profit are lost.

§ 2.8 HOW THE COMMERCIAL ASSET MANAGEMENT SYSTEM FUNCTIONS

To illustrate how the asset management system functions, let's suppose that the asset manager has learned that a major tenant is delinquent in its rental payment and thus sufficient cash is not available to meet the monthly mortgage payment due in 10 days.

Through a structured asset management system, the asset manager would have been informed of this tenant delinquency from the following sources:

- Property manager (through property meetings).
- Property accountant (advised the asset manager or property manager).
- The sources/uses statement (report prepared monthly).
- The monthly aging report.

If the system of checks and balances is effective, this event would have triggered the following actions:

1. The collections department should have automatically sent a delinquent notice to the tenant within a predefined number of days after the rental due date (usually five days depending on the lease terms and asset type) with a copy of the notice to the property manager and lease administrator.
2. The property manager should have contacted the tenant to determine if there has been an error or oversight. If there is not an error

or oversight, and the tenant is aware of the delinquency, then the property manager should review the lease to ascertain the actions of the tenant and landlord in this situation. The lease may state that a penalty can be charged, or other specific actions. Pending the circumstances (if the tenant regularly pays late or if this is a first time), give the tenant a grace period to pay.

3. If the tenant still has not paid after the grace period, then the property manager should advise the asset manager to determine how to go forward, or notify the legal department and determine the next course of action. Usually a default notice is the next step. The statutes governing the procedure to handle a delinquent tenant vary from state to state. In addition, the manager must advise accounting/accounts receivable.

The outcome of the efforts to collect the delinquent payment will determine the action plan of the asset manager. Depending on the circumstances, the asset manager may take the following actions:

- Instruct the controller to contact the lender and advise of the deficiency. The asset manager may request a grace period; however, he or she should ascertain if a penalty is due under the terms of the loan agreement.
- Determine potential sources of cash to fund the mortgage payment. The asset manager may (as a last option) contact the owner to determine if a cash contribution is necessary to fund the deficiency.
- Through the property manager, ascertain the purpose of the delinquency and if feasible, coordinate a payment plan with the tenant.
- Meet with the leasing agent to determine the marketability of the space. If the space is not marketable, then a workout with the tenant may be the best course of action. If the space is marketable or better economic terms could be achieved from a new tenant, then the asset manager may decide to evict the tenant unless all arrearages are paid.
- Through the property manager, authorize the attorney to commence eviction proceeding.

One event, the failure of the tenant to pay rent, initiated actions from the various professionals. This example illustrates how the asset management system works to coordinate the information flow between the various professionals involved in the successful operation of the property. In this case, remedying the situation involved professionals in the following areas:

1. Asset management.
2. Property management.

3. Collections.
4. Legal counsel.
5. Lending institution.
6. Leasing.
7. Lease administration.
8. Accounting—accounts receivable.
9. Accounting—accounts payable.

Numerous professionals were motivated to remedy this situation because it threatened the profitability of the asset, as well as their positions. Thus, because tangible performance measurements (including profitability) exist, the various professionals are motivated to deliver a superior performance and ensure that the profitability is protected.

The structure of the asset management system will vary depending on the asset type, circumstances of the asset manager, and overall legal structure of the asset. However, as demonstrated, *the system* channels information to the appropriate people in the organization. By delineating and delegating the responsibility of these specialized professions, the environment tends to maximize profit. Through an effective asset management system, the asset manager should coordinate the various professions to achieve the specific goals of the owner in an effective and orderly manner.

§ 2.9 RISK/REWARD AND THE PURSUIT OF PROFIT

Real estate investment by third parties follows the risk/reward theory of investing. The investor assumes a level of risk in exchange for an equivalent (as measured in the market) economic return. Theoretically, knowledge/information is the factor balancing risk/reward. If complete information necessary to accurately measure risk were available to all parties, then risk would equal reward with no discrepancies. But because perfect information is rarely available, sophisticated investors build wealth by pursuing profit where the reward is higher than the risk assumed. So what does this have to do with your corporation? Everything, if you want to take advantage of a unique opportunity.

An inherent risk is associated with real estate investment by a third party. Risk in this investment sense is merely a function of the unknown. For example, a building with a long-term lease to a corporation that has had a triple-A credit rating for 20 years is perceived as having a lower risk factor due to the relatively stabilized and predictable income stream over the term of the lease. On the other hand, the same lease to a start-up venture with minimal capital would be perceived as an enormous risk.

The corporation, in utilizing the asset, is very much in control of a large portion of the risk assumed by a third-party investor, risk in which the return is measured, and on balance, demanded by the third-party investor. So why not capitalize on this risk/reward phenomenon and keep the profit for the shareholders?

Through the long-term planning function, the corporation can control its real estate needs. If the needs are long-term, then it may be advantageous for the firm to develop its own facilities and capitalize on the value of a long-term lease. On the other hand, if the needs are short-term, it may be economically feasible to lease space from a third party rather than undertake a large capital expenditure. The real estate executive should coordinate the corporation's real estate needs with a focus on achieving profits.

The profit-motivation environment greatly alters how the asset is managed and how profits are realized. Real estate ownership has no prejudice; the corporate owner's management of the asset can achieve the same profit potential as that of the commercial investor owner. The difference is the level and quality of management service and techniques used to achieve and measure profitability.

The first step in achieving profit is to desire profit. Thus corporations wishing to capitalize on this potentially profitable endeavor should begin by recognizing the importance of establishing management policies that will approach the corporate real estate assets as a profit opportunity center.

Once these policies are established, firms can set goals and authorize properly trained, motivated personnel with expertise in commercial asset management to operate this profit-opportunity center. The next step would be to develop strategic plans to achieve these goals. The ingredients are all there, all you have to do is go forward!

§ 2.10 THE NEW REAL ESTATE ASSET MANAGEMENT INDUSTRY

This chapter has addressed the linkages between national economic factors of change; industry factors of change; the profit-oriented asset management techniques of the commercial asset manager *and* the unmistakable shift toward downsizing, decentralization, and outsourcing by corporate America.

As a result of these trends, the real estate industry is evolving from a "project-oriented" to a "process-oriented" business. Exhibit 2.5 illustrates this change, from the perspective of marketing, finance, and the overall organization.

The real estate industry has evolved from a higher profit-oriented development and brokerage environment to one based on the fee-service

EXHIBIT 2.5 Moving from a Project-Oriented to a Process-Oriented Business

Project Oriented	Process Oriented
Marketing	
One project at a time	Continuous stream of business
No guarantee of follow-on projects	Repeat business generally assured if customer satisfied
Higher margins	Lower margins
Higher risk	Lower risk
Finance	
Unique deal structure	More uniform contract structure
Constantly changing financing markets	More or less consistent financing
Project-by-project financing	Corporate financing potential
Limited access to public equity market	Broader access to public equity market
Potential for major surprises; constant restructuring of financing vehicles	More stable financing structure
Organization	
Job shop	Assembly line
Barely contained anarchy	Efficient
Exciting and ever changing	Consistent
Fighter pilots	Ship's crew
High turnover	Stable work force

business. The service side, which was considered secondary, is now primary for survival in both the short-term and long-term future of a third-party real estate company. Experts in the real estate field all agree that the basic development/brokerage concept was too narrow in focus. In addition, the ease of credit provided the industry with less than qualified talent to produce an easy and substantial profit. Revised strategies for some of the more prominent development/brokerage companies indicate that they view themselves no longer as in the development/brokerage business but more broadly, as in the real estate business. There is a recognition in the industry that the "easy days" are over and the need exists for talented people to perform tasks on a high-quality service basis in a highly competitive environment. As a result of these structural industry shifts corporate users are seeking and purchasing additional services.

The strategic planning process used by the corporation (see Chapter One) is a first-rate guide to assessing these corporate needs. The approach includes answering the following basic questions:

- How do you identify potential client needs?
- How do you assess your internal and external strengths and weaknesses?
- How should you be organized for optimum service and profit opportunities?
- What services can you offer realistically?
- Where do you need to strengthen internal and external capabilities to really be "full service"?
- How much additional operating expense (overhead) will be required?
- Do you really need and want the corporate client business?

Many traditional real estate companies are searching for the answers and eagerly courting the business. The answers are all in this book.

Chapter Three presents information on the corporate environment within which the real estate executive functions and makes the decisions that impacts new and profitable opportunities facing the traditional full-service real estate company.

Three

An Overview of Corporate and Commercial Real Estate Performance Measurement

§ 3.1 INTRODUCTION

Corporate real estate executives are paid for superior performance. Their success depends on their ability to manage a diverse organization, to motivate key personnel and functions, and to make firm, judicious, and productive business decisions based on the analysis of performance measurements. Risk is always present, because choosing among alternatives requires the assumption of risk. Corporate real estate executives get paid for taking risks and, on balance, making money.

Managing a real estate operation with a line or profit center attitude can produce handsome bottom-line results. The extra dollars earned are "found money," since by definition, the company already owns or leases the necessary property; like it or not, the firm is already in the real estate business.

The first step in implementing profit-oriented real estate management is to measure current performance.

§ 3.2 PERFORMANCE MEASUREMENT

When dealing with real estate within a business, there are two tiers of performance measurement: occupancy cost, which measures utilization of the real estate; and corporate profit, which measures real estate department performance relative to the overall profitability of the company. This performance is ultimately reflected on the company's return to the shareholders. Inefficient operations will diminish that return, whereas efficient streamlined real estate operations can result in more dollars to the shareholders—the ultimate performance measurement by the marketplace.

The two measurements are interrelated. Efficiency on the occupancy cost level is a function of efficient policy decisions on the corporate level.

(a) OCCUPANCY COSTS

Occupancy costs are defined as follows: *any and all costs associated with owning and/or leasing corporate facilities, whether by virtue of a contract or incident, for the purpose of housing company operations and personnel.*

In today's environment, U.S. corporations are struggling to find opportunities for increased profitability at every corner. Many have begun to realize that efficiently utilizing their real estate assets, which as we have said before, generally comprise 25 percent to 40 percent of total corporate assets, can dramatically affect corporate returns. To illustrate; a $1 decrease in occupancy costs will translate into a $1 increase in corporate profitability. As a point of comparison, assuming a company generates a 10 percent return on sales, a $1 increase in profits will require a $10 increase in sales. Managing occupancy costs from an opportunistic perspective has some very interesting implications.[1]

- During the 1980s, many corporate managers made real estate commitments without regard to corporate strategy. In most cases, these commitments involved long-term leases or outright purchases. These managers failed to realize that once the documents are signed, fixed costs increase accordingly for an extended time period. Consequently, management must constantly keep in mind the strategic direction of the company to evaluate ramifications with respect to corporate real estate. Without such constant attention, the utilization of real estate assets becomes increasingly inefficient.
- The fragmentation of real estate markets makes location a prime determinant of occupancy costs. For example, rent differentials between center city and suburban locations can be as much as 100 percent for similar quality office space. With respect to layout, decisions should be made by corporate business professionals and based on an analysis of needs and value, rather than by building professionals who generally focus primarily on aesthetic appeal, which tends to drive up costs. In terms of leasing, lessees often believe that the lowest cost lease is the one with the most abatements and concessions. However, the more practical manager will realize that total lease costs have many quantitative and nonquantitative aspects that are not immediately clear to the novice.

  Consequently, effective rent is the proper indicator of total lease costs. Compounding these factors, managers and employees may get so enamored with a particular facility or location that they fail to scrutinize the true value of the facility. Such a condition leads to breaking one of the "cardinal rules" of real estate acquisition and investment, which is "never let yourself get emotionally attached to the real estate." Breaking this rule has caused the fall of many companies and investors. Further, like any initiative, the corporate real estate executive, with the support of senior

[1] Numerous articles have been written on this subject. The interested reader may wish to review Joel R. Parker, "Managing Occupancy Costs: Opportunities and Challenges," Industrial Development Research Council, *Industrial Development,* April 1991.

management, must be the champion of such an initiative, if it is to be truly successful.

- Total occupancy costs are driven by the costs of capital, operations, and administration. Capital costs typically range from 15 percent to 50 percent of total occupancy costs and are made up of costs to finish and equip the facility that are incurred under either a lease or purchase decision. The cost of operation will generally range from 30 percent to 80 percent of total occupancy costs and are driven by costs including rent, financing, escalations, pass-throughs, and so on. Unfortunately, many times leases are viewed as an operating expense which takes a short-term perspective on what amounts to a long-term decision. To efficiently control occupancy costs, managers must realize that a lease commitment amounts to a long-term strategic investment. Administrative costs, which usually range within 5 percent to 10 percent of occupancy costs, cover all personnel, internal and external, who devise, implement, and control the occupancy cost process.
- Regrettably, many corporate managers do not attempt to correlate space utilization with its value to corporate profitability. In fact, many managers view occupancy costs as a small part of total operating expenses. This common perspective appears to be a function of not understanding and/or not having data, that reflect true occupancy costs. To control occupancy costs efficiently, management must have the desire and the information to do so. In most cases, the quickest way to get managers to focus on an issue is to make the outcomes of their decisions with respect to the issue have an effect on their personal pockets. The structure of these objectives must be carefully thought out, however. Otherwise, managers will focus on immediate occupancy cost reduction efforts at the expense of the future.

Based on a particular organization's perspective of the preceding principles and their business segment(s), there is a significant range of occupancy costs. Exhibit 3.1 shows the results of a survey conducted in 1988 and 1989 that attempted to benchmark this range.[2]

The survey results clearly imply that efficient occupancy cost management could significantly improve an organization's competitive position by reducing its total fixed costs. In a micro level, performance is based on the utilization of the real estate asset in a maneuver that will minimize the occupancy cost associated with the utilization of the asset, maximize productivity, and reduce overall costs.

[2] The study was authored by Edmond P. Rondeau, Principal, Rondeau & Associates, Atlanta, Georgia, under the sponsorship of the Chevron Corporation.

EXHIBIT 3.1 Ranges for Occupancy Costs

	1988	1989
Occupancy Costs		
Minimum	$0.03 billion	$0.05 billion
Maximum	$1.00 billion	$1.00 billion
Occupancy Costs as a % of Expenses		
Minimum	0.30	0.26
Maximum	8.57	7.85
Revenue per Employee		
Minimum/S.F.	$ 303	$ 306
Maximum/S.F.	$5,493	$5,998
Occupancy Costs		
Minimum/S.F.	$15.42	$15.19
Maximum/S.F.	$50.57	$48.28
Occupancy Costs/S.F. as a % of Revenue/Employee		
Minimum	94.03	92.93
Maximum	99.72	99.75

Let's examine how to measure the economic performance of real estate assets on the micro level and discuss strategies for better utilizing those assets by minimizing costs and maximizing income.

The first step in cost minimization is to *define* the cost components associated with the assets. The most common costs are:

- Rental expense
- Cost of capital
- Electricity
- Water/sewer opportunity cost
- Natural gas
- Telecommunications
- Cleaning
- Property taxes
- Insurance
- Roof
- Structure
- Landscape

- Parking lot
- Handicap elevator

Depending on the legal structure defining your rights to utilize the asset (i.e., whether you lease or own), there can be various costs for which your organization is not responsible. If you lease, some of these costs may be the responsibility of the landlord; thus, it is your responsibility to fully understand the lease agreement to ensure that you are paying only those costs for which you are responsible. Often, tenants incorrectly assume costs of the landlord. Once you have identified your costs, you must measure them and determine whether they reflect efficient management practices that will maximize bottom-line profit.

As a general rule, the rent, utility, and property tax expenses are the largest expenses associated with real estate utilization. They should be closely monitored so that they remain in line with the market standard. Logically, if your organization is paying more per square foot to lease warehouse space than your competitor across the street, it should be easy to figure out who will have the competitive advantage, assuming all other factors are equal.

To ensure that your operating costs are in line with the market, periodically compare these expenses with the market; more specifically, with good substitute properties. For example, say you own a 100,000-square-foot warehouse in Atlanta, Georgia, with the following annual costs:

Rent	$ 279,000
Electricity	137,000
Water/Sewer	50,000
Taxes	75,000

Then your per-square-foot costs are:

Rent	$ 2.79
Electricity	1.37
Water/Sewer	.50
Taxes	.75

Based on these costs, you can research the market for comparable properties to ensure your costs are in line. You can then supplement this information with your own market analyses and explore procedures to further reduce costs. For example, you may learn that rental rates for comparable buildings are $2.25/sf. You may want to bring this to your landlord's attention to determine if there are ways to cut your annual rental expense. If your lease is up for renewal, the lessor may be willing to renew it at a lower rate or give incentives. Or, you may want to consider relocating your business, or possibly purchasing the building if your cost of capital is lower than the cost of rent and the long-term cost of capital is likely to be lower than the cost of rent and the asset.

Other sources can provide comparable studies to measure the cost performance of your asset (see §§ 3.1(b)–(c)). The local taxing authority can give information on standard tax costs and the procedure to contest tax expense if it is too high. This point is discussed more extensively in Chapter Seventeen.

If your utility costs are high for the market or your utilization of the asset, the local utility companies may be able to suggest ways to minimize these costs such as insulation, light refit, window treatments, and/or revised company policy regarding the turning off of lights, and other energy-consuming devices when not in use.

If the company leases or owns real estate assets that are not 100 percent utilized, then you should explore alternatives to achieve income on the nonutilized portions. As a lessee, you may want to sublet a portion or all of the asset to another user and in effect assume the role of a landlord, your own lease permitting. Or your analysis of the market may suggest that you can maximize by selling an asset.

(b) COMMERCIAL PROPERTY REFERENCE MATERIALS[3]

An outstanding service that the Building Owners and Managers Association (BOMA)[4] and the Institute of Real Estate Management (IREM)[5] provide to the office building industry are their annual operating expense reports. BOMA publishes the *Experience Exchange Report,* and IREM publishes the *Income/Expense Analysis, Office Buildings, Downtown and Suburban.*

The BOMA *Experience Exchange Report* is a compilation of information on office buildings of all types throughout the United States. The report compares buildings by size, age, location, and specific characteristics. Income and expenses are broken down into categories and then compared on the basis of the highest cost, the lowest cost, and the median for that item. Costs are also stated on the basis of cents per square foot.

The Institute of Real Estate Management's *Income/Expense Analysis* is an annual publication analyzing office buildings' income and expenses in every metropolitan area and suburban area. Operating expenses and vacancy trends are analyzed in chart and graph formats. It is always helpful and enlightening to compare buildings with similar characteristics when

[3] See also Alan A. Alexander and Richard F. Muhlebach, *Managing and Leasing Commercial Properties* (New York: John Wiley & Sons, 1988).

[4] BOMA, 1250 Eye St., NW, Suite 200, Washington, DC 20005, (202) 289-7000.

[5] IREM, 430 North Michigan Avenue, Chicago, IL 60611-4090, (312) 661-1930.

setting the budget for a proposed or new building, preparing the operating budgets of an existing building, and evaluating expenses at year's end. These reports are also helpful in evaluating whether the building's property tax assessment is correct and in appealing the assessment. Both BOMA and IREM publish several other informative publications.

The best comparative measure of tenant over costs (and sales) in the shopping center industry is *Dollars and Cents of Shopping Centers,* published every three years by the Urban Land Institute. This book has excellent comparative figures on various aspects of retail leases of interest to the shopping center manager. The book is organized by center types, geographic areas, and tenant types. It provides store size ranges, sales ranges and medians, percentage rental rate ranges and medians, and occupancy cost ranges and medians. By comparing a center's or tenant's sales with those in *Dollars and Cents,* the property manager can gauge how well the tenants are performing. It is often necessary to extrapolate and interpret the information in light of individual situations, but the guide is helpful in analyzing existing tenants as well as prospective tenants.

In summary, defining the specific cost components associated with owning or leasing real estate assets is the first step toward controlling them.

§ 3.3 ASSETS, LIABILITIES, AND CASH FLOWS

Assets refer to those things that a company owns (cash, securities, patents, inventory, property, plant, and equipment) or has a right to (accounts receivable, leased property). Liabilities refer to those things that a company owes (accounts payable, bank notes payable, mortgage notes payable). Assets can be used to pay, reduce, or retire liabilities. Accordingly, there is a significant relationship between assets and liabilities and a practical necessity for maintaining this relationship in some form of healthy balance. Therefore, asset management refers to organized activities and efforts to identify and sustain a predefined equational balance between assets and liabilities. A balance sheet displays the results of these efforts in corporate financial (monthly, quarterly, and annually) reports, which when properly prepared and audited, tell the educated reader about the quality of the real estate management. (Also see Chapter Thirteen.)

(a) MEASUREMENT VIA THE BALANCE SHEET

Exhibit 3.2 shows the 1992 consolidated balance sheet of Home Depot, Inc. It describes the status of the company's asset base and reflects the positive impact of the real estate department on the company's asset management program.

EXHIBIT 3.2 Sample Consolidated Balance Sheets

	February 2, 1992	February 3, 1991
LIABILITIES AND STOCKHOLDERS' EQUITY		
CURRENT LIABILITIES:		
Accounts Payable	$ 293,958	$ 235,267
Accrued Salaries and Related Expenses	92,531	63,547
Sales Taxes Payable	34,387	26,806
Other Accrued Expenses	89,305	76,381
Income Taxes Payable	22,288	8,800
Current Installments of Long-Term Debt (note 2)	1,842	1,906
Total Current Liabilities	534,311	412,707
LONG-TERM DEBT, excluding current installments (notes 2 and 6)	270,575	530,774
OTHER LONG-TERM LIABILITIES	7,126	4,415
DEFERRED INCOME TAXES (note 3)	7,068	8,205
STOCKHOLDERS' EQUITY (notes 2 and 4):		
Common stock, par value $.05. Authorized: 250,000,000 shares; issued and outstanding – 211,112,000 shares at February 2, 1992 and 177,099,000 shares at February 3, 1991	10,556	8,855
Paid-in Capital	1,032,598	261,349
Retained Earnings	666,471	439,770
	1,709,625	709,974
Less Notes Receivable From ESOP (note 6)	18,413	26,572
Total Stockholders' Equity	1,691,212	683,402
COMMITMENTS AND CONTINGENCIES (notes 5 and 8)		
	$2,510,292	$1,639,503

	February 2, 1992	February 3, 1991
ASSETS		
CURRENT ASSETS:		
Cash and Cash Equivalents	$ 218,549	$ 107,895
Short-term Investments, including current maturities of long-term investments (note 7)	176,650	29,401
Accounts Receivable, Net	79,472	49,325
Merchandise Inventories	662,257	509,022
Other Current Assets	21,320	17,931
Total Current Assets	1,158,248	713,574
PROPERTY AND EQUIPMENT, at cost:		
Land	386,453	262,560
Buildings	444,249	272,095
Furniture, Fixtures and Equipment	253,831	186,025
Leasehold Improvements	178,460	160,760
Construction in Progress	120,390	82,179
	1,383,383	963,619
Less Accumulated Depreciation and Amortization	128,609	84,889
Net Property and Equipment	1,254,774	878,730
LONG-TERM INVESTMENTS (note 7)	64,268	–
COST IN EXCESS OF THE FAIR VALUE OF NET ASSETS ACQUIRED, net of accumulated amortization of $4,523 at February 2, 1992 and $3,891 at February 3, 1991	20,768	21,400
OTHER	12,234	25,799
	$2,510,292	$1,639,503

See accompanying notes to consolidated financial statements.

From Exhibit 3.2, we can see that net property assets (before depreciation and amortization) of Home Depot, Inc., total $1.383 billion, with real estate assets (land, improvements, and buildings) totaling $1.129 billion, or 82 percent of the net property assets. If we include related real estate assets (furniture, fixtures, and equipment), then real estate and related assets represent 100 percent of Home Depot, Inc.'s total fixed assets.

If we extend the analysis to the bottom of Exhibit 3.2—to shareholders' equity—you can see that corporate real estate assets equal approximately 67 percent of this vital statistic, while including the real estate related assets discussed above pushes the level to 75 percent.

Home Depot's debt ratio is indeed enviable at just over 10 percent of total assets. Further, it has a very solid liquidity position as evidenced by both its cash and working capital positions. What does this have to do with corporate real estate? First, Home Depot's senior management has indicated it has a 50:50 target ratio of leased versus owned stores. Because of Home Depot's high level of liquidity, a significant portion of the 50 percent-owned store target can be capitalized with cash. Second, Home Depot's primary method of issuing debt is through long-term subordinated debentures. This allows the company to match long-term assets with long-term liabilities. More importantly, however, such a vehicle provides an extremely attractive coupon rate of interest (usually 60 percent of the market rate for a standard corporate debenture) as well as an equity conversion feature. Consequently, to the extent debt is used to finance expansion (real estate in reality), such expansion is capitalized at a low cost and decreased risk to the company. This strategy successfully reduces to a manageable level the concern many corporations express over the ownership of real estate—the effects on the balance sheet.

Home Depot utilizes such a strategy because management realizes that its tremendous growth and success is not only a function of its product but, equally as important, a function of the "franchise value" that it creates at its locations. Therefore, Home Depot is just as much in the real estate business as it is in the "do-it-yourself home improvement business."

(b) MEASUREMENT VIA STATEMENT OF CASH FLOWS

Exhibit 3.3, also taken from the Home Depot 1992 annual report, provides further insights into the importance of effective asset management and into the critically important contribution the corporate real estate executive can make to a company's economic vitality.

Among other things, Exhibit 3.3 shows that sales of property were minimal. The exhibit also shows that Home Depot expended $432 million capital dollars for property additions during 1991. Note that Home Depot reports real estate under cash flows from "investment activities" in accordance with generally accepted reporting requirements.

EXHIBIT 3.3 Sample Statement of Cash Flows

	Fiscal Year Ended		
	February 2, 1992	February 3, 1991	January 28, 1990
CASH PROVIDED FROM OPERATIONS:			
Net Earnings	$249,150	$163,428	$111,954
Reconciliation of Net Earnings to Net Cash Provided by Operations:			
Depreciation and Amortization	52,283	34,358	21,107
Deferred Income Tax (Benefit) Expense	(2,082)	688	(2,880)
Increase in Receivables, Net	(30,147)	(10,392)	(16,063)
Increase in Merchandise Inventories	(153,235)	(127,570)	(87,178)
Increase in Accounts Payable and Accrued Expenses	108,180	111,059	99,106
Increase (Decrease) in Income Taxes Payable	28,063	16,496	(2,067)
Other	14,405	(7,371)	(7,220)
Total	17,467	17,268	4,805
Net Cash Provided by Operations	266,617	180,696	116,759
CASH FLOWS FROM INVESTING ACTIVITIES:			
Capital Expenditures, Net of $538, $2,100 and $14,728 of non-cash capital expenditures in 1991, 1990 and 1989, respectively	(431,660)	(398,105)	(190,244)
Proceeds from Sale of Property and Equipment	831	229	719
(Purchase) Sale of Short-term Investments, Net	(132,124)	36,455	(65,856)
Purchase of Long-term Investments	(85,844)	–	–
Proceeds from Maturities of Long-term Investments	6,451	–	–
Advances Secured by Real Estate	–	(7,389)	–
Net Cash Used in Investing Activities	(642,346)	(368,810)	(255,381)
CASH FLOWS FROM FINANCING ACTIVITIES:			
Repayments Under Revolving Line of Credit, Net	–	–	(71,000)
Proceeds from Long-term Borrowings	5,200	230,000	258,750
Cash Loaned to ESOP	–	(19,655)	(345)
Repayments of Notes Receivable from ESOP	8,159	7,428	6,000
Principal Repayments of Long-term Debt	(7,141)	(1,567)	(5,871)
Proceeds from Sale of Common Stock, Net	502,614	23,113	13,146
Cash Dividends Paid to Stockholders	(22,449)	(12,835)	(8,386)
Net Cash Provided by Financing Activities	486,383	226,484	192,294
Increase in Cash and Cash Equivalents	110,654	38,370	53,672
Cash and Cash Equivalents at Beginning of Year	107,895	69,525	15,853
Cash and Cash Equivalents at End of Year	$218,549	$107,895	$ 69,525
SUPPLEMENTAL DISCLOSURE OF CASH PAYMENTS MADE FOR:			
Interest (net of interest capitalized)	$ 16,366	$ 21,138	$ 11,831
Income Taxes	$119,901	$ 78,427	$ 69,016

See accompanying notes to consolidated financial statements.

Several notes to these financial statements give an even better idea of the real estate asset manager's contribution.

Note 5, Leases (Exhibit 3.4), indicates that total lease expenses for the year ending February 2, 1992, are $87,750,000. Assuming this represents a 10 percent return to the lessor, this indicates $877.5 million of real estate value. Since these leases are triple net, the indicated value represents additional real estate inventory that is being managed by Home Depot's real estate department. Note 10, Subsequent event, indicates that the company issued $805 million of Convertible Subordinated Notes at par and that the dollars raised will be primarily utilized to fund future store expansion. Assuming the company continues with its strategy to use 50 percent ownership and 50 percent leases for store operations, the indications are the corporate real estate department will be responsible for the management of $1.6 billion of real estate assets over and above its $2 billion current responsibilities (fixed assets plus indicated property value implicit in the operating leases).

§ 3.4 MEASURING CURRENT PERFORMANCE

The financial statements represent only a static report of events gone by, cash generated, and obligations assumed. They do not answer the question, "How can I track present activity, be informed of future profit goals, and measure performance on a current basis?"

We will illustrate answers with two kinds of reports—the Status Report and the Quota Report. In its annual status report, the real estate department details its activities, particularly those relating to the disposition of surplus properties and the concurrent cash flow into the corporate coffers. In its quota report, the real estate department indicates to top management the department's prospects for the coming year and how those prospects relate to the corporation's operational and financial objectives.

These reports stress dispositions rather than acquisitions, and this is only natural, since sales mean "cash in" and purchases mean "cash out." While we do not minimize the necessity for skillful negotiations and so forth, for purposes of central information transmission, the reports should stress those elements that have the most dramatic impact on the company's fiscal posture.

(a) THE STATUS REPORT

The specific format for this kind of report is a matter of personal preference, but it should provide the top corporate leadership with a logical and concise presentation of action information. This report probably represents the best opportunity to evaluate the real estate department's current status and its activities during the past performance period.

EXHIBIT 3.4 Sample Note to Consolidated Financial Statements

LEASES

The company leases certain retail locations, office space, warehouse and distribution space, equipment and vehicle operating leases. As leases expire, it can be expected that in the normal course of business, they will be renewed or replaced. Total rent expense, net of minor sublease income, for the fiscal years ending February 2, 1992, February 3, 1991, and January 28, 1990, amounted to $87,750,000, $68,691,000 and $48,515,000, respectively. Real estate taxes, insurance, maintenance and operating expenses applicable to leased property are obligations of the Company under the building leases. Certain of the store leases provide for contingent rentals based percentages of sales in excess of specified amounts. Contingent rentals for fiscal years ended February 2, 1992, February 2, 1991, and January 28, 1990, were approximately $4,381,000, $3,328,000 and $2,072,000 respectively.

SUBSEQUENT EVENT

On February 3, 1992, the Company issued, through a public offering, $805 million of its 4 1/2% Convertible Subordinated Notes at par, maturing February 15, 1997. The notes are convertible into shares of common stock at any time prior to maturity, unless previously redeemed, at a conversion price of $77.50 per share, subject to adjustment under certain conditions. The notes may be redeemed in whole or in part during the period beginning March 3, 1995, and ending on February 14, 1996, at 101.125% of their principal amount and thereafter at 100% of their principal amount. The notes are not subject to sinking fund provisions. The net proceeds of $796,000,000 from the sale of the notes will be used principally for the company's capital expenditure programs over the next several years, including store expansions and renovations.

Exhibit 3.5 illustrates an acceptable format. Following a dated title page, the report gives a short summary of the real estate inventory. This summary should state the total land acreage, the amount of properties owned and leased, the dollars involved in lease commitments, and the amount of square footage managed. The report should then present a detailed analysis of the dollar amount of surplus properties marketed within the last fiscal year as well as the total consideration received by the company and, most importantly, the net book gain or loss. The purpose is to indicate the impact of these transactions, not only on cash flow but also on corporate earnings. The report cannot show how these transactions have improved the operations of the various divisions, but the company should be cognizant of such benefits.

The report can also compare the dollar figures involved in surplus property sales with the real estate departmental budget in order to indicate the rate of return on assets. The status report should also emphasize the management aspects of lease activity because it is a vital part of the total real estate management function and represents significant future dollar commitments.

EXHIBIT 3.5 Sample Status Report Format

Annual Status Report

1. Title page: Identify real estate department, sender, recipient, and date.
2. Inventory status:
   a. Number of acres owned
   b. Number of square feet of building space
   c. Number of square feet leased
   d. Number of leases
   e. Remaining dollar commitment
   f. Number of manufacturing plants, sales offices, warehouses, and service centers.
3. List of surplus properties sold:
   a. Direct sales of real estate by property description, consideration received, net book value, division identification, date of closing
   b. Real estate included in sales of businesses (same information as for direct sales of real estate).
4. Maps identifying sale locations.
5. Lease activity information:
   a. New organizations
   b. Renewals
   c. Expansions.
6. Maps identifying lease activity.
7. Surplus real estate disposal report:
   a. Properties approved for disposition
   b. Likely prospects for disposition.

(b) THE QUOTA, OR ANTICIPATED PERFORMANCE, REPORT

Corporate operating divisions and groups generate annual operating plans (AOPs) and long-range plans (LRPs) concerning certain stated objectives and the dollars necessary to meet those objectives. In much the same manner, the real estate department should file its own "annual operating plan," indicating that certain corporate assets are going to be committed to the pursuit of certain operational objectives. Corporate real estate executives should require such a report as a matter of course. As shown in Exhibit 3.6, the report should take a specific position; that is, the real estate department should state that based on the stock of inventory it expects to manage, it will achieve certain objectives within the fiscal year. Thus, the department can be evaluated consistently in the same way as any other operating unit.

Senior management can compare the status report with the quota report to see whether or not the department has obtained the anticipated level of activity. Thus, the quota report permits management to judge the attitude *and* performance of department personnel.

(c) THE MONTHLY ACTIVITY REPORT

The last item in Exhibit 3.5 indicates a surplus real estate disposal report is included in the annual status report. Actually, the surplus property report should be revised on a monthly basis as part of a continuing monitoring of department activity. Exhibit 3.7 shows a good example of a surplus property report. This type of form should clearly depict the current status of the surplus real estate sales effort, the opportunities for cash generation that it provides, and the pre-tax and after-tax effect of each potential sale. Note especially that the surplus real estate disposal report should provide some advance information on contemplated dispositions.

EXHIBIT 3.6 Sample Quota Report Format

Quota Report

1. Title page: Identify real estate department, sender, recipient, and date.
2. Organization chart: Personnel, title, report channels, and budget information.
3. Operating objectives for coming fiscal year.
4. Financial objectives for coming fiscal year.
5. Identification by property of anticipated fiscal year sales: Identify division, net book value, and anticipated sales price.

EXHIBIT 3.7 Sample Surplus Property Report

S: Sell
L: Lease
SL: Sublease

Date ________
Page ____ of ____

Div./ Oper.	Property Location	Owned/ Leased	Bldg. Size Land Area	Date Avail.	Est. Mkt. Value	Current Net Book Value	Annual Real Estate Tax	Appropriation/ Request Approval Date	Objective (sell or lease)	Disposal Status

This report should be supplemented by a narrative description of all department activities. This information is generally provided by the staff members involved in the projects.

After preparation of a detailed monthly report for internal department circulation, the highlights are reproduced in a transmittal document that goes to the responsible senior-level executive, such as the vice president-operations, with subjects capsulized under the headings "Accomplishments, Information, Problems" (A-I-P). The full report can serve as backup, should clarification and amplification of the summary report be needed.

The monthly activity report should stress the beneficial effects that real estate actions have on operating divisions. For example, the real estate department may have negotiated a utility easement at little or no cost with a local power company servicing one of the company's manufacturing plants. Although the financial impact of this transaction is negligible, the power line may have permitted the plant to increase its production capacity significantly—a real operational benefit.

(d) THE BOARD OF DIRECTORS REPORT

The acquisition and disposition of land and buildings—or the acquisition and disposition of debt in the case of mortgages or capital leases—affects the corporation's financial stability. The board of directors, mentioned in Chapter One, provides overall policy guidance and is directly accountable to the shareholders. Consequently, the board should have a keen interest in real estate transactions, because these directly affect the balance sheet. The real estate department should be required by the board to report significant real estate transactions, sales, acquisitions, leases, and so on, based on a dollar figure "cutoff." Exhibit 3.8 illustrates the format for such a report.

In summary, you can certainly monitor, measure, and evaluate the operating performance of a real estate department. If the department has been delegated the authority necessary for effective performance and is, in fact, operating productively, it occupies a unique niche in the traditional staff category because its results can be measured in dollar terms. It is at least one staff function that needs no defense as a "corporate burden"!

§ 3.5 GAAP REPORTING

Generally accepted accounting principles (GAAP) create a standardized reporting method so that financial statements provide objective and verifiable measures, with minimum subjectivity. Such standards maximize financial statement comparability. Under GAAP, assets are recorded

EXHIBIT 3.8 Real Estate Department Report to Board of Directors—Acquisitions/Sales/Leases over $500,000—First and Second Quarters, Fiscal Year 1992

Location/Description	Consideration Total Lease Commitment	Seller/Lessor	Buyer/Lessee	Closing	Net Book Value	Remarks

based on their original costs, with periodic adjustments to account for physical, technical, and economic obsolescence.

Regrettably, no consideration is given to the unique characteristic of real estate assets; namely, that their value is likely to appreciate, rather than depreciate, over time. As a result, the fair market value of the real estate asset can gradually increase, while its book value decreases. If a corporation holds a real estate asset for an extended period, the gap between its fair market value and its book value may become exceedingly large. This creates the following problems:

- The market value of the corporation is understated since the traditional stock price valuation model does not reflect this discrepancy.
- It is impossible for the market to make this adjustment to the stock valuation model, since GAAP-based financial statements do not provide the necessary information to determine either the current or possible future value of corporate real estate assets.

§ 3.6 THE FINANCIAL ACCOUNTING STANDARDS BOARD (FASB)

The Financial Accounting Standards Board is the body designated by the American Institute of Certified Public Accountants (AICPA) to establish generally accepted accounting principles. The FASB issues *Statements of Financial Accounting Standards* (SFAS). This section briefly describes those Statements that relate specifically to real estate assets.

- *SFAS No. 5, "Accounting for Contingencies," issued March 1975.* This Statement defines a contingency as an existing condition, situation, or set of circumstances involving uncertainty as to a possible gain or loss, and which will be resolved when one or more future events occur or fail to occur. This SFAS specifies how to account for such possible gain or loss. An estimated loss is accrued by a charge against income if both of the following conditions are met:
  - It must be probable that one or more future events will occur, which will confirm the fact that a loss has occurred.
  - The amount of the loss can be reasonably estimated.

  With respect to a potential gain, disclosure is made in the financial statement, using sufficient care to avoid misleading implications as to the likelihood of the realization.
- *SFAS No. 13, "Accounting for Leases," issued November 1976.* Although this SFAS covers a host of different issues, the most

important one for the corporate real estate professional is the establishment of criteria to classify a lease as a capital lease, rather than an operating lease, for financial reporting purposes. A lease may be deemed a capital lease if it satisfies any one of the following criteria:

- The lease transfers ownership of the property to the lessee at the end of the lease term.
- The lease contains a bargain purchase option, defined as a purchase option that may be exercised by the lessee at below the fair market value of the leased property.
- The lease term is equivalent to 75 percent of the asset's economic life. This criterion does not apply if the lease term falls within 25 percent of the total remaining economic life of the asset.
- The present value of the minimum lease payments, at the beginning of the lease term, equal or exceed 90 percent of the fair market value of the leased property.

To the extent that any of the preceding criteria are found to hold true, the lease is treated as a capital lease. Otherwise, it is treated as an operating lease.

- *SFAS No. 34, "Capitalization of Interest Cost," issued October 1979.* This Statement establishes standards for capitalizing interest costs as part of the historical cost of acquiring certain assets. The eligible interest cost is restricted to interest cost recognized on indebtedness. The amount of interest cost that may be capitalized is restricted to the cost incurred during the period it takes to ready the asset for its intended use. To the extent interest expense is incurred subsequent to the period of readying the asset for use, then such cost will be an expense.
- *SFAS No. 57, "Related Party Disclosures," issued March 1982.* This Statement provides reporting guidelines for the disclosure in financial statements of a reporting entity that has participated in related party transactions that are material, individually or in the aggregate. The disclosure should include the following:
  - The nature of the relationship(s).
  - A description of the transaction(s), sufficient in detail to determine their effect on the financial statement.
  - The dollar volume of transaction(s).
  - Amounts due from related parties and, if not otherwise apparent, the terms and manner of settlement.
- *SFAS No. 66, "Accounting for Sales of Real Estate," issued October 1982.* This Statement deals with the timing of profit recognition

involving the sale of a real estate asset. In general, profit on the sale of a real estate asset may not be recognized unless the following conditions are met:

- A sale has been consummated. That is, all conditions precedent for a closing have taken place.
- To the extent a receivable has been created for the seller, the buyer's initial and continuing investments are sufficient to demonstrate a commitment to satisfy the receivable.
- The seller's receivable is not subject to future subordination.
- The seller has transferred title to the buyer and the seller's future involvement in the property is nominal.

- *SFAS No. 67, "Accounting for Costs and Initial Rental Operations of Real Estate Projects," issued October 1982.* This Statement establishes the treatment of costs associated with acquiring, developing, constructing, selling, and renting real estate projects. In general, these costs will be treated as capital costs, until the property is fully operating. The project will be considered fully operating no later than one year after the cessation of major construction activities. At that time, costs should no longer be capitalized. Rather, they will be operating expenses.
- *SFAS No. 91, "Accounting for Non-Refundable Fees and Costs Associated with Originating and Acquiring Loans and Initial Direct Costs of Leases," issued December 1987.* This Statement requires lessors to amortize initial direct lease costs (those costs incurred by the lessor that are incidental to the specific lease transaction), over the term of the lease. Treating these costs as an expense is no longer permitted.
- *SFAS No. 94, "Consolidation of All Majority-Owned Subsidiaries," issued December 1988.* This Statement requires financial statement consolidation of all majority-owned subsidiaries with the majority owner's financial statement. Consolidation is required even if the operation is nonhomogenous, a large minority interest, or a foreign location.
- *SFAS No. 98, "Accounting for Leases: Sale-Leaseback Transactions Involving Real Estate, Sales Type Leases of Real Estate, Definition of Lease Term, and Initial Direct Costs of Direct Financing Leases," issued May 1988.* This Statement specifies the accounting by a seller-lessee for a sale-leaseback transaction involving real estate. The Statement provides that:
  - The sale must qualify as a sale under SFAS No. 66.
  - The definition of lease term under SFAS No. 13 is amended to include all renewal periods during which there is a purchase money mortgage outstanding.

§ 3.7 CONCLUSION

A number of major U.S. Corporations have comprehensive real estate asset management programs staffed by true professionals. These programs are, however, the distinct minority compared with the legion of companies that are only beginning to recognize the unparalleled benefits of effective corporate real estate management. As a result, they are seeking first class corporate real estate executives for *both* in-house and out-sourced positions. The issues of accurate performance measurement are central to a successful real estate asset management program because benchmarks are required to evaluate the performance of *both* in-house and out-sourced personnel. We have begun the process of creating performance evaluation guidelines, but much remains to be done. The typical corporation has little historical experience with evaluating in-house staff and they, in turn, are only now learning how to choose and measure the performance of the third-party firm.

Four

The Nature of Real Estate Operations

§ 4.1 RESPONSIBILITIES AND OBJECTIVES OF THE REAL ESTATE FUNCTION

As discussed in Chapter One, the real estate function of a corporation supports strategic and operational objectives in the form of facilities planning as well as specific analytical and transactional activities, which it provides to both senior and line management. These services enable the corporation to acquire, manage, and dispose of the real estate interests it requires within acceptable time and cost parameters. While the objectives of the real estate function tend to focus on cost minimization, they extend also toward broader strategic matters.

Senior management is beginning to acknowledge the substantial role of real estate in corporate affairs. With real property interests representing such a substantial portion of corporate book and, particularly, market value, real estate personnel must continue to inform senior management as to how corporate real estate can substantially impact corporate profitability, strategy, and organization. The effect on corporations of the inflationary period of the 1970s, followed by the generous tax environment of the early and mid-1980s, was to substantially increase the market values of corporate real estate. Suddenly, corporations began to recognize the vast reservoir of untapped wealth, salable or mortgageable, in their real estate. If they did not, others did, transforming unobservant corporations into acquisition targets. Some corporations, hoping to cash in on such unrealized equity, even went into real estate development—temporarily. By the end of the 1980s, times changed for real estate and, consequently, the attitude of senior management toward real estate.

The lesson learned by senior management from the past 20 years is that real estate can have a significant effect—either positive or negative—on corporate value and strategy. Therefore, changes in the real estate market require a prompt management response. Because the risks and rewards for the corporation can be so substantial, the real estate function must provide management with accurate information regarding real estate market changes, their impact on the corporation, and strategy recommendations relating thereto.

Although many corporations emphasize that "they are not in the real estate business," virtually every corporation is *invested* in real estate, in some cases, to the extent of billions of dollars. Therefore, the present or forecasted impact of real estate on the corporation, as developed by the real estate function, should be presented in an annual *strategic facilities plan,* described later in this chapter. For example, this plan might recommend, based on observed real estate market activity, that the corporation should acquire or lease, on a long-term basis, property in specific submarkets due to historically low values being transacted at the time. In so doing, the corporation, while modifying its balance sheet, may be able to secure long-term cost advantages over its competitors, or at least retain competitive occupancy costs. In other situations, it may be advantageous to dispose of property due to the specter of litigation and consequent major financial losses and contingent liabilities stemming from, for example, persons occupying buildings that contain asbestos. Finally, the real estate department might recommend forming or spinning off a real estate subsidiary to deal with either risk avoidance or profit opportunities. The real estate function can, in all these instances, affect the organizational structure, financial profile, and profitability through its interface with senior management.

Corporate real estate personnel typically spend most of their time and resources on servicing line management at operational levels. In connection with these responsibilities, the real estate function acquires, manages, and disposes of the real estate required to pursue the objectives of the corporation's strategic business units. Real estate personnel may also contribute to divisional operating plans and the capital budgeting process with respect to real estate acquisition/disposition and operating costs. Such planning and analytical activities are becoming increasingly important to the real estate function's interactive, rather than reactive, role in corporate operations. Generally, real estate personnel should try to perform such tasks in a manner that adds value to the activities of the strategic business units.

Value may be added by minimizing costs and offsetting costs, the latter by creating or augmenting cash inflows, for example, by the enhancement of property value prior to disposition. More often, however, cost minimization is of principal importance to the corporation's strategic business units and will influence all property acquisition and management activities. The disposal of real estate no longer required by the corporation is often underappreciated by line management, who may be inclined to just "get rid of it." In that situation, real estate personnel might minimize costs by transferring a property no longer needed by one division to another division that needs such facilities, thus avoiding higher new acquisition costs.

It is sometimes difficult for corporate real estate personnel to acknowledge that minimizing acquisition costs or enhancing property values does not always translate into increased corporate profitability. An inexpensive, but poorly located, site could require the corporation to incur additional transportation costs; or a low-cost building might, due to its configuration, limit the equipment that could be used therein, thus increasing equipment costs or inhibiting productivity. In the example cited earlier, a property considered disposable by one corporate division might generate a substantial profit if sold but could be a very cost-effective acquisition for another division. Although selling the property at a substantial profit might bring special recognition to both the selling division and the real estate function, transferring the property to the other division might minimize overall corporate cash requirements, especially since it would avoid payment of capital gains taxes. In executing their responsibilities, real estate personnel must acknowledge the distinction between realizing real estate values and corporate profitability.

An additional distinction between traditional profit-oriented real estate activity and the corporate management of real estate is the form in which economic benefits of real estate holdings are derived and reported on financial reports. This is an important concept: In all their activities, corporations are concerned both with when economic benefits are obtained and with when and how those benefits are reported. Whether the corporation is publicly or privately held, even closely held, reports concerning the corporation's financial performance and status will be frequently examined by others including banks, equity investors, regulatory agencies, credit rating agencies, and securities firms. All these outside entities are agents in determining the corporation's future. The financial statements they examine, and upon which they will rely, are almost always prepared according to Generally Accepted Accounting Principles (GAAP). The principle of conservatism that, in part, directs the recognition of profit (and, to some extent, losses) in GAAP financial statements can heavily influence or even dictate corporate behavior, particularly at the level of the individual with bottom-line responsibility. This effect is most striking with respect to the recognition of gains and losses on the disposition of realty, and the effect of such recognition on the measured performance of management.

Corporate management is typically rewarded for performance measured at quarterly or annual intervals. As noted earlier, corporations, by virtue of requiring a location in which to conduct business, are invested in real estate. Changes in the value of real estate, however, typically occur rather slowly. Current income from realty investments, through rental activity, is often nominal and can take years to substantially change a property's market value. Furthermore, the increased value is not recognized under GAAP until the property is sold. Therefore, appreciation of real estate values rightly tend to be of less concern to line management than how properties can contribute to current earnings. Over the long run, returns from real estate investments have generally not exceeded corporate earnings. Also, those returns tend to be based, in part, on the ability of real estate investments to shelter a certain amount of cash flow from taxation as ordinary income, converting some ordinary income to capital gains. While the 1986 Tax Act eliminated much of the tax sheltering available through real estate investments, the nature of economic gains in real estate has not changed.

There are additional reasons why management, or at least managers with bottom-line responsibility, might not want to sell properties even though it might be beneficial to the corporation. For example, rather than being unconcerned about realizing value appreciation, line management might be very concerned about reporting a loss on a sale of realty. Land held by a corporation for expansion purposes may no longer be needed. Furthermore, its market value over time may have decreased below its acquisition costs. In fact, if the value of the property were continuing to decrease, selling as soon as practicable might avoid a greater loss. However, if sold, a loss would be reported and, if sizable, might seriously affect a division's financial performance (as reported in the short-term). Consequently, the general manager of the division might be very reluctant to act to minimize real economic losses. Still, the reporting of the reduced economic value of such a property asset might be reported in spite of management's reluctance to act. Under GAAP, and according to the Financial Accounting Standards Board (FASB) in the Statement of Financial Accounting Standards (SFAS) No. 33, the corporation's auditors might be required to report the loss of value, recognizing an unrealized loss based on the present value of the property's future cash flows (fair rental value).

Another example of management's reluctance to sell property, whether at a profit or loss, arises from the manner in which operating profits or cash flows are claimed and held at some corporations by senior management or parent organizations. If operating profits or cash inflows are subject to claim by, say, a parent company of a subsidiary with surplus real estate, management of that subsidiary may prefer to keep the asset rather than to lose control of it and whatever potential benefits it might represent. If a subsidiary sends the proceeds from a disposition upstream to its parent in one year, and in the next year needs those same funds to acquire new property, it will have to make a specific appropriations request for the funds represented by the value in the property it recently owned. While the subsidiary may want to sell the property and retain the proceeds for immediate reinvestment, such capital spending plans and activity (above preset limits) are usually part of the formal capital allocation process, thereby short-circuiting the subsidiary's autonomy.

Furthermore, the timing and amount of proceeds from prospective sales of real property are sometimes difficult to forecast and are therefore unlikely to be included as a source of funds in the formal capital expenditures plan that the operating subsidiary submits to its parent. As a result, a property may not be formally declared surplus, making it unavailable for sale. Alternative strategies respecting surplus land might be to (1) execute a land lease to another party, (2) contribute the property to a development joint venture, or (3) exchange the property (perhaps in a tax-deferred exchange) for another parcel that better meets the subsidiary's operating requirements. Alternatives 1 and 2 would not prohibit a later sale or exchange for other realty (as in 3), as long as the joint venture was structured as a tenancy in common, as opposed to a partnership. Consequently, an exchange of real estate (two-way or three-way) can be a useful way to handle surplus property.

As can be seen in the foregoing, a corporation's real estate function must be cognizant of the needs of different levels of management as well as the inclinations of individual managers, each of whom may have somewhat differing interests. Therefore, it is likely that the real estate function's objectives and responsibilities will depend on its own reporting responsibilities and location within the organization, as a centralized or decentralized function. This also applies to outside consultants, who will need to balance objectivity with the goals of the individuals who retain advisory services.

§ 4.2 BASIC PRACTICES IN CORPORATE REAL ESTATE ASSET MANAGEMENT

In the rest of this chapter, and in many of the following chapters, we will discuss particular practices corporate real estate personnel use to accomplish their objectives. As already stressed, strategic planning is the most important concern. As discussed in Chapter One, strategic planning pertains to the exchange of information and proposed strategies between comprehensive corporate planning and specific facilities planning. This section will examine strategic planning for corporate real estate in three ways. First, we identify several ways in which real estate can significantly affect the strategic or financial posture of the entire corporation. The two items that follow, managing values and managing risk, exist something like the yin and yang of oriental philosophy: Each complements and is necessary for the other, and each is in some way contained in the other, even though they also serve as polar opposites. In § 4.3, we will discuss the corporation's strategic facilities plan.

(a) STRATEGIC PLANNING

The responsibilities and objectives of the real estate function should be identified through strategic planning, from which all other real estate plans and action should emerge. The strategic planning process should not operate solely in a "top-down" fashion. Doing so would ignore the very valuable input of the real estate function regarding market knowledge, inventory status, and the risks and opportunities associated with its real estate asset base. The real estate function's relationship with other corporate functions (especially senior management) in the strategic planning process is interactive, and, in many instances, a proactive process, generating valuable information and recommendations for comprehensive corporate strategic planning. Moreover, the contributions of the real estate function can extend into fundamental corporate concerns, such as capital accumulation.

The ability to raise capital is fundamental to operating any business—an entirely new venture, an initial public offering (IPO), or even the recapitalization of an existing corporation. Businesses need to secure funds, and a corporation's real estate assets can contribute significantly to that objective. Corporations typically obtain additional funds in three ways: retained earnings and issuance of debt or stock securities. If managed properly, real estate assets can significantly enhance retained earnings through gains realized upon sale. Rather than sell real estate assets, a corporation might elect to leverage its net worth as augmented by the unrealized equity it holds in real estate assets. Again, if properly managed, real estate assets may allow a corporation to issue additional debt or stock in amounts that significantly enhance its strategic posture. In fact, if management does not act on the unrealized equity in its real estate, others may force it to, as witnessed by the takeover activity of the late 1980s.

The real estate function can be a key player in identifying such opportunities, or necessities, and can initiate corporate actions to recapitalize or to ward off a takeover attempt. On the other hand, the real estate function can also play a key role in identifying and evaluating acquisition opportunities for its own corporation, based on market values and capacity utilization. In addition, real estate personnel might recommend acquiring realty that could be beneficial to the corporation, such as specific locations that might increase the value of property or the corporation as a whole. Finally, real estate personnel might identify opportunities to maintain or enhance a corporation's product or service market share by securing key sites (especially for retail or service companies and facilities) that might preclude or counterbalance competitor activity.

Risks also are everpresent. Keeping a close watch on the factors affecting real estate can help the corporation avoid the adverse effects of general or local hazards. For example, it might be beneficial for the corporation to divest certain real property interests in anticipation of changes in the corporate environment such as hazardous waste regulation, plant-closing legislation, historic preservation laws, escalating energy costs, trends toward "nuisance" challenges relating to major installations in various communities or states, and evolving worker-safety regulations affecting facility designs (expensively reconfigured). The corporation's strategic facility plan should address these concerns through the application of principles that involve the management of both real estate values and risks.

(b) MANAGING REAL ESTATE MARKET VALUES AND PRODUCTIVITY

The principal value of real estate to a corporation is its ability to provide productive facilities for the manufacture of goods or provision of services. Therefore, whatever the real estate function can do to cost-effectively maintain and enhance the productivity of the facility will augment its value. However, once the site has been selected and the facility constructed, it is often difficult to implement a major productivity enhancement program without incurring major capital expenditures. Consequently, the usual key to high productivity is good initial design and location, along with adequate maintenance of the physical plant and prudent risk management measures.

Most financial benefits attributable to real estate investment are typically available only upon disposition of the property. Indeed, substantial gains might become available to the corporation through the sale of certain real estate. Unfortunately, while land values typically rise, the improvements (e.g., a building) built on a site usually experience some degree of obsolescence. Generally, there are three kinds of obsolescence: physical deterioration, functional obsolescence, and external obsolescence. Some degree of physical deterioration is to be expected, with the greatest amount usually coming in a building's first few years. Functional obsolescence pertains to the degree of utility present with the improvements, while external obsolescence refers to things external to the site that affect its utility and value.

Since improvements often represent 70 to 80 percent of the market value of a newly improved property (to its highest and best use), it is quite important in managing property values to anticipate and attempt to offset functional obsolescence, which is measured by the degree of utility in the marketplace, as attributed by the typical buyer of such property. Unless the productivity of a facility is threatened, it is unlikely that substantial funds would be allocated to attend to and cure increased functional obsolescence. Therefore, it is necessary to try to anticipate and prevent functional obsolescence without compromising operating productivity or the capital budget. The cost-benefit analysis involves anticipating the course of functional obsolescence, with and without remedial measures, and comparing the costs for prevention of some degree of obsolescence with the present value of the incremental proceeds from a future disposition. The facility characteristic that provides the greatest payback, for both continuing operations and future disposition, is flexibility. Flexibility in the improvements often provides greater long-term utility to the corporation and increases the property's marketability in terms of a larger universe of potential buyers, as well as a shorter marketing period. Flexibility is discussed again in Chapter Six.

While improvements may represent the larger portion of total property value when new, the site on which they are built is more likely to maintain or increase its value. However, the site can also decrease in value, often because of external obsolescence. On the other hand, if the value of a site goes down due to a configuration that gradually is becoming less usable for a range of potential uses, the decrease in value is considered to be functional obsolescence. Causes of external obsolescence, on the other hand, exist outside the site and are locational in nature: Changes in the character of the neighborhood, loss of access to a major freeway, increases in traffic congestion, or various kinds of pollution are examples. To counter such obsolescence, the corporation must either act to prevent these changes through political involvement, legal action, or, perhaps, additional "off-site" investment; or minimize the chance of encountering these negative factors by selecting a site that is less likely to experience such changes. The principles of site selection are discussed in Chapter Seven.

(c) RISK MANAGEMENT

Each of the foregoing real estate asset management activities is intended to enhance earnings per share and corporate market value. Such activities must be supported by risk management practices. It is often said that any average manager can exploit an opportunity; the exceptional manager is one who can envision and manage risks. Risk management practices, for our purposes, fall under two major headings: assessment (including identification and measurement) and control (including elimination and management). While a larger corporation may well have an entire department devoted to risk management, the real estate function still holds much of the information required by a risk management department. Furthermore, some risks, especially real estate market risks, are the sole responsibility of the corporate real estate function.

(1) Assessment

The identification of certain risks related to real estate are fairly apparent. Buildings can burn; storms can blow out windows; earthquakes can shake buildings apart; visitors can slip on an icy sidewalk; building maintenance workers can fall from ladders. These risks are generally not the concern of corporate real estate management on a regular basis. However, as was the case with managing value, managing real-estate-related risks may require attention to these issues at the initial stages of securing and developing a property. The location of a site and the design of the improvements thereon often have much to do with minimizing such risks and reducing insurance premiums. Therefore, to minimize facility operating costs (e.g., insurance premiums), and enhance productivity, the real estate function should assess the traditional categories of risk. Nevertheless, to the extent that the real estate function also oversees facility management and maintenance functions, operational safety concerns will necessarily require attention.

There are, however, other kinds of risks about which the real estate function should be routinely concerned. One kind is financial risk, that is, the management and reliability of the cost and timely provision of items other than space, such as services or products required in the operation of corporate facilities. While the risk management department is not usually involved here, both the purchasing and legal departments typically support the real estate function. In acquiring such items from other parties, the financial objective is always to "fix the future" to the extent possible. "Fixing the future" means establishing and agreeing to a cost on which you can rely for a particular item to be available, at a particular time and place, for the lowest cost. The purchasing department is usually responsible for securing items at the lowest cost. The legal department is often responsible for providing or approving the terms of the agreement or contract involved. Still, the real estate function is the key player here in that it must identify the item required (its specifications), the time and place for delivery, the manner of delivery, and furthermore, the consequences due to any departure from the result anticipated. Here, no other party can identify the risks involved as thoroughly as the real estate function.

The most critical area for the identification of risk by the real estate function is real estate market risk including the future acquisition cost of property (purchased or leased), as well as its value prior to and upon disposition. However, such risk also involves the availability of the property when desired, as well as the presence of a market for it at the time of disposition. No other department within the corporation can address this issue. It is the sole responsibility of the real estate function. Even though real estate personnel may be able to secure the assistance of market experts (brokers, etc.), the ultimate responsibility for this issue is fully on their shoulders. Furthermore, brokers and other outside parties will not have all the information necessary for such matters. Additional information will have to be secured from the current users of the corporation's existing inventory of facilities. This area is at the heart of the strategic facilities plan and plan assembly process to be outlined in the next section.

Measuring the risks present in relation to corporate real estate involves a variety of concerns. With respect to casualty losses, a determination of replacement cost or market value, whichever is of concern to the corporation, can be made. Downtime, however, can be even more significant. Even though replacement costs might be relatively low, replacing critical production bottlenecks, no matter how inexpensive, can seriously impair profitability. Therefore, such costs should be identified and measured, say, in units per day. Financial losses due to contract problems can be estimated in terms of direct and consequential money losses, including the cost to cure the problem.

The ability to calculate future market losses in the real estate market is very limited. Nobody's crystal ball is clear enough to make that determination with any degree of reliability. Indeed, insurance companies do not insure market risks since they have no actuarial basis. Nevertheless, the risk is very real. Furthermore, since much real estate (i.e., location) is considered nonfungible, the risk can, at times, be substantial. This is why the management of market risk is an intrinsic component of the real estate function. Other types of loss, once identified and measured, can be converted into an amount of probable loss, based on the likelihood of the amount of possible total loss.

(2) Control

A corporation has two basic alternatives for dealing with risks: it can either eliminate the risk or retain and manage it. Eliminating various risks is often prohibitively expensive or effectively impossible. Therefore, to remain active in a certain business, corporations have to manage most risks. There are three basic management approaches: Assume the risk, attempt to control the risk, or transfer all or a part of the risk. Assuming the risk means to be prepared to accept the full loss if it occurs, thus becoming actively or passively self-insured. Controlling the risk means to minimize it to the extent feasible: the costs to control not exceeding the probable benefits available. Finally, transferring risk is possible; this is the function of insurance contracts. Insurance companies are usually quite willing to insure most casualty risks, as well as general liability, and even ownership of property (e.g., title insurance). Aggressive legal representation is key to managing the risks of contract agreements. This leaves real estate market risks, the management of which is a principal responsibility of the real estate function.

Real estate market risks revolve around price and availability, at the time of both acquisition and disposition. Management of market risks is based on information and technique. Generally, the amount of the information required and available will determine the technique employed. It may be possible to avoid certain risks, which usually requires having the correct, and sometimes, expensive, information. For example, the potential for the beneficial or adverse rezoning of land under consideration for acquisition may require extended contact with city planners, citizens, and elected officials, possibly consuming a great deal of time and money. As just noted, leasing, as opposed to purchasing real estate, helps avoid certain risks. However, much real estate risk is simply managed.

With respect to real estate, our focus is on three risk management techniques: diversification, space banking, and joint venture. Diversification is a standard technique of portfolio management and also has a degree of utility in corporate real estate. However, the need for specific locations for corporate activity is generally determined in a manner that precludes the geographic diversification techniques employed by those managing investment real estate portfolios. Instead, corporate real estate managers often develop a policy of diversifying by identifying an "optimal" mix of owned-versus-leased facilities. Through leasing, the manager can further spread risk by contracting with more than one lessor. This can be of substantial importance in leasing space in multitenant buildings, when the financial strength of the owner can significantly affect building operations, maintenance, and tenant relations. Also, staggering lease terms so that the expiration dates do not all fall in the same year will help the corporation avoid incurring unfavorable lease terms in a suddenly "tight" market.

Land and space banking is another risk management technique that functions in two ways. First, banking space (say, office space) helps to ensure that the space will be available when needed. Space banking can also operate to secure a particular, and acceptable, cost for the space desired. Land and space banking can be accomplished either through holding the rights to current and future occupancy of the space (through ownership or lease), or by securing only the future right to occupy the needed space, through options to purchase or lease space. Holding existing space through ownership or lease that is not currently required by the corporation for its own needs can, in some instances, be a very costly alternative. Therefore, many corporations turn toward leasing or subleasing space not currently required for operations as a means of offsetting the holding costs. Such partial divestment requires a market for the space and the lease terms the corporation is prepared to provide. A discount from the market price is often required to interest potential occupants, thus creating the price for managing the risk. At times, the current market price for space the corporation desires to lease is above its cost to the corporation creating an arbitrage opportunity.

Finally, a joint venture arrangement can function as a risk management technique for the corporation's real estate. The corporation identifies another party to assume a portion of the risk. A joint venture arrangement can serve the corporation during any phase of real estate ownership: acquisition, holding and management, and disposition. Such joint ventures are typically arranged with companies active in the real estate business as investors or developers. For example, in the acquisition of property, it may become necessary for a corporation to establish a "buffer" zone around a major facility such as a manufacturing plant.

Rather than acquire buffer-zone land that might simply remain vacant, a corporation might be able to develop the buffer zone with uses that are compatible with its facility and capable of providing a transition to existing land uses. In this case, a joint venture with a developer of industrial parks might help the corporation to attain the development as well as generate a profitable return on the investment in the extra land. Since the corporation is not in the development business, the joint venture with a developer would moderate the risk involved.

As noted earlier, many corporations have a policy of maintaining a particular mix of owned and leased property. During the period of ownership, the corporation, to maintain the mix, may need to divest itself of certain real property ownership. This can also be accomplished through an effective joint venture in which a partial or full interest in the property is sold to another party, say, a real estate investment fund. The property sold would then be leased back by the corporation at some preestablished rate. This joint venture arrangement gives rise to what is known in the real estate industry as a "sale-leaseback" transaction. However, to avoid a host of legal issues, the corporation must avoid structuring the arrangement as a partnership. With such a sale-leaseback arrangement, the corporation is able to maintain the mix and real estate risk profile set forth in its policies.

When a corporation finally declares a facility "surplus," it is usually so that the property can be sold. However, over time, the value of the site may have increased to the point where, if the property were sold "as is," a substantial amount of profit might be forfeited. Keep in mind that it is the value of the site that has appreciated, rather than the improvements, which may contribute little, if any value to the site. Redevelopment is necessary to realize the profit potential of the site. Again, it might be prudent to arrange a joint venture with an experienced developer, who can redevelop the site into its highest and best use. Substantial development activity should not dilute the principal purposes of the real estate function, unless a such formal strategy is declared. Again, employing a joint venture will moderate the risks of return on invested capital and the energies of the real estate function, while still obtaining greater value for the land.

§ 4.3 THE STRATEGIC FACILITIES PLAN

Strategic planning with respect to the corporation's facilities is at the heart of an effective real estate function. The information and strategy exchange noted earlier is essential to producing a useful document and game plan. While a purely "top-down" approach should be avoided, it is critical to carefully observe and integrate corporate policy into the strategic facilities plan. This can include policies such as make-or-buy preferences (revolving around the corporation's strategic competencies), investment focus (e.g., research and development, inventory, facilities), and customer service. Information should be gathered from every appropriate source. Some of the best sources include the operating plans for the corporation's strategic business units, the corporation's general policies and business plan, as well as historical data for the corporation and its various interfaces. No two strategic facilities plans are alike, nor should they be. Therefore, the following material provides a menu of important items, from which the corporate real estate executive can structure a plan best suited for his or her corporation.

(a) ISSUES TO ADDRESS IN A STRATEGIC FACILITIES PLAN

1. Capacity requirements forecast.
2. Facility location, relocation, expansion, and consolidation.
3. Facility acquisition, utilization, and divestiture.
4. Life-cycle costing and productivity incorporating perspectives on trade-offs.
5. Facilities financing, including the capital budgeting plan.
6. Financial statement effects of real estate organizational structure, management policies, and action.
7. Implementation policies and procedures.
8. Facilities standards.

(b) INFORMATION REQUIRED TO DEVELOP THE STRATEGIC FACILITIES PLAN

1. Marketing distribution plans, inventory management, and sales forecasts by product/service type.
2. Financial objectives including funding, profitability, and profile.
3. Organizational structure for operating, regulatory, and liability management.
4. Human resources, as related to site specific operating costs and relocations.
5. Real estate inventory and utilization data, historical and forecasted.
6. Strategic and operating requirements for each strategic business unit.
7. Ancillary services related to facility operations (utilities, amenities, etc.).
8. Market information respecting the commodity (space and location).

9. Corporate policies related to or involving facilities including:
   - Real property interest preferences (fee or leaseholds).
   - Facility type: location (foreign?), risks (environmental, financial, market).
   - Financing methods—internal, seller financing, third-party (e.g., banks), or leases.
   - Financial statement objectives—asset, liability, or expense recognition and timing.
   - Cash flow impact.
   - Management of financial risk, market and legal risks, and contingencies.
   - Strategic aspects of real estate (i.e., image, worker morale, environmental protection, etc.).

(c) THE PLANNING PROCESS

1. Parties involved in the development of the strategic facilities plan:
   - CEO and CFO, and an executive committee representing senior management.
   - Representatives of departmental functions (e.g., human resources, finance, etc.).
   - Representatives of the strategic business units operating within the corporation.
   - Corporate real estate department manager and facilities managers.
2. Corporate strategy input:
   - Product and packaging impact—changing consumer acceptance.
   - Marketing strategy impact—changing customer location.
   - Manufacturing technology selection.
   - Materials sourcing program.
   - Production planning and control—changes in volume.
   - Logistical strategy—purchasing, packaging, shipment.
   - Inventory planning—demand and factors variation.
   - Capital funding.
   - Organizational design.
   - Human resources program (labor pool, benefits, etc.).
3. Operations management—the dynamics of the environment and potential for:
   - Changes in demand.
   - Changes in supply (competition).

- Changes in technology.
- Changes in management methods (e.g., "just-in-time").
- Changes in management objectives (e.g., "total quality").
- Changes in organizational objectives/structure.
- Changes in labor pool size or quality.

4. Physical plant inventory management.
   - Impact on corporate profitability and risk profile.
   - Schedule and delivery date coordination.

(d) IDENTIFICATION OF SPACE REQUIREMENTS

1. Present—this operating period.
2. Future—short-term and long-term.
3. Space requirements affected by:
   - Employee efficiency.
   - Technology used in operations—telecommunications, etc.
   - Land and building costs.
   - Development or land banking potential for proposed or adjacent sites.
   - Timing considerations.
   - Legal and/or environmental considerations.
   - Locus of decision-making ability and acquisition authority.
   - Evaluation of alternatives, especially short- versus long-term solutions.
   - Single-purpose versus multiple-purpose solutions.
   - Image and prestige considerations.

(e) ASSEMBLY OF A STRATEGIC FACILITIES PLAN

1. Statement of corporate objectives for the upcoming period players, timetable, resources, constraints.
2. Identification of specific facilities requirements per strategic business unit (type, amount, where, when, budget, linkages):
   - Definition of the objective(s) of the function requiring a facility.
   - Identification of relationships and contributions of other corporate functions.
   - Establishment of space requirements.
   - Identification and evaluation of alternative facility plans.
   - Selection and implementation of the plan.
   - Reprogramming of the facility in step with operational objectives.

- Identification of existing inventory and capacity of facilities in relation to policies addressing utilization and performance standards.

3. Identification of alternative solutions to accommodate the objectives, with specific notation as to the related costs, benefits, tradeoffs, risks, impact, and externalities. This will require the input of the various staff and operating personnel.
4. Identification of a comprehensive and integrated set of recommendations and rationale for the actions proposed, constituting a basic strategic facilities plan.
5. Senior management review and adoption (with modifications).
6. Development of implementation plans and procedures for corporate real estate personnel as well as the strategic business units and staff departments involved in executing the action plans.
7. Implementation monitoring, notation of feedback, and realignment of plan details as necessary.

(f) IMPLEMENTATION PROGRAM

1. Capital allocation requests and acquisitions.
2. Land and space banking.
3. Divestitures.
4. Inventory redeployment.
5. Cost management measures.
6. Refinancing of real property interests.
7. Pursuit of cost-offsetting opportunities.
8. Relocation.

§ 4.4 PRINCIPAL ANALYTICAL AND TRANSACTIONAL ACTIVITIES

Corporations, through their real estate function, buy/lease, hold and sell/sublet property. Specific actions in these areas should be directed by the strategic facilities plan. Real estate personnel, however, can employ a range of methods to accomplish their objectives. Many such methods are available; we will mention only the most important. The following discussion is divided into the three principal postures the corporation can take with respect to its real estate: acquisition, management of its portfolio, and disposition.

(a) ACQUISITIONS

What real estate service should be acquired and where it should be located are covered in Chapters Six and Seven, respectively. The focus here is on how it should be acquired: whether by purchase or lease, and whether by building new facilities or occupying existing facilities. The corporation's decision to pursue one of these alternatives rests on its ability to provide the desired utility at the lowest possible cost. Some trade-offs are likely to be part of the decision-making process, unless there are no alternatives, due either to specification requirements or the lack of market alternatives. Also, decisions regarding financing, such as whether to fund an acquisition through the capital budgeting process, using mortgages, or using an operating lease, will usually be made separately, by the finance function. Still, real estate acquisitions can often be considered investment decisions, rather than decisions only about how to fund the cost of consuming an acquired resource, as with most equipment financing decisions. Therefore, the real estate function, with its unique access to information about the real estate market, must examine the typical "financing" decision in light of the relevant market conditions. This is true of the basic lease-versus-buy decision.

The decision to lease, rather than buy, space should be based on a lower net cost to the corporation, all other things being equal. However, all other things are usually not equal. For reasons of flexibility, timeliness, economies of scale, and the availability of funds, leasing property may make better sense, or simply be necessary. Otherwise, this decision is based on the present value of the cash flows related to the two alternatives. An example of such an analysis is presented in Exhibit 4.1. The selection of a discount rate is often a critical factor. For most true financing decisions, the after-tax cost of debt is usually used. However, for investment decisions, which may be the case for certain real estate acquisitions, the preferred discount rate would be the after-tax cost of capital. In instances of pure cost (where funds are being consumed), where the only cash flows being considered are negative, the lowest net present value of the cash flows related to each alternative indicates the more advantageous alternative; otherwise, the highest net present value indicates the more advantageous alternative.

The decision to acquire and occupy existing facilities versus constructing new facilities is based on an analysis similar to the lease-versus-buy analysis, with an important additional component. That item is whether the same real estate service, or utility for the user, is available with facilities not originally designed for the prospective user. The lack of utility is roughly equivalent to the functional obsolescence concern noted earlier. The cost to cure the obsolescence must also be identified and added to the acquisition cost of the existing facility to compare apples with apples. Unfortunately, not all obsolescence can be cured, which might adversely affect productivity. Therefore, in considering existing facilities for acquisition, an additional analysis will have to be performed to determine the impact on productivity and, therefore, the implicit additional costs of the existing facility. Thereafter, the analysis is virtually identical to the one set forth

EXHIBIT 4.1 Lease versus Buy Analysis*

Assuming:

Corporate Tax Rate of	34.00%
Discount Rate	10.00%
Depreciation	31.5 years
Borrowing Rate	8.00%
Land Value at Purchase	20.00%

	Acquisition	Years 1–5	Years 6–10	Disposition
LEASE				
Net Rent Paid	0	(2,000,000)	(2,100,000)	0
Operating Expenses	0	(1,250,000)	(1,312,500)	0
Taxable Expenses	0	(3,250,000)	(3,412,500)	0
Tax Shield	0	1,105,000	1,160,250	0
Net Cash Flow	0	(2,145,000)	(2,252,250)	0
Discounted Cash Flow	0	(1,626,248)	(1,060,260)	0
Net Present Value	(2,686,508)			
PURCHASE				
Operating Expenses	0	(1,250,000)	(1,312,500)	0
Depreciation	0	(634,921)	(634,921)	0
Interest Expense		(2,000,000)	(2,000,000)	
Taxable Expenses	0	(3,884,921)	(3,947,421)	0
Tax Shield		1,320,873	1,342,123	
Depreciation		634,921	634,921	
Borrowings	5,000,000			
Purchase Price	(5,000,000)			
Reversion Value				5,000,000
Selling Costs				(150,000)
Capital Gains Taxes				(380,746)
Principal Balance				(5,000,000)
Net Cash Flow	0	(1,929,127)	(1,970,377)	(530,746)
Discounted Cash Flow	0	(1,462,582)	(927,567)	(204,626)
Net Present Value	(2,594,774)			

* See Chapter 9 for an elaboration of the lease versus buy technique.

in Exhibit 4.1. Since so many markets are heavily oversupplied from time to time (as in the early 1990s), it is likely that the costs to acquire and cure the obsolescence of existing facilities will be the less costly alternative. This may not be true, however, for the need for very specialized facilities, such as research and development, headquarters, and specialized manufacturing property (high-tech or heavy industry). Bargains, if available, are likely to be found in markets offering rather homogeneous space, for example, administrative office and warehouse facilities.

(b) PORTFOLIO MANAGEMENT

Active management of a corporation's real estate holdings—its real estate "portfolio"—is essential to maintaining and enhancing the overall value of the corporation. Managing the value of a corporation's real estate and related risks were discussed earlier. This discussion focuses on managing the *existing* inventory of space and land held by the corporation as a specific collection of assets. Portfolio management, as distinguished from property management, involves manipulating a corporation's inventory of real estate to achieve the most beneficial asset mix. The essence of portfolio management can be characterized as follows: If a property is not contributing in a manner that maximizes the profitability or strategic position of the corporation, the asset should be redeployed (put to a better use) or sold (perhaps requiring the acquisition of, better, substitute property). The contributory value of each parcel, in terms of corporate strategy and profitability, must be analyzed. Therefore, by identifying the contributory value of current specific assets vis-à-vis the entire portfolio, corporate real estate personnel can decide and act to hold, redeploy, or divest particular holdings.

First and foremost, a corporation's real estate must support its strategic and operational objectives. If a particular parcel cannot provide the service required by a strategic business unit, it should be either redeployed within the corporation, replaced by another property, or sold. A decision to act on one of these alternatives is driven by factors essentially internal to the corporation. The only significant external factors in the decision-making process are the cost and availability of the real estate required. Those factors are market driven and imply a need to respect real estate market values and conditions. What emerges from this picture is the further need to identify and achieve a balance between a utility and value of a corporation's real estate that will maximize the firm's profitability and strategic posture.

Maximizing the contribution of a corporation's real estate portfolio requires employing each parcel to its highest and best use. The concept of "highest and best use" is familiar to those in commercial and investment real estate. For commercial real estate, the highest and best use of property is generally considered to be that use which is physically possible, legally permissible, financially feasible, and maximally productive (or profitable). The highest and best use for corporate real estate is very similar, except that the property's contribution to corporate strategy and profitability must be compared with the determination of maximal productivity within the context of the real estate marketplace. Because a property may have more than one potential use either within the corporation or in the marketplace, it is necessary to determine and compare the potential profitability of each to determine the highest and best use. This should be done periodically, depending on the rate of change in both the corporation and the real estate marketplace. The resulting determination will indicate what kind of action (redeployment, disposition, land banking, etc.) will be in the best interests of the corporation. Consider the following example.

> In 1970, ABC Corporation acquired a 10-acre parcel of industrially zoned land for a manufacturing/warehouse facility, not all of which was developed, though it did have a rail spur. Since that time, the market for products manufactured at this facility has grown substantially, and is expected to continue to grow. To continue meeting production targets in the short-term, the facility needs to be modernized and expanded. The anticipated expansion would result in the site being fully developed. When acquired, the parcel was located in the urban fringe. However, the metropolitan area has grown substantially since that time, and the neighborhood in which the facility is located has continued to mature. The neighborhood's residential land is 75 percent developed, and its commercially zoned land is fully built-out (albeit not always to its highest and best use). There is currently a fairly high demand for land that could support additional retail development to accommodate the neighborhood's growing residential base. Therefore, the value of the manufacturing site has increased substantially, though the contributing market value of its buildings is now marginal. Brokers have inquired whether the property might be made available for sale and have suggested that new industrial sites are available a little further out. The operations housed in this facility are not very location-sensitive, and most product is currently shipped by truck. Furthermore, some of the operations at this facility could be relocated separately, though some economies of scale are available in aggregating the operations. A decision regarding these facilities must be made before ABC Corporation risks losing its competitive position.

This kind of situation and decision is not uncommon; it is the natural result of the passage of time in business operations and real estate markets. To resolve the matter, it is necessary to ask the following question: What real estate asset(s) can best support the strategic and profit objectives of the corporation? The alternatives are as follows: (1) Modernize and expand at the existing location; (2) sell the existing facility and relocate the entire operation; (3) bifurcate the operations, relocating only a part to another facility; (4) bifurcate the operations, relocate one part, and also expand at the existing site; (5) relocate all or part of the facility's operations to another location or facility already owned by the corporation, if there are any. Obviously, if relocation is considered, there must be a further consideration of building versus buying versus leasing new facilities. Furthermore, the decision must be considered in view of both short-term (e.g., immediate production requirements) and long-term factors (e.g., market growth, the rate of facility obsolescence, and future real estate market values).

Alternative courses of action, such as the preceding ones, must be evaluated to resolve the question: What real estate asset(s) can best support the objectives of the corporation? The evaluation serves as the "highest and best use" analysis, incorporating both operational and real estate market data and considerations. To the extent that the analysis can be quantified (i.e., put into dollar terms), the best alternative will be that which provides the greatest net present value to the corporation through the continuation or termination/initiation of operations at one or more facilities. The analysis must include all gains and costs, both actual and effective, such as relocation costs, taxes, commissions, shipping cost differentials, and operational (in)effeciencies. The format for the highest-and-best-use determination is similar to that employed in the lease-versus-buy analysis, except that there will usually be more than two alternatives, and the items of cash flow will have to be expanded to include the overall impact on operations.

Turnover of space in terms of its use, especially in administrative facilities, is a phenomenon that occurs much more frequently than the large-scale relocations or redeployment of space just described. For example, from time to time, the particular use of administrative space might change from executive offices, to general office space, to idle or vacant space, to data processing, and to records storage. This kind of change is of neither the magnitude nor character of the prior relocation example and requires a different kind of management. Such change is a normal characteristic of space utilization, and should be accommodated within the portfolio of real estate assets secured for the corporation on the basis of its strategic facilities plan. In other words, it does not function as a principal determinant of portfolio management. It does raise the issue, however, as to when vacant space should be considered surplus, which will be examined in the next section.

In the course of normal space utilization, certain properties, or portions thereof, will become vacant or go idle. The corporation may have a future need for the space—though it may not arise for months or even years. The space (or land) could be disposed of (i.e., sold or leased). However, if the corporation's need arises sooner than expected or is only, perhaps, one year off, it may not make economic sense to sell or lease it to another party. In the first place, such short-term lessees are unlikely to be available. Secondly, the net cost to reacquire the property in the future might exceed the interim holding costs (property taxes, maintenance, insurance, security, etc.). If so, the corporate real estate executive should recommend or act to hold, or bank, the idle property until it is needed.

Another type of land or space banking may occur when there is a forecasted or anticipated future need for a specific kind of space, yet no such space is currently held by the corporation. In that case, the corporate real estate executive might find it desirable to preacquire space or land so as to meet the future need on a timely and/or cost-effective basis. Again, the decision to bank land or space in anticipation of a future need should be determined on the basis of the present value of the costs incurred in each alternative, assuming or "costing-out" the condition of the availability of such space when required. This is a form of hedging, and functions as a kind of space insurance—and may serve as a tool of risk management (discussed earlier). To profitably bank space, the real estate executive needs to have reliable information available on corporate capacity planning as well as current and likely future real estate market conditions.

One of the most important considerations in profitable space banking is leasing or subleasing the idle property. Chapter Five deals with leasing or subleasing space as a partial disposition of realty. It should be considered, first and foremost, as a method of offsetting holding costs, thus increasing the net present value of the acquisition. On the other hand, it may be possible to generate a positive cash flow during the time the property is banked. In this case, the income from leasing or subleasing the property would exceed the actual or imputed lease cost of leased or owned property, respectively. Such an opportunity requires a sophisticated understanding of local market conditions and the special terms of an interest transfer by (sub)lease.

A further method of offsetting real estate costs is "lease arbitrage," which takes advantage of the differential between market and contract lease rates for property the corporation either holds or can acquire (note that one acquires a lease interest as well as a fee, i.e., ownership interest). Leased property can be transferred temporarily by sublease, or permanently by an assignment. Of course, only a sublease that conveys a term shorter than the primary lease can function as a tool for offsetting the costs of banking space. An assignment cannot so function, since it conveys the corporation's entire interest in the leased premises.

(c) DISPOSITIONS

Property that is deemed unnecessary to the pursuit of the corporation's objectives should be identified as surplus and the corporation's interest therein divested. This rule should have no exceptions. For example, if a new property will better serve the corporation, the old property should not be ignored, but should be considered surplus and sold; the preceding discussion on portfolio management covered this issue. On the other hand, if the corporation does not need a property for current operations, yet determines that it should be held for future use, the property is not surplus but is an example of land or space banking. And if, on the basis of enhancing corporate profitability, a corporation determines that it should lease or sublease idle space for which it has identified no current or future use, that space is *not* surplus. It is a key asset in the corporation's (presumably) new business mission, effectively or in fact. In this situation, however, the corporation either has or should make a clear statement of its intention to be active in the business of real estate investment (at least with respect to this property), since it is now competing in a new marketplace for profitability, rather than for income that might offset the cost of carrying idle property held for a separate purpose.

The determination that a property is surplus should be made as quickly as possible, for the cost of carrying idle assets can be exorbitant. Moreover, the proceeds from the disposition of surplus property can be substantial, and of considerable aid to the corporation's cash position. Therefore, in addition to absorbing the out-of-pocket carrying costs of surplus real estate, the actual carrying cost also includes the cost of the capital not realized by virtue of the continued holding and investment in unproductive property. Finally, once the surplus determination is made, the corporation should also act quickly to dispose of the property in the most profitable manner.

There are several ways of disposing of surplus owned or leased real estate. (See Chapter Five for a detailed listing of the various available options.)

Often, it is worth exploring the merits of several alternatives. In disposing of property, there will always be some costs involved (e.g., commissions, carrying costs, deferred maintenance). Therefore, to obtain a net benefit, some form of cost-benefit analysis should be implemented (using present value methods, if necessary). Attempting to convey an interest real estate for some reasonable amount of consideration (i.e., money, or other items of value) may also require marketing savvy. Disposing of property is much more than putting up a "For Sale" sign. Even the most straightforward disposal can be a complicated matter. Considerations such as broker selection and even splitting the fee with cooperating brokers currently have received much examination in the literature. The relevant issues surrounding a marketing effort are discussed in Chapter Five.

While the prompt (though not hasty) disposition of surplus property is always in order, the real estate function should be aware that, from time to time, there may be certain constraints to disposing of property. The most obvious is the simple lack of a strong enough market, in which buyers are few or marketing time is long. Sometimes, due to the nature of the property, its location, or the improvements thereon, there are no ready buyers, even in an otherwise strong general commercial market. For example, in a suburb of a major metropolitan area, a massive mid-rise brick and concrete slaughterhouse stood idle for many years following the termination of operations. While hundreds of thousands of square feet were available, the cost to convert it to another use was prohibitively expensive. In addition, while the site constituted a valuable location for an industrial park, the cost to raze the mid-rise structure, having been built very sturdily to accommodate the production process, was more than the land value. The only buyer ended up being the local development authority, which acquired the property at a questionable price and incurred the cost to raze the structure simply to stimulate development in an area that was deteriorating as a result of this long-idle property.

The specter of environmental liability under federal or state legislation enacted over the past two decades has also posed serious realty divestment problems for certain corporations (see Chapter Sixteen). In earlier years, it was not uncommon, even for the federal government, to dispose of toxic waste by putting it in the ground at or near the site where it was produced. In most instances, the waste can no longer be recovered or treated, except at extraordinary expense. Nobody wants to buy trouble. Therefore, even if the property may no longer be of use to its owner, it is unlikely that it will ever be sold. Asbestos located in buildings poses a similar problem. Many investors will not acquire properties that contain asbestos. Even willing buyers typically approach the matter prudently by requiring that the seller remove the asbestos at its own cost as part of a buy/sell agreement. If the cost to cure the asbestos problem exceeds the property's value, which can happen, selling the property may not be cost-effective.

Finally, even though a property may be both marketable and in demand, there may be legal hurdles or prohibitions to disposition. Perhaps the most common prohibition is the right to sublet or assign leased space. Lease clauses, reasonably constructed, which restrict the corporate lessee from subleasing or assigning a lease to a third party by requiring the lessor's consent are often upheld if challenged in court or ignored. The court's rationale respects the lessor's interest in protecting the value and income stream from the property, which might be jeopardized by an unwelcome tenant. While corporate property owned in fee simple may generally be sold in spite of "alienation" restrictions included in the deed, other hurdles can still complicate the disposal. For example, in joint ventures, where the corporation owns, say, a 50 percent interest in the realty it occupies, such an interest may prove difficult to market, depending on the character of the remaining owner or probable buyer(s)—apart from market considerations—but particularly if the selling corporation will no longer occupy space in the property. Limitations on the sale of interests in partnerships that own corporate (occupied) real property can be even more severe and enforceable, for legal reasons alone, though such are beyond the scope of this text. Of course, the best time to examine these limitations is not when property is declared "surplus," but instead, before it is acquired.

Five

Marketing Corporate Real Estate

§ 5.1 INTRODUCTION

Corporations change management or direction, grow or decline. In going through these cycles, your corporation may vacate leased space or own property that has become surplus and is unrelated to the corporation's immediate business plans. If there is or will be a business need for the surplus property in the near future, the corporation or customer may be willing to pay the ongoing costs to keep the unused space.

If there are no business plans to use the vacant leased space or surplus owned property, the large monthly carrying expenses and the accompanying legal issues will usually dictate its timely disposal. The corporation should review the financial, legal, and marketing issues with legal counsel and a real estate broker and then develop a marketing strategy and tactical plan to dispose of the excess real property.

§ 5.2 MARKETING

"Marketing" means two things in the corporate environment. In the narrower sense, marketing simply represents the act of selling something. In this view, marketing is synonymous with sales activity and such a definition cannot provide long-term prosperity for any company. Although selling has an obvious beneficial impact on the corporate growth curve, there is much more to marketing than the sale of the end product.

The second definition of marketing—the one stressed in this book—is that marketing in its most profit-related sense is the function whereby a goods-producing organization (1) determines consumer's needs, real or potential, (2) develops concepts and products that meet them, and (3) distributes and sells these products at a profit that reflects a fair return on the invested capital.

- Marketing strategy is the basis for evolving the preceding objectives—a design for the firm's commitment of resources to achieve marketing's three-fold goals.
- Marketing tactics are the steps taken to implement strategy.[1]

To apply this definition to the marketing of your surplus real assets and the maximizing of profit, you must think of your surplus property as a new product that the professionals in your corporate real estate department are considering launching: Analyze its potential uses and users; identify the potential market on the basis of a time-related cost/benefit study; choose your target; prepare marketing literature; and be flexible and responsive to changing market opportunities.

(a) MARKETING STRATEGY: IDENTIFYING USES AND USERS

A surplus property provides a rare opportunity for the objective analysis of an asset that is no longer committed to a specific use. Potential options for disposing of property *owned* by the corporation include the following:

- Identify another related division or related corporate entity that could use and purchase the property.
- Sell the property "as is."
- Sell the property after enhancing its value by:
  - rezoning.
  - development analysis and planning.

[1] "Marketing Decisions," Bulletin 525 (New York: Conference Board, 1971), p. 15.

    - premarketing.
    - securing key adjacent parcels.
- Partially divest owned property through leasing as a landlord.
- Donate the property to a governmental agency, a nonprofit organization, or a university or college to create a tax credit that could benefit the corporation.
- Abandon otherwise unmarketable property, letting ownership revert to the state by escheat.
- Contribute the property for an interest in another business.
- Exchange the property, in a tax-deferred transaction, for another property the corporation can either use currently or justify banking.

The following are potential options for disposing of property *leased* by the corporation:

- Identify another related division or related corporate entity that could use and lease via assignment or sublease.
- Sublease all or a part of the space (in which the corporation conveys less than its full leasehold interest).
- Assign the lease, conveying all of its rights, interest, and legal obligations in the property to another in-house company or to another corporation as approved by the landlord.
- Donate the leasehold interest, if permitted, to obtain any tax benefit.
- Abandon the premises, which would typically revert to the landlord under the law (this action in some leases, could put your company in default and possibly subject it to damages).
- Contribute the property for an interest in another business.
- Exchange the property, perhaps in a tax-deferred exchange, for another lease or other *personal* property the corporation can either use currently or justify banking (a leasehold is an item of personal property, not real property).
- Buy out the lease and legal obligation at an effective price lower than the present value of the remaining lease payments.

Whatever course of action the corporation chooses, disposing of property will require that you, as the real estate professional, assume the role of property owner or landlord and market the property. To accomplish the strategic disposal of this real property, you must understand, develop, implement the tactical marketing plan, and review the financial and legal requirements in marketing the property.

(b) COST/BENEFIT ANALYSIS[2]

A cost/benefit analysis provides a useful financial process to review the possible uses and users for your marketing plan.

(1) Marketing Alternative I-A: Sale to a Similar User

The logical first place to turn in a disposition program for a major plant is to companies in your industry that could utilize your layout, labor pool, and at least some of the equipment in place. The drawback is that these companies will usually reject such a plant for the same reasons that you are closing it. In this discussion, we assume that the corporation has already explored, and rejected, selling the plant as a going business to its employees or to another company. It has therefore decided to sell the real estate either to another company in its industry or to whomever makes the best offer.

Experience has shown that 90 percent of the deals made for a surplus plant to another company in the same industry are well under way within 30 days of the announcement of the closing. If you decide to pursue this alternative, you should have an answer quickly. A word of caution: A property is usually most marketable when it first becomes available. How you handle the first weeks of the program can be critical to the final outcome. In addition to the value of the time, which you risk losing, your early actions will set the tone for the program for the first year. A good building that gets a negative response from other companies in its industry can give the property a label of "unwanted," which is difficult to change.

Therefore, you should pursue selling the property solely to some other company in your industry only if your analysis shows there is a significant chance that the firm will be interested. To determine whether your property would be likely to interest to another company in your industry, answer the following questions:

1. Why are you closing this facility?
   - ___ Inefficient operation
   - ___ Uncompetitive labor costs
   - ___ Labor shortage
   - ___ Labor relations

[2] This section is based on materials prepared by the professional staff of Howard P. Hoffman Associates, Inc., which specializes in providing corporate clients with marketing strategy and implementation consultation on surplus real estate problems. Used by permission.

____ Large modernization expense required for which the return is uncertain
____ Weakness in the market for the products produced at the facility
____ High operating costs
____ New governmental restrictions, such as pollution control, make continued operation uneconomical
____ Corporate decision to combine operation into another plant.

2. What benefits does the facility offer another company in your industry?
____ A layout specifically tailored to its operation
____ A good location
____ Low operating costs
____ Highly productive labor force
____ Likely strong governmental aid for new industry
____ Machinery in place
____ Favorable regional trends.

2a. What is the recent history of propery acquisitions by other companies in your industry?

____

____

Why? ______________________________

3. List those companies that should be interested in your facility?

- Company ______________________________
  Operation ______________________________
  Advantages to it ______________________________
- Company ______________________________
  Operation ______________________________
  Advantages to it ______________________________
- Company ______________________________
  Operation ______________________________
  Advantages to it ______________________________
- Company ______________________________
  Operation ______________________________
  Advantages to it ______________________________
- Company ______________________________
  Operation ______________________________
  Advantages to it ______________________________

4. If your roles were reversed, and you were making the decision for one of the preceding companies, how long would it take for you to obtain full corporate approval to proceed? _____ Months
5. What is the book value of this facility? $ _____

5a. How do you feel that this book value relates to the facility's likely selling price in today's market?
Realistic _____ Unrealistic _____

6. Based on this analysis, do you consider it likely that one of the companies listed could become strongly interested in this acquisition in the next 30 days? Yes _____ No _____
   - If Yes, proceed to Marketing Alternative I-B to determine the facility's potential selling price to such a company.[3]
   - If No, continue with question 7.
7. Are the benefits of your facility listed in question 2 strong enough to attract a single user from a different industry to your facility within a reasonable period of time? Yes _____ No _____
   - If you answered Yes to question 7, proceed to Marketing Alternative I-B.
   - If you answered No to both questions 6 and 7, you have determined that a program aimed solely at a single user will run a high degree of risk. However, proceed to Marketing Alternative I-B to determine the facility's potential selling price, since this number plays an important role in other alternatives.

(2) Marketing Alternative I-B: Sale to a Single User

Whether the sale is to a company in your industry or to a company in a totally different business, this can be the simplest of all transactions. Unless, however, the sale is made to a company in your industry, or unless your facility is fairly modern and adaptable—with a prime location—the extended period of time that it can take to achieve a sale can significantly reduce the value of the property. Properties that exceed 100,000 square feet[4] pose additional problems because the few companies looking for existing facilities of that size know that they are functioning in a buyer's market. Time is on their side, and they will use it to their advantage.

[3] This price is for facility's real estate alone. In addition, there will be an increment of value for the equipment in place above what your company would receive if it were to sell the equipment separately.

[4] A recent study has indicated that less than 12 percent of the companies seeking space are considering existing facilities of 100,000 square feet or more.

8. Total building(s) size (square feet) ____
9. Unusable area (square feet) ____
10. Net usable area (square feet) (line 8 minus line 9) ____
11. Based on your company's operating experience, what total annual rental could be justified to run a similar operation profitably? $ ____

    Take into account the operating expenses of the property and the benefits from its layout.
12. Estimate the annual real estate taxes, building insurance and utility costs that are included in the total rental above. $ ____
13. Effective net annual rental likely from real estate (line 11 minus line 12)[5] $ ____
14. How long do you think it would take to find a company looking to relocate to a facility of this size (in months)? ____ Months
15. Once found, how long do you think it would take the company to get all the necessary corporate approvals (including time to complete the necessary studies) to purchase your facility after the company becomes aware of it (in months)? ____ Months
16. Total months to carry empty (line 14 plus line 15) ____ Months
17. Total carrying costs while empty (line 16 divided by line 12, times line 16) $ ____
18. Sales price (based on what net rental cost of real estate would be) $ ____
    A. Capitalize line 13 at 10 percent for high-credit-rated company, 12 percent for medium-credit-rated company, 14 percent for low-credit-rated company[6] $ ____
    B. Required capital expenditures for occupancy $ ____
    C. Sales price (line 18A minus line 18B) $ ____
    D. Marketing costs (6% of line 18C)[7] $ ____
    E. Net return from sale (line 18C minus 18D) $ ____
19. Net return to corporation (line 18E minus line 17) $ ____

[5] An actual lease may be drawn for a gross rental, but for simplicity of calculation, all rental figures should be figured on a net basis.

[6] Capitalization rates can range from 8 to 20 percent depending upon the credit strength (rating) of the company concerned. To simplify the calculation here, we have utilized the rates that apply in the majority of cases at the three different levels of credit rating.

[7] Marketing costs can vary from 1 to 10 percent, according to the area and the difficulty of completing the transaction. Experience has shown that, in the majority of cases, approximately 5 percent of the sales price will cover the brokers' commissions, advertising, brochures, and so on.

20. Present value of net return to corporation (capitalize line 19 at corporate discount rate for the number of months in line 16) $ ______

Enter the figure from line 20 on line 61, and proceed to Marketing Alternative II.

(3) Marketing Alternative II: Sale to a Speculator

If the corporation's goal is to dispose of the facility regardless of price—or the length of time required—this may prove to be an acceptable method. The speculator might buy a property in exchange for a deep discount below its potential selling price.[8] For the corporation, it could mean an end to carrying costs. Keep in mind, however, that speculators do not buy real estate—they tie it up, first with lengthy negotiations and then by taking title with a low down payment until they can find a buyer. If their efforts are unsuccessful, they default, and the company is once again in its initial position.

If the property is obsolescent or poorly located, its high carrying costs may make it impossible to attract a speculator at any price. Assuming that your property is salable to a speculator, utilize the following list to quickly outline a potential selling price to such a buyer.

21. Eventual net return to corporation upon sale of a fully leased building (line 19) $ ______

22. Sales price to a speculator (present value of line 21, discounted at 50% per year-use time period from line 16) $ ______

23. Terms

A. Likely down payment (10% of line 40) $ ______

B. Purchase money mortgage (90% of line 40) $ ______

24. Sales price of purchase money mortgage to an investor (75% of line 23B) $ ______

25. Marketing costs: commissions on sale (6% of line 22) $ ______

26. Total net return to corporation (line 23A plus line 24 minus line 25 plus 6 months of carry) $ ______

A. Present value of net return (line 26 at corporate discount rate for 6 months)[9] $ ______

[8] This discount will usually be calculated to provide a net return to the speculator at least equivalent to what would be expected by an investor in a venture capital situation.

[9] Negotiation periods, from the time a speculator is found, generally range from 3 to 12 months, with 6 months being the average.

Enter the figure from line 26A on line 62, and proceed to Marketing Alternative III.

(4) Marketing Alternative III: Preparing Subdivision Plans and Selling to a Speculator

With this alternative, the corporation packages its property to present a program for much greater return. Rather than leave this factor for the purchaser to figure out, the company undertakes research and analysis of the property to show potential buyers the property's best uses.

The company can answer all questions about structural and mechanical systems and possible alterations in the building and also has a specific pro forma income projection. In this way, a speculator is able to see the potential of the property more clearly. The program reduces risk and gives the speculator something to start on right away.

Thus, the corporation can demand a price more in line with its full potential selling price, increasing its return from the sale of the facility by at least 50 percent. The corporation, however, is still dealing with a speculator, not an investor. The sale is not final. The speculator will pay a better price in exchange for the marketing plan and very liberal mortgage terms from the corporation. Should he or she fail in implementing the plan, the corporation will be forced to take back the facility.

27. Usable square feet (line 10 minus 5%)[10] _____

28. Anticipated annual net rental per square foot to a single user (line 13 divided by line 10) $ _____

29. Higher per square foot rents paid by smaller tenants (line 28 plus 40% of line 28, or a minimum of 75 cents per square foot[11]) $ _____

30. Annual net income (line 28 times line 29) $ _____

31. Vacancy and management expenses (10% of line 30) $ _____

32. Effective annual net income (line 30 minus line 31) $ _____

33. Eventual sales price to an investor, fully leased (capitalize line 32 at 12%)[12] $ _____

34. Reduced time period anticipated to lease building to multiple tenants (line 16 minus line 33) _____

[10] In most cases where no space is lost to demolition, 5 percent of the total space will cover the amount needed for subdivision walls and additional access. Where demolition is likely or there is unusual space, a higher percentage should be used.

[11] In cases where the anticipated net rental of the building in its entirety is 50 cents per square foot or less, the likely rental income from subdivided units would be greater than 40 percent more than the income would be from a single tenant.

[12] This percentage is used because it is the minimum acceptable return in the majority of cases.

35. Carrying costs (line 17 minus line 33) $ ____
36. Estimated subdivision costs (line 20 times $2.65)[13] $ ____
37. Marketing costs: commissions for lessor (line 30 times 6% times 5 years) $ ____
38. Marketing costs: commissions on sale (3% of line 33)[14] $ ____
39. Net return from sale from subdivision and leasing program (line 33 minus lines 35, 36, 37, and 38) $ ____
40. Sales price to speculator (line 39 discounted 25% for time period in line 34) $ ____
41. Terms
    A. Likely down payment (10% of line 40) $ ____
    B. Purchase money mortgage (90% of line 40) $ ____
42. Sales price of purchase money mortgage to an investor (75% of line 41B) $ ____
43. Marketing costs: commissions on actual sale (6% of line 40) $ ____
44. Total net return to corporation (line 41A plus line 42 minus line 43 carrying costs for 6 months) $ ____
    A. Present value of net return (line 44 at corporate discount rate for 6 months)[15] $ ____

Enter the figure from line 44A on line 63, and proceed to Marketing Alternative IV.

(5) Marketing Alternative IV: Subdividing and Leasing, Then Selling to an Investor

By carrying out the program prepared in Marketing Alternative III, the corporation converts its property from a corporate discard to an income-producing investment. The company now has a product of interest to the group who traditionally pay the highest amount for any property—the real estate investors. This is also the largest and most easily identifiable group of potential customers.

Second, in its leasing program the company is appealing to the largest potential group of quality tenants, the medium-size users. Thus the market for the building is broadened to include multiple as well as

[13] Subdivision costs in a typical building can range from $1 to $6 per foot and in rare cases even more. Most building subdivisions can be completed for $2.50 per square foot, and planning at 15 cents or more per square foot.

[14] In the sale of a leased building to an investor, the only likely sales marketing cost is a small brokerage commission, if any.

[15] In determining the time period, three months has been allowed to complete the planning and three months to complete the negotiations with the speculator.

single tenants, lessees as well as user-purchasers. Therefore, the disposition period should be reduced dramatically over the likely disposition period in a single-user search.

45. Net return to corporation on sale to an investor (line 39) $ ______

46. Full net return to the corporation (50% of line 32 plus line 45 less 3 months of carrying costs)[16] $ ______

47. Present value of net return (line 46 at the corporate discount rate for the period estimated in line 34 plus 3 months for planning and 2 months for negotiations with investor) $ ______

Enter the figure from line 47 on line 64, and proceed to Marketing Alternative V.

(6) Marketing Alternative V: Leasing Small Units, Obtaining Financing, and Then Selling to an Investor

This step adds one more increment of profit by offering a complete package, fully leased and financed. It takes the last bit of delay and uncertainty out of the disposal process by eliminating the need for the buyer to look for and arrange financing. It also presents an opportunity to further enhance the selling price of the property through the negotiation of advantageous mortgage terms.

48. Annual net income from property (line 32) $ ______

49. Mortgage (75% of line 33) $ ______

50. Annual mortgage payments (line 49 times mortgage constant, see Exhibit 5.1)[17] $ ______

51. Pretax cash flow—return on equity investment (line 48 minus line 50) $ ______

52. Investor's cash payment for net cash flow (line 51 capitalized at 10%)[18] $ ______

53. Investor's total payment for property (line 49 plus line 52) $ ______

[16] During the leasing period, the rental income generated could equal as much as 50 percent of the final annual rental figure. A speculator will not pay for even a discounted value of this.

[17] Assume a 20-year mortgage at an interest rate 1 percent above the current AA corporate bond rates.

[18] This percentage has been used since it is a likely return requirement to equity from a fully leased building with financing.

EXHIBIT 5.1 Mortgage Constant Table (20-Year Term Self-Liquidating)

Interest Rate	Factor Obtained from Any Readily Available Mortgage Constant Table	Constant Annual Percent
8	______	10.04
8¼	______	10.23
8½	______	10.42
8¾	______	10.61
9	______	10.80
9¼	______	11.00
9½	______	11.19
9¾	______	11.39
10	______	11.59
10¼	______	11.78
10½	______	11.99
10¾	______	12.19
11	______	12.39
11¼	______	12.60
11½	______	12.80
11¾	______	13.01
12	______	13.22

54. Income generated during leasing period (50% of line 32) $ ______

55. Carrying costs plus 3 months (line 35) $ ______

56. Estimated subdivision costs (line 36) $ ______

57. Cost to obtain mortgage (1% of line 49) $ ______

58. Marketing costs: on sale to investor (3% of line 33)[19] $ ______

59. Net return to company on sale to investor (line 53 plus line 54 minus lines 55, 56, 57, and 58) $ ______

60. Present value to company at corporate discount rate (use time period in line 34 plus 3 months to obtain financing) $ ______

[19] Because of the relative ease of finding purchasers for income-producing property, commission expenses should not exceed 3 percent, which is approximately one half of the figure in line 18.

(7) Summary

61. Present value of sale to a single user (line 20) $ ____
62. Present value of sale to a speculator (line 26) $ ____
63. Present value of sale to a speculator with subdivision plan (line 44) $ ____
64. Present value of subdividing and leasing, then selling to an investor (line 47) $ ____
65. Present value of subdividing, leasing, and financing, and then selling to an investor (line 60) $ ____

In the hypothetical numbers have been applied to the foregoing analyses to give you an idea of the dollars involved in the available alternatives. You must choose the approach that best suits your company's pattern and willingness to commit funds for generating that extra profit.

(c) DETERMINING THE DOLLAR-PRODUCING CAPABILITY OF AN INDUSTRIAL FACILITY[20]

Based on five different marketing approaches, here is how to determine the present value of a hypothetical 200,000-square-foot industrial facility. Assume the carrying costs while empty to be $0.60 per square foot; the current market rent for large space, $0.80 per square foot; and the market rent for small space, $1.10 per square foot.

(1) Quick Sale "As Is"

A study by researchers at the University of Georgia in 1987 found that of the 228 executives who responded to the survey, 92.5 percent stated that they attempted to dispose of property "as is."[21] The buyer will probably be a speculator who wants to buy very cheaply, "lease-up" the property, and then sell it as an income producer to an investor. To arrive at a purchase price, the speculator discounts the eventual selling price and deducts projected carrying costs during the lease-up period. The eventual selling price will be the capitalized value of the expected income when the building is fully leased. The speculator will usually want terms from the owner.

[20] These data were prepared by Irving E. Cohen. *Source:* C. Lincoln Jewett, "How to Market Surplus Real Estate," *Harvard Business Review*, January–February 1977, p. 7.

[21] See Hugh O. Nourse and Dorothy Kingory, "Survey of Approaches to Disposing of Surplus Corporate Real Estate," *The Journal of Real Estate Research*, 2, 1, (Fall, 1987).

Income potential (200,000 sq. ft. × $0.80)	$ 160,000
Eventual selling price to an investor (income capitalized at 11%)	$1,455,000
Present value of $1,455,000 discounted at 25% for 3 years (lease-up period)	745,000
Less estimated three years' carrying costs	360,000
Price speculator will pay, and thus present value to company	$ 385,000

(2) Lease "As Is"

This approach places the company in an entrepreneurial role. To arrive at a present value, the company applies a lower discount rate than does the speculator.

Eventual selling price to investor	$1,455,000
Less estimated three years' carrying costs	360,000
Net return to company on sale to investor in three years	1,095,000
Present value to company (15% corporate discount rate assumed)	$ 720,000

(3) Preparing Subdivision Plans and Selling to a Speculator

With this approach, the owner makes the facility more marketable because of the larger market and the premium generally attached to the rent of small units. A speculator can pay a higher price based on the premium rents and the shorter period needed to lease-up the facility.

Income potential (200,000 sq. ft. × $1.10)	$ 220,000
Eventual selling price to an investor (income capitalized at 11%)	2,000,000
Present value of $2 million discounted at 25% for one year (lease-up period)	1,600,000
Less estimated one year of carrying costs	120,000
Less estimated costs to subdivide (at $2 per sq. ft.)	400,000
Price speculator will pay, and thus present value to company	$1,080,000

(4) Subleasing and Leasing, Then Selling to an Investor

As in the second situation, the corporation takes an entrepreneurial role and launches a leasing program.

Eventual selling price to an investor	$2,000,000
Less estimated one year of carrying costs	120,000
Less estimated costs to subdivide (at $2 per sq. ft.)	400,000
Net return to company on sale in one year	1,480,000
Present value to company (15% corporate discount rate assumed)	$1,290,000

(5) Leasing Small Units, Obtaining Permanent Financing, and Then Selling to an Investor

Obtaining permanent financing on the income-producing property further enhances the eventual resale price to an investor. (This calculation includes a permanent mortgage of $1,700,000—85% of the $2 million value—with terms of 30 years at 9%.)

Income from property (200,000 square feet × $1.10)	$ 220,000
Less mortgage payments	163,000
Pretax cash flow	57,000
Investor's cash payment of $520,000 for the pretax cash flow (capitalized at 11%), plus the mortgage	2,200,000
Less estimated one year carrying costs	120,000
Less estimated fix-up costs (at $2 per sq. ft.)	400,000
Less costs to obtain mortgage	20,000
Net return to company on sale to investor in 1¼ years (extra 3 months for financing)	1,600,000
Present value to company (15% corporate discount rate assumed)	$1,400,000

(d) Other Disposition Alternatives

There are other disposition alternatives, depending on the corporation's operating requirements and tax position, the condition of the property and its market potential, and the political nature of the business environment. These alternatives are *sublease, donation, sale to a liquidator, installment sale, buy-out,* and *joint venture.*

(1) Sublease

If another in-house user cannot be located, listing the space with a real estate broker may be part of the disposal strategy. You should choose the listing real estate broker with the same care that you choose the leasing or purchase real estate broker because the corporation has now become a landlord; the space is competing with that of other landlords in the local market. A subleasing model of before tax income or loss should be developed according to corporate policies and procedures and what you, your customer, and listing broker agree is realistic based on market conditions (see Exhibit 5.2).

The timing and associated economic/real estate activity will indicate whether this is a "seller's" or a "buyer's" market. When you are subleasing space, market conditions and the corporation's desire to divest the space will often be a function of the *time* it will take to dispose of the asset. The expense items to be considered for subleasing property will include items such as:

- Lease payments for the remaining term of the obligation.
- Insurance.
- A percentage commission for the listing real estate broker.
- Space planning fee.
- Permits.
- Allowance for construction and depreciation costs.
- Income taxes.

Once you have found a tenant to sublease your surplus leased property, a Sublease Agreement (see Exhibit 5.3) should be prepared based on your prime lease and the landlord's approval.

EXHIBIT 5.2 Sublease Analysis

The Sublease Analysis spreadsheet shown on page 125 was specifically designed as a tool using LOTUS 1-2-3 or any other comparable spreadsheet software to help develop a model income or (loss) for a sublease property based on the local real estate market, competition, and the size/remaining time left on the current lease. The model can then be used to run numerous iterations against the model to help the user (sublandlord) develop a subleasing strategy and run a pro forma against each particular proposal for each proposed subtenant to help make an informed management and real estate decision.

EXHIBIT 5.2 *(Continued)*

This analysis was developed as a spreadsheet file within Lotus 1-2-3, and can be used to test your understanding of the sublease analysis results and to create your own sublease analysis spreadsheets tailored to your company's current sublease requirements. To use the analysis, you should have a basic knowledge of Lotus 1-2-3 and of the modification and/or development of the analysis formulas. Also, you should be familiar with the real estate terminology used and with lease and sublease analysis techniques.

The analysis has been set up based on subleasing office space. You must be able to provide all the variables in the items in the upper part of the spreadsheet.

- If some of the items do not apply to a particular analysis, a "0" (zero) should be entered in the variable cell in lieu of leaving a blank.
- If an item or items do not appear on this spreadsheet and you want to include them as a separate line item (i.e., electricity or real estate taxes), new items can be added. You must be aware of how these items will impact the existing formulas and the analysis results. Items in the spreadsheet below the lines of ****** should also be modified to suit each particular analysis.
- If the sublease term is less than 6 years, which most are, it will be necessary to modify the initial year formula to reflect the specific starting month and date of the sublease. The sixth-year formula assumes a partial year, which will need to be modified to meet the particular sublease termination date.
- Each year of the analysis starting date may need to be modified manually to reflect the particular lease term.

The spreadsheet formulas use the variable information that is contained within the variable cells at the top of the spreadsheet. Please note that the variable information must be entered within the cell width and in the proper Lotus format for formula use to obtain a meaningful analysis.

Based on the variable items and the modifications to the cell formulas, the spreadsheet analysis will take place automatically as the input variables are entered. It is recommended that initial results be checked manually to ensure that modifications to the formulas reflect the correct sublease terms and expected results of income or (loss).

The Subleasing Analysis spreadsheet was designed to help provide an organized methodology to establish a subleasing program for each property to be subleased and to help users understand the impact of each sublease against the cash flow and income or (loss) that will impact the company's bottom line. You will need to spend some time reviewing the formulas, how the spreadsheet works, and how best to tailor modifications to take advantage of the power and speed of the computer-aided real estate tool.

EXHIBIT 5.2 *(Continued)*

LOTUS 1-2-3 SUBLEASE ANALYSIS SPREADSHEET

XYZBLDG1.WK1
PAGE 1

SUBTENANT: C.O.D. CORPORATION - SUBLEASING P & L
SUBLANDLORD: ABC COMPANY - FINANCIAL ANALYSIS #1

(NAME OF PREPARER)
(DATE ANALYSIS MADE)

Building & Address: XYZ BUILDING, 1234 MAIN STREET
City, St. & Zip: CHICAGO, IL. 50515-1234
Sublease Fl.(s): 7TH FLOOR (SUITE 703)
Subleased Area: 17,022 Rentable Square Feet (R.S.F.)
15,000 Usable Square Feet (U.S.F.)
Subl. Start Date: NOVEMBER 1, 1991
Subl.Term/End Date: 72 MONTHS - OCTOBER 31, 1997
Sublease Rate: $20.00 /R.S.F.
Subl. Allowances: $15.00 /R.S.F. For Upfit
Subl. Rent Increase: 103.50% PER SUBLEASE YEAR
Subl.Rent Abatement: 12 MOS. - RENT STARTS NOV. 1, 1991.
2 MOS. IN 1991
10 MOS. IN 1992
# of Parking Spaces: 45 Cost/Sp./Mo $30 THRU 10/92

ABC COMPANY Lease Information:
Lease Ends: OCTOBER 31, 1997
Total Leased Area: 25,250 Rentable Square Feet (R.S.F.)
Rentable To 22,250 Usable Square Feet (U.S.F.)
Usable Factor: 88.119%
Current Lease Rate: $19.00 /R.S.F.
Lease Rent Increase: 104.50% Per Lease Year
Income Tax Rate: 0.34 % Of Before Tax Income Or (Loss)
Net Present Value: 0.08 %
Sublandlord Upfit: $0.00 /RSF For Multi-Tenant Construction
Brokerage Commission 6.00%
Space Planning, Etc. $0.75 /RSF
Park. Sp. Cost Incr. 103.50% Per Lease Year
# of Parking Spaces: 67 Cost/Sp./Mo. $30 Thru 10/92

	Year 0 Costs	1991 (2 MO.)	1992 (12 MO.)	1993 (12 MO.)	1994 (12 MO.)	1995 (12 MO.)	1996 (12 MO.)	1997 (10 MO.)	TOTAL (6 YRS 0 MO)
Sublease Revenues:									
Rent Income		$56,742	$342,435	$354,421	$366,825	$379,664	$392,952	$336,956	$2,229,996
Parking Income		$2,700	$16,295	$16,865	$17,455	$18,066	$18,698	$16,034	$106,112
Less Rent Abatement		($56,742)	($283,708)	$0	$0	$0	$0	$0	($340,449)
NET REVENUES		$2,700	$75,022	$371,285	$384,280	$397,730	$411,651	$352,990	$1,995,659
EFFECTIVE RENT $19.54 /R.S.F.									
Tenant Part Of Upfit Cost:	$0								
ABC COMPANY EXPENSES:									
Space Planning, Etc.	$12,767								$12,767
Brokerage Fee	$113,373								$113,373
Upfit/Depreciation	$255,337	$7,093	$42,556	$42,556	$42,556	$42,556	$42,556	$35,463	$255,337
Rent & Oper Expense	N/A	$53,904	$325,853	$340,516	$355,839	$371,852	$388,585	$335,874	$2,172,424
Parking Expense	N/A	$2,700	$16,295	$16,865	$17,455	$18,066	$18,698	$16,034	$106,112
TOTAL EXPENSES	$381,477	$63,697	$384,703	$399,937	$415,851	$432,474	$449,840	$387,371	$2,660,013
NET EFF. RENT $16.91 /R.S.F.									
CUM. BEFORE TAX INC.(LOSS):	($126,140)	($187,137)	($496,818)	($525,470)	($557,040)	($591,784)	($629,973)	($664,354)	
CUM. YEARLY INCOME (LOSS):	$0	($187,137)	($309,681)	($28,652)	($31,570)	($34,744)	($38,189)	($34,382)	
BEFORE TAX INCOME OR (LOSS):									($664,354)
INCOME TAXES:									$225,880
NET INCOME OR (LOSS):									($438,474)
Tenant Improvements:	($255,337)								
Add Back Depreciation:		$7,093	$42,556	$42,556	$42,556	$42,556	$42,556	$35,463	$255,337
NET CASH FLOW:	($255,337)	$7,093	$42,556	$42,556	$42,556	$42,556	$42,556	$35,463	($183,137)
NPV (THRU 10/31/95) =	($157,010)								

PROJECTED INCOME OR (LOSS) = ($664,354)
INITIAL MODEL FOR 7TH FLOOR PROJECTED INCOME OR (LOSS) = ($670,354)

ADDITIONAL INCOME OR (LOSS) = $6,000

EXHIBIT 5.3 Sublease Agreement Sample for ABC Company

AGREEMENT OF SUBLEASE

This Sublease Agreement is made and entered into this 5th day of December, 1994, by and between ABC Company, a Delaware corporation, ("Landlord"), and Ross, Jones and Smith, Inc., a Delaware corporation ("Tenant").

WITNESSETH:

WHEREAS, Landlord is itself a tenant under that certain Lease dated August 10, 1993 entered into between ABC Company and West Wacker Towers, L.P. (Prime Landlord);

WHEREAS, Article 7 of the Prime Lease permits Landlord to sublease all or a portion of the demised premises on the prior express written consent of the Prime Landlord; and

WHEREAS, Tenant and Landlord desire to obtain the Prime Landlord's consent hereto:

NOW THEREFORE, in consideration of the agreements hereinafter set forth, the parties hereto mutually agree as follows:

1. DEMISED PREMISES. Landlord hereby leases to Tenant, and Tenant hereby leases from Landlord, certain space (the "demised premises") on the second floor of the Building (the "Building") situated at 4425 West Wacker Drive, Chicago, Cook County, Illinois 60630, assigned Suite #201 (outlined on Exhibit A attached hereto). The demised premises constitute approximately 2,000 square feet of net rentable area which constitutes approximately 1,800 square feet of net usable area.

2. TERM. This Sublease agreement shall be for a term of two (2) years and three (3) months beginning on the Sublease Commencement Date, which shall be January 1, 1995, and ending on March 31, 1997 (the "Expiration Date"), provided, however, that in the event the demised premises are not substantially completed in accordance with the provisions of Article 6 by said date, for any reason or cause, then the Sublease Commencement Date shall be earlier of (i) the date the demised premises are occupied by Tenant or (ii) the day which is fifteen (15) days after Landlord has certified in writing to Tenant that all work to be performed by Landlord pursuant to Article 6 has been substantially completed, in which event Landlord shall not be liable or responsible for any claims, damages, or liabilities by reason of such delay, nor shall the obligations of Tenant hereunder be affected. In the event the demised premises are occupied by Tenant prior to the Sublease Commencement Date, such tenancy shall be deemed to be by the day, and Tenant shall be responsible for payment of monthly rental, for each day of such occupancy prior to the Sublease Commencement Date. Within thirty (30) days after the Sublease Commencement Date, Landlord and Tenant shall execute Exhibit D attached hereto and made a part hereof by reference confirming the dates of commencement and expiration of the term of this Sublease Agreement in accordance with the provisions of this Article 2.

3. USE. Tenant will use and occupy the demised premises solely in accordance with the terms of the Prime Lease. Tenant will not use or occupy the demised premises for any unlawful, disorderly, or hazardous purpose, and will not manufacture any commodity or prepare or dispense any food or beverage therein, without Landlord's and Prime Landlord's written consent. Tenant shall comply with all present and future laws, ordinances, regulations and orders of all governmental authorities having jurisdiction over the demised premises.

4. RENTAL. Tenant shall pay to Landlord an annual rental of Forty Thousand Dollars ($40,000.), payable in monthly installments, in advance, on the first day of each calendar month during the term of this Sublease, equal to Three Thousand Three Hundred Thirty-Three and 33/100 Dollars ($3,333.33) per month for the period beginning with the Sublease Commencement Date through September 30, 1995. Beginning on the first anniversary date of the Sublease Commencement Date and at each anniversary date thereafter, the annual rental due each year Shall be increased by 4.5%. If the Sublease Commencement Date occurs on a day other than the first day of a month, rent from the Sublease Commencement Date until the first day of the following month shall be prorated at the rate of one-thirtieth (1/30th) of the monthly rental for each such day, payable in advance on the Sublease Commencement Date. Tenant will pay said rent without demand, deduction, set-off or counter-claim by check to Landlord at 4425 West Wacker Drive, Suite 200, Chicago, IL. 60630 or to such other party or address as Landlord may designate by written notice to Tenant. If Landlord shall at any time or times accept said rent after it shall become due and payable, such acceptance shall not excuse delay upon subsequent occasions, or constitute a waiver of any or all of Landlord's rights hereunder.

EXHIBIT 5.3 *(Continued)*

5. DEPOSITS. Upon execution of this Sublease, Tenant shall deposit with Landlord the sum of Three Thousand Three Hundred Thirty-Three and 33/100 Dollars ($3,333.33) as a deposit to be applied against the first month's rent. In addition, Tenant shall pay to Landlord as a security deposit the sum of Three Thousand Three Hundred Thirty-Three and 33/100 Dollars ($3,333.33). Such security deposit (which shall bear interest at the then market rate) shall be considered as security for the performance by Tenant of all of Tenant's obligations under this Sublease. Upon expiration of the term hereof, Landlord shall (provided that Tenant is not in default under the terms hereof) return and pay back such security deposit including interest to Tenant, less such portion thereof as Landlord shall have appropriated to cure any default by Tenant. In the event of any default by Tenant hereunder, Landlord shall have the right, but shall not be obligated, to apply all or any portion of the security deposit to cure such default, in which event Tenant shall be obligated to deposit with Landlord upon demand therefor the amount necessary to restore the security deposit to its original amount and such amount shall constitute additional rent hereunder.

6. WORK LETTER AGREEMENT. Landlord will finish the demised premises in accordance with the provisions set forth in Exhibit B attached hereto and made a part hereof. Landlord shall have no obligation to make any alterations or improvements to the demised premises except as set forth in Exhibit B.

7. MAINTENANCE BY TENANT. Tenant shall keep the demised premises and the other fixtures and equipment therein in clean, safe and sanitary condition, will take good care thereof, will suffer no waste or injury thereto, and will, at the expiration or other termination of the term of this Sublease, surrender the same, broom clean, in the same order and condition in which they are on the commencement of the term of this Sublease, except for ordinary wear and tear and damage by the elements, fire and other casualty not due to the negligence of the Tenant, its employees, invitees, agents, contractors and licensees: and upon such termination of this Sublease, Landlord shall have the right to re-enter and resume possession of the demised premises. Tenant shall make all repairs to the demised premises caused by any negligent act or omission of Tenant, or its employees, invitees, agents, contractors and licensees.

8. ALTERATIONS. Tenant will not make or permit anyone to make any alterations, additions or improvements, structural or otherwise (hereinafter referred to as "Alterations"), in or to the demised premises or the Building, without the prior written consent of Landlord and Prime Landlord which consent shall not be unreasonably withheld. If any mechanic's lien is filed against the demised premises, or the Building for work or materials done for, or furnished to, Tenant (other than for work or materials supplied by Landlord), such mechanic's lien shall be discharged by Tenant within ten (10) days thereafter, at Tenant's sole cost and expense, by the payment thereof or by the filing of any bond required by law. If Tenant shall fail to discharge any such mechanic's lien, Landlord may, at its option, discharge the same and treat the cost thereof as additional rent hereunder, payable with the monthly installment of rent next becoming due and such discharge by Landlord shall not be deemed to waive the default of Tenant in not discharging the same.

Tenant will indemnify and hold Landlord and Prime Landlord harmless from and against any and all expenses, liens, claims or damages to person or property which may or might arise by reason of the making by Tenant or any Alterations. If any Alteration is made without the prior written consent of Landlord and Prime Landlord, Landlord may correct or remove the same, and Tenant shall be liable for all expenses so incurred by Landlord. All Alterations in or to the demised premises or the Building made by either party shall immediately become the property of the Landlord and shall remain upon and be surrendered with the Demised Premises as a part thereof at the end of the term hereof; provided, however, that if Tenant is not in default in the performance of any of its obligations under this Sublease, Tenant shall have the right to remove, prior to the expiration of the term of this Sublease, all movable furniture, furnishings or equipment installed in the demised premises at the expense of Tenant, and if such property of Tenant is not removed by Tenant prior to the expiration or termination of this Sublease, the same shall at Landlord's option, become the property of the Landlord and shall be surrendered with the demised premises as a part thereof. Should Landlord elect that Alterations installed by Tenant be removed upon the expiration or termination of this Lease, Tenant shall remove the same at Tenant's sole cost and expense, and if Tenant fails to remove the same, Landlord may remove the same at Tenant's expense and Tenant shall reimburse Landlord for the cost of such removal together with any and all damages which Landlord may sustain by reason of such default by Tenant, including cost of restoration of the premises to their original state, ordinary wear and tear excepted.

9. INDEMNITY AND PUBLIC LIABILITY INSURANCE. Tenant will indemnify and hold harmless Landlord from and against any loss, damage or liability occasioned by or resulting from any default hereunder or any willful or negligent act on the part of Tenant, its agents, employees, contractors, licensees, or invitees. Tenant

EXHIBIT 5.3 *(Continued)*

shall obtain and maintain in effect at all times during the term of this Sublease, a policy of comprehensive public liability insurance naming Landlord, Prime Landlord and any mortgagee of the Building as additional insureds, protecting Prime Landlord, Landlord, Tenant and any such mortgagee against any liability for bodily injury, death or property damage occurring upon, in or about any part of the Building or the demised premises arising from any of the items and coverage as set forth in the Prime Lease against which Tenant is required to indemnify Landlord with such policies to afford protection to the limits and coverage as set forth in the Prime Lease.

10. RIGHT OF LANDLORD TO CURE TENANT'S DEFAULT: LATE PAYMENTS. If Tenant defaults in the making of any payment or in the doing of any act herein required to be made or done by Tenant, then after ten (10) days' notice from Landlord, Landlord may, but shall not be required to, make such payment or do such act, and the amount of the expense thereof, if made or done by Landlord, with interest thereon at the rate of the prime interest rate charged by the Chicago National Bank during the period of such default plus two percent (2%) per annum (hereinafter referred to as the "Default Interest Rate"), from the date paid by Landlord, shall be paid by Tenant to Landlord and shall constitute additional rent hereunder due and payable with the next monthly installment of rent; but the making of such payment or the doing of such act by Landlord shall not operate to cure such default or to estop Landlord from the pursuit of any remedy to which Landlord would otherwise be entitled. If Tenant fails to pay any installment of rent on or before the first day of the calendar month when such installment is due and payable, such unpaid installment shall bear interest at the rate of the Default Interest Rate, from the date such installment became due and payable to the date of payment thereof by Tenant. Such interest shall constitute additional rent hereunder due and payable with the next monthly installment of rent. In addition, Tenant shall pay to Landlord, as a "late charge", five percent (5%) of any payment herein required to be made by Tenant which is more than ten (10) days late or cover the costs of collecting amounts past due.

11. NO REPRESENTATION BY LANDLORD. Neither Landlord, Prime Landlord nor any agent or employee of Landlord or Prime Landlord has made any representations or promises with respect to the demised premises or the building except as herein expressly set forth, and no rights, privileges, easements or licenses are granted to Tenant except as herein set forth. Tenant, by taking possession of the demised premises, shall accept the same "as is" and such taking of possession shall be conclusive evidence that the demised premises are in good and satisfactory condition at the time of such taking or possession.

12. BROKERS. Tenant represents and warrants that it has not employed any broker other than Professional Brokerage Company and Mid-Town Realty, Inc. in carrying on the negotiations relating to this Sublease. Tenant shall indemnify and hold Landlord harmless from and against any claim for brokerage or other commission arising against any claim for brokerage or other commission arising from or out of any breach of the foregoing representation and warranty. Any representation or statement by a leasing company or other third party (or employee thereof) engaged by Landlord as an independent contractor which is made with regard to the demised premises or the Building shall not be binding upon Landlord or serve as a modification of this Lease and Landlord shall have no liability therefor, except to the extent such representation is also contained herein or is approved in writing by Landlord.

13. NOTICE. All notices or other communications hereunder shall be in writing and shall be deemed duly given if delivered in person or sent by certified or registered mail, return receipt requested, first class, postage prepaid, (i) if to Landlord: ABC Company
4425 West Wacker Drive
Suite 200
Chicago, IL 60630
Attention: Vice President of Corporate Real Estate

and (ii) if to Tenant: Ross, Jones and Smith, Inc.
4425 West Wacker Drive
Suite 201
Chicago, IL 60630
Attention: President

unless notice of change of address is given pursuant to the provisions of this Article 13.

EXHIBIT 5.3 *(Continued)*

14. COVENANTS OF LANDLORD. Landlord covenants that it has the right to make this Sublease and that if Tenant shall pay the rental and perform all of Tenant's obligations under this Sublease, Tenant shall, during the term hereof, freely, peaceably and quietly occupy and enjoy the full possession of the demised premises without molestation or hindrance by Landlord or any party claiming through or under Landlord. In the event of any sale or transfer of Landlord's interest in the demised premises, the covenants and obligations of Landlord hereunder accruing after the date of such sale or transfer shall be imposed upon such successor-in-interest (subject to the provisions of Article 22 of the Prime Lease) and any prior Landlord shall be freed and relieved of all covenants and obligations of Landlord hereunder accruing after the date of such sale or transfer.

15. LIEN FOR RENT. Tenant hereby grants to Landlord a lien on all property of Tenant now or hereafter placed in or on the demised premises (except such part of any property as may be exchanged, replaced, or sold from time to time in the ordinary course of business) and such property shall be and remain subject to such lien of Landlord for payment of all rent and all other sums agreed to be paid by Tenant herein or for services or costs relating to the demised premises that Tenant may hereafter agree to pay to Landlord. Said lien shall be in addition to and cumulative of the Landlord's lien rights provided by law.

16. PARKING. Landlord grants to Tenant the right to park six (6) automobiles for no additional monthly rental for the first year of the Prim Lease term and Landlord grants to Tenant the right to park one (1) automobile for no additional rental for the balance of the Sublease term on parking levels 1, or 2 as set forth in Exhibit E. Starting January 1, 1995 through the balance of the term of the Sublease, Landlord grants to Tenant the right to park five (5) automobiles for additional rent which shall be the then market rate for comparable parking in a Class A office building in the Chicago, IL metropolitan area. Nothing herein shall be construed to grant to tenant the exclusive right to a particular parking space, and at such appropriate, Landlord may rearrange parking spaces or may provide assigned spaces, and may provide attendant parking or such other system of management of parking as it deems necessary. Landlord shall not be liable to Tenant, its invitees, employees or guests because of failure to promptly remove snow, ice or water from the parking area and/or structure or because of any injury or damage that may be sustained due to holes of defects that may develop or arise in the parking areas or due to any inconvenience that may arise due to temporary closure of parking areas for repair, maintenance or snow, ice or water removal.

17. ENTIRE AGREEMENT. This Sublease, together with the Exhibits and any Addenda attached hereto, contain and embody the entire agreement of the parties hereto, and no representations, inducements, or agreements, real or otherwise, between the parties not contained in this Sublease, Addenda (if any) and Exhibits, shall be of any force or effect. This Sublease may not be modified, changed or terminated in whole or in part in any manner other than by an agreement in writing duly signed by both parties hereto.

18. DEFINED TERMS. All terms used herein which are defined in the Prime Lease shall have the same meaning as in the Prime Lease.

19. ASSUMPTION OF OBLIGATIONS BY TENANT. Tenant hereby expressly assumes each and every obligation of Landlord set forth in the Prime Lease (Exhibit G) with respect to the demised premises to the same extent as if Tenant had directly entered into a lease with the Prime Landlord for said demised premises. Notwithstanding the foregoing, Landlord acknowledges its continuing obligation to the Prime Landlord under the Prime Lease with respect to the demised premises.

20. LANDLORD'S CONSENT REQUIRED. Notwithstanding anything to the contrary contained herein, this Sublease shall be null and void, and of no force and effect whatever, unless executed by the Prime Landlord in the space provided. Prime Landlord's execution of the Sublease signifies its consent to every provision contained herein and permits Landlord to sublease the demised premises in accordance with its rights to do so under the Prime Lease.

21. SPECIAL STIPULATIONS. Landlord and Tenant agree to the following special stipulations to this Sublease which shall take precedence over other Articles in this Sublease:

(1) With Prim Landlord's consent, Landlord shall provide to the Tenant, at no additional rental for the term of the Sublease, use of the Building's 250 square foot Conference Room which Landlord shall construct at no

EXHIBIT 5.3 *(Continued)*

additional cost to the Tenant. The Conference Room shall be located on the first floor of the Building adjacent to the public rest rooms, as shown and specified on Exhibit F, and shall be available for Tenant use on a first come basis from 7:30 AM to 6:00 PM (CST) Monday through Friday and from 7:30 AM to 12:30 PM (CST) on Saturday.

(2) Landlord shall provide the Tenant with one (1) Option to renew the Sublease for an additional two (2) year and Nine (9) month term which shall commence on April 1, 1997 and terminate on December 31, 1999. Tenant shall notify the Landlord a minimum of 180 calendar days in advance of the beginning of the Option date should Tenant choose to exercise this Option to extend the Sublease.

(3) Landlord shall provide the Tenant with one (1) month of Rental Abatement commencing on January 1, 1995 and ending on January 31, 1995. Tenant shall pay as monthly rental during this Rent Abatement period Tenant's share of 1995 Operating Expenses which are $6.45 per rentable square feet which shall be One Thousand Seventy-Five and 00/100 Dollars ($1,075.00) per month.

In WITNESS WHEREOF, Tenant and Landlord have each executed this Lease as of the day and year first above written.

TENANT:
Ross, Jones and Smith, Inc.

Attest:

By: ______________________

Title: President

____
(Corporate Seal)

LANDLORD:
ABC Company

Attest:

By: ______________________

Title: Vice President

____
(Corporate Seal)

ACCEPTED AND AGREED TO THIS _____ DAY OF _________, 1995.

PRIME LANDLORD:
West Wacker Towers, L.P.

By: ______________________

Name: ______________________

Title: General Partner

EXHIBIT 5.3 *(Continued)*

EXHIBIT A

FLOOR PLAN - SUITE 201

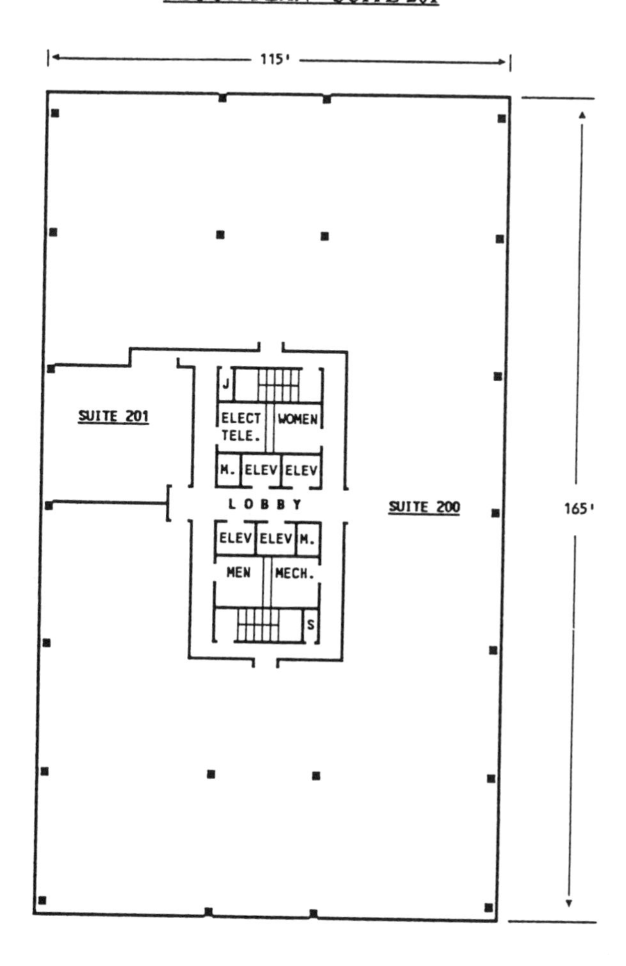

EXHIBIT 5.3 *(Continued)*

EXHIBIT "B"

WORK LETTER AGREEMENT

In consideration of the terms and conditions of the Sublease, the work shown in Exhibit "A" to this Sublease Agreement and in the terms and conditions hereinafter contained, Landlord and Tenant agree as follows:

A. Landlord's Standard Work

1. Landlord has selected certain building standard materials and building standard designs provided by the Prime Landlord for the Premises (hereinafter "Landlord's Standard Work"). Except as provided in Section B of this Work Letter Agreement, Landlord shall furnish and install Landlord's Standard Work in the Premises. Landlord's Standard Work shall include the following:

   a. **Partitions** - (number of) lineal feet of floor-to-finished-ceiling drywall partitions with 5/8" gypsum board and 4" vinyl cove base molding.

   b. **Painting** - Two (2) coats on partitions throughout the Premises, in colors selected by Tenant from Prime Landlord's standard paint colors and not more than two (2) colors in any one (1) room or space.

   c. **Ceilings** - Suspended 2' x 2' tegular acoustical ceiling installed in accordance with the building standard design. Ceiling height 9' - 0".

   d. **Lighting Fixtures** - (number of) recessed 2' x 4' fluorescent lighting fixtures installed in accordance with the building standard lighting design with three (3) fluorescent tubes per fixture.

   e. **Sprinkler System** - A sprinkler system including recessed sprinkler heads in accordance with the building standard sprinkler design and with City of Chicago Bureau of Buildings requirements.

   f. **Heating, Ventilating and Air-Conditioning (HVAC)** - A heating, ventilating and air conditioning system, including ducts, supply distribution and return air plenum. The Building Standard mechanical and electrical system is designed to accommodate loads generated by lights and equipment up to a maximum of 3.5 watts per square foot in specific areas (e.g. word and data processing areas, copying rooms, mail rooms, kitchens, special equipment areas) in the Premises.

   g. **Doors** - (number of) 3' - 0" wide x 8' - 6" high x 1 3/4" thick full height, solid core, oak veneer faced doors with frames, hinges, doorstops and latch sets. The entrance door to the Premises and all public corridor doors shall each have a lock set and closer.

   h. **Electrical and Telephone Outlets** - (number of) 120 volt duplex electrical outlets and (number of) telephone outlets not including wiring, equipment or fixtures customarily furnished by telephone suppliers. A single floor mounted device may contain one duplex electrical outlet, one telephone outlet, two duplex electrical outlets, two telephone outlets, or one duplex electrical outlet and one telephone outlet. Although provided through a single device, each shall be counted separately for purposes of determining the number of outlets Landlord is obligated to provide. Telephone conduit provided by Landlord is minimum 3/4" and maximum 1" in diameter. Landlord has not included any work, outlets or conduit in this Work Letter for Tenant's computer cabling. Should Tenant require additional outlets for computer cabling, Landlord shall charge Tenant a separate fee for such outlets. Tenant or Tenant's independent contractor shall provide and install computer cabling and where such cabling is in the return air plenum, Tenant shall ensure that such computer cable meets the City of Chicago's fire and smoke rating requirements.

   i. **Carpeting** - Carpeting throughout the Premises shall be of a type and color selected by the Tenant from Prime Landlord's standard types and colors.

   j. **Sun Control** - Landlord through Prime Landlord shall provide 1" aluminum horizontal blinds on all exterior windows. All such blinds shall be manufacturer's standard design, style and color as selected by the Prime Landlord.

EXHIBIT 5.3 *(Continued)*

k. **Public and Core Areas** - Landlord through Prime Landlord shall provide public and core areas within the Building as outlined in Exhibit "A", and finished in accordance with plans and specifications for the Building.

l. **Floor** - Landlord shall provide finished concrete prepared to receive floor covering. Floor loading capacities: 50 pounds per square foot live load, 20 pounds per square foot partition load or per square foot in non-partitioned areas.

B. Tenant's Non-Standard Work

1. Tenant may request work in addition to or different from Landlord's Standard Work (hereafter "Tenant's Non-Standard Work").

2. Landlord shall, upon Tenant's request in accordance with Sections C and D of this Work Letter Agreement, install the following Tenant's Non-Standard Work:

   a. Quantities and qualities of Landlord's Standard Work in excess of those provided by Landlord.

   b. Lighting fixtures, sprinklers and/or any mechanical equipment in other than Building standard design locations due to the location of partitions.

   c. Additional mechanical and electrical equipment and controls required by Tenant's design or use of the Premises generating loads in excess of those described in subparagraph A.1.f. of this Work Letter Agreement.

   d. Tenant's computer and telecommunication equipment, cabinets, modems, switching units, consoles and terminal boards.

   e. Tenant may request Landlord to install any other Tenant's Non-Standard Work in accordance with Section C and D of this Work Letter Agreement including by not limited to substitution of materials or change in design from Landlord's Standard Work. Any such request shall be subject to the written approval of Landlord, which Landlord may reasonably withhold.

   f. Landlord shall, upon Tenant's request and at Tenant's expense, alter, remove and/or replace acoustical ceiling tiles or exposed mechanical suspension system after initial installation due to installation of Tenant's computer, telephone or intercommunication system.

   g. All Tenant's Non-Standard Work shall be located within the Premises except were permitted by the Landlord and Prime Landlord in writing.

3. Improvements Constructed by Tenant: If any Work is to be performed in connection with improvements to the Premises by Tenant or Tenant's contractor:

   a. Such work shall proceed upon Landlord's and Prime Landlord's written approval of (i) Tenant's contractor, (ii) public liability and property damage insurance carried by Tenant's contractor, and (iii) detailed plans and specifications for such work.

   b. All work shall be dome in conformity with a valid building permit when required, a copy of which shall be furnished to Landlord and Prime Landlord before such Tenant's work is commenced, and in any case, all such work shall be performed in accordance with all applicable governmental regulations. Notwithstanding any failure by Landlord and/or Prime Landlord to object to any such work, Landlord and/or Prime Landlord shall have no responsibility for Tenant's failure to meet all applicable regulations.

   c. All work by Tenant or Tenant's contractor shall be done with Union labor in accordance with all Union Labor agreements applicable to the trades being employed.

   d. All work by Tenant or Tenant's contractor shall be scheduled through Landlord and Prime Landlord.

EXHIBIT 5.3 *(Continued)*

e. Tenant or Tenant's contractor shall arrange for necessary utility, hoisting and elevator service with Prime Landlord and Landlord's Contractor and shall pay such reasonable charges for such services as may be charged by Landlord's Contractor.

f. Tenant's entry to the Premises for any purpose, including without limitation, inspection or performance of Tenant construction by Tenant's agents, prior to the Sublease Commencement Date as specified in Paragraph 2 of the Sublease shall be subject to all the terms and conditions of the Sublease except the payment of Rent. Tenant's entry shall mean entry by Tenant, its officers, contractors, licensees, agents, employees, guests, invitees or visitors.

g. Tenant shall promptly reimburse Landlord upon demand for any extra expense incurred by Landlord by reason of faulty work done by Tenant or its contractors, or by reason of any delays caused by such work, or by reason of inadequate clean-up.

C. Responsibilities Of Landlord And Tenant

1. Time is of the essence with regard to the responsibilities of Landlord and Tenant under this Work Letter Agreement.

2. On or before (month, day, year) hereinafter known at the Preliminary Plan Delivery Date, Tenant shall provide Landlord with all necessary information, including all specifications and requirements for any Tenant's Non-Standard Work, to enable Landlord and/or Landlord's Architect to prepare a fully dimensioned floor plan and a reflected ceiling plan showing the location of the following:

   a. Partitions, doors, electrical, telephone and computer outlets;
   b. Equipment requiring electrical power, such as copiers, appliances, word processors, computers, printers, computer related equipment, and clocks;
   c. Furniture, fixtures, including trade fixtures, refrigerators, ice makers, coffee makers, microwave ovens, ovens, range hoods, can openers, water coolers, disposers, stoves, vending machines, cabinets and counters;
   d. Plumbing fixtures;
   e. Lighting;
   f. Special finishes to floors, walls and ceilings; and
   g. Special mechanical, electrical, or structural requirements, special features, facilities or additions.

3. From the information provided by Tenant, Landlord and/or Landlord's Architect shall prepare a fully dimensioned preliminary floor plan and reflected ceiling plan which Landlord shall submit to Tenant.

4. Tenant shall have ten (10) calendar days to review and approve the preliminary plans. Tenant shall also, at or prior to the time of approval, select paint color(s) and carpet type(s) and color(s) from Landlord's standard types and colors, and provide Landlord with any additional information Landlord needs in order to prepare working drawings and specifications.

5. Following Tenant's approval of the above preliminary plans and selections, and Landlord's receipt of necessary information, Landlord and/or Landlord's Architect and Engineer shall prepare working drawings and specifications which Landlord shall submit to Landlord.

6. Tenant shall have five (5) calendar days to review and approve the working drawings and specifications. Tenant shall also, at or prior to the time of approval, select paint color(s) and carpet type(s) and color(s) from Landlord's standard types and colors, and provide Landlord with any additional information Landlord needs in order to prepare working drawings and specifications.

7. Following Tenant's approval of the above working drawings and specifications and if Tenant has not requested Tenant's Non-Standard Work, Landlord shall, authorize Landlord's Contractor to commence construction.

8. If Tenant has requested and Landlord has granted necessary approvals for Tenant's Non-Standard Work, Landlord have the requested work incorporated into the working drawings and specifications and Landlord shall obtain a firm price for the Tenant's Non-Standard Work from the Landlord's Contractor. Landlord

EXHIBIT 5.3 *(Continued)*

will provide Tenant the firm price for the above Work and Tenant shall review and approve Landlord's Contractor's price within five (5) calendar days. Upon Tenant's written approval of Landlord's Contractor's price, Landlord with Prime Landlord's approval shall authorize Landlord's Contractor to commence construction. In the absence of such written approval, Landlord shall not be required to authorize commencement of construction.

9. Tenant shall be responsible for delays in completion of the Premises and additional costs in Landlord' Standard Work and Tenant's Non-Standard Work caused by:

   a. Tenant's failure to provide information or approvals in a timely manner;
   b. Request for materials, finishes or installations other than Landlord's Standard Work;
   c. Tenant's changes in any plans, drawings or specifications; and
   d. Inaccuracies, omissions, or changes in any information provided by Tenant.

   Delay in completion of Landlord's Standard Work or Tenant's Non-Standard Work for any of the foregoing reasons shall be considered the fault of Tenant and shall not serve to extend the Commencement Date under Paragraph 2 of the Lease.

10. If Tenant shall request any change after construction commencement, Tenant shall request in writing to Landlord and such request shall be accompanied by all plans and specifications necessary to show and explain changes from the approved working drawings and specifications. After receiving this information, Landlord shall give Tenant a written estimate of the maximum cost of engineering and design services to prepare working drawings and incorporate the changes in accordance with such request. If Tenant approves such estimate in writing, Landlord shall have such working drawings prepared and Tenant shall reimburse Landlord for the cost thereof not in excess of such estimate. Promptly upon completion of such working drawings, Landlord shall obtain a cost, if any, for the change from Landlord's Contractor and Landlord shall notify Tenant in writing of the cost, if any, which will be chargeable or credited to Tenant for such change, addition or deletion. Tenant shall within fine (5) calendar days notify Landlord in writing to proceed with such change addition or deletion. In the absence of such notice, Landlord shall proceed in accordance with the working drawings and specifications prepared pursuant to the previously approved working drawings and specifications.

11. No Landlord's Standard Work or Tenant's Non-Standard Work shall be performed by Tenant or Tenant's contractor unless approved in writing by Landlord and Prime Landlord.

D. Financial

1. If Tenant does not request any Tenant's Non-Standard Work, Landlord shall install and furnish Landlord's Standard Work at Landlord's expense, including expense related to preparation of the fully dimensioned preliminary floor plan, reflected ceiling plan, and the working drawings and specifications.

2. If Tenant requests Tenant's Non-Standard Work, Tenant shall pay Landlord all costs related to Tenant's Non-Standard Work, including but not limited to:

   a. The cost of professional services (including services of architects, interior designers, engineers and consultants) required to incorporate Tenant's Non-Standard Work into the working drawings and specifications;
   b. The cost of materials other than Landlord's Standard Work materials and the cost of installing such materials; and
   c. The cost of structural changes in the Building.

   Whether or not Tenant requests Tenant's Non-Standard Work, Tenant shall not be entitled to an credits whatsoever for Landlord's Standard Work not utilized by Tenant.

3. Following commencement of construction, Landlord shall bill Tenant monthly for the cost of Tenant's Non-Standard Work. Tenant shall pay Landlord the entire amount of each statement within ten (10) calendar days after receipt.

EXHIBIT 5.3 *(Continued)*

4. **Notwithstanding Paragraphs 6 and 9 of the Lease, any sums payable by Tenant to Landlord under this Work Letter Agreement which shall not be paid upon the due date shall bear interest at a rate equal to the Prime Rate as determined by First Bank of Chicago plus one (1) percentage point, as the rate may vary from time to time.**

LANDLORD:
ABC COMPANY

By:______________________________

Title: Vice President

Date:______________________________

TENANT:
Ross, Jones, and Smith, Inc.

By:______________________________

Title: President

Date:______________________________

ACCEPTED AND AGREED TO THIS ____ DAY OF ____________, 1995

PRIME LANDLORD:
West Wacker Towers, L.P.

By:______________________________

Name:______________________________

Title: General Partner

EXHIBIT 5.3 *(Continued)*

EXHIBIT "C"

RULES AND REGULATIONS

1. **Common Areas.** The sidewalks, halls, passages, exits, entrances, elevators, and stairways of the Building shall not be obstructed by any of the tenants or used by them for any purpose other than for ingress to and egress from their respective premises. The halls, passages, exits, entrances, elevators and stairways are not intended for use by the general public and Landlord shall in all cases retain the right to control and prevent access thereto of all persons whose presence in the judgment of Landlord would be prejudicial to the safety, character, reputation or interest of the Building, Landlord or tenants, provided that nothing herein contained shall be construed to prevent access by persons with whom any tenant normally deals in the ordinary course of its business, unless such persons are engaged in illegal activities.

2. **Use and Occupancy of Premises.** For the safety, efficiency and protection of the tenants and the Building, Tenant shall not, nor permit any employee, agent, or invitee of Tenant to use its Premises for:

   a. Storage of merchandise held for sale to the general public;

   b. Lodging;

   c. Cooking except for private use by Tenant or its employees with Underwriters Laboratory approved equipment for brewing coffee, tea or hot chocolate. Such limited quantities shall be only stored in containers approved by appropriate regulatory agencies;

   d. Use or keeping or storing any kerosene, gasoline or inflammable or combustible fluid or material other that limited quantities thereof reasonably necessary for the operation or maintenance of office equipment, foul or noxious gas or substance;

   e. The business of stenography, typewriting, printing or photocopying or any similar business for the service or accommodation of occupants of any other portion of the Building, unless specifically authorized in the Lease:

   f. Any use which would be reasonably offensive to other tenants or Landlord or which would tend to create a nuisance or damage the reputation of the Premises or Building.

3. **Prohibited Activities.** Tenant shall not, nor permit any employee, agent or invitee of Tenant to:

   a. Interfere in any way with other tenants or those having business in the Building:

   b. Use in its Premises of ice, drinking water, beverages, or catering service except at such reasonable hours and under such reasonable regulations as may be fixed by Landlord;

   c. Bring into the Building or keep within its Premises any birds or animals other than seeing eye dogs and like animals;

   d. Load any floor beyond the point considered safe by a competent engineer or architect selected by the Landlord.

   e. Use any method of heating or air conditioning other than that provided by the Landlord;

   f. Attach or install curtains, draperies, blinds, shades, sun control devices, screens on or adjacent to any window or glass situated within its Premises without Landlord's written consent which shall not be unreasonably withheld.

   g. Use in the Building or its Premises any hand trucks except those equipped with rubber tires and side guards or such other material handling equipment without Landlord's prior written consent;

   h. Operate any television, radio, recorder or sound system in such a manner as to cause a nuisance to any other tenant of the Building;

EXHIBIT 5.3 *(Continued)*

i. Engage in any activity which would make it impossible to insure the Premises against casualty, would increase the insurance rate, or would prevent Landlord from taking advantage of any ruling of the State and local regulatory insurance agencies and Landlord's insurance company, unless Tenant pays the additional cost of insurance.

4. **Tenant Requirements.** Tenant shall, and shall require its employees and agents to:

   a. Keep window coverings in its Premises closed when the effect of sunlight or cold weather would impose unnecessary loads on the Building's heating or air conditioning system;

   b. Keep the doors to Building corridors closed at all times except for ingress and egress and ensure that the doors of its Premises are closed and locked and that all water faucets, water apparatus and utilities are shut off before leaving the Premises each day; and

   c. Store all its trash and refuse within its Premises. No material shall be placed in trash boxes of receptacles if such material is of such nature that it may not be safely disposed of in the customary manner of removing and disposing of office build trash and refuse in the City of Chicago without being in violation of any law or ordinance governing such disposal. All trash and refuse disposal shall be made only through entrances and elevators provided for such purposes and at such times as Landlord shall designate.

5. **Keys and Locks.** Landlord will furnish each tenant two keys to each entry door lock to its Premises. Landlord may make a reasonable charge for any additional keys. Tenant shall not have any such keys duplicated. Tenant shall not alter any lock, install a new or additional lock or any bolt on any door of its Premises. Upon the Termination of the lease, Tenant shall deliver to Landlord all keys to Premise doors.

6. **Janitorial Service.** Tenant shall not employ, authorize or permit any person, persons or firm other that the janitor of the Landlord for the purpose of cleaning its Premises. Landlord shall not be responsible to any tenant for any loss of property on the premises, however occurring, or for any damage done to the effects of any tenant by the janitor or any other employee or any other person. Janitor service will not be furnished on nights when rooms are occupied after 6:00 P.M. unless, by prior agreement in writing, service is extended to a later hour for specifically designated rooms.

7. **Use of Service Elevator.** The Landlord shall designate appropriate entrances and a "service" elevator for deliveries or other movement to or from the Premises of equipment, materials, supplies, furniture or other property, and Tenant shall not use any other entrances or elevators for such purposes. The service elevator shall be available for use by all tenants in the Building, subject to such reasonable scheduling as Landlord at its discretion shall deem appropriate.

8. **Movement of Equipment.** All persons employed by the Tenant who have the means or methods to move equipment, materials, supplies, furniture or other property in or out of the Building must be approved by Landlord prior to any such movement. Landlord shall have the right to prescribe the method of protection to the Building, lobbies, corridors, elevator and Premises to be provided by the Tenant before such movement and prescribe the maximum weight, size and positions of all equipment, materials, furniture or other property brought into the Building. Heavy objects shall, if considered necessary by Landlord, stand on a platform of such thickness as is necessary to properly distribute the weight. Landlord will not be responsible for loss of or damage to any such property from any cause, and all damage done to the Building by moving or maintaining such property shall be repaired at the expense of the Tenant.

9. **Building Services.** Landlord establishes the hours 8:00 A.M. to 6:00 P.M. (CST) of each weekday and 8:00 A.M. to 1:00 P.M. (CST) on Saturdays, as reasonable and usual business hours for the purposes of this Lease. If Tenant requests heat or air conditioning during any hours other than the above and if Landlord is able to provide the same, Tenant shall pay Landlord such charges as Landlord shall establish from time to time for providing such services during such hours. Any such charges which Tenant is obligated to pay shall be deemed to be additional rent under this Lease, and should Tenant fail to pay the same within twenty (20) days after demand invoice, such failure shall be a default by Tenant under this Lease.

10. **Access to Building After Hours.** Landlord reserves the right to exclude from the Building all persons who do not present identification acceptable to Landlord between the hours of 6:00 P.M. and 7:00 A.M. (CST) and at all hours on Saturdays, Sundays and legal holidays. Tenant shall provide Landlord with a list of all persons

EXHIBIT 5.3 *(Continued)*

authorized by Tenant to enter its Premises and shall be liable to Landlord for all acts of such persons. Landlord shall in no case be liable for damages for any error with regard to the admission to or exclusion from the Building of any person. In the case of invasion, mob, riot, public excitement or other circumstances rendering such action advisable in Landlord's opinion, Landlord reserves the right to prevent access to the Building during the continuance of the same by such action as Landlord may deem appropriate.

11. **Building Directory.** A building directory will be provided for the display of the name and location of tenants and a reasonable number of the principal officers and employees of tenants. Landlord reserves the right to restrict the amount of directory space utilized by any tenant.

12. **Rest Room Use.** Rest rooms and all fixtures and apparatus located therein shall not be used for any purpose other than that for which they were constructed.

13. **Tenant's Requests.** Special requests of tenants will be considered only upon receipt of a written and signed application on Tenants letterhead stationary addressed to the Landlord. Landlord reserves the right to deny and such special requests. Employees of Landlord shall not perform any work or do anything outside of their regular duties unless under special instructions from Landlord.

14. **Canvassing in the Building.** Canvassing, soliciting, distribution of handbills or any other written material and peddling in the Building are prohibited, and Tenant shall cooperate to prevent the same.

15. **Signs.** No sign, placard, picture, name, advertisement or notice visible from the exterior of any tenant's premises shall be inscribed, painted, affixed or otherwise displayed by any tenant on any part of the Building without the prior written consent of Landlord. Landlord will adopt and furnish to tenants general guidelines relating to signs inside the Building. Tenant agrees to conform to such guidelines. All approved signs or lettering on doors shall be printed, painted, affixed or inscribed at the expense of the Tenant by a person approved by Landlord. Material visible from outside the Building will not be permitted without the prior written consent of Landlord.

16. **Building Name and Street Address.** Landlord shall have the right, exercisable without notice and without liability to any tenant, to change the name or street address of the Building.

17. **Landlord Access.** Landlord shall, at reasonable hours, have the right to enter premises leased to tenants, to examine same or to make such alterations and repairs as may be deemed necessary, or to exhibit the same to prospective tenants.

18. **Noise and Building Utilization.** Tenants shall not make or permit any improper noises in the Building, or otherwise interfere in any way with other tenants, or person having business with them.

19. **Rules and Regulations.** Landlord may waive any one or more of these Rules and Regulations for the benefit of any particular tenant or tenants, but no such waiver by Landlord shall be construed as a waiver of such Rules and Regulations in favor of any other tenant or tenants, or prevent Landlord from thereafter enforcing any such Rules and Regulations against any or all of the tenants of the Building. These Rules and Regulations are in addition to, and shall not be construed to in any way modify or amend, in whole or in part, the agreements, covenants, conditions and provisions of any lease of premises in the Building. Landlord reserves the right to make such other rules and regulations as in its judgement may from time to time be needed for the safety, care and cleanliness of the Building, for the preservation of good order therein, and to meet and require tenants to observe and comply with additional Federal, State and local regulations as they pertain to the tenant's occupancy of the Building and the tenant's Premises.

■

EXHIBIT 5.3 *(Continued)*

EXHIBIT "D"

LEASE COMMENCEMENT DATE

An Agreement made this ______ day of ________________, 199__, by and between ____________________ ____________________________ (hereinafter called "Landlord") and ______________________________________ (hereinafter called "Tenant").

WITNESSETH:

WHEREAS on ____________________, 199__, Landlord and Tenant entered into a Sublease (the "Sublease") relating to certain office premises located at ____; and

WHEREAS the term of the Sublease has commenced, pursuant to Section ____ of the Sublease; and

NOW, THEREFORE, in consideration of the mutual covenants herein contained, Landlord and Tenant agree as follows:

1. The Term Commencement Date of the Sublease is ________________________________.
2. Tenant's obligation to pay Rent under the Sublease commenced on ____________________.
3. The Term Expiration Date of the Sublease is ________________________________.
4. The execution of this Agreement shall not constitute the exercise by Tenant of any option it may have to extend the term of the Sublease.
5. The Lease and Sublease is in full force and effect and is hereby ratified and confirmed.

IN WHEREAS WHEREOF, Landlord and Tenant have caused this Agreement to be duly executed on the date first written above.

Landlord: ______________________________ Tenant: ______________________________

EXHIBIT 5.3 *(Continued)*

EXHIBIT "E"

LEVELS 1 AND 2 PARKING PLAN

....

EXHIBIT 5.3 **(continued)**

EXHIBIT "F"

CONFERENCE ROOM PLAN

....

EXHIBIT 5.3 **(continued)**

EXHIBIT "G"

PRIME LEASE

(2) Donation

A division of the EMR Corporation had purchased a tract of land for new facility expansion. The tract, 160 acres in area, was to be utilized as follows: 20 acres for immediate use; 25 acres for future plant expansion; 115 acres for resale at a later date. Of the 115 acres, 60 acres were occupied by a small "feeder" airport with a 4,000-foot asphalt runway; 40 acres were occupied by "T" hangars and used as an aircraft tie-down area; and 15 acres, at the rear of the property, were unused.

After the land purchase, the former owner remained as an airport operator on a month-to-month lease with EMR Corporation. With the exception of the 20 acres for EMR's new facilities, the land remained committed as before and, based on state statute, all land used for airport purposes (60 acres plus 40 acres) was exempt from local property taxes, thus significantly reducing EMR's holding costs.

Several years passed without incident. Then a number of changes occurred. First, the former owner/airport operator died, and EMR was faced with operating the airport—not a bright prospect given its lack of experience and enthusiasm for the job. Second, a large number of small manufacturers located in the vicinity of the airport used it for a growing fleet of company aircraft. The airport became a vital economic asset for the community. Third, the runway and other facilities had deteriorated so that they were in need of $300,000 in repairs. Fourth, the airport land acquired significant market value for light industrial/distribution use. Fifth, and this became an element in the business decision reached, another division of EMR manufactured general aviation aircraft in a location far removed from the subject airport.

There was little doubt that EMR wanted to divest itself of the airport, realize a profit from the sale of its land, and go on about its manufacturing business. But the potential negative public relations effect of a sale and the closing of the airport hovered over the decision like a buzzard over a dying steer. The local community would have suffered from the closing—and EMR now had a large fixed asset investment there. An adverse impact on EMR's aircraft division was also a possibility.

The problem of dealing with the 115 acres targeted for resale was solved by donating 25 acres of the 60-acre airport site to a county airport agency that already operated two other airports and that, by virtue of its public charter, qualified for matching fund grants from state and federal agencies. The balance of the airport site, 35 acres, was sold at fair market value to the county for use as an aircraft storage area and as the site of a new terminal location, and EMR entered into a year-to-year lease with the county for the remaining 55 acres (to provide transition time for the construction of hangars and the terminal). The local community was able to keep its airport without having to absorb the financial burden of repairs and maintenance, the county was happy to acquire another airport; and, most importantly, EMR emerged a hero—*and made money on the deal.* Here is how it worked.

Under Section 170 of the Internal Revenue Code (IRC), the basic rule with respect to a donation of property to a governmental unit is that the gift be made for exclusively public purposes without any strings attached. Thus EMR's donation qualified for a tax deduction.

On the acreage sale, EMR estimated an after-tax gain of $7,000, and on the donation, an after-tax loss of $72,000. Therefore, a net after-tax loss of $65,000 was anticipated. However, offsetting the loss was an estimated property tax savings of $100,000 by the avoidance of taxes on the acreage sold and on the leased land area, which would be held for anticipated market appreciation. The reconditioning and modernizing of the airport facilities were viewed as a "plus" for future land sales by the corporate real estate department. Three years after the donation and relocation of airport support facilities, the lease was terminated by mutual agreement, and EMR sold the remaining 55 acres in two parcels for $2,775,000, at an approximate after-tax gain of $1,120,000.

(3) Sale to a Liquidator

The Wheels and Widgets Manufacturing Company declared a manufacturing facility surplus. It had the following characteristics:

- Age of building: 32 years.
- Building area: 170,000 square feet.
- Land area: 12 acres.
- Zoning: Heavy manufacturing.
- Ceiling height: 25-foot clearance.
- Other features: Sprinklered, 12 cranes (1½–6 ton), rail spur, low-pressure gas heaters, four truck doors, high labor rates.

The property was appraised at $260,000. The recent sale of a comparably sized facility in a comparable location in the same city, for $1 per square foot, influenced the value estimate. The real estate department's evaluation supported the value estimate even though the depreciated net book value (NBV) of the facility equaled $400,000. An initial asking price of $450,000 was established, with marketing to be handled by the corporate real estate department and no brokerage listing agreements. Prospects for achieving a sale at or above NBV appeared dim. The operating division was having difficulty maintaining its annual operating profit (AOP) and could not readily afford a sale at much less than book value.

The facility still contained a good deal of machinery and equipment after intradivision and interdivision redeployment transfers. The W&W real estate department recommended that the company seek bids on the whole package—machinery, equipment, and real estate—rather than sell the remaining machinery and equipment on a bid basis. The real estate department maintained contact with used machinery and equipment dealers throughout the country. A list of potential buyers was prepared, and invitations to view the merchandise were issued. Subsequently, an asset list was distributed to a reduced list of prospects and sealed competitive bids were requested.

The company accepted the high bid of $735,000. Through advantageously allocating value between real estate and machinery and equipment, the division avoided a loss and garnered a significant gain on the fully depreciated machinery and equipment.

(4) Installment Sale

The IRS requirements for installment sales of real estate should be considered. Our emphasis here is on the business strategy rationale for electing this type of sale. Use the installment sale to maximize profit (usually in the form of long-term capital gains) or minimize a loss, or both. Your decision will be affected by:

- Your general operating plan.
- The relative marketability of the property.
- Your current and forecast tax position.
- Your ability to wait for future payments.
- The creditworthiness of the proposed buyer as determined by your finance department.

The installment sale is a viable disposition alternative when, on balance, your evaluation of the preceding factors is positive.

(5) Lease Buy-Out

A buy-out of the lease is another viable option if the lessor needs your space for an existing tenant or for a new tenant. If the facility has too much vacant space, if there is an overabundance of similar space, or if you are currently paying market or above-market rent, the landlord usually will not consider a lease buy-out.

But if the landlord needs cash, has a highly qualified tenant ready to take over your space at a higher rate than you are paying or can provide a more marketable space or contiguous floor area to sign a new tenant, a buy-out of your lease may be possible. The buy-out must provide an economic benefit to the landlord, and usually the tenant must make the initial offer on the buy-out amount. This cash buy-out should take into account the:

- Remaining value of the space at the current rate times the time remaining on the lease.
- Plus or minus the remaining value of the space at today's market rate times the time remaining on the lease.
- Plus a recapture of the value of the remaining undepreciated improvements made by the landlord.
- Plus a recapture of a value for a pro rata amount of any other costs or cash inducements (moving costs, etc).
- Plus a recapture of the value on the pro rata number of months of free rent (if any).
- Plus a recapture of a pro rata value of design and project management fees.
- Plus a recapture of a pro rata value of the real estate commissions paid by the landlord.
- Plus an estimated marketing cost to acquire a new tenant, which is added to the preceding and totaled.

The net present value (NPV) of the total will indicate today's value or the "time value of money" of the total and is the *breakeven point* in the proposed buy-out. To obtain the NPV, you will need to determine the financial value of money today. This financial value is the percentage of interest that your company or the landlord would usually have to pay to borrow money from a financial institution.

The breakeven point *can* provide a beginning figure on which to base your initial buy-out offer. This offer may or may not be acceptable depending on the market, the landlord's immediate need for cash, and his or her estimate of what your company is willing to pay to get out of the lease. Your negotiation skills and strategy, as well as help from your real estate broker, can help to establish your initial offer, subsequent offers, and final offer.

A lease buy-out can be very beneficial to your customer and corporation in removing a legal and financial obligation from today's balance sheet. It is important that you and your legal counsel review this document carefully to ensure that the buy-out is the *final* payment and that the corporation will have *no* further obligations to the landlord for this space. This document should remove all liability for *all* past or future additional rents, costs, expenses, liens, fees, taxes, or assessments. After the buy-out is complete, it is not unusual to receive a bill(s) later for additional operating expenses, fees, or taxes for the space; your buy-out document should provide protection from such demands.

Example. ABC Company currently is a tenant in the XYZ building in a downtown mid-rise building. The company is planning to relocate the operation in the XYZ building to another city that will provide considerable marketing and income opportunities. At the time of relocation, however, 36 months will remain on the current 5-year lease. The company does not want to sublease the space but wishes to buy out the remaining lease commitment. The local real estate market surrounding the XYZ building is soft, and the building is 30 percent vacant. Nevertheless, the landlord of the XYZ building needs cash and may consider a buy-out of the lease, but will not make an offer. What offer could (should) you make to the landlord?

Before making such an offer, you will need to take into account the issues that the landlord will consider. Based on the lease agreement, the following is one approach to looking at the remaining investment in the lease space:

Total Leased Area: 25,550 Rentable Square Feet (RSF)
Current Lease Rate: $18.00/RSF
Lease Rent Increase: 3% Per Year
NPV Rate: 8%
ABC Company Expenses:

	1993 (9 mo.)	1994 (12 mo.)	1995 (12 mo.)	1996 (3 mo.)	TOTAL (3 yrs. 0 mo.)
Upfit/Depreciation	$ 24,388	$ 32,518	$ 32,518	$ 8,130	$ 97,554
Rent and Operating Expense	374,165	513,852	529,268	133,288	1,550,573
Total Expenses	$398,553	$546,371	$561,786	$141,417	$1,648,127

Recapture Expenses:

	1993 (9 mo.)	1994 (12 mo.)	1995 (12 mo.)	1996 (3 mo.)	TOTAL (3 yrs. 0 mo.)
Undepreciated Improvements	$ 8,130	$ 32,518	$ 32,518	$ 8,130	$ 81,295
6 Months' Free Rent and 4 Months' Marketing Exp.	$337,357				337,357
Fees and Commissions	6,676	27,252	27,997	8,858	70,783
36 Months' Recapture Costs					489,435
Total Possible Buy-Out Obligation					$2,137,562

The remaining rent and depreciation on premises improvement due to the landlord over the 36-month period is $1,648,127. The recapture of prior expenses and projects expenses totals $489,435. So the total possible obligation may be approximately $2,137,562 in future dollars to buy out the lease obligation. Using a net present value rate of 8 percent of the cash requirements for each year, we can determine the current total dollar value that the future $2,137,562 represents today.

Once we have the possible buy-out breakeven number, this becomes the basis for the initial buy-out offer. It is not uncommon to offer a landlord half or less of the breakeven number as an initial buy-out offer and then based on the landlord's response, continue with negotiations or call off the tenant buy-out process. Some landlords will negotiate and some will not depending on what the tenant is paying, their vacancy rate, cash flow situation, current debt service requirements, relationship with their mortgage lender or financial partner, and marketing prospects for the building and for leasing the space in question at a higher rate than is currently being paid.

(6) Joint Venture

This subject is covered in detail in Chapter Eight. We mention it here just as another possible disposition alternative. There are times when a community can effectively block the disposal of property. For example, the New York Institute of Technology in Brookville, New York, wanted to sell its 100-acre Long Island campus to Cannon Corporation as a site for its corporate headquarters. After over a year of work and meeting with local residents and community groups, Cannon found that the major preoccupation in the area was preserving what is commonly referred to as "a way of life." Cannon even agreed to build on only five acres, place parking underground and preserve 95 acres of the campus lawns, oaks, and weeping willows. The final decision from Brookville relied on a special exception from the residential zoning previously granted to the school that could *not* be extended to Cannon. Here the property owner was effectively blocked from this joint venture, which would have also placed the property back on the property tax roles—the 100-acre school site was exempt from property taxes.[22]

§ 5.3 WHO SHOULD MARKET YOUR REAL ESTATE?

You will be dollars ahead if an internal real estate department merchandises your real estate. Such a department will have your best interests at

[22] "Village Rebuffs Big Corporate Office and Long Island Worries over Price," *The New York Times*, August 23, 1992, p. 18.

heart, save you dollars that would otherwise be spent on commissions, and protect the privacy of your operating plans.

But perhaps you are not ready to establish a real estate department, do not have enough real estate/facility activities to make such a department worthwhile, or have downsized your real estate department and rely on outsourcing to provide the majority of the marketing services. In that event, the chances are good that you will turn to the real estate brokerage community for assistance.

(a) REAL ESTATE BROKER EXPERTISE

The hard-won experience of a well-qualified, professional real estate broker can provide you with counsel that will probably not be available from your legal counsel, customer, or anyone within your corporation.

The real estate broker serves as your expert and resource on the health and availability of real estate in the local geographical market (see Exhibits 5.4 and 5.5). His or her knowledge and contacts for the type of real estate you are dealing with can help you successfully identify potential real estate sites and acquire or dispose of real estate in a timely manner.

Traditionally, the broker's commission for services has been paid by the landlord (leased property) or by the seller (purchased property). The broker's commission for leased property is often a percentage of the total rent to be paid over the term of the lease. For purchased property, it is often a percentage of the total purchase price. There is also a growing number of tenant representation brokers who market their services as a consultant. These brokers will represent you for a fee for services in lieu of the landlord or seller paying them a commission. A number of companies also market their services as real estate counselors or corporate real estate advisory services; these consultants usually work on very large, complex requirements to lease, sublease, acquire, or dispose of property.

But the brokerage community is evolving—large regional and national real estate brokerage firms are moving toward partnerships with corporations and corporate real estate departments, sometimes grudgingly, as market rate commissions give way to prenegotiated fees, contingent commissions change into salaried and performance bonus compensation packages, and the isolated deal becomes a part of the larger corporate business strategy. These changes are profound for the traditional real estate brokerage/development industry and, in particular, for the street broker. The real estate broker is becoming more corporate and a member in partnership with the corporate real estate executives of the emerging "new guard."[23]

[23] Robert Kevin Brown, "Corporate Staff Changes Herald Changing of the Guard," *National Real Estate Investor,* October 1988, p. 42.

EXHIBIT 5.4 Lease Property Market Survey

MARKET SURVEY ITEMS	BLDG. 1	BLDG. 2	BLDG. 3	BLDG. 4	BLDG. 5
Building Name	Park Plaza	191 Union Tower	Westfield Place	Sutton Building	1 Crown Square
Building Quality (A, B, or C)	A	A	B	C	A
Landlord	Main St. Ltd.	Wright & Partners	Associated Developers	Metro Properties	Brown & Thomas
Financial Partner	Major Life Insurance	Western Casualty	Chicago Nat'l. Bank	Metro Properties	Teacher's Pension Fund
Total Building Rentable Sq. Ft.	258,000	487,400	281,500	110,700	879,550
Building Occupancy %	78.3%	85.2%	67.8%	59.6%	62.4%
Available Rentable Sq. Ft.	55,986	72,137	90,562	44,723	330,711
Available Contiguous R.S.F.	43,000	23,210	31,760	27,610	201,040
Floor Plate Size (R.S.F.)	21,500	23,210	18,750	18,450	25,150
Number of Floors	12	21	15	6	35
Efficiency Factor (rsf/usf)	1.143	1.112	1.136	1.162	1.122
Rate Per Rentable Square Foot	$18.00	$20.50	$15.00	$12.00	$23.00
Rent Escalation	5% / yr.	C.P.I.	3% / yr.	$.15/rsf/yr	7% / yr.
Operating Expense Cost Per RSF	$8.10	$7.05	$6.50	$7.73	$9.12
Blocks From ABC Building	Adjacent	2 North	1 South	3 East	2 West
Building Age	6 yrs.	7 yrs.	10 yrs.	14 yrs.	6 mos.
Floor to Ceiling Height	9' - 0"	8' - 6"	8' - 6"	8' - 3"	9' - 0"
Improvement Allowance/U.S.F.	$22.00	Turnkey	$15.00	Work Ltr.	$27.50
Free Rent On Five Year Term	12 months	9 months	10 months	5 months	12 mos.
Expansion Options	Yes	No	Yes	Yes	Yes
Cancellation Option Available	No	Unknown	Yes	Yes	No
Building Security	Card Access	Sign In/Out	Key and After Hrs.	After Hrs. Only	24 Hrs./On Site
Sprinklered	Yes	Yes	Yes	No	Yes
Conference Room/Facility	No	Yes	No	No	Yes
On Site Parking Available	Yes	No	Yes	Yes	No
Available Parking Cost/Space	$3.15/day	$2.25/day	$2.75/day	No cost	$3.50
Food Service	Yes	Yes	No	Yes	Yes
Computer Room Available	Yes/5th Fl.	No	Yes/Bsmt.	Yes	No
Freight Elevator	Yes	Yes	No	No	Yes
Loading Dock	Yes/3 bays	Yes/2 bays	Yes/2 bays	No	Yes/4 bays

Additional Market Survey Information:

Building 1 - Landlord has been aggressively marketing the building as a number of the 1st five year tenants have left the building. Building includes a quality sit down sandwich shop and is frequented by building tenants and tenants from adjacent buildings. No asbestos.

Building 2 - Landlord's Financial Partner has previously taken 3 to 6 months to review each proposal and 2 to 4 months to sign off on the lease for this quality building. A new property management company has been hired and building janitorial services have improved. No asbestos.

Building 3 - A major corporation which occupies 4 floors will be moving out of the building in 60 days. This space includes a 3,000 square foot computer room with 12" raised floor and a 2 hour UPS System in the building basement. Landlord has been marketing the space and may be close to leasing 2 floors. No asbestos.

Building 4 - Landlord has a good reputation and has numerous office properties throughout Chicago. Building is in good repair and lobby/elevator has recently been renovated. One of the tenants is a small competitor of ABC, Inc. and has three years remaining on there lease. Asbestos has been partially abated.

Building 5 - This is a landmark design and is the newest office building in town. A major corporation has leased 50% of the building for 15 years. There is a lunch/dinner club on the top floor, the ground floor contains a number of food and retail shops, and the conference facility will accommodate 50 in a classroom setting.

EXHIBIT 5.5 Purchase Property Market Survey

MARKET SURVEY ITEMS	PROP. 1	PROP. 2	PROP. 3	PROP. 4	PROP. 5
Building Name	132 Union Center	Summitview Terrace	832 Ridgecrest	4420 Main Street	1st Nat'l. Bank Bldg.
Prop./Bldg. Quality (A, B, or C)	B	A	C	B	A
Property Owner	Associated Developers	Brown & Thomas	Smith Properties	Teacher's Pension Fund	Sumitzu Bank & Trust
Acreage Available	6.112	4.231	5.568	3.827	2.969
Site Terrain	Sloping	Level	Sloping	Level	Sloping
Bldg. Size (Gross Sq. Ft.)	77,848	253,000	127,680	375,138	372,806
Number of Floors	4	10	7	18	14
Gross Square Feet Per Floor	19,462	25,300	18,240	20,841	26,629
Efficiency Factor (gsf/usf)	1.123	1.142	1.109	1.136	1.157
Blocks From ABC Building	1 West	2 South	4 North	Adjacent	3 East
Sale Price For Property/Sq. Ft.	$7.00	$12.00	$10.00	$15.00	$17.00
Total Property Sale Price	$1,597,400	$2,211,600	$2,425,450	$2,500,000	$2,198,600
Sale Price For Building/GSF	$78.00	$93.00	$69.00	$82.00	$104.00
Total Building Sale Price	$6,072,144	$23,529,000	$8,809,920	$30,761,316	$38,771,824
Total Property/Building Sale Price	$7,669,544	$25,740,600	$11,235,370	$33,261,316	$40,970,424
Building Age	8 yrs.	5 yrs.	12 yrs.	10 yrs.	16 yrs.
Building Occupancy %	72.8%	0%	87.2%	77.6%	62.4%
Operating Cost Per GSF	$6.96	$8.21	$7.24	$8.47	$9.91
On Site Parking Spaces/1,000 GSF	3.11	1.13	2.2	2.5	None
Number Of Mos. On The Market	3	6	10	7	9
Previous Office Use	Spec.	Corp. HQ.	Spec.	Spec.	Bank/Spec
Floor To Ceiling Height	8' - 8"	9' - 0"	8' - 2"	8' - 6"	9' - 0"
Building Security	Sign In/Out	Card Access	Key and After Hours	After Hours Only	24 Hrs./On Site
Asbestos/Structure	No/Steel	No/Steel	Yes/Steel	No/Concrete	No/Concrete
Computer Room	Yes/1st Fl.	Yes/Bsmt.	No	No	Yes/Bsmt.
Sprinklered	Yes	Yes	Partial	Yes	Yes
Food Service	Yes	Yes	No	No	Yes
Loading Dock	Yes/1 Bay	Yes/2 Bays	Yes/1 Bay	Yes/2 Bays	Yes/3 Bays
Freight Elevator	Yes	Yes	No	No	Yes

Additional Market Survey Information:

Property 1 - Seller is slowly leasing the building after a major tenant moved out to Building 5. Majority of leases have 3 or less years until termination. Seller is very interested in selling for cash.

Property 2 - A major corporation headquarters has left town and the building is vacant. This building includes a 5,000 square foot computer room with 18" raised floor, a 4 hour UPS System and an emergency generator in the building basement.

Property 3 - Seller has a good reputation and has numerous office properties throughout Chicago. Building is in good repair and lobby/elevator has recently been renovated.

Property 4 - A new brokerage company has just listed the building and is known for getting "top dollar" for sellers.

Property 5 - This is an older landmark design and a major bank is in the process of relocating to a new building. There is a full service restaurant on the ground floor which also contains a number of retail shops, and a health facility which can accommodate 100 members at a time.

(b) REAL ESTATE BROKER SELECTION PROCESS

Selecting, training, and using the *right* real estate broker is a very important process that you should complete ideally *before* you need help on a real estate assignment. The selection process in many ways is similar to that used to select a design firm or general contractor for ongoing facility management requirements.

Each major metropolitan area will have a number of qualified, professional, commercial real estate brokerage firms who understand the local market and have contacts in other metropolitan areas if you have an out-of-town requirement. Ask other corporate real estate managers, bankers, and landlords to identify real estate brokerage firms who have the *best* real estate and customer service reputation. If you are currently using a brokerage firm that you "inherited" or that your customer wishes to use, is it providing the services you need and does your poll indicate it is one of the best?

The object of this research is to identify a firm that will increase your capabilities and effectiveness, save you time, and increase your efficiency. Develop a "Request for Proposal for Real Estate Brokerage Services" (RFP) including presentation format requirements, and invite a number of the superior brokerage firms you have identified to make presentations, including the following materials:

- Customer service orientation.
- Available in-house services, such as research capability, real estate financial analysis capability, marketing skills, sales, leasing, subleasing, property management, construction management, specializations (office, industrial, warehouse, etc.).
- Contacts with other brokers in other cities.
- History and ownership of the brokerage company.
- Experience as brokers.
- Financial capability.
- Follow-up procedures.
- Request for Proposal (RFP) capability.
- Methods of compensation for services, including percentage fee from the landlord and consulting fee from the corporate customer.
- Means of measuring their performance and service.
- Reputation and references.

After studying these presentations, select the best two or three firms using the following guidelines:

- Be selective and tailor your choice to your particular marketing needs. Check the broker's references and track record with other clients. A small local firm may be better in certain circumstances than a large national firm, and vice versa. A joint listing by two real estate firms may enable you to attract local prospects and also to obtain the broader exposure that the marketing of your property may require.
- Have any listing agreements, especially exclusive ones, reviewed by your legal counsel (see Exhibit 5.6). If you object to something in a listing agreement, change it! After all, you are giving the broker a commodity to sell and without goods he or she is out of business.

EXHIBIT 5.6 Exclusive Right Letter

(DATE)

(BROKER NAME)
(BROKER COMPANY NAME)
(BROKER COMPANY ADDRESS)
(BROKER COMPANY SUITE #)
(BROKER COMPANY CITY, STATE, ZIP)

Dear (BROKER NAME):

On behalf of ABC Company, the (BROKERAGE COMPANY NAME) is hereby appointed our sole broker and granted the exclusive right to obtain a lease (or sale and purchase) for _________ rentable (or usable) square feet of ___________________ (general office) space on our behalf in the (city name) area, commencing on the date of this instrument, continuing through execution of a lease, or ending upon our written notification to you of our desire to terminate this arrangement.

You will enlist the best efforts of your firm to secure a location satisfactory to us, and if you deem it necessary, you will also solicit the cooperation of other real estate brokers. We will refer all inquiries and offerings received by us either from principals, brokers, agents or others to you, and all negotiations shall be conducted solely by you and under your direction, subject to our final approval.

You will acquire the details on all contemplated or presently available locations and carefully select and present to us, at a time convenient to us, those which in your opinion are the most suitable for our occupancy. If and when we decide on a location, you will negotiate the terms of the lease (or sale and purchase) on our behalf and in our interest, taking advantage of your knowledge of the real estate market and the terms of the numerous leases (or purchases) previously negotiated by your firm.

Unless otherwise agreed, you will look only to the landlord (or property owner), as the situation may be, for your commission or fee. Subsequent to the termination of this agreement, we shall continue to recognize you as our exclusive broker, in accordance with the terms hereof, with respect to any prospective locations which you have submitted to us during the term of this agreement.

Please signify your agreement to the terms set forth herein by executing the enclosed copy of this letter and returning it to the undersigned.

Sincerely,

(WRITER'S NAME)
(WRITER'S TITLE)

cc: (as appropriate)
(Project file)

Accepted and Agreed to this ____ day of _______________, 19__

(Broker Company Name)

By: ______________________________

Title: ____________________________

- Remember that all aspects of the listing agreement—*including commission rates*—are negotiable.
- Be wary of lengthy exclusive listing terms (anything over six months) unless you have confidence in the broker.
- Do not pay a broker "up-front" money for the preparation of brochures unless those fees are reimbursable to you upon the successful consummation of a sale. At that, scrutinize carefully any initial financial or other commitments that the broker requires to facilitate the sale of your property. Be obligated to pay a commission only *after* the consummation (closing) of a sale or after the tenant or subtenant has moved in.
- Select a mature and experienced individual rather than a firm and insist that he or she handle the proposed disposition personally. There are differences in attitude and capability in all activities, including those of real estate brokerages. If you enjoy a profitable (for you) relationship with a broker, do repeat business with him or her. If you have a problem in a distant location, ask the broker for a recommendation. In short, look for the person who understands your method of operation (another reason for creating your own department), appreciates your business, and performs.
- Be frank about what you or your client needs and answer the broker's ongoing questions during the interview and evaluation process.
- Respond as appropriate to a considered, well-thought out phone call or letter requesting an appointment.
- Be willing to make decisions on behalf of your client and company.
- Take responsibility for gathering project information and developing a complete program at the appropriate stage.
- Be straightforward as to selection procedure—is it or is it not an opportunity for the broker.
- Have a standard RFP and format for evaluating and interviewing brokers—have a set of rules that all competing brokerage firms must play by.
- Create a reference list of local, regional, and national brokers firms; give a new brokerage firm a chance to sell him- or herself as time permits.
- Understand the broker's role in the total team—to act as a bridge and facilitator between you, your client, the brokerage community, and the landlord.
- Be an owner or tenant, not a broker or landlord.
- Be a constructive, technically competent team member dedicated to solving your client's real estate and facility requirements.

- Be honest about the reality of a possibility of working together.
- Be honest about what services you expect and the fees to be charged.
- Maintain continuity by having the same key staff in control/attendance on your behalf throughout the interview process and real estate project.
- Limit your interviews. Even if you have a great many firms under consideration, limit the number of interviews to approximately five.
- Even if a brokerage firm has had a substantial history of doing comparable real estate projects, check whether the people with that specific experience are still with the firm and will be available for your real estate requirement.
- Check references with prior clients, with chief executives, heads of real estate, facilities, and users.
- If you are an owner or are going to be subleasing company office space, define the scope of work consistently to each firm. Your object is to select the brokerage firm that is most likely to respond effectively to you and your tenant's or subtenant's unique needs.
- Where possible, stay with your decisions regardless of "corporate pressure."
- Spend sufficient time checking out references and the specific brokerage work that a firm had done that may relate to your client's work at hand.
- Be accessible, open and direct—treat everyone professionally.
- Offer the opportunity to conduct "generic interviews" involving several decision makers from the corporation.
- Offer an opportunity to continue conversations over an extended period of time in order to get to know a brokerage firm better.
- Define what is unique about your organization, interests, and your real estate requirements.
- Be willing to fully share information about needs and concerns with those you interview.
- Clarify—state as clearly as possible your needs, objectives, and constraints, including budget and schedule demands.
- Be consistent—establish and convey your priorities and job criteria consistently; you will then ensure more responsive and comparable submissions.
- Define in advance the services you want, need, and expect. If unsure, your real estate broker should be experienced and willing to help you define the scope of work.
- Allow sufficient time for you and your prospective brokers to exchange information. The brokers will better understand your wants

and needs and be in a position to clearly identify areas of their expertise that are most responsive.

- Focus fee negotiations on those firms that meet fully your stated criteria. The selection will result in a relationship that can either be rewarding to you, your client, and company or will require a change if expectations are not met.
- If you are not sure about what the prospective broker has told you, if a statement gives you some anxiety or concern, ask for clarification.
- Before the selection process, be sure that your real estate requirement is really ready to go. As appropriate, verify market support, program definition, site acquisition and/or allocation of corporate funds. A false start can damage your credibility as well as that of your organization and your project.

When you feel confident that one or possibly two of these firms can provide the real estate services you require, make a selection and begin the commitment and investment process between you, the brokerage firm, and the broker you have chosen. You and they must agree to invest the time necessary to learn about each other and your corporation. This can include the history of your corporation, the corporation's business and how it is organized, the decision-making process, its position in the marketplace and the competition.

Your broker should clearly understand your mission and your department's services to the corporation and your customers, as well as your quality, excellence, and service requirements including performance measurement and standards of service. You should also thoroughly review the broker's role and the services you expect.

As with any project, the real estate requirement must be managed through strong lines of communication between all members of the team so that everyone understands the mission, what is to be accomplished, and who is responsible for specific actions based on an established schedule.

§ 5.4 APPRAISALS

Many companies have policies that dictate the use of one or more appraisals in real estate acquisition/disposition activities. Many company dollars are spent on appraisal fees. Here, as elsewhere in this book, our focus is on making a profit from operations-related real estate activities. We are concerned about appraisals for several reasons, not the least of which is the overreliance on appraisals by companies that do not understand what appraisals are and how they can be truly helpful in making sound real estate marketing decisions.

(a) THE REVIEW PROCESS

Appraisals of real property are usually requested by corporations for three purposes:

1. To provide bench work input before a corporation establishes the asking price for surplus property.
2. To assist a corporation in evaluating the price of proposed purchase.
3. To help a corporation establish fair market value for donation and tax purposes.

Your corporate real estate staff is responsible for both securing *and* reviewing appraisals. However, we are focusing here on the review function.

Upon receiving the completed appraisal, the review appraiser will first consider these questions: "What are we really looking for in this appraisal? Has the appraiser, using accepted and professionally recognized procedures, adequately addressed the issues in arriving at a final value estimate? Does the appraiser, as represented by the analyses and comments in his report, demonstrate a sensitivity to the market and its true value components?"

In all cases, the value opinion received by the corporation is fed into a decision-making mechanism that will eventually trigger a disposal decision. Unlike the real estate investor/developer, whose potential profit comes from real estate, the corporate user looks for its profit from the service, product, or distributed product that is marketed and sold from a real estate facility. Consequently, the motives of the corporation in acquiring and disposing of real property may be quite different from those of the real estate investor/developer.

It is critically important for the appraisers to understand the non-real estate influences that frequently surround the supposed "real estate decision" of the corporation. The lack of such knowledge can manifest itself in misdirected and misleading interpretations of market behavior and, hence, of market value.

The answer to the first question, "What are we really looking for in this appraisal?" is that corporations are looking for direction and guidance in making decisions that will help implement a corporate service, production, or distribution objective. The appraiser not only must understand that goal but also be able to adequately "read" a market composed of similar users. Although such hopes are not always realized, the understanding of market study is improving and that consequent shifts in applications of appraisal theory are occurring.

(b) THE APPRAISAL PROCESS REDEFINED[24]

The primary shift in appraisal process theory is away from highly regimented, mechanical number techniques, typified by the cost approach, and toward a greater intrinsic understanding of the market and of such strange-sounding concepts as supply demand analyses, resource allocation, risk management, and impact studies. It is a movement toward the same type of applied economic forecasting that corporations use in charting business strategies. You should make certain that your real estate staff is cognizant of these changes.

The market or direct sales approach is a second case in point. If an appraisal contains a value estimate that has been derived by translating *past* sales into present value (and therefore future use) without identifying and analyzing the supply-demand forces that will influence value in the *present* and *future* markets, the document is deficient and unsuitable for sound business decision making.

Example. The real estate department of Company S was given the assignment of divesting a real estate inventory of approximately 1,500 acres of land. It comprised approximately two-thirds of a southeastern town and contained 1,800,000 square feet of manufacturing space (not included in the disposal analysis), an airport, a nine-hole private golf course, the municipal sewage system, several dozen automobile garages, a rod-and-gun club, and 1,100 acres of vacant land in various zoning classifications. The company-owned high-pressure steam heating system provided heat to several municipal buildings.

As a first step, the company elected to dispose of the unimproved property, including the airport and the golf course. Next an appraiser was selected to provide the company with an opinion of the value of this part of the inventory. In addition to possessing impressive professional credentials, he had years of experience in the local market area. Moreover, he had done excellent work for the company on other assignments.

Subsequent to receiving and reviewing his opinion, the company proceeded cautiously with its first marketing efforts, with acreage asking prices somewhat above the appraised values. They anticipated a three-year selling effort because the town had experienced an economic slowdown and decreasing employment—virtually paralleling a downturn in the company's business there, since it was the only significant employer in the community.

[24] James R. Cooper and Robert Kevin Brown, "Valuing Nonperforming Investment Real Estate," Research Monograph No. 104 (0-88406-256-2), Georgia State University, October 1992. This important monograph examines extensively the necessity for reexamining the basic principals underlying the appraisal process.

Surprisingly, the properties began to sell readily—*at the asking prices!* The marketing program was suspended while an analysis began of the now observed real supply-demand forces. Clearly the company and the appraisers had missed something.

What had happened? The town had been created over a period of years by a predecessor corporation. The corporation had acquired land whenever it was available, as a means of environmental control, and consequently, little land was ever sold except to company employees at reduced prices; other land was developed only for company-related purposes. In retrospect, it seems clear that *no* market existed at the time of the appraisal. Value inferences in the appraisal were based on data relating to sales in nearby markets that, as it turned out, were not relevant to the company's situation.

The company discovered that there was significant pent-up demand for property in the town. Accordingly, after consulting with the appraiser, the company adjusted their prices upward as the market began to develop and to reach a supply-demand equilibrium plateau. The first phase, originally designed for three years, was completed in 18 months, with prices yielding 112 percent above the original estimate of value. That experience certainly moved the appraiser and the corporate real estate department, as review appraisers, upward on the mutual learning curve.

(c) SHORTCOMINGS OF THE TRADITIONAL APPROACH

The traditional view of the appraisal process begins with purposes and assumptions, continues through data collection and analysis within the separate and equal three approaches to correlation, and concludes with the final value estimate. This approach places heavy emphasis on technique and data manipulation and attaches little weight to an awareness of intrinsic market forces. The appraisal process is normally portrayed as a very systematic, straightforward, and comfortable sequential flow, such as that depicted in Exhibit 5.7.

As mechanical market reporting gradually shifts to applied economic forecasting, a graphic portrayal of the appraisal process will begin to look more like Exhibit 5.7, with heavy emphasis on understanding all of the market phenomena previously cited.

We have already questioned the traditional approach for basing appraisals of current values on an analysis of past sales that may have occurred in a market environment that no longer exists. The traditional way of arriving at a preliminary estimate of value via the cost, or summation, approach is also problematic. In this method, the buildings and other improvements are evaluated separately from the land, the value of which is then ascertained in the market and added to the depreciated

EXHIBIT 5.7 Steps in Arriving at Value Estimates

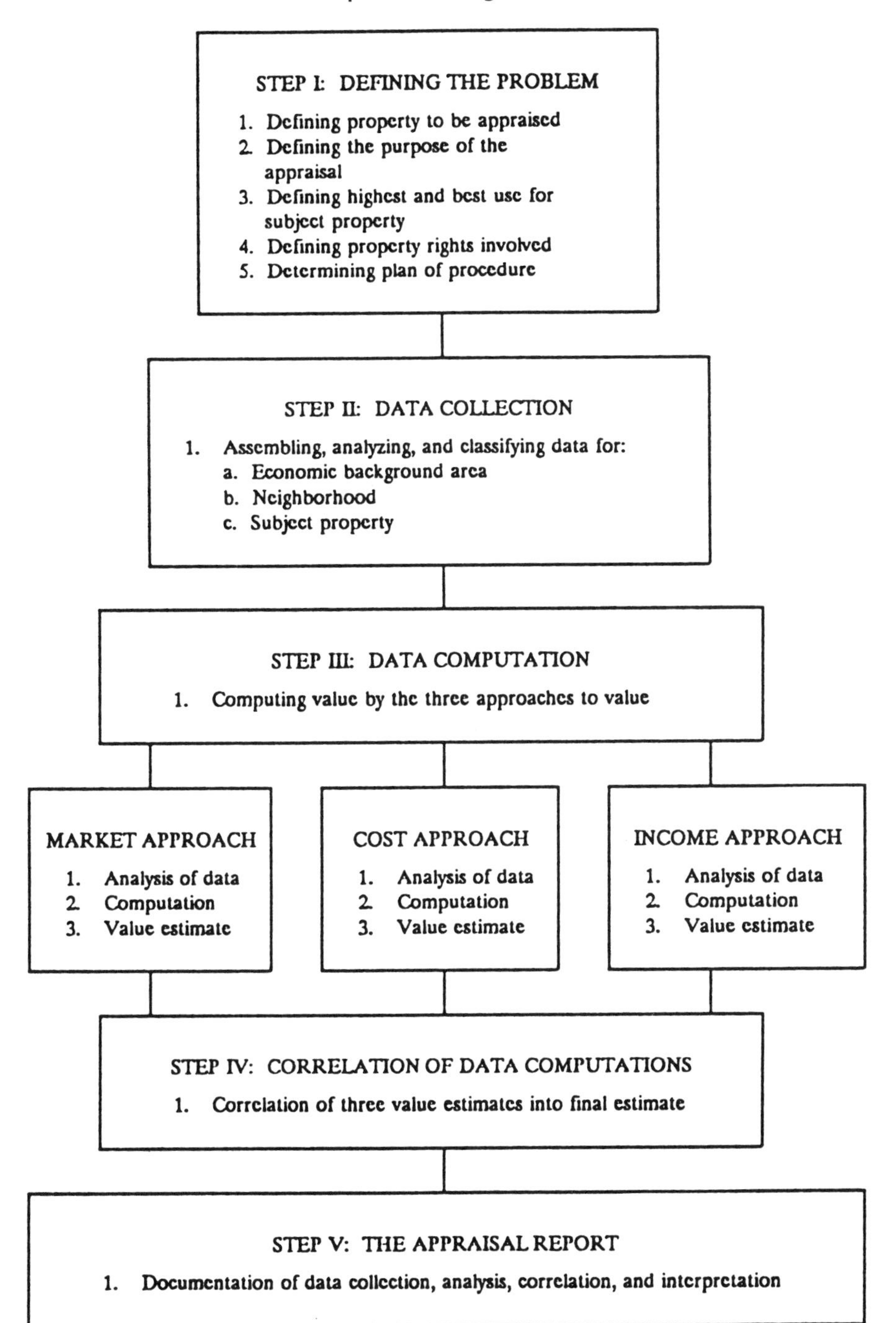
STEP I: DEFINING THE PROBLEM
1. Defining property to be appraised
2. Defining the purpose of the appraisal
3. Defining highest and best use for subject property
4. Defining property rights involved
5. Determining plan of procedure
STEP II: DATA COLLECTION
1. Assembling, analyzing, and classifying data for:
a. Economic background area
b. Neighborhood
c. Subject property
STEP III: DATA COMPUTATION
1. Computing value by the three approaches to value
MARKET APPROACH
1. Analysis of data
2. Computation
3. Value estimate
COST APPROACH
1. Analysis of data
2. Computation
3. Value estimate
INCOME APPROACH
1. Analysis of data
2. Computation
3. Value estimate
STEP IV: CORRELATION OF DATA COMPUTATIONS
1. Correlation of three value estimates into final estimate
STEP V: THE APPRAISAL REPORT
1. Documentation of data collection, analysis, correlation, and interpretation

value estimate of the improvements. How accurate can such an approach be, because buildings are seldom, if ever, actually sold without supporting land? Conversely, how can vacant, unencumbered land sales properly give value parameters to a tract clearly encumbered by improvements? Although it may be easier to calculate with assumptions, the procedure is useless unless the assumptions are realistic.

Because the real estate industry in the early 1990s is in an alarming state of market disequilibrium, the industry needs more precise differentiation of product, especially among nonperforming assets. The focus is now on the valuation of distressed properties, and proposals have been made to adopt standards that improve the quality of the knowledge base for decision makers who are forced to act today. Improving the flow of information used to estimate the value of real estate will achieve a higher velocity of trade, expansion of real estate credit, and improved liquidity.

Useful appraisals provide essential weaponry for you and your real estate department. Pure self-survival, if no more altruistic motive can be found, should prompt your efforts to obtain insightful appraisals that truly reflect existing and forecasted market conditions.

§ 5.5 CONCLUSION

One final caveat: Although we have not discussed the legal document aspects of marketing surplus real estate, legal instruments, such as options, sales contracts, deeds, easements, and title policies, are essential ingredients in the marketing process. Your corporation's legal and real estate departments must have a clear, in-depth understanding of their use in negotiations and marketing implementation. You should have that understanding right now.

The same point can be made for the understanding of lease agreements, which we will examine in Chapter Ten.

Six

Determining Space Requirements

§ 6.1 THE ROLE OF FACILITIES PLANNING

The bartender noticed the fish and inquired, "So, what can I get you?" The fish looked squarely at the bartender and replied, "*Water!*" Sometimes we overlook the obvious. Those responsible for securing corporate real estate must be aware of certain important issues. Suppose the division president wants to market a product to a new group of consumers. In all probability, this new venture will require new or expanded facilities to house the related production, distribution, and administrative activities. The principal question is, What physical characteristics do for these facilities require? Certainly, there will be accommodations for factory, warehouse, and office functions. But how much space for each? How should each area be configured for maximum productivity? Where, generally speaking, should these facilities be located? When must they be "on line?" And, finally, are the corresponding costs fairly close to budget? Answers to these questions are necessary before the corporation's real estate personnel can secure the required facilities.

This information-seeking process is the *facilities planning function.* Facilities planning is defined as those activities that identify the optimum location, configuration, and life-cycle cost of the land and buildings required by corporations to pursue their strategic objectives. Facilities planning focuses on the required physical characteristics, *not* on financing, legal requirements, nor the impact on risk and portfolio management. The most conspicuous need for facilities planning arises when facilities are required for new ventures. However, facilities planning activities also become essential if the capacity of existing facilities is inadequate for planned or current operation requirements. Other changes may also precipitate the need for facilities planning, such as improvements in production technology, relocation of suppliers or customers, and movement to a new stage in a product cycle. Not every permutation in the corporate environment will require a formal facilities planning effort. However, when significant changes do occur, facilities planning will be essential in acquiring the necessary information to secure the proper facilities.

(a) THE ASSET MANAGEMENT FUNCTION

The responsibility for securing the facilities required by the firm is assigned to the real estate function, which manages the acquisition, utilization, and disposition of the corporation's real estate assets. This is the corporation's real estate *asset management* function, discussed in earlier chapters. Information developed in the facilities planning process is incorporated into the asset management function, and vice versa. These two activities might be handled by different departments, or perhaps by the same person, depending on the size of the corporation. Logically, the facilities planning function should be subordinate to the asset management function because the facilities planning function is a technical discipline, reactive and supportive of corporate strategy; whereas the asset management function is involved in strategy formation and incorporates facilities planning information into its contributions. Regardless of corporate organization, the information exchange between these functions is critical to securing facilities that meet the firm's strategic, operational, and financial objectives.

(b) THE FACILITIES MANAGEMENT FUNCTION

Another real estate function that complements the facilities planning and asset management functions is *facilities management* (see Chapter Twelve). It includes the activities that maintain the productive capacity of a corporation's facilities in their current location and configuration, as directed by asset management strategies. While operationally subordinate to the other functions, facilities management contributes significantly to facilities planning by collecting information on historical and current utilization levels and operating costs. Thus, it can provide life-cycle-cost data that are critical to designing and locating future facilities. Even more importantly, this function can supply information that will indicate the extent of the need to increase the firm's capacity.

When items such as facility capacity or cost-effectiveness become an issue, the facilities planning function is likely to become involved. Although corporate facilities planning includes determining the optimal design, general location, and related costs of the land and buildings required for operations, sometimes optimal designs, preferred locations, and budgeted costs are not attainable. Occasionally, desired features are unavailable, or trade-offs may be necessary to satisfy the facility's array of requirements. An overall strategy is essential to develop workable solutions for all the facilities specifications of the corporation.

(c) THE STRATEGIC FACILITIES PLAN

To achieve these solutions, corporations establish a *strategic facilities plan* (see Chapter Four). This plan can range from a formal, detailed planning document at the senior management level (more common in larger organizations) to a generalized, unarticulated notion as to the adequacy of the current facilities profile (more likely in smaller firms). Because facilities have a substantial impact on a firm's profitability and risk profile, a strategic facilities plan should be part of all corporate planning. The tools to develop strategic facilities plans have come primarily from the fields of operations management (in business schools) and industrial engineering (in engineering schools). Together, these academic disciplines provide a range of useful theory and technique for those involved in corporate real estate functions.

This chapter provides an overview of facilities planning topics related to the acquisition, utilization, and eventual disposal of corporate real estate, using the perspective found in business school courses in operations management. The issue of capacity planning serves as the point of departure for exploring the basic components of facilities planning, namely, location analysis and facility design. Much of the following material supplements the discussion of strategic facilities plans in Chapter Four. Since real estate personnel need not be expert in the technical areas of facilities planning, some issues have been developed more thoroughly than others. Basic architectural planning issues and materials have also been included.

§ 6.2 TRIGGERING THE FACILITIES PLANNING FUNCTION

A corporation will routinely engage in facilities planning in connection with an identified need for a specific facility. This primary role may be handled formally or informally. The facility planning function can also support the corporation's continual process of self-examination either through periodic management audits, or through the day-to-day management activity of the firm. Information that affects facilities planning is continuously generated and channeled through various reporting mechanisms, such as the facilities management function discussed earlier, and sometimes has significant diagnostic potential. Facilities planning issues may also rise in connection with broader management concerns at both strategic and operational planning levels. Such concerns may ripple through the firm's activities to impact decisions regarding the acquisition, redeployment, or disposal of certain types of facilities.

Strategic planning issues that can have a significant impact on the corporation as a whole and its facilities in particular include product design and development, resource and requirements planning, and production process analysis and design. Operations management typically addresses these concerns. Since there will always be considerable overlap among such issues, they must be considered in a comprehensive manner. For example, the design of a product will certainly impact the production process employed to turn raw materials into a finished product. If the corporation decides to assemble a product with "off-the-shelf" components to accelerate a market entry date, the research and development (or product development) activity might become more limited, thus reducing the need for more R&D facilities, at least for the time being. A similar impact will occur if the corporation decides to incorporate new production technology, such as robotics, to improve overall production efficiency. Adding robotics is likely to alter the need for the existing materials handling systems, materials storage locations, employee support areas (e.g., lunchrooms, locker rooms) and parking requirements and, therefore, will affect the overall plant layout. These examples demonstrate the impact of strategic issues on facilities planning within the context of operations management, the field most directly related to facilities issues.

A wide range of fundamental strategic planning issues can require facilities planning attention, which must then take a more comprehensive and long-term perspective, at least with respect to the corporation's strategic business units. The following issues are likely to influence the corporation's needs for certain kinds of space at certain locations.

- The corporation's strategy with respect to growth or contraction will affect facilities decisions: If the product or industry is in a declining stage, the corporation should respond, or be prepared to respond, by downscaling production. It may be appropriate to reorient a division toward customer service to maintain customer loyalty in anticipation of the introduction of new products or services.
- The corporation may intend to increase market share: Facilities should be designed and located to minimize costs while meeting strategic objectives (e.g., capturing market share).

- The corporation may intend to broaden product lines or, alternatively, to shift to a niche market focus.
- The corporation's facilities should correspond, particularly in terms of capacity, to the life-cycle stage of the product or industry.
- Facilities should be designed so that new, more productive technology (one of the most important strategic resources) can be incorporated without undue outlay of time and money.
- The corporation might expand vertically or horizontally, or, perhaps, merge with or acquire other related or diversified businesses.
- The corporation might be downsizing organizationally by trying to sell a line or subsidiary as a viable entity, or by liquidating the related assets altogether and focusing on the corporation's remaining lines.
- The firm and its facilities should be properly positioned to modify its operating posture in terms of flexibility (operational adaptability) and liquidity (convertibility into other resources).
- The firm could decide to divest itself of any physical plant, regardless of its utilization, if the gains from disposition are greater than those that could be realized through their use in production or service activity.

Also having a significant impact on the corporation and its facilities are operational level planning concerns such as aggregate production planning, scheduling and control, materials requirement planning and management, inventory policy (which can also be a strategic consideration), job design, and quality control. This class of issues operates at a somewhat more standard operational level in corporate affairs. While evaluating the design or location of a $50,000,000 facility might not seem "standard" to many, the distinguishing characteristic of this class of issues is that design, location, or cost issues are usually considered apart from the strategic issues noted earlier. The following issues are likely to require an evaluation of the design, location, and cost efficiency of a corporation's facilities:

- Facilities should be acquired and retained at acceptable acquisition and operating costs, relative to their contribution to revenues or gains upon disposition. It should be determined whether the corporation's facilities should and can be reconfigured or operated more efficiently to reduce managerial and maintenance costs.
- Facilities should be configured to minimize handling costs. Handling costs can refer to physical items (e.g., conveyor systems in manufacturing companies) or to items of information (e.g., computer networks in service firms).
- Since energy has become one of the most expensive "raw materials" in the production of goods and services, energy conservation,

utilization, and recycling measures should be incorporated into facilities design and location efforts to enhance the corporation's profitability.

- The corporation's facilities should have a positive (or at least non-negative) impact on employee attitudes and productivity. New (or existing) employee health concerns and health-related regulatory compliance are likely to have an impact on facilities.
- Risk-management measures related to the following should affect facilities: employee, invitee (and even trespasser) safety including protection from fire, flood, and natural disaster, as well as rebellion and war (especially for overseas facilities); security matters related to such items as burglary, vandalism, pilferage, terrorism, and espionage.
- Federal, state, and local pollution control and waste disposal regulations (present and future) will impact facilities. These concerns range from hazardous waste storage to the need for interior air recirculation (the lack of which gives rise to the "sick building syndrome").
- Production processes may create community relations problems (e.g., neighborhood aesthetics, noise, and congestion) that require an alteration in the physical plant, its operation, or management plans related thereto (e.g., expansion or conversion to a new use).

The preceding issues, both in the strategic and operational (or tactical) areas, illustrate that virtually every other function within the corporation—marketing, production, finance, legal affairs, risk management, human resources, or even the boardroom—can and usually does affect the corporation's facilities and, therefore, the facilities planning function. Hence, communication and coordination between these various corporate functions, including the real estate function, are of paramount importance and are often achieved through the *strategic facilities plan* (see Chapter Four). However, despite all these issues (and many others not discussed), the need for facilities is still driven primarily by the need to house the present or future capacity required by the corporation.

§ 6.3 CAPACITY PLANNING

Capacity planning addresses in broad terms the amount of each factor of production required to meet stated objectives, including raw materials, employee labor, equipment, and facilities. *Capacity* is usually defined as the potential amount of output during a specified amount of time for one or more operations or facilities. Capacity planning supports corporate strategic planning for resolution of issues involving the scale of the operation and the required investment(s). Capacity planning is one of the most fundamental inputs for developing a strategic facilities plan and establishing the scale of any particular facility. Since decisions regarding facilities usually involve large, often illiquid, long-term investments, determining the optimal scale and capacity for an operation and the facilities required to support it is most critical. Those decisions will depend on various factors, some of which are of particular concern to the facilities planning function.

In considering significant capacity issues, there is a critical distinction between the two major categories of business in our economy: manufacturing and service industries. A physical product is the output in manufacturing industries; whereas in service industries, the output is a service, which is virtually impossible to inventory. While it is feasible to build up a backlog of orders in service businesses, it is not possible (or profitable) to "warehouse" a significant portion of the finished "product" (i.e., service) for any real length of time. Indeed, customers of some service businesses expect the output to be available the instant after placing their order, as in the telecommunications industry. Consequently, planning for capacity and providing the facilities to accommodate that capacity can be significantly different from industry to industry. Therefore, the following capacity factors should be evaluated in relation to the specific industry involved.

(a) VOLUME

Once the corporation determines the product or service it intends to provide, the most important issue to resolve is the projected volume of that product or service. For the purposes of facilities planning, volume usually translates into the scale of the facility or facilities required to accommodate the proposed operation(s). If volume remained constant over a long period, determining the configuration of the required facilities would be much simplified. But volume typically varies substantially over time. A product or service usually has a "life cycle" that can differ substantially from one product or service to the next. The normal life cycle is described by low volume when the product (or service) is introduced into the marketplace, followed by volume growth as the cycle heads toward maturity (where volume may "plateau" for a while), after which volume typically declines to a point where the product or service is discontinued. This curve is perhaps the most fundamental reason for variation in volume over time. Understanding a product's life cycle—the expected life span and shape of the volume curve—is critical to planning facilities that correspond to overall (average) demand over time.

In addition to life-cycle variations, volume may also change because of general economic cycles or conditions, though increasingly shorter life cycles may alter the nature of this impact. Volume might also vary on a seasonal basis (e.g., major household appliances are purchased in greater quantities during the home building seasons). Volume may also vary with promotional campaigns executed by the corporation or its competitors. Competitor activity in all its forms may significantly affect volume of output. Changes in technology and productivity can alter production costs, and therefore prices, further affecting competitor activity and buyer behavior. Buyer behavior, which is the foundation for volume expectations, is very complex. It is the responsibility of marketing personnel to forecast the expected sales volume over time to provide a demand profile which indicates the degree of reliability for various levels of sales over time. This profile will help to optimize the required facilities by avoiding a scale that is necessary only to meet sometimes tenuous demand levels. Overbuilding a facility can substantially increase the risk of underutilization and decrease the corporation's return on assets.

(b) OTHER CAPACITY ISSUES

As capacity planning resolves a wide range of strategic issues, these resolutions are synthesized into a set of operating plans—the strategic facilities plan—for various activities of the corporation. Key capacity issues include resource requirements, technology and labor utilization, and what is often termed *aggregate planning*. Each strategic consideration can influence capacity planning. For example, resolution of the corporation's resource requirements can indicate the need for stockpiling raw materials (due to concerns about interruptions in supply), which may call for more storage capacity. If the corporation decides to build, rather than buy, a component of a product, substantial additional production (and other) capacity may be required. Advances in production technology might increase production speed, thereby negating the need for additional space to meet production goals. A shift to a continuous operating mode in, say, a data processing facility, might eliminate the need for additional (office) space, even though capacity is increased 25 percent. Aggregate planning, including production scheduling, inventory management, and materials handling and logistics, can have a similar impact on capacity planning. Such factors may suggest alternatives to expanding (or contracting) facilities to accommodate capacity. These approaches are discussed in the following section.

Generally, to accommodate significant changes in capacity, it will be necessary to increase the scale of the facilities, especially if the current capacity is inadequate. More specifically, if a production facility is already operating at 100 percent of capacity (or nearly so), it will be necessary to expand, usually by building or otherwise acquiring new facilities. However, the costs associated with building or even acquiring an existing facility can be enormous (let alone the costs of relocation). Before incurring such costs, the corporation should examine whether it is possible to accommodate additional capacity at the corporation's existing facilities.

Identifying the most cost-effective alternative for the capacity requirements is the Holy Grail of facilities planning.

(c) ALTERNATIVES TO ACQUIRING NEW FACILITIES OR MAKING MAJOR MODIFICATIONS

There may be room to expand or reconfigure the existing facilities at the current location without compromising production efficiencies. If not, perhaps only a portion of the new capacity needs to be established in a new location. In either case, it must be determined which alternative(s) is (are) economically feasible, most profitable, and potentially obtainable by the time such capacity is required (what are the respective delivery dates)?

(1) Alternatives Addressing Only the Facilities

- Identify idle or underutilized space.
- Optimize production or administrative spatial juxtapositions to minimize space consumption for physical traffic and information flow.
- Optimize vertical space utilization.
- Reconfigure existing space to maximize overall utility and minimize costs (e.g., instead of relocating all manufacturing space, expand manufacturing activity into adjacent warehouse space and acquire additional warehouse space, which may be much less costly).
- Consolidate or decentralize corporate facilities to take advantage of or create opportunities in the marketplace (an effort led by the asset management function, which is likely to identify such opportunities).

(2) Alternatives Addressing Resource Utilization Other than Facilities

- Increase labor input with additional hours (e.g., overtime, extra shifts, part-timers, temporaries).
- Install more productive technology and equipment.

(3) Alternatives Addressing Management Practices

- Implement more efficient production management methods.
- Build inventory levels to avoid production backlogs and the need to expand manufacturing facilities to meet peak demand (with resultant lower utilization in off-peak times).

- Examine order-processing mechanisms and better manage information flows to reduce production backlogs.
- Backlog demand (if possible).
- Redesign distribution policies or systems (e.g., employ just-in-time methods).
- Examine and modify production control mechanisms, including standards, feedback channels, and authorization.

(4) Alternatives Addressing Strategic Issues

- Modify product design, components, and assembly (and even shift assembly responsibility, or part of it, to the customer).
- Reduce customer service or quality levels to minimize the facility requirements.
- Identify value-adding activities, retaining those that maximize profitability relative to investment in facilities.
- Acquire new facilities (or even other corporations) that offer greater productivity relative to the investment in facilities.
- Address demand (elastic) directly, perhaps reducing it through pricing to the point of maximum profitability, rather than maximum revenue; otherwise, do not supply some of the existing or future demand for a product or service.
- Limit product or service lines to the ones that are most profitable.

§ 6.4 LOCATION ANALYSIS

Another fundamental component of facilities planning is *location analysis,* which identifies the best geographic location for the corporation's facilities (see Chapter Seven). The "best" location for a facility depends on its purpose and the effect of a particular location's geographic attributes on corporate operations and profitability. Traditionally, important geographic attributes include proximity to the factors of production and the cost of those factors in a given location or community, proximity to markets and potential additional revenue capture, related administrative (in)efficiencies, and incremental transportation and communication costs. Often, the focus attributes in a location analysis will include local labor costs and taxes associated with a particular community, together with transportation costs associated with the flow of inputs and outputs between a prospective location and its geographic interfaces. Therefore, the focus of location analysis is on the region and the community, defined as that area providing the same basic cost or revenue factors for any number of potential "sites."

(a) LOCATION ANALYSIS VERSUS SITE SELECTION

Location analysis revolves around the nature of corporate operations, rather than real estate. Location analysis must be distinguished from *site selection,* which is concerned with identifying a particular parcel of land that may be improved with buildings the corporation can use. Location analysis is not site specific, but user specific; site selection is both site and user specific. It is axiomatic that some locations are better than others, with respect to the needs of a specific firm. An "optimum" location should be maximally profitable for the corporation. What methods should be used to identify an optimum location, and what criteria should be considered? A particular location may enhance revenues or reduce costs, or both. Therefore, the first step in location analysis is to identify all the significant locational factors that contribute to potential revenue enhancement and the costs of conducting operations at a particular location.

In practice, it is admittedly difficult to perform location analysis and site selection efforts separately. Consequently, this text will present a unified treatment of both location analysis and site selection in Chapter Seven. This chapter will be limited to an introductory discussion of the impact of location per se on corporate operations.

(b) SINGLE AND MULTIPLE LOCATION ANALYSIS

Only a very small business is likely to have only one location for corporate activity. In this "pure" case of a solitary location, the importance of operational interfaces with customers and suppliers becomes clearer. The required proximity to either customers or suppliers depends on the nature of the interface and the cost to transfer product or information in and out of the corporation's operating location. A mail-order business does not generally have any face-to-face contact with its customers. Therefore, proximity to customers is not a crucial concern. On the other hand, a photo-processing business offering one-hour or same-day service must certainly be located close to customers.

The facilities planning concerns of a growing or larger business are likely to involve more than one location. Still, a large service business, such as a credit bureau, that receives, processes, and delivers information via telecommunications can operate wherever telephone lines, electricity, and employees are available. This situation differs dramatically from that faced by manufacturers or retailers producing or providing a physical product. In that case, distribution of both operations and the physical product become a substantial consideration in the location of corporate activity. The scale of localized activity and management of transportation costs become the principal determinants of location and should be addressed jointly. The following example illustrates distribution systems and transportation costs:

> A manufacturer in Pittsburgh produces and distributes a product across the country to various retailers, some of which are located in the western states. The manufacturer could transport the product from the manufacturing facility in Pittsburgh to each retailer in response to each order. However, such orders are sometimes relatively small and may occur irregularly. Distributing the product in this manner is likely to increase order processing significantly and (especially) transportation costs per unit of product. The "less-than-full-load" and "back-haul" shipment conditions may account for a substantial portion of elevated transportation costs and are a common and ever-present problem for many corporations. If sales levels in the western states do not justify an additional manufacturing facility (minimum scale requirements being the limiting factor), the product will continue to be shipped from Pittsburgh, particularly if that location has underutilized capacity. It may become evident to the corporation that distribution costs could be reduced if warehouse space were secured in the western region of the country. This might reduce transportation costs by minimizing the per-unit transportation costs resulting from less-than-full-load shipments, since the warehouse could inventory large amounts of product for more efficient redistribution. The justification for this new warehouse is based on the projected feasibility of this new operating posture, which constitutes a basic effort in facilities planning, including capacity planning and location analysis. Again, feasibility would be based on the impact on overall profitability.

Assuming that a warehouse in the western states is feasible, where should it be located? This location analysis scenario shows that there must be a concurrent effort to locate the warehouse geographically so as to minimize distribution system costs. Evaluating the corporation's operating posture and analyzing transportation costs are both necessary to determine the full impact on profits and the corporation's new location profile. The analysis of transportation costs involves an inquiry into the logistics leading to a distribution system design. Though a full treatment of logistics is required to fully appreciate the significance of its impact on location, such is beyond the scope of this text. We will, however, provide a brief overview.

(c) LOGISTICS

Logistics is defined as the management of all activities related to the distribution and storage of product. In addition to transportation modes and costs, product mix, order processing, inventory levels, and customer service must also be considered. The two corporate functions of production and marketing are often at odds as to how to resolve these issues. Production would prefer having limited product mix to achieve greater production efficiency by handling fewer items. Marketing would contend that a broader product mix captures more customers. Maintaining high inventory levels would ensure that customer orders could always be filled. However, investing in high inventory levels can be very expensive. Furthermore, manufacturing would have to schedule many smaller production runs to maintain continuously elevated inventory levels. Large manufacturing facilities cannot operate efficiently in such a mode. Operating several smaller, product-dedicated production facilities might be possible, but smaller facilities might not be as efficient, and retooling each at the end of the product life cycle could also be expensive. Marketing would prefer to have rapid customer service, though moving the product closer to the customer would require more manufacturing sites or, alternatively, distribution centers (i.e., warehouses). Each strategy has a different need for space. The potential trade-offs require a massive balancing act between the various interests throughout the logistical universe.

(d) METHODOLOGY

Management science has provided an array of methodologies for dealing with these issues. The most commonly employed method relies on the mathematical tool known as *linear programming*. Linear programming maximizes and minimizes quantifiable values related to the production and distribution of one or more items. It is intended to identify optimal solutions to well-defined (quantitative) problems. Not all problems can be fully quantified, and therefore optimal solutions may only be partial or generalized solutions. Two of the generic labels for applications of linear programming are "the transportation problem" and "the assignment problem." The first application attempts to minimize transportation costs incorporating those factors that can be quantified. The second application attempts to maximize the productivity of the corporation by assigning the production or inventory of product(s) to various facilities. Many of these techniques have been computerized, in order to deal effectively with many variables and copious mathematics. The "center-of-gravity" method has been used with some success. This method minimizes the distance between a warehouse, manufacturing facilities, and destinations. This method is rather limited, however, since it only considers the weight of the product transported for various distances, and not transportation costs and modalities.

One solution that has been developed to distribute products efficiently in a large product mix is known as a "material-management center." These facilities are warehouses where inventory and orders for various products can be consolidated so that the corporation can take advantage of full truckload or containerload quantities, thereby achieving lower per-unit shipping costs. Still, there may be some offset to this cost savings because order processing costs might increase. Also, providing each material-management center with a full complement of product might involve a somewhat higher investment in inventory, as well as warehouse facilities. Balancing the interests of various corporate functions and areas of investment is required in every instance of facilities location; virtually every aspect of corporate operations is involved. This is also true of the design of individual facilities, as will be seen in the next section. The facility planner's ability to resolve these issues might well rival the wisdom of Solomon.

§ 6.5 DESIGN REQUIREMENTS AND LAYOUT

The design of a facility can have a substantial impact on productivity and profitability. The issue of capacity planning, discussed earlier, is intimately involved in determining the physical size of a facility. The focus of this section is on the layout of facilities, for both manufacturing and service firms, apart from their size. This issue will certainly arise when a new facility is being constructed, but it can also come up when there is a significant change in production volume, product, or product mix, as well as technology or production methods. Optimization or productivity analysis might also lead to an examination of a facility's design relative to maximizing production volume and control; minimizing production equipment investments and operating costs (e.g., handling and work-in-process inventory); and even enhancing corporate image and worker productivity. In addition, facility layout may become an issue when space utilization is suboptimal.

(a) CORPORATE FUNCTIONS AND DESIGN REQUIREMENTS

Corporations engage in a wide variety of activities. Different functions within the corporation will require different kinds of space, as summarized in Exhibit 6.1. Some of these functions will be conducted in or on solitary facilities with a single-purpose design. Many more are likely to be juxtaposed within the same building shell, exist in proximity (say on a "corporate campus"), or even operate within the same space. The latter alternative is being pursued by many companies that are now trying to return management (and their administrative office functions) to the shop floor—to provide for better awareness, communication, and productivity.

The location of the internal functions of a corporation must also provide for overall operating efficiency, which again, is measured by its impact on overall corporate profitability. As the critical internal

EXHIBIT 6.1 Design Requirements for Corporate Functions

Function	Space Required
Administrative	Executive offices General office Supporting office
Manufacturing	Fabrication/assembly Processing/refining
Utilities	Electrical generation and transmission Telecommunications switching cable lines, microwave stations
Extraction	Mines and wells
Agriculture	Farmland Timberlands
Distribution	Warehouses Ports Pipelines
Selling	Wholesale marts Retail Office (services, etc.)

linkages must be identified and coordinated in the physical design and layout of a facility, so must the linkages between internal functions and external interfaces be coordinated. For example, showroom space in a showroom/office/warehouse facility is located to provide customers with ready access; the facility's warehouse space is positioned to accommodate truck or rail deliveries.

Perhaps one of the most notable aspects of economic conditions since the 1960s has been the increase in the rate of change, particularly in two respects: the length of product life cycles and the development of technology. Consequently, manufacturing and service firms need to provide for flexibility in their space design to allow for changes in product types, design, and volume, as well as the transformation processes applied thereto. Provisions for change in operations should include the manner in which facilities function as an input of production. This can be accomplished, in part, by incorporating wider spans between columns and walls, higher ceilings, floors with greater weight-bearing capacity, oversized chases, and less permanent methods of attaching personality.

Not only should buildings be designed with flexibility, the building site should also feature this characteristic. While each aspect of site selection should be considered for flexibility (transportation, energy, and water supplies, etc.), the ability to expand at an existing location is of principal importance. Incorporating flexibility is not only important for current operations but also for unrelated subsequent users (future purchasers) of the same facility. Adaptability to a large number of potential users is likely to increase the facility's residual value and establish greater value in the marketplace. In real estate appraisal parlance, such facilities are said to have greater functional utility. Therefore, flexibility may increase the corporation's return on assets, depending on the incremental costs (initial and continuing) involved in providing that additional flexibility.

In addition to the general methods of space programming discussed later in this chapter, there are certain special determinants for manufacturing space layout. Much corporate space (e.g., office, warehouse, and retail space) can be reused (with relatively minor modifications) by subsequent users. However, manufacturing or processing facilities are a frequent exception because such facilities are constructed to house certain product-related production/transformation processes that are not generally standardized between products. Consequently, the product lines or product mix manufactured at a facility will substantially determine its configuration. Taken a step further, production methods, technology, and so forth, will be selected or required on the basis of several factors: the stage of the product life cycle and its impact on the scale of the operation; the manufacturing processes used; the handling systems required; and materials storage requirements. The manufacturing processes used include nonrepetitive (fixed-position) processes (e.g., airplane production), intermittent processes (e.g., sequential and differentiated batches, typical of job shops), assembly lines (e.g., most automobile production), or processing/refinement operations (e.g., oil refining, grain, and chemical industries). Each of these processes, technology types, and production methods and ancillary activities requires a different layout. The array of layout permutations generated by these different production requirements is responsible for the wide variation in facility configuration and is a major consideration in facility planning.

(b) DETERMINING FACILITY SCALE AND LAYOUT

This section discusses the process used by the facilities planner to estimate the company's space requirements. As used in the context of facilities planning, space requirements refer to the volume, type, and design of space required to achieve corporate goals and objectives. The term *space* includes both site and building considerations. Most of the work of space programming, however, focuses on the building elements. These requirements are translated into site selection and facilities design criteria. The process is often referred to as *space programming.* Most often, an examination of the corporation's space requirements precedes a specific action the company intends to take—add a new production or support activity, expand into a new region, consolidate two or more existing operations, and so on. Space requirements are also examined and forecast for the firm as a whole in the preparation of a strategic facilities plan. Even if the focus is on a single facility, the impact of that facility on other corporate facilities must be considered. The process of establishing space requirements involves four basic steps, as follows:

1. Identification and analysis of activities to be accommodated.
2. Establishment of the basis and criteria for space utilization.
3. Development and application of space standards.
4. Calculation of space requirements for the activity and for the firm.

Depending on the planning effort, these steps might be broken down into several smaller steps to address specific project concerns. Each of these steps will be discussed in order, followed by an example of their application.

(1) Identification and Analysis of Activities to Be Accommodated

This step requires identifying each activity to be performed in a facility, describing its nature and role in the productive activities of the firm, and considering its relationship to other activities. The analysis starts with a charge to plan for space-consuming corporate activities and the facilities to house those activities. To prepare a forecast of space requirements, the space planner must understand the nature of the activities to be housed in planned facilities over the next period (or within the planning horizon, if it extends over several periods). The starting point is to examine corporate documents (the strategic planning documents, if they are available) that establish expectations of corporate production and growth. The key elements to examine are:

1. Revenue forecasts for each productive activity—to ascertain the level of production expected and the relative importance of that activity to the financial health of the corporation.
2. Type and scale of activities required to support the revenue forecasts—to establish the identity of the productive and support activities to be accommodated and their interrelationships.
3. Forecasts of the number of employees by type of activity—to establish a basis for planning the type and quantity of workstations and support facilities and services.
4. Productivity forecasts, such as amount of revenue per employee or workstation—to serve as one basis for establishing relative importance of activities and budget constraints.

5. Other statements or data that give direction to the space planning effort—to use in setting design standards, budget allowances, and so on.

Once the basic activities and corporate criteria for space planning have been identified, the activities need to be detailed into subactivities, and the interrelationships of each subactivity examined. One tool for accomplishing this task is adjacency diagrams. Adjacency diagrams use "bubbles" and other geometric forms to illustrate schematically where activities and subactivities are conducted in space. The linkages between activities are shown as connecting lines between the geometric forms.

(2) Establishment of the Basis and Criteria for Space Utilization

After identifying activities and evaluating their spatial relationships, the facilities planner must specify the amount and type of space each activity will need. This process begins with an examination of each type of activity in the plan to isolate characteristics that require space or special design features.

Two procedures are typically required for this task. First, a technical analysis is performed listing and describing spatial characteristics. Then, inputs from occupants or potential occupants of the space need to be obtained to help ensure the space will function adequately.

Following is a list of terms normally included in the technical analysis:

1. Number of employees by activity area and type of work activity. For each employee, develop information about:
   a. The individual work space required.
   b. Exclusive support required for the tasks performed in that work space.
   c. Shared support required for the tasks performed in that work space.
2. Equipment and furnishings required in the work space.
3. Work activity characteristics that require special design or spatial solutions (noise, temperature control, special security, limited accessibility, special utility connections, etc.).
4. Accessibility features. Type and frequency of access needed for:
   a. Other internal activities.
   b. Visitor and core function areas.
   c. External entrances and exits.
   d. Loading and utility areas.

5. Core functions required to support work areas. These include:
   a. Reception and visitor areas.
   b. Rest rooms, lounges, and rest areas.
   c. Cafeterias, kitchens, and eating areas.
   d. Passageways, vertical transportation devices, and emergency exits.
   e. Utility and building support areas.
   f. Other common areas or special features (recreation and exercise areas, day-care facilities, etc.).

When the technical analysis is completed, it is often desirable to test the conclusions with those who will actually occupy the space. Inputs from occupants may be elicited from either corporate employees, potential occupants who might lease or purchase the space, and occupants of comparable space elsewhere. The last two groups of respondents constitute samples from the market and will provide information about market expectations and market norms. Information about the following issues may be gathered using either an interview or written questionnaire format:

1. Security features.
2. Privacy requirements.
3. Special accessibility requirements.
4. Special support functions needed.
5. Personal preferences, where applicable.
6. Work environment characteristics.
7. Other spatial design elements.

The results of the technical analysis and the inputs from occupants are used in developing specifications for the quantity, quality, and special design features needed in the facility.

(3) Development and Application of Space Standards

The two basic components of space standards are design standards and quantity of space, or spatial, standards. The design standards are, by far, the more technical and more complicated.

Design standards for particular types of space can be found in architectural and engineering manuals, and these are usually used at least as a starting point. Design standards may also be derived from previous facilities planning experience, both within the company or from other companies or consulting groups. These standards can then be modified to reflect specific corporate requirements or other considerations derived from the technical analysis and inputs from occupants. Essentially, the design standards developed and used in a particular facilities plan reflect:

1. Minimum requirements from architectural/engineering standards, local and state codes, and any relevant federal requirements (OSHA requirements, handicapped design requirements, etc.).
2. Special corporate requirements imposed on the particular activity or facility, or on all facilities of the company.
3. Requirements derived from user/occupant input.
4. Budget constraints.

Spatial standards specify the quantity and/or dimensional requirements. These standards are often specified as the square feet of floor area per employee, work space, or activity space. Sometimes the cubic volume of space may be needed, and in other situations the floor area plus ceiling heights may be required to determine adequacy. Dimensional requirements may be more important than unit measures for some types of operations, such as some production line processes or the stage area of an auditorium. The most common measure used in spatial standards is the number of square feet of floor area by type of activity.

(4) Calculation of Space Requirements

The last two tasks in the process of estimating space requirements are performed simultaneously and flow from the prior tasks. The calculation of space requirements takes each activity and subactivity in the facilities plan and establishes the quantity of space required by applying the appropriate spatial standard. Space allocations are provided by assigning square footage requirements to the various activities. Identifying and classifying the activities and the space required is the allocation mechanism. Once space for the principal activities has been allocated, it is also necessary to allocate space for support areas and core functions.

Spatial standards are usually established on the basis of net floor area. To convert the space allocations to usable measures for cost estimation and other planning purposes, two conversions are necessary. First, net floor area needs to be converted to gross floor area. This usually involves taking into consideration exterior and interior wall thicknesses. It may involve more a detailed analysis if the building has exterior elements such as attached loading docks, storage sheds, or utility rooms.

The second conversion is to establish minimum site requirements for the facility. The space required for all buildings and structures to be placed on the site must be allotted and the footprints of the buildings placed in exact locations. A site plan must then be developed that provides the most advantageous access for the building, all the on-site circulation requirements, adequate parking, and other site elements as needed or specified. Ratios of site area to building area for various types of facilities, which are sometimes used to estimate site requirements may suffice for rough estimates but should not be relied on for detailed plans. Only a well-thought-out site plan can take into consideration such factors as irregular site configuration, unusual access features, or such natural features as topography, vegetation, and drainage.

In summary, a forecast for corporate space requirements involves the following actions:

1. Summation of activity space requirements.
2. Addition of space requirements for core functions and accessibility features.
3. Conversion of net floor area to gross floor area.
4. Conversion of building area to minimum site requirements to accommodate:
   a. Buildings and other structures on the site.
   b. General access and circulation requirements.
   c. Loading, utility, and service access requirements.
   d. Specialized transportation features (rail, docking facilities, etc.).
   e. Parking.
   f. Landscaping, recreational, and signage requirements.

(c) BUILDING COST ESTIMATES

Corporations require cost estimates for purposes related to the construction, renovation, conversion, and reconfiguration of facilities. Such cost estimates are a necessary element of the capital budgeting process, the development of annual operating plans, and the calculation of corporate performance. Even if a corporation acquires existing buildings, making no changes to the building shell or structural components, it is most likely that the interior space will have to be modified to make it usable. Furthermore, if a facility provides no utility whatsoever to the corporation or others, it may need to be razed to make the underlying land reusable and/or marketable, and this would require a cost estimate (which could be substantial if, for example, the structure contained asbestos). Securing cost estimates is typically the responsibility of the facilities planning function. These estimates might be preliminary or developed in some detail by architects, engineers, or construction contractors (perhaps with bids). Some corporations can justify maintaining this expertise inhouse.

Different types of costs estimates are required for different purposes. Preliminary or detailed cost estimates can be developed or obtained for the following:

- Initial construction costs, including "hard" costs (such as materials and labor and construction management) and "soft" costs (such as professional fees, permits, construction period interest, and taxes) to construct new space or to modify existing space.
- Operating costs, including items such as utilities, maintenance, and repairs; property taxes; property management; and property insurance (casualty and liability, if not covered under a corporate umbrella).
- Retirement or salvage costs, including all costs necessary to decommission and dispose of buildings and other improvements to land.

Some facilities can have fairly low initial costs, yet experience elevated operating costs, and vice versa. Integrating the costs of constructing, operating, and retiring a facility into a single, present-valued amount results in what is termed its *life-cycle cost.* Identifying this cost is very useful for capital budgeting, projecting corporate performance, and especially for comparing one facility alternative with another. However, cost and resulting value must be considered together in determining which alternative is or was more profitable for any accomplished or planned corporate activity. Identifying financial values (market value, value in use, residual value) is not part of the facility planning function. Value estimation is a responsibility of the larger real estate function, for which the facilities planning function will develop cost estimates.

(d) SPACE PROGRAMMING ILLUSTRATED[1]

The following example illustrates the application of the principles involved in space programming, discussed earlier in this section. In this example, a specific project—a combined office and R&D facility—is identified following the establishment and confirmation of overall corporate objectives and strategic planning documents. Subsequently, the determination of space requirements is initiated by analyzing corporate intent for a specific physical facility. Corporate goals and objectives for this facility are then established, along with facilities design criteria, also termed space programming. In this case, seven sequential steps are pursued as follows:

1. The context of space programming for building and site requirements is determined and presented in Exhibit 6.2.

[1] The example used in this subsection to illustrate space programming has been provided by Roger D. Roslansky, AIA, a registered architect residing in La Crosse, Wisconsin.

2. Project goals, a personnel listing, and site influences for this project are developed as follows:

Project Goals:

a. Develop a building organization with appropriate internal relationships to use all spaces efficiently.
b. Provide comprehensive, "state-of-the-art" laboratory space.
c. Develop a creative "high technology" image that relates to corporate headquarters.
d. Provide effective interior space that is sympathetic to human resources and promotes productivity.
e. Recognize the site influences, develop the site to its "highest and best use."
f. Relate the project to adjacent properties, the community, and environmental concerns.
g. Employ energy conservation methodologies in all disciplines of architecture and engineering, including life-cycle costing.
h. Meet the construction budget target, set at $5,565,000.
i. Meet the schedule of phase completion points, reviews, and approvals, plus the required occupancy date.
j. Provide for a reasonable degree of flexibility, plus the ability to expand the space by 50 percent (or more).

Personnel Listing (not including future growth or expansion):

Department	Personnel
Administration	2
Operations—North America	20
Operations—International	2
Product Marketing	29
Human Resources	7
Finance	41
Engineering	26
Technology and Plant	41
Summary Total	166

Site Influences (key factors that will affect the design concept):

a. Site area and configuration—Amount and shape of the land available to support the site requirements, plus the building footprint.
b. Topography—The slope of the land and drainage aspects.
c. Existing vegetation—Locations and areas of existing trees.

EXHIBIT 6.2 Implementation Process

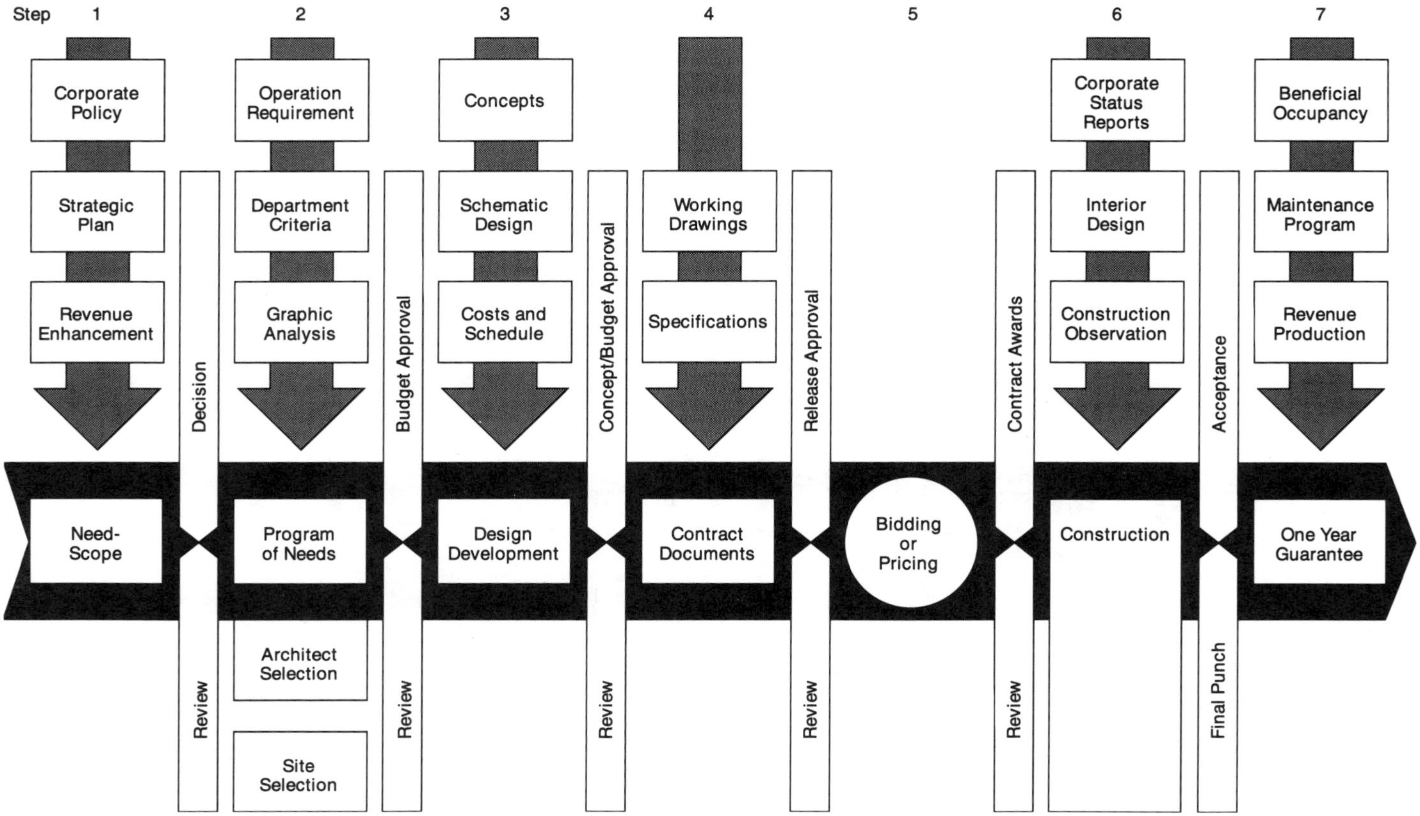

d. Freeway noise—Traffic noise generated by nearby interstate highway.
e. Site access—Vehicular routes of access to the site.
f. Adjacent land—Use of parcels adjacent to the site.
g. Location—Position of site in the area and community in terms of visibility and potential image.
h. Sun and wind—Climatalogical conditions.
i. Views—Vistas outward from the site.

3. A summary list of spaces by departments or major components is compiled, and supplemented or amplified by an expanded and detailed list of spaces for each department. The schedules included in Exhibit 6.3 illustrate this important compilation of items, presenting both the project summary and the details for each of the departments. To complete each department calculation, and eventually arrive at the total area required, a circulation factor must be included for conversion from net assignable feet (NASF), to gross square feet (GSF). Often a relative sizes diagram is included as a comparative device for initial scope understanding and space perception (Exhibit 6.4).

EXHIBIT 6.3 Project Summary and Detailed Schedules

BUILDING AREA SUMMARY

Department	Area, SF
Administration	736
Operations—North America	2,515
Operations—International	331
Product Marketing	4,047
Human Resources	4,658
Finance	5,986
Engineering	4,885
Subtotal (Office Space)	23,158 SF
	× 1.2 Building Gross Factor
	27,790 GSF
Technology/Laboratory	18,514 SF
	× 1.2 Building Gross Factor
	22,217 GSF
Experimental Plant	4,950 SF
	× 1.2 Building Gross Factor
	5,940 GSF
	88,888 GSF
Total Building	55,947 GSF

EXHIBIT 6.3 *(Continued)*

DEPARTMENT AREA SUMMARY

Administration

Space	Quantity	Planning Standard	Net Area	Net/ Gross	Dept. Gross	Comments
President	1	320	320	1.1	352	Closed office
Executive Secretary	1	96	96	1.25	120	includes file space
Conference Room	1	240	240	1.1	264	Closed conference area
Total Area:					736 SF	

OPERATIONS—NORTH AMERICA

Space	Quantity	Planning Standard	Net Area	Net/ Gross	Dept. Gross	Comments
Vice President	1	192	192	1.1	211	Closed office
Executive Secretary	1	96	96	1.25	120	Includes file space
Managers	4	144	576	1.1	634	Closed office
Engineers	5	96	480	1.2	528	
Safety Supervisor	1	96	96	1.2	115	
Clerks	6	64	384	1.2	461	
Director	1	192	192	1.1	211	Closed office
Purchasing Agent	1	64	64	1.2	77	
Vendor Interview	1	144	144	1.1	158	Closed conference area—adjacent lobby
Total Area:					2,515 SF	

OPERATIONS—INTERNATIONAL

Space	Quantity	Planning Standard	Net Area	Net/ Gross	Dept. Gross	Comments
Vice President	1	192	192	1.1	211	Closed office
Executive Secretary	1	96	96	1.25	120	Includes file space
Total Area:					331 SF	

EXHIBIT 6.3 *(Continued)*

Product Marketing

Space	Quantity	Planning Standard	Net Area	Net/ Gross	Dept. Gross	Comments
Vice President	1	192	192	1.1	211	Closed office
Executive Secretary	1	96	96	1.25	120	Includes file space
Managers	6	144	864	1.1	950	Closed office
Product Managers	4	144	576	1.1	634	Closed office
Marketing Specialist	1	128	128	1.2	154	
Pricing Representative	1	64	64	1.2	77	
Engineers	7	96	672	1.2	806	
Customer Service Reps	6	64	384	1.2	461	
Planners	2	64	128	1.2	154	
Conference Room	1	400	400	1.2	480	Closed conference area
Total Area:					4,047 SF	

HUMAN RESOURCES

Space	Quantity	Planning Standard	Net Area	Net/ Gross	Dept. Gross	Comments
Director	1	192	192	1.1	211	Closed office
Executive Secretary	1	96	96	1.25	120	Includes file space
Manager	1	144	144	1.1	158	Closed office
Loading Dock/ Staging Area	1	1,000	1,000	1.1	1,100	Two loading areas
Clerks	2	64	128	1.2	154	
Mailroom	1	440	440	1.1	484	
Lunch Room	1	1,000	1,000	1.1	1,100	Include vending machines, microwave, refrigerator
Interview Room	1	100	100	1.1	110	
Reception/Waiting	1	320	320	1.25	400	
Copy Room	1	92	92	1.1	101	
Men's Lockers/ Showers	1	300	300	1.2	360	Adjacent exterior access
Women's Lockers/ Showers	1	300	300	1.2	360	Adjacent exterior access
Total Area:					4,658 SF	

EXHIBIT 6.3 *(Continued)*

FINANCE

Space	Quantity	Planning Standard	Net Area	Net/ Gross	Dept. Gross	Comments
Vice President	1	192	192	1.1	211	Closed office
Executive Secretary	1	96	96	1.25	120	Includes file space
Managers	7	144	1008	1.1	1,109	Closed office
Controller	2	144	288	1.1	317	Closed office
Director Information Systems	1	192	192	1.1	211	Closed office
Asst. Controller/ Specialists	2	64	128	1.2	154	
Accounting	13	64	832	1.2	988	
Credit Representatives	4	64	256	1.2	307	
Coordinators	4	64	256	1.2	307	
Computer Operators	2	64	128	1.2	154	
Data Center	1	1,480	1,480	1.1	1,628	Raised flooring
Personal Computer Stations	4	64	256	1.2	307	
Conference	1	144	144	1.2	173	Open conference area
Total Area:					5,986 SF	

ENGINEERING

Space	Quantity	Planning Standard	Net Area	Net/ Gross	Dept. Gross	Comments
Director	1	192	192	1.1	211	Closed office
Executive Secretary	1	96	96	1.25	120	Includes file space
Managers	5	144	720	1.1	792	Closed office
Engineers	14	96	1,344	1.2	1,613	
Designer/Draftsman	3	96	288	1.2	346	
Secretary	2	64	128	1.2	154	
Conference Room	1	216	216	1.1	238	Closed room shared with technology group
Personal Computer Stations	3	64	192	1.2	230	
Engineering Storage	1	300	300	1.2	360	
Blueprint & Copy Machine	1	240	240	1.2	288	
Library	1	300	300	1.2	360	
Conference	1	144	144	1.2	173	Open conference area
Total Area:					4,885 SF	

EXHIBIT 6.3 *(Continued)*

TECHNOLOGY/LABORATORY

Space	Quantity	Planning Standard	Net Area	Net/ Gross	Dept. Gross	Comments
Director	2	192	384	1.1	422	Closed office
Executive Secretary	2	96	192	1.25	240	Includes file space
Manager Offices	5	144	720	1.1	792	Closed office
R&D Chemist or Engineer	12	96	1,152	1.2	1,382	
Analytical Lab Chemist or Technician	12	96	1,152	1.2	1,382	
International Technologies Chemist or Technician	7	96	672	1.2	806	
Personal Computer Stations	3	64	192	1.2	230	
Conference	1	144	144	1.2	173	Open conference area
Secretary	1	64	64	1.2	77	
Library	1	300	300	1.2	360	
Laboratory Space	1	11,000	11,000	1.1	12,100	Area for R&D & analytical lab space included for manager office 144 SF
Lab Support	1	500	500	1.1	550	Storage area for labs
Total Area:					18,514 SF	

EXPERIMENTAL PLANT

Space	Quantity	Planning Standard	Net Area	Net/ Gross	Dept. Gross	Comments
Experimental Plant	1	4,500	4,500	1.1	4,950	
Total Area:					4,950 SF	

EXHIBIT 6.4 Comparative Department Size/Scope

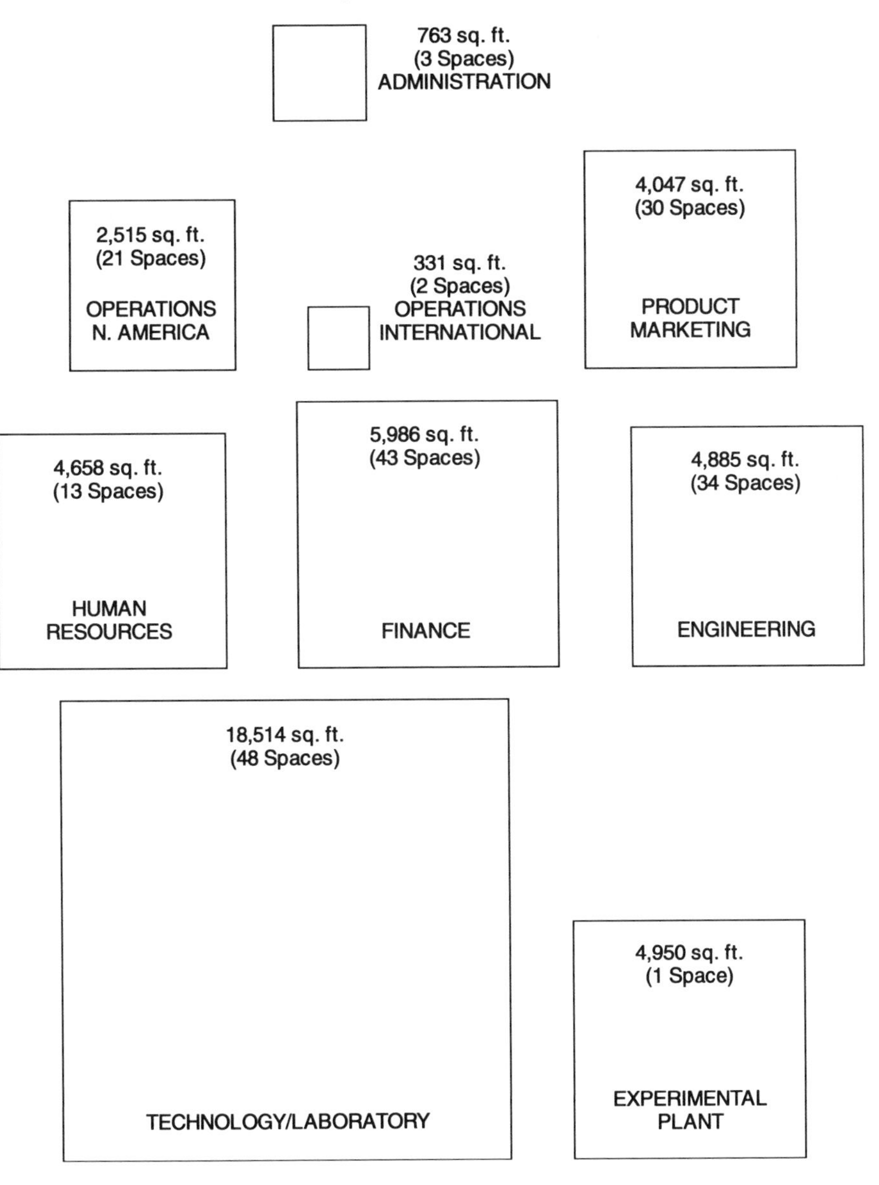

4. A list of site requirements is developed, often accompanied by site use diagramming, as shown in Exhibit 6.5. Site design requirements are as follows:
   a. Provide parking for 10 visitors and 150 staff, and future space for 75 additional automobiles, using the essentially level areas in the center of the site relating to access points.
   b. Locate service access from the east, near the northeast corner, due to topography. Provide a definite service zone away from the main entry.
   c. Locate the main entry from the west on Oak Street.
   d. Consider the building location or footprint centralized on the site, with the potential of two levels utilizing the terrain, and a northerly direction to gain a portion of the knoll.
   e. Take advantage of the existing trees for locational purposes and the "near views," plus the "long views" to the northeast, east and southeast.
   f. Use the existing vegetation and sufficient setback to achieve barriers for the interstate freeway noise.
5. Overall project organization, using the major departments or components, is described in a diagram similar to Exhibit 6.6. Often, it is advisable and helpful to show relationships in a matrix chart as well, which is shown in Exhibit 6.7.
6. Each department or major component is then broken down and described graphically with its significant relationships, as shown in Exhibit 6.8. Occasionally, supplemental analysis diagrams are used to visually depict certain other planning aspects, such as movement of people and services, flow of materials handling, manufacturing process, communications, robotic configurations, and security barriers.
7. Finally, the space programming or "Building and Site Programming of Needs" also presents the first opportunity to develop sufficient information for a preliminary estimate of probable construction costs. The cost estimate analysis must account for all items to establish the economic parameters, or the "Project Budget." Depending on the time frame for implementation, escalation factors to the midpoint of construction should be included. The schedule in Exhibit 6.9 presents a summary of the pertinent cost factors for the project, exclusive of certain "soft costs," such as financing and legal costs and fees.

(e) SPACE UTILIZATION MEASURES

The facilities planning function is often concerned with *space utilization measures.* Such measures, typically ratios, gauge the performance

EXHIBIT 6.5 Site Conditions and Analysis

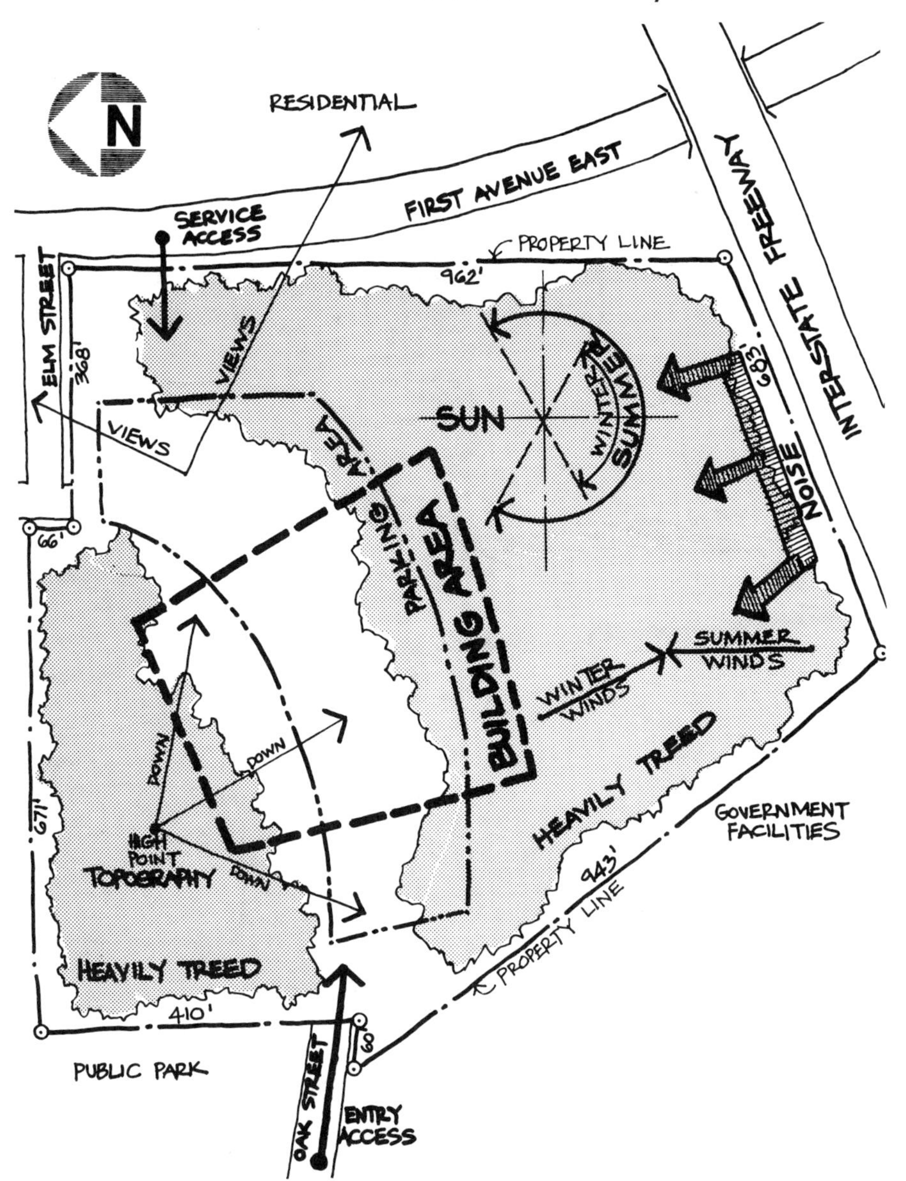

EXHIBIT 6.6 Project Organization and Relationships

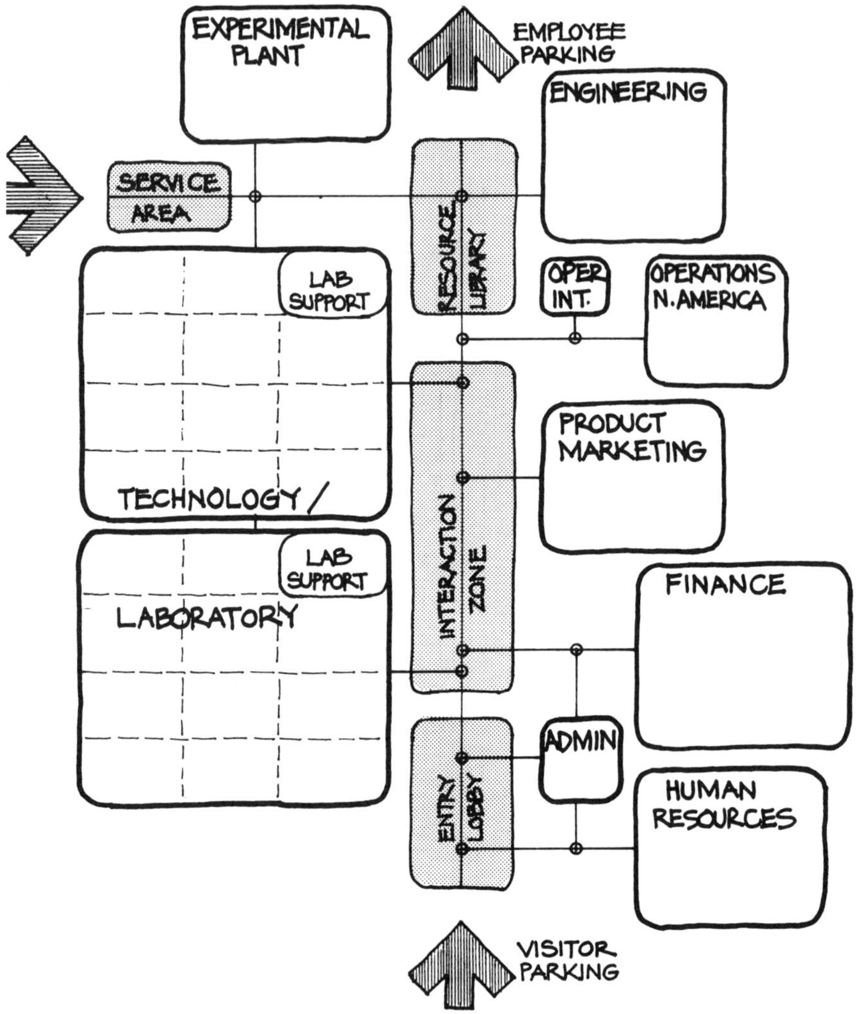

of facilities design and operations. The standards of performance are generally set forth as objectives relating to the decision to acquire, reconfigure, or operate a facility. Standards may be calibrated either with data internal to the corporation or through industry benchmarking. Therefore, evaluation of performance is either against project or operational goals, most of which can be based on competitive concerns. The evaluation of performance against the established standard can identify immediate remedial requirements or determine appropriate objectives for future facilities (and the planning therefor). To the extent that

EXHIBIT 6.7 Relationships Matrix—Major Components

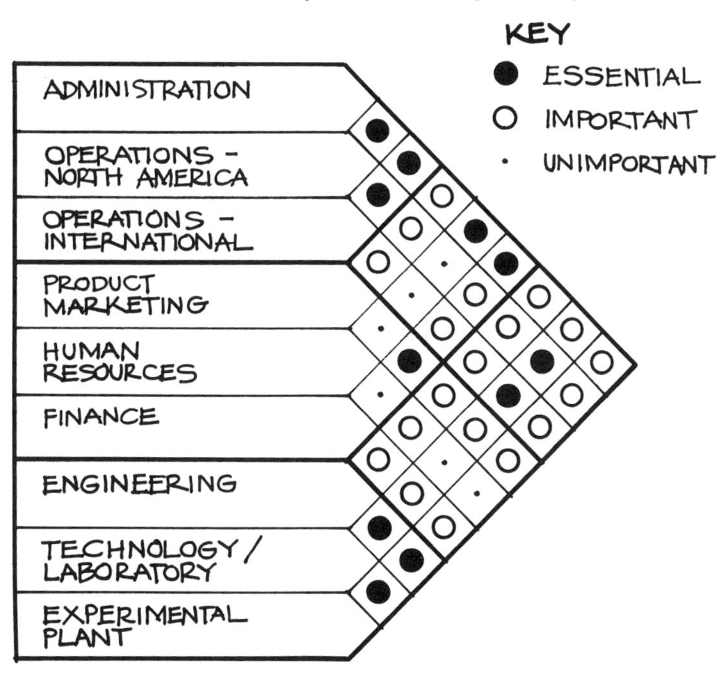

individual responsibility can be assigned to various facility performance measures, they may also serve for employee performance evaluation.

There are two classes of space utilization measures: (1) those that measure physical performance and (2) those that measure financial performance. The principal difference between the two classes is the management level at which each conveys performance data. Physical performance measures originate within the facilities planning function and are rarely conveyed beyond reports to those involved in real estate asset management, except in cases in which management of operating divisions are concerned with production quotients. Financial performance measures may originate within the facilities planning function, though it is more likely that the asset management personnel will participate in developing these measures, some of which will be included in reports to senior management. Financial measures are generally concerned with the impact of facilities on revenue and expenses. They are specifically concerned with two issues: corporate productivity and the consumption of resources (e.g., operating funds). Physical measures are generally concerned with functional efficiency, which is typically equated with profitability, though this can be a presumption worth examining when the effect of the trade-offs made to achieve efficiency is uncertain.

EXHIBIT 6.8 Departmental Graphic Analysis

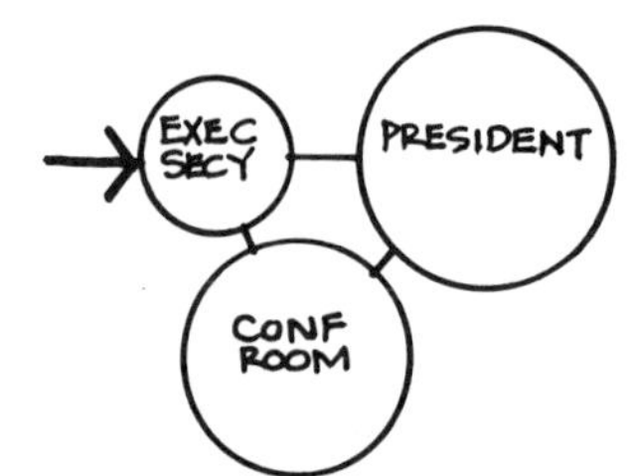

ADMINISTRATION · 736 SF · 2 STAFF

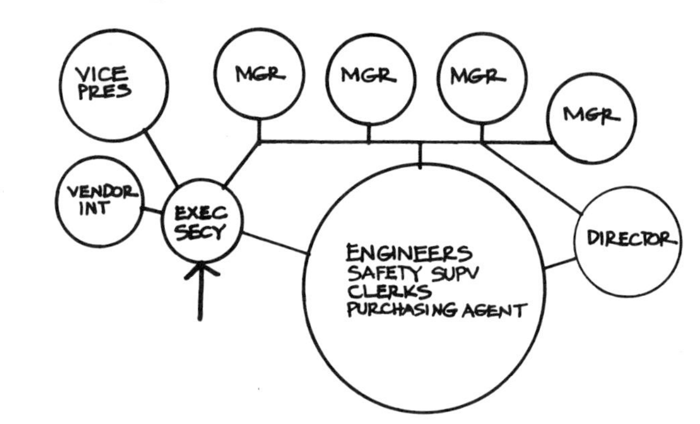

OPERATIONS-NORTH AMERICA · 2515 SF · 20 STAFF

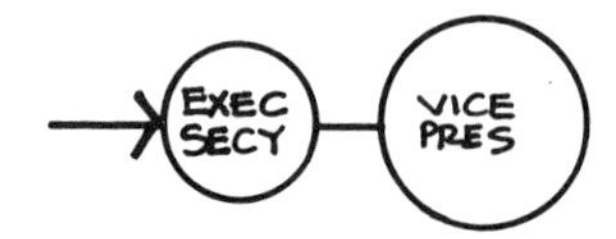

OPERATIONS-INTERNATIONAL · 331 SF · 2 STAFF

Examples of physical performance measures include items such as (1) the number of square feet per employee and (2) the ratio of net to gross building area. These two examples might look somewhat familiar; they should, since each measure was used to plan the building project discussed in the previous section. These types of measurement describe different types of functional efficiency. But, recall the caveat noted earlier, regarding functional efficiency: There are almost always trade-offs involved. Minimizing the number of square feet per employee is likely to adversely affect worker morale and productivity. Therefore, maximizing such measures of functional efficiency should not be the only goal. Rather, such measures should be used as diagnostic tools to identify potential symptoms of problems that may require greater definition. Still, an ounce of prevention is worth a pound of cure, and that is why facility planners utilize such measures in planning new facilities. Guidelines,

EXHIBIT 6.9 Cost Summary

PROJECT: ABC CORPORATION TECHNICAL CENTER
DATE: OCTOBER 1, 1992
FILE NUMBER: 920 0115
PHASE: PROGRAM

$ 50,000	Site Clearing, Removal and Demolition
384,513	Site Development—Estimated 10% of Building Cost
3,845,130	Building Construction
	$1,667,400 Office 27,790 GSF @$60/SF
	$1,999,530 Lab 22,217 GSF @$90/SF
	$ 178,200 Plant 5,940 GSF @$30/SF
	(Average) 55,947 GSF @$68.73/SF
50,000	Elevator—2 Stop Hydraulic
25,000	Utility Connections from Off-Site
384,513	Fixed Equipment—Estimated 10% of Building Cost
461,416	Moveable Equipment/Furnishings—Estimated 12% of Building Cost
(Not Included)	Additive Options—Provisions for Expansion, Skywalk Connections, Additional Site Improvements, Special Appointments or Other Amenities
$5,200,572	Subtotal
364,040	Contingency—Estimated 7% of Subtotal
$5,564,612	TOTAL CONSTRUCTION COST
333,877	Architectural/Engineering, Professional Fees @6%
25,000	Miscellaneous Costs
	Property Survey
	Soils Testing
	Plans and Specs
	Agency Reviews
	Environment Assessment
225,000	Land Acquisition
$6,148,489	TOTAL PROJECT COST

rules of thumb, or industry standards can often suggest the measures that will work to the corporation's overall benefit and profitability in a facility design. However, after a new facility is up and operating, the operations it houses continue to evolve. Therefore, it is advisable to measure its physical performance periodically to determine whether any changes may be in order to enhance corporate profitability.

Examples of financial performance measures focus on two aspects of corporate facilities: how facilities consume resources, and how they contribute to the creation of value. With this perspective on both input and output, these measures can form the basis for a cost-benefit analysis of corporate facilities. The most common measures of resource consumption include facility operating costs per square foot, and facility operating costs as a percentage of incremental value attributable to the use of a facility (as in revenues or sales). The degree of incremental value just noted is also the ordinary measure of value contribution, the other financial measure. However, except for retail (or some service) facilities, it is often difficult to determine an amount of value contribution for facilities such as office space, warehouses, and factories, though a value-added factor might be established for some facilities as a measure of value contribution. The usual denomination for all these financial measures is dollars per square foot, which allows facilities to be compared with one another.

Using the facilities of a corporation's competitors to compare and evaluate the corporation's own performance is termed *benchmarking*. Benchmarking usually involves the participation of several companies that are interested in obtaining similar performance data. This practice can be done within an industry or across industries, provided the facilities themselves are reasonably comparable. Benchmarking is becoming an increasingly popular approach to performance measurement. The special benefit that accounts for this popularity is the group participants' ability to identify the management and design practices used by the facilities that appear to be performing better than their own. Consequently, a corporation may be able to improve its performance by adopting specific established and tested practices. An outside consultant may facilitate and coordinate the information exchange, which is accomplished on a confidential basis.

§ 6.6 CONCLUSION

The facilities planning function is generally responsible for facilities location, design, and cost estimation. Its role is to support the corporate real estate asset management function. It is a technical discipline, incorporating skills and information from operations management, industrial engineering, architecture, and construction. There is always a need for this function in a corporation, though many firms will find it cost-effective to outsource some or all of these tasks. The scope of the information requirements and outputs of the facilities planning process can be considerable, as can be the task of overseeing this function. However, recall one of the variations of Murphy's Laws: "If everything seems to be going right, you've obviously overlooked something." Overlooking a significant item in the facilities planning process could seriously impair the competitiveness of the firm, since individual facility costs are sometimes enormous and difficult to recapture, at least in the short term.

Seven

Development of Locational Strategies for Corporate Operations

§ 7.1 INTRODUCTION

Changes in facilities are constantly being planned as economic conditions fluctuate and companies adapt their level of business and production to new market circumstances. Locational decisions must be made whenever a new facility is contemplated or an existing facility is relocated, expanded, reduced in size, or shut down. Facility changes that involve locational factors include:

1. On-site expansion or contraction of existing facilities.
2. Expansion of an existing facility onto an adjacent site.
3. Branch plant acquisition, which may require integrating acquired facilities with existing operations at other locations.
4. Relocation of existing facilities to a new site or location.
5. New facility location, either through construction or acquisition of improvements.
6. Closure and disposition of existing facilities.

Whenever a facility location is considered, the geographic context of the decision must also be addressed. Essential geographic components are:

1. International, national, regional, or statewide factors that impact business relationships and/or the specific facility.
2. Community-level factors affecting the cost and operation of the facility.
3. Site-specific factors involving alternative site locations within a particular community.
4. Site-specific factors involving on-site expansion, reconfiguration, and/or expansion onto adjacent sites.

This chapter explains how to make locational decisions by analyzing critical factors and describes the impact of locational decisions on the company and its operations.

§ 7.2 DIMENSIONS OF THE LOCATIONAL DECISION

The locational decision for a corporate facility starts with the requirements for the facility itself, such as the general type of land use, space requirements, and architectural needs. Other factors, such as the relationship of the facility to adjacent or nearby activities or the corporate image to be achieved, are also involved. These basic considerations establish the context for making the locational decision.

(a) USE AND FUNCTION OF THE REAL ESTATE

The facilities planner first identifies the types of land uses and the functions the facility and its attendant site and improvements will play in achieving corporate objectives. "Use" in this context means that the type and scale of activities planned for the facility need to be classified into the general land use categories employed in the real estate and planning communities. The company may need residential, retail, office, industrial, or warehouse space in its operations, depending on its product or service as well as its market area. To start, the company and the specific activities proposed for the location need to be described using the appropriate Standard Industrial Classification (SIC) code. Exhibit 7.1 shows general land use needs normally associated with different types of companies.

This exhibit illustrates how the typical manufacturing firm requires three types of land uses—industrial, office, and storage. Some manufacturing firms will also require special purpose land uses such as dump sites and/or excavation sites in addition to a processing plant. A nonmanufacturing firm, such as a financial or business service provider, typically requires only two types of land use—office and storage space.

The corporation's intended functional activities provide a second dimension for the locational decision. Manufacturing firms need land and space for production, for shipping and receiving purposes, and for storage of both inputs and outputs, as well as employee parking and other support functions. These functions involve building improvements and

EXHIBIT 7.1 General Land Use Needs by Type of Company

	Land Use Needs					
Type of Company:	Industrial	Special Purpose	Office	Storage	Retail	Residential
Manufacturing	X		X	X		
Transportation		X	X	X		
Communications		X	X	X		
Utilities		X	X	X		
Wholesaling			X	X		
Warehousing	X		X	X		
Retailing			X	X	X	
Finance/Insurance/ Real Estate			X		X	
Business services	X		X	X	X	
Other services			X		X	
Construction	X	X	X	X		

site improvements for open land uses and support facilities. For example, production will occur in a plant, but receiving, shipping, and storage can be either an indoor or outdoor function depending on the product. Employee parking is typically an outdoor, on-site function for a manufacturing plant.

Companies using only office space may house all activities, such as provision of the service, receiving/shipping, and storage, in a single structure. On-site surface-level parking may be feasible if the office building is freestanding, with available surface space. On-site parking may also be accommodated in a parking deck constructed next to or on lower floors of the office building. Alternatively, some situations may allow off-site parking.

The third and most technical step is translating the use and function data to more specific site requirements. To do this, the corporate real estate executive must describe the requirement in fairly precise terms, and then identify, in quantifiable terms, the standards for construction or operational adequacy. For example, assume a corporate real estate executive is evaluating a site for a manufacturing facility that contains 25 acres zoned industrial along Oakwood Industrial Boulevard. The site is rectangular with 900 feet of road frontage along Oakwood Industrial Boulevard and 1,210 feet along Hickory Drive. It is generally level with a dense tree cover on the northern perimeter of the site but with sparse tree and brush growth elsewhere. One curb cut can be put along Oakwood Industrial Boulevard and two curb cuts along Hickory Drive. Left-hand turns are not permitted from Oakwood Industrial Boulevard, but a signalized intersection with a left-turn signal is located at the intersection, and left-hand turns are permitted anywhere along Hickory Drive. All utilities needed for a manufacturing operation are available at reasonable cost. Using this information, the corporate real estate executive must determine if the site is worthy of additional consideration and further negotiation.

The decision to go forward will be based on the executive's conclusions regarding how well the site meets minimum requirements for size, dimensions, parking and loading, accessibility and visibility standards, utilities and service, and aural and visual buffers, as well as how well it will accommodate the structures to be built there. So, the executive must envision the minimum standards to ensure operating adequacy for the facility, and understand how flexible these standards are and what penalties are attached to violations of minimum standards.

In addition to site standards, other locational standards also enter into the decision. The site being evaluated is one mile south of an interstate interchange with Oakwood Industrial Boulevard and is also within five miles of 70 percent of the potential employees' homes. No rail sidings are available, but a piggyback rail facility is 12 miles away, and a commercial airport with both passenger and air freight service is 8 miles away. The corporate real estate executive, then, must marry locational standards to site standards in determining if the site will be adequate.

(b) IDENTIFYING SPACE NEEDS

Identifying a firm's space needs is a dynamic, not a static, activity. Space needs change over time as the market for the firm's product or service changes, and as the firm's corporate structure evolves. Consequently, the real estate executive must first measure the firm's current space needs and then set out possible scenarios for the future in developing the firm's potential requirements. At both points in time, the need for space should be matched to the firm's present inventory of space. Chapter Six describes procedures for completing this task.

(1) Current Needs versus Current Inventory

The initial focus for identifying space needs is the relationship between the firm's current needs and its actual holdings or utilization of space. The question is, are the actual land and space holdings in balance with the need for that land and space? An office-space-oriented firm may have 15,000 square feet of space leased, but there is a great deal of crowding; actual need exceeds current holdings. The company has an unmet demand for space.

A manufacturing plant has a 15-acre (653,400 sq. ft.) site divided into a 150,000-square-foot production facility; a 200,000-square-foot outdoor space for receiving, shipping, and storage; and a 200,000-square-foot parking area. The parking area and the receiving, shipping, and storage area are not used to capacity. In this instance, the company's actual land and space holdings meet current needs leaving some excess capacity, and there are 103,400 square feet of excess land.

(2) Future Needs versus Future Inventory

The 103,400 square feet of land classified as excess acreage under current conditions will more than likely change in the future. First, if the output from that plant declines, land in the parking area as well as in the storage area can also be reclassified as excess acreage. On the other hand, if production increases, the current excess acreage will be needed for some economic purpose.

Because of the need to match future needs to future inventory, the corporate real estate executive should be integrally linked to the company's strategic planning process. This link should be direct; the real estate executive should serve on the strategic planning committee because the specific input concerning the site is part of his or her responsibilities. For example, the real estate executive might identify that the excess land would be usable to expand storage and parking when a second shift is added to the plant, or that the excess land could not be effectively used without reconfiguring the site. If the excess land is on the opposite side of the plant from the existing parking and storage area, part of the original parking area may have to be moved and reconstructed to that location. The old parking deck could then be reassigned and redesigned to serve as part of the storage facility.

(3) Spatial Aspects of Space Needs and Inventory

In addition to the temporal dimension of the analysis, the geographic location of the space needs and the inventory must be investigated. The current space needs may perfectly balance with current inventory, but the need may be in the West while the plant is in the Northeast. In another example, the inventory of retail space may be downtown, but the market is in the suburbs.

The real estate executive must be informed about the changes that the company is experiencing from shifts in the market, production costs, distribution costs, input procurement costs, and so on. Effects of these changes and the company's reaction to them in the strategic plan can be incorporated into the needs versus inventory analysis.

(c) IDENTIFYING THE LOCATION STRATEGY

A firm's location strategy reflects the analysis of its temporal and spatial needs versus its space inventory. An existing company generally faces one of several types of situations that require locational choices:

- *New Facility Construction/Acquisition.* The firm opens a new operation on a site not previously owned or occupied by the company by acquiring an existing property ready to house the operation or by acquiring a site and constructing a facility. The location may mark a new presence for the company, requiring an introductory locational strategy. Alternatively, other company operations may already be present, requiring an integrative locational strategy to coordinate the new operation with local corporate activities.
- *On-Site Expansion/Contraction.* The firm either expands or contracts existing facilities on a site or sites that are currently in inventory by changing the magnitude of a space function in relation to any excess land, such as adding or reducing production space while keeping the other space functions constant. It may also reassign space among various functions. An integrative locational strategy should be followed.
- *Adjacent Site Expansion.* The original facility is used but expansion occurs by acquiring additional land that is nearby or adjacent to

the site. Only an integrative locational strategy may be necessary. But contraction of operations on adjacent sites can also occur. Then excess acreage or buildings are sold off. In this instance, a combined integrative and exiting locational strategy should be pursued to accommodate a smaller company presence.

- *Relocation.* The company closes the original facility and moves to another facility, either a newly constructed or existing building. The relocation can be a short move (the company moves to another facility in the same general area or in the same community) or a long move (the company moves to another community, another part of the state, another state, another region, or even another country). Any one strategy or combination of them may have to be employed.
- *Branch Plant Acquisition.* The company keeps the original facility and continues to use it while acquiring another facility in a different location. Both an introductory and integrative locational strategy may be needed for the acquired facility.
- *Closure and Disposition.* The company shuts down an existing operation and does not have an immediate internal reuse. A disposition decision must be made to sell, lease, or otherwise dispose of the property, or to keep it in inventory for future corporate use. An exiting and/or integrative locational strategy is needed to guide the disposition decision.

The real estate executive matches the location strategy to the changing needs of the company. For example, if the company establishes an objective of expanding the sale of its product to another geographic market, such as in the West, and its current production facility is still cost-efficient, then the location strategy will more than likely involve a branch plant acquisition. It could also be an on-site or adjacent site expansion. The production and transportation cost numbers will identify the location strategy to take. If, on the other hand, the current production facility is obsolete and cost-inefficient, the strategy could involve a relocation to a site that is somewhat centrally located between the current market and the emerging market.

The location strategy that is actually undertaken is determined by comparing the economic and noneconomic costs of the possible alternative location opportunities. The corporate real estate executive should help generate these figures as a member of the company team or committee that undertakes the analysis and renders a recommendation. If there is a need to avoid locational bias, all or parts of the analysis can be contracted to a consultant.

(d) BENEFITS AND COSTS IN THE LOCATION STRATEGY

The analysis of a location strategy includes an examination of both quantifiable and qualitative factors. Quantifiable factors can be directly or explicitly measured in a numeric sense. Qualitative factors generally must be described to be analyzed but can usually be implicitly measured with a nominal or ordinal scale. In any event, the financial analysis must take into account and reflect their effect. The real estate executive must be familiar with the nature and techniques of the analysis to properly use the results.

(1) Quantifiable Costs

Quantifiable costs include the following factors:

- *Site and Space Acquisition and Operational Costs.* Both acquisition and operational costs of the facility will vary among different sites and different locations. Prices of existing properties, land costs, construction costs, and rental rates will fluctuate among and within different markets. Similarly, property taxes, insurance rates, utility rates, maintenance and repair costs, and other operating costs can vary. All these costs must be calculated on a site-specific basis.
- *Production Costs.* The cost to produce the product or provide the service will be different for each site and each location examined. A principal component is the geographic difference in labor cost, which can be expressed by a wage rate difference if the productivity of the labor force is constant between the sites. But differences in productivity also need to be estimated to the get complete picture. Another cost savings can arise because one location has a pool of skilled labor that can easily be hired, or because the school system teaches students better general and vocational skills. These factors can reduce company training expenses. In addition, cost savings can arise because one location has specialized firms that can provide services to the company on a contract or fee basis while another location may require the firm to internalize those costs as employee wages and salaries.
- *Procurement Costs.* The cost to acquire the material inputs into the production process, that is, the cost to transport these materials is the dominant factor in this category. The cost is determined by the distance over which the material input is being transported, the nature of the material being shipped, the freight rate structure, and the availability of alternative or competing modes of transport.
- *Distribution Cost.* This is the cost to send the finished product to either its consumer or industrial market. It can also be interpreted as the cost of travel for company personnel who are providing services. The cost to transport the product or person is determined by the distance the product or person is being transported, the nature of the product, the transport rate structure, and the availability of alternative or competing modes of transport.

(2) Quantifiable Benefits

Choice of location can affect the revenues a firm generates from the sale of its product or service. For example, users of the product or service may increase the volume of their orders if the production facilities are reasonably close. In addition to the increase in gross sales, total profits can also increase from economies of scale as average costs of production decline with increased output levels.

(3) Qualitative Benefits and Costs

Qualitative benefits and costs are discussed in more detail under the headings of business climate and quality-of-life studies, which are discussed in §§ 7.7 and 7.8 of this chapter.

§ 7.3 THE LOCATION SELECTION PROCESS

The location selection process revolves around the calculation of the financial and other benefits the company may gain from expansion, relocation, branch plant acquisition, or the like. The company, with the explicit involvement of the real estate executive, identifies its current and future needs for space, and then matches its future inventory to those future needs.

This process starts with the creation of a short list of major locational criteria that should reflect the company's specific needs. The following are typical locational objectives:

1. Close proximity to the market.
2. Reduction in the cost of labor without loss of productivity so as to maintain or improve current profit margins.
3. Maintenance or improvement of the quality of life for management, other key personnel, and personnel recruited from outside the local area.
4. A site with a predetermined set of physical characteristics (e.g., adequate site size and configuration, level topography).
5. A site with a predetermined set of accessibility characteristics (e.g., proximity to an interstate system for trucking, rail, and air access, adequate community facilities).
6. A location close to bulky natural resources or producers of critical inputs to the production process. Those requirements arise when items cannot be transported economically over long distance or require special handling and/or storage. The product could be fragile, perishable, or high valued relative to its weight or volume.

The transport mode could be air cargo or water carrier necessitating proximity to airports or harbors.

This short list can be used to identify a general location. Several communities or labor markets in the general area could qualify, and each community could contain several possible sites.

At this point, the acquisition and operational attributes of each possible site are evaluated in two stages to determine benefits and revenues as well as costs. First, a more detailed set of key characteristics can be used to reduce the number of potential sites. It may include such items as:

1. The percentage of skilled production line workers needed from the existing labor force.
2. Requirements that potential sites must be in an industrial park, and minimum characteristics for industrial park locations.
3. The minimum level of industrial services and facilities available in the community, such as solid waste treatment facilities, fire protection equipment, and so on.
4. The minimum population base and other standards for the community to ensure adequate housing choice, educational opportunities, and shopping.

Once a manageable set of potential locations has been identified, each site is evaluated on the basis of the quantifiable costs and benefits as well as the qualitative elements identified in the preceding section. The quantitative evaluation can focus on an estimate of profit, using either a profit maximization or profit satisfaction orientation.

The search team can incorporate the qualitative elements as an add-on factor to the profit measure, or by means of a comparative ranking and weighting system.

To illustrate how such a system can be used to evaluate qualitative factors for a locational decision, consider the following hypothetical example. A company wants to expand its specialized computer operations by establishing a facility to perform research and development on software and hardware for specialized financial applications. The new facility will employ about 50 executive and professional personnel and have a technical and production staff of about 100. After an initial locational analysis, the company has narrowed down the search to Site A in North Carolina and Site B in Tennessee.

The following standards were established to guide the locational and site selection process:

- Basic Research and Development Needs
  - To be relatively close to other computer manufacturing operations that may use the software and hardware products.

    - To be relatively close to other computer R&D operations that will provide valuable relationships for research personnel and contractual services.
- Basic Market Needs
    - To be located in a community with a metropolitan population of 500,000 or more with a significant regionally oriented financial community.
    - To be located in a community with good air transportation links to major cities with financial communities of national significance.
- Basic Production Needs
    - To have an available labor force with a relatively high educational level and good technical skills.
    - To have a plentiful, high-quality water supply and a reliable source of relatively inexpensive electrical power.
- Basic Site Environment Needs
    - To have a relatively high level of site amenities in an organized industrial park that provides adequate privacy, a proper image, and adequate support facilities for the operation and its research-oriented personnel.
    - To be located in a part of the community that is reasonably proximate to amenable housing areas preferred by executive and professional personnel and with supporting commercial facilities nearby.

Research by the facilities planning division revealed the following information about the two final sites. Site A was in a new industrial park located on the outskirts of a city of 100,000 but within a three-county metropolitan region of 900,000. The financial community contained several regional and nationally ranked banks and insurance companies. A new airport provided direct flights to virtually all national cities. A small number of computer parts producers operated in the area, but computer-oriented research and development operations were developing at a fairly rapid pace. The labor force exhibited adequate technical skills, but the educational level was below the national average. A plentiful water supply was available but water quality was only average, and electric power in the area was generated by coal-fired plants with high rates that were expected to increase in the future. Site amenity levels in the industrial park were excellent, and there were adequate shopping facilities nearby. However, the site was at least a 20-minute commute from the closest high-quality neighborhoods.

Site B was in a city of 50,000 situated about 20 miles from a larger city of 200,000. The two-county metropolitan area contained about 700,000 people. There were a number of regional and state-wide banks and insurance companies in the larger city, but air connections to most large national or international centers were available only through Atlanta, Cincinnati, or New York. Relatively frequent flights to these cities, however, were available. There were a few computer parts operations in the area, but only a handful of complimentary research and development operations were operating locally. There was a skilled labor force available but mostly trained in assembly-line operations, and the educational level was below national norms. However, there was a plentiful supply of high-quality water, and electric power, generated with substantial hydroelectric facilities, was reliable and relatively cheap. The site had excellent privacy and amenities with shopping facilities nearby, but there would be a relatively long commute required from most of the higher quality neighborhoods in the metropolitan area.

Exhibit 7.2 contains the ranking and weighting system used to evaluate these factors for Sites A and B. Although several different weighting and ranking systems could have been used, a 1-to-5 system provides an order of magnitude measure that is sufficient for most major distinctions, particularly when used in conjunction with another measuring system to develop a point scale. A 1-to-10 system is useful when finer distinctions are needed. A −2 to +2 scale can be used in lieu of a 1-to-5 scale when positive and negative measurements are made above a neutral standard represented by 0. However, a scale containing positive and negative values can be used only for one part of the system if more than one scale is used to develop a point system.

The following sections present issues related to the locational decision process including linkages, site requirements, community selection factors, business climate, quality-of-life issues, and employee relocation issues. Each of the topics will be discussed separately although they are interrelated parts of a whole.

§ 7.4 LINKAGES IN THE LOCATIONAL DECISION

The locational decision requires an analysis of the numerous relationships between the site location for a corporate facility and the many entities in the community with whom the newly located corporate operation must relate. These entities include consumers of the product or service, the suppliers of inputs into the production process, the employees of the company, utility companies, and any other persons or activities that are important in the operation of the business. This analysis must be performed for each potential community and each potential site on the company's short list.

These relationships between the company and these community-based entities are referred to as *linkages.* A linkage is a relationship or

EXHIBIT 7.2 Ranking and Weighting of Locational Factors

Factor	Weight[a]	Rank[b]		Overall	
		Site A	Site B	Site A	Site B
R&D Needs					
Complimentary production facilities	3	0	0	0	0
Complimentary R&D facilities	4	+1	−1	+4	−4
Production Needs					
Labor force characteristics	3	+1	0	+3	0
Water and power availability	5	0	+2	0	+10
Test Market Needs					
Local community characteristics	3	+1	0	+3	0
Air links to national centers	5	+2	+1	+10	+5
Environmental Needs					
Site amenities and environment	4	+2	+2	+8	+8
Commuting routes and conditions	2	+1	0	+2	0
Total Weighted Score				+30	+19

[a] *Weighting System*
1 = Relatively unimportant.
2 = Of minor importance.
3 = Important.
4 = Very important.
5 = Extremely important.

[b] *Ranking System*
−2 = Ranks well below the standard.
−1 = Ranks somewhat below the standard.
0 = Achieves the standard.
+1 = Ranks somewhat above the standard.
+2 = Ranks well above the standard.

interdependency between a land use (the corporate facility) and another land use or activity in the surrounding community—consumers, input suppliers, utility providers, and so on.

The location strategy involves minimizing the economic and noneconomic costs of maintaining each of the linkages as well as the overall linkage pattern. The following are the basic steps of a linkage analysis:

1. Identification of all important linkages the corporate facility requires.
2. Estimation of the current and future economic and noneconomic costs to maintain each linkage.
3. Determination of the quality of each linkage, by examining the distance, route structure, and environment; importance or significance of the relationship; whether or not it is inward or outward oriented; and other measurable features.
4. Evaluation of the cost to maintain linkage patterns for each of the communities and the sites on the short list.
5. Inclusion of the results from the analysis and costs of the linkage patterns into the information base for the location decision.

To illustrate a pattern of linkages, consider the critical linkages for a manufacturing site. Manufacturing firms have many characteristics that differentiate one company's operation from another, even in the same industry. Some of these are:

1. The nature of the product.
2. The market in which the product is sold, including:
   a. Geographic submarkets.
   b. Market characteristics (e.g., consumer vs. industrial market).
3. The degree of capital intensity in the production process and subsequent skill levels needed by employees.
4. The transportation mode used for inputs and outputs.
5. The nature of production inputs.

The linkage pattern of the firm must reflect many, if not all these differentiating features. Linkages for a manufacturing plant using preassembled components are used in the following example.

(a) LINKAGE TO THE MARKET

The linkage between the manufacturing plant and the market is facilitated by both the local street system and the interstate highway system if the plant ships its product to market by truck. This linkage is evaluated by examining the distance and travel time between the plant and the market, the number of truck trips required over a fixed period of time, and the conditions (route structure) affecting travel time, currently and in the future. The relationship of the plant to the closest interstate highway interchange is important. Excellent access to distant markets may be available via the interstate highway system, but the site might require costly crosstown travel to get to that interstate.

The cost to maintain the link is the full estimate of distribution cost.

(b) LINKAGE TO INPUT SUPPLIERS

The local street system and the interstate highway system also facilitate the linkage between the manufacturing plant and its input suppliers. The plant may receive inputs by either truck or railroad. As in the case of the linkage to the market, the input linkage is evaluated by investigating the distance and travel time between the plant and the input supplier, the number of truck trips required over a fixed period of time, and the route structure.

The cost to maintain the link is the full estimate of procurement cost.

(c) LINKAGE TO THE LABOR MARKET

The availability and skills of a local labor pool (which saves on recruiting and training costs) is an important criterion on a short list. The critical linkage is the relative location of the plant to the pool of skilled labor. If the labor pool is uniformly distributed over the entire community, the plant should seriously evaluate a centrally located site. If, on the other hand, the skilled labor pool is concentrated in a single section of the community, the best plant location would be a site directly accessible from that area.

The objective for the location decision is minimization of employees' commuting costs, in both monetary and nonmonetary terms. Total travel time for the whole employee pool is reduced if the firm is located near the residential areas where most employees live.

(d) LINKAGE TO MANAGEMENT AND EXECUTIVE HOUSING

The link between the plant and residential areas for top management is also important. Managerial personnel will be more effective if their commuting problems are minimized, so accessibility from upper income housing areas is also desirable.

Which is more important—proximity to executive housing or to employee housing? Many times, as in the following example, the location decision has been almost totally skewed in favor of proximity to executive housing:

> We want this site search to be completely objective. We're stuck with a plant in this city, because the division president wanted it here. He left the company three years after we built it, and for the past 10 years we've had to live with the problems of trying to operate here. I don't ever want that to happen again.

Or, in another case:

> We built our new plant in a large metropolitan area. The recommended site was on the south side of the city, but the plant manager we hired wanted it closer to his home on the north side. Three months after we opened the north-side plant, we had to fire the man. It's a lousy situation because we employ a lot of low-skilled people who tend to quit after they realize how long the commute from their houses really is. We should have known better.[1]

The warning implicit in these examples is that this linkage should receive consideration but should not be assigned an inordinate amount of importance.

(e) LINKAGE TO MANAGEMENT TRAVEL

The managers of the plant must periodically travel to many destinations—to the corporate headquarters, to plants and/or distribution centers of input suppliers, to plants of buyers of the output from the plant, and to distributors who are providing the output into the consumer market. In addition, the management from other firms will make reciprocal trips to the plant. So, access to public transportation facilities must also be convenient.

The linkage that has to be maintained is usually stated as the distance and travel time to the airport. Even though this statement is true, it is not undimensional. The airport could be a major regional or municipal airport, but it could also encompass the small private airport with no commercial service. This linkage is especially important if plant management typically travels in a company airplane. The linkage could also involve auto travel in which the interstate system is a critical feature. In some areas of the country, rail travel would be an important form of management travel.

§ 7.5 SITE REQUIREMENTS

Site requirements for a particular corporate facility are established as a logical extension of establishing spatial standards, discussed in

[1] Charles F. Harding, "Company Politics in Plant Location," *Industrial Development* (September/October 1982), p. 19.

Chapter Six. The requirements of the company, the buildings and activities associated with the corporate operation being planned, and all the ancillary activities must be accommodated on the site. Additional site requirements may be imposed by community standards, federal or state regulations, or by the environment in which a site is situated. For example, a manufacturing plant in a warm, sprawling desert town, where land is plentiful and flat, may have very different site requirements from the same operation located in a congested eastern metropolis with hilly terrain and a cold climate. Like space requirements, site requirements form a basis for the comparative analysis of community and site alternatives, both in the initial analysis and for the short list.

The most efficient way to handle site requirements for corporate facilities planning purposes is to develop a comprehensive site factors checklist for each type of facility. This checklist can then be used to establish minimum standards for each site factor and to list the range of acceptable limits. It can also be used to evaluate alternative sites using a ranking and weighting system for each site factor in much the same fashion as locational factors were evaluated in Exhibit 7.2. The site factors checklist should be divided into at least two components—physical factors and legal/regulatory factors. This checklist can be integrated with other checklists containing locational factors, financial factors, and other forms of comparative analysis.

There are numerous sources of information for development of a site factors checklist. Publications from the Society of Industrial and Office Realtors, the National Association of Industrial and Office Parks, and other organizations contain information about site factors for office and industrial uses.

Legal and regulatory requirements and their impact on site requirements have not been well addressed but are receiving more attention from many industry groups. This issue will be discussed in subsequent chapters.

Exhibit 7.3 is a checklist of major site factors commonly considered for most types of office and industrial uses. Many of these same site factors would appear on a checklist for retail uses as well, but more attention to such items as accessibility, visibility, parking, and loading and unloading facilities would be needed. Standards for retail development would need to be closely attuned to the market norms for the local area for the site to be competitive with other retail facilities.

§ 7.6 COMMUNITY SELECTION FACTORS

When a company selects to locate in a particular community, how the community's characteristics will affect the company and its operations is of paramount concern. Other impacts, such as the community's

EXHIBIT 7.3 Site Characteristics Checklist

Physical Conditions

Site Size
Site Configuration
Site Dimensions
- Depth
- Width
- Frontage

Significant Vegetative Cover
- Predominant coverage
- Percentage covered

Topography
- Average slope
- Percent with critical slope

Hydrology
- Drainage adequacy
- Percent with flood hazard
- On-site retention needs

Soil Characteristics
- Types of soils
- Vulnerability to erosion
- Special features

Geologic Characteristics
- Surface features
- Subterranean features
- Weight-supporting capability
- Depth to bedrock

Infrastructure Conditions

Utilities
- Electric Power
  - Available sources
  - Deliverable capacity
- Water
  - Available sources
  - Water quality
  - Sanitary sewers
- Sanitary Sewer
  - Available sources
  - Treatment capacity
- Natural Gas
- Waste Collection/Disposal
  - Trash and garbage
  - Solid wastes
  - Liquid wastes
  - Special features
- Fire Protection Services
- Security Services

Support Facilities

Access Features
- Abutting Thoroughfares
  - Number
  - Design capacities
  - Traffic conditions
- Abutting Minor Streets
  - Number
  - Traffic conditions
- Site Entrances
  - Number
  - Location
  - Capacity
  - Conditions
- Site Exists
  - Number
  - Location
  - Capacity
  - Conditions

Parking/Loading Facilities
- Parking Spaces
  - Employees
  - Executives
  - Visitors
  - Others
- Loading/Unloading Spaces

Other Support Facilities
- Landscaping Needs
- Visibility Requirements
  - Signage
  - Site entrances
  - Building entrances

EXHIBIT 7.3 *(Continued)*

Legal/Regulatory Conditions

Contractual Constraints
- Title Conditions
- Deed Covenants/Restrictions
- Easements
  - Type
  - Location
- Existing Leases
  - Type
  - Effective rents
  - Duration
  - Conditions of repossession
- Restrictions Imposed by Lenders

Public Regulations
- Zoning Conditions
  - Existing zoning
    - Use restrictions
    - Development standards
  - Needed zoning
    - Use restrictions
    - Development standards
    - Time required for rezoning
- Development Requirements to Obtain Permits
  - Site improvements required
  - Site design standards required
  - Dedication/reservation requirements
  - Impact fee requirements
  - Other development exactions

Other Regulatory Requirements
- Environmental Requirements
- Other Requirements

effect on the employees' quality of life and the effect of the company on the community, appear in a later chapter.

This analysis focuses on factors that affect the cost structure of the firm. Relevant factors used in community selection affect production costs and administrative costs. The community selection factors include legal/regulatory, economic, political, demographic/social, and physical characteristics.

A distinction needs to be made between and among three interrelated studies dealing with community impacts. The quality-of-life study focuses on how conditions in the community affect employee well-being and attitudes, consequently productivity. The business climate study, on the other hand, deals with how the attitudes of community leaders, other business operators, and citizens, as perceived by the corporate entity, affect company operations. This distinction is highlighted by the following:

> Business climate measures the attitudes of the population and its elected and appointed officials toward business. These studies generally focus on issues that can be controlled by the population and its government, such as laws, regulations, tax expenditures, union elections and strike activity.[2]

[2] Charles F. Harding, "Business Climate Studies: How Useful Are They," *Industrial Development* (January/February 1983), p. 22.

A community analysis concentrates on the business' attitude concerning the community and what it can offer the business.[3]

The following list shows major community selection factors.

Community Characteristics

- Labor Force Concerns
  - Wage rates
  - Productivity
  - Availability of required skills
  - Unionization
  - Educational level and training available
- Property Taxation
  - Rates and assessment practices
  - Tax abatements, concessions, etc.
  - Personal property tax
  - Special tax districts
- Corporate Income Taxation: State and Local
  - Rates
  - Allowable deductions
  - Credits and concessions
- Other Forms of Taxation: State and Local
  - Unemployment premiums
  - Workmen's compensation premiums
  - Inventory tax
- Fees and Charges
  - Impact fees
  - Water and sewer hookup fees
  - Applications and permit charges
  - Special assessments
- Regulations and Development Controls
  - Zoning requirements
  - Subdivision regulations
  - Construction codes
  - Occupancy codes and licensing requirements
  - Growth management restrictions—utility extension, sewer moratorium, development or population caps, timing controls, etc.

[3] Joseph Rabianski, "Business Climate Studies: Do We Agree on What They Are and Why We Need Them?" *Industrial Development* (August 1990), p. 20.

- Utilities and Public Services
  Quantity and quality of street system
  Quantity and quality of utilities—electric power, natural gas, water, sewerage
  Quantity and quality of fire and police services
  Quantity and quality of educational facilities for employees and their families
  Quantity and quality of medical facilities
  Quantity and quality of parks and recreation facilities
  Quantity and quality of public cultural facilities
- Transportation Services
  Availability of trucking, railroad, and air cargo services for shipping and receiving outputs and inputs
  Availability of air transport service for executive travel
  Availability of port or barge facilities
  Availability of mass transit facilities
  Condition and plans for regional thoroughfare system

Community Attitudes

- Name recognition of the community and the industrial area or business park in which the site is located
- Age and condition of the industrial area or business park in which the site is located
- Compatibility of land users in the immediate area to the company
- Absence of negative externalities such as litter, noise, and air pollution
- Perception of the safety of the area for both employees and property.[4]
- Receptivity of political leaders and leaders and service providers in the business community

The objective of establishing and evaluating community selection factors is twofold. To find a proper fit between the corporate operation and a community, the company needs to focus on how the community will, first of all, affect the capital and operational costs for the corporate facility. Then a longer term perspective is taken in evaluating how the community will affect productivity, both at the facility being located and for the company as a whole. This latter task involves looking at how efficiently the company will be able to orchestrate inputs and

[4] See Rabianski, "Business Climate Studies," p. 20, for an earlier version of this discussion.

outputs, how marketing of the product or service will be affected, how well the company will be able to do business with others, both locally and elsewhere, as well as how the location will affect morale of corporate personnel and the company's strategic image and role.

One of the initial concerns of the company is to determine if the community offers an adequate human resource environment. The two principal sets of factors examined for this analysis are labor force concerns and community attitudes. A detailed examination of the availability of labor resources, skills, and training available, attitudes and historic productivity levels, and other aspects of the labor force provides a picture of the costs and difficulty the company will have in procuring an adequate pool of employees. The company's reception in the community by those who will provide services, do business with it, and provide the social environment for the enterprise is also a critical concern. Many locational strategies often overlook the relevant detail needed for this analysis.

Initial community selection criteria can then be established as a basis for obtaining more specific information. The next round of analysis usually deals with the sources, availability, and quality of facilities and services—both commercial and public—the company will need to conduct its operation. This information is developed by carefully examining utilities and public services, transportation services, and the regulatory environment affecting acquisition and use of sites. The availability and quality of needed business services are also taken into consideration, although the company is usually able to supply those services not available in the community from providers elsewhere. This part of the analysis reveals a great deal about how critical a specific requirement may be. It helps to establish the relevancy and importance of specific facilities and services in a comparative analysis of competing communities.

In the final analysis, the company must be able to establish the facility on a cost-effective basis. No matter how attractive a community may be for other reasons, it will not meet the company's community selection criteria if cost thresholds cannot be achieved. For this reason, a very careful study should be conducted of the tax environment and conditions and of the types of development charges and hookup fees involved. A critical examination of the regulatory environment is also in order to determine if there are hidden risks and costs in complying with all the procedures and standards required. Time delays and meeting discretionary requirements imposed by regulators can significantly affect costs.

The next sections deal with analyzing a community's business environment, the quality of life it offers, and difficulties employees may have in relocating there. These issues can also make or break a locational decision.

§ 7.7 THE BUSINESS CLIMATE STUDY

The business climate study considers the attitude of the community toward the newly located facility as a physical entity, toward the management personnel as business operatives in the community, and toward the company as a whole. In general terms, it asks and answers the question, "How will the company and its leading representatives be treated after the business moves into the community?"

(a) FOCUS OF THE STUDY[5]

The business climate study is a survey of the attitudes of government officials, business leaders, and social organizations in the community. The information sought focuses on how the company will be treated in the following matters:

- *The Property Assessment Process.* Will the company be treated adversely by continual overvaluation of the property?
- *The Provision of Public Services.* Will the company face delays and/or hostility in the provision of necessary services now and in the future? Items of particular concern are repairs and expansion of utilities, enhanced security and police protection, and continued adequacy of fire protection services.

The business climate study also focuses on how existing business leaders in the community treat the firm's management team. Will they be welcomed and invited to participate in business-sponsored events, or will they be ostracized?

In addition, the business climate study also examines the attitude of the general population toward the firm and its managers. Will personnel be able to find friends in the community who are not employees of the firm? Will they receive invitations to join social and civic organizations?

(b) PUBLIC ATTITUDES IN THE BUSINESS CLIMATE STUDY[6]

Usually an analysis of public attitudes focuses on residents' attitudes toward business in general. The focus rather should be the public atti-

[5] The material in this section was adapted from Joseph Rabianski and Neil G. Carn, "Selecting Industrial Locations, Sites," *The National Real Estate Investor* (August 1991), p. 24.

[6] An earlier version of this discussion appears in Rabianski, "Business Climate Studies," pp. 21–22.

tude toward the specific business that is considering the community as a possible location.

No two firms are identical. First, they can be very dissimilar industries. People will more than likely react differently to different types of firms as well as different companies in the same business. For example, a rock quarry operation will be viewed and may be treated differently from an electronic instrument assembly plant. Further, a nationally known company may be viewed quite differently from a local company, even if they are in the same business.

Second, two firms are in the same industry may be applying contrasting production processes or technologies. Firm A could be utilizing a capital-intensive production process, while Firm B follows a more labor-intensive production process. This disparity translates into the type and amount of labor the firm will require from the community's labor pool. Firm A may be treated with indifference by a community in which the laborers are not sufficiently skilled to obtain employment while simultaneously being seen as a source of high tax revenue by the community government. Firm B may be welcomed as a neighbor by that same community especially if it has been suffering with high unemployment.

Third, the management of the same firm could be treated differently by the public in various locations. Consider the situations that a firm in a "smokestack" industry might face. Community A has high unemployment in a labor force with the skills for direct employment (low training time and cost) in that firm. This community could welcome the upper management of the firm into the community by opening the door to various social and fraternal organizations. On the other hand, Community B, which has low unemployment and primarily a white-collar labor force, could exhibit the reverse reaction. Here, the firm is viewed as undesirable; since the management team is operating an undesirable facility, the members are viewed as undesirable themselves.

Charles Harding recognizes the significance of these firm-specific and community-specific issues because he said that "a businessman seeking a location must understand how these public attitudes affect *his* business." However, his subsequent discussion turned to more general points.

Harding identified two very important factors that are affected by the public's attitude. First, if a company is viewed as a major contributor to a state's or a community's economic health, it will more than likely be treated in "a fair and even-handed manner." If it is seen as a detriment, "when new taxes are required, industry is likely to be hit most heavily." When industry carries the heaviest tax burden, a major consideration is to examine the relative burden of the property tax on different land users—residential versus commercial versus industrial.

When considering a location, the general attitude matters to a company because although the community may not be able overtly to discriminate against a specific firm, there are many ways to hinder an unwelcome firm within the letter of the law. First, its assessed value can be disproportionately higher and the public services provided to it disproportionately lower than for other firms in the community. Second, public attitude can affect legal rulings, and thus the damages assessed, against industry in workers' compensation cases in the local judicial system. Cases can be decided on the basis of sympathy for a sick (or injured) worker rather than on the legitimacy of the claim against the employer creating a serious cost burden for a small company. On the other hand, firms with a good public image may face fewer proceedings and/or pay lower damage values than firms perceived to be dangerous, unhealthy, unsafe, or dirty, or just unwelcome in the community.

In addition to these effects, several other manifestations of public opinion can affect a firm after it decides to locate in a community. First, when raw land is purchased for development in the future, the community can reflect a negative attitude in the development approval process. Second, the construction activity of a site can be hampered or the construction period lengthened by the local officials involved in the permitting and inspection processes. Third, zoning or code variances required for on-site expansion may meet with government resistance.

Fourth, the community's attitude toward government indebtedness can affect the firm through the tax assessment policy and procedures. The firm specifically, or local industry in general, may be seen as a "cash cow," and the tax assessor may establish a disproportionate assessed value to repay that indebtedness. This situation can occur if the tax assessor establishes a higher assessed value for the undesirable firm in relation to other more desirable firms; or if the tax assessor shifts the burden of meeting the budget onto the local industry by establishing more than a proportionate assessed value on plant, equipment, and inventory in relation to single-family homes and retail property.

Fifth, the community's attitude toward government indebtedness can affect the firm through the policy and procedures of providing public services. An initial willingness shown by the community to maintain, and possibly upgrade, public services may be sharply curtailed as the level of debt increases. This change in attitude can be directed at the undesirable firm specifically or at the local industry in general.

Sixth, the community's attitude toward the firm and its management personnel can affect the costs of operating the plant and thereby the cost of producing the product. Salaries of plant management and other key personnel may have to be increased to retain these people if they are excluded from social and community activities because of being viewed as undesirable. If salaries do not provide sufficient incentives, then extra expense will be incurred from the turnover of these personnel.

(c) USE OF THE STUDY IN SITE SELECTION

The preceding factors make business climate studies an important aspect of a site selection. Such studies can lead to an understanding of significant future impacts on the cost structure of the firm including public attitudes that can strongly affect the bottom line in the future.

§ 7.8 THE QUALITY-OF-LIFE STUDY

The quality-of-life study attempts to identify the positive differential in personal satisfaction that current managerial and key production employees will experience by making a geographic move with the company. This study should be a part of any employee relocation plan. Its findings can be reflected in the financial arrangements surrounding employee relocation.

(a) FOCUS OF THE STUDY[7]

The quality-of-life study has a specific focus on perceptions as well as quantifiable factors and a specific orientation toward the relocation of employees.

Humphrey Taylor pointed out that the typical quality-of-life study focuses on measurable variables while ignoring the more important perceptual questions.[8] "Quality of life means different things to different people. . . . (It) is in the eye of the beholder."[9] This same point was also made by another author, who said, "Most researchers have relied solely on objective or hard data and totally neglected the psychological aspect."[10]

Given its importance, perception should be covered in quality-of-life studies, although it can be handled in different ways. The approach discussed by Taylor focuses on a survey in which a cross section of Americans described what they thought the words *quality of life* meant. Their

[7] An earlier version of this discussion appears in Joseph Rabianski, "How to Specify a Quality-of-Life Study," *Industrial Development* (February 1989), pp. 18–19.

[8] Ibid.

[9] Ibid.

[10] Naomi Bailin Wish, "Are We Really Measuring the Quality of Life?" *American Journal of Economics and Sociology* (January 1986), p. 95; and Rosen, Sherwin, "Wage-Based Indexes of Urban Quality of Life," *Current Issues in Urban Economics,* P. Mieszkowski and M. Strasheim, eds. (Baltimore: Johns Hopkins Press, 1979), p. 92.

primary responses were, in essence, "getting good things, living well and enjoying peace, security, and happiness."[11]

The conclusion is that quality of life from a perceptual perspective differs from quality of life as measured by quantifiable variables. Individual "well-being" and "getting good things" connote economic security for oneself and one's family. The number of jobs in the community indicates, to some degree, the opportunities to find a satisfactory job but denotes nothing more. Which perspective is more relevant—perception or hard figures? Logically, the perceptual focus is more relevant: Quantitative studies merely establish proxy variables in attempting to identify the thoughts and desires of people.

Furthermore, the location decision maker who uses quality-of-life studies is very often considering the quality-of-life opinions of the wrong people. The general population of Americans is not the correct set of people to study to get a set of relevant perceptions. The people who are going to be affected by the relocation are the appropriate group to examine.

(b) KEY ISSUES[12]

The quality-of-life study considers the following key issues:

1. Cost-of-living differentials.
2. Employee preferences for natural and man-made amenities.
3. Journey-to-work costs.
4. Price versus quality aspects of housing opportunities.
5. Public services versus taxation relationship.

The study should start by interviewing the management personnel and the key production employees who are subject to relocation. This will provide data for comparing what they have at their current location with what they desire (or will accept) at the new location. Notice that the orientation of the study is person-specific, not location-specific. It compares an individual's needs and desires, not the difference between the characteristics of two points in space.

The price/quality of housing study considers what the employee can acquire at the current location for a specific salary with what that individual can acquire at the new location for the same salary. This would

[11] Dale D. Wheeler, "Have World Headquarters; Will Travel," *Industrial Development, 147,* 2 (March/April 1978), p. 15.

[12] The material in this section was adapted from Joseph Rabianski and Neil G. Carn, "Selecting Industrial Locations, Sites," *The National Real Estate Investor* (August 1991), p. 24.

include any finance cost differentials that may arise by forgoing a low-interest-rate loan in the move.

The cost-of-living study considers differences in acquisition costs of employees' household necessities as well as the luxury items. Other cost differentials considered include home ownership costs, both for selling and buying houses, differences in rental costs, and complimentary costs of housing, such as utilities and insurance. The analysis also includes changes in tax bites—state and local income tax, property tax, state and local tax, and so on.

The monetary and nonmonetary costs of commuting from the most likely employee housing areas can be evaluated and compared, including the monetary costs of fuel, maintenance and repair, and insurance, as well as any price differentials in car prices. The nonmonetary costs would include travel time differentials as well as aggravation factors such as poor roads. This study is a subset of the cost-of-living study, but the differentials in commuting time add an important dimension.

Individual preferences for natural and man-made amenities reflect the employee's desires and lifestyle factors. Individual preferences for scenery and recreational activities can be surveyed and compared. For example, a multitude of golf courses in the new community will mean nothing to a man who spends his leisure time fishing, whereas absence of a good trout stream may make him very unhappy.

An additional dimension of the price/quality of housing study is the focus on the neighborhood and the public services. Relocating from a current home to the new destination may entail moving children from high-quality to fair-quality public schools. The difference in educational opportunities may only be resolved by the use of private schools at added expense.

(c) PERFORMING A QUALITY-OF-LIFE STUDY[13]

Assuming that the company wants a large percentage of its current employees to transfer, the study should use the following procedures. First, identify the specific employees or group(s) of employees that the company has targeted for special consideration during the move. Notice that a listing of quantitative variables for alternate locations is not the starting point for the study, but rather the identification of the employees, managerial and nonmanagerial, who will be affected by the move. These people are then surveyed to determine what quality of life means to them.

Taylor stresses an important point about relocation: "Most people tend to like what they have and the places in which they live. Wherever

[13] An earlier version of this discussion appears in Joseph Rabianski, "How to Specify a Quality-of-Life Study," *Industrial Development* (February 1989), pp. 18–19.

they live. Most Americans think that the quality of life which they enjoy is better than that of other people living in other parts of the country."[14]

The questioning process can start with general, open-ended questions that are directed not only to the employee, but also to that employee's family. The researcher can let the employee speak for the spouse and the family, or the spouse and family members can be surveyed separately. These general questions can include the following items:

- What would the alternative locations have to offer that you do not find in the neighborhood, community, and general location where you live?
- What location amenities do you currently use? Golf courses? Tennis clubs and courts? Swimming pools, public and private? Parks and nature areas?
- What type of housing would you prefer at the alternative location? Price range? Style? Condition/age?
- What public services would you expect from the community? Types of schools and educational opportunities? Types of recreation areas? Quality of police and fire protection? Kinds of cultural facilities?
- What climate and weather would you prefer at the alternative locations?

The answers to these open-ended inquiries will highlight the quality-of-life factors employees value and can also reveal the features that may have to be available at the new location to overcome the reluctance and uncertainty engendered by the move. The study focuses on both quantitative and qualitative aspects of the employees' quality of life.

Next, the researcher can design a set of more specific questions to ask the employees. These follow-up questions should focus on current behavior and circumstances primarily and attitude secondarily. For example:

- What is the current market value of your house? Is this based on a professional appraisal, or your opinion? Is the house meeting your current needs? If not, is it too big or too small? What size and price of housing would you like in the alternative location?
- Do you have school-age children? If yes, are they going to a public or private school?
- What recreational facilities do you and your family currently use, and how often to you use them?
- Does your spouse work? Will that job need to be maintained at the new location? What is the nature of the job? What are the annual earnings?

[14] Taylor, p. 2.

These questions will provide specific information about the factors that will be viewed as an improvement in existing quality of life. This information can now be developed further through subsequent rounds of surveying. Answers to the subsequent survey questions can then be used to differentiate among the alternative locations for the plant or the headquarters office from the quality-of-life perspective.

Although the evaluation process does not start with a stipulated list of factors, there is advance knowledge about what a relevant list of factors could contain. This knowledge helps the researcher using survey techniques to develop a relevant list of quantitative factors and the employees' perceptions about those factors.

Each group of employees will differ because of economic, demographic, and psychographic features. And each potential location is unique. Therefore, any quality-of-life studies not specifically designed for a given company are only marginally beneficial. Even if the company is considering "Greattown" and "Fairtown" as its two potential locations, Greattown's higher ranking on a general list of places may have no significance to the affected employees.

No other single completed study can be more helpful in determining the company's and the employees' needs and desires than the quality-of-life study. Moreover, the corporate decision on retention of a work force through the relocation process adds another dimension to that study.

(d) SPATIAL SPECIFICATIONS

When quality of life is studied, the geographical area of consideration is typically the metropolitan statistical area (MSA). This focus on the metropolitan area assumes away all differences within the defined geographic area although various areas of an MSA may differ in their levels of total employment, employment distribution across standard industrial classification (SIC) codes, and employment growth rates. Consequently, a single employment indicator value for the MSA cannot do justice to the economic position of an MSA subarea. On this point, Wish has written, "Any aggregate statistic that largely obliterates these differences (between subareas of an MSA) is of questionable validity."[15]

This same reasoning can be applied to other quality-of-life factors such as housing and recreational amenities. This difficulty also occurs when using the Consumer Price Index (CPI) as a measure of the cost of living. In many quality-of-life studies, the researcher uses the CPIs calculated for specific MSAs and then compares across the MSAs in the study, a practice that also contains concept error.

When the U.S. Department of Labor (DOL) gathers CPI data at one of its 85 locations in 23 metropolitan area, it uses random-sampling techniques to represent that MSA. Even if the DOL is totally successful in

[15] Wish, p. 96.

its attempts, the use of that data to represent a subsector of the MSA is subject to concept error. For example, the CPI for the whole MSA may increase 4 percent, while the CPI for the subsector of the MSA site under evaluation may go up by 10 percent.

(e) PERCEPTUAL ASPECTS OF A GEOGRAPHIC AREA

The previous discussion concerning the spatial measurement is the "where" aspect of quality of life. Based on the quantitative variables, quality of life can vary greatly over space within a predefined area. However, to complicate the analysis, the perceptual aspect can create an even more perplexing situation.

For example, a subarea in a MSA could be rated very highly on quantitative amenities because of the number of golf courses, tennis facilities, and swimming pools; but the individuals moving with the plant or headquarters relocation may not play golf or tennis, and they may find the chlorine level of public swimming pools to be unbearable. To this group, the area may be a barren wasteland because there are no hiking trails, bike paths, and quiet public parks.

(f) TIME HORIZON CONSIDERATIONS

The typical quality-of-life study focuses on the present and ignores the future. The list of quantifiable variables for one place is checked against those of another place, and one is found to be superior to the other. This approach is short-sighted for at least two reasons. First, individuals' perceptions of quality of life change over time.[16]

Secondly, these studies do not consider the negative externalities that can, and often do, arise in areas with a current high rating. The quality of life in a community can deteriorate for transferees as the quality of life they valued changes. For example, an easy commute to work and easy assess to the workplace can disappear as growth brings the traffic congestion employees tried to escape five years ago. Open space and scenic vistas disappear as development occurs, and the extent of their disappearance is worse in areas with poor local controls on the development process.

So, an evaluation of quality-of-life factors for the relocating employee should not be frozen in the present. Two areas can be equally attractive today, but the prospect for undesirable change may be greater in one than another. This temporal consideration of anticipated benefits should enter the evaluation process.

Analyzing alternative local development controls can help the decision maker to evaluate the prospects for change. These factors include the

[16] Ibid., p. 95.

community planning process, community involvement, the zoning ordinance, the subdivision regulations, and the administration of the zoning ordinance and subdivision regulations.

(g) USE OF THE STUDY IN SITE SELECTION

The quality-of-life study and its constituent parts allow the corporation to evaluate the full cost of the move for its key personnel by revealing an order of magnitude for compensation differentials that may have to be paid to get the desired people to relocate. The analysis may make the transition easier for both the employee and the corporation.

The quality-of-life study is a natural for outsourcing because both employees and management should see an independent consultant as unbiased and thus are more likely to accept his or her conclusions.

§ 7.9 EMPLOYEE RELOCATION ISSUES

When relocating a plant or initiating a branch plant, the company will consider relocating management and key technical as well as production personnel. The real estate executive should understand the reasons labor migrates, which are essentially the same reasons people move. In simple terms, labor migrates because the benefits to be achieved from the move outweigh its costs. The real estate executive needs to identify these benefits and costs.

The benefits of labor migration include employment-related factors, the cost-of-living differential, and quality-of-life factors. The costs of labor migration include moving costs, potential loss of equity in the family home, additional travel expenses, and personal dislocation.

(a) BENEFITS FROM MIGRATION

The fully array of benefits—both immediate returns and those that accrue over time—include economic as well as noneconomic or psychic returns. The following subsections discuss the various benefits.

(1) Job Retention

Many employees will accept a transfer to the new location just to retain their job, and will personally incur whatever immediate expense or loss is necessary. These expenses are usually the cost of moving the family and its belongings, the cost of return visits if the family is temporarily separated, and any loss of equity that results from selling the family's home.

However, the most highly valued employees of a company may have other options when faced with a move. If these people are valuable to the company, they most likely will be recognized as valuable to other companies in the local area. These people will resign and accept another position to avoid a move. Consequently, the relocation of key personnel may, and typically does, involve the company providing a package of benefits to offset the costs of the move.

(2) Employment-Related Benefits

Labor will favorably consider a change in their promotion and earnings status. If the employee sincerely believes that chances for advancement and promotion in the company will be significantly better after the move than before, this is an economic benefit. A relocation that is accompanied by a pay raise or any other compensation factor creating a positive differential in earnings is also an economic benefit. This last point could include a better health care package, a reduction in state income tax withholdings, an improved vacation package, and the prospects for more overtime.

(3) Housing Costs

A reduction in the cost of living that occurs after the move is also a benefit. To establish whether this benefit exists, or if the difference is negative and therefore a cost of the move, it is necessary to measure the cost of living at each location on the company's short list of potential communities and sites.

These studies can be performed in house or by an outside consultant. The first task is to determine the key factors in the employee's life-style. The most obvious factor is the cost of comparable housing. Can the employee replace the present home with a highly comparable house in the new community? The answer involves understanding the "elements of comparison" that are taught to appraisers. These elements include the physical characteristics of the employee's current home site and structure, the quality of the neighborhood, and the financial aspects of the house, such as equity, mortgage payment, property tax level, utility costs, and any other relatively large expenditures.

The physical and neighborhood factors are used to identify housing possibilities in the new location. These features will reveal the price of the alternative housing. The financial characteristics are then investigated to see what impact the move and the replacement of the current home will have on the employee's financial position.

(4) Retail Expenditures

In addition to the cost of housing, the other big aspect of the cost of living is the cost of retail goods and services. An investigation of the employees' life-styles will reveal the nature of the "market basket" that is being consumed. The investigation focuses on the cost of groceries, clothing, entertainment, recreation, and so on. For example, a week's worth of grocery purchases can be priced in the two locations using the lowest priced grocery chain. This differential can be as great as 10 to 15 percent. The same comparisons can be made for clothing, movie tickets, greens fees at public golf courses, membership fees at country clubs, average restaurant bills, and gasoline prices.

The significance of these measures needs to be put into perspective. First, the costs of housing can range from a low of 30 percent to a high of 45 percent of annual earnings. Retail expenditures typically average 40 percent of annual earnings. The remaining 25 percent of annual earnings consists of savings, insurance payments, taxes, and so on. If the transferred employee earns $30,000 per year and has had housing costs of 35%, and if total living costs at the new location are 10 percent greater, the employee will suffer an approximate $2,250 loss ($30,000 × [35% + 40%] × 10%). This is a 7.5 percent reduction in real income ($2,250 ÷ $30,000).

(5) Quality of Life

In addition to the specific housing cost factors, the analyst should consider the cost impact of all of the other quality-of-life concerns expressed earlier in this chapter. Neighborhood analysis in the housing cost analysis could have considered differences in recreational amenities, quality of schools and public services, and availability of shopping alternatives. But there may still be an array of amenities that are not classified as "being in the neighborhood," such as cultural and sporting events, recreational areas (e.g., the seashore, the mountains, national and state parks), public facilities (e.g., a zoo, an aquarium, museums), climate, and scenery.

These quality-of-life factors may be difficult to measure in economic terms but they can be identified and compared between locations on the basis of their availability and the expenditure of time and effort to obtain them. For example, if the family enjoys major league baseball and the nearest team is 500 miles away at the original location and 30 miles away at the new location, this is a positive quality-of-life difference.

(b) COSTS OF MIGRATION

The full array of costs includes immediate outlays and those that can accrue. Again, there are economic as well as noneconomic or psychic costs. The various costs are discussed in the following subsections.

(1) The Cost to Move Family and Belongings

These costs are generally well understood and typically easy to quantify. The typical family may have 20,000 to 30,000 pounds of appliances, furniture, and personal effects. How much does it cost to transport this 600 miles? How much will it cost to drive the family or fly the family between the locations? These moving costs are front-end, nonrecurring outlays.

(2) Loss of Equity in the Family Residence

Often, relocation requires the sale of the family home in order to buy its replacement in the new community. This creates pressure for a quick sale, which could result in a loss in the equity in the property.

To avoid such a loss, the company may purchase the house from the employee and remarket the property. Or, the company could guarantee the equity in the house by subsidizing the difference between the sales price of the house and its appraised market value.

(3) Additional Travel Costs and Personal Dislocation

The major psychic cost of a relocation is the separation from family and friends. For some employees, this cost is so great that they will not even consider a relocation. But for other employees, the additional costs of travel to return for periodic visits and the increased telephone bills can be minimized by providing a relatively small wage or salary differential, which should be specifically identified (e.g., "The company is also increasing your salary by $50 per month to cover some of your costs to keep in touch with and to return to visit your family"). This annual stipend can be worth a multiple in terms of an enhanced attitude toward the company.

(4) An Employee Relocation Plan

Successful relocation of key personnel requires the corporate real estate executive and the personnel manager to understand the motivations affecting that employee's willingness to relocate. To offer a financial package that will improve the employee's total situation, company personnel must carefully evaluate all the components including the prospects for promotion. Some of the tasks may be more amenable to "outsourcing." Having an external consultant make an unbiased determination of the differences in financial costs as well as quality-of-life factors is critical when the move occurs from a high cost-of-living area to a low-cost-of-living area. The result may be an offer at the existing wage or a nominal salary increase, which is a sizable increase in real terms.

Eight

Development of Multipurpose Facilities

§ 8.1 REAL ESTATE DEVELOPMENT BY BUSINESS FIRMS

In many corporate boardrooms, the words *real estate development* trigger shivers of doubt or worrisome remembrance. During the past few decades, numerous firms learned some hard lessons from their unsuccessful pursuit of profit dollars through real estate development. Nevertheless, real estate development is a potential profit generator; we have included this chapter for two primary reasons:

1. You may have an opportunity to become involved in a real estate development project, or you may already be involved in one.
2. The pursuit of profit furnishes the logic and thrust of real estate development. Even if the personality, players, and market environment of another company described in this chapter differ from those of your company, there is still a strong opportunity for knowledge transfer, particularly when you view your corporate real estate activity as an almost limitless collection of profit opportunities.

There are three methods that a corporation can employ in moving aggressively into the investment and development business:

1. Acquiring a successful company.
2. Engaging in a joint venture with an existing real estate developer.[1]
3. Building its own real estate group (see also Chapter Three).[2]

(a) THE ACQUISITION OF A SUCCESSFUL COMPANY

In this approach, the corporation's properties and capital are combined with the assets of the acquired company creating a highly autonomous subsidiary.

[1] See § 8.2 for more information on joint ventures.

[2] This section is based on an article by Donald R. Riehl, "Caveats for Corporate Real Estate Development," *Urban Land News and Trends in Land Development* (April 1970). Copyright 1970 by Urban Land Institute. Used by permission.

Example. A privately held development company is purchased by a Fortune 100 corporation (parent corporation). The parent corporation may or may not combine the purchased company's assets with its own assets. Also, the purchased company name may be changed to the parent corporation name, but often for tax and regulatory reporting reasons, the purchased company remains a separate profit center and is an autonomous subsidiary with its own management group. This provides the parent corporation with operational flexibility and simple divestment should the acquisition prove unprofitable.

Advantages to the Corporation

- The corporation immediately acquires a knowledgeable management team that can implement the development of corporation properties as well as other real estate opportunities.
- The acquired management team should have sufficient credibility and self-confidence to operate autonomously.
- Through acquisition, a corporation may gain the talent of one or more able real estate entrepreneurs.

Disadvantages to the Corporation

- A strong, independent, autonomous real estate team may not fit well in a traditional corporate management hierarchy.
- The acquiring corporation's major commitment to a new field, will be difficult to reverse.
- Without immediate and continued activity, coupled with relative autonomy, it is virtually impossible to hold together a newly acquired management team.
- The salary and fringe benefit schedules for such a team are likely to exceed those of personnel who hold comparable positions in other corporate divisions.

(b) JOINT VENTURE WITH AN EXISTING REAL ESTATE DEVELOPER[3]

There are four types of joint ventures:

1. A single-purpose joint venture on a new development, in which the corporate partner provides the capital and the development partner provides the know-how.

Example. A support subsidiary of a Fortune 500 corporation had a strategic requirement to acquire regional warehouses throughout the

[3] See § 8.2 for more information on joint ventures.

United States but had no expertise or experienced staff to implement and manage this growth requirement. Management identified and retained a development company with unique regional and national expertise and political savvy to develop these projects within a specific time frame and budget. When the warehouse development program was complete, the joint venture relationship was dissolved.

2. A continuing joint venture, in which the partners provide the necessary people and capital to create a new ongoing jointly owned company for development. The joint venture may continue over considerable time and/over geographic areas to provide service wherever the corporate partner requires a facility. The jointly owned company is often 49 percent owned by the corporation and 51 percent owned by the parent development company.

Example. A corporation was disappointed in cost overruns and time delays to its ongoing national expansion program. A joint venture development company was established with a development company to share the development risk, costs, and profits to satisfy an ongoing facility need. Also, selected experienced real estate staff in the joint venture development company became licensed to provide exclusive real estate brokerage services for the corporation in selected states, thereby earning a real estate commission for the joint venture development company.

3. A single-purpose joint venture on a specific piece of a corporation's property, in which the corporation provides the land and capital or the land only and the developer provides the know-how. This joint venture is becoming more common where the corporate partner does not wish to take all the risk and seeks a development partner to manage the design, construction, interior construction, and leasing activity.

Example. A major bank owned a prime location for many years and considered relocating its corporate headquarters to this site. Location, value, and size dictated a high-rise landmark building as the highest and best use for the site. But the total square footage of the proposed building provided over twice the space required by the bank. The balance of the space in this landmark building could be leased to other tenants, however, and the bank could grow into additional space when needed. The bank had no in-house expertise in developing, financing, constructing, or leasing up such a landmark facility and turned to a regional development company to share in the development, leasing, and management risk. In this single-purpose joint venture, the bank provided the land and some capital, and the development company provided high-rise development and leasing expertise and the balance of the capital; obtained construction financing; and implemented a leasing and property management program. The bank agreed to provide permanent financing and would be the owner of the building. When construction was completed, the joint venture development company was dissolved, but the joint venture leasing and property management arm remained in place as a profit center with minority ownership by the bank and majority ownership by the development company.

4. The sale of specific property to a developer at wholesale prices, with the corporation retaining a participation in the development profits. The corporation's equity in the property becomes the basis of its participation and risk in the development.

Example. Adjacent to a major interchange, a manufacturing company owned a site that had been purchased in the late 1950s and used for over 30 years as a warehouse and distribution center before development of the interchange encouraged major development around the distribution site. Zoning for the sites surrounding the interchange had been changed to retail, and traffic congestion had severely increased travel time into and out of the site. Also, the local railroad distribution facility, which was the receiving point for the large majority of the distribution center's inventory, had been relocated thereby adding receiving and shipping time. The manufacturing company decided to relocate its distribution center to an acceptable site near the railroad distribution facility. A local office park developer proposed a joint venture: The manufacturing company would sell its site to the developer at a wholesale price that was considerably more than book value. The manufacturing company, in turn, would be compensated by a percentage of the development profits equal to the ratio of the wholesale price to the mutually agreed upon appraised retail value of the site. The developer secured the site at a substantially reduced price, leveraged the site for its retail value, provided the manufacturing company with cash in purchasing the site, and provided the manufacturing company with additional cash when the development was profitably sold. The total cash realized was substantially more than the retail value of the site, and the manufacturing company was able to pay off its new site and the cost of the new distribution center.

Advantages to the Corporation

- The basic framework is provided, enabling the corporation to limit its involvement and exposure.
- By working with an existing knowledgeable group, the passive partner (in this case, the corporation) has no need to create its own organization.

- By exposure to the decision-making process in the joint venture, a corporation can educate itself regarding real estate development.
- With respect to real estate, the corporation can maintain a relatively clean balance sheet on behalf of a parent.
- If the corporation provides services or products to the federal government, the corporation cannot charge the cost of ownership but can charge leasing costs.

Disadvantages to the Corporation

- The company does not necessarily gain an ongoing new-business diversification.
- The company has very little control or expertise over the joint venture.
- If the project should fail, the corporation could inherit, through its partnership interest, a sick project and would be ill-equipped to provide the talent and know-how to rescue the joint venture partner, with its own substantial financial risk.
- The corporation will have neither acquired nor built its own real estate management team.
- Communication and understanding between such a subsidiary and staff engaged in normal corporate activity may be a problem.

(c) BUILDING A REAL ESTATE GROUP

In this approach, the corporation decides to develop an internal group of real estate professionals who are intimately aware of the people, products, services, policies, procedures, culture, history, and strategic direction of the corporation. They will have the leadership and communication skills necessary to manage the priorities, budgets, schedules, technical details, and administrative requirements for the corporation.

Advantages to the Corporation

- Top management can control the growth and direction of the emerging real estate function.
- There could be close rapport and communication among the real estate group and the operating divisions and a corporate staff.

Disadvantages to the Corporation

- Building one's own real estate group is the slowest way to create a team that can compete successfully in the development business.
- It is difficult to attract topflight real estate entrepreneurs into the normally sluggish corporate machine.

- The traditional approaches to corporate management do not generally provide a good background for real estate developers.
- Building a real estate staff with untrained or inappropriately trained or skilled staff may result in having to correct expensive faulty decisions, and the learning curve can be extensive and expensive.
- This method is least likely to provide outstanding success, unless the company has already adopted a profit-center attitude toward real estate activities.

The corporate real estate department plays an important role in the acquisitions or divestments of a going business since physical assets are always involved in such transactions, even when they involve only transfers of stock. It is always necessary to establish for the record the value of the real property or leaseholds, or both, in a proposed acquisition or disposition. Beyond the matters of good title, asset value, and legal description, included in an acquisition, the corporate real estate executive also wants to be assured of continuing operation in the same apparent manner as observed (i.e., that there are no title defects or nonconforming uses). One company, for example, bought another company only to discover that the main manufacturing facility was operating as a nonconforming use, contrary to existing zoning. Legal notice was served to the acquiring company soon after the sale, and the new owner was forced to relocate, at a considerable cost in moving expense and lost profit potential. There are many reasons and counterbalancing pitfalls behind the decisions to acquire or divest.[4] The expertise of a corporate real estate department can narrow the odds in the company's favor.

(d) THE FUNDAMENTALS OF SUCCESSFUL CORPORATE REAL ESTATE ACTIVITY

Regardless of the final approach taken, two ingredients are essential to the creation of a successful corporate real estate activity:

1. The activity must be headed by an experienced, able, and aggressive real estate person with a proven record. This is not a job for the outstanding division manager in a manufacturing company or for the chief financial officer, nor, for that matter, is the job of directing a company's ongoing manufacturing-related real estate activities.
2. Performance objectives should be clearly delineated and understood by all the parties involved. These objectives should be limited

[4] See, for example, Parmanand Kumar, "Corporate Growth through Acquisitions," *Management Planning* (July/August 1977), pp. 9–39, for a well-referenced treatment of acquisitions.

primarily to investment performance over specific periods of time. Beyond that, the real estate team should be given a free hand, unencumbered to the greatest extent possible by reviews, planning, conferences, staff meetings, presentations, and so forth.

The "people aspects" of corporate real estate development have been emphasized. But another, equally important facet should be explored and completely understood at the corporation's top level—the financial aspects of corporate real estate development. Many astute corporate managers have entered the real estate development field with a limited comprehension of its financial aspects. Without a thorough analysis and a detailed financial plan, management must constantly reevaluate and redirect its course as one problem after another is encountered.

A thorough review of the company's financial structure and tax planning program as they related to the real estate program should be guided by a person who is completely knowledgeable in major real estate and financial activity. It should focus on the leverage and tax demands of real estate development in the context of the corporation's overall objectives. Debt is an essential element in achieving a high return on invested capital in real estate. It may be difficult to balance real estate debt needs against certain existing indenture restrictions. Occasionally, such problems have required restructuring or reorganizing of the real estate entity to permit a full utilization of debt without placing the parent in default.

How the corporation maintains its records for tax purposes and reporting purposes must be considered, to be certain that the objectives for real estate profits are consistent with the corporation's tax and reporting policies. The value of assets such as real estate and facilities appears in corporate statements and reports. These assets should be accounted for in a manner that best serves the needs of the corporation and stockholders while remaining within IRS, FASB, and other commonly accepted accounting guidelines and regulations.

Finally, the manner in which the legal entity or entities created for real estate development are constituted should be analyzed against the requirements of the organizational and administrative objectives, the profit and cash flow objectives, the tax objectives, and the financial objectives. Ideally, profits generated by the real estate entity should help the parent company, while losses can be sheltered from the parent company balance sheet and thereby not be a detriment to shareholder value.

Taking these steps during the planning stages can minimize later problems in successfully integrating real estate activities into the overall corporate operating system.

(e) THE PHILOSOPHY OF THE DEVELOPMENT MARKET

The philosophy of the development market is best captured in a series of relationships that tend to exist between the practical demands of the development market and the participants in that market. The following relationships form a circular, interdependent set of forces and counterforces that combine positively in a successful project and negatively in an unsuccessful one:

- The success of a real estate development project will depend in the first instance on its location and on a realistic assessment of the facility proposed for that particular economic environment using a generic design and construction that will not become obsolete in the short term.

  Real estate facilities are very much the creatures of their environment, since the land is immovable and the improvements, because of their cost and their physical characteristics, are virtually immovable.
- The success of a development project will depend on the developer's success in identifying the potential market demand and matching that demand with the projected revenues that the project will need to generate a net profit.

  The identification of market demand is not an abstract concept, but must be done for the particular contemplated use contained in the development plan. For example, suppose that we can identify $100 million of purchasing power within the projected primary and secondary markets of a projected shopping center and that we anticipate capturing 60 percent of this potential. If, however, our land and development costs require $100 million in gross revenue for success, our projected share of the market will not be sufficient to warrant going ahead with the project. Or the prevailing rentals in the market area may not be high enough to justify going ahead with the project even if we could increase the market share.
- The success of a project will depend on the developer's ability to select the best combination of costs, including financing charges, and revenues.

  In the preceding example, the developer may be able to command a higher than customary rent or reduce the development costs by changing the design—or both. In either case, the adjustment in cost or revenue will affect the feasibility of the proposed project.
- The success of a project will depend on the ability of the developer's architect to design a facility that will be consistent with the projected costs and revenues. The design must also meet the needs of the potential user and must be flexible to ensure that it will not quickly become functionally obsolescent.

  Since the architect is in a position to control costs and to keep them within a projected development budget, there is a critical relationship between the architect and the developer and the marketplace. This relationship should be developed as early as possible so that the architect can provide cost input information for determining initial project feasibility. The developer has an equal duty to provide the architect with cost and design guidelines.

- The success of a project will depend on the developer's ability to develop the project within the budget, according to previously established costs and specifications.

  This relationship, following from the preceding item, indicates the primary responsibility of the developer. Bringing the project to market on budget is essential if the cost-revenue relationship is to have any validity. This is probably the most vexing part of any project, particularly during times of inflation, and especially when a large project is being developed over a period of years. The other side of the process, shown during the early 1990s, is that a large project developed over a long period may be completed as planned, but a radical change in the economy may make income projections invalid and unobtainable for some years.
- The success of a project will depend on the developer's ability to properly and economically finance each of its phases, including the provision of interim and permanent financing.
- The success of a project will depend on the ability of the developer to operate it efficiently once it becomes a functioning unit in the competitive marketplace. The project has been created as a real estate resource. In the essential relationship that exists between costs and revenues, efficient operation will influence the revenue side of the equation.
- The success of a project will depend on the developer's ability to market it successfully, whether it be a facility created for lease, such as an office building, or a facility created for sale, such as a condominium project.

It would be impossible to overstate the importance of marketing for the success of a project. So, although this relationship is mentioned last, it really provides the key to successful real estate development. These relationships are self-reinforcing in a development project, and the successful implementation of each depends on the implementation of all the others. For example, failure to market or operate the facility properly will have an adverse effect, even if all the other relationships have been carefully implemented.

(f) THE IDENTIFICATION OF RISKS

Risks may be classified as pure risks or speculative risks. A *pure risk* involves only the possibility of loss, whereas a *speculative risk* involves the possibility of either gain or loss. Real estate projects are more appropriately classified as speculative risks. The evaluation of the risks inherent in a real estate project is termed *sensitivity analysis*. The sources of possible variability are found in the internal rate of return (IRR), the principal measure of project feasibility, in social, physical, and economic phenomena. Risks from any source are reflected in the variability of one or more factors that determine the internal rate of return. For example, inflation might affect income and expenses, taxes, and reversion value.

The first step in sensitivity analysis is to identify the key variables that might be affected by risks that cannot be prevented, controlled, or transferred. For most projects, such as apartments, shopping centers, and commercial and industrial buildings, the crucial variables are:

- The level of effective rent (asking rates less concessions, etc.).
- The vacancy rates.
- The annual increase in rental income.
- Expenses as a percentage of rental income.
- The holding period.
- The resale price.

Construction costs can usually be eliminated as a source of possible variability in a project's internal rate of return. If a cost-plus contract is effected, however, there is a strong possibility that cost overruns during inflationary periods will reduce the internal rate of return. Variations in mortgage terms will affect the internal rate of return.

The second step in sensitivity analysis is to estimate mathematically the impact of possible changes in the key variables on the project's internal rate of return.

(g) MEASURING RISK VIA THE INTERNAL RATE OF RETURN

The traditional method of calculating the yield on a real estate project involves dividing the expected benefits by the initial investment. For example, if a $20,000 investment in a duplex yields $2,000 in benefits per year, then the apparent equity dividend rate is 10 percent.

There are several objections to the traditional method. First, the term *benefits* may be defined as net income on a pretax basis or as the cash flow from the project.[5] Second, regardless of which definition of net income is employed, there is the question of whether to use first-year benefits or the average benefit level over the holding period of the project. Third, the term *initial investment* may be defined as the initial equity investment or as the initial equity plus the debt. Fourth, neither of these

[5] *Cash flow* is defined as net income plus depreciation less mortgage payments, income tax, and so on.

definitions takes into account changes in the equity position over the holding period of the project. Finally, none of the possible combinations of numerators and denominators cited here take into account the *time value of money,* that is, the concept that the value of the promise to receive a dollar this year is worth more than the value of the promise to receive a dollar in future years.

(h) THE INTERNAL RATE OF RETURN METHOD

Recognition of the time value-of-money concept led to the development of the internal rate of return (IRR) method of calculating investment yields. The *internal rate of return* is defined as the interest rate that equates the present value of the expected future benefits from an investment to the cost of the investment. The equation for calculating the internal rate of return is:

$$C = \frac{R_1}{(1+r)^1} + \frac{R_2}{(1+r)^2} + \ . \ . \ . \ + \frac{R_n}{(1+r)^n}$$

C is the cost of the investment outlay; R is the annual benefits; and r is the internal rate of return, or the discount rate that equates the sum of the present values of the annual benefits to the initial capital outlay. Because the expected annual benefits are discounted, recognition is given to the time value of money.

The internal rate of return may be found quite readily by using a financial calculator or a table of present values. The table shows the present value of $1 at various interest rates and for various periods of time. Using a discount rate of 9 percent, the present value of $1 due one year hence is $0.917. That is, $0.917 invested at 9 percent will grow to $1 in one year. Thus, to find the present value of any sum due at some time in the future, multiply that sum by the present value factor for the time period involved.

Example. The present value of $10,000 due five years hence is $6,210. Suppose that an investor is evaluating the purchase of an apartment complex that costs $100,000 and that will yield annual benefits of $10,000 for five years. Assume further that the investor believes that this investment could be sold for $100,000 at the end of the fifth year. What is the internal rate of return for this project?

The first step in calculating the internal rate of return is to select an arbitrary interest rate to discount the expected flow of benefits. Then compare the sum of the present values with the investment's cost. If the sum of the present values is greater, select a higher interest rate; if the sum of the present values is lower, select a lower interest rate. When each of the expected benefits is discounted at 9 percent, the net present value is $8,890. Using a discount rate of 11 percent, the investment has a negative net present value of $3,740. At 10 percent, the sum of the present values is equal to the cost of the investment. Thus, the internal rate of return for the proposed investment is 10 percent. This type of analysis is useful, then, because it provides a common denominator for the ranking of several investment project proposals.

(i) FINANCIAL LEVERAGE

Thus, the internal rate of return is the discount rate that equates the stream of cash benefits from a project with the equity investment in the project. The internal rate of return may be raised by increasing income and the resale price and by lowering expenses. A project's internal rate of return may also be raised through financial leverage, which is the use of fixed-cost funds to raise the internal rate of return on the project. Lengthening the maturity of the note for the borrowed funds also raises the internal rate of return and, hence, may be included in a broader concept of financial leverage.

Financial leverage is favorable when the internal rate of return is above the opportunity cost of equity capital and is unfavorable when the internal rate of return falls below the opportunity cost of equity capital. Favorable financial leverage magnifies the internal rate of return considerably, and conversely, unfavorable financial leverage greatly magnifies the loss on equity investment.

(j) MEASURING DOLLAR IMPACT

The facility investment impact will be one of two types, or a combination of both, depending on the company's operating attitude and posture. If the facility is built and owned on company-owned land, one system of measurement will be used. If the company decides to lease from an owner-developer of the land, the dollar investment impact will appear as rent expense (assuming that the lease is not capitalized) and will be measured accordingly.

If you, the corporate real estate executive, are considering a purchase of the fee and investment of your own money, the invested capital dollars (land, buildings, and site improvements) will be totaled and inputed into a manual or computerized budget model that contains information relating to the anticipated volume of business, projected operating expenses, patterns of distribution, advertising costs and coverage, and so forth, to create a realistic relationship between cost and benefit. The potentials will then be evaluated by using an internal "hurdle rate," and, in similar fashion, the internal rate of return (IRR) system of evaluation.

The system of investment evaluation in this case should be identical to the existing, accepted pattern of evaluating capital investments. On the other hand, an analysis of a build-to-suit on someone else's land or

EXHIBIT 8.1 Investor's After-Tax Return on Cash Assuming a 12 Percent Rent

	1 INITIAL	2 FIRST YEAR	3 SECOND YEAR	4 THIRD YEAR	5 FOURTH YEAR
COST OF ACQUISITION:					
1. LAND	70,000.00				
2. BUILDING	92,500.00				
3. TOTAL	162,500.00				
4. CASH	40,625.00				
5. FINANCING	121,875.00				
34. BASE RENT		19,500.00	19,500.00	19,500.00	19,500.00
6. RENTAL INCOME		19,500.00	19,500.00	19,500.00	19,500.00
LESS EXPENSES:					
7. DEPRECIATION		6,938.00	6,417.00	5,938.00	5,491.00
9. INTEREST		11,486.00	11,273.00	11,039.00	10,782.00
11. TOTAL EXPENSES		18,424.00	17,690.00	16,975.00	16,272.00
12. INCOME BEF TAX		1,076.00	1,810.00	2,525.00	3,228.00
13. TAX		538.00	905.00	1,262.00	1,614.00
14. INCOME AFT TAX		538.00	905.00	1,262.00	1,614.00
7. ADD: DEPR		6,928.00	6,417.00	5,936.00	5,491.00
15. GROSS CASH FLOW		7,476.00	7,322.00	7,198.00	7,104.00
16. DEBT SERVICE		2,146.00	2,359.00	2,593.00	2,851.00
17. NET CASH FLOW	-40,625.00	5,329.00	4,963.00	4,605.00	4,254.00
18. CUM CASH FLOW	-40,625.00	-35,296.00	-30,333.00	-25,728.00	-21,474.00
19. PV FACTOR	1.000	0.893	0.797	0.712	0.636
20. DISC CASH FLOW	-40,625.00	4,758.00	3,956.00	3,278.00	2,703.00
31. RET ON INV (%)	12.30				

Memo items key:
(1) LAND INC: Estimated annual percent rate of appreciated land value.
(2) FIN RATE: Annual percent rate of interest on initial financing.
(3) FIN MAT: Lifetime in years over which financing is amortized.
(4) FIN SCHED: Assumed number of finance payments per year.

a sale-leaseback to an investor-developer of a completed facility on company-owned land involves an additional consideration—the alternatives of the investor-developer.

Example.[6] Before negotiating the rent on a sale-leaseback deal with an investor, a corporate real estate executive should prepare for the negotiations by estimating the present value of the after-tax cash flows from the cash invested in the proposed deal, based on the investor's tax

[6] David P. Segal, Vice-President, Real Estate and Construction, Dunkin' Donuts of America, Inc., provided the basics of this example.

EXHIBIT 8.1 *(Continued)*

6 FIFTH YEAR	7 SIXTH YEAR	8 SEVENTH YEAR	9 EIGHTH YEAR	10 NINTH YEAR	11 TENTH YEAR
19,500.00	19,500.00	19,500.00	19,500.00	19,500.00	19,500.00
19,500.00	19,500.00	19,500.00	19,500.00	19,500.00	19,500.00
5,079.00	4,898.00	4,625.00	4,625.00	4,625.00	4,625.00
10,499.00	10.188.00	9,845.00	9,470.00	9,057.00	8,603.00
15,578.00	14,868.00	14,471.00	14,095.00	13,682.00	13,228.00
3,922.00	4,614.00	5,029.00	5,405.00	5,618.00	6,272.00
1,961.00	2,307.00	2,515.00	2,702.00	2,909.00	3,136.00
1,961.00	2,307.00	2,515.00	2,702.00	2,909.00	3,136.00
5,079.00	4,698.00	4,625.00	4,625.00	4,625.00	4,625.00
7,040.00	7,005.00	7,140.00	7,327.00	7,534.00	7,761.00
3,134.00	3,445.00	3,786.00	4,162.00	4,575.00	5,029.00
3,906.00	3,560.00	3,353.00	3,165.00	2,939.00	2,732.00
-17,567.00	-14,007.00	-10,654.00	-7,439.00	-4,530.00	-1,798.00
0.567	0.507	0.452	0.404	0.361	0.322
2,217.00	1,804.00	1,517.00	1,278.00	1,067.00	879.00

(5) DEPR LIFE: Lifetime over which building is depreciated.
(6) DEPR FACTOR: Percentage multiplier for "variable declining balance" depreciation calculations—for 150% declining balance use 150.
(7) DISC RATE: Annual percent used in calculating PV factor and discount cash flows.
(8) TAX RATE: Sum of federal and state corporation income taxes paid expressed as a percent.

bracket. These results can then be compared with possible alternative investments, such as those typically available in the bond market.

Assume that an investor is asking for a fixed rental equivalent to 12 percent of the original project cost. The cash flow of this hypothetical deal is based on the following data: As shown in Exhibit 8.1, the investor's after-tax return, assuming the preceding facts, is 12.3 percent on the $40,625 cash invested. This analysis shows the advantages afforded by real estate because of its high degree of financial leverage and because of the availability of tax shelters that are not always available in other forms of investment.

EXHIBIT 8.1 *(Continued)*

****

	12	13	14	15	16
	11TH	12TH	13TH	14TH	15TH
	YEAR	YEAR	YEAR	YEAR	YEAR

THE ABOVE REINVESTED RATE OF RETURN ASSUMES CASH FLOWS FROM THIS INVESTMENT

Memo items:					
21. LAND INC (%/YR)	4.20 (1)				
22. FIN RATE (%/YR)	9.50 (2)				
23. FIN MAT (YR)	20.00 (3)				
24. FIN SCHED (P/YR)	12.00 (4)				
27. DEPR LIFE (YR)	20.00 (5)				
28. DEPR FACTOR (%)	150.00 (6)				
30. DISC RATE (%)	12.00 (7)				
40. TAX RATE (%)	30.00 (8)				
41. LAND VALUE ($)	70,000.00	72,940.00	76,003.00	79,196.00	82,522.00
37. BLDG VALUE ($)	92,500.00	85,563.00	79,145.00	73,209.00	67,719.00
42. TOT ASSET VAL. ($)	162,500.00	158,503.00	155,149.00	152,406.00	150,241.00
51. R.O.I. (%)	12.30				

COST OF ACQUISITION:					
1. LAND					
2. BUILDING					
3. TOTAL					
4. CASH					
5. FINANCING					
34. BASE RENT	19,500.00	19,500.00	19,500.00	19,500.00	19,500.00
6. RENTAL INCOME	19,500.00	19,500.00	19,500.00	19,500.00	19,500.00
LESS EXPENSES:					
7. DEPRECIATION	4,625.00	4,625.00	4,625.00	4,625.00	4,625.00
9. INTEREST	8,104.00	7,555.00	6,952.00	6,289.00	5,560.00
11. TOTAL EXPENSES	12,729.00	12,180.00	11,577.00	10,914.00	10,185.00
12. INCOME BEF TAX	6,771.00	7,320.00	7,923.00	8,586.00	9,313.00
13. TAX	3,388.00	3,660.00	3,962.00	4,293.00	4,657.00
14. INCOME AFT TAX	3,388.00	3,660.00	3,962.00	4,293.00	4,657.00
7. ADD: DEPR	4,625.00	4,625.00	4,625.00	4,625.00	4,625.00
15. GROSS CASH FLOW	8,011.00	8,295.00	8,587.00	8,218.00	9,282.00
16. DEBT SERVICE	5,529.00	6,077.00	6,680.00	7,343.00	8,072.00
17. NET CASH FLOW	2,428.00	2,208.00	1,906.00	1,575.00	1,210.00
18. CUM CASH FLOW	684.00	2,891.00	4,797.00	6,372.00	7,582.00
19. PV FACTOR	0.287	0.257	0.229	0.205	0.183
20. DISC CASH FLOWS	714.00	567.00	437.00	322.00	221.00
41. LAND VALUE ($)	110,063.00	114,588.00	119,503.00	124,522.00	129,752.00
37. BLDG VALUE ($)	34,817.00	30,192.00	25,567.00	20,942.00	16,317.00
42. TOT ASSET VAL.($)	144,880.00	144,870.00	145,070.00	145,464.00	146,069.00

EXHIBIT 8.1 *(Continued)*

****

17 16TH YEAR	18 17TH YEAR	19 18TH YEAR	20 19TH YEAR	21 20TH YEAR	22 TOTAL

ARE INVESTED AT 12.00%.

17	18	19	20	21	22
85,988.00	89,599.00	93,362.00	97,284.00	101,270.00	105,627.00
62,640.00	57,942.00	53,317.00	48,692.00	44,067.00	39,442.00
148,628.00	147,541.00	146,679.00	145,975.00	145,975.00	145,059.00
					70,000.00
					92,500.00
					162,500.00
				-159,625.00	-118,762.00
					121,875.00
19,500.00	19,500.00	19,500.00	19,500.00	19,500.00	390,000.00
19,500.00	19,500.00	19,500.00	19,500.00	19,500.00	390,000.00
4,625.00	4,625.00	4,625.00	2,442.00		92,500.00
4,759.00	3.378.00	2,910.00	1,848.00	676.00	150,774.00
9,384.00	8,503.00	7,535.00	4,288.00	676.00	242,274.00
10,115.00	10,997.00	11,965.00	15,212.00	18,824.00	146,725.00
5,058.00	5,498.00	5,982.00	7,606.00	9,412.00	73,363.00
5,058.00	5,498.00	5,982.00	7,606.00	9,412.00	73,363.00
4,625.00	4,625.00	4,625.00	2,442.00		92,500.00
9,683.00	10,123.00	10,507.00	10,048.00	9,412.00	165,863.00
8,873.00	9,734.00	10,722.00	11,788.00	12,956.00	121,875.00
810.00	359.00	-115.00	-1,738.00	153,853.00	182,780.00
8,392.00	8,761.00	8,645.00	8,908.00	162,750.00	
0.163	0.146	0.130	0.116	0.104	0.000
132.00	54.00	-15.00	-202.00	16,156.00	1,218.00
135,202.00	140,880.00	146,797.00	152,962.00	159,387.00	159,387.00
11,692.00	7,067.00	2,442.00			
146,093.00	147,947.00	149,239.00	152,962.00	159,387.00	159,387.00

These after-tax returns to the investor can be compared in two ways: first, to the pretax returns from real estate that are currently acceptable to investors; and second, to alternative investment opportunities that are available in the bond market.

To calculate the alternative investment, we will consider the tax-free bond at 5 percent. This alternative is equivalent to a bond earning 10 percent before taxes to the investor in the 50 percent tax bracket. The investor also earns a true present value rate of the 5 percent return after taxes only when the initial capital is returned.

However, to earn 12 percent after taxes from a bond that the company negotiator could offer from the lease deal, as shown in Exhibit 8.1, this investor would need a bond paying 24 percent before taxes—not, typically, an available alternative.

An investor's decision to commit to a long-term lease is also influenced by such considerations as the long-term viability of the location (i.e., its likely residual value after 20 years), the financial strength of the company guaranteeing the rent, the probable continued acceptance of the company's business concept and of its ability to compete in the market, and the caliber of the design and construction of the property. In addition, how attractive the deal appears may also determine the probability that the property can be sold or refinanced when the after-tax cash flows decline in future years.

On the other hand, the attractiveness of the bond alternative over the short term may depend on whether or not interest rates are likely to go up. Although a bond is more liquid than real estate, should interest rates increase, the value of the bond as reflected in the market would decline. Although both the bond principal and the theoretical value of the lease may decline as interest rates increase, the market value of real estate is unlikely to decline as much because of its appreciation potential.

(k) THE FRAMEWORK FOR DETERMINING PROJECT FEASIBILITY

Project feasibility analysis involves three separate but highly related activities:

1. A market analysis.
2. A feasibility analysis.
3. A master development plan, together with a development strategy program.

(1) A Market Analysis

A market analysis is undertaken to determine the types and quantities of additional real estate resources that can be absorbed by a given market area over a predetermined span of time. The analyst, then, is trying to determine the level of basic economic strengths before applying these general findings to a particular parcel or tract of land. There is a high degree of similarity between this effort and those that the corporate real estate department would undertake in a site selection search (see Chapter Seven).

The sequential logic of a market analysis can be illustrated by the following series of steps.[7]

- *Define the Objective.* Clearly, the market analysis should begin with a clear definition of its objective. For example, the objective could revolve around the following types of potential venture projects:
  - To determine the base market support for a planned unit development (PUD) containing 800 acres in a community that falls within a metropolitan area with a population of 550,000.
  - To determine the market support for a 100,000-square-foot shopping center in a community of 26,000.
  - To determine the market support for an apartment complex of 56 units in a community of 65,000 with an existing vacancy rate of 7 percent.
  - To determine the market support for a condominium project in a resort area with a seasonal economy and with existing, competitive projects marketing units at $52 per square foot per unit.

  When the precise objective has been identified, a plan of attack can be formulated for a definitive array of professional services, and estimates can be made of the personnel, out-of-pocket support, and related expenses required for the research effort.
- *Examine the Economic Base.* Obtain information about the economic base of the area under study—its economic activities, employment characteristics and stability, past economic trends, and future economic prospects.
- *Examine the Population Base.* Social, economic, geographic, and demographic profiles of the persons within the predefined study area provide useful information about buying habits.
- *Examine the Environment.* Under this category, the analyst will include the physical conditions of the study area, such as the terrain, road network, land uses, zoning regulations, land access patterns,

[7] Supermarket chains, operating through the Super Market Institute, have probably been the research leaders in the retail field. William Applebaum, of the Harvard Business School, has been the innovator and the influential force in their research program. This sequence of store location strategy steps is based on materials prepared by Mr. Applebaum.

climate, and geologic features. Additionally, he or she will examine the existing competition and inventory the developers of existing competitive projects to determine their experience. This information should be related, ultimately, to the subject site, since real estate creations are very much captives of their environment.

- *Inventory the Competition.* At best, the real estate market is exceedingly fragmented, with little market activity information. None is available on the national level, and little more is found on the local market level except for field information gathered by the analyst relating to the market experience of competing projects. Developing reliable, current data about those projects that vie for the same general share of the consumer's disposable dollar provide one half of the equation necessary to accurately predict community absorption for a proposed project. The other half will have been provided by the population and income analysis of the community.
- *Study Consumer Attitudes.* The proposed project will ultimately be marketed to buyers, and their demonstrated product preferences will have a major bearing on the success or failure of the proposed project. Consumer attitude surveys have not been used to any great extent in the real estate development market, though they offer a means for ascertaining product acceptability, particularly when a new real estate product is to be introduced into a market area where competitor experience cannot be determined. Properly analyzed, the results from this type of survey can provide important guidelines for predicting the success/failure prospects for a proposed development.
- *Study Your Own Market Coverage and Penetration.* Experience is the best teacher, so the saying goes, and no one's experience can be more valuable to the analyst than that of his or her own client. Although this aspect of the market study is probably particularly applicable to the retail sales business, any experience gained by the client in a particular market area—or a similar market area—should be utilized as an additional measure of market acceptability for the client's product.
- *Look for Market Opportunities.* Thus far, we have stressed the market study aspects of a predetermined type of project. Sometimes, however, the type of proposed project has not been established and the analyst looks for the best use or combination of uses for a site. Indeed, the analyst may be involved in just identifying unmet market needs without having a specific site or type of use in mind.
- *Consider Your Competitor's Probable Development Moves.* Every important competitor has notions for growth by providing real estate facilities within a given market area. Development planning, there-

fore, cannot be conducted in a vacuum, as if the proposed project will be an island unto itself. If development opportunities can be identified for one developer, they can also be identified for others. The essence of development success is to identify an unmet market need and then be the first to meet that need successfully.

- *Create a Development Strategy Program.* Each of the previous steps plays an important role in providing input into the development program.

(2) The Feasibility Analysis

Feasibility analysis requires bringing together all the factors required to determine a proposed project's market worthiness in financial terms that are extended over the projected development term. Having accumulated the necessary market data, the analyst now infuses relevant financial information into the development program. The sum of these activities will be presented in two documents: a *financial pro forma* for the project and a *cash flow chart* that will indicate the expected balance between project costs and revenues over the development term. To prepare these documents, the analyst will prepare financial information in five categories:

1. *The Projected Costs of Capital Improvements.* This category of financial information will be prepared by architects and engineers familiar with costs and specifications and will be based on project land use configurations formulated in the market study. Each projected type of use, assuming that the analyst is concerned with a multiuse project, will be analyzed individually prior to the determination of a maximum project budget.
2. *Revenue and Operating Expense Estimates.* This is another key relationship. Projected revenue will have been determined by the market study, and operating expenses will be estimated from the analyst's experience with comparable properties—normally those within the same market area as the subject property.
3. *Financing Terms and Conditions.* The analyst will need information on current trends in the financial markets pertaining to the proposed project. Items such as loan term, interest rates, special charges, interim and permanent financing charges, and so forth, must be determined for input into the financial analysis. The analyst who is not thoroughly conversant with these terms should consult a reliable mortgage banker or a lender for information.
4. *Land Cost or Value.* A determination of the basis for utilizing project land will have to be made. Normally the private developer

will "take" the land into the project on its appraised value, based on market comparables, because the land basis will probably provide some built-in equity that can be transferred into project value.

5. *Land Development Costs.* Estimates of these costs will ordinarily be prepared for the entire project as well as its component parts if it is a multiuse project. The costs will include site preparation costs, the costs of installing utilities and major roads, and any special land preparation and other land development costs that the developer will absorb as the project unfolds. Where possible, such costs should be allocated to each phase of the proposed project.

(3) The Master Development Plan and the Development Strategy Program

The master development plan, be it conceptual or detailed, embodies graphically the land use recommendations of the analyst. The preparation of a master development plan should be based on the following closely interrelated planning and marketing objectives:

- The plan should maximize the apparent development potentials of the subject property; that is, the end product of final development should have produced the maximum possible revenue, assuming the highest and best land use commitments *at a specific time.*
- The plan should be flexible enough to permit alterations in broad land use concepts if changing market patterns and circumstances present unique development opportunities at certain points during the development program.
- Potential revenues are most likely to be maximized if anticipated uses are interrelated with existing and projected areawide land uses. This statement is based on the premise that the development will be assessed on its total yield over a reasonable span of time. An observable relationship exists between economic yield and compatibility with community development trends.

The evolution of an individual package of market, financial, and graphic materials relating to a specific project has the concept of "strategy" intertwined throughout the exercise. As stated earlier, a real estate development venture depends for its success on a series of essential relationships, each of which depends on the others. The project-feasibility analysis should clearly identify as many of these essential relationships as possible, so that the risks of the development venture can be realistically assessed.

(l) LEGAL ENTITIES

One of the most important decisions affecting the financial and tax planning of a real estate development venture is the selection of the proper form of legal organization. The basic forms of legal organization that are adaptable to real estate ventures are:

1. Corporations.
2. General partnerships.
3. Limited partnerships.
4. Tenancy in common.
5. Real estate syndicates.
6. Real estate investment trusts.
7. Cooperatives.
8. Condominiums.

Since each of these forms has special attributes, the objectives of the investor/developer must be analyzed before choosing a particular form. However, two comments are applicable to real estate ventures in general:

1. The corporate form of legal organization is most often utilized when a venture is substantial in size and is expected to last for a long time. Further, the corporate form does offer a number of advantages not provided by other business organizations. For example, a corporation is organized under specific statutes and occupies the position of a legal person. It can sue, be sued, buy, sell, own property, and commit crimes. Persons investing in it have limited legal liability for its acts. Its life is said to be permanent. This characteristic permits the investor to invest without fear that the venture will be disrupted if the owner should die and also permits the investor to transfer ownership without interrupting the venture.
2. Other forms of organizations are normally utilized when a proposed venture is expected to last for only a short time; where, for example, property is being held for speculative appreciation in a rising real estate market. Most of these forms of business organization are easier to create than a corporation. In a general partnership, unlike a corporation, each participant has unlimited liability and is therefore responsible for the partnership's actions and debts.

Each form of business organization has both advantages and drawbacks. The legal ramifications surrounding the ownership of real estate development projects are complex, detailed, subject to changing interpretations, and potentially explosive for the uninitiated or uninformed, so the corporate legal department should be involved in the negotiations as early as possible.

§ 8.2 JOINT VENTURES

In a joint venture which is normally created between a developer and a corporate landowner, the developer will offer the corporate landowner one of two postures: Either the developer will have the in-house capability to furnish all the necessary development services, or will offer the necessary skills as a development project organizer (a bringer together, if you will, of the ingredients for a successful project). The corporate landowner will usually offer a parcel or tract of land that is largely or entirely unencumbered, so that the equity in it can be used as leverage for development purposes. The developer will be seeking a percentage split of profits as well as compensation for his or her development skills, while the landowner will be seeking a fair purchase price for its land and a split of profit, the sum total of which would exceed the profit from an outright sale.

This type of joint venture will require a meeting of the minds on many essential points. Probably the most critical element will revolve around the method of payment for corporate land—a method that must permit the developer leverage latitude, or the essential reason for the joint venture will not exist. The basics of the agreement between the two parties can usually be spelled out in a letter of agreement or intent and then elaborated upon in a formal written agreement prepared by attorneys representing each side. The wording of the hypothetical letter of intent shown in Exhibit 8.2 illustrates one method for expressing the relationship between the parties—in this instance, a full-service development company and a landowner with unencumbered land.

EXHIBIT 8.2 Letter of Intent

1. The basic vehicle for property ownership, development, and management will be a limited partnership, with the Owner or its designees owning a __________ percent (______%) interest therein, and Venture Development, or its designees, owning the remaining __________ percent (______%) interest therein. The Owner shall hold its interest as a limited partner, and Venture Development shall hold its interest as a limited partner and/or a general partner, with one or more of its principals acting as additional general partners.
2. Agreement as to the master development plan and all the basic decisions in connection with the development of the proposed project prior to the execution of the partnership agreement shall be made by a designee of the Owner and a designee of Venture Development. Following the execution of the

EXHIBIT 8.2 *(Continued)*

partnership agreement, the general partners shall be responsible for obtaining and supervising the planning, design, financing, construction, and marketing of the proposed dwelling units, facilities, and appurtenances in the development.

3. Upon the execution of the limited partnership agreement, the Owner shall convey to the limited partnership title to that property, agreed upon in accordance with paragraph 2 above, to be developed as Phase I of the project. Additional properties in phase development shall be deeded into the partnership when the general partners deem it an appropriate time to start the development of the additional phases. The agreed-upon value of all the properties deeded into the partnership for any phase shall be ________ dollars ($______) per acre, which amount shall be evidenced by a partnership note secured by a mortgage subordinated to the lien of any institutional lender or lenders furnishing funds for the development of the property. Said note shall provide for interest at the rate of ________ percent (______%) per annum, commencing on the date of conveyance, but payments being deferred until proceeds from sales of dwelling units (cash flow) allow such payments. Interest payments shall be junior only to partnership debts owed to third-party creditors.
4. Upon execution of the partnership agreement, the costs theretofore incurred by the Owner and/or Venture Development in obtaining the services of ________ for the investigation of the development potential of the subject property shall become an obligation of the partnership.
5. Venture Development agrees to accept a partnership note in payment of its services rendered to the partnership, which note shall bear interest and be repaid in like manner as the Owner is repaid for his land (i.e., in proportion on a ______–______ basis), so that Venture Development shall be paid its compensation no later than the Owner is paid for his land.

   The above notes shall be subordinated, if requested by the partnership, to all other debts of the partnership, and shall be repaid in full before there is any distribution of profits to the partners from the development. Venture Development's estimated cost of developing each phase is ______.______ percent of the total development cost (exclusive of land). In the event that the compensation due Venture Development exceeds this estimate, said excess shall be paid by the partnership, as are the other expenses of the partnership. In the event that said compensation is less than the estimated amount of said note, said savings shall accrue to the benefit of the partnership and shall be reflected in profits. Venture Development shall give the partnership credit against its development compensation for Phase I in an amount equal to that paid by the partnership in fees for the market and feasibility study and the cost of acquiring utilities and proper zoning (said fees presently estimated to be a maximum of $______). It is understood that the above-mentioned deferred compensation arrangement with Venture Development does not include the services, if any, rendered to the partnership by ________ or any of its subsidiaries, which services shall be contracted for and paid for, as are obligations to all other third parties to the partnership.

The wording of this agreement attempts to address the underlying principle of participation, that is, equity among the parties. Although limitless variations are possible, this example illustrates the types of legal relationships that joint venture participators will enter into *for the lure of higher yield.* The key, then, is to adequately assess the realities of an equation that begins with the corporate operating structure and profit philosophy and ends with an estimate of risk and offsetting potential gain (see Exhibit 8.3).

The A. B. Dick Company, for example, has developed an interesting wrinkle to joint venturing. Operating through its real estate subsidiary

EXHIBIT 8.3 Estimated Yield from a Joint Venture

A Joint Venture Between
ABC COMPANY & METRO DEVELOPERS

DISTRIBUTION CENTER
Perimeter Business Park
7645 Warehouse Drive
Chicago, IL

Building Area: 32,000 RENTABLE SQUARE FEET
33,546 GROSS SQUARE FEET

Office - 1,500 Square Feet
Warehouse - 30,500 Square Feet

Ext. Storage Area: 85,378 SQUARE FEET (Fenced)

Property Area: 5.1783 ACRES

Lease: LEASE COMMENCEMENT - December 1, 1993

LEASE EXPIRATION - November 30, 2013

BASIC RENT AMOUNTS -

Lease Year	Rate Per Sq. Ft.	Rents
Year One	$ 7.00	$ 224,000.00
Year Two	$ 8.28	$ 264,960.00
Year Three	$ 8.75	$ 280,000.00
Year Four	$ 8.88	$ 284,160.00
Year Five	$ 9.34	$ 298,880.00
Year Six	$ 9.81	$ 313,920.00
Year Seven through Ten	$10.09	$ 322,880.00
Year Eleven through Fifteen	$11.79	$ 377,280.00
Year Sixteen through Twenty	$14.14	$ 452,480.00
	Total Rental Commitment	**$7,106,240.00**

Option To Purchase: End of Year Five - $3,395,000.00
End of Year Eight - $3,500,800.00

Expansion Option: Lease an additional 2 acres within one year of Certificate of Occupancy (December 1, 1994).

(A. B. Dick Realty Corporation) the company develops multitenant buildings for branch sales offices or product distribution centers. Some space is leased by the parent, normally for a 20-year term, and the balance is made available for lease to any other bona fide tenant. Ownership is usually vested in a general partnership in an arm's-length joint venture involving the parent company's real estate subsidiary. The resulting projects are fully leveraged, resulting in little or no equity investment, and the joint venture can either enjoy the advantages of ownership or sell the completed and leased facility without disturbing the basic leases. The interesting aspect, however, is not the financing methods or legal organization, but rather the fact that A. B. Dick invites other corporate space users with similar geographic requirements to participate in the joint venturing with it.

§ 8.3 PROFIT MANAGEMENT FOR THE CORPORATE FRANCHISOR

Many large corporations, such as General Mills, Pepsico, Heublein, Pillsbury, Ralston Purina, TWA, and Pet Foods have all bought or tried to buy into the franchise business. This major profit-making industry (McDonald's earned $70 billion in 1992) includes real estate logistics and management as vital and integral elements.

Mention the word franchise, and "fast food" comes immediately to mind: McDonald's, Dunkin' Donuts, Arby's, Burger King, Kentucky Fried Chicken, Church's, Wendy's, and Pizza Hut are often-mentioned industry leaders.

(a) TWO APPROACHES TO FRANCHISING

There are two approaches to franchising: The choice has a material bearing on the manner in which profit performance is measured where the total volume is divided between company-owned and franchisee-owned operations. The former, or more traditional, approach is known as "product and trade name" franchising; the latter approach is called "business format" franchising. In the former, the franchiser uses someone else's money for facilities and looks for profit from the sale of product supplies; in the latter, the franchiser uses its own money and looks for profit from the total operation including an active interest in the real estate aspects of company investment.

Despite the preponderance of franchisee-owned operations, the trend is toward company-owned operations. McDonald's has made recent efforts to repurchase franchises from franchisee owner-operators and has now entered the investment real estate market vigorously to accelerate the repurchase program. Many of the franchises, particularly the older, more established ones, have appreciated fantastically in value and any sale for cash would bring with it a significant capital gains burden—so the owner-operators are understandably reluctant to sell. If, however, an acceptable substitute investment property can be found, McDonald's will purchase it and arrange a tax-free exchange with the owner-operator. Real estate investment opportunities and complexities unquestionably have come full bore to the franchising business.

Real estate value and investment considerations impinge on franchising in two primary ways: first, by the current and prospective value of the real estate, based on its location and the resulting market environment; second, by the actual or projected capital investment in facilities and its relation to overall profitability.

(b) SITE LOCATION ANALYSIS PROCEDURES[8]

Exhibit 8.4 is an example of a field inspection survey checklist used by a real estate representative looking for a potential location. The checklist provides base data for the narrowing down of choices as subjective evaluation begins. Exhibit 8.5 illustrates a subjective rating system that assigns values to site location factors. This rating system is based on 100 points determined by evaluating 25 factors as being excellent (4), good (3), fair (2), or poor (0). The following definitions are guidelines for the rating and the factors:

Excellent (4) The factor being evaluated is without a flaw. For example, if an evaluator were to indicate that the proximity to employment concentration is excellent, the situation probably could not be better.

Good (3) Most of the factors relative to a successful operation will fall in this category. A location is good if it has adequate access, ingress, egress, and visibility identification, and is in a neighborhood that experience indicates to be a desirable opportunity.

Fair (2) The given factor is marginal or "just passing." For example, a fair check for visibility would indicate that there are obstructions from one or two directions, but the visibility is reasonably good from at least two directions.

Poor (0) The situation is unacceptable. For example, if accessibility to the subject property were rated as poor, this might mean that the property cannot be reached by a public thoroughfare.

[8] Norbert F. Wall, President, American Realty Consultants, contributed to the insights on site selection factors contained in this section.

EXHIBIT 8.4 Field Inspection Survey

1. Unit No. ________

2. Location ____
3. (a) Volume ____________________
   (b) Franchised ________________ System-owned ____________________

   _____ ______________________ __________
   _____ ______________________ __________

   _____ ______________________ __________
   _____ ______________________ __________

4. Site:
   a. Storefront ____ Free-standing ____ Interior or corner lot _____
   b. Type of Road: Highway _____ Boulevard _____ Main arterial _____ Secondary arterial _____
   c. Speed Limit _____ Number of lanes _____ Traffic volume __________
   d. Lot size: ______________ (estimated) Booths available __________
   e. Parking: On-street (no. of spaces) _____ Off-street (no. of spaces) _____ Paved _____
   f. Visibility: From

	E	G	F	P	Comment
North	E	G	F	P	Comment __________
South	E	G	F	P	Comment __________
East	E	G	F	P	Comment __________
West	E	G	F	P	Comment __________

   g. Building appearance E G F P Comment __________
   h. Accessibility (general) ____
5. Adjacent land use:
   a. Residential _____ Industrial _____ Institutional _____ Commercial _____ Office _____ Parks ___
      Comments: ____
      ____
   b. Nearby occupation: ____
      ____
6. Locational environment:
   a. Neighborhood: Age _____ Condition __________ Trend ____________________
   b. Type of residence: Single family _____ 2-3 flats _____ Low-rise apartments _____
      High-rise apartments _____
   c. Dominant ethnic group ______________ Income Group: Upper _____ Middle __________
      Upper-middle _____ Lower-middle ______
      Low _____
   d. Nearby schools/institutions/parks ____
      ____
   e. Nearby industry: ____
      ____
   f. Nearby complementary recreational facilities ______________________________
      ____
   b. Nearby traffic generators (department stores, supermarkets, etc.) ____________
      ____
      ____

Exhibit 8.5 scores the following factors:

1. *Accessibility*
   a. *Proximity to major traffic artery.* Access to subject property is critical. It is essential to locate the facility on a high-volume major traffic artery that provides good access for persons either residing in nearby neighborhoods or going to and from work. The facility should also provide identity and exposure for the passing motorist.

EXHIBIT 8.5 Site Scoring Sheet

Site Scoring Sheet

Unit No. ________________

Location ____

Volume ____________ Month ____________ Year ____________ Score ____________

	Excellent (4)	Good (3)	Fair (2)	Poor (0)
1. Accessibility a. Proximity to major traffic artery b. Moving traffic lanes c. Local congestion at peak buying periods				
2. Ingress and egress at site a. Favorable speed limit b. Proximity to stoplight or stop sign c. Favorable circulation (left and right turn)				
3. Immediate or adjacent properties a. Degree of compatibility (commercial, etc.) b. Identifiable commercial location c. Appearance or condition of adjacent uses				
4. Visibility and exposure a. Directional visibility b. Sign dominance				
5. Neighborhood characteristics a. Age of residents b. Condition and trend of neighborhood c. Density (high or low) d. Income (E = $10,000 - $20,000; G = $20,000 - $25,000; F = over $25,000 and under $10,000) e. Ethnic composition (G = mixed transition; F = contemporary caucasian; P = international stock)				
6. Site a. Ingress and egress b. Parking space				
	Excellent (4)	Good (3)	Fair (2)	Poor (0)
7. Proximity to employment concentrations (factories, offices, etc.)				
8. Proximity to institutions (schools, hospitals, military installations, etc.) or recreational facilities (shows, bowling, golf, etc.)				
9. Proximity to major traffic generators (department stores, discount stores, supermarkets, etc.)				
10. Competitive Analysis a. Complementary b. Direct competition				
11. Appearance of store (type of unit - image, nonimage, etc.)				
12. Traffic volume at or near site (high to low)				
Total				

b. *Moving traffic lanes.* At least four traffic lanes are required to move sufficient traffic to generate a high sales volume. Anything less reduces the sales potential considerably.
c. *Local congestion at peak buying periods.* Local congestion at peak buying periods implies two things: (1) More than half the total traffic occurs between 11:00 A.M. and 7:30 P.M.; (2) on Sunday evenings, traffic is not backed up because of some other activity.

2. *Ingress and Egress at Site*

a. *Favorable speed limit.* In an urban area, a speed limit in excess of 45 mph makes it difficult for motorists to stop. Speed limits will generally range between 35 and 45 mph, averaging about 40 mph in suburban areas and 30 mph in the central city. The speed limit provides sufficient traffic movement to carry heavy numbers of cars.
b. *Proximity to stoplight or stop sign.* A corner location at a stop sign or stoplight is highly desirable. A location set back from the intersection at a stoplight or a stop sign can be both favorable and unfavorable. It is favorable in the sense that traffic is slowed and therefore exposed for a longer time. Furthermore, it can be easier to get into or out of the site. However, on heavily traveled traffic arteries, stop signs and stoplights tend to back up traffic and as a result can make turning into the property extremely difficult, which is a deterrent rather than a benefit. Each site must be evaluated separately.
c. *Favorable circulation (left and right turns).* The ability to make both a left and a right turn into the property is essential to a high-volume location. A site that provides both a corner location and the ability to turn into and out of the property reasonably frequently would represent an excellent check. Roads with median strips and no provision for breaks do not allow a left turn. Such locations should be avoided because they substantially reduce accessibility.

3. *Immediate or Adjacent Properties*

a. *Degree of compatibility.* This represents the degree to which other uses in the general vicinity are compatible with that of the subject location. For example, retail stores and commercial complexes, office buildings, and industrial facilities are compatible with most fast-food operations. A deleterious use might be that of industrial facilities with almost no activity on the weekends. Quite often, other food outlets represent a compatible use.
b. *Identifiable commercial location.* The highest volume of use outside the inner-city and high-rise apartment areas exists

at identifiable commercial locations such as regional shopping centers, office complexes, and industrial and medical parks. A location in proximity to an identifiable commercial location would be in an intercepting position to this traffic movement.

c. *Appearance or condition of adjacent uses.* The appearance or condition of adjacent uses indicates the physical trend of the neighborhood or community. For example, the decline of neighborhoods or communities is quickly reflected in the commercial facilities located therein. Viable and growing communities indicate a strong, well-kept community area, which is also reflected in the commercial facilities. The condition of the adjacent uses is not as important in the inner city.

4. *Visibility and Exposure*

a. *Directional visibility.* This is the ability of the potential customer to see the facility. An excellent situation would be the visibility of the facility from all directions. Two-directional visibility is a must; anything less is poor.

b. *Sign dominance.* This is the same as directional visibility in that it is rated on the basis of a person's ability to see the signs from the approaching direction.

5. *Neighborhood Characteristics*

a. *Age of residents.* The older the residents of an area are, and the fewer children there are, the fewer the purchases that are required. Consequently, the age of the residents of an area is important in determining its viability.

b. *Condition and trend of neighborhood.* An improving condition or trend naturally indicates the longevity of a neighborhood, whereas a declining condition or trend can indicate a neighborhood in transition.

c. *Density (high or low).* In general, high density is a favorable factor in potential site selection, assuming that all the other necessary characteristics are present, because more people mean more possibilities to sell. Low density can be a favorable feature if incomes are high and family size offsets the low density.

d. *Income.* Our studies, as well as studies conducted by advertising agencies, indicate that a person with an income of from $10,000 to $20,000 represents the best customer for fast-food operations. We have, therefore, designated that as excellent; $20,000 to $25,000, as good; and $25,000 to $30,000, as fair.

e. *Ethnic composition.* The ethnic composition of an area can have a direct relationship to volume. Generally, first-generation residential areas have a poor record of fast-food purchasing.

6. *Site*

a. *Ingress and egress.* This refers to the ability of the consumer to get into and out of the parking lot easily. A corner location without median strips would represent excellent ingress and egress. Access with ease to and from a major traffic artery would be good.

b. *Parking space.* This relates to the adequacy of the available parking space to handle the average amount of business at a particular location. Lot size is also considered. Minimum and maximum frontage can be evaluated only in a relative sense, since this is greatly affected by other factors. For example, a small area would be adequate in an urban location approached by customers on foot, whereas a highway location would require a much greater area for adequate parking space.

7. *Proximity to Employment Concentrations.* Employment concentrations, such as factories, office buildings, and industrial parks, represent desirable nearby facilities since they not only generate exposure and identity to people traveling to and from these areas, but they also increase the opportunity for luncheon business.

8. *Proximity to Institutions.* Schools, hospitals, military installations, recreational facilities, and other institutional type operations represent desirable and compatible neighbors. Naturally, each of these operations, as well as the types of traffic that it generates, has to be evaluated. The stronger the activity and its compatibility, the higher the rating.

9. *Proximity to Major Traffic Generators.* Major retail traffic generators attract considerable numbers of people. Good locations are usually found in interceptor positions. Proximity to a major retail generator is excellent if it intercepts the traffic flowing toward the major traffic generator. This proximity is good if it is near enough to take some advantage of the traffic; it is fair if it is on the opposite side of the traffic, even though it represents a smaller portion of the overall exposure; and it is poor if it is located several blocks away.

10. *Competitive Analysis*

a. *Complementary.* Complementary competition includes other fast-food facilities. A location in proximity to other successful uses is usually desirable.

   b. *Direct competition.* Direct competition relates to comparable service facilities. The more there are, the better the location.

11. *Appearance of Store.* This relates to an image unit or a nonimage unit with respect to attractiveness, maintenance, and other factors.
12. *Traffic Volume at or Near the Site.* The significance of the traffic passing a site has great significance, although the relative significance of traffic counts varies among cities. The volume of traffic will reflect the success of surrounding activities.

All the preceding factors relate to site specifics. A further consideration relates to locations in different types of neighborhoods and, consequently, market environments. Here the choice would usually be one between suburban and central city locations. A listing of the major site criteria would look something like this:

1. *Suburban Locations*
   a. *Highway.* Such locations should be on major traffic arteries (heavily traveled) at or near an intersection. They should provide adequate turning (no median, or if median exists, should have break). It is desirable to be near an identifiable commercial, industrial, or institutional complex and along recognized driving patterns. Other factors to consider are exposure and identity, ingress and egress, and adequate lot size.
   b. *Central business district or major road.* The location should be as close as possible to major magnets and where suburban commuter service is available, should be in proximity to the station or on major traffic route to and from the station. It should also be visible from commuter trains. It should have adequate turning lanes, be at a corner intersection, and offer exposure and identity. Other desirable factors are a recognized travel pattern, adequate ingress and egress, and adequate lot size.
2. *Urban Locations*
   a. *Inner city.* Excellent locations are on a major traffic artery, have good identity and exposure, and are near identifiable commercial complexes or places of employment, along transit routes, or at or near a transfer point.
   b. *Central city.* These locations need to be in or near an identifiable commercial complex, provide adequate turning lanes, and be along established travel patterns. They should offer adequate ingress and egress on an adequate size property with satisfactory exposure and identity. It is helpful to be near as many industrial, institutional, and recreational

facilities as possible or near a high-rise apartment area (single persons and childless couples), on a major street through that area, especially at or near an intersection.

The preceding criteria orient the site selector toward successful commercial areas because shoppers tend to move in a habitual manner toward such areas. Sites along these routes minimize the possibility of site selection error. The trend, particularly for fast-food outlets, is toward "Phase I" locations, either on site or adjacent to major suburban shopping centers. This is particularly true of chains entering new markets and seeking market identity. Once market acceptance has been established, the chain then seeks less expensive "Phase II" locations that fit a predetermined location/distribution plan.

§ 8.4 CONCLUSION

Whether your company ever becomes an active participant in the development game, the opportunities (or the pressure) to do so will undoubtedly increase. Many companies have financial and personnel resources available, and control highly desirable land.

Changes are occurring that indicate permanent shifts in the manner of developing private real estate resources:

1. Enormous market opportunities have emerged for full-scale projects, usually located in or adjacent to major metropolitan concentrations. The scale of the development opportunities—matched by the scale of the required financial resources—has attracted capital supported by rather sophisticated analytic talent.
2. The environmental movement and the desire to seek a better balance between the physical and the aesthetic aspects of living environments have generated a larger scale perspective on the part of developers, their financial counterparts, and the ultimate purchasers.
3. New capital resources have been attracted to the real estate development market, particularly through joint ventures, and this trend should intensify.
4. A wide variety of public programs have been created to achieve public purposes by assisting private real estate development projects.
5. New nationally based real estate corporations, including development subsidiaries of manufacturing corporations and financial corporations, have been bringing tested systems and financial management into the development marketplace. They have imposed structured growth, profit, and market forecasting

techniques on otherwise highly unstructured real estate development activities.

6. There have been significant shifts in the life-styles of the traditional real estate consumers, prompting major efforts to satisfy market segments that were largely ignored a generation ago. For example, the shelter and recreation requirements of the elderly that were once satisfied by old-age homes are now being met by whole communities. Also, the shortened workweek and the rise of leisure-time activities have fostered a significant boom in second-home recreational communities. The increasing social responsibility concept of corporate citizenship may also involve more active participation in development projects.

We will close this chapter with one more example—a retail-oriented franchise deal—to highlight the value of imaginative and resourceful real estate professionals.

Example.[9] The site selection team of A Corporation had identified a portion of a 15-acre site as its prime candidate for the location of a franchise outlet. Ideally, the company was interested in acquiring three acres of the site. It had discussed its choice with an investor-developer who had indicated his desire to provide the site and a facility on an agreed-upon net, net rental basis, assuming that he could acquire ownership and/or control of the site.

The 15-acre site, one of the prime undeveloped sites in the market area, was owned by Mrs. Smith, a widow, and had a current market value of approximately $2 million. Mrs. Smith had inherited the site ten years previously, and at that time a value of $500,000 had been placed on it for estate tax purposes.

The investor-developer approached Mrs. Smith and offered to pay the full current market value for the site. Mrs. Smith's tax attorney advised against the sale because of the extremely heavy potential capital gains tax. The investor-developer then suggested that Mrs. Smith lease the land to him with a subordinated land lease (that is, allow him to subordinate her claim for repayment below that of a first mortgagee, since he could not finance an unsubordinated land lease). Mrs. Smith was reluctant to do so because, plainly, her potential subordinate position made this risky. Further, even if everything worked well, her income from the subordinated lease would be considered ordinary income, placing her in a higher, more uncomfortable tax bracket.

The answer to achieving a successful deal was found in the creation of a limited partnership, in which the investor-developer became the general partner and Mrs. Smith a limited partner. Under the terms of the

[9] Frank M. Mihalik, President, Commercial Realty Marketing, Inc., provided the facts for this example.

partnership agreement, Mrs. Smith agreed to deed her land into the partnership when the construction loan on the entire project was closed. This loan included the three-acre portion for the franchise operation (the balance was to be occupied by a major triple A discounter). Upon surrendering the deed, Mrs. Smith received, by partnership agreement with her investor-developer general partner, $2 million, the full market value of her land. This sum was nontaxable. Further, as a limited partner in the development venture, Mrs. Smith was to receive income from the project according to the terms of the partnership agreement. This continuing income stream, again based on terms contained in the partnership agreement, was to be offset by an allocation of project expenses and depreciation. In the meantime, the investor-developer, as the general partner, would continue to oversee the management of the entire project and to be legally responsible for that effort.

This relationship did not escape the watchful eye of the Internal Revenue Service. In June 1978, however, the U.S. Tax Court held that the contribution of an owner's land into such a partnership arrangement was for capital contribution purposes and that since the other partner's contribution was his good credit rating, the land represented the partnership's only capital.[10]

How was this deal put together, given the desire of the company to acquire a prime franchise location; the desire of the investor-developer to satisfy that need and at the same time acquire the fee title of the entire site for total development; and the desire of the landowner to sell her interest and minimize the adverse tax burden? The investor-developer and the landowner entered into a limited partnership agreement. Under the terms of the agreement, the investor-developer, as the general partner, agreed to:

1. Lend his expertise and good credit rating to the established partnership.
2. Provide working capital to the partnership for whatever period necessary, prior to the start of construction funding.
3. Advance all the planning, engineering, architectural, legal, and mortgage commitment fees necessary for the development of the premises, provided, however, that such fees would be included in the cost of development as set forth in the agreement and reimbursed to the investor-developer (general partner) upon the commencement of the principal term.
4. Be responsible for all bank accounts, books, and records of the partnership.

[10] *John H. Otey, Jr., and Bettye G. Otey v. Commissioner of Internal Revenue,* Respondent Docket No. 1203-76. 70 T.C. 28 (filed May 23, 1978).

In turn, the owner, as the limited partner, agreed to:

1. Contribute a small stipulated sum ($100) upon the execution of the agreement.
2. Deliver a good marketable, insurable title to the premises upon the commencement of the principal term.
3. Receive full payment for the land from the construction loan proceeds.
4. Share in any net profits and losses of the partnership on an agreed-upon basis over and above the payment for land value.

Regardless of future events, however, one truism remains firm in our mind, and we hope in yours also. Real estate is a profit-seeking business. You should run your company's real estate business on this basis, whatever your attitude toward or your previous experience in the "development" end of the game. You are absolutely right—real estate is a fascinating business with particular benefits for you!

Nine

Tenure Decisions and Control-of-the-Space Concerns

§ 9.1 INTRODUCTION

Corporations buy or lease property and facilities for many reasons: business requirements, necessities of the time and place, and occasionally, for development and investment. This chapter will review these reasons and the financial concepts that are used by corporations in making their decisions.

For long-term business operations—especially larger manufacturing, assembly, utilities, automotive and financial institutions—corporations generally choose to own property and facilities because they will usually be making a significant, long-term investment in capital fixed equipment and support infrastructure. These investments in fixed equipment and support infrastructure can far surpass the initial capital cost of property and facilities. Corporations must rely on their continued use of the property and facilities that house the fixed equipment to generate a continuous stream of product or service for sale. By owning uniquely designed and developed property and facilities, the corporation significantly reduces the risk of outside influences disrupting production or services. Also, corporations often own property and facilities because they cannot find a readily available vacant property with a suitable facility to lease or prefer to locate in an area that has few or no "speculative" facilities of the size required to lease. Unless the site is in a major metropolitan area, developers are seldom willing to build a unique industry-specific facility for lease to a major corporation; if the lease is not renewed, the developer may be stuck with a property and facility that has no ready tenant or prospective purchaser without substantial modification or a major discount in the lease or sale price.

Example. A telecommunications company invests $20 million in land and buildings, and $40 million in fixed equipment and support infrastructure to generate $300 million in sales each year. With this major investment in a location, there would not be any business advantage to lease a property. Even on a long-term lease, the corporate investment and service to customers could be held at risk should the property owner choose not to negotiate a new lease or be unable to perform the obligations of a landlord. Also, at the end of the lease term the corporation could be faced with the prospect of having to negotiate acceptable lease terms. At this point in their development, some corporations seek to purchase the property or decide to purchase other property and build a facility to avoid disruptions to production or services and to establish fixed property costs in lieu of variable lease costs.

Corporations that provide a product or service which is rapidly expanding or shrinking in sales and staff, usually have not made a substantial investment in fixed equipment. Such corporations can live with a variable lease cost and will most likely choose to lease versus own property and facilities. These corporations—often smaller manufacturing, retailers, or service providers—tend to seek three- to five-year lease commitments, use cash for operations, do not invest heavily in equipment, can be mobile in their geographical service area, must remain flexible in their business operations, and must be able to reduce lease occupancy expenses when required.

Example. A local accounting firm is one of the largest in town. It leases 20,000 square feet in the downtown area in a major office building and 7,500 square feet at a satellite office 9 miles from the downtown office in a developing office-park area. The firm has grown rapidly in the past two years from 10,000 square feet (1/2 floor) to its present size and needs an additional 4,000 square feet in the next 6 months. Furnishings, including records storage, telephones, copier, fax, and computer equipment, represent the firm's investment in fixed assets. The firm has no fixed investment in equipment in either space. The firm is people-intensive and uses cash to pay the rent and office supplies, salaries and bonuses, purchased or leased furniture, equipment, and other ongoing miscellaneous expenses, such as telephone, business licenses, and income taxes. By leasing, the firm remains flexible in its ability to grow or contract in the local marketplace, and uses income to support the business and the needs of the owners. This accounting firm can work from almost any location and currently sees no financial or business advantage to own property or its own building.

Most corporations have a policy—either in writing or in practice—to own, lease, or a combination of both. The economic recession of the early 1990s has provided corporations with an opportunity to purchase property and facilities at discount, but they must also look at the opportunities to lease versus buy to ensure they are making the best financial and business decision. This chapter is designed to assist the corporate real estate executive in making property analysis and acquisition decision recommendations to management.

§ 9.2 OWNERSHIP ANALYSIS AND DECISIONS—BUY/BUILD DECISIONS

A number of key financial and business items must be considered in analyzing buy/build decisions. Other items may need to be included if they are unique to a specific corporation's financial, business, and legal requirements.

- Balance outstanding on first and/or second mortgage.
- Requirements to satisfy the financial partner if one exists.
- Date for closing of the sale.
- Occupancy date or certificate of occupancy date.
- Options to purchase additional property. If yes, number of options, years for each option period, and dates options begin and end.
- Amount of option period cost—fixed, consumer price index (CPI), percentage per year.
- Amount of earnest money deposit required, refundable under what circumstances, and whether applied to purchase price.
- Seller or purchaser to pay for all, a share or part of the closing costs, attorney fees, prorated property taxes, prorated insurance, prorated municipal special assessments, boundary surveys, legal descriptions, easements, environmental audits, soil testing, soil borings, soil engineering, zoning fees, filing and recording fees.

The sale and purchase should be contingent upon certain conditions that must be completed to the satisfaction of the purchaser and may include:

- Closing to take place only after permission for the work has been obtained from local governmental authorities.
- Initial and final approval of the parent company.
- Existing required zoning suitable for proposed use.
- Letter from local utility providers and local governmental authorities that the quantity and quality of utility and site services (water, sewer, natural gas, electricity, fire protection, etc.) are available for the specific purchaser's project at the time required.
- The seller and purchaser to meet certain key dates to complete preliminary plans, design development and construction permits, obtain construction or permanent financing or mortgage, and so on.
- A bonus/penalty, which may be monetary, if certain key dates or events are not met by either party.

- Obtaining of a General Warranty Deed.
- The removal of liens, back taxes, easements or items that prohibit or cloud clear title to the property.
- Clear title and title insurance for the property.
- Written confirmation from an independent testing firm that the site and adjacent sites (subsurface, surface, and airborne) do not contain soil pollutants, hazardous waste, or buried obstructions.
- Soil investigation report stating that the soil beneath the proposed improvements can support proposed traffic and building loads and/or site use.
- Ability of the purchaser to obtain insurance.
- Limit on purchaser's initial property taxes for a specified period of time.
- Purchaser's ability to obtain a specified mortgage at a specified percentage rate.
- Purchaser's ability to obtain favorable financing or waiver of taxes from the local governmental authority.
- Acceptance of restrictive covenants and site developments including utilities, roads and services by the local governmental authorities before closing.
- Procurement of an inspection and a bond from a local pest control company that the facility is free from specific pests (termites, mice, rats, ants, etc.).
- Procurement of continued warranties for major building mechanical and electrical systems.

Other factors for consideration are:

- On-site parking for staff, visitors, and reserved parking.
- Cost for parking if there is no on-site parking (if not free, try to lock in a long-term rate).
- Total purchase commitment.
- Cost per square foot of property and/or building.
- Mortgage payment per month, mortgage percentage for a specified period of time and total mortgage cost per year.
- Availability of local municipal development bonds or industrial development revenue bonds.
- Operating expenses per month.
- Size of property area in square feet and acres to 3 decimal places.
- Common area maintenance costs especially for site utilities, landscaping, and insurance.

EXHIBIT 9.1 Geographical Analysis for ABC Company, June 18, 1993

	FAC #	ZIP	CITY	ST	LAND COST PSF	SITE DEV COST PSF	FEES & BLDG COST PSF	TOTAL DEV COST PSF	REAL PROP TAXES PSF	ELECT PSF	GAS PSF
1	82	351	PHOENIX CITY	AL	$0.22	$6.00	$26.70	$32.92	$0.25000	$0.400	$0.200
2	95	302	THOMASTON	GA	$0.12	$6.00	$26.70	$32.82	$0.20000	$0.400	$0.200
3	81	300	ATLANTA	GA	$2.00	$7.50	$30.00	$39.50	$0.35000	$0.400	$0.200
4	83	088	NEWARK	NJ	$6.88	$6.90	$31.30	$45.08	$0.55000	$0.420	$0.550
5	80	122	ALBANY	NY	$1.15	$6.90	$31.30	$39.35	$1.53000	$0.370	$0.300
6	101	120	JOHNSTOWN	NY	$0.05	$6.90	$31.30	$38.25	$1.48000	$0.370	$0.300
7	87	641	KANSAS CITY	MO	$1.75	$6.00	$28.00	$35.75	$0.83000	$0.410	$0.150
8	98	633	ST. CHARLES	MO	$0.80	$5.10	$24.70	$30.60	$0.55000	$0.380	$0.150
9	94	982	BELLEVUE	WA	$1.75	$6.90	$31.30	$39.95	$0.65000	$0.320	$0.240
10	99	982	BURLINGTON	WA	$1.50	$6.90	$31.30	$39.70	$0.62000	$0.320	$0.240
11	84	907	ANAHEIM	CA	$10.00	$6.90	$31.30	$48.20	$0.54000	$0.340	$0.400
12	86	917	ONTARIO	CA	$6.00	$6.90	$31.30	$44.20	$0.54000	$0.340	$0.400
13	85	924	SAN BERNADINO	CA	$3.00	$6.90	$31.30	$41.20	$0.54000	$0.340	$0.400
14	100	923	VICTORVILLE	CA	$1.50	$6.90	$31.30	$39.70	$0.54000	$0.440	$0.400

Notes:

1. Includes grading, utilities, yard fence, yard crusher run, bldg. shell, paving & interior finish.
2. Land cost psf is the estimated cost of an improved industrial site ready for bldg. and bldg. cost psf assumes a base building cost for tilt-up construction.

- Total building square footage (sq. ft.) being purchased and how it is calculated by the seller (as defined by BOMA [Building Owners and Managers Association] or the commonly accepted/recognized local method).
- Rentable square feet (rsf) and usable square feet (usf) per floor in the facility.
- Total usable square footage (usf) in the facility and how it was calculated by the seller (as defined by BOMA or the commonly accepted/recognized local method).
- Common area factors in the facility (as defined by BOMA or the commonly accepted/recognized local method).
- Last year's, this year's, and estimated taxes for next year.
- Tax advantages:
  - No local or business taxes
  - No local or state income taxes
  - State revenue bonds for historical restoration, etc.
- Occupancy or Use Tax (established by local government).
- Insurance costs.
- Porter service and costs if any.

EXHIBIT 9.1 *(Continued)*

WATER & SEWER PSF	TOTAL OPER COST PSF	SQUARE FOOT VALUES: 10 ACRES BUILDING 200,000 SF 56,000 SF	10 ACRES BUILDING 150,000 SF 40,000 SF	7 ACRES BUILDING 100,000 SF 35,000 SF	4 ACRES BUILDING 60,000 SF 20,000 SF	4 ACRES BUILDING 30,000 SF 10,000 SF	NOTES
$0.050	$0.900	$2,791,032	$2,063,832	$1,601,582	$932,333	$485,333	1, 2 & 3
$0.050	$0.850	$2,747,472	$2,020,272	$1,571,090	$914,909	$467,909	1, 2 & 3
$0.050	$1.000	$4,051,200	$3,196,200	$2,409,840	$1,398,480	$873,480	1, 2 & 3
$0.052	$1.572	$6,129,728	$5,283,928	$3,883,350	$2,238,771	$1,718,771	1, 2 & 3
$0.050	$2.250	$3,633,740	$2,787,940	$2,136,158	$1,240,376	$720,376	1, 2 & 3
$0.050	$2.200	$3,152,402	$2,306,602	$1,799,221	$1,047,841	$527,841	1, 2 & 3
$0.050	$1.440	$3,530,300	$2,782,300	$2,113,610	$1,224,920	$764,920	1, 2 & 3
$0.050	$1.130	$2,751,680	$2,101,480	$1,618,436	$939,392	$539,392	1, 2 & 3
$0.050	$1.260	$3,895,100	$3,049,300	$2,319,110	$1,344,920	$824,920	1, 2 & 3
$0.050	$1.230	$3,786,200	$2,940,400	$2,242,880	$1,301,360	$781,360	1, 2 & 3
$0.050	$1.330	$7,488,800	$6,643,000	$4,834,700	$2,782,400	$2,262,400	1, 2 & 3
$0.050	$1.330	$5,746,400	$4,900,600	$3,615,020	$2,085,440	$1,565,440	1, 2 & 3
$0.050	$1.330	$4,439,600	$3,593,800	$2,700,260	$1,562,720	$1,042,720	1, 2 & 3
$0.050	$1.430	$3,786,200	$2,940,400	$2,242,880	$1,301,360	$781,360	1, 2 & 3

3. $6.00 psf of bldg. cost are fees for:
   Legal costs, etc. ($.50 psf).
   Programming, arch., eng., surveying, & inspection ($2.50 psf).
   General contingency ($2.00 psf).
   Landscaping and irrigation ($1.00 psf).

- Written statement from seller that the site and/or building contains *no* subsurface, surface or airborne friable asbestos, hazardous waste, or soil pollutants, and meets ADA requirements.
- Environmental site audit acceptable to the purchaser.

With few exceptions, a corporation purchases property for a specific requirement. Exhibits 9.1 and 9.2 provide information that may need to be obtained before proceeding with an analysis. Exhibit 9.1 provides geographical cost information for different locations in the United States for a specific application. Exhibit 9.2 is a purchase property market survey for a specific office location with specific survey items. Each property must be evaluated in light of this requirement and how the corporation will use and improve the property. As discussed in detail in the following sections, the corporation may:

1. Acquire improved property and modify the property and existing facilities.
2. Acquire land and make all improvements through new construction.
3. Acquire a developed property and facility through a build-to-suit via a turnkey acquisition.

EXHIBIT 9.2 Purchase Property Market Survey

MARKET SURVEY ITEMS	PROP. 1	PROP. 2	PROP. 3	PROP. 4	PROP. 5
Building Name	132 Union Center	Summitview Terrace	832 Ridgecrest	4420 Main Street	1st Nat'l. Bank Bldg.
Prop./Bldg. Quality (A, B, or C)	B	A	C	B	A
Property Owner	Associated Developers	Brown & Thomas	Smith Properties	Teacher's Pension Fund	Sumitzu Bank & Trust
Acreage Available	6.112	4.231	5.568	3.827	2.969
Site Terrain	Sloping	Level	Sloping	Level	Sloping
Bldg. Size (Gross Sq. Ft.)	77,848	253,000	127,680	375,138	372,806
Number of Floors	4	10	7	18	14
Gross Square Feet Per Floor	19,462	25,300	18,240	20,841	26,629
Efficiency Factor (gsf/usf)	1.123	1.142	1.109	1.136	1.157
Blocks From ABC Building	1 West	2 South	4 North	Adjacent	3 East
Sale Price For Property/Sq. Ft.	$7.00	$12.00	$10.00	$15.00	$17.00
Total Property Sale Price	$1,597,400	$2,211,600	$2,425,450	$2,500,000	$2,198,600
Sale Price For Building/GSF	$78.00	$93.00	$69.00	$82.00	$104.00
Total Building Sale Price	$6,072,144	$23,529,000	$8,809,920	$30,761,316	$38,771,824
Total Property/Building Sale Price	$7,669,544	$25,740,600	$11,235,370	$33,261,316	$40,970,424
Building Age	8 yrs.	5 yrs.	12 yrs.	10 yrs.	16 yrs.
Building Occupancy %	72.8%	0%	87.2%	77.6%	62.4%
Operating Cost Per GSF	$6.96	$8.21	$7.24	$8.47	$9.91
On Site Parking Spaces/1,000 GSF	3.11	1.13	2.2	2.5	None
Number Of Mos. On The Market	3	6	10	7	9
Previous Office Use	Spec.	Corp. HQ.	Spec.	Spec.	Bank/Spec
Floor To Ceiling Height	8' - 8"	9' - 0"	8' - 2"	8' - 6"	9' - 0"
Building Security	Sign In/Out	Card Access	Key and After Hours	After Hours Only	24 Hrs./On Site
Asbestos/Structure	No/Steel	No/Steel	Yes/Steel	No/Concrete	No/Concrete
Computer Room	Yes/1st Fl.	Yes/Bsmt.	No	No	Yes/Bsmt.
Sprinklered	Yes	Yes	Partial	Yes	Yes
Food Service	Yes	Yes	No	No	Yes
Loading Dock	Yes/1 Bay	Yes/2 Bays	Yes/1 Bay	Yes/2 Bays	Yes/3 Bays
Freight Elevator	Yes	Yes	No	No	Yes

Additional Market Survey Information:

Property 1 - Seller is slowly leasing the building after a major tenant moved out to Building 5. Majority of leases have 3 or less years until termination. Seller is very interested in selling for cash.

Property 2 - A major corporation headquarters has left town and the building is vacant. This building includes a 5,000 square foot computer room with 18" raised floor, a 4 hour UPS System and an emergency generator in the building basement.

Property 3 - Seller has a good reputation and has numerous office properties throughout Chicago. Building is in good repair and lobby/elevator has recently been renovated.

Property 4 - A new brokerage company has just listed the building and is known for getting "top dollar" for sellers.

Property 5 - This is an older landmark design and a major bank is in the process of relocating to a new building. There is a full service restaurant on the ground floor which also contains a number of retail shops, and a health facility which can accommodate 100 members at a time.

(a) ACQUIRING AN IMPROVED PROPERTY AND MODIFYING IT

There are a number of key financial and business items to consider in analyzing the acquisition and modification of improved property. Other unique items should be included as necessary, but the following are basic factors:

- Size of property in acreage, up to three decimal places, and in square feet.
- Cost per acre and per sq. ft.
- Date for schedule of completion and occupancy.
- Total land purchase price.
- Total improvements purchase price and cost to modify.
- Total land and improvements purchase price.
- Total closing costs, taxes, commissions, title insurance, or other fees.
- Purchase options, if any.
- Closing date.
- Construction start date.
- Certificate of Occupancy date.
- Cost of financing:

  Financing for construction alterations

  Permanent financing for construction alterations if required

  Financing for fixtures, furniture, and equipment (FF&E).
- Building operating expense in $/square feet with increases of %/year.
- Site operating expense in $/square feet with increases of %/year.
- Existing building depreciation asset life after modifications/alterations (31.5 years?).
- Corporate tax rate (34%).
- Alteration costs ($/sq. ft.).

(b) LAND ACQUISITION WITH CONSTRUCTION

There are a number of key financial and business items to consider in analyzing the acquisition of land and construction of a facility. Other items should be included if they are unique to a corporation's financial, business and legal requirements.

- Property acreage, up to three decimal places, and in square feet.
- Cost per acre and per sq. ft.
- Date for schedule of completion and occupancy.
- Total land purchase price.
- Total improvements purchase price.
- Total land and improvements purchase price.
- Total closing costs, taxes, commissions, title insurance, or other fees.

- Purchase option:

  Appropriate wording—"A sale and purchase option for approximately _____ adjacent acres to construct approximately _____ square feet of additional office space. The option shall be available to the Purchaser for a period of _____ (____) months after the initial property Closing Date."

  Proposed per-square-foot cost, the proposed number of square feet, and the total purchase price of the property exclusive of closing costs, taxes, commissions, title insurance, or other fees.
- Closing date.
- Construction start date.
- Certificate of Occupancy date.
- Cost of financing:

  Construction financing

  Permanent financing for construction

  Financing for fixtures, furniture, and equipment (FF&E).
- Operating expense in $/sq. ft. with increases of %/year.
- New building asset life (31.5 years).
- Corporate tax rate (34%).
- Construction cost ($/sq. ft.).

(c) BUILD-TO-SUIT CONCERNS (TURNKEY ACQUISITION)

Sometimes, corporate management desires to develop a facility but lacks the expertise and/or the initial capital. A build-to-suit turnkey process has become an advantageous solution for some corporations who can provide performance specifications and obtain a completed facility without having to manage the details of real estate acquisition, design, construction, and inspection. The premise of this process is that the developer or developer/general contractor, who has major expertise and purchasing resources, provides all services for the project and then, on completion of the project, turns over the keys to the corporation. The developer provides:

- Property—properly zoned and sub-divided.
- Architectural, interior, and landscape design and engineering services.
- Construction schedules and documents.
- Construction financing, bonds, and payments to subcontractors.
- Project utilities, permits, and insurance.
- Site and building construction, finishes, supervision, and coordination for corporate-furnished items.

- Interim construction payments, inspections, and the Certificate of Occupancy.
- As-built drawings, completed punch-list work, lien waivers, warranty, and final construction payments.
- Training on building systems and the building keys at closing.

Reasons corporations choose the build-to-suit option include:

- *Lack of Capital Funds.* Because the corporation lacks funds to finance property acquisition and construction, the developer purchases the property and obtains financing. The corporation and developer have agreed on a specific price and delivery date, which eliminates the corporation's development risk while working to obtain the best financing for the permanent mortgage or the cash required at closing.
- *Timing Issues.* The corporation does not have the total amount of funds available to begin the project at a specific time, needs the facility in a timely manner for business requirements, and will have the necessary funds at closing.
- *Business Implications.* Cash is needed for specific business operations or delay of a major expenditure or financing will in the short term help the balance sheet.
- *Tax Implications.* The corporation may be able to defer taxes or depreciation to a more favorable tax period, especially where closing takes place just after the start of the new tax year and the corporation will have a full year of depreciation.
- *Lack of Available Sites.* It may be difficult to find sites that have utilities, zoning, or completed infrastructure (roads, stoplights, utilities, etc.). The build-to-suit developer has, controls or has the political know-how to promptly secure the necessary site requirements, permits, and approvals. In some areas of the country, local developers control the more desirable sites and often have the "connections" to move the project through the state or local bureaucratic maze.
- *Difficulty in Doing Business in the Location.* Should the corporation try to direct the acquisition and development of the property, there may be considerable delay while corporation staff try to determine local ways and timing of doing business. The developer may be able to acquire an option on additional adjacent property for an attractive price, whereas the corporation's "deep pockets" may inflate the adjacent property owner's expectations.
- *Lack of Expertise within the Corporation.* Because development is not an ongoing operation, the corporation does not wish to deal with development details. Many corporations may build a major

facility once in 10 years and do not have skilled or experienced staff readily available to manage the project on a day-to-day basis. The developer is hired to provide an acceptable solution.

- *Need to Remain Flexible.* Corporate resources that were scheduled to finance the project have been transferred to other requirements, and this solution provides a means of continuing with the project, but deferring fund requirements to a later date. There may also be other business issues pending; until they are resolved, flexibility remains an immediate corporate requirement.
- *Requirement Not to Own the Project.* The corporation may prefer not to own the property until certain other events or timing takes place. Again, balance sheet expenditures and asset disclosures may be more advantageously deferred to a later time and in some cases under other corporate leadership.

Advantages to the corporation may include:

- Corporation is not the owner until the project is complete.
- Corporation can "walk" (within reason) if the developer cannot deliver the project as specified.
- Corporation has leveraged its resources by using other people's money (capital).
- Burden of zoning, utilities, etc., is the responsibility of the developer.
- Corporation retains its capital for other interim purposes.
- Options to purchase additional property later at a specific price can be included.
- "Turn-key" concept provides a fixed cost for the corporation to finance at closing.
- Corporation obtains a site and a facility that are developed to its specifications.
- Developer can provide project to the corporation on a fast-track basis.
- Corporation has not had to staff up for the project.

Disadvantages to the corporation may include:

- Corporation is not the owner until closing.
- Time frame may be critical, and corporation has no direct control of schedule.
- Project could be more costly.
- Paying for the use of other people's money could be substantially more costly.

- Financial ability and stability of build-to-suit developer may be unknown.
- Quality of construction may be more difficult to control with lack of available and qualified staff.
- Corporation will have to develop a very detailed RFP.

Exhibit 9.1 provides a geographical analysis of various proposed warehouse sites around the United States. The key variables are land cost, site development cost, fees and building cost, taxes, and utility/operating costs for each location. The right-hand section provides a variety of land acreages and building sizes to obtain a total land acquisition and capital/building cost. This analysis provides basic locational cost information for a review of possible sites. Remember that these costs are only for development of the facility. The cost of living, availability of a trained work force, transportation, housing, income taxes, and many other business and operational issues must also be obtained and included before making a final selection.

Exhibit 9.2 is a Purchase Property Market Survey prepared on a number of office buildings and sites for sale in a particular section of a metropolitan area. The Survey provides competitive information on five office buildings and objectively compares items that are important in making an evaluation. The additional information at the bottom of the survey provides subjective information about each site and the seller.

Exhibit 9.3 provides 10-year spreadsheet analysis of a Cash Flow for a 10-Year Mortgage. The analysis assumes a rental income stream and expenses to determine a net operating income. The analysis also shows the Cash Flow before Taxes and the Cash Flow after Taxes. The bottom section of the analysis provides the basis for determining the gain on a sale and the proceeds from the sale.

§ 9.3 LEASE ANALYSIS AND DECISIONS

(a) COST ISSUES AND ITEMS FOR REVIEW AND ANALYSIS

Responses to a Request for Proposal (RFP) (see Chapter Eleven) to lease property or space may not follow the requested response format or provide the requested information. The corporation will need to develop an "apples to apples" comparative financial analysis of the responses. Depending on the size of the requirement, and the complexity of the RFP, the "apples to apples" financial analysis may be very straightforward or very complex.

The financial analysis should be provided in a format that the concerned parties can recognize and understand. All responses should be listed with each item quantified and responses addressed in the same

EXHIBIT 9.3 Spreadsheet Analysis

CASH FLOW FOR 10 YEAR MORTGAGE

	YEAR 1	YEAR 2	YEAR 3	YEAR 4	YEAR 5	YEAR 6	YEAR 7	YEAR 8	YEAR 9	YEAR 10
1 GROSS RENTAL INCOME	10,000	10,500	11,025	11,576	12,155	12,763	13,401	14,071	14,775	15,513
2 OTHER INCOME	0	0	0	0	0	0	0	0	0	0
3 EFFECTIVE RENTAL INCOME	10,000	10,500	11,025	11,576	12,155	12,763	13,401	14,071	14,775	15,513
4 VAC & CREDIT LOSSES	0	0	0	0	0	0	0	0	0	0
5 GROSS OPERATING INCOME	10,000	10,500	11,025	11,576	12,155	12,763	13,401	14,071	14,775	15,513
6 OPERATING EXPENSE	2,000	2,000	2,000	2,000	2,000	2,000	2,000	2,000	2,000	2,000
7 NET OPERATING INCOME	8,000	8,500	9,025	9,576	10,155	10,763	11,401	12,071	12,775	13,513
8 INTEREST FIRST MORTGAGE	4,820	4,416	3,991	3,544	3,074	2,580	2,061	1,515	941	338
9 INTEREST SECOND MORTGAGE	0	0	0	0	0	0	0	0	0	0
10 INTEREST THIRD MORTGAGE	0	0	0	0	0	0	0	0	0	0
11 COST RECOVERY - IMPROVEMENTS	794	794	794	794	794	794	794	794	794	794
12 COST RECOVERY - PERS PROP.	0	0	0	0	0	0	0	0	0	0
13 AMORTIZATION OF LOAN POINTS	0	0	0	0	0	0	0	0	0	0
14 PARTICIPATION PAYMENTS	0	0	0	0	0	0	0	0	0	0
16 TAXABLE INCOME BEFORE ADJ.	2,386	3,290	4,241	5,239	6,288	7,389	8,547	9,763	11,040	12,382
17 MARGINAL TAX RATE	33%	33%	33%	33%	33%	33%	33%	33%	33%	33%
18 TAX LIABILITY ON REAL ESTATE	787	1,086	1,399	1,729	2,075	2,438	2,820	3,222	3,643	4,086
19 NET OPERATING INCOME	8,000	8,500	9,025	9,576	10,155	10,763	11,401	12,071	12,775	13,513
20 ANNUAL DEBT SERVICE	4,820	4,416	3,991	3,544	3,074	2,580	2,061	1,515	941	338
21 PARTICIPATION PAYMENTS	0	0	0	0	0	0	0	0	0	0
22 CASH FLOW BEFORE TAXES	3,180	4,084	5,034	6,033	7,081	8,183	9,340	10,556	11,833	13,175
23 TAX LIABILITY ON REAL ESTATE	787	1,086	1,399	1,729	2,075	2,438	2,820	3,222	3,643	4,086
24 INVESTMENT TAX CREDIT	0	0	0	0	0	0	0	0	0	0
25 CASH FLOW AFTER TAXES	2,392	2,998	3,635	4,304	5,006	5,745	6,520	7,335	8,190	9,089

	YEAR 1	YEAR 2	YEAR 3	YEAR 4	YEAR 5	YEAR 6	YEAR 7	YEAR 8	YEAR 9	YEAR 10
PRINCIPAL BALANCE 1ST MORTGAGE	92,767	84,489	75,788	66,642	57,028	46,922	36,299	25,132	13,395	1,056
PRINCIPAL BALANCE 2ND MORTGAGE	0	0	0	0	0	0	0	0	0	0
PRINCIPAL BALANCE 3RD MORTGAGE	0	0	0	0	0	0	0	0	0	0
TOTAL UNPAID PRINCIPAL	92,767	84,489	75,788	66,642	57,028	46,922	36,299	25,132	13,395	1,056
PRINCIPAL REDUCTION 1ST MORG	7,233	8,278	8,701	9,146	9,614	10,106	10,623	11,167	11,738	12,338
PRINCIPAL REDUCTION 2ND MORG										
PRINCIPAL REDUCTION 3RD MORG										
TOTAL YEARLY PRINCIPAL PAID	7,233	8,278	8,701	9,146	9,614	10,106	10,623	11,167	11,738	12,338
CUMULATIVE PRINCIPAL REDUCTION	7,233	8,278	8,701	9,146	9,614	10,106	10,623	11,167	11,738	12,338

CASH FLOW FOR 10 YEAR MORTGAGE

CALCULATION OF ADJUSTED BASIS

1 BASIS OF ACQUISITION	500,000
2 CAPITOL ADDITIONS	0
3 LESS COST RECOVERY TAKEN	7,937
4 ADJUSTED BASIS OF SALE	492,063

CALCULATION OF EXCESS C.R.

5 TOTAL COST RECOVERY TAKEN	0
6 STRAIGHT LINE COST RECOVERY	0
7 EXCESS COST RECOVERY	0
8 EXCESS COST RECOVERY C.O.	0
9 TOTAL EXCESS COST RECOVERY	0

CALCULATION OF GAIN ON SALE

10 SALE PRICE	1,000,000
11 COST OF SALE	70,000
12 ADJUSTED BASIS OF SALE	492,063
13 PARTICIPATION PAYMENTS	0
14 TOTAL GAIN	437,937
15 EXCESS COST RECOVERY	[illegible]

16 SUSPENDED LOSSES	0
17 CAPITAL GAIN OR (LOSS)	437,937

CALCULATION OF TAX LIABILITY

18 EXCESS COST RECOVERY	0
19 CAPITAL GAIN	437,937
20 TAXABLE INCOME FOR SALE	437,937
21 TAX BRACKET	33%
22 TAX LIABILITY ON SALE	144,519

CALCULATION OF SALE PROCEEDS

23 TOTAL SALE PRICE	1,000,000
24 COST OF SALE	70,000
25 PARTICIPATION PAYMENTS	0
26 MORTGAGE BALANCE(S)	1,056
27 SALE PROCEEDS BEFORE TAXES	928,944
28 TAX LIABILITY ON SALE	144,519
29 RECAPTURE OF I T C	0

YEAR	CASH FLOWS
0	(50,000)
1	2,392
2	2,998
3	3,635
4	4,304
5	5,006
6	5,745
7	6,520
8	7,335
9	8,190
10	793,514

INTERNAL RATE OF RETURN (IRR) = 34.9%

comparative format (see Exhibits 9.4, 9.5, and 9.6). As shown in the following example, each response may quote different rentable square feet (rsf) while the usable square feet (usf) number, which is a function of the efficiency (eff) of the floor and building design, is quoted as requested.

Example

Location	usf	eff	rsf		Rent/rsf		Rent/Yr.		Rent for 5 Yrs.
Building A	13,500	10.0%	15,000	×	$15	=	$225,000	=	$1,125,000
Building B	13,500	12.5%	15,429	×	$15	=	$231,435	=	$1,157,175
Building C	13,500	15.0%	15,882	×	$15	=	$238,230	=	$1,191,150

This analysis shows that based on rentable square feet (rsf) alone and assuming that all landlords quoted a $15/rsf rental rate, the corporation (tenant) would be paying over $6,000 more per year at Building B than at Building A and over $13,000 more per year at Building C than at Building A. The total rent for the 5-year term assuming a constant $15 per rsf would amount to more than $30,000 in savings at Building A over Building B, and more than $66,000 at Building A over Building C.

But the analysis must also look at many additional items such as:

- The upfit allowance and what it includes in real dollars based on new or existing space.
- Comparing and equating floor-to-ceiling or floor-to-bottom of structure costs with landlord's improvement allowance or workletter.
- In-place or to-be-installed mechanical, electrical, ceiling, and sprinkler systems.
- The rental rate, including escalations and free rent.
- Parking costs.
- ADA compliance, operating expenses, etc.

A number of variables must be compared to reach an "apples to apples" analysis in determining the Net Present Value (NPV) and Effective Level Rent for each property. The results of the analyses, the reputation of the landlords, and their responses to the RFP form the basis for site recommendation.

(b) LEASE COMPONENTS

The business and legal terms of the lease are discussed in detail in Chapter Ten. When analyzing the terms of the lease, the following financial and business items are the key lease components to consider before making a final recommendation or selection.

(1) Rent

- The rate per rsf, total rent per year and monthly amount $________ and ______/100 dollars ($______.____) due to the landlord, usually by the first day of the month, including the name the rent check is made payable to and the rent payment address.
- What is or is not included in the rent payment (i.e., rent, utilities, insurance, taxes [real property/personal/other], maintenance) and whether any of these are defined as "additional rent."
- The penalties/interest for late payment.

(2) Escalations

Escalations, that is, provisions for increases in the rent, are very important as they establish future rents and specify what is being escalated. Escalations vary by type, base year, and when they will take effect. These increases usually occur yearly and may include the following adjustments to the base rent and/or to the operating expenses:

- A specific percentage increase per year.
- The Consumer Price Index (CPI) or a percentage of the CPI with a cap or a minimum and a maximum increase.
- An additional $________.____ cost per rsf.
- A set amount based on a specific $________.____ cost per rsf as a cap.
- A combination of the above.
- Whatever can be negotiated, which can include no increase in the rent and/or operating expenses.

(3) Operating Expenses

Operating and common area maintenance expenses per month are often expressed in an amount-per-square-foot for a specific year as a "peg" or "expense stop." Since this can be a very complicated and expensive item, it should be thoroughly detailed in the lease, especially with regard to the percentage of expense pass-thru, the base amount and base year, and so on. Common area maintenance expenses per month are often found at warehouse properties where the site maintenance is managed by the landlord and the tenants pay utilities, janitorial costs, and so on for their space.

Operating expenses in a lease may be full service or net and the tenant's right to audit all operating expenses should be fully described to ensure access to landlord operating expense records. The full service lease includes ______. The net lease includes ______. Operating expenses may include:

- Maintenance cost.
- Repairs and replacement.
- Management expenses.
- Utilities.
- Janitorial/housekeeping costs.
- Capital costs.
- Miscellaneous expenses/property taxes/special assessments.

(4) Allowances

Allowances can include the costs for the design and construction of the premises that may be required before the tenant can take occupancy. The cost of this work will be paid for by either the landlord or the tenant, or may be prorated between the landlord and the tenant. As part of the negotiating process, who will pay and is responsible for what work, at what cost and within what design and construction schedule must be identified in writing before the lease is executed. The construction allowance can take one of the following forms as an exhibit attached to the lease:

- A landlord's workletter and construction schedule, which includes design and construction completion dates, cost, and work the landlord will pay for before the premises is delivered to the tenant; the cost and work that the landlord will do but the tenant will pay for; and the work that the tenant will pay for and do during or after the landlord finishes its work.
- A dollar allowance per usable square foot provided by the landlord where the landlord will schedule all design and construction work to provide the space as requested, pay all design and permit fees, and pay for all construction work; the tenant will reimburse the landlord for any costs over the total allowance amounts.
- A dollar allowance per usable square foot provided by the landlord where the tenant will be responsible for obtaining all design work, paying for permits and fees, scheduling the work, hiring a general contractor, completing and paying for all work, and requesting reimbursement from the landlord for all costs up to the total allowance amounts.

The cost, responsibility, design and construction schedule should specify in detail:

- Landlord coordination or management fees.
- Design and/or engineering firm/fees/services.
- Design and construction documents/changes.
- Work to be completed by the landlord.
- Work to be completed by the tenant.
- Access to the premises.
- The definition of substantial completion tied to receipt of the certificate of occupancy.
- Improvement schedule/milestone dates.
- Change order procedures.
- Insurance.
- Lien Waivers.
- Permitting and Certificate of Occupancy.
- Bonus/Penalty or Late Penalty Clause.

Other allowances can include a dollar amount per rentable (preferable) or usable square feet for design and/or engineering fees, moving, telecommunications, carpet, and furnishings. These nonconstruction allowances can be paid to the tenant in the form of cash, usually as a reimbursable expense. Should the allowance not be totally expended, negotiations should include the tenant's option to take the balance due in cash, or apply to rent or operating expenses.

(5) Concessions

Concessions are items that are unique to the tenant's business and/or the lease, such as:

- Purchase option with the total cost, date to notify landlord, or date of purchase.
- Density of employees restriction where, for example, the landlord requires that the tenant's premises can only accommodate one employee for every 200 rentable square feet. If additional employees reduce the ratio, then the landlord could find the tenant in default of the lease terms.
- Pro rata share of property taxes if these are not included in the operating expenses.
- Local occupancy or use taxes that the tenant must pay and that are not included in the operating expenses.
- Tenant conference room, with projection, coat, and storage facilities, provided by the landlord to the tenant at no initial cost or use fee for the term of the lease.

- Lease renewal options with the amount of rent for the option period(s) either fixed, consumer price index (CPI), percentage per year, or market, upfit allowance per option for painting, carpet, etc.
- An option or option(s) for additional space within the property, and/or the right of first refusal for specific floors or space.

Rent abatement is another concession that should be considered in a lease analysis. In today's rental markets, a number of months of free rent may create a financial benefit and reduce the effective rental rate. The rent abatement concession should include the:

- Starting date.
- Number of months of free rent.
- The value of the free rent.
- When the first rent payment is due.
- Whether or not operating expense payments are included in the rent abatement period. Landlords usually require the tenant to pay operating expenses regardless of the amount or length of free rent.

(6) Other Important Lease Terms

Contingency or special stipulation clauses may be included for special requirements such as:

- Permissions for the work.
- Possession of a Certificate of Occupancy.
- Approval of the parent company.
- Existence of required zoning for the proposed use.
- Letter from local utility providers that the amount and quality of services are available for the specific project.
- Key dates in qualifying landlord for a bonus/penalty (monetary, additional days of free rent, delay of the start of the lease effective date, etc.).
- After-hours HVAC and cost.
- Basement or tenant storage cost.

(c) PRESENT VALUE ANALYSIS—ANNUAL WEIGHTED COST FACTORS

Effective Level Rent translates a net present value of periodic lease payments into an annualized dollar amount per square foot. A new present value calculation is one of the few ways in which all the dollar values of the concession package are taken into account while allowing for the alternative cost of money leasehold. The advantage of using a constant payment as the net effective rent is that it is easier to compare in different transactions and is close to the actual rent that would be paid on an annualized basis.

Example. Showing the mechanics of this calculation is the best way to explain the concept of Effective Level Rent:

Alternative 1

1,000 sq. ft.

One year free rent

$10.00 per sq. ft. for Years 2–5

9% discount rate

In this alternative, the net present value at 9% equals $29,722.20. The level annual payment for five years at 9% using this net present value equals $7,641.35. Thus, the Effective Level Rent per square foot equals $7.64.

Alternative 2

1,000 sq. ft.

No free rent

$8.00 per sq. ft. for five years

9% discount rate

Here, the net present value at 9% equals $31,117.21. The level annual payment for five years at 9% using this net present value equals $8,000.00. Thus, the Effective Level Rent per square foot equals $8.00.

Both scenarios would yield the same amount of gross dollars, $40,000 and, as quoted by the landlords, the same effective rent at $8.00. However, because of the present value impact of the timing of the lease payments, Alternative 1 has a lower Effective Level Rent (this lease analysis computes the present value using monthly lease payments with the payment made at the beginning of the month).

(d) LEASE AGREEMENTS

The following sections provide checklists for the major kinds of lease agreements.

(1) Lease

Premises

____ Approximately _____ rentable sq. ft. initially with the option to lease approximately _____ contiguous rentable sq. ft. within one year of the initial lease date.

____ Approximately ______ usf of the leased space will comprise a Computer Room.

Term

____ ______ (____) years.

Term Commencement Date

____ ______ ____, 19____.

Term Ending Date

____ ______ ____, 199____.

Rental Rate

____ $______/rsf.

Escalation and Any Other Rental Adjustment Clause(s)

____ Rental Rate: ______.____% year.

____ Operating Costs Rate: ______.____% max./year.

Tenant Improvements

____ $______.____ per usf for construction ("slab-to-slab" or "below-a-finished ceiling" construction allowance).

____ $______.____ per usf for design fees.

____ $______.____ per usf for relocation.

____ $______.____ per usf for telephone system.

Expansion Option(s)

____ ______ rsf will be required at the end of the initial lease year.

____ ______ years' expansion option term.

____ ______ days' notice required.

____ $______.____ rental rate per rsf.

____ $______.____ improvement/renovation allowance.

Renewal Option(s)

____ ______ consecutive ______ year renewal options.

____ ______ days' notice required.

____ $______.____ rental rate per rsf.

____ $______.____ improvement/renovation allowance.

Parking

____ $______.____ per parking space for ______ year(s).

(2) Ground Lease

Premises/Property

____ ______.____ acres.

____ ____________ sq. ft.

Term

____ ______ years.

Term Commencement Date

____ ______ ____, 199____.

Term Ending Date

____ ______ ____, 199____.

Rental Rate

____ $______/acre.

____ $______/sq. ft.

Escalation and Any Other Rental Adjustment Clause(s)

____ Rental Rate: ______.____% year.

Expansion Option(s)

____ ______ sq. ft. of property will be required at the end of the initial lease year.

____ ______ years' expansion option term.

____ ______ days' notice required.

____ $______.____ rental sq. ft.

Renewal Option(s)

____ ______ consecutive ______ year renewal options.

____ ______ days' notice required.

____ $______.____ rate per sq. ft.

Purchase Option

____ $______.____/acre.

____ $______.____/sq. ft.

____ Total purchase price: $__________.

____ Purchase option date: ______ ____, ______.

____ Closing date: ______ ____, ______.

(3) Build-to-Lease Arrangement

Premises/Building

____ Approximately ______ rentable square feet initially with the option to lease approximately ______ contiguous rentable sq. ft. within one year of the initial lease date.

____ Approximately ______ usf of the leased space will comprise a Computer Room.

Term

____ ______ (____) years.

Term Commencement Date

____ ______ ____, 19____.

Term Ending Date

____ ______ ____, 19____.

Rental Rate

____ $______/rsf.

Escalation and Any Other Rental Adjustment Clause(s)

____ Rental Rate: ______.____% year.

____ Operating Costs Rate: ______.____% max./year.

Tenant Improvements

____ $______.____ per usf for construction. ("slab-to-slab" or "below-a-finished ceiling" construction allowance)

____ $______.____ per usf for design fees.

____ $______.____ per usf for relocation.

____ $______.____ per usf for telephone system.

Expansion Option(s)

____ ______ rsf will be required at the end of the initial lease year.

____ ______ years' expansion option term.

____ ______ days' notice required.

____ $______.____ rental rate per rsf.

____ $______.____ improvement/renovation allowance.

Renewal Option(s)

____ ______ consecutive ______ year renewal options.

____ ______ days' notice required.

____ $______.____ rental rate per rsf.

____ $______.____ improvement/renovation allowance.

Parking

____ $______.____ per parking space for ______ year(s).

Premises/Property

____ ______.____ acres.

____ ____________ sq. ft.

Term

____ ______ years.

Term Commencement Date

____ ______ ____, 19____.

Term Ending Date

____ ______ ____, 19____.

Rental Rate

____ $______/acre.

____ $______/sq. ft.

Escalation and Any Other Rental Adjustment Clause(s)

____ Rental Rate: ______._____% year.

Expansion Option(s)

____ ______ sq. ft. of property will be required at the end of the initial lease year.

____ ______ years' expansion option term.

____ ______ days' notice required.

____ $______._____ rental sq. ft.

Renewal Option(s)

____ ______ consecutive ______ year renewal options.

____ ______ days' notice required.

____ $______._____ rate per sq. ft.

Purchase Option

____ $______._____/acre.

____ $______._____/sq. ft.

____ Total purchase price: $____________.

____ Purchase option date: ______ _____, ______.

____ Closing date: ______ _____, ______.

(4) Sale-Leaseback

Sale Price

____ $______._____/acre.

____ $______._____/sq. ft.

____ Total purchase price: $____________.

____ Purchase Agreement date: ______ _____, ______.

____ Closing date: ______ _____, ______.

Premises/Building

____ Approximately ______ rentable square feet initially with the option to lease approximately ______ contiguous rentable sq. ft. within one year of the initial lease date.

Term

____ ______ (____) years.

Term Commencement Date

____ ______ _____, 19____.

Term Ending Date

____ ______ ____, 19____.

Rental Rate

____ $______/rsf.

Escalation and Any Other Rental Adjustment Clause(s)

____ Rental Rate: ______.____% year.

____ Operating Costs Rate: ______.____% max./year.

Renewal Option(s)

____ ______ consecutive ______ year renewal options.

____ ______ days' notice required.

____ $______.____ rental rate per rsf.

____ $______.____ improvement/renovation allowance.

Parking

____ $______.____ per parking space for ______ year(s).

Premises/Property

____ ______.____ acres.

____ ____________ sq. ft.

Term

____ ______ (____) years.

Term Commencement Date

____ ______ ____, 19____.

Term Ending Date

____ ______ ____, 19____.

Rental Rate

____ $______/acre.

____ $______/sq. ft.

Escalation and Any Other Rental Adjustment Clause(s)

____ Rental Rate: ______.____% year.

Renewal Option(s)

____ ______ consecutive ______ year renewal options.

____ ______ days' notice required.

____ $______.____ rate per sf.

Exhibit 9.4 is a Lease Property Market Survey prepared on a number of office buildings for lease in a particular section of a metropolitan area. The survey provides competitive information on five office buildings and objectively compares items that are important for an

EXHIBIT 9.4 Lease Property Market Survey

MARKET SURVEY ITEMS	BLDG. 1	BLDG. 2	BLDG. 3	BLDG. 4	BLDG. 5
Building Name	Park Plaza	191 Union Tower	Westfield Place	Sutton Building	1 Crown Square
Building Quality (A, B, or C)	A	A	B	C	A
Landlord	Main St. Ltd.	Wright & Partners	Associated Developers	Metro Properties	Brown & Thomas
Financial Partner	Major Life Insurance	Western Casualty	Chicago Nat'l. Bank	Metro Properties	Teacher's Pension Fund
Total Building Rentable Sq. Ft.	258,000	487,400	281,500	110,700	879,550
Building Occupancy %	78.3%	85.2%	67.8%	59.6%	62.4%
Available Rentable Sq. Ft.	55,986	72,137	90,562	44,723	330,711
Available Contiguous R.S.F.	43,000	23,210	31,760	27,610	201,040
Floor Plate Size (R.S.F.)	21,500	23,210	18,750	18,450	25,150
Number of Floors	12	21	15	6	35
Efficiency Factor (rsf/usf)	1.143	1.112	1.136	1.162	1.122
Rate Per Rentable Square Foot	$18.00	$20.50	$15.00	$12.00	$23.00
Rent Escalation	5% / yr.	C.P.I.	3% / yr.	$.15/rsf/yr	7% / yr.
Operating Expense Cost Per RSF	$8.10	$7.05	$6.50	$7.73	$9.12
Blocks From ABC Building	Adjacent	2 North	1 South	3 East	2 West
Building Age	6 yrs.	7 yrs.	10 yrs.	14 yrs.	6 mos.
Floor to Ceiling Height	9' - 0"	8' - 6"	8' - 6"	8' - 3"	9' - 0"
Improvement Allowance/U.S.F.	$22.00	Turnkey	$15.00	Work Ltr.	$27.50
Free Rent On Five Year Term	12 months	9 months	10 months	5 months	12 mos.
Expansion Options	Yes	No	Yes	Yes	Yes
Cancellation Option Available	No	Unknown	Yes	Yes	No
Building Security	Card Access	Sign In/Out	Key and After Hrs.	After Hrs. Only	24 Hrs./On Site
Sprinklered	Yes	Yes	Yes	No	Yes
Conference Room/Facility	No	Yes	No	No	Yes
On Site Parking Available	Yes	No	Yes	Yes	No
Available Parking Cost/Space	$3.15/day	$2.25/day	$2.75/day	No cost	$3.50
Food Service	Yes	Yes	No	Yes	Yes
Computer Room Available	Yes/5th Fl.	No	Yes/Bsmt.	Yes	No
Freight Elevator	Yes	Yes	No	No	Yes
Loading Dock	Yes/3 bays	Yes/2 bays	Yes/2 bays	No	Yes/4 bays

Additional Market Survey Information:

Building 1 - Landlord has been aggressively marketing the building as a number of the 1st five year tenants have left the building. Building includes a quality sit down sandwich shop and is frequented by building tenants and tenants from adjacent buildings. No asbestos.

Building 2 - Landlord's Financial Partner has previously taken 3 to 6 months to review each proposal and 2 to 4 months to sign off on the lease for this quality building. A new property management company has been hired and building janitorial services have improved. No asbestos.

Building 3 - A major corporation which occupies 4 floors will be moving out of the building in 60 days. This space includes a 3,000 square foot computer room with 12" raised floor and a 2 hour UPS System in the building basement. Landlord has been marketing the space and may be close to leasing 2 floors. No asbestos.

Building 4 - Landlord has a good reputation and has numerous office properties throughout Chicago. Building is in good repair and lobby/elevator has recently been renovated. One of the tenants is a small competitor of ABC, Inc. and has three years remaining on there lease. Asbestos has been partially abated.

Building 5 - This is a landmark design and is the newest office building in town. A major corporation has leased 50% of the building for 15 years. There is a lunch/dinner club on the top floor, the ground floor contains a number of food and retail shops, and the conference facility will accommodate 50 in a classroom setting.

evaluation. The additional information at the bottom of the survey provides subjective information about each site and the seller.

Exhibit 9.5 provides a Lease Analysis for ABC Company at Building X including several important items to consider in an evaluation such as the Total Gross Cash Outlay and the Net Present Value of the Cash Outlay shown at the bottom of the exhibit.

EXHIBIT 9.5 Lease Analysis

```
                                   ABC CORPORATION                              AT: BUILDING X

                      ( Assumes Proportionate 1st year escalation based on commencement date)

      Commencement Date -            2 /90          Rentable to Usable
                              -------------                    Factor             1.1200
VARIABLES:                                                                   -----------
-----------
  RENT:
      Initial Sq. Footage          22,321          Initial Sq. Footage           25,000
            (Usable)          ------------              (Rentable)           -----------
      Lease Term (months)            120 months
                              ------------
      Initial Rental Rate         $21.28 / Sq.Ft.  Initial  Rental Rate      $19.00 / Sq.Ft.
            (Usable)          ------------              (Rentable)           -----------
ESCALATIONS:

CPI-    % of CPI                     60%           Fixed Rate                        0%
                              -----------                                    -----------
      Assumed CPI                     5%           Basis for Fixed Rate  $        0.00 Usable
                              ------------                                   -----------
      CPI or Fixed begins            11 months from commencement.
                                   -----
 PRO RATA-
      Base or 1st Year Op. Exp    $6.72 / Sq. Ft.  Base Year R.E. Taxes          $0.00
      (Usable S.F.)           ------------                                   -----------
      Assumed % Increase              6%           Assumed % Increase                0%
                              ------------                                   -----------
      Expense Stop(Usable)        $6.72
                              ------------
      PR/Tax Escalation begin        11 months from commencement.
                              -----------
  LANDLORD CONTRIBUTION & TENANT COSTS:

      Rent Abatement Period          24 months     Moving Allowance     $        37,500
                              ------------                                   -----------
      Rent Abatement Sq. Ft.       22,321 Sq.Ft. Usable
                              ------------
      Total Construction Cost$     21.28 / Sq. Ft.  $    475,000
                              ----------- (Usable)  -----------

      Less Const. Allowance  $     20.16 / Sq.Ft.   $    450,000     Plus    $            0    Equal    $     25,000
                              ------------(Usable)  -----------              -----------              -----------
      Tenant Current                        Less:  Landlord's
       Lease Obligation      $    175,000          Rent Assumption      $       150,000
                              ------------                                   -----------             PARKING :
                                                                                                     '# of spaces
      Re-Location Costs      $          0          Moving Costs         $        50,000
                              ------------                                   -----------             Cost per Spa

  ANALYSIS FACTOR:                                                                                   Monthly Cost

      Analysis Discount Rate      10.00 %                                                            Annual Incre
                              ------------

                                                           Cash Outlay
                                                          -------------
                              Total Gross           $ 5,020,352    Net Present Value  $  2,806,953    Gross
                                                    ===========                       ===========
                              Average Gross Cost                   Effective Level Rent                 NPV
                              Per S.F. Per Year     $     22.49    Per S.F. Over      $       19.78 / Usable S.F
                                                    ===========    Lease Term           ===========
                                                        $20.08 Rentable                     $17.66 /Rentable SF
                                                    ===========                         ===========
```

Exhibit 9.6 provides a comparative analysis of 5 different buildings and the lease and capital costs for each location. The notes section at the bottom of the page provides subjective information obtained from the various landlords' proposals and from research on each location. This analysis provides objective bottom-line comparisons that become part of the information to use in making a selection.

Exhibit 9.7 is a Site Evaluation Matrix showing three sites that have been evaluated. This spreadsheet format provides an objective ranking of site evaluation criteria that have been weighted. Each ranking is then scored by the prospective tenant and the average ratings and scores for each site are shown. Notes at the bottom of the page are for weighting and site upfit, and also provide general information to assist in the decision-making process.

EXHIBIT 9.6 Analysis of 24-Month Proposals for the Relocation of ABC Company

June 18, 1993

Proposed Location/Term	Rate/ R.S.F.	Esc./ Year	Total R.S.F.	Total U.S.F.	First Years Rent	Upfit Allow./ U.S.F.	Total Allow.	Estimated Total Improve. Cost	Total Rent	Total Commitment = Total Rent + Total Improve. Cost	Estimated Balance Of Improve. Cost Paid By XYZ CO.	Remarks
1. 1245 Wacker Avenue, 3rd & 4th Floor												
24 Months	$17.75	4%	50,000	44,000	$875,500	$5.00	$250,000	$480,000	$1,798,500	$2,278,000	$230,000	Note 1
2. 769 Michigan Drive, 4th Floor & partial 2nd, 5th & 8th Fls.												
24 Months	$19.50	3%+	45,000	40,284	$877,500	$8.00	$322,272	$445,000	$1,782,000	$2,227,000	$122,800	Note 2
30 Months	$19.50	3%+	45,000	40,284	$877,500	$10.00	$402,840					Note 2
36 Months	$19.50	3%+	45,000	40,384	$877,500	$12.00	$484,608					Note 2
3. 849 Wacker Avenue, 5th & 6th Floors												
18 Months	$12.00	Fixed	47,743	45,481	$572,916	$1.00+	$ 45,481					Note 3
24 Months	$12.15	Fixed	47,743	45,481	$580,078	$1.00+	$ 45,481	$446,600	$1,160,200	$1,606,800	$204,700	Note 3
4. 982 Michigan Drive, 14th & 15 Floors, with Basement/Computer Rm.												
18 Months	$15.00	Fixed	49,439	44,754	$741,585	$4.47	$200,000					Note 4
24 Months	$15.00	Fixed	49,439	44,754	$741,585	$6.70	$300,000	$380,400	$1,483,200	$1,863,600	$ 80,400	Note 4
5. 1200 Richards Street, 8th & 9th Floors												
18 Months	$14.66Net	Market	47,000	43,519	$806,500	$8.00	$348,152					Note 5
24 Months	$12.00Net	Market	47,000	43,519	$681,500	$8.00	$348,152	$522,300	$1,397,100	$1,919,400	$174,200	Note 5

Notes:

1. 1245 Wacker Avenue did not make an 18 month proposal, but they stated that this would not be a deal-breaker. Proposal provided an option for an additional 18 months and included the Landlord providing preliminary and working drawings.
2. 769 Michigan Drive did not make an 18 month proposal, and again, they expressed a serious interest in ABC Co. If 18 months is required, the upfit allowance would be $0.00 (i.e. that cost would be totally ABC Co.'s). Rent would be $20.10 for year 2 and $20.70 for year 3.
3. 849 Wacker Avenue proposal provides for recarpeting and repainting and an additional upfit allowance of $1.00 per usf. The lease term may be extended to a total of 60 months at a rental rate of $13.00/rsf at the end of the initial lease term.
4. 982 Michigan Drive proposal recognized the possible need to alter 60% of the space and has provided for a renewal term of 36 or 42 months at $16.00/rsf. This is the only proposal to include a computer room which meets ABC Co.'s needs without having to build one from scratch. This proposal includes our subleasing and using the current major tenant's facilities including food service, catering, vending, parking, security, and card access, and includes space planning, construction drawings, building permits, and certificate of occupancy. The above yearly rental includes an existing Computer Room of 3,878 rsf and not all of this space has to be leased.
5. 1200 Richards Street proposal is a *net* of janitorial and utilities which are estimated to be $2.00 to $2.50/rsf. Existing space will be vacated by Jan. 15, 1992 by the current tenant and because of the age of the building and wear on the space, the entire inside of the existing office/warehouse will require *gutting* and is included in the $8.00/rsf. Proposal includes one preliminary drawing and one completed set of construction documents.

EXHIBIT 9.7 Site Evaluation Matrix

ABC COMPANY RELOCATION - NORTHERN CHICAGO, IL.

Evaluation Date: JUNE 18, 1993
Evaluation By: BILL ROBERTS, SUSAN ADAMS, AND WALTER LITTLE.

OFFICE LOCATION/LANDLORD EVALUATION CRITERIA	WEIGHT	SUMMERFIELD/GLENV'. MAYFIELD INVEST. Rating	Score	RICHLAND/NILES FAIRFIELD DEVELOP. Rating	Score	WESTLAKE/SKOKIE WESTLAKE & ASSOC Rating	Score
Total Cost/Value	9.0	9.5	85.5	9.0	81.0	9.0	81.0
Land Cost/Value	7.0	9.0	63.0	8.5	59.5	5.0	35.0
Upfit Cost/Value	8.0	9.5	76.0	8.5	68.0	9.5	76.0
Location	8.0	10.0	80.0	9.0	72.0	8.5	68.0
Building Configuration	6.0	10.0	60.0	8.5	51.0	8.5	51.0
Amenities (Food Service,)	10.0	9.5	95.0	8.5	85.0	8.5	85.0
Free Parking	9.0	9.5	85.5	9.5	85.5	7.0	63.0
Building Services & Security	8.0	9.5	76.0	9.0	72.0	6.0	48.0
Collocation With XYZ Corp.	6.0	6.0	36.0	9.5	57.0	6.0	36.0
Bus Route To & From Site	8.0	9.0	72.0	8.0	64.0	8.0	64.0
Courier Service Available	10.0	9.0	90.0	8.5	85.0	8.5	85.0
Real Property, etc. Taxes	6.0	8.0	48.0	8.0	48.0	8.5	51.0
Housing/Local Labor Market	6.0	8.5	51.0	8.0	48.0	8.0	48.0
Operational Cost Savings	7.0	9.0	63.0	8.0	56.0	8.0	56.0
Human Resources Issues	7.0	8.0	56.0	8.0	56.0	8.0	56.0
Ability To Meet Schedule	10.0	9.5	95.0	9.0	90.0	10.0	100.0
Landlord Resources Avail.	9.0	9.5	85.5	9.5	85.5	10.0	90.0
Overall Landlord Exper.	9.0	9.5	85.5	9.0	81.0	9.0	81.0
Overall Evaluation	8.0	9.5	76.0	9.0	72.0	8.5	68.0
TOTAL SCORE:			1379.0		1316.5		1242.0

Evaluation Notes:
1. Weights are between 0 and 10 (10 being best)
2. Rates are between 0 and 10 (10 being best)
3. Ratings x weights = score

Upfit Notes:
1. Full Turnkey Construction. — $38.00 Per Sq. Ft. For Office & $95.00 For Computer Room. — Full Turnkey Construction.

Information Notes:

	NILES (City & County)	GLENVIEW (City) and SKOKIE (City)
1. TAXES:		
Real Estate	$1.38/$100 + Fire & Rescue Levy	$0.88/$100
Personal Property	$3.75/$100	$4.20/$100
	No Merchants Capital Tax	No Merchants Capital Tax
	Gross Receipts Tax In Effect	Gross Receipts Tax In Effect
2. HOUSING COSTS		
2 Bedroom (Median-1992)	$99,500	$136,000
3 Bedroom (Median-1992)	$107,000	$193,000
2 Bedroom - Rental	$570 per month	$690 per month

§ 9.4 OWN VERSUS LEASE COMPARISON: RISK/RETURN IMPACTS

(a) ORGANIZATIONAL CRITERIA

Historically, senior management has paid little attention to this aspect of company performance, but that attitude is gradually improving.

During the past few years, a number of factors have forced senior managers to look more closely at asset management programs—or the lack thereof—and to recognize their need for corporate real estate professionals.

- Companies became fat and sloppy during the post-World War II period, with major management emphasis on cash flow and expansions and little management emphasis on the asset aspects of production facilities and manufacturing implements. The recession of the 1970s and early 1990s brought a lot of companies back to earth. Many of them were cash poor, and they began to look for ways to trim operations, improve return on assets (ROA) and cash flow—and survive.
- Statement of Financial Accounting Standards No. 13, "Accounting for Lease" (see Chapter 10), issued in November 1976 by the Financial Accounting Standards Board (FASB), changed the manner in which lease obligations could be reported and materially affected the "numbers game" that management and Wall Street traditionally like to play. Management was now forced to consider intently the "lease versus buy" consequences of facility acquisition, and this circumstance increased management visibility for the asset manager.
- Section 388 of the Internal Revenue Code, on investment tax credits, provides a basis for significantly improving a corporation's bottom-line tax position. As a prerequisite to reaping these benefits, however, the corporation must be thoroughly familiar with the rules and, in particular, with specific depreciation and credit allowances and the assets to which they apply. As an article in *Dun's Review* pointed out:

> The most common error is failing to accurately analyze new buildings for their full tax benefits. Under Internal Revenue Service rules, a building generally has a long depreciation life (40 to 45 years) and thus is slow in recovering costs. And, of course, a building itself isn't allowed an investment tax credit.
>
> But under other IRS regulations, many components of a new building do qualify for the 10% tax credit and for much faster depreciation—

machinery connections and foundations, electrical wiring and piping, lighting systems, process temperature controls and plumbing fixtures, to name only a few. Frequently, however, building contractors and subcontractors do not submit fully itemized lists of all these individual parts. As a result, accounting departments often do not get essential information for calculating the company's tax returns.[1]

- Finally, the Securities and Exchange Commission established a requirement (Rule 190), effective in 1976, that all companies with assets of $100 million or over report the current replacement cost of their assets, as well as their historical costs. This requirement has prompted an intensive look at the asset inventory; once again, greater management attention is being given to the asset manager.

Whether the real estate department should be considered a legitimate investment or profit center[2] depends on management's attitude toward accountability, staff-line relationships, profit sharing via performance bonuses, the concept of "captive business," and so forth. Issues relating to organizational and performance measurement have been discussed in previous chapters. The real estate function is unique in the corporate staff structure since its performance is easily capable of measurement. The profit potentials inherent in having a professional real estate department, invite the idea of profit-center accountability and rewards for corporate real estate operations.

The issue of who should own real estate relates to two issues, the first one being the traditional manner in which control of physical assets is assigned to an operating division or group and the resulting return on assets is used as a measure of performance.

In this context, the asset base becomes a critical element in investment center evaluation and sometimes creates a detrimental, short-term attitude toward effective asset management. The general manager may yield to the temptation of surplusing an asset (particularly if a potential capital gain exists) to improve his annual ROA, without adequately considering longer term implications or overall corporate benefits.

On the other hand, the general manager may object to holding a currently unneeded asset on the books to provide for long-term corporate growth considerations.

[1] *Dun's Review,* December 1977, p. 98.

[2] There is a difference between the terms *investment center* and *profit center.* For a more complete discussion of the subject and its applicability to performance measurement, see James S. Reece and William R. Cool, "Measuring Investment Center Performance," *Harvard Business Review* (May–June 1978), pp. 38–154.

Thus, the traditional system tends to foster opportunities for unsound economic discussions and family discord. The disparity in operating objectives becomes significantly more acute in those cases where the operating division or group is required to absorb losses on asset sales but receives no binding cash claim or asset sale gains, with the cash going directly into the general corporate coffers.

The second issue relates to measures that are being taken to blunt the apparent disparities in the traditional asset allocation system. Short-term solutions would include direct credits to division/group managers for asset sale gains and the concurrent opportunity for reinvestment of sale dollars in other business ventures. They could also include a system for asset transfer (at the division/group's request) to the corporate books when a conflict arises between division/group business plan objectives and longer term corporate growth objectives.

For a longer term solution to the problem of corporate real estate ownership, we recommend investigating the merits of a wholly owned, unrestricted, fully consolidated real estate subsidiary that can operate within corporate guidelines and yet show entrepreneurship and profitability to the corporation and its shareholders.

In any event, line operating executives should concentrate on "making their plan" by manufacturing and marketing product lines—*not* by real estate sales.

(b) FINANCIAL ANALYSIS

There are times when management could choose either to own or lease a facility. Within the corporation, the decision is often a factor of corporate policy, politics, operational need, and financial resources. Outside the corporation, the financial, real estate, and construction marketplace may provide a financial opportunity to choose owning rather than leasing. Interest rates may be low, rental rates may be low, and construction costs may be lower than recent historical costs. Changing conditions may dictate a financial opportunity or may confirm previous policies.

If there is a slumping real estate market, low interest rates, low inflation, and low construction costs, an own versus lease feasibility analysis may show that the net cost/break-even point may be over 10 years. In this case, although it is less expensive to lease a facility for 10 years, it may make better business sense to own because of the ongoing capital investments to be made in the facility over the next 10 years that could be lost at the end of a 10-year lease term. But if interest and inflation rates are high and rental rates are moderate, the break-even point for leasing may be at 5 years and the advantage to a long-term lease would be readily apparent.

A shorter time frame break-even point for owning versus leasing may make owning very attractive financially, especially with low interest rates. There may also be a substantial cash difference after the break-even point, and this cash could be used for other business or operational purposes. The longer the time frame to the break-even point, the more likely either decision could prove to be acceptable assuming the corporation has the financial resources and time to select either alternative. But some corporations will not consider a lease scenario unless a 15-year or longer lease term with options can be obtained.

There are a number of variables to consider in the own versus lease comparison. An analysis completed today can be quite different from an analysis made 5 years ago or 5 years in the future depending on the cost of financing, rent payments, operating expenses, escalations, and construction costs. These numbers will not be exactly the same for two similar corporations and should be based on the corporation's financial condition and particular financial leverage in the financial, real estate and construction marketplace.

Example. Exhibit 9.8 reviews a lease versus buy financial analysis for ABC Company's Perimeter Park Site. The Real Estate Analysis includes:

- Using 10% financing.
- Market rate of $15.50/sq. ft.; years 1–5, $21/sq. ft.; year 6, with increases of 2.5%/yr.
- Assumes no land & FF&E.
- Asset life = 31.5 years.
- Tax rate = 34%.
- Operating expense of $5.50/sq. ft. with increases of 2.5%/yr.
- Construction cost = $100/sq. ft.

As you can see in Exhibit 9.8, the break-even point for the "Total Cost/Sq Ft (Before Tax)" occurs during the 5th year. At that point, the cost of ownership becomes less expensive than leasing. The 6th year cost for leasing increases to $21.00/sq. ft., and the cost of ownership is down to $17.91 and dropping. By the 10th year, the cumulative cost savings in owning is over $1,342,000, and the savings continue to increase.

When the variables previously discussed change, the analysis findings and previous conclusions may or may not remain valid. A number of feasibility analyses should be made with a variety of assumptions to review how the changes in variables and assumptions would impact the financial and business decision. To lock in variable costs, the feasibility analysis should be re-run with hard numbers from the finance and facility/construction departments to ensure that the current and/or previous own or lease decision remains valid.

Not included in this analysis is the value of the facility at the end of its asset life (31.5 years) compared with the value of the lease. In some marketplaces, the value of the building at the end of its asset life may

EXHIBIT 9.8 Lease versus Buy Analysis

Assumptions:

- Using 10% Financing
- Market rate of $15.50/sq ft; years 1-5, $21/sq ft; year 6, Incr 2.5%/yr
- Operating expense of $5.50/sq ft; incr 2.5%/yr
- Asset life = 31.5 years
- Tax rate = 34%
- Construction cost = $100/sq ft
- Assumes no land & F F & E

LEASE MODE (Full service lease)	1	2	3	4	5	6	7	8	9	10	11	12	13	14	15
105,000 sq. ft.	1628	1668	1710	1753	1796	2205	2260	2317	2375	2434	2495	2557	2621	2687	2754
PRE TAX COST	1628	1668	1710	1753	1796	2205	2260	2317	2375	2434	2495	2557	2621	2687	2754
TAXES	553	567	581	596	611	750	768	788	807	828	848	869	891	913	936
NET COST	1074	1101	1129	1157	1186	1455	1492	1529	1567	1606	1647	1688	1730	1773	1817
TOTAL COST/SQ FT (Before Tax)	15.50	15.89	16.28	16.69	17.11	21.00	21.53	22.06	22.61	23.18	23.76	24.35	24.96	25.59	26.23
10 YR CUM COST (Before Tax)										20145					
OWNERSHIP MODE															
INTEREST (@ 10%)	1050	1017	983	950	917	883	850	817	783	750	717	683	650	617	583
OPERATING COSTS (beg. @ $5.50/sq ft)	578	592	607	622	637	653	670	686	704	721	739	758	777	796	816
DEPRECIATION	333	333	333	333	333	333	333	333	333	333	333	333	333	333	333
PRE TAX COST (Equivalent Rent)	1961	1942	1923	1905	1887	1870	1853	1836	1820	1805	1789	1774	1760	1746	1733
TAXES	667	660	654	648	642	636	630	624	619	614	608	603	598	594	589
NET COST	1294	1282	1269	1257	1246	1234	1223	1212	1201	1191	1181	1171	1162	1152	1144
TOTAL COST/SQ FT (Before Tax)	18.67	18.49	18.32	18.15	17.98	17.81	17.65	17.49	17.34	17.19	17.04	16.90	16.76	16.63	16.50
10 YR CUM COST (Before Tax)										18803					
NBV AFTER 10 YEARS	10500	10167	9833	9500	9167	8833	8500	8167	7833	7167 7500	7167	6833	6500	6167	5833

have appreciated substantially if it has been well maintained and has been kept clean, current with enhanced building systems, and aesthetically competitive. The market value of the asset above its book value in an appreciating real estate market could provide an opportunity for substantial capital gain and nonoperational income to improve the corporation's bottom line. The corporate finance and operations management departments must exercise great care in choosing how to report such a capital gain and income, both internally and externally.

§ 9.5 CONCLUSION

You have seen throughout this chapter the need for quality information. This information is needed by all levels of corporate management to ensure that well thought out and detailed ownership and leasing decisions are made based on an objective review of the facts surrounding your real property requirements.

EXHIBIT 9.8 *(Continued)*

ABC COMPANY - PERIMETER PARK SITE
REAL ESTATE ANALYSIS
LEASING VS. BUILDING A NEW FACILITY
($000)

B. Smith
7-15-93

YEAR

16	17	18	19	20	21	22	23	24	25	26	27	28	29	30	31	32	TOTAL
2823	2893	2965	3040	3116	3193	3273	3355	3439	3525	3613	3703	3796	3891	3988	4088	2095	90,056
2823	2893	2965	3040	3116	3193	3273	3355	3439	3525	3613	3703	3796	3891	3988	4088	2095	90,056
960	984	1008	1033	1059	1086	1113	1141	1169	1199	1228	1259	1291	1323	1356	1390	712	30,619
1863	1909	1957	2006	2056	2108	2160	2214	2270	2327	2385	2444	2505	2568	2632	2698	1383	59,437
26.88	27.55	28.24	28.95	29.67	30.41	31.17	31.95	32.75	33.57	34.41	35.27	36.15	37.06	37.98	38.93	19.95	
550	517	483	450	417	383	350	317	283	250	217	183	150	117	83	50	17	17,067
836	857	879	901	923	946	970	994	1019	1045	1071	1097	1125	1153	1182	1211	621	27,186
333	333	333	333	333	333	333	333	333	333	333	333	333	333	333	333	167	10,500
1720	1707	1695	1684	1673	1663	1653	1644	1636	1628	1621	1614	1608	1603	1598	1595	804	54,753
585	580	576	573	569	565	562	559	556	553	551	549	547	545	543	542	273	18,616
1135	1127	1119	1111	1104	1098	1091	1085	1080	1074	1070	1065	1061	1058	1055	1052	531	36,137
16.38	16.26	16.15	16.04	15.94	15.84	15.75	15.66	15.58	15.50	15.43	15.37	15.32	15.27	15.22	15.19	7.66	
5500	5167	4833	4500	4167	3833	3500	3167	2833	2500	2167	1833	1500	1167	833	500	167	

In the past, we have often seen corporations use inadequate, incorrect or mis-leading information to tie up substantial corporate resources. The corporate real estate executive has now become a central figure in corporate real estate development and with this responsibility comes the challenge to perform at higher and higher levels of expertise. We trust that the financial responsibilities described and provided herein and throughout this book will support your career goals and your corporations' success as we move toward and into the 21st century.

Ten

Acquiring Real Property

§ 10.1 INTRODUCTION

In 1989, *The Wall Street Journal* sited a study by the Roulac Real Estate Consulting Group of Deloitte & Touche that reported, "Corporations account for almost 75 percent of the nation's real estate capital . . . with $2.6 trillion of equity in plants, warehouses, land and office buildings. . . . [Corporations] are selling some assets and decreasing their vast holdings. They are likely to be much more active in real estate transactions in the future."[1]

Arthur Andersen & Company's Real Estate Services Group reported in 1991, "More than seven billion square feet of building space and four quadrillion square feet of land are owned by corporate America. It is often the most valuable asset on U.S. company balance sheets. As the nation's businesses continue to undergo a fundamental restructuring—through mergers and acquisitions, decentralization, new technologies, changing markets and tightening profits—the pressure is on to better manage corporate real estate and make those assets work harder."[2]

With $2.6 trillion in equity, more than seven billion square feet of building space, and four quadrillion square feet of land owned by corporate America, it appears reasonable that the acquisition of corporate real estate resources and assets should follow certain basic business, real estate, and asset management principles. This chapter presents real estate information about the acquisition of leased and owned corporate assets. As local, national, and global economies and services change, the ability to make informed and financially sound leasing and purchasing decisions becomes more important in protecting acquisitions and assets, and in improving the value of the corporation.

§ 10.2 LEASING REAL PROPERTY

Lease obligations, either present payments or future commitments, represent a considerable financial and legal investment. Corporate real estate staffs probably spend more time negotiating leases and managing a portfolio of existing leases than performing any other single department activity.[3] Skillful performance of this work can save a company many dollars in the leasing function and, just as important, reduce future exposure through lease contract language negotiations.

[1] "The Flow of Money Into Real Estate," *The Wall Street Journal*, July 24, 1989.

[2] Arthur Andersen & Company, Real Estate Services Group, 1991 marketing publication.

[3] See Chapter Three for details of lease portfolio management procedures.

(a) DEFINITIONS AND DISTINCTIONS

A lease may be defined as a legal contract that transfers the right to the use and enjoyment of real property. This contract may be oral or written. In some states, if the use is to continue for more than one year, the contract must be in writing to be enforceable. In other states, a lease for a period of over three years must be in writing. This formality is required by the Statute of Frauds, which, except as modified by state legislation, continues to be the law of the country at large.

The person who leases out property is known as the *landlord,* and the contract is a demise of his or her lands. The person who takes such property is known as the *tenant,* and such a contract is his or her *lease.* A *leasehold,* therefore, is the interest in the real property of the landlord that the tenant acquires through the lease. The landlord is also known as the *lessor,* and the tenant as the *lessee.* Each lease is made for a definite period of time, or term, such as a month, a year, or several years. Such a contract implies that a landlord intends to give up the use and enjoyment of the property to the tenant for the stated length of time. It does not merely imply the use of the property for a particular occasion, for that kind of use is granted by a license and not a lease. A lease must also be distinguished from a simple agreement which contemplates that the parties at some future time will enter into the relationship created by a lease.

A *sublease* is a contract between the original tenant and a subsequent tenant who subleases the property from the original tenant rather than the landlord. The sublease may be for all or a part of the property that the tenant has acquired, but only for a part of the term. It creates a new interest in the premises.

An *assignment* of a lease, however, is a transfer by the original lessee of all or part of the premises for the whole of the term. It creates new interest, but it transfers an existing interest into new hands. The distinction between a sublease and an assignment depends entirely on the duration, not the extent, of the transferred interest (see Exhibit 10.5 for additional lease definitions and distinctions).

(b) SHORT-TERM AND LONG-TERM LEASES

Short-term leases include leasing for a month, or from month to month, or from year to year, or in some cases, for a certain number of years. The amount of time that constitutes the dividing line between a short-term and a long-term lease is indefinite. Custom and usage, however, have generally considered leases that run for but a few years, such as three, five, or seven years, as short-term, whereas leases that run for 10 years, 21 years, 99 years, or 999 years, or any multiple thereof, are always considered long-term leases.

In addition, the long-term lease differs from the short-term lease in form, content, and legal effect. The long-term lease will often be longer and contain more clauses than the short-term lease, and will explain in detail a relationship between two parties that will continue over a long period of time. The term may be so long that neither of the original parties will be alive when it ends. Further, the law tends to imbue the long-term lessee with certain quasi-ownership characteristics, particularly in the case of 99-year leases. Some states require the recording of long-term leases, much in the manner that deeds are recorded. Corporate lease "flexibility" requirements for divisional and regional offices in the late 1980s and 1990s have tended toward the shorter term lease (3 to 5 years) with multiple renewal options. Short-term leases with cancellation (buy-out) clauses for short-term corporate business reasons have also become more evident in the real estate marketplace throughout the United States.

(c) THE FORM OF LEASES AND CONTENT OF LEASE CLAUSES

No prescribed form is necessary in drawing a short-term or long-term lease, and no set arrangement of the various clauses is required. In the last analysis, what is written into a lease is an appropriate wording of previous oral conversations and understandings regarding each particular item of a transaction between the parties. The lease should be prepared by your corporate real estate department and approved by the legal department. Like any other real estate instrument, it is subdivided into different parts. These parts consist of an introductory statement; a description of the property; the term of the lease; details as to the amount of rent and its manner of payment; provisions as to renewals, deposits, and security; and special clauses concerning the rights and liabilities of the parties and the use of the premises. The lease concludes with the signatures, seal, and acknowledgment. The statement includes the date and a proper designation of the parties. A lease between individuals should use their full names; leases between corporations often insert a reference to their places of incorporation. The property description is best set forth by lot number or by metes and bounds and should include (when applicable) the building name, street address, suite number, city, state, and zip code. The term is expressed by giving the total number of years for which the lease is to continue, followed by its beginning and expiration dates.

Most owners try to insert clauses that provide for every possible contingency that may occur over a long period of years to ensure that the lease will never be a cause of loss or danger to themselves or to those who succeed to the title. Such clauses, which should be intelligently and fairly negotiated, deal with the following subjects:

- Option to purchase/options for additional space.
- Constructing buildings.

- Repairs and insurance.
- Condemnation.
- Subordination.
- Assignments and subletting.
- Restrictions.
- Arbitration.
- Terminations and renewals.
- Right to mortgage leasehold.
- Payments of taxes.
- Compliance with municipal ordinances.
- Bankruptcy.
- Use and care of premises.
- Liens and waste.
- Escalations (operating expenses).
- Alterations during lease term.
- Rent commencement.
- Rent abatement.

We will discuss the more important clauses later in this chapter.

(d) THE ADVANTAGES OF LONG-TERM LEASES TO THE OWNER AND THE TENANT

The trend toward the long-term leasehold and away from outright purchase has become very marked for some corporations located in the more valuable sections of the larger cities of this country. In some neighborhoods, the cost of acreage is so high that no improvement erected on the land would produce a sufficiently attractive income unless it were figured over a long period of years. Many owners do not care to part with the title to their property but are unable or unwilling to improve it adequately. Leasing for a long term provides the owner with an immediate and sure source of income. Since the owner is not liable for taxes, assessments, or water charges on the land or building, income from the property is net. He or she retains title and obtains adequate improvements, together with the usual privilege of revaluing the site after a reasonable time and thus increasing the net return. There is no dissipation of the owner's estate, and many such ownerships, retained because of sentimental reasons, remain in a single family for generations. The income thus made available proves a permanent investment for dependents of the owner.

On the other hand, the individual or organization (lessee/tenant) that obtains the property under lease for the purpose of improvement is saved a large capital investment in the land. In this way, the lessee's funds can be employed most effectively toward the contemplated improvement. Corporate tenants are quick to see that obtaining a long-term lease is like borrowing directly from the owner, with interest being paid in the form of rent. This method provides the logical site for improvement, freeing the lessees from short tenancies that have to be renewed, often at increased rentals. Then, too, as the location increases in importance, it becomes more valuable, and the tenant may be able to realize a good profit by selling the lease.

(e) THE LEASING DECISION

The leasing of space is rooted in the same type of philosophy as any other business judgment. Once the primary decision has been made that space is required for facilities, the corporate real estate department will negotiate to fulfill that operating need in the most favorable manner. Exhibit 10.1 depicts the typical logic flow in space acquisition decisions.

It looks simple, we know, but let us stress three decision points in Exhibit 10.1 and illustrate their relationship to the LRP, AOP, and AR procedures discussed in Chapter Three and the site selection procedures discussed in Chapter Seven.

(1) Location Criteria

These considerations (item (1) of Exhibit 10.1) are the primary responsibility of the requester division; the decision is based on criteria described in Chapter Seven. The location decision is usually made separately from the selection of a financing method. That is, the need must first be justified by business plan requirements; the choice of acquisition method follows and is normally a finance department decision based on input from the real estate department and on the corporation's internal cash position.

(2) Lease versus Buy[4]

The acquisition decision is based on study of alternatives (item 2 in Exhibit 10.1), the company's relative cash and tax positions and preferred leased/owned property ratio, the anticipated term of use of the facility, asset risk management factors, the desirability of flexibility, and so

[4] In the mid-1970s, Motorola, Inc., created an innovative lease versus buy program for quick analysis called BOLD (*b*uy *o*r *l*ease *d*ecision making) that is still useful today. See Daniel C. Przybylski, *Buy vs. Lease Decision: Motorola's Approach to Financial Decision Making*, Research Report 18 (Atlanta: Industrial Development Research Council, August 1977).

EXHIBIT 10.1 Logic Flow in Space Acquisition Decisions

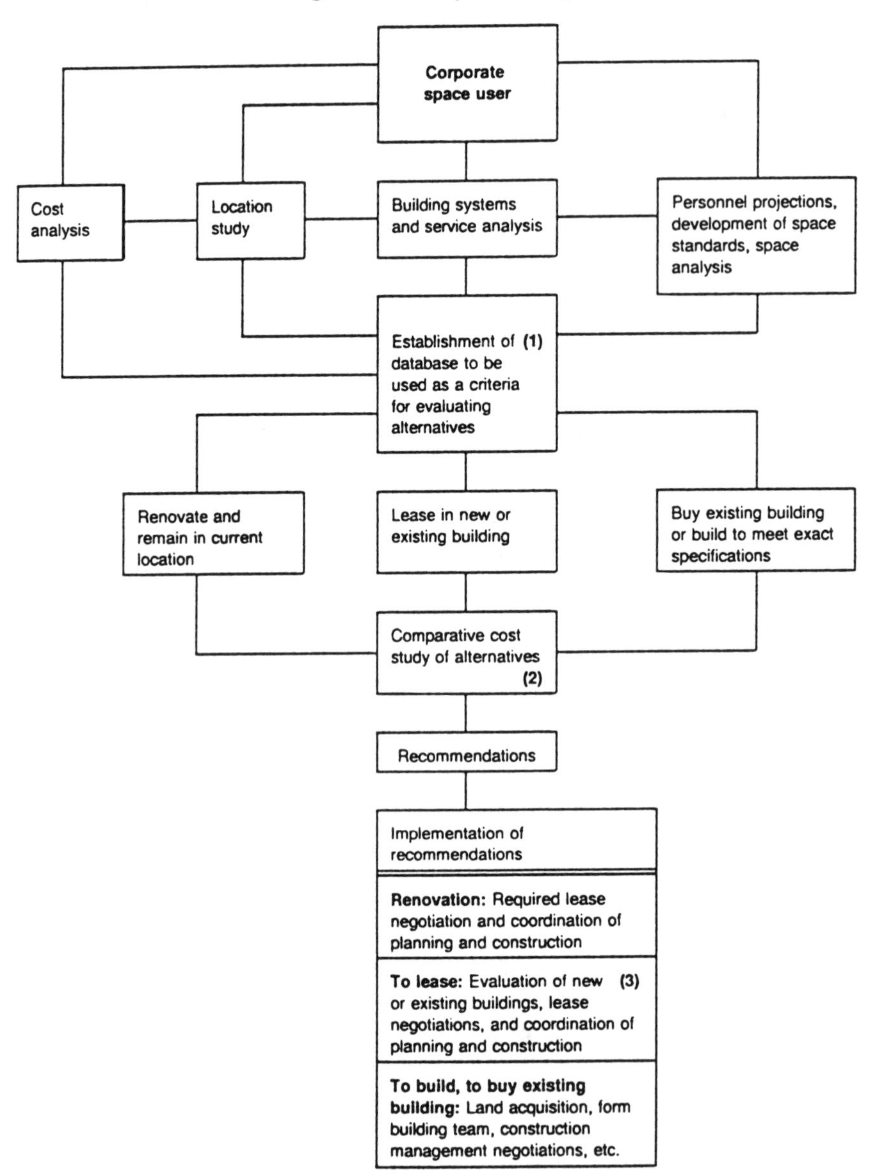

* Items 1, 2, and 3 are critical decision points that are discussed in detail in the text.

forth. Traditionally, facility acquisition through financing leases is most advantageous when the following conditions exist:

- *Tax Shelters.* When the lessee cannot take advantage of additional tax credit and the lessor can, thereby affecting the terms of the lease.
- *Cash Flow.* When the lessee is willing to pay a premium to lease in order to minimize cash outflow or to utilize a fixed cash allocation for other purposes.
- *Cost of Capital.* When a highly developed lessor has a lower cost of capital than does a lessee who is not highly leveraged.
- *Opportunity Cost.* When the yield on the lease provides a good return to the lessor and when more profitable opportunities than buying are available for the funds of the lessee.
- *Asset Appreciation.* When the probability of value appreciation is low or there is decreasing demand for the specific type of asset.
- *"Priceless Asset."* When the lessor is unwilling or unable to sell the asset due to personal desires or legal restrictions.
- *Asset Appraisal.* When testing or experience with the use of an asset is required to provide data for economic evaluation.

The lease versus buy decision involves both qualitative and quantitative analysis. Qualitative decisions are discussed in detail in Chapter Thirteen. The quantitative information requirements include the impact of the asset on the balance sheet, the income statement, the RONA (return on assets) base, and the discounted cash flow.

(3) Capital Leases versus Operating Leases

We mentioned SFAS No. 13 in Chapter Three. It has had an impact on lease versus buy decisions that transcends the objective financial evaluation of the two alternatives and requires in-depth treatment in this chapter.

In November 1976, the Financial Accounting Standards Board (FASB) issued Statement of Financial Accounting Standards No. 13, "Accounting for Lease." This accounting standard requires that leases entered into on or after January 1, 1977, that meet one of the following four criteria must be capitalized:

1. The lease transfers ownership of the property.
2. The lease contains a bargain purchase option.
3. The lease term (the "fixed noncancelable term of the lease") is equal to 75 percent or more of the estimated economic life of the property.

4. The present value of the minimum lease payments (the *noncancelable* rental payments that a company is required to make) is equal to 90 percent or more of the fair value of the leased property, less any related investment credit retained by the lessor.

In addition, this accounting standard requires that leases entered into prior to January 1, 1977, which meet one of these four criteria, must be capitalized by January 1, 1981, if such leases have a material impact on a company's financial statements. Until 1981, when such leases must be capitalized, the standard requires an additional footnote disclosure in a company's annual report.

The following terms are applicable to a capital lease:

- *Bargain Purchase Option.* A provision in the lease allowing a company to buy the property being leased at a price sufficiently lower than the price that would be paid in an arm's-length transaction at the date the provision became exercisable, so that it would be a company's intention at the beginning of the lease to exercise that option.
- *Estimated Economic Life of Leased Property.* The period of time for which a property is expected to be "economically usable" by a company or another user, assuming normal repairs and maintenance, for the purpose intended by the company at the beginning of the lease, ignoring the lease term.
- *Fair Value of the Leased Property.* The price that a company would pay for the leased property in an arm's-length transaction with an unrelated party.

Capitalization criteria 1 and 2 are self-explanatory, and their existence can be determined by examination of the actual lease agreement. Criteria 3 and 4 are more complex and are illustrated in the following simplified examples. In these examples, it has already been determined that the lease does not transfer ownership of the property to the company and that there is no bargain purchase option. The facts for both examples are as follows:

Property Leased	Office building
Lease Term	25 years, 01/01/1994 to 12/31/2019, noncancelable
Lease Payment	$10,000 per year, due January 1 Economic life: 45 years
Fair Value	$185,000

Example 1. Determine whether the lease term is equal to 75 percent or more of the estimated economic life of the property.

$$\frac{\text{Lease term}}{\text{Economic life}} = \frac{25\text{ years}}{45\text{ years}} = 56\%$$

56 percent is less than 75 percent, and therefore the lease term does not qualify it as a capital lease.

Example 2. Determine whether the present value of the minimum lease payments is equal to 90 percent or more of the fair value of the property leased, less any related investment credit retained by the lessor.

$$\frac{\text{Lease term}}{25\text{ years}} \times \frac{\text{Annual rental payment}}{\$10{,}000} = \frac{\text{Minimum lease payments}}{\$250{,}000}$$

The present value of the $250,000 at the inception of the lease, assuming a 6 percent "incremental borrowing rate," would be $128,000.

$$\frac{\text{Present value of the minimum lease payment}}{\text{Fair value}} \quad \frac{\$128{,}000}{\$185{,}000} = 69\%$$

Since 69 percent is less than the 90 percent required by the criterion, the present value of the minimum lease payments does not qualify the lease as a capital lease. In the hypothetical lease used here none of the four characteristics of a capital lease are present, and therefore the lease would be treated as an operating lease.

Most corporate accounting departments have had experience in differentiating between capital and operating leases (current reporting requirements include all companies with $100 million or more in annual sales).

Exhibit 10.2 is designed to assist companies in compiling and maintaining information on leased inventory. We recommend that the accounting department and real estate department coordinate this activity on a continuing basis, whether or not the company is currently required to report the dollar value of capital leases because it adds vigor to lease administration activities.

(4) Lease Negotiations

After looking at a number of locations and making a preliminary choice, the company will receive a proposal letter (*s*ee Exhibit 10.3) that lists the business terms for a lease agreement. This begins the "nuts and bolts" phase of facility acquisition through the negotiation of a lease (item 3 of Exhibit 10.1).

Exhibit 10.4 illustrates a typical tenant-drawn lease for occupancy in a multi-tenant complex. We will go over provisions of the lease and note the most important aspects of the provision to a corporate tenant. The

EXHIBIT 10.2 Lease Information Sheet: Lease No. ______

1. Is this a sale and leaseback arrangement? Yes ____ No ____

2. Who is the lessor? ______________________________

3. What is the lease number? ______________________________

4. Describe the leased property and the company's use of it. ______________________________

   ______________________________.

5. What is the "estimated economic life of the property" in years? ______________________________

6. What interest rate is specified in the lease? ______________________________%

7. If no interest rate is specified, what was the prime rate at the inception of the lease? ______________%

8. Lease term information - furnish the month and year.

	Original lease period	*Renewal option period*
A. Execution date of the lease (when the company signed the lease or exercised the option)..................................	____________	____________
B. Date when the first rental payment was made...............	____________	____________
C. Date when the renewal option may be exercises...........	____________	____________
D. Expiration date of the lease or option...........................	____________	____________
E. Months remaining in the lease or option.......................	____________	____________

9. Is there a cancellation option in the lease? Yes ____ No ____

10. What is the earliest date that such cancellation option may be exercised by the company? ______________

11. What amount of penalty payment or payments is required upon exercise of such a cancellation penalty?

    $ ______________________________ and ______/100 ($ ____________________.______)

12. Has the lease been assigned or the entire property subleased? Yes ____ No ____

13. Is a purchase option available to the company? Yes ____ No ____
    If yes, give the date when the purchase option may be exercised and corresponding purchase price as specified in the lease.

    Date............................... ______________

    Purchase Price................$ ______________

14. Does the lease transfer ownership of the property to the company by the end of the lease?
    Yes ____ No ____

15. What was the fair market value of the leased property at the date that the company entered into the lease?

    $ ______________________________ and ______/100 ($ ____________________.______)

16. Attach any explanation or additional information deemed necessary.

EXHIBIT 10.3 Lease: Sample Proposal Letter

WEST WACKER TOWERS, L.P.

4425 West Wacker Drive
Suite 2100
Chicago, IL 60630
(312) 555-3400

June 30, 1993

Ms. Sandra K. Broker
Vice President - Brokerage
Professional Brokerage Company
304 E. Wacker Drive
Suite 2210
Chicago, IL 60630

Re: West Wacker Towers
Second Floor Lease Proposal
4425 W. Wacker Drive
Chicago, IL 60630

Dear Ms. Broker:

In response to your Request For Proposal dated June 18, 1993, I have been authorized by Westland Development Company, Inc. (Landlord) to submit the following proposal to your client, ABC Company (Tenant), for the leasing of new office space at the referenced location:

PREMISES: Approximately 16,535 rentable square feet (15,683 usable square feet) on the second (2nd) floor known as Suite 200 and as shown in the enclosed Exhibit "A".

COMMENCEMENT: October 1, 1993.

LEASE TERM: Five (5) years - October 1, 1993 to September 30, 1998.

RENEWAL OPTIONS: Two (2) options for five (5) years for each option. Landlord must be notified in writing one hundred eighty (180) days in advance of the end of the current lease term if Tenant elects to remain in the lease space.

RENTAL RATE: $21.00 per rentable square feet which includes a Base Rental component of $13.41 per rentable square foot and an Operating Expense component (expense stop) of $7.59 per rentable square foot.

ESCALATION: On the first day of each lease year, commencing October 1, 1994, the Base Rental component shall be increased by four and one half percent (4.5%). Option period Base Rent and Operating Expense component shall be market.

IMPROVEMENTS: Landlord shall provide to the Tenant an allowance of $17.00 per rentable square feet toward the Tenants improvement of the space. Should Tenant elect to take the option to extend the lease term, Landlord shall provide Tenant an allowance of $ 8.00 per rentable square feet at the beginning of each option period for painting, carpeting and minor alterations.

EXHIBIT 10.3 *(Continued)*

Ms. Sandra K. Broker
June 30, 1993
Page 2

RENT ABATEMENT:	Tenant shall receive twelve (12) free months of Base Rent abatement starting on October 1, 1993 and will begin Base Rental payments effective October 1, 1994. Operating Expenses shall be paid for the term of the lease.
PARKING:	Landlord shall provide to the Tenant three (3) parking spaces per thousand rentable square feet at $10 per month per space through September 30, 1994. Landlord shall provide Tenant five (5) reserved and free spaces for the initial term of the lease on the 1st parking level.
CONF. FACILITIES:	Landlord's 600 square feet conference facilities on the first floor shall be available for reservation by the Tenant at no additional cost.
HEALTH FAC.:	Landlord shall provide five (5) Executive memberships in the West Wacker Towers Health Club at no cost to the Tenant through the end of the initial term of the lease. Landlord shall provide up to seventy-five (75) Standard memberships for Tenant employees in the Health Club at $40 per month per member through September 30, 1994 when these memberships are paid by the Tenant.
SECURITY DEPOSIT:	One (1) month's rent to be held for the term of the lease.
ASBESTOS:	Landlord warrants to the Tenant that the space, building systems and the building contain no friable asbestos.

If the terms and conditions set forth in this proposal are acceptable, please have the proposal executed by your client where indicated below and return one executed copy to my attention not later than 5:00 P.M. (CT), July 6, 1993. Should you have any questions please do not hesitate to contact me.

Sincerely,

Robert A. Thompson
Vice President
Property Management

enclosures

cc: Linda B. Stone (w/enclosures)
W. Wacker/ABC Co. file (w/enclosures)

AGREED AND ACCEPTED:
ABC Company

By:_______________________ Date:_______________

Title:_______________________

EXHIBIT 10.3 *(Continued)*

Exhibit "A"

FLOOR PLAN

(Floor Plan Inserted Here)

EXHIBIT 10.4 Specimen Lease Agreement for ABC Company

LEASE AGREEMENT

This Lease Agreement is made and entered into this 10th day of August, 1993, by and between West Wacker Towers, L.P. an Illinois Limited Partnership ("Landlord"), and ABC Company, a Delaware Corporation ("Tenant").

In consideration of the agreements hereinafter set forth, the parties here to mutually agree as follows:

(1.) DEMISED PREMISES. Landlord hereby leases to Tenant, and Tenant hereby leases from Landlord, certain space (the "demised premises") on the second floor of the Building (the "Building") situated at 4425 West Wacker Drive, Chicago, Cook County, Illinois 60630, assigned Suite #200 (outlined on Exhibit A attached hereto). The demised premises constitute approximately 16,535 square feet of net rentable area.

(2.) TERM. This lease agreement shall be for a term of five (5) years and no (0) months beginning of the Lease Commencement Date, which shall be October 1, 1993, and ending on September 30, 1998 (the "Expiration Date"), provided, however, that in the event the demised premises are not substantially completed in accordance with the provisions of Article 6 by said date, for any reason or cause, then the Lease Commencement Date shall be earlier of (i) the date the demised premises are occupied by Tenant or (ii) the day which is fifteen (15) days after Landlord has certified in writing to Tenant that all work to be performed by Landlord pursuant to Article 6 has been substantially completed, in which event Landlord shall not be liable or responsible for any claims, damages, or liabilities by reason of such delay, nor shall the obligations of Tenant hereunder be affected. In the event the demised premises are occupied by Tenant prior to the Lease Commencement Date, such tenancy shall be deemed to be by the day, and Tenant shall be responsible for payment of monthly rental, for each day of such occupancy prior to the Lease Commencement Date. Within thirty (30) days after the Lease Commencement Date, Landlord and Tenant shall execute Exhibit H attached hereto and made a part hereof by reference confirming the dates of commencement and expiration of the term of this Lease Agreement in accordance with the provisions of this Article 2.

(3.) USE. Tenant will use and occupy the demised premises solely for general purposes, such other purposes as Landlord consents to in writing in advance, and as a part of its present business operations and for uses incidental thereto in accordance with the use permitted under applicable zoning regulations, and for no other purpose. Tenant will not use or occupy the demised premises for any unlawful, disorderly, or hazardous purpose, and will not manufacture any commodity or prepare or dispense any food or beverage therein, without Landlord's written consent. Tenant shall comply with all present and future laws, ordinances, regulations and orders of all governmental authorities having jurisdiction over the demised premises.

(4.) RENTAL. Tenant shall pay to Landlord an annual rental, payable in monthly installments of Twenty-Eight Thousand Nine Hundred Thirty-Seven and 25/100 Dollars ($28,937.25), in advance, on the first day of each calendar month during the term of this Lease, equal to Three Hundred Forty-Seven Thousand Two Hundred Forty-Seven and 00/100 Dollars ($347,247.00) per year for the period beginning with the Lease Commencement Date through September 30, 1992. Beginning on the first anniversary date of the Lease Commencement Date and at each anniversary date thereafter, the annual rental due each year Shall be increased by 4.5%. If the Lease Commencement Date occurs on a day other than the first day of a month, rent from the Lease Commencement Date until the first day of the following month shall be prorated at the rate of one-thirtieth (1/30th) of the monthly rental for each such day, payable in advance on the Lease Commencement Date. Tenant will pay said rent without demand, deduction, set-off or counter-claim by check to Landlord at 4425 West Wacker Drive, Suite 2100, Chicago, IL. 60630 or to such other party or address as Landlord may designate by written notice to Tenant. If Landlord shall at any time or times accept said rent after it shall become due and payable, such acceptance shall not excuse delay upon subsequent occasions, or constitute a waiver of any or all of Landlord's rights hereunder.

5. DEPOSITS. Upon execution of this Lease, Tenant shall deposit with Landlord the sum of Twenty-Eight Thousand Nine Hundred Thirty-Seven and 25/100 Dollars ($28,937.25), as a deposit to be applied against the first month's rent. In addition, Tenant shall pay to Landlord as a security deposit the sum of Twenty-Eight Thousand Nine Hundred Thirty-Seven and 25/100 Dollars ($28,937.25). Such security deposit (which shall bear interest at the then market rate) shall be considered as security for the performance by Tenant of all of Tenant's obligations under this Lease. Upon expiration of the term hereof, Landlord shall (provided that Tenant is not in default under the terms hereof) return and pay back such security deposit including interest to Tenant, less such portion thereof as Landlord shall have appropriated to cure any default by Tenant. In the event of any default by Tenant hereunder, Landlord shall have the right, but shall not be obligated, to apply all or any portion of the security deposit to cure such default, in which event Tenant shall be obligated to deposit with Landlord upon demand therefor the amount necessary to

EXHIBIT 10.4 *(Continued)*

restore the security deposit to its original amount and such amount shall constitute additional rent hereunder. In the event of the sale or transfer of Landlord's interest in the Building, Landlord shall have the right to transfer the security deposit to such purchaser or transferee, Tenant shall look solely to the new Landlord for the return of the security deposit and the transferor Landlord shall thereupon be released from all liability to Tenant for the return of such security deposit.

6. WORK LETTER AGREEMENT. Landlord will finish the demised premises in accordance with the provisions set forth in Exhibit B attached hereto and made a part hereof. Landlord shall have no obligation to make any alterations or improvements to the demised premises except as set forth in Exhibit B.

7. ASSIGNMENT AND SUBLETTING. Tenant may not assign, transfer, mortgage or encumber this Lease, nor shall any assignment or transfer of this Lease be effectuated by operation of law or otherwise, without the prior written consent of Landlord which consent shall not be unreasonably withheld. Tenant may not sublet (or permit occupancy or use of demised premises, or any party thereof) without the prior written consent of Landlord which shall not be unreasonably withheld. If at any time during the term of the Lease, the legal or beneficial ownership in Tenant of fifty percent or more of any of the stockholders, partners or other beneficial owners of Tenant should change, or if the legal entity through which Tenant does business should change, by reason of sale, assignment, transfer, encumbrance, operation of law, reorganization, merger, consolidation, bankruptcy, other disposition or other event, such change shall be deemed and shall constitute an assignment, transfer, mortgage or encumbrance of the Lease, and shall require the prior written consent of the Landlord. If such change of ownership is done without the prior written consent of the Landlord, then Tenant expressly agrees that such change shall be deemed and shall constitute a default of Tenant under the Lease and Landlord may, at its sole option, elect to pursue any of the remedies set forth in Article 20 of this Lease. In the event that Tenant defaults hereunder, Tenant hereby assigns to Landlord the rent due from any subtenant of Tenant and hereby authorizes each such subtenant to pay said rent directly to Landlord. The consent by Landlord to any assignment, transfer, or subletting to any party shall not be construed as a waiver or release of Tenant from the terms of any covenant or obligation under this Lease, not shall the collection or acceptance of rent from any such assignee, transferee, subtenant or occupant constitute a waiver or release of any covenant or obligation contained in this Lease, nor shall any assignment or subletting be construed to relieve Tenant from obtaining the consent in writing of Landlord to any further assignment or subletting.

(8.) MAINTENANCE BY TENANT. Tenant shall keep the demised premises and the other fixtures and equipment therein in clean, safe and sanitary condition, will take good care thereof, will suffer no waste or injury thereto, and will, at the expiration or other termination of the term of this Lease, surrender the same, broom clean, in the same order and condition in which they are on the commencement of the term of this Lease, except for ordinary wear and tear and damage by the elements, fire and other casualty not due to the negligence of the Tenant, its employees, invitees, agents, contractors and licensees; and upon such termination of this Lease, Landlord shall have the right to re-enter and resume possession of the demised premises. Tenant shall make all repairs to the demised premises caused by any negligent act or omission of Tenant, or its employees, invitees, agents, contractors and licensees.

(9.) ALTERATIONS. Tenant will not make or permit anyone to make any alterations, additions or improvements, structural or otherwise (hereinafter referred to as "Alterations"), in or to the demised premises or the Building, without the prior written consent of Landlord which consent shall not be unreasonably withheld. If any mechanic's lien is filed against the demised premises, or the Building for work or materials done for, or furnished to, Tenant (other than for work or materials supplied by Landlord), such mechanic's lien shall be discharged by Tenant within ten (10) days thereafter, at Tenant's sole cost and expense, by the payment thereof or by the filing of any bond required by law. If Tenant shall fail to discharge any such mechanic's lien, Landlord may, at its option, discharge the same and treat the cost thereof as additional rent hereunder, payable with the monthly installment of rent next becoming due and such discharge by Landlord shall not be deemed to waive the default of Tenant in not discharging the same.

Tenant will indemnify and hold Landlord harmless from and against any and all expenses, liens, claims or damages to person or property which may or might arise by reason of the making by Tenant or any Alterations. If any Alteration is made without the prior written consent of Landlord, Landlord may correct or remove the same, and Tenant shall be liable for all expenses so incurred by Landlord. All Alterations in or to the demised premises or the Building made by either party shall immediately become the property of the Landlord and shall remain upon and be surrendered with the Demised Premises as a part thereof at the end of the term hereof; provided, however, that if Tenant is not in default in the performance of any of its obligations under this Lease, Tenant shall have the right to remove, prior to the expiration of the term of this Lease, all movable furniture, furnishings or equipment installed

EXHIBIT 10.4 *(Continued)*

in the demised premises at the expense of Tenant, and if such property of Tenant is not removed by Tenant prior to the expiration or termination of this Lease, the same shall at Landlord's option, become the property of the Landlord and shall be surrendered with the demised premises as a part thereof. Should Landlord elect that Alterations installed by Tenant be removed upon the expiration or termination of this Lease, Tenant shall remove the same at Tenant's sole cost and expense, and if Tenant fails to remove the same, Landlord may remove the same at Tenant's expense and Tenant shall reimburse Landlord for the cost of such removal together with any and all damages which Landlord may sustain by reason of such default by Tenant, including cost of restoration of the premises to their original state, ordinary wear and tear excepted.

10. SIGNS, SAFES AND FURNISHINGS. No sign, advertisement or notice shall be inscribed, painted, affixed or displayed by Tenant on any part of the outside or the inside of the Building except on the doors of offices, and then only in such place, number, size, color and style as is approved by Landlord, and if any such sign, advertisement or notice is exhibited, without Landlord's approval which approval shall not be unreasonably withheld, Landlord shall have the right to remove the same and Tenant shall be liable for any and all expenses incurred by Landlord by said removal. Any such permitted use, including directories and name plates, shall be at the sole expense of Tenant. Landlord shall have the right to prescribe the weight and position of safes and other heavy equipment or fixtures that Tenant desires to install in the demised premises. Any and all damage or injury to the demised premises or the Building caused by moving the property of Tenant into or out of the demised premises, or due to the same being on the demised premises, shall be repaired by and at the sole cost of Tenant. No furniture, equipment or other bulky matter of any description will be received into the building or carried in the elevators except as approved by Landlord. All moving of furniture, equipment and other material within the public areas shall be at such times and conducted in such manner as Landlord may reasonably require in the interests of all tenants in the Building. Tenant agrees to remove promptly from the loading docks and sidewalks adjacent to the Building any of Tenant's furniture, equipment or other property.

11. ENTRY FOR REPAIRS AND INSPECTION. Unless due to an emergency, Landlord will provide reasonable notice for Tenant to permit Landlord, or its representatives, to enter the demised premises, without diminution of the rent payable by Tenant, to examine, inspect and protect the same, and to make such alterations and/or repairs as in the judgement of Landlord may be deemed necessary, or to exhibit the same to prospective tenants during the last one hundred twenty (120) days of the term of this Lease.

12. INSURANCE RATING. Tenant will not conduct or permit to be conducted any activity or place any equipment in or about the demised premises, which will, in any way, increase the rate of insurance premiums on the Building; and if any increase in the rate of insurance premiums is stated by the insurance company or by the applicable Insurance Rating Bureau to be due to any activity or equipment in or about the demised premises, such statement shall be conclusive evidence that the increase in such rate is due to such activity or equipment and as a result thereof, Tenant shall be liable for such increase, as additional rent hereunder, and shall reimburse Landlord therefor.

(13.) TENANT'S FIXTURES AND EQUIPMENT. Tenant will not install or operate in the demised premises any electrically operated equipment or other machinery, other than electric typewriters, adding machines, radios, televisions, tape recorders, calculators, dictaphones and clocks, without first obtaining the prior written consent of Landlord, which consent shall not be unreasonably withheld, who may condition such consent upon the payment by Tenant of additional rent in compensation for such excess consumption of utilities (including additional air conditioning costs) and for the cost of additional wiring, if any, as may be occasioned by the operation of said equipment or machinery. Tenant shall not install any other equipment of any kind or nature whatsoever which may necessitate any changes, replacements or additions to, or in the use of, the water, heating, plumbing, air conditioning, or electrical systems of the Building without first obtaining the prior written consent of Landlord which consent shall not be unreasonably withheld. Business machines and mechanical equipment belonging to Tenant which cause noise or vibration that may be transmitted to any part of the Building to such a degree as to be objectionable to Landlord or to any tenant in the Building shall be installed and maintained by Tenant, at Tenant's expense, on vibration eliminators or other devices sufficient to eliminate such noise and vibration.

(14.) INDEMNITY AND PUBLIC LIABILITY INSURANCE. Tenant will indemnify and hold harmless Landlord from and against any loss, damage or liability occasioned by or resulting from any default hereunder or any willful or negligent act on the part of Tenant, its agents, employees, contractors, licensees, or invitees. Tenant shall obtain and maintain in effect at all times during the term of this Lease, a policy of comprehensive public liability insurance naming Landlord and any mortgagee of the Building as additional insureds, protecting Landlord, Tenant and any such mortgagee against any liability for bodily injury, death or property damage occurring upon, in or about any part of the Building or the demised premises arising from any of the items set forth in this Article 14

EXHIBIT 10.4 *(Continued)*

against which Tenant is required to indemnify Landlord with such policies to afford protection to the limit of not less that Five Hundred Thousand Dollars ($500,000) with respect to bodily injury or death to any one person, to the limit of not less than One Million Dollars ($1,000,000) with respect to any one accident, and to the limit of not less than Five Hundred Thousand Dollars ($500,000) with respect to damage to the property of any one owner. Such insurance policies shall be issued by responsible insurance companies licensed to do business in the State of Illinois. Neither the issuance of any insurance policy required under this Lease, nor the minimum limits specified herein with respect to Tenant's insurance coverage, shall be deemed to limit or restrict in any way Tenant's liability arising under or out of this Lease. The term "Landlord" as used in this Article 14, shall be deemed to include in all instances not only West Wacker Towers, L.P., but also Universal Financial Life, Inc. and its assigns as the owner of the Building.

(15.) SERVICES AND UTILITIES. As long as Tenant is not in default under any of the provisions of this Lease, Landlord shall provide the following facilities and services to Tenant without additional charge to Tenant (except as otherwise provided herein):

(1) Automatically operated elevator service.

(2) Restroom facilities and necessary lavatory supplies, including hot and cold running water, at those points of supply provided for general use of other tenants in the Building, and routine maintenance, cleaning, painting, and electric lighting service for the Building in the manner and to the extent that is standard for first-class office buildings in the Chicago, Illinois metropolitan area.

(3) Heating, ventilating, air conditioning and electricity as is customary in first-class office buildings in the Chicago, Illinois metropolitan area, provided that it is understood that heating, air conditioning and ventilation may be operated only during the hours from 7:30 A.M. to 6:00 P.M (CT) Monday through Friday, exclusive of generally recognized holidays and on Saturdays from 7:30 A.M. to 12:30 P.M. (CT).

(4) Access to the demised premises on a full-time, twenty-four hour basis, subject to such reasonable regulations Landlord may impose for security purposes.

(5) Provide janitorial services after 5:00 P.M. weekdays exclusive of generally recognized holidays.

Any failure by Landlord to furnish the foregoing services as a result of governmental restrictions, energy shortages, equipment breakdowns, maintenance, repairs, strikes, scarcity of labor or materials, or from any cause beyond the control of Landlord, shall not render Landlord liable in any respect for damages to either person or property, nor be construed as an eviction of Tenant nor work an abatement of rent, nor relieve Tenant from Tenant's obligations hereunder. If the Building equipment should cease to function properly, Landlord shall use reasonable diligence and make best efforts to repair the same promptly.

16. RESPONSIBILITY FOR DAMAGE TO DEMISED PREMISES. All injury or damage to the demised premises or the Building caused by Tenant or its agents, employees, contractors, licensees, and invitees, shall be repaired by Tenant at Tenant's sole expense. If Tenant shall fail to do so upon reasonable demand, Landlord shall have the right to make such repairs or replacements, and any cost so incurred by Landlord shall be paid by the installment of rent next becoming due under the terms of this Lease. All injury or damage to the demised premises or the Building caused by the willful or negligent act of Landlord, or its agents or employees, shall be the responsibility of Landlord and shall be repaired with due diligence and as soon as practicable, at Landlord's sole expense, and in no event shall Tenant be liable for any such injury or damage caused by the willful or negligent act of Landlord.

17. LIABILITY FOR DAMAGE TO PERSONAL PROPERTY AND PERSON. All personal property of Tenant, its employees, agents, contractors, licensees, and invitees in the demised premises shall be and remain at their sole risk. Landlord shall not be liable for any damage to or loss of such personal property arising from any act or negligence of any person, or from any cause other than any damage or loss resulting directly from the negligence of Landlord. Landlord shall not be liable for any interruption of loss to tenant's business, and shall not be liable for any personal injury to Tenant, its employees, agents, contractors, licensees, or invitees, arising from the use, occupancy and condition of the demised premises other than from the negligence of Landlord. Notwithstanding the foregoing, Landlord shall not be liable to Tenant for any loss or damage to personal property, or injury to person, whether or not the result of Landlord's negligence to the extent that Tenant is compensated therefor by Tenant's insurance.

EXHIBIT 10.4 *(Continued)*

(18.) FIRE AND OTHER CASUALTY DAMAGE TO DEMISED PREMISES. If the demised premises shall be damaged by fire or other casualty, other than the willful fault or neglect of Tenant, Landlord shall as soon as practical after such damage occurs repair such damage (taking into account the time necessary to effectuate a satisfactory settlement with any insurance company) at the expense of Landlord, and the rent shall be reduced in proportion to the extent the demised premises are rendered untenantable until such repairs are completed. No compensation or reduction of rent will be allowed or paid by Landlord by reason of inconvenience, annoyance, or injury to business arising from the necessity of repairing the demised premises or any portion of the Building.

19. BANKRUPTCY OR INSOLVENCY. If a petition shall be filed, either by or against Tenant, in any court or pursuant to any federal, state or municipal statute, whether in bankruptcy, insolvency, for reorganization or arrangement, for the appointment of a receiver of Tenant's property or because of any general assignment made by Tenant of Tenant's property for the benefit of Tenant's creditors, then after the happening of any such event or in the case of an involuntary petition, then (if such petition is not discharged within sixty (60) days from the filing thereof), Landlord shall have the right, at its option, to terminate this Lease by sending written notice to Tenant, in which event Landlord shall be entitled to immediate possession of the demised premises and to recover damages from Tenant in accordance with Article 20 thereof.

(20.) DEFAULT OF TENANT. If Tenant shall fail to pay any monthly installment of rent as aforesaid or shall violate or fail to perform any of the other conditions, covenants or agreements herein made by Tenant, and if such violation or failure shall continue for a period of ten (10) days after written notice thereof to Tenant by Landlord, or if Tenant shall abandon or vacate the demised premises before the Expiration Date of this Lease, then and in any of said events Landlord shall have the right, at its election, then or at any time thereafter while such event of default shall continue, either:

(i) To give Tenant written notice that Landlord has elected to terminate this Lease on the date of such notice or on any later date specified therein, and on the date specified in such notice Tenant's right to possession of the demised premises shall cease and this Lease shall thereupon be terminated; or

(ii) Without demand or notice, to re-enter and take possession of the demised premises, or any part thereof, and reposes the same as of Landlord's former estate and expel Tenant and those claiming through or under Tenant and remove the effects of both or either, by summary proceedings, or by action at law or in equity or by force (if necessary) or otherwise, without being deemed guilty of any manner of trespass and without prejudice to any remedies for arrears of rent or breach of covenant. If Landlord elects to re-enter under this clause, Landlord may terminate this Lease, or from time to time, without terminating this Lease, may relet the demised premises, or any part thereof, as agent for Tenant for such term or terms and at such rental or rentals and upon such other terms and conditions as Landlord may deem advisable, with the right to make alterations and repairs to the demised premises. No such re-entry or taking of possession of the demised premises by Landlord shall be construed as an election on Landlord's part to terminate this Lease unless a written notice of such intention is given to Tenant under clause (i), above, or unless the termination thereof be decreed by a court of competent jurisdiction at the instance of the Landlord. Tenant waives any right to the service of any notice of Landlord's intention to re-enter provided for by any present or future law.

If Landlord terminates this Lease pursuant to this Article 20, Tenant shall remain liable (in addition to accrued liabilities) for (i) the (A) rent and all other sums provided for in this Lease until the date this Lease would have expired had such termination not occurred, and (B) any and all reasonable expenses incurred by Landlord in re-entering the demised premises, repossessing the same, making good any default of Tenant, painting, altering or dividing the demised premises, putting the same in proper repair, protection and preserving the same by placing therein watchmen and caretakers, reletting the same (including any and all attorney's fees and disbursements and brokerage fees incurred in so doing), and any and all expenses which Landlord may incur during the occupancy of any new tenant; less (ii) the net proceeds of any reletting prior to the date when this Lease would have expired if it has not been terminated. Tenant agrees to pay to Landlord the difference between items (i) and (ii) of the foregoing sentence with respect to each month during the term of this Lease, at the end of such month. Any suit brought by Landlord to enforce collection of such difference for any one month shall not prejudice Landlord's right to enforce the collection of any difference for any subsequent month. In addition to the foregoing, and without regard to whether this Lease is terminated, Tenant shall pay to landlord all costs incurred, including reasonable attorney's fees with respect to any successful lawsuit or action taken instituted by Landlord to enforce the provisions of this Lease. Landlord shall have the right, at its sole option, to relet the whole or any part of the demised premises for the whole of the unexpired term of this Lease, or longer, or from time to time for shorter periods, for any rental then obtainable, giving such concessions of rent and making such repairs, alterations, decorations and paintings for

EXHIBIT 10.4 *(Continued)*

any new tenant as Landlord, in its sole and absolute discretion, may deem advisable. Tenant's liability as foresaid shall survive the institution of summary proceeding and the issuance of any warrant thereunder. Landlord shall be under no obligation to relet the demised premises but agrees to use reasonable efforts to do so. If Landlord terminates this Lease pursuant to this Article 20, Landlord shall have the right, at any time, at its option, to require tenant to pay Landlord, on demand, as liquidated and agreed final damages in lieu of Tenant's liability for damages hereunder, the rent and all other charges which would have been payable from the date of such demand to the date when this Lease would have expired the demised premises for the same period. If the demised premises shall have been relet for all or part of the remaining balance of the term by Landlord after a default but before presentation of proof of such liquidated damages, the amount of rent reserved upon such reletting, absent proof to the contrary, shall be deemed the fair rental value of the demise premises for purposes of the forgoing determination of liquidated damages. Upon payment of such liquidated and agreed final damages, Tenant shall be released from all further liability under this Lease with respect to the period after the date of such demand. For purposes of this Article 20, the term rent shall include monthly rental, additional rent and all other charges to be paid by Tenant under this Lease. All rights and remedies of Landlord under this Lease shall be cumulative and shall not be exclusive of any other rights and remedies provided Landlord under applicable law.

21. WAIVER. If under the provisions hereof Landlord shall institute proceedings and a compromise pr settlement thereof shall be made, the same shall not constitute a waiver of any covenant herein contained nor of any of Landlord's rights hereunder. No waiver by Landlord of any breach of any covenant, condition or agreement herein contained shall operate as a waiver of such covenant, condition, or agreement itself, or of any subsequent breach thereof. No payment by Tenant or receipt by Landlord or a lesser amount than the monthly installments of rent stipulated shall be deemed to be other than on account of the earliest stipulated rent nor shall any endorsement or statement on any check or letter accompanying a check for payment of rent or any other amounts owed to Landlord be deemed an accord and satisfaction and Landlord may accept such check or payment without prejudice to Landlord's rights to recover the balance of such rent or other amount owed or to pursue any other remedy provided in this Lease. No re-entry by Landlord, and not acceptance by Landlord of keys from Tenant, shall be considered an acceptance of a surrender of this Lease.

22. ATTORNMENT. Tenant understands that Universal Financial Life, Inc., as Owner of the Building, has mortgaged the Building to the Fidelity National Bank, Limited (Mortgagor), San Francisco Branch. Tenant further understands that Owner and any future mortgagee will agree not to disturb Tenant's rights and possession so long as Tenant is not in default hereunder, and that any purchaser and of said property under foreclosure of other suit or proceeding shall take said property subject to this Lease. Tenant further agrees to execute such subordination and attornment agreements or other similar instruments as may be required by Landlord or such mortgagee. It is further understood and agreed that in the event of default of Owner under its mortgage with Mortgagor, Mortgagor or any other party who becomes landlord hereunder by virtue of any such default may, at such party's sole option, require Tenant to pay as additional rent for each year of the lease commencing with the year of default its proportionate share (being the percentage that the square feet of net rentable space occupied by it bears to the entire rentable space in the Building) of any increase in operating expenses and real estate taxes for the base year. For this purpose, the base year is defined to be the calendar year 1991, and such base year costs and rental year costs shall be as determined by Owner's accountant. In the event the final lease year does not coincide with the base year, Tenant shall pay a percentage of such proportionate part equal to the number of days occupancy divided by the number of days in the year.

23. CONDEMNATION. If the whole or a substantial part of the demised premises shall be taken or condemned by any governmental authority for a public or quasi-public use or purpose, then the term of this Lease shall cease and terminate as of the date when title vests in such governmental authority, or if earlier, the date of occupancy by such authority, and the rent shall be abated on such date. If less that a substantial part of the demised premises is taken or condemned by any governmental authority for any public or quasi-public use or purpose, the rent shall be equitably adjusted on the date when title vests in such governmental authority and this Lease shall otherwise continue if full force and effect. For purposes hereof, a substantial part of the demised premises shall be considered to have been taken if more than fifty percent (50%) of the demised premises are unusable by Tenant. In the case of any such taking or condemnation, whether or not involving the whole or a substantial part of the demised premises. Tenant shall have no claim against Landlord or the condemning authority for any portion of the amount that may be awarded as damages as a result of such taking or condemnation or for the value of any unexpired term of this Lease, and Tenant hereby assigns to Landlord all its rights, title and interest in and to any such award; provided, however, that Tenant may assert any claim that it may have against the condemning authority for compensation for any fixtures owned by Tenant and for any relocation expenses compensable by stature, and receive such awards therefor as may be allowed in the condemnation proceeding if such

EXHIBIT 10.4 *(Continued)*

awards shall be made in addition and state separately from the award made for the land and the Building or the part thereof so take.

24. RULES AND REGULATIONS. Tenant, its agents, employees, invitees, contractors, and licensees shall abide by and observe the rules and regulations attached hereto as Exhibit C. Tenant, its agents, employees, invitees, contractors, and licensees shall abide by and observe such other rules or regulations as may be promulgated from time to time by Landlord for the operation and maintenance of the Building provided that the same are in conformity with common practice and usage in similar buildings and are not inconsistent with the provisions of the Lease and a copy thereof is sent to Tenant. Nothing contained in the Lease shall be construed to impose upon Landlord any duty or obligation to enforce such rules and regulations, or the terms, conditions or covenants contained in any other lease, as against any other tenant, and Landlord shall not be liable to Tenant for violation of the same by any other tenant, its employees, agents, contractors, invitees, or licensees.

(25.) RIGHT OF LANDLORD TO CURE TENANT'S DEFAULT: LATE PAYMENTS. If Tenant defaults in the making of any payment or in the doing of any act herein required to be made or done by Tenant, then after ten (10) days' notice from Landlord, Landlord may, but shall not be required to, make such payment or do such act, and the amount of the expense thereof, if made or done by Landlord, with interest thereon at the rate of the prime interest rate charged by the Chicago National Bank during the period of such default plus two percent (2%) per annum (hereinafter referred to as the "Default Interest Rate"), from the date paid by Landlord, shall be paid by Tenant to Landlord and shall constitute additional rent hereunder due and payable with the next monthly installment of rent; but the making of such payment or the doing of such act by Landlord shall not operate to cure such default or to estop Landlord from the pursuit of any remedy to which Landlord would otherwise be entitled. If Tenant fails to pay any installment of rent on or before the first day of the calendar month when such installment is due and payable, such unpaid installment shall bear interest at the rate of the Default Interest Rate, from the date such installment became due and payable to the date of payment thereof by Tenant. Such interest shall constitute additional rent hereunder due and payable with the next monthly installment of rent. In addition, Tenant shall pay to Landlord, as a "late charge", five percent (5%) of any payment herein required to be made by Tenant which is more than ten (10) days late or cover the costs of collecting amounts past due.

26. NO PARTNERSHIP. Nothing contained in this Lease shall be deemed or construed to create a partnership or joint venture of or between Landlord and Tenant or to create any other relationship between the parties hereto other than that of Landlord and Tenant.

27. NO REPRESENTATION BY LANDLORD. Neither Landlord nor any agent or employee of Landlord has made any representations or promises with respect to the demised premises or the building except as herein expressly set forth, and no rights, privileges, easements or licenses are granted to Tenant except as herein set forth. Tenant, by taking possession of the demised premises, shall accept the same "as is" and such taking of possession shall be conclusive evidence that the demised premises are in good and satisfactory condition at the time of such taking or possession.

28. BROKERS. Tenant represents and warrants that it has not employed any broker other than Professional Brokerage Company in carrying on the negotiations relating to this Lease. Tenant shall indemnify and hold Landlord harmless from and against any claim for brokerage or other commission arising against any claim for brokerage or other commission arising from or out of any breach of the foregoing representation and warranty. Any representation or statement by a leasing company or other third party (or employee thereof) engaged by Landlord as an independent contractor which is made with regard to the demised premises or the Building shall not be binding upon Landlord or serve as a modification of this Lease and Landlord shall have no liability therefor, except to the extent such representation is also contained herein or is approved in writing by Landlord.

29. NOTICE. All notices or other communications hereunder shall be in writing and shall be deemed duly given if delivered in person or sent by certified or registered mail, return receipt requested, first class, postage prepaid, (i) if to Landlord: West Wacker Towers, L.P.
4425 West Wacker Drive
Suite 2100
Chicago, IL 60630
Attention: Vice President - Property Management

EXHIBIT 10.4 *(Continued)*

and (ii) if to Tenant: ABC Company
4425 West Wacker Drive
Suite 200
Chicago, IL 60630
Attention: Vice President of Corporate Real Estate

unless notice of change of address is given pursuant to the provisions of this Article 29.

30. ESTOPPEL CERTIFICATE. Tenant agrees, at any time and from time to time, upon not less than five (5) days prior written notice by Landlord, to execute, acknowledge and deliver to Landlord a statement in writing (i) certifying that this Lease has been unmodified since its execution and is in full force and effect (or if there have been modifications, that this Lease is in full force and effect, as modified, and stating the modifications), (ii) stating the dates, if any, to which the rent and sums hereunder have been paid by Tenant, (iii) stating whether or not to the knowledge of Tenant, there are then existing any defaults under this Lease (and, if so, specifying the same), and (iv) stating the address to which notices to Tenant should be sent. Any such statement delivered pursuant hereto may be relied upon Landlord or any prospective purchaser or mortgagee of the Building or any part thereof or estate therein. Tenant also agrees, at any time or times after Tenant has assumed possession of the demised premises, upon not less than five (5) days' prior written notice by Landlord, to execute, acknowledge and deliver to West Wacker Towers, L.P. an "estoppel statement" in the form attached hereto as Exhibit D inserting the appropriate information in the blank spaces therein and making any changes thereto (if any) that are necessary to make the statements contained therein letter correct.

(31.) COVENANTS OF LANDLORD. Landlord covenants that it has the right to make this Lease and that if Tenant shall pay the rental and perform all of Tenant's obligations under this Lease, Tenant shall, during the term hereof, freely, peaceably and quietly occupy and enjoy the full possession of the demised premises without molestation or hindrance by Landlord or any party claiming through or under Landlord. In the event of any sale or transfer of Landlord's interest in the demised premises, the covenants and obligations of Landlord hereunder accruing after the date of such sale or transfer shall be imposed upon such successor-in-interest (subject to the provisions of Article 22 hereof) and any prior Landlord shall be freed and relieved of all covenants and obligations of Landlord hereunder accruing after the date of such sale or transfer.

32. LIEN FOR RENT. Tenant hereby grants to Landlord a lien on all property of Tenant now or hereafter placed in or on the demised premises (except such part of any property as may be exchanged, replaced, or sold from time to time in the ordinary course of business) and such property shall be and remain subject to such lien of Landlord for payment of all rent and all other sums agreed to be paid by Tenant herein or for services or costs relating to the demised premises that Tenant may hereafter agree to pay to Landlord. Said lien shall be in addition to and cumulative of the Landlord's lien rights provided by law.

33. HOLDOVER. In the event that Tenant continues to occupy the demised premises after the expiration of the term of this Lease, with the written consent of Landlord, such tenancy shall be from month to month at 125% of the yearly rental at the end of the term of the Lease and shall not be a renewal of the term of this Lease or a tenancy from year to year.

34. PARKING. Landlord grants to Tenant the right to park fifty (50) automobiles for no additional monthly rental for the first year of the Lease term and Landlord grants to Tenant the right to park five (5) automobiles for no additional rental for the balance of the Lease term on parking levels 1, 2 and 3 as set forth in Exhibit E. Starting October 1, 1993 through the balance of the term of the Lease, Landlord grants to Tenant the right to park forty-five (45) automobiles for additional rent which shall be the then market rate for comparable parking in a Class A office building in the Chicago, IL metropolitan area. Nothing herein shall be construed to grant to tenant the exclusive right to a particular parking space, and at such appropriate, Landlord may rearrange parking spaces or may provide assigned spaces, and may provide attendant parking or such other system of management of parking as it deems necessary. Landlord shall not be liable to Tenant, its invitees, employees or guests because of failure to promptly remove snow, ice or water from the parking area and/or structure or because of any injury or damage that may be sustained due to holes of defects that may develop or arise in the parking areas or due to any inconvenience that may arise due to temporary closure of parking areas for repair, maintenance or snow, ice or water removal.

35. GENDER. Feminine or neuter pronouns shall be substituted for those of masculine form, and the plural shall be substituted for the singular number, in any place or places herein in which the context may require such substitution.

EXHIBIT 10.4 *(Continued)*

36. BENEFIT AND BURDEN. The provisions of this Lease shall be binding upon and inure to the benefit of the parties hereto and each of their permitted successors and assigns. Landlord may freely and fully assign its interest hereunder.

37. ENTIRE AGREEMENT. This Lease, together with the Exhibits and any Addenda attached hereto, contain and embody the entire agreement of the parties hereto, and no representations, inducements, or agreements, real or otherwise, between the parties not contained in this Lease, Addenda (if any) and Exhibits, shall be of any force or effect. This Lease may not be modified, changed or terminated in whole or in part in any manner other than by an agreement in writing duly signed by both parties hereto.

(38.) COMPLIANCE WITH GOVERNMENTAL REQUIREMENTS. Tenant agrees that Tenant has received and will keep the demised premises and all appurtenances thereto, in good, safe, tenantable, and sanitary conditions; that Tenant will promptly comply with and carry out all laws, ordinances, rules, regulations, and requirements (including zoning by all federal, state, municipal, and county governments) relating to the demised premises and /or the business conducted therein; and that Tenant will indemnify Landlord against any and all liability for damage to person and property caused by the breach of any covenant or agreement of Tenant contained in this lease. Tenant recognizes that neither Landlord nor Agent makes any representation, expressed or implied, that the demised premises are zoned for the uses(s) contemplated by Tenant and expressed in this lease, Tenant being satisfied before executing and delivering this lease that the demised premises can be used for such purpose.

(39.) OPTION TO RENEW. Landlord shall provide the Tenant with one (1) Option to renew the Lease for an additional five (5) year term which shall commence on October 1, 1998 and terminate on September 30, 2003. Tenant shall notify the Landlord a minimum of 180 calendar days in advance of the beginning of the Option date should Tenant choose to exercise this Option to extend the Lease. Should Tenant choose to exercise this Option, Tenant shall pay a monthly rental equal to the then market rate for a Class A office building with a one mile radius of the Building. Should Tenant choose to exercise this Option, Landlord shall provide to Tenant a painting and carpet allowance of $5.00 per usable square foot to be completed by Tenant within one year of the Option date.

(40.) TAXES. Landlord shall pay (before delinquent) all real property taxes and general special assessment ("real property taxes") levied and assessed against the premises.

Tenant shall pay before delinquency all taxes, assessments, license fees, and other charges ("taxes") that are levied and assessed against Tenant's personal property installed or located in or on the premises, and that become payable during the term. On demand by Landlord, Tenant shall furnish Landlord with satisfactory evidence of these payments.

Tenant shall pay its *pro rata* share (7.8 percent) of the increase in real property taxes over a base year, calculated as follows: the base year on the unimproved land assessment will be in 1991, and the base year on the improvements thereto when occupied at 80 percent of building capacity. Tenant shall pay this share of taxes within 15 days after receipt of a copy of the tax bills from the Landlord.

41. SPECIAL STIPULATIONS. Landlord and Tenant agree to the following special stipulations to this Lease which shall take precedence over other Articles in this Lease:

(1) Tenant shall pay to Landlord as additional monthly rent the direct cost of additional of operating and providing above Building standard air conditioning and electrical services to the Tenant's Computer Room in Space 231. This additional rent shall be determined by multiplying the gallons of additional chilled water provided to Tenant's Computer Room air conditioning units times a cost of chilled water not to exceed $0.05 per gallon for the first year of the Lease and electrical usage within the Computer Room for all items except general purpose lighting and general purpose electrical wall outlets shall be on a separate electrical meter and billed to Tenant at the Landlord's cost.

(2) Landlord shall provide to the Tenant, at no additional rental for the term of the Lease, use of the Building's 250 square foot Conference Room which Landlord shall construct at no additional cost to the Tenant. The Conference Room shall be located on the first floor of the Building adjacent to the public rest rooms, as shown and specified on Exhibit F, and shall be available for Tenant use on a first come basis from 7:30 AM to 6:00 PM Monday through Friday and from 7:30 AM to 12:30 PM on Saturday.

EXHIBIT 10.4 *(Continued)*

(3) Landlord shall provide to the Tenant, at no additional rental for the term of the Lease, use of the Buildings unattended Fitness Facility which shall be available for Tenant use on a first come basis from 6:00 AM to 8:00 PM Monday through Friday and from 7:00 AM to 4:30 PM on Saturday and Sunday. The Fitness Facility is located on the ground floor of the Building as shown on Exhibit G.

(4) Landlord shall provide the Tenant with nine (9) months of Rental Abatement commencing on October 1, 1993 and ending on June 30, 1994. Tenant shall pay as monthly rental during this Rent Abatement period Tenant's share of 1993 Operating Expenses which are $6.45 per rentable square feet which shall be Eight Thousand Eight Hundred Eighty-Seven and 56/100 Dollars ($8,887.56).

In WITNESS WHEREOF, Tenant and Landlord have each executed this Lease as of the day and year first above written.

TENANT:
ABC Company

Attest: By: ______________________

______________________ Its: Vice President

(Corporate Seal)

LANDLORD:
WEST WACKER TOWERS, L.P.

Attest: By: ______________________

______________________ Its: General Partner

EXHIBIT 10.4 *(Continued)*

EXHIBIT "A"

FLOOR PLAN(S)

(Insert Floor Plan(s) Here)

EXHIBIT 10.4 *(Continued)*

EXHIBIT "B"

WORK LETTER AGREEMENT

In consideration of the terms and conditions of the Lease, the work shown in Exhibit "A" to this Lease Agreement and in the terms and conditions hereinafter contained, Landlord and Tenant agree as follows:

A. **Landlord's Standard Work**

1. Landlord has selected certain building standard materials and building standard designs for the Premises (hereinafter "Landlord's Standard Work"). Except as provided in Section B of this Work Letter Agreement, Landlord shall furnish and install Landlord's Standard Work in the Premises. Landlord's Standard Work shall include the following:

   a. **Partitions** - (number of) lineal feet of floor-to-finished-ceiling drywall partitions with 5/8" gypsum board and 4" vinyl cove base molding.

   b. **Painting** - Two (2) coats on partitions throughout the Public Areas, Core and Premises, in colors selected by Tenant from Landlord's standard paint colors and not more than two (2) colors in any one (1) room or space.

   c. **Ceilings** - Suspended 2' x 2' tegular acoustical ceiling installed in accordance with the building standard design. Ceiling height 9' - 0".

   d. **Lighting Fixtures** - (number of) recessed 2' x 4' fluorescent lighting fixtures installed in accordance with the building standard lighting design with three (3) fluorescent tubes per fixture.

   e. **Sprinkler System** - A sprinkler system including recessed sprinkler heads in accordance with the building standard sprinkler design and with City of Chicago Bureau of Buildings requirements.

   f. **Heating, Ventilating and Air-Conditioning (HVAC)** - A heating, ventilating and air conditioning system, including ducts, supply distribution and return air plenum. The Building Standard mechanical and electrical system is designed to accommodate loads generated by lights and equipment up to a maximum of 3.5 watts per square foot in specific areas (e.g. word and data processing areas, copying rooms, mail rooms, kitchens, special equipment areas) in the Premises.

   g. **Doors** - (number of) 3' - 0" wide x 8' - 6" high x 1 3/4" thick full height, solid core, oak veneer faced doors with frames, hinges, doorstops and latch sets. The entrance door to the Premises and all public corridor doors shall each have a lock set and closer.

   h. **Electrical and Telephone Outlets** - (number of) 120 volt duplex electrical outlets and (number of) telephone outlets not including wiring, equipment or fixtures customarily furnished by telephone suppliers. A single floor mounted device may contain one duplex electrical outlet, one telephone outlet, two duplex electrical outlets, two telephone outlets, or one duplex electrical outlet and one telephone outlet. Although provided through a single device, each shall be counted separately for purposes of determining the number of outlets Landlord is obligated to provide. Telephone conduit provided by Landlord is minimum 3/4" and maximum 1" in diameter. Landlord has not included any work, outlets or conduit in this Work Letter for Tenant's computer cabling. Should Tenant require additional outlets for computer cabling, Landlord shall charge Tenant a separate fee for such outlets. Tenant or Tenant's independent contractor shall provide and install computer cabling and where such cabling is in the return air plenum, Tenant shall ensure that such computer cable meets the City of Chicago's fire and smoke rating requirements.

   i. **Carpeting** - Carpeting throughout the Premises shall be of a type and color selected by the Tenant from Landlord's standard types and colors.

   j. **Sun Control** - Landlord shall provide 1" aluminum horizontal blinds on all exterior windows. All such blinds shall be manufacturer's standard design, style and color as selected by the Landlord.

EXHIBIT 10.4 *(Continued)*

k. **Public and Core Areas** - Landlord shall provide public and core areas within the Building as outlined in Exhibit "A", and finished in accordance with plans and specifications for the Building.

l. **Floor** - Landlord shall provide finished concrete prepared to receive floor covering. Floor loading capacities: 50 pounds per square foot live load, 20 pounds per square foot partition load or per square foot in non-partitioned areas.

B. Tenant's Non-Standard Work

1. Tenant may request work in addition to or different from Landlord's Standard Work (hereafter "Tenant's Non-Standard Work").

2. Landlord shall, upon Tenant's request in accordance with Sections C and D of this Work Letter Agreement, install the following Tenant's Non-Standard Work:

   a. Quantities and qualities of Landlord's Standard Work in excess of those provided by Landlord.

   b. Lighting fixtures, sprinklers and/or any mechanical equipment in other than Building standard design locations due to the location of partitions.

   c. Additional mechanical and electrical equipment and controls required by Tenant's design or use of the Premises generating loads in excess of those described in subparagraph A.1.f. of this Work Letter Agreement.

   d. Tenant's computer and telecommunication equipment, cabinets, modems, switching units, consoles and terminal boards.

   e. Tenant may request Landlord to install any other Tenant's Non-Standard Work in accordance with Section C and D of this Work Letter Agreement including by not limited to substitution of materials or change in design from Landlord's Standard Work. Any such request shall be subject to the written approval of Landlord, which Landlord may reasonably withhold.

   f. Landlord shall, upon Tenant's request and at Tenant's expense, alter, remove and/or replace acoustical ceiling tiles or exposed mechanical suspension system after initial installation due to installation of Tenant's computer, telephone or intercommunication system.

   g. All Tenant's Non-Standard Work shall be located within the Premises except were permitted by the Landlord in writing.

3. Improvements Constructed by Tenant: If any Work is to be performed in connection with improvements to the Premises by Tenant or Tenant's contractor:

   a. Such work shall proceed upon Landlord's written approval of (i) Tenant's contractor, (ii) public liability and property damage insurance carried by Tenant's contractor, and (iii) detailed plans and specifications for such work.

   b. All work shall be dome in conformity with a valid building permit when required, a copy of which shall be furnished to Landlord before such Tenant's work is commenced, and in any case, all such work shall be performed in accordance with all applicable governmental regulations. Notwithstanding any failure by Landlord to object to any such work, Landlord shall have no responsibility for Tenant's failure to meet all applicable regulations.

   c. All work by Tenant or Tenant's contractor shall be done with Union labor in accordance with all Union Labor agreements applicable to the trades being employed.

   d. All work by Tenant or Tenant's contractor shall be scheduled through Landlord.

   e. Tenant or Tenant's contractor shall arrange for necessary utility, hoisting and elevator service with Landlord's Contractor and shall pay such reasonable charges for such services as may be charged by Landlord's Contractor.

EXHIBIT 10.4 *(Continued)*

f. Tenant's entry to the Premises for any purpose, including without limitation, inspection or performance of Tenant construction by Tenant's agents, prior to the Lease Commencement Date as specified in Paragraph 2 of the Lease shall be subject to all the terms and conditions of the Lease except the payment of Rent. Tenant's entry shall mean entry by Tenant, its officers, contractors, licensees, agents, employees, guests, invitees or visitors.

g. Tenant shall promptly reimburse Landlord upon demand for any extra expense incurred by Landlord by reason of faulty work done by Tenant or its contractors, or by reason of any delays caused by such work, or by reason of inadequate clean-up.

C. Responsibilities Of Landlord And Tenant

1. Time is of the essence with regard to the responsibilities of Landlord and Tenant under this Work Letter Agreement.

2. On or before (month, day, year) hereinafter known at the Preliminary Plan Delivery Date, Tenant shall provide Landlord with all necessary information, including all specifications and requirements for any Tenant's Non-Standard Work, to enable Landlord and/or Landlord's Architect to prepare a fully dimensioned floor plan and a reflected ceiling plan showing the location of the following:

   a. Partitions, doors, electrical, telephone and computer outlets;

   b. Equipment requiring electrical power, such as copiers, appliances, word processors, computers, printers, computer related equipment, and clocks;

   c. Furniture, fixtures, including trade fixtures, refrigerators, ice makers, coffee makers, microwave ovens, ovens, range hoods, can openers, water coolers, disposers, stoves, vending machines, cabinets and counters;

   d. Plumbing fixtures;

   e. Lighting;

   f. Special finishes to floors, walls and ceilings; and

   g. Special mechanical, electrical, or structural requirements, special features, facilities or additions.

3. From the information provided by Tenant, Landlord and/or Landlord's Architect shall prepare a fully dimensioned preliminary floor plan and reflected ceiling plan which Landlord shall submit to Tenant.

4. Tenant shall have ten (10) calendar days to review and approve the preliminary plans. Tenant shall also, at or prior to the time of approval, select paint color(s) and carpet type(s) and color(s) from Landlord's standard types and colors, and provide Landlord with any additional information Landlord needs in order to prepare working drawings and specifications.

5. Following Tenant's approval of the above preliminary plans and selections, and Landlord's receipt of necessary information, Landlord and/or Landlord's Architect and Engineer shall prepare working drawings and specifications which Landlord shall submit to Landlord.

6. Tenant shall have five (5) calendar days to review and approve the working drawings and specifications. Tenant shall also, at or prior to the time of approval, select paint color(s) and carpet type(s) and color(s) from Landlord's standard types and colors, and provide Landlord with any additional information Landlord needs in order to prepare working drawings and specifications.

7. Following Tenant's approval of the above working drawings and specifications and if Tenant has not requested Tenant's Non-Standard Work, Landlord shall, authorize Landlord's Contractor to commence construction.

8. If Tenant has requested and Landlord has granted necessary approvals for Tenant's Non-Standard Work, Landlord have the requested work incorporated into the working drawings and specifications and Landlord

EXHIBIT 10.4 *(Continued)*

shall obtain a firm price for the Tenant's Non-Standard Work from the Landlord's Contractor. Landlord will provide Tenant the firm price for the above Work and Tenant shall review and approve Landlord's Contractor's price within five (5) calendar days. Upon Tenant's written approval of Landlord's Contractor's price, Landlord shall authorize Landlord's Contractor to commence construction. In the absence of such written approval, Landlord shall not be required to authorize commencement of construction.

9. Tenant shall be responsible for delays in completion of the Premises and additional costs in Landlord' Standard Work and Tenant's Non-Standard Work caused by:

   a. Tenant's failure to provide information or approvals in a timely manner;

   b. Request for materials, finishes or installations other than Landlord's Standard Work;

   c. Tenant's changes in any plans, drawings or specifications; and

   d. Inaccuracies, omissions, or changes in any information provided by Tenant. Delay in completion of Landlord's Standard Work or Tenant's Non-Standard Work for any of the foregoing reasons shall be considered the fault of Tenant and shall not serve to extend the Commencement Date under Paragraph 2 of the Lease.

10. If Tenant shall request any change after construction commencement, Tenant shall request in writing to Landlord and such request shall be accompanied by all plans and specifications necessary to show and explain changes from the approved working drawings and specifications. After receiving this information, Landlord shall give Tenant a written estimate of the maximum cost of engineering and design services to prepare working drawings and incorporate the changes in accordance with such request. If Tenant approves such estimate in writing, Landlord shall have such working drawings prepared and Tenant shall reimburse Landlord for the cost thereof not in excess of such estimate. Promptly upon completion of such working drawings, Landlord shall obtain a cost, if any, for the change from Landlord's Contractor and Landlord shall notify Tenant in writing of the cost, if any, which will be chargeable or credited to Tenant for such change, addition or deletion. Tenant shall within fine (5) calendar days notify Landlord in writing to proceed with such change addition or deletion. In the absence of such notice, Landlord shall proceed in accordance with the working drawings and specifications prepared pursuant to the previously approved working drawings and specifications.

11. No Landlord's Standard Work or Tenant's Non-Standard Work shall be performed by Tenant or Tenant's contractor unless approved in writing by Landlord.

D. Financial

1. If Tenant does not request any Tenant's Non-Standard Work, Landlord shall install and furnish Landlord's Standard Work at Landlord's expense, including expense related to preparation of the fully dimensioned preliminary floor plan, reflected ceiling plan, and the working drawings and specifications.

2. If Tenant requests Tenant's Non-Standard Work, Tenant shall pay Landlord all costs related to Tenant's Non-Standard Work, including but not limited to:

   a. The cost of professional services (including services of architects, interior designers, engineers and consultants) required to incorporate Tenant's Non-Standard Work into the working drawings and specifications;

   b. The cost of materials other than Landlord's Standard Work materials and the cost of installing such materials; and

   c. The cost of structural changes in the Building.

   Whether or not Tenant requests Tenant's Non-Standard Work, Tenant shall not be entitled to an credits whatsoever for Landlord's Standard Work not utilized by Tenant.

EXHIBIT 10.4 *(Continued)*

3. Following commencement of construction, Landlord shall bill Tenant monthly for the cost of Tenant's Non-Standard Work. Tenant shall pay Landlord the entire amount of each statement within ten (10) calendar days after receipt.

4. Notwithstanding Paragraphs 6 and 9 of the Lease, any sums payable by Tenant to Landlord under this Work Letter Agreement which shall not be paid upon the due date shall bear interest at a rate equal to the Prime Rate as determined by First Bank of Chicago plus one (1) percentage point, as the rate may vary from time to time.

TENANT:
ABC COMPANY

By:____________________________

Title: Vice President

Date:____________________________

LANDLORD:
WEST WACKER TOWERS, L.P.

By:____________________________

Title: General Partner

Date:____________________________

EXHIBIT 10.4 *(Continued)*

EXHIBIT "C"

RULES & REGULATIONS

1. **Common Areas.** The sidewalks, halls, passages, exits, entrances, elevators, and stairways of the Building shall not be obstructed by any of the tenants or used by them for any purpose other than for ingress to and egress from their respective premises. The halls, passages, exits, entrances, elevators and stairways are not intended for use by the general public and Landlord shall in all cases retain the right to control and prevent access thereto of all persons whose presence in the judgment of Landlord would be prejudicial to the safety, character, reputation or interest of the Building, Landlord or tenants, provided that nothing herein contained shall be construed to prevent access by persons with whom any tenant normally deals in the ordinary course of its business, unless such persons are engaged in illegal activities.

2. **Use and Occupancy of Premises.** For the safety, efficiency and protection of the tenants and the Building, Tenant shall not, nor permit any employee, agent, or invitee of Tenant to use its Premises for:

   a. Storage of merchandise held for sale to the general public;

   b. Lodging;

   c. Cooking except for private use by Tenant or its employees with Underwriters Laboratory approved equipment for brewing coffee, tea or hot chocolate. Such limited quantities shall be only stored in containers approved by appropriate regulatory agencies;

   d. Use or keeping or storing any kerosene, gasoline or inflammable or combustible fluid or material other that limited quantities thereof reasonably necessary for the operation or maintenance of office equipment, foul or noxious gas or substance;

   e. The business of stenography, typewriting, printing or photocopying or any similar business for the service or accommodation of occupants of any other portion of the Building, unless specifically authorized in the Lease:

   f. Any use which would be reasonably offensive to other tenants or Landlord or which would tend to create a nuisance or damage the reputation of the Premises or Building.

3. **Prohibited Activities.** Tenant shall not, nor permit any employee, agent or invitee of Tenant to:

   a. Interfere in any way with other tenants or those having business in the Building:

   b. Use in its Premises of ice, drinking water, beverages, or catering service except at such reasonable hours and under such reasonable regulations as may be fixed by Landlord;

   c. Bring into the Building or keep within its Premises any birds or animals other than seeing eye dogs and like animals;

   d. Load any floor beyond the point considered safe by a competent engineer or architect selected by the Landlord.

   e. Use any method of heating or air conditioning other than that provided by the Landlord;

   f. Attach or install curtains, draperies, blinds, shades, sun control devices, screens on or adjacent to any window or glass situated within its Premises without Landlord's written consent which shall not be unreasonably withheld.

   g. Use in the Building or its Premises any hand trucks except those equipped with rubber tires and side guards or such other material handling equipment without Landlord's prior written consent;

   h. Operate any television, radio, recorder or sound system in such a manner as to cause a nuisance to any other tenant of the Building;

EXHIBIT 10.4 *(Continued)*

i. Engage in any activity which would make it impossible to insure the Premises against casualty, would increase the insurance rate, or would prevent Landlord from taking advantage of any ruling of the State and local regulatory insurance agencies and Landlord's insurance company, unless Tenant pays the additional cost of insurance.

4. **Tenant Requirements.** Tenant shall, and shall require its employees and agents to:

   a. Keep window coverings in its Premises closed when the effect of sunlight or cold weather would impose unnecessary loads on the Building's heating or air conditioning system;

   b. Keep the doors to Building corridors closed at all times except for ingress and egress and ensure that the doors of its Premises are closed and locked and that all water faucets, water apparatus and utilities are shut off before leaving the Premises each day; and

   c. Store all its trash and refuse within its Premises. No material shall be placed in trash boxes of receptacles if such material is of such nature that it may not be safely disposed of in the customary manner of removing and disposing of office build trash and refuse in the City of Chicago without being in violation of any law or ordinance governing such disposal. All trash and refuse disposal shall be made only through entrances and elevators provided for such purposes and at such times as Landlord shall designate.

5. **Keys and Locks.** Landlord will furnish each tenant two keys to each entry door lock to its Premises. Landlord may make a reasonable charge for any additional keys. Tenant shall not have any such keys duplicated. Tenant shall not alter any lock, install a new or additional lock or any bolt on any door of its Premises. Upon the Termination of the lease, Tenant shall deliver to Landlord all keys to doors in the Premises.

6. **Janitorial Service.** Tenant shall not employ, authorize or permit any person, persons or firm other that the janitor of the Landlord for the purpose of cleaning its Premises. Landlord shall not be responsible to any tenant for any loss of property on the premises, however occurring, or for any damage done to the effects of any tenant by the janitor or any other employee or any other person. Janitor service will not be furnished on nights when rooms are occupied after 6:00 P.M. unless, by prior agreement in writing, service is extended to a later hour for specifically designated rooms.

7. **Use of Service Elevator.** The Landlord shall designate appropriate entrances and a "service" elevator for deliveries or other movement to or from the Premises of equipment, materials, supplies, furniture or other property, and Tenant shall not use any other entrances or elevators for such purposes. The service elevator shall be available for use by all tenants in the Building, subject to such reasonable scheduling as Landlord at its discretion shall deem appropriate.

8. **Movement of Equipment.** All persons employed by the Tenant who have the means or methods to move equipment, materials, supplies, furniture or other property in or out of the Building must be approved by Landlord prior to any such movement. Landlord shall have the right to prescribe the method of protection to the Building, lobbies, corridors, elevator and Premises to be provided by the Tenant before such movement and prescribe the maximum weight, size and positions of all equipment, materials, furniture or other property brought into the Building. Heavy objects shall, if considered necessary by Landlord, stand on a platform of such thickness as is necessary to properly distribute the weight. Landlord will not be responsible for loss of or damage to any such property from any cause, and all damage done to the Building by moving or maintaining such property shall be repaired at the expense of the Tenant.

9. **Building Services** . Landlord establishes the hours 8:00 A.M. to 6:00 P.M. (CST) of each weekday and 8:00 A.M. to 1:00 P.M. (CST) on Saturdays, as reasonable and usual business hours for the purposes of this Lease. If Tenant requests heat or air conditioning during any hours other than the above and if Landlord is able to provide the same, Tenant shall pay Landlord such charges as Landlord shall establish from time to time for providing such services during such hours. Any such charges which Tenant is obligated to pay shall be deemed to be additional rent under this Lease, and should Tenant fail to pay the same within twenty (20) days after demand invoice, such failure shall be a default by Tenant under this Lease.

10. **Access to Building After Hours.** Landlord reserves the right to exclude from the Building all persons who do not present identification acceptable to Landlord between the hours of 6:00 P.M. and 7:00 A.M. (CST) and at all hours on Saturdays, Sundays and legal holidays. Tenant shall provide Landlord with a list of all persons authorized by Tenant to enter its Premises and shall be liable to Landlord for all acts of such persons. Landlord shall in no case be liable for damages for any error with regard to the admission to or exclusion from the

EXHIBIT 10.4 *(Continued)*

Building of any person. In the case of invasion, mob, riot, public excitement or other circumstances rendering such action advisable in Landlord's opinion, Landlord reserves the right to prevent access to the Building during the continuance of the same by such action as Landlord may deem appropriate.

11. **Building Directory.** A building directory will be provided for the display of the name and location of tenants and a reasonable number of the principal officers and employees of tenants. Landlord reserves the right to restrict the amount of directory space utilized by any tenant.

12. **Rest Room Use.** Rest rooms and all fixtures and apparatus located therein shall not be used for any purpose other than that for which they were constructed.

13. **Tenant's Requests.** Special requests of tenants will be considered only upon receipt of a written and signed application on Tenants letterhead stationary addressed to the Landlord. Landlord reserves the right to deny and such special requests. Employees of Landlord shall not perform any work or do anything outside of their regular duties unless under special instructions from Landlord.

14. **Canvassing in the Building.** Canvassing, soliciting, distribution of handbills or any other written material and peddling in the Building are prohibited, and Tenant shall cooperate to prevent the same.

15. **Signs.** No sign, placard, picture, name, advertisement or notice visible from the exterior of any tenant's premises shall be inscribed, painted, affixed or otherwise displayed by any tenant on any part of the Building without the prior written consent of Landlord. Landlord will adopt and furnish to tenants general guidelines relating to signs inside the Building. Tenant agrees to conform to such guidelines. All approved signs or lettering on doors shall be printed, painted, affixed or inscribed at the expense of the Tenant by a person approved by Landlord. Material visible from outside the Building will not be permitted without the prior written consent of Landlord.

16. **Building Name and Street Address.** Landlord shall have the right, exercisable without notice and without liability to any tenant, to change the name or street address of the Building.

17. **Landlord Access.** Landlord shall, at reasonable hours, have the right to enter premises leased to tenants, to examine same or to make such alterations and repairs as may be deemed necessary, or to exhibit the same to prospective tenants.

18. **Noise and Building Utilization.** Tenants shall not make or permit any improper noises in the Building, or otherwise interfere in any way with other tenants, or person having business with them.

19. **Rules and Regulations.** Landlord may waive any one or more of these Rules and Regulations for the benefit of any particular tenant or tenants, but no such waiver by Landlord shall be construed as a waiver of such Rules and Regulations in favor of any other tenant or tenants, or prevent Landlord from thereafter enforcing any such Rules and Regulations against any or all of the tenants of the Building. These Rules and Regulations are in addition to, and shall not be construed to in any way modify or amend, in whole or in part, the agreements, covenants, conditions and provisions of any lease of premises in the Building. Landlord reserves the right to make such other rules and regulations as in its judgement may from time to time be needed for the safety, care and cleanliness of the Building, for the preservation of good order therein, and to meet and require tenants to observe and comply with additional Federal, State and local regulations as they pertain to the tenant's occupancy of the Building and the tenant's Premises.

■

EXHIBIT 10.4 *(Continued)*

EXHIBIT "D"

ESTOPPEL CERTIFICATE

____, of

____, the Tenant, gives

this estoppel certificate to ____,

of ____, the Purchaser. The

Tenant has entered into a lease dated ______________, with ______________________________,

as Landlord, for the following space: ____

____.

The Purchaser has requested the information and representations in this certificate with regard to the Lease because it wishes to acquire an interest in the property known as ______________________________, which includes the property that is subject to the Lease. The Tenant acknowledges that the Purchaser intends to rely on the information and representations the Tenant makes in this certificate in Purchaser's acquisition of the property.

The Tenant stated as follows:

1. A copy of all documents that constitute its Lease are attached to this certificate, and there are no understandings or verbal agreements that affect or amend the terms of the Lease.

2. The monthly Base Rate payments under the Lease are $ ______________________, with additional rent due under the Lease as follows: ____

____.

3. The Lease term ends on ______________________________, with the following renewal options:

____.

4. To the best knowledge of Tenant, no notice has been received by Tenant of any default which has not been cured.

5. The Lease is in full effect.

Dated: ______________________________ ______________________________

Tenant

EXHIBIT 10.4 *(Continued)*

EXHIBIT "E"

PARKING PLANS FOR LEVELS 1, 2 AND 3

(Insert Parking Plans Here)

EXHIBIT 10.4 (continued)

EXHIBIT "F"

CONFERENCE ROOM PLAN

(Insert Conference Room Plan Here)

EXHIBIT 10.4 (continued)

EXHIBIT "G"

FITNESS FACILITY PLAN

(Insert Fitness Facility Plan Here)

EXHIBIT 10.4 *(Continued)*

EXHIBIT "H"

COMMENCEMENT DATE AGREEMENT

An Agreement made this ______ day of ________________, 19____, by and between __________________ ____________________________ (hereinafter called "Landlord") and ____________________________________ (hereinafter called "Tenant").

WITNESSETH:

WHEREAS on ____________________, 19_____, Landlord and Tenant entered into a lease (the "Lease") relating to certain office premises located at ____; and

WHEREAS the term of the Lease has commenced, pursuant to Section ____ of the Lease; and

NOW, THEREFORE, in consideration of the mutual covenants herein contained, Landlord and Tenant agree as follows:

1. The Term Commencement Date of the Lease is ____.
2. Tenant's obligation to pay Rent under the Lease commenced on ______________________________.
3. The Term Expiration Date of the Lease is ____.
4. The execution of this Agreement shall not constitute the exercise by Tenant of any option it may have to extend the term of the Lease.
5. The Lease is in full force and effect and is hereby ratified and confirmed.

IN WHEREAS WHEREOF, Landlord and Tenant have caused this Agreement to be duly executed on the date first written above.

Landlord: ________________________________ Tenant: ____

numbers accompanying each lease clause discussed in the text refer to the corresponding numbers on clauses in the specimen lease, Exhibit 10.4. Exhibit 10.5 reviews a number of clauses not covered in this specimen lease form, such as cancellation penalty.

Under *Demised Premises* (1) and *Term* (2) it is important that the premises actually leased be adequately defined and that you and the landlord agree on the definitions. This provision should include information on whether the space is to be leased as is, whether leasehold improvements are to be installed, or whether the space is to be built to suit your specifications. In the last two instances, the timing for the completion of construction must be set forth. If the construction or installation of leasehold improvements is to be completed within the specified period, excluding causes beyond the control of the landlord, it is imperative to obtain the right to walk away from the lease before the lease is executed. Penalties for excessive delays have also been imposed on landlords to reimburse tenants as "damages" for costs that the tenants have probably incurred in anticipation of the promised occupancy date. If a lease concerns a build-to-suit facility, a letter of acceptance or commencement addendum executed by both parties should set forth the commencement and termination dates of the lease. The company should not execute such a document until the premises have been fully readied for the start of business, since the document indicates acceptance of the premises. The corporate real estate executive should make certain that all inspections have been made, that the completion items on the company's "punch list" have been satisfied, and that signing authority has been delegated appropriately.

Every landlord desires the *Use* (3) clause to be as specific as possible to eliminate problems with his or her insurance carrier, but it is to the advantage of a large corporate tenant to demand that the use allowance be as broad as possible to permit possible changes in the scope of the tenant's operations and possible subleases. Therefore, any landlord should accept a change from, say, "to be used for the sales and repair of *power tools*" to "to be used for the sales, storage, and repair of *tenant's products.*" If the landlord accepts such a change, it is essential that the tenant be assured that existing zoning laws permit such uses.

When drafting a lease on behalf of a tenant, it is important to delete any restriction against withholding *Rental* (4) in order to induce the landlord to maintain the premises. If the landlord insists that such a restriction be in the lease, and if needed structural repairs are not made by the landlord after the tenant has given notice and after the landlord has been given a reasonable amount of time in which to make such repairs, it is worthwhile in many instances for the tenant to make the necessary *minimum* repairs and to withhold the amounts expended from future rentals. We do not advocate doing this except in instances where the landlord's neglect poses a threat to human life or has caused considerable damage to the tenant's personal property.

EXHIBIT 10.5 Lease Components

The following are additional items that should be considered while reviewing your lease agreement to ensure that your customer, the Tenant, and your corporation are equally represented and protected. Other items should be considered and may be required by your corporation's legal counsel which are unique to your business and/or location.

Lease agreement date:

Landlord (Lessor) name, a (State) corporation or limited partnership, etc.:

Tenant (Lessee) name, a (State) corporation:

Rental agreement: Total rentable sq. footage (R.S.F.), R.S.F. per floor being leased, and how it is calculated by the landlord (as defined by BOMA or the commonly accepted/recognized local method). Total usable sq. footage (U.S.F.), U.S.F. per floor, and how it is calculated by the landlord (as defined by BOMA or the commonly accepted/recognized local method). The common area factors (as defined by BOMA or the commonly accepted/recognized local method). The property area in sq. ft. and acres if this is a ground lease. The property street address, suite #(s), county, city, zip code.

Location of premises: Where the premises are located (often the legal description of the property included as Exhibit "B").

Parking: Parking that is provided by the landlord is often expressed ____________ (___) per 1000 square feet of usable office space. Parking for visitors, reserved parking (ideally at no cost), and the cost of parking (if not free for the term of the lease, try to lock in the rate for the term and option periods) should be included here.

Term: Effective or commencement date, occupancy date, termination date and total initial term of lease in years/months/days.

Base rental: Rental rate per rentable square foot, total rent per year and monthly amount - $ ________________ and _____/100 dollars ($_______________.___) - due to the landlord usually by the first day of the month including the name the rent check is to made payable to and the rent payment address.

Operating and common area maintenance expenses: Operating expenses per month are often expressed to an amount per square foot for a specific year as a "peg" or "expense stop" and can be a very complicated and expensive item which should be thoroughly detailed in the lease, especially with regard to the percentage of expense pass-thru, the base amount and base year, etc. Common area maintenance expenses per month are often found at warehouse properties where the site maintenance is managed by the landlord and you pay utilities, janitorial, etc. for your space.

Rental adjustment: Sometimes called rent escalation, these increases are very important as they establish future rents with specific information on what is being escalated. These increases usually occur yearly and may include increases to the base rent and/or to the operating expenses by:

- A specific % increase or
- The CPI or a % of the CPI with a minimum and a maximum increase or
- An additional $______.___ cost per rentable square foot or
- A set amount based on a specific $______.___ cost per rentable square foot or
- A combination of the above or
- Whatever you negotiate.

Use: What your customer will be legally doing in the space.

Landlord repairs and services included in the lease: Such as:

- None
- Janitorial
- Plumbing Repair
- HVAC
- Grounds /CAM
- Lightning
- Electricity

EXHIBIT 10.5 *(Continued)*

- o Roof
- o Exterior/Window Repair
- o Snow Removal
- o Window Washing Schedule
- o Parking Lot Repair
- o After hours HVAC and cost.
- o Hours of normal HVAC service. Is Saturday morning included?
- o Building holidays of property?
- o Service elevator hours.
- o Porter service and costs.
- o Loading dock hours and trash disposal.
- o Security: Guards, access card (cost), cameras, parking, after hour access, fire stair access, keys, etc.
- o Fire and life safety.
- o Basement or tenant storage.
- o Interior Signage: Suite, lobby directory, etc.

Repairs by the tenant: Such as repair of construction within the tenant's premises.

Possession: Lessor may or may not warrant that your customer can occupy the space on the commencement date of the lease.

Inspection: Usually require that the landlord give the tenant 24 hour prior notice to enter the premises at reasonable hours to inspect the premises to see that the tenant is complying with all of the tenant's obligations.

ADA Compliance: The lease property meets the requirements of the federal American Disability Act (ADA) and any other state and local rules and regulations.

Default: States what will happen if the tenant fails to pay the rent within a specific time period thereby defaulting on the terms of the lease.

Reletting by landlord and other remedies: Usually states that if tenant is in default the landlord can rent the space to another tenant and that by doing so the landlord has not waived the right to seek further legal action against the original tenant.

Exterior signs: States whether or not the tenant can place an exterior sign on the building wall, roof or grounds. If this is permitted, then a description of what can be installed and where, the approval process, and who will pay for the sign would be included.

Removal of fixtures: Tenant is usually permitted at the end of the lease term to remove tenant owned furnishings and removable items not included as part of the base building. This should be carefully reviewed especially if your customer will be spending their capital funds to install a computer room and associated systems to ensure that they can take the raised floor, HVAC units, fire suppression, alarm system, etc. when they move.

Assignment and subletting: Ability to assign or sublease the lease and what restrictions, landlord approval if any? Your customer should be able to sublease the space to any similar operation division without having to secure the landlord's approval.

Destruction or damage: Addresses what happens to the lease agreement if the building is destroyed or damaged by fire.

Condemnation by governmental authorities: Addresses what happens to the lease if the premises or the building is permanently taken or condemned by a governmental authority.

Alterations and improvements: Often stipulates that the tenant can make no alterations in or to the premises without first obtaining the landlord's prior written consent. This can also be less restrictive where the tenant can redecorate, repaint, move a partition, re-carpet, make non-structural changes and changes which to do not effect the building mechanical, electrical, plumbing, and life safety systems of the space and building without first obtaining the landlord's prior written consent. Some landlord's are using this section to try to "require" tenant's to use the landlord's construction services and charge a management fee for any alterations or improvements to the space.

EXHIBIT 10.5 *(Continued)*

Attorney's fee: Usually requires that the tenant agrees to pay all attorney's fees and expenses the Landlord incurs in enforcing any of the tenant's obligations of the lease.

Waiver of subrogation: Briefly, the landlord and tenant waive all rights to recover against each other or against any other tenant or occupant of the building for any loss or damage arising from any cause covered by any insurance required to be carried by each of the parties or any other insurance actually carried by the landlord or the tenant.

Indemnification: Briefly, this usually provides that the tenant will indemnify the landlord, its agents, and employees against, and hold the landlord, its agents and employees harmless from, any and all demands, claims, causes, fines, damages, etc. arising from the tenant's occupancy of the premises arising at any time unless damage or injury results from the negligence of the landlord where the tenant is negligent, or violates the terms of the lease causing harm to any party. If any action or proceeding is brought against the landlord, it agents, or employees by reason of any such claim, tenant, upon notice from the landlord, will defend the claim at tenant's expense with counsel reasonably satisfactory to the landlord.

Rules and regulations: Landlords adopt rules and regulations for the building operation and safety of their tenants and are usually attached as an Exhibit to the lease. These can be fairly restrictive, should be carefully reviewed, and changes or modifications should be requested and approved by the landlord in writing before or when the lease is executed. For example, the rules and regulations may prohibit drink machines in tenant suites. If your customer plans to have a drink machine for the exclusive use of their employees in their break room, an exception in writing should be requested for approval by the landlord during lease negotiation.

Holding over: Can the tenant stay on in the premises after the end of the lease on a month-to-month basis and if yes, will the monthly rental increase and if yes by how much? This can range from no increase to 200% of the monthly rental.

Surrender of the premises: At the termination of the lease, the tenant shall surrender the premises and keys to the landlord in the same condition as at the commencement of the term, natural wear and tear, fire or other casualty only excepted. This can be used by the landlord to withhold the return of a deposit where when the tenant vacated the premises, substantial abuse to the space became readily apparent and would need major repair.

Notice: Tenant and Landlord correspondence notification address are the legal addresses where each party must send their formal notices when informing the other party of an issue that is informational or legal in nature.

Parties: The Landlord or "Lessor" is usually used in the lease as the first party. The Tenant or "Lessee" is usually used in the lease as the second party.

Mortgages: The tenant's rights shall be subject to any bona fide mortgage or deed to secure debt which may be placed upon the building by the landlord. The tenant has a right to remain at the premises under the terms of the lease regardless of default on the mortgage by the landlord.

Late charges: If the tenant is late in the payment of rent, a specific late charge is often required in the form of the greater of a minimum dollar amount or a maximum % of the amount due would be due for every _______(___) days the rent payment was late.

Cancellation penalties: If your customer (the tenant) desires to cancel the lease at a specific time(s) during the term of the lease, an amount should be negotiated with the landlord and included in this section.

Tenant's insurance: Landlord's require that their tenant's provide a certificate of insurance for minimum amounts of coverage specified in the lease with the landlord named as an insured in the tenant's public liability policies

Options: If your customer believes they would like to have a specific option to stay in their space a number of options with years for each option period and dates that the options will begin and end including the number of days required to notify landlord to take option, option for other space within the property with amount of space being optioned, the amount of rent for the option period(s) either fixed, consumer price index (CPI), percentage per year, or market, specific option information which may be unique to your location, and the Right of First Refusal of specific floors or space, etc. should be included in the lease.

EXHIBIT 10.5 *(Continued)*

Deposit: Is a deposit required? Your company may adopt or have a policy NOT to pay a deposit as the deposit represents risk which your company may not pose to a landlord. If a deposit cannot be negotiated out of the deal, ideally the deposit should be no more that one month's rent with interest to your company on the deposit.

Rent abatement: In today's rental markets, a number of months of free rent is an appropriate method to gain financial benefit and reduce the effective rate to your company/your customer.

Improvements to the premises: The design and construction of the premises your customer will occupy will often require some work to get it ready before it can be occupied. The cost of this work will either be paid for by the landlord, the tenant or the cost will be prorated between the landlord and the tenant. As part of the negotiating process, who will pay and is responsible for what work, at what cost and within what design and construction schedule must be identified in writing before the lease is executed. The cost, responsibility, design and construction schedule often take one of the following forms of an Exhibit attached to the lease as:

- o A landlord's workletter and construction schedule which includes design and construction completion dates, cost, and work the landlord will pay for before the premises is delivered to the tenant, the cost and work which the landlord will do but the tenant will pay for, and the work which the tenant will pay for and do during or after the landlord finishes its work.
- o A dollar allowance per usable square foot provided by the landlord where the landlord will schedule all design and construction work to provide the space as requested, pay all design and permit fees, pay for all construction work, and the tenant will reimburse the landlord for any costs over the total allowance amounts.
- o A dollar allowance per usable square foot provided by the landlord where the tenant will be responsible for all design work, permits and fees, scheduling the work, hiring a general contractor, completing and paying for all work, and requesting reimbursement from the landlord for all costs up to the total allowance amounts.

Contingencies or special stipulations: There may be items which are unique to your business or this lease which may be included such as:

- o **A Written statement from the Landlord that the building and site contains NO friable asbestos or other airborne, suface or sub-surface environmetal contaminates.**
- o **A Written statement from the Landlord that the building and site conforms to the ADA - "Americans with Disabilities Act of 1990" and other federal, state and local rules and regulations.**
- o Purchase option. If yes, cost and date to notify landlord or date of purchase.
- o Density of employees restriction where for example the landlord requires that your customer's premises can only accommodate one employee for every 200 rentable square feet. If additional employees are assigned to the premises that reduce the ratio then the landlord could find your customer in default of the lease terms.
- o Prorata share of property taxes if these are not included in the operating expenses.
- o Occupancy or Use Tax that have been established by local governments that you must pay either to the local government or to the landlord and is not included in the operating expenses.
- o Business non-competitive tenants where the landlord cannot lease space within the building to your customer's competition without their approval.
- o Food service, type, location, hours of operation, etc. which the landlord agrees to provide in the building or site.
- o Change and vending machines provided by the landlord by type and location to be serviced ___ times per week?
- o Statement if there are no smoking areas or policies for the building, a floor, etc.
- o A tenant conference room that will hold ___ people with a projection, coat and storage room which the landlord will provide within the building to the tenant at no initial cost or use fee for the term of the lease.
- o A health/fitness center which the landlord will provide within the building or on site to include: (specify requirements).
- o Retail services: Bank, copy center, laundry, etc.
- o Mail or postal facility in the building or on site.
- o Access to the building: Pedestrian, vehicular and services.
- o Handicapped parking, access, rest rooms, etc.
- o Shared telephone switch, telephone services, etc.

Commissions: Any and all commissions, compensations or other broker or finder fee expenses as part of this lease shall be paid by the landlord unless stipulated otherwise.

EXHIBIT 10.5 *(Continued)*

Changes to the agreement: No term or condition of the agreement will be considered to have been waived or amended unless expressed in writing, agreed to by both parties and shall be binding upon the parties, their heirs, succors or assigns.

Execution of the lease agreement: Space should be provided for the:

- o Signature(s) of the landlord, and a witness signature, a notary public seal and signature and the landlord's corporate seal if appropriate
- o Signature(s) of the landlord's agent if required, and a witness signature, a notary public seal and signature, and the agent's corporate seal where appropriate
- o Signature(s) for the tenant's corporate officer(s), and a witness signature, a notary public seal and signature, and the tenant's corporate seal.

Exhibits: These are attached to the lease and often some or all of the following depending on the lease term and complexity of the business terms and legal requirements by both parties:

- o Floor and/or site plan(s)
- o Workletter or upfit allowance agreement including landlord and tenant change order responsibilities
- o Lease terms and definitions
- o Building standard finishes definitions
- o Landlord rules & regulations
- o Lease contingency requirements
- o Definition of environmental audit and landlord and tenant requirements
- o Definition of certificate of occupancy requirements
- o Bonus and penalty requirements
- o Estoppel certificate
- o Commencement date agreement
- o Rent escalation agreement and example
- o Operating expense definitions, agreement and example
- o Common area maintenance definitions, agreement and example
- o Parking plan and specifications
- o Security specifications
- o Janitorial specifications
- o Building, HVAC System, Electrical, and Maintenance specifications
- o After business hours HVAC and electrical service specifications and agreement
- o Building signage specifications
- o Option to lease additional space schedule, description and specifications
- o Lease cancellation specifications and agreement
- o Option to purchase agreement

Most standard or printed leases do not allow *Assignment and Subletting* (7) without the landlord's written consent. Such leases should be revised to require the landlord "not to unreasonably withhold permission."

The largest problems that surface during negotiations for a new lease concern the provisions dealing with *Maintenance by Tenant* (8) and *Services and Utilities* (15). If these provisions are meticulously and artfully drafted, no repairs should be required during the term of the lease that are not clearly allocated to either party. Due to the excessive costs of many repairs, many landlords strapped for money are aggressively refusing to make repairs once thought of as being entirely the responsibility of the landlord. Since the courts have been sympathetic with the plight of the landlord, they have been finding repeatedly in favor of the landlord where the maintenance obligations are the least bit vague. Although obstinate and unreasonable behavior in a landlord is uncommon, it creates enough of a problem to require that landlord–tenant obligations be thoroughly defined. The standard definition of landlord's structural repairs, typically set forth as ". . . the roof, foundation, walls, columns . . . ," has been held to be too vague. Generally, a good rule to follow is that the more tenants there are in a building, the less you will be expected to be responsible for.

To protect the interests of both landlord and tenant with regard to any *Alterations* (9) (e.g., partitioning, additional electrical capacity, air-conditioning, carpeting) that are necessary for the tenant's use of a given building, all such alterations should be attached as an exhibit to the lease, either in the form of an appropriately marked building layout or as a list detailing the nature and extent of such alterations. The performing party and responsibility for payment of the alterations should either be spelled out in the lease or indicated on the exhibit. During the term of the lease, the tenant should be allowed to make minor additional alterations without the consent of the landlord. If any alterations were installed and paid for by the tenant, he or she should be allowed to remove or be reimbursed for the alterations at termination of the lease.

Tenant's Fixtures and Equipment (13) should be removable at any time during the lease term if these are installed by the tenant.

A common net lease usually provides that the landlord will carry *Indemnity and Public Liability Insurance* (14) but that the tenant will pay a specified share of the annual premium. Liability and contents insurance are made the responsibility of the tenant, and in most corporations, this is covered under a blanket policy. The landlord may want to be named as the coinsured. In negotiating a lease, many parties will hold up the document in haggling about indemnification from the tenant to the landlord. But regardless of what the lease says, landlords are liable for their negligence.

Services and Utilities (15) is the standard phrasing used for a net lease where the tenant assumes the obligation for paying utility bills. In the case of a *gross* lease, the landlord would assume the obligation and the lease language would be changed to reflect this shift of responsibility.

When the tenant's premises are destroyed by *Fire and Other Casualty Damage to Demised Premises* (18), the landlord should have the obligation to rebuild within a reasonable time if the damage is under 75 percent, during which time the rent should abate. During the last year of the term, the landlord should not be obligated to repair or rebuild unless the tenant renews. If the damage exceeds 75 percent and the premises cannot be repaired within 120 days, both parties should have the option of terminating the lease. The same logic applies to condemnation. Here the tenant should be given the opportunity to remain in a reduced space at a proportionately reduced rental.

Default of Tenant (20) provisions are fairly standard; the tenant should not be found in default unless (1) notice has been given to the tenant by the landlord and (2) the alleged default has not been cured within a reasonable time (30–60 days).

Any *Right of Landlord to Cure Tenant's Default: Late Payments* (25) should also extend to the tenant, giving him or her the opportunity to make the landlord's payments under any of the landlord's obligations (for example, fire insurance, repair, and mortgage payments).

The lease should always provide in the *Covenants of Landlord* (31) that the person or persons signing it are the owners and/or have the right to lease the property. Whether the landlord be a trustee, a partnership, or a corporation, it is essential that all the persons authorized and required to execute the lease do so.

Compliance with Governmental Requirements (38) should be the responsibility of the tenant only insofar as the tenant's use of the demised premises is concerned.

The *Option to Renew* (39) will be discussed in § 10.2(e)(7).

The *Taxes* (40) clause is fraught with peril for the inexperienced tenant who may agree to innocent-sounding but punitive wording in a lease form. A tenant with a net lease can be made to pay taxes in two ways:

1. The taxes are established for a base year, and in new construction the property will probably be assessed as "unimproved." For example, a new shopping center has a tax bill of $20,000 in the base year. Then the tenant is required to pay his share of the taxes on the property. We will use 7.8 percent as the tenant's percentage share of the property tax bill. Thus the tenant's tax bill for the first year after base is $1,560. The second year the property gets fully taxed at $80,000, and the tenant's tax bill is $6,240. The tax bill for the third year is $82,000, and the tenant's share is $6,396. For the three years, $14,196 is payable by the tenant.
2. If we used the same figures and the tenant paid only his share (7.8 percent) of the increase in taxes for the base year—the "base year"

being defined as the year in which the building is fully assessed—the tenant would have a payment due of $4,680 during the second year and of $4,836 during the third year. The total for three years would be $9,516, a saving of $4,680.

Therefore, the two most significant matters to be negotiated with regard to tax escalation provisions are:

1. The base that will be used to determine the increases chargeable as tax escalation.
2. The manner in which the total increase in the real estate tax on the property will be allotted to a particular tenant.

In negotiating the base from which increased taxes will be charged, taxes are generally compiled on a fiscal year basis and the assessment for any given fiscal year may be determined considerably in advance of the tax year. Consideration must also be given to the significant difference between tax assessments on buildings that have been completed for some time and tax assessments on newly completed buildings.

Different formulas are utilized to allocate tax increase percentages among tenants. These must also be closely examined, because landlords who use a formula based on the tenant's projected occupancy in relation to that of the total building will often try to reduce the formula denominator in determining the percentage.

Unless you concentrate careful attention on the extremely technical area of taxes, you may well experience unnecessary tax escalations during your tenancy.

(5) Escalations

The negotiation of escalation clauses in commercial leases threatens to supplant baseball or football as the real national pastime. The inclusion of escalation clauses for property taxes and operating expenses has been accepted as a norm in most commercial leases. We have already looked at the real estate tax escalation clause. Operating expense escalation clauses are structured in much the same manner, and the same words of caution apply.

Numerous formulas are followed to establish the basis on which tenants pay increased costs associated with the operation of a building. Many of these formulas produce additional profit for the landlord. The base period on which operating expense escalation will be determined can also earn additional income for the landlord—particularly when new construction is involved. Inadequate protection in this area can increase a tenant's base rental significantly, so be on guard.

The following wording is appropriate for an escalation clause:

> Base rate for space leased initially and under all renewal and expansion options shall be $_____ per rentable square foot on all floors, computed on a BOMA rentable, single- or multi-tenant rate as applicable (See Exhibit _____). The rent will include all utilities and services.
>
> Rentals shall be subject to an agreed-upon escalation rate for operating expenses above those of the base year. Increases in real estate taxes shall be paid when such taxes surpass the assessment made for the building as fully completed.
>
> The base year for operating expenses will be the first full year of building operation. Adjustment will be made to increase the base amount to reflect costs which would have been incurred had the original equipment not been under warranty by the manufacturer or supplier and to reflect the costs of a ninety-five (95) percent occupied building.
>
> The established base for real estate taxes and operating expenses will apply to base rentals for expansion space and the renewal term.
>
> Rentals and terms for right of first refusal space will be negotiated at the time the tenant elects to exercise the right of first refusal.

Landlords have been seeking additional protection against inflation through the inclusion of cost-of-living escalator clauses that are designed to increase rentals at a rate consistent with the annual rate of inflation. These efforts have been most successful in markets that are short of space, but tenants have resisted the inclusion of escalator clauses wherever possible. When an escalator clause is included in a lease, tenants should strive for a cap on the maximum allowable annual increase, regardless of the projected inflation rate, and should also attempt to negotiate a cap on total annual rent obligations, including base rent and all escalations.

(6) Additional Space

Tenants need to protect themselves against the possibility of needing additional space in an office building (particularly a new one) by inserting wording similar to the following in the lease:

> Tenant will have the right to lease additional space on the next contiguous floor on the same terms and conditions for at least six months after commencement of the term to allow for expansions in the initial requirement which may develop after lease execution.
>
> Expansion space options:
>
> (a) 3rd lease year _____________ square feet
> (b) 5th lease year _____________ square feet
> (c) 7th lease year _____________ square feet
> (d) 9th lease year _____________ square feet
> (e) 11th lease year _____________ square feet
> (f) 13th lease year _____________ square feet

(g) 15th lease year ___________ square feet
(h) 17th lease year ___________ square feet

All space is to be contiguous and in accordance with the expansion layout shown on attached Exhibit _____ to this lease agreement. Requirement based on lease renewal after the 10th and 15th years. The dates for delivery of the expansion space will be determined during negotiations on a "no later than _____" date basis.

After the first full year of the lease, Landlord will be required to offer Tenant, in writing, any space that becomes available in the building. Such space is to be available to Tenant on short term or, if practicable, for the remainder of the lease term.

Tenant will reply in writing within fifteen (15) business days, and if the space is rejected, Tenant has no further right to the space offered. However, this right of first refusal shall in no way affect the Tenant options for expansion shown herein. Space not leased to another tenant within six (6) months shall be offered in writing to Tenant on the terms outlined in this paragraph.

(7) Additional Rights and Provisions

- *The Option to Renew.* The purpose of an option to renew is to legally give the tenant the right to remain on the premises after the termination of a lease. This does not mean that a firm rental rate has to be set forth. An option to renew differs from a right of first refusal in that a tenant can exercise a right of first refusal only if the landlord is willing to lease, whereas an option to renew is a firm commitment by the landlord.
- *Sale-Leasebacks.* Sale-leasebacks come in many shapes and sizes. In concept, the technique has been developed primarily as a financing vehicle to allow the seller-tenant to take capital dollars out of a facility, obtain locational flexibility, and at the same time create a long-term investment vehicle for the buyer-landlord. Since such a transaction obviously requires the construction of a lease document satisfactory to both parties, as well as negotiated financial terms and conditions, our general comments about leases also apply to sale-leasebacks.

There are many variations of sale-leasebacks, but their general rationale can be illustrated with the following example.

Example. A food-processing concern owned an 800,000-square-foot facility in a well-located industrial area of a southeastern city. The building had been constructed in stages over a period of approximately 20 years, the newest addition being 2 years of age. There were 2,600 employees in the facility. Approximately 180,000 square feet of the facility was refrigerated, since the facility was used to store and distribute food. The property was debt free. The company was anxious to acquire the dollars represented by its investment in this asset and to use them in manufacturing operations. Accordingly, it sought a party that would be willing to negotiate a sale-leaseback with it. Ultimately a deal was struck.

The book value of the facility was $8 million. Its estimated current market value was approximately $11 million. The sale-leaseback was arranged on the basis of a purchase price at a book value of $8 million. The manufacturing concern leased the facility back on a firm 18-year-lease term at a rental constant of 9.08, with 10 five-year options for renewal at the same rate, beginning at the expiration of the original 18-year lease term. The rental rate on a net net basis approximated 91 cents per square foot. The current going market rental rate for this type of space was approximately $1.30 per square foot net net. Finally, the manufacturing concern also had the right to sublease the facility at any time during the firm initial 18-year term.

Immediate advantages of the sale-leaseback to the manufacturing concern seem rather obvious. First, it freed $8 million in cash for use in the manufacturing operation, and since the facility was sold at its book value rather than at its current fair market value, no capital gains tax burden was assumed by the manufacturing concern. Further, if the concern had sold the property at its current fair market value, the buyer, in turn, would have had to quote a rental rate significantly higher than the agreed-upon rental rate. In other words, the selling concern did not have a capital gains tax burden and was not obligated to pay rent on a capital gains tax burden for at least 18 years. If the manufacturing concern elected to exercise all its options, it could have 68 years of occupancy at a significantly reduced rental rate and would have to face up to the issue of paying or not paying a fair market rental rate only after that. Further, it had the freedom to sublease the facility if the facility should no longer be needed; assuming that it could find another tenant, it could thus get out of the burden of the initial lease.

The arrangement also had appeal for the buyer—in this case a large institutional investor with long-term portfolio management objectives. The seller-tenant represented excellent credit, and the rent constant, although low by the standards of the real estate market, was higher than the buyer's alternative long-term investment opportunities. And, of course, the reversionary value of the real estate, even 68 years later, held appeal since the property was well located and seemed to have an excellent appreciation potential.

The sale-leaseback satisfied the needs of both parties and provided the basis for a bilateral good deal for the investor and the manufacturer.

§ 10.3 PURCHASING REAL PROPERTY

Just as a corporation may choose to lease property, there are times when it will make economic sense to purchase real property. Corporate policy, available resources and funding, timing, investment in building and equipment, business and economic climate, competition, operational requirements, and tax consequences will all drive a purchase decision. There will be times when leasing may prove to be more economical, but business issues and corporate strategies will dictate the purchase decision.

Many of the same steps to acquire leased property are required to purchase a location. A main difference is that if the corporation owns property, it must maintain, manage, and be legally responsible for the actions occurring on the site. When the lease is up, the corporation can choose to vacate and realize an expense savings. With owned property, ongoing expenses, maintenance, taxes, and insurance must be identified and budgeted until and when the corporation sells the property.

(a) CONTINGENCIES

All contingencies items must be satisfied before closing on the property, for once title changes hands and the deed is recorded, the corporation has very little recourse to return the property to the seller. The corporate legal department must be part of the acquisition to ensure that corporate property acquisition policies and requirements as well as all legal issues have been addressed before closing takes place. The corporation's obligation to purchase real property could be contingent on being able to obtain items such as an acceptable environmental audit, licenses, permits, zoning, utilities, tax abatements and/or incentives, completion and approval of site development and subdivision approvals, mortgage financing, development bids within agreed upon amounts, and other authorizations including parent company approval. If the company cannot obtain all necessary licenses, permits, and other authorizations within a specific number of days, the corporate legal department should ensure that the sale and purchase agreement provides that either party can terminate the contract and all earnest money deposit and any additional funds in escrow will be returned.

(b) SALE AND PURCHASE AGREEMENT

The following items should be included in the sale and purchase agreement to ensure that the purchaser and seller are equally represented and protected (see Exhibit 10.6 for a Sample Letter of Intent and Exhibit 10.7 for a Sample Sale and Purchase Agreement). Other items unique to a business or location should be considered and may be required by the corporation's legal counsel.

- *Seller Name, Address, City, Zip Code.*
- *Purchaser Name, Address, City, Zip Code.*

EXHIBIT 10.6 Purchase Property: Sample Letter of Intent

This Letter of Intent is made and entered into this 15th day of September, 1993, by and between ABC Company ("Purchaser") and Warehouse Developers, Inc. ("Seller").

In consideration of the agreements herein after set forth, the parties hereto mutually agree as follows:

1. Seller agrees to sell and Purchaser agrees to purchase the property located at 2548 West Wacker Drive, Chicago, IL. 60638, in the County of Cook, State of Illinois, as more specifically described in Exhibit A, which is attached hereto and incorporated herein by this reference, together with all rights and appurtenances thereto and all rights, title and interest of Seller in and to any and all roads and streets bounding such property. A more definitive description shall be provided by the Seller to the Purchaser from an accurate boundary and topographic survey acceptable to the Seller and Purchaser, at Seller's cost to be reimbursed by Purchaser at closing.

2. The purchase price shall be as agreed to by the Seller and Purchaser based upon an appraisal of the property not later than 90 days from the date of this Letter of Intent by a minimum of three (3) appraisers retained by the Purchaser and approved by the Seller. Seller and Purchaser agree that the purchase price shall not exceed $ 6.60 nor be less than $ 5.15 per square foot of the appraised and surveyed property. Failure to agree on a reasonable purchase price shall render this Letter of Intent null and void.

3. Conveyance of the property shall be by general warranty deed and shall be covered by a fully paid title insurance policy.

4. Purchaser proposes to use the property for the construction and operation of a free-standing warehouse distribution center with outside storage. In the event that the property is restricted in any way which prohibits, limits or restricts the use of the property for such purpose, Seller shall obtain appropriate authorization so that the property may be used for the purposes described above. In the event Seller is unable to secure the authorization necessary for utilizing the property within 180 days from the date of this Letter of Intent, Purchaser may so notify Seller in writing, whereupon this Letter of Intent shall become null and void.

5. Further, Purchaser's obligation to purchase is also subject to the following within 180 days from the above date:
   a. Purchaser's obtaining approval and funding of the purchase of the property and construction of the warehouse distribution center from their parent company, XYZ Corporation;

   b. Seller's acquisition of clear title to an entrance way to the property from the adjacent property owner (whereby the adjacent property owner will exchange a portion of the adjacent property to create an entrance way to the subject property in exchange for a portion of the subject property which borders West Wacker Drive and 4th Avenue and the adjacent property);

   c. Seller grant's Purchaser access to the site, and the right to physically investigate the site. Purchaser, as part the due deligence and contingency phase of the agreement, shall be completely satisfied before closing shall take place that the site and/or building are free and clear of any and all current airborne, surface, and sub-surface environmental contaminates and/or wetland restrictions which effect the current and possible future use of the site and/or building. Purchaser shall employ an environmental audit process to make this determination which includes but is not limited to retaining a qualified consulting organization to investigate and research the site and adjacent sites, obtain and analyze samples of site materials and soil via borings, investigate wetland issues and restrictions to the site, and provide a written report satisfactory to the purchaser that the site and/or building is free and clear of contaminates and the site and/or building use(s) are not limited by wetland restrictions. If the environmental audit process through the above report or other Purchaser investigation does not provide the Purchaser with a "clean" and "usable" site, the Purchaser may at the Purchaser's option cancel the Sale and Purchase Agreement without penalty.

   d. Seller shall provide the Purchaser with a written statement that the site and/or building meets the requirements of the federal "Americans With Disabilities Act of 1990" (ADA) and all other federal, state and local rules and regulations. The Purchaser shall have the option to investigate the site and/or building to verify the Sellers claim.

   e. Purchaser's obtaining the necessary licenses, permits and other authorizations, including curb cuts for reasonable traffic access;

EXHIBIT 10.6 *(Continued)*

Letter of Intent
Page 2

f. Seller's obtaining letters of service and supply from the appropriate agencies for water, gas, electricity, sanity sewer, storm sewers, and any other necessary public utilities stating that the services and supply are immediately on or contiguous to the subject property and are available to the Purchaser for a connection fee for all such utilities at the time of occupancy; and

g. Purchaser's obtaining title insurance binder, title insurance, and a general warranty deed.

6. Real estate taxes for the current year shall be prorated as of the date of closing.

7. The closing of the herein described purchase and sale shall be subject to the conditions set forth in this Letter of Intent and shall be scheduled at a mutually agreeable time and date on or after 180 days following the date of this Letter of Intent.

In WITNESS WHEREOF, the Seller has caused this Letter of Intent to be executed on the date noted above.

Witness:

SELLER:
WAREHOUSE DEVELOPERS, INC.

____

By: ____________________
Walter H. Simpson
Its: President

In WITNESS WHEREOF, the Purchaser has caused this Letter of Intent to be executed on the date noted above.

Witness:

PURCHASER:
ABC COMPANY

____

By: ____________________
Robert C. Wilson
Its: President

■

EXHIBIT 10.7 Sale and Purchase Agreement: Sample for ABC Company

SALE AND PURCHASE AGREEMENT

Rayson Development Company, hereinafter "Seller," whose address is 550 South Madison Avenue, Suite 900, New York, NY 20246-1234, hereby agrees to sell, and ABC Company, hereinafter "Purchaser," whose address is 235 East Wacker Drive, Suite 1700, Chicago, IL 60634-6578, or its assigns, agrees to purchase the following described property at 334 East Wacker Drive, Chicago, IL 60634-6578 in the County of Cook, State of Illinois, and as more commonly described in Exhibit A (Site Plan) and legally described by frontage, dimensions and square footage as shown on Exhibit B (Legal Description) together with all rights and appurtenances thereto belonging or in anywise appertaining and all right, title and interest of Seller in and to any and all roads, streets, alleys and ways, bounding such property.

A more definite description as shall be obtained by Purchaser from an accurate boundary and topographic survey acceptable to Purchaser, at Purchaser's cost to be reimbursed by Seller at closing.

1. The purchase price shall be Eight Million Sixty-Five Thousand Four Hundred Thirty-Two and 01/100 Dollars ($8,065,432.01), with an earnest money deposit in the amount of Fifty Thousand and 00/100 Dollars ($50,000.00) at the time of the execution of this Agreement by the Purchaser, which shall be considered as a portion of the purchase price. The balance of the purchase price shall be payable in cash at closing. In the event Purchaser fails or refuses to consummate the subject sale for any reason whatsoever, and through no fault of the Seller, then all earnest money shall be paid to the Seller as full, complete and final liquidated damages sustained by the Seller and Seller shall have no other recourse or remedy.

2. Conveyance shall be by deed of general warranty. All municipal, county, state and federal transfer taxes shall be paid by Seller at the time of closing. The conveyance shall be free from dower or statutory rights, taxes, assessments and all other liens and encumbrances of any kind, without exceptions, unless otherwise specified herein, so as to convey to the Purchaser good and marketable title. Recording of the deed will be at Purchaser's expense.

3. Purchaser proposes to use the property for the constructions and operation of a free standing office building, including off-street parking incident thereto and the erection of its standard identification sign. In the event that the property is restricted by any state, county, municipal or other government ordinance, rule or regulation, including limited access rules, restrictions or regulations (hereinafter collectively called "zoning") which prohibit, limit or restrict the use of the property for such purposes Purchaser shall undertake at Seller's expense to be reimbursed at closing, to make good faith effort to secure rezoning, special use permits or variances hereinafter "Authorizations", so that the property may be used for the purposes hereinabove set forth. Seller hereby agrees to cooperate fully with Purchaser in securing such Authorizations and hereby grants permission to Purchaser to make application for such Authorizations in the name of Seller. In the event Purchaser is unable to secure the Authorizations necessary for utilizing the property for the purposes hereinabove set forth within the prescribed time, Purchaser may notify Seller in writing of such fact, whereupon this Agreement shall become null and void, Purchaser shall not be obligated to complete the purchase of the property and Seller shall promptly return to Purchaser the consideration paid to Seller. The determination of the necessity for obtaining such Authorizations or the adequacy of the Authorizations granted shall be within the sole discretion of Purchaser.

4. Purchaser's obligation to purchase is contingent on Purchaser being able to obtain the necessary licenses, permits, and other authorizations, including curb cuts for reasonable traffic access. Reasonable traffic access shall include:

(a) two accesses to a major highway at least one of which shall be a left turn access;

(b) one access for each secondary highway. Access in each instance shall be for ingress and egress.

In the event Purchaser is unable to obtain all the necessary licenses, permits, curb cuts, or authorizations within 180 days, or as may have been extended, from the last date of execution by Purchaser and Seller, either party may terminate the contract and the Purchaser shall be entitled to the return of the earnest money deposit and additional funds in escrow, and the Seller shall be entitled to the return of his deed or other instruments placed in escrow and the parties shall be released from further liability. Closing shall take place within ten (10) days after all of the contingencies of the contract have been fulfilled and vacant possession of the property shall be delivered to Purchaser at time of closing. Risk of loss to said property and improvements thereon prior to closing shall remain with Seller.

EXHIBIT 10.7 *(Continued)*

5. Within 180 days from the date of last execution of this contract Seller shall permit Purchaser to enter upon the subject property to make a topographic and boundary survey; determine the location of utilities; perform engineering studies, and to conduct soil tests and borings on the property (except where buildings if any, are now located) to determine the property's suitability for Purchaser's proposed improvements. If such survey, studies, soil borings or tests indicate conditions unsuitable to Purchaser for such proposed improvements or Purchaser's contemplated use, then Purchaser may terminate this Agreement whereupon both parties shall be released from further performance hereunder and the earnest money deposit shall be returned to Purchaser.

6. If prior to closing any part of the property is condemned or appropriated by public authority or any party exercising the right of eminent domain, or is threatened thereby, or if the buildings and improvements on the above-described property shall be destroyed or materially damaged by fire, windstorm, explosion or other casualty, then this Agreement shall, at the election of Purchaser, become null and void, whereupon the consideration paid by the Purchaser to or for the benefit of the Seller shall be promptly repaid. Should the Purchaser elect not to terminate this contract the purchase price shall be reduced by the amount of the Seller's
award.

7. As a material inducement to Purchaser entering into this Agreement Seller represents that water, gas, electricity, sanitary sewers, storm sewers, and other necessary public utilities are immediately on or contiguous to the subject property and are available to Purchaser for a connection fee not to exceed Twelve Thousand Dollars ($12,000) for all such utilities. In the event that any of such utilities are not so available Purchaser shall have the right to terminate this Agreement and the earnest money deposit returned.

8. (a) Purchaser shall order a title insurance binder on the property prepared by a title insurance company acceptable to Purchaser. Seller shall provide a current abstract of title to the title insurance company, if required, and shall pay for any costs incurred in title searches. At closing Seller will convey a good and marketable title to the property, and except as provided for herein, free, clear and unencumbered.

(b) In the event the title insurance binder shall reflect title defects or other conditions which were not as represented by Seller, then upon notification of such defects or conditions, the Seller shall immediately and diligently proceed to cure same and shall have a reasonable time within which so to do. If after the exercise of all reasonable diligence Seller is unable to clear the title or defects of the property, then Purchaser may accept the title and defects in its then condition or Purchaser may terminate this Agreement, whereupon both parties shall be released from further performance hereunder and the earnest money deposit shall be returned to Purchaser.

9. Seller grant's Purchaser access to the site, and the right to physically investigate the site. Purchaser, as part the due deligence and contingency phase of the agreement, shall be completely satisfied before closing shall take place that the site and/or building are free and clear of any and all current airborne, surface, and sub-surface environmental contaminates and/or wetland restrictions which effect the current and possible future use of the site and/or building. Purchaser shall employ an environmental audit process to make this determination which includes but is not limited to retaining a qualified consulting organization to investigate and research the site and adjacent sites, obtain and analyze samples of site materials and soil via borings, investigate wetland issues and restrictions to the site, and provide a written report satisfactory to the purchaser that the site and/or building is free and clear of contaminates and the site and/or building use(s) are not limited by wetland restrictions. If the environmental audit process through the above report or other Purchaser investigation does not provide the Purchaser with a "clean" and "usable" site, the Purchaser may at the Purchaser's option cancel the Sale and Purchase Agreement without penalty.

10. Seller shall provide the Purchaser with a written statement that the site and/or building meets the requirements of the federal "Americans With Disabilities Act of 1990" (ADA) and all other federal, state and local rules and regulations. The Purchaser shall have the option to investigate the site and/or building to verify the Sellers claim.

11. Any and all commissions, compensations or other broker or finder fee expenses incident to this sale shall be paid by the Seller to Professional Brokerage Company and Simpson Realty, Inc.

12. Real estate taxes for the current year shall be prorated as of the date of closing. Seller shall pay all certified liens and make allowance for all pending liens which represent work which is actually in progress or completed on the date of closing, but which have not as yet been certified as a lien. Purchaser shall assume all pending liens representing improvements which have not as yet commenced. Seller shall give the Purchaser at closing credit for future assessments, even if called in the nature of "taxes" for improvements completed.

13. Seller shall deliver to Purchaser at closing an affidavit of vacant possession stating that there are not unrecorded leases or agreements upon the property, and an affidavit certifying that there are no mechanic's or

EXHIBIT 10.7 *(Continued)*

statutory liens against the property. Seller will execute as Purchaser's request as many deeds as Purchaser deems desirable to divide the property into more than one parcel.

14. No term or condition of this Agreement will be deemed to have been waived or amended unless expressed in writing, and the waiver of any condition or the breach of any term will not be a waiver of any subsequent breach of the same or any other term or condition. This Agreement constitutes the entire Agreement of the parties which incorporates prior written or oral understandings. This Agreement shall be binding upon the parties, their heirs, successors or assigns.

15. As a material inducement for the Purchaser to enter into this Agreement the Seller covenants that no property presently owned or hereafter acquired by the Seller contiguous or adjacent to the within described property shall be used or occupied for a business activity which consists of the sale, for on premises consumption, of so called retail automotive items. This covenant on the part of the Seller shall survive the closing for a period of ten (10) years.

16. Closing of the herein described purchase shall be subject to final acceptance by the Purchaser's parent company, XYZ Corporation.

IN WITNESS WHEREOF, the Seller has caused this instrument to be executed and sealed this 4th day of January, 1994.

Witness:

____________________________ By: ____________________________

Philip A. Goodman, President

Attest: ____________________________

Richard D. Rayson, Secretary

SELLER (SEAL)

IN WITNESS WHEREOF, the Purchaser has caused this instrument to be executed and sealed this 5th day of January, 1994.

Witness:

____________________________ By: ____________________________

Jane M. Simpson, President

Attest: ____________________________

Philip S. Miller, Secretary

PURCHASER (SEAL)

STATE OF ILLINOIS
COUNTY OF COOK

BEFORE ME, the undersigned authority, personally appeared ________________________ to me well known and known to me to be the individuals described in and who executed the foregoing instrument as __________ President and _________ Secretary of __________, __________ corporation, and severally acknowledged to and before me that they executed such instrument as such __________ President and __________ Secretary respectively of said corporation and that the seal affixed to the foregoing instrument is the corporate seal of said corporation, and that it was affixed to said instrument by due and regular corporate authority, and that said instrument is the free act and deed of WITNESS my hand and official seal this ____ day of ________, 19_.

____

(SEAL) Notary Public

My Commission Expires:

EXHIBIT 10.7 *(Continued)*

STATE OF ILLINOIS
COUNTY OF COOK

BEFORE ME, the undersigned a Notary Public in and for said County and State, on this day personally appeared ____ to me known and known to me to be the person(s) whose name(s) is (are) subscribed to the foregoing instrument, and acknowledged to me that he executed the same for the purposes and considerations therein expressed.

WITNESS my hand and official seal this _______ day of _________, 19__.

____

(SEAL) Notary Public

My Commission Expires:

STATE OF ILLINOIS
COUNTY OF COOK

BEFORE ME, the undersigned authority, personally appeared ______________________________to me well known and known to me to be the individuals described in and who executed the foregoing instrument as ______________ President and ____________ Secretary of ________________, ______________ corporation, and severally acknowledged to and before me that they executed such instrument as such ________________ President and _____________ Secretary respectively of said corporation and that the seal affixed to the foregoing instrument is the corporate seal of said corporation, and that it was affixed to said instrument by due and regular corporate authority, and that said instrument is the free act and deed of WITNESS my hand and official seal this _____ day of _________, 19_.

____

(SEAL) Notary Public

My Commission Expires:

STATE OF ILLINOIS
COUNTY OF COOK

BEFORE ME, the undersigned a Notary Public in and for said County and State, on this day personally appeared ____to me known and known to me to be the person(s) whose name(s) is (are) subscribed to the foregoing instrument, and acknowledged to me that he executed the same for the purposes and considerations therein expressed.

WITNESS my hand and official seal this _______ day of _________, 19__.

____

(SEAL) Notary Public

My Commission Expires:

EXHIBIT 10.7 *(Continued)*

EXHIBIT "A"

SITE PLAN

(Insert Site Plan Here)

....

EXHIBIT 10.7 (continued)

EXHIBIT "B"

LEGAL DESCRIPTION

(Insert Legal Description Here)

- *Property Address Including Street, County, City, Zip Code.*
- *Site Information.* This includes total acreage, frontage, dimensions, and square footage of land, building (sometimes attached as Exhibit A).
- *Property Legal Description* (often attached as Exhibit B).
- *Boundary and Topographic Surveys.* Purchaser is to obtain an accurate boundary and topographic survey acceptable to purchaser (cost may be paid by the purchaser or negotiated to be reimbursed by the seller at closing). This may be attached as an Exhibit.
- *Purchase Price.* State the purchase price __________ and __________ /100 dollars ($__________) and that earnest money deposit __________ and __________ /100 dollars ($__________) shall be considered as a portion of the purchase price.
- *Mortgage.* If applicable, note mortgage term, monthly payments, payable to, payment address, and mortgage correspondence notification address.
- *Conveyance of the Deed.* The deed will usually be in the form of a general warranty, special warranty, grant, quitclaim, or other deed.
- *Taxes.* Seller pays prorated taxes at closing.
- *Recording of the Deed.* This is usually at the purchaser's expense.
- *Zoning Jurisdiction.* What city or county has authority for zoning?
- *Zoned.* State the zoning of the affected area. Occasionally, a community will impose prohibitive restrictions on signage, building setbacks, and curb cuts. Local sign and building codes vary, site densities vary, so it is important to examine all applicable ordinances *before* acquiring a property. It may be necessary to consult with an attorney, architect, and/or engineer prior to selecting and closing on a site. It is a good idea to buy a copy of the community's zoning code/ordinances to study all site requirements. It may be appropriate to include a clause in the purchase contract making the closing of the sale contingent upon the company's obtaining a construction permit (see below).
- *Site Plan Agreement or Subdivision of Property Agreement.* This may be attached as an Exhibit.
- *Property Covenants and Restrictions.* These may be attached as an Exhibit.
- *Roads and Site Improvements Dedicated to the Municipality.* This may be a statement or attached as an Exhibit.
- *Proposed Use of the Property.* State purchaser's proposed use of the property and authorization and agreement by the seller to cooperate fully with the purchaser in providing access to the property, and in applying for and obtaining any necessary rezoning, variances,

permits, and utilities. If the purchaser cannot obtain use of the property for its proposed use, the purchaser may notify the seller in writing of the fact and the agreement will become null and void.

- *Purchase Contingencies.* Purchaser's obligation to purchase is contingent on being able to obtain licenses, permits, and other authorizations.
- *Environmental Audit.* The purchaser must have the right to physically investigate the site and/or building and verify, before closing, that the site and/or building are free of all environmental contaminants and/or wetland restrictions that would affect its current and possible future use. This environmental audit process should include but is not limited to retaining a qualified consulting organization to research the site and adjacent sites, investigate wetland issues and restrictions to the site, and provide a satisfactory written report. If the investigation does not verify a "clean" and "usable" site, the purchaser may cancel the Sale and Purchase Agreement without penalty.
- *Closing.* State the date of closing and for taking possession of the property.
- *Condemnation.* Condemnation of the property by a public authority before closing can, at the election of the purchaser, cause the agreement to become null and void.
- *ADA Compliance.* The seller provides the purchaser with a written statement that the site and/or building meets the requirements of the federal "Americans With Disabilities Act of 1990" (ADA) and all other federal, state, and local rules and regulations. The purchaser has the option to verify the seller's claim.
- *Utilities.* Water, gas, electricity, sanitary sewers, storm sewers, site drainage and site storm water retention, and other necessary public utilities must be immediately on or contiguous to the subject property and available to the purchaser for a connection fee. If these utilities are not available, the purchaser has the right to terminate the agreement and receive the earnest money deposit.
- *Title Insurance.* Purchaser orders a title binder on the property. At closing, the seller will convey a good and marketable title to the property. If title defects are present and seller cannot cure the defects, the purchaser may accept the title and defects or may terminate the agreement. The title insurance policy should be issued and on hand at closing.
- *Commissions.* Any and all commissions, compensations, or other broker or finder fee expenses are paid by the seller.

- *Taxes and Liens.* Real estate taxes for the current year are prorated as of the date of closing and seller pays all current and pending certified liens.
- *Affidavit of Vacant Possession.* The seller's affidavit of vacant possession states that there are no unrecorded leases, agreements, or liens on the property.
- *Changes to the Agreement.* All changes must be in writing, agreed to by both parties, and binding on the parties, their heirs, succors, or assigns.
- *Competitive Business in an Adjacent or Contiguous Property.* If the corporation is sensitive to adjacent neighbor businesses, it may wish to include a clause that restricts the seller's uses for contiguous properties.
- *Special Stipulations.* These may be items unique to a particular business.
- *Parent Company Approval.* Closing of the purchase must receive final approval from the parent company. This provides the corporation a final out if business or strategic plans change before closing.
- *Execution of the Purchase Agreement.* Space should be provided for the date, signature(s) of the seller(s), two witness signatures, with a seller's corporate seal if appropriate, and space for the date, signature(s) for the purchaser's corporate officer(s), and two witness signatures with the purchaser's corporate seal.
- *Exhibits.* These are attached to the sale and purchase agreement and include some or all of the following, depending on the complexity of the business terms and legal requirements by both parties:
  - Site, plot, and floor plan(s)
  - Legal description
  - Easements
  - Purchase contingency requirements
  - Title binder, title insurance, and closing requirements
  - Definition of the environmental audit process and seller and purchaser requirements
  - Payoff of existing mortgage(s)
  - Closing date definition and agreement
  - Common area maintenance definitions, agreement, and example
  - Approval by parent company including corporate resolution, appraisal, financing, deed, title, and title insurance requirements

- Option to purchase additional property schedule, description, plan(s), and specifications.

§ 10.4 CONCLUSION

In presenting the complex subject of leases and sale-purchase agreements, this chapter has stressed certain fundamental operating strategies and tactics that relate to other real estate asset management issues in this book.

Previous chapters have pointed out the desirability of maintaining corporate headquarters control over all real estate activity. Real estate control should be a centralized activity, a nondelegated corporate function. This admonition applies with special vigor to the negotiation and execution of leases and sale-purchase agreements.

Exhibits 10.8 and 10.9 show forms devised to assist a company in the control and administration of leasing and purchase property activity. The forms should be filled in by the requesting division and submitted to the real estate department for further action. It puts the real estate department on notice that an operational need exists and permits the department to check for financial approvals and maintain control of the proposed action.

The following guidelines will help in the administration and control of leases and sale-purchase agreements:

- Most printed lease and sale-purchase forms are "landlord" or "owner" forms, so be wary of every word. You would be well advised to create your own lease and sale-purchase forms if possible.
- There isn't much that is legally sacred in a printed lease or sale-purchase form, so don't be afraid to throw out anything objectionable—or at least bargain to have it removed.
- Be constantly cognizant of the total dollar volume of your future lease and purchase commitments. Such commitments have a way of innocently mounting up, much like a department store charge account.
- Pay increasing attention to the *capital* versus *operating* character of leases. Even if you do not report capital leases now, you probably will in the future, so be prepared.
- Give some thought to the owned/leased facilities ratio experience of your company so that your responsiveness to market conditions will be sufficiently flexible.
- All lease and purchase arrangements, regardless of term, should be committed to writing. Remember that properly negotiated written lease and sale-purchase agreements protect your interests as well as those of the landlord or owner.

EXHIBIT 10.8 Proposed Lease Real Estate Summary

RE FILE NO.:	DATE SUBMITTED:	NEW LEASE/EXTENSION/RENEWAL:
LESSOR:		
LESSEE:		
TYPE OF FACILITY:		
LOCATION:		
LEGAL REVIEW BY:		DATE:
FINANCIAL REVIEW BY:		DATE:
A/R REQUIRED: YES NO	A/R APPROVED: YES NO	IL ONLY: YES NO IF YES, DATE:

TERM OF LEASE

EFFECTIVE:	OCCUPANCY:		TERMINATION:
TOTAL TERM:	YEARS:	MONTHS:	DAYS:
HOLDOVER:	RENT/PENALTY:		
OPTIONS: FOR YEARS	NOTICE REQUIRED:	DAYS	
CANCELLATION/PENALTY:			

RENTAL INFORMATION

BASIC LEASE TERM: $	PER MONTH	($ PER SQ. FT. PER MONTH)	
TOTAL COMMITMENT: $	ANNUAL COMMITMENT: $	QUITCLAIM:	GRANT:
OPTION PERIOD:	OR OTHER:		
ESCALATION: $			
TOTAL AREA:	SQ. FT.	RENTABLE AREA:	SQ. FT.
USABLE AREA:	SQ. FT.	OFFICE AREA:	SQ. FT.
ADDITIONAL AREA AFFECTED:	SQ. FT.	LAND:	ACRES

LESSOR/LESSEE RESPONSIBILITIES

TAXES:	INSURANCE:
MAINTENANCE/REPAIR:	UTILITIES:

COMMENTS:

DIVISION APPROVAL:	DATE:	SECTOR APPROVAL:	DATE:
CORPORATE APPROVAL:	DATE:	VACANCY APPROVAL:	DATE:

EXHIBIT 10.9 Proposed Purchase Real Estate Summary

RE FILE NO.:	DATE SUBMITTED:
SECTOR:	

PROPERTY INFORMATION

LOCATION NAME:				
CITY:	COUNTY:	STATE:	COUNTRY:	ZIP:
TYPE OF FACILITY:		ZONED:		
ACREAGE - LAND:		BUILDING:	SQUARE FEET	
TOPO AVAILABLE:	DATE:	SURVEY/PLOT PLAN AVAILABLE:	DATE:	PICTURES AVAILABLE:
APPRAISED VALUE:			APPRAISAL DATE:	

TITLE INFORMATION

DEED DATED:	RECORDED:	DEED BOOK VOLUME:	PAGE:
GENERAL WARRANTY:	SPECIAL WARRANTY:	QUITCLAIM:	GRANT:
GRANTOR:		GRANTEE:	
PURCHASE PRICE: $	LAND VALUE: $	BOOK VALUE: $	DATE:
EASEMENTS:			
COMMENTS:			
DIVISION APPROVAL:	DATE:	SECTOR APPROVAL:	DATE:
CORPORATE APPROVAL:	DATE:	VACANCY APPROVAL:	DATE:

The lease approval process can take from a few weeks to many months. The process phases and the lease document steps are critical. Exhibit 10.10 identifies the process phases.

Process phases[5] (see Exhibit 10.10) include:

- Lease Document Prepared by the Landlord or Tenant.
- Queue Time with a focus on reducing iterations and changes to the signature process.
- Business Terms with a focus on a more detailed RFP.
- Normal Coordination with Legal.
- Transfer of Documents, Automation, Communication and Word Processing.
- Cycle of the lease document process including the number of iterations.
- External & Internal Requirements which the Tenant and Landlord must address.
- Process Time with a focus on the development and use of a Lease Document Log to record and document process time.

Lease Document Steps[6] (see Exhibit 10.11) include the following:

- The Pre-Negotiated Document or Model Lease, which incorporates a business Term Sheet and can be developed between the tenant and the landlord and/or can be developed for the real estate industry to resemble standard contract documents that other business areas have developed and use regularly (e.g., engineering, design, architectural services, general construction). The Model Lease may pose a problem with some corporate legal counsel who may insist that each document have their "imprint." Corporate legal counsel may want a say in the drafting of the document, no matter how minor. If this happens, the use of a Model Lease by corporate real estate may not be beneficial.
- Administration of the lease through word processing, communications via electronic mail, modem or corporate network; the ability via software to red-line changes to the lease; and a readability index 40 so that the lease can be read and understood before and after the lease is signed.
- Local legal requirements that are unique and could impact the rights and responsibilities of either or both parties to the lease.

[5] *Source:* Benchmarking Research Study on "The Office Lease Approval Process" by Edmond P. Rondeau for the Industrial Development Research Foundation (IDRF), June 1992.

[6] Ibid.

EXHIBIT 10.10 Office Lease Approval Process: *Lease Document Steps*

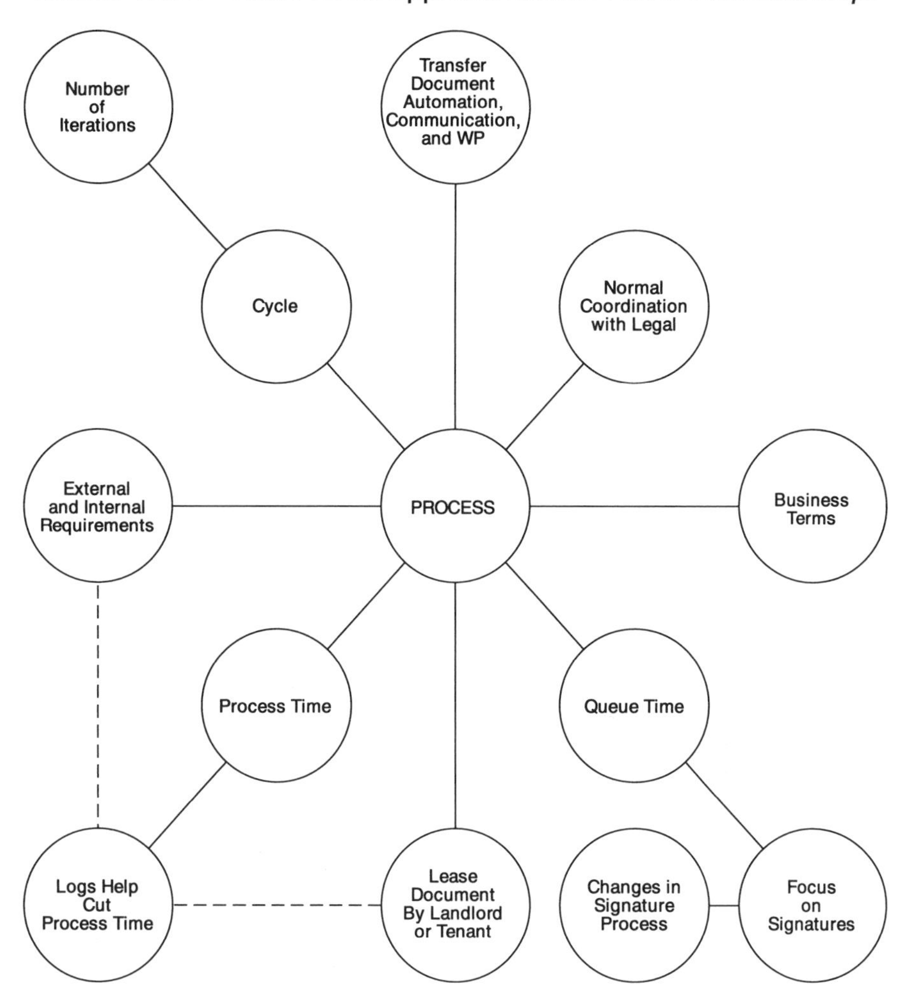

EXHIBIT 10.11 Office Lease Approval Process: *Process Phases*

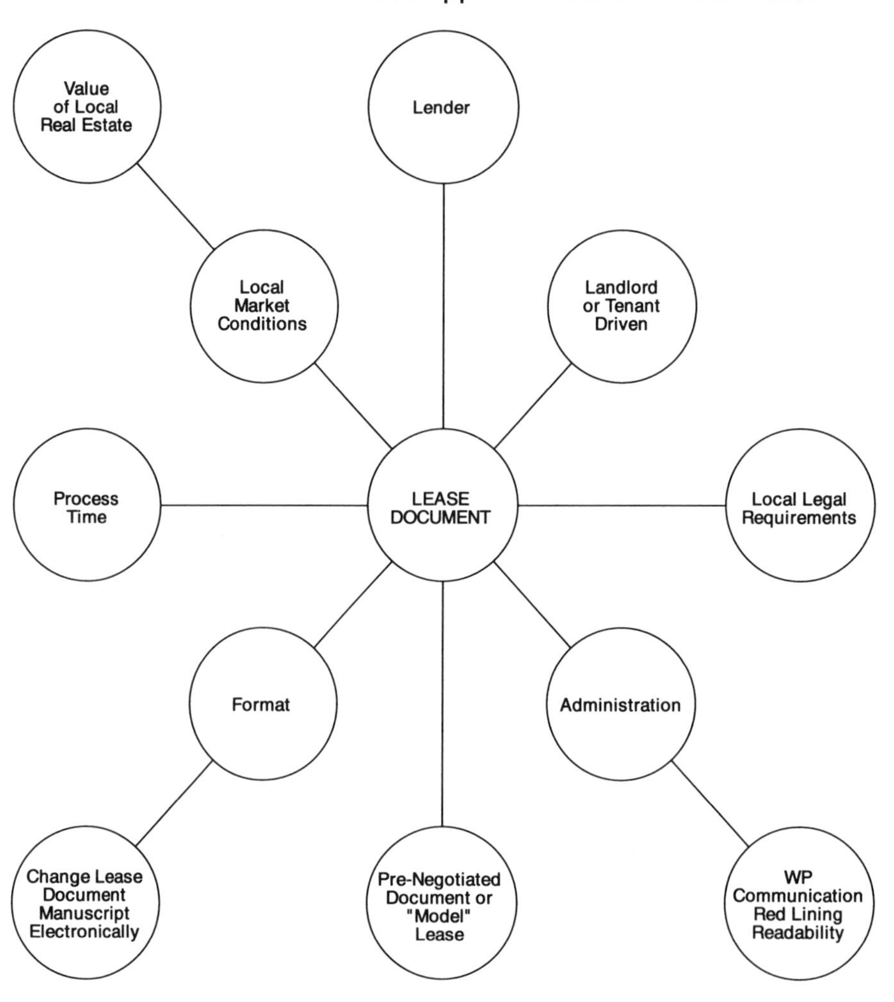

- Landlord or tenant driven business, legal requirements, and contingencies to complete the lease.
- Lender or financial partner whose financial interest may become a major obstacle or opportunity to completing the lease agreement. Ideally, the lender's legal and business requirements should be understood before all business terms are agreed upon.
- Local market conditions where the local real estate economy or business terms of the lease reflect local real estate values concerning such items as concessions, rents, operating expenses, upfit, and free rent.
- Process Time, including all the steps and time required to develop the lease document from the agreement of the business terms to the execution of the lease document. Reducing process time can improve productivity.
- Format, which standardizes the business and lease terms, contents and wording, arrangement, and the ability to make and receive changes to the lease document manuscript electronically.

Exhibit 10.12 provides a flow chart of the office lease approval process from the tenant's perspective and Exhibit 10.13 provides a process flow chart from the landlord's perspective.

An Ideal Flow Chart for the office lease approval process is shown in Exhibit 10.14. The flow chart includes the queue time before the next activity (step) and the time to review the document at the activity is included within the activity box.

The Ideal Flow Chart (Exhibit 10.14) incorporates the use of a Model Lease document with a business terms document, and an attached boiler plate legal requirements document which would provide the opportunity for both parties to spend their time focusing on the business aspects of the lease. Legal issues unique to local requirements would be addressed as revisions only to those boiler plate items which need to be revised. When the processing time is reduced by almost 80 days with only two iterations, the tenant and the landlord can execute the lease sooner and provide (ideally with a Model Lease) a quality product where both parties are protected.

EXHIBIT 10.12 Office Lease Approval Process: Tenant's Perspective

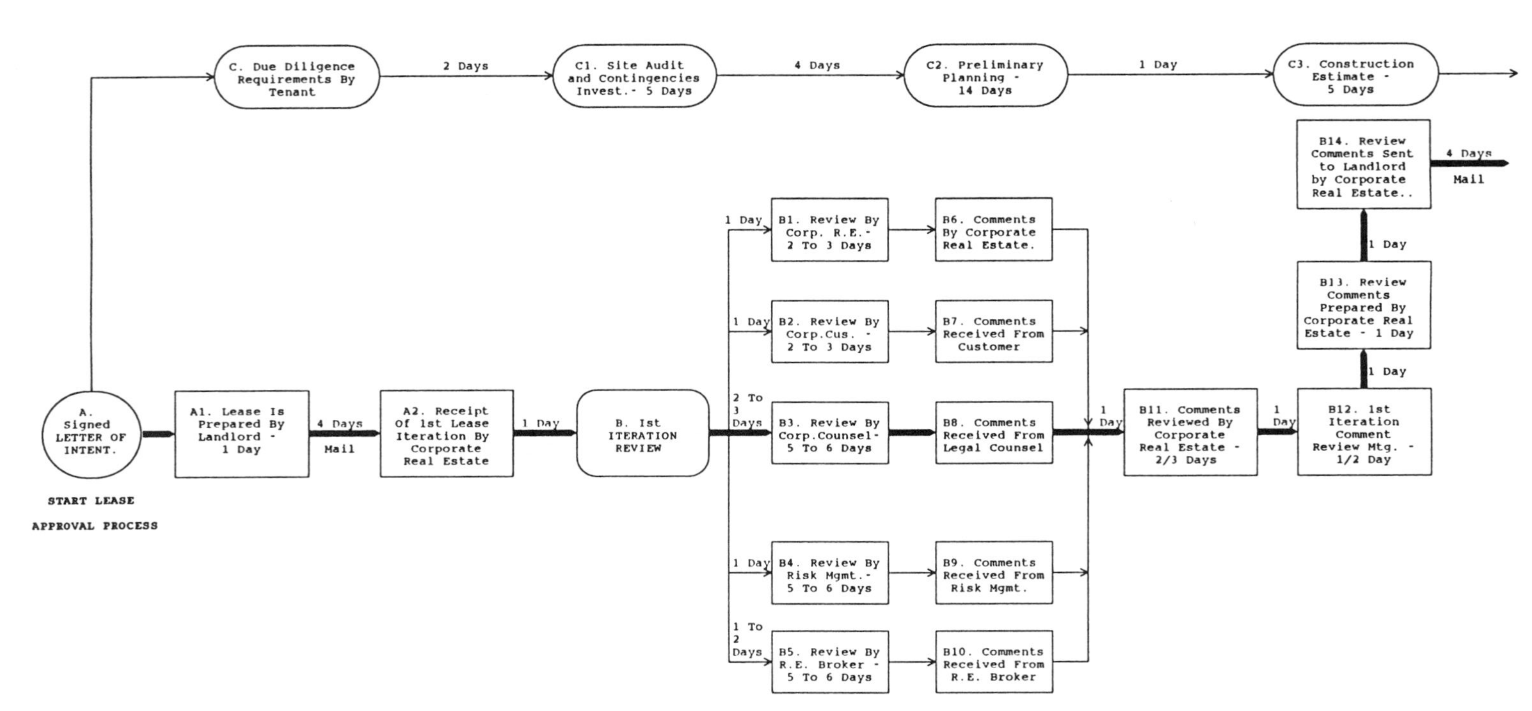

EXHIBIT 10.12 *(Continued)*

ACTUAL FLOW CHART FOR ABC COMPANY

Lease Prepared By Landlord

Page 2 of 3

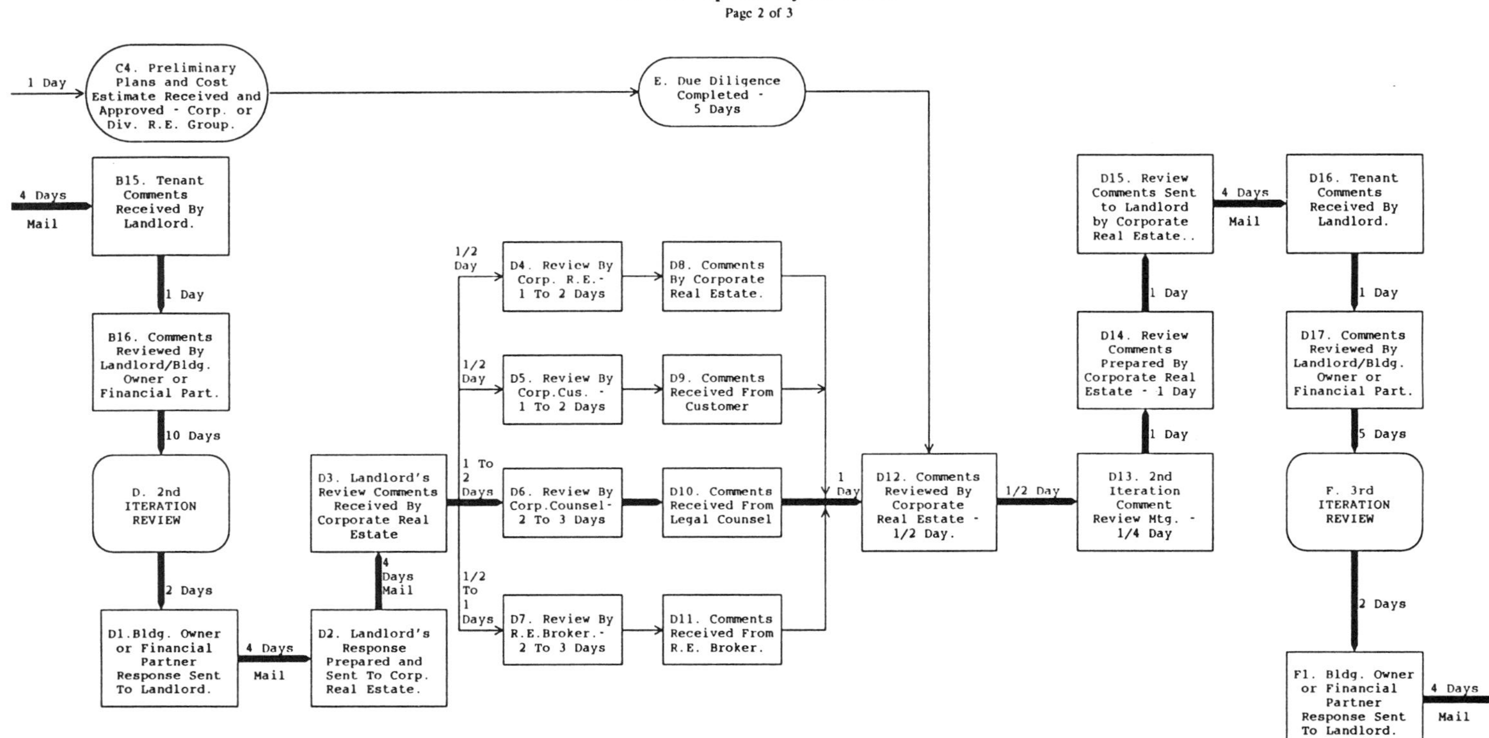

EXHIBIT 10.12 *(Continued)*

ACTUAL FLOW CHART FOR ABC COMPANY

Lease Prepared By Landlord

Page 3 of 3

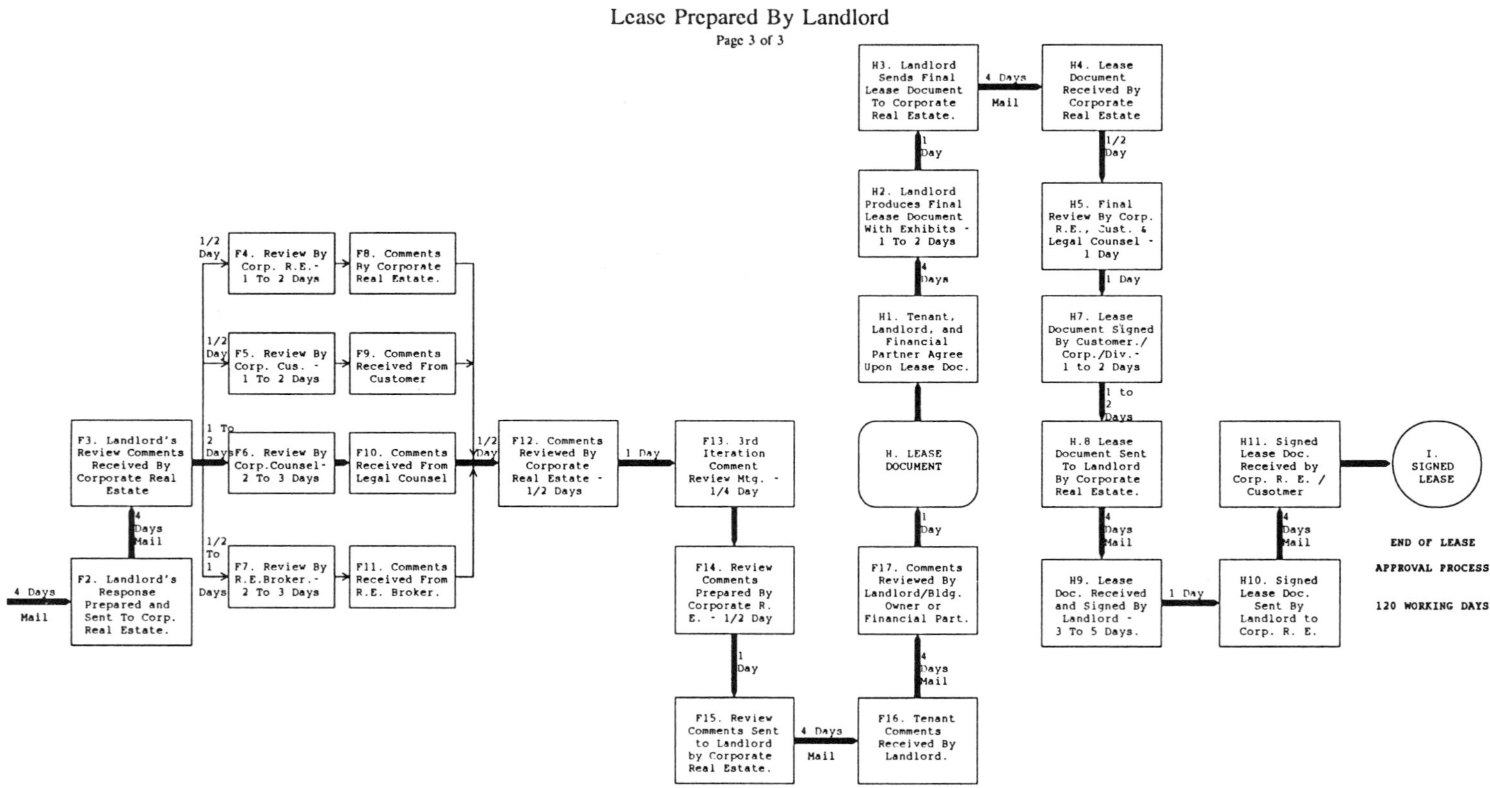

EXHIBIT 10.13 Office Lease Approval Process: Landlord's Perspective

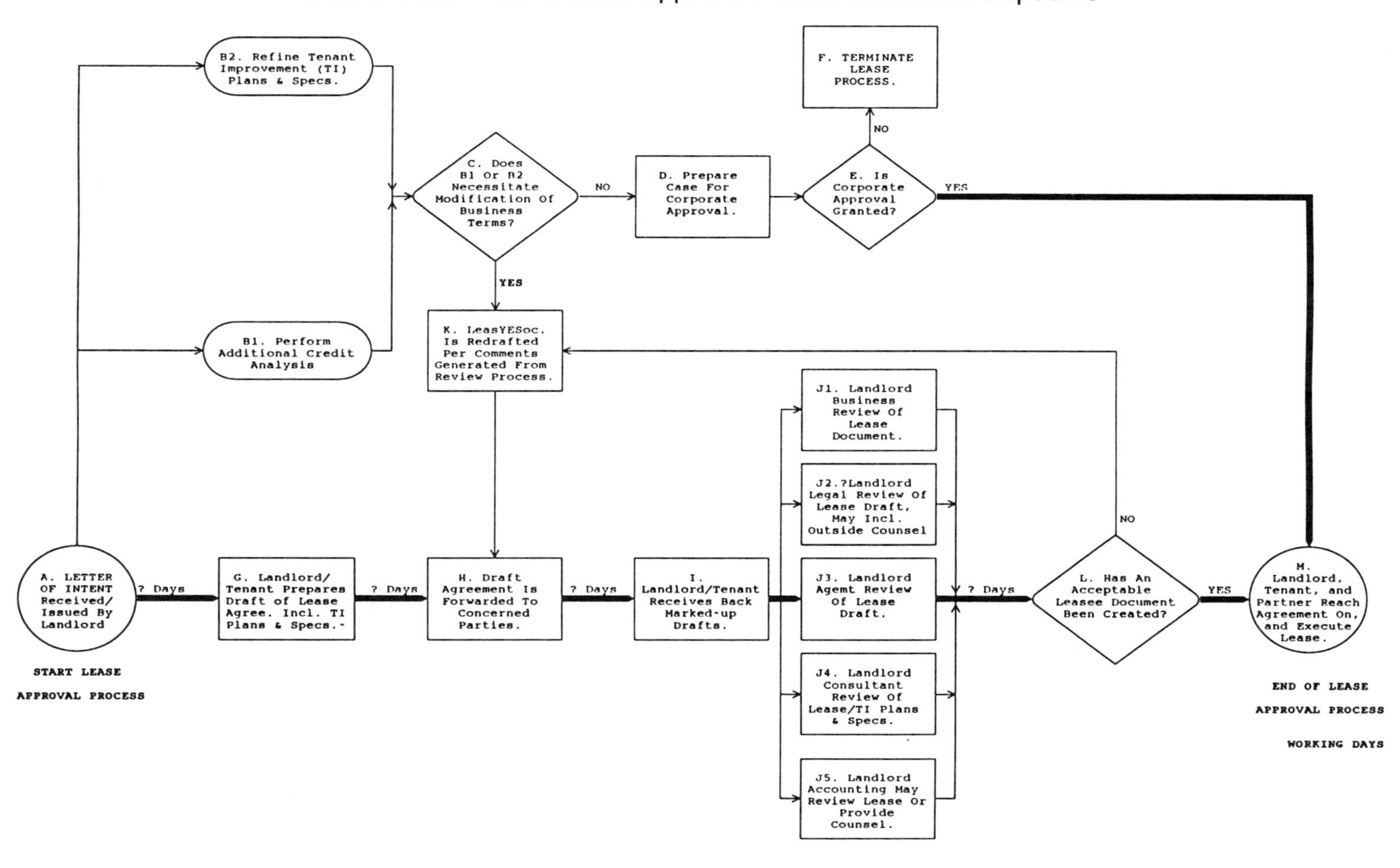

EXHIBIT 10.14 Office Lease Approval Process: Ideal Flow Chart

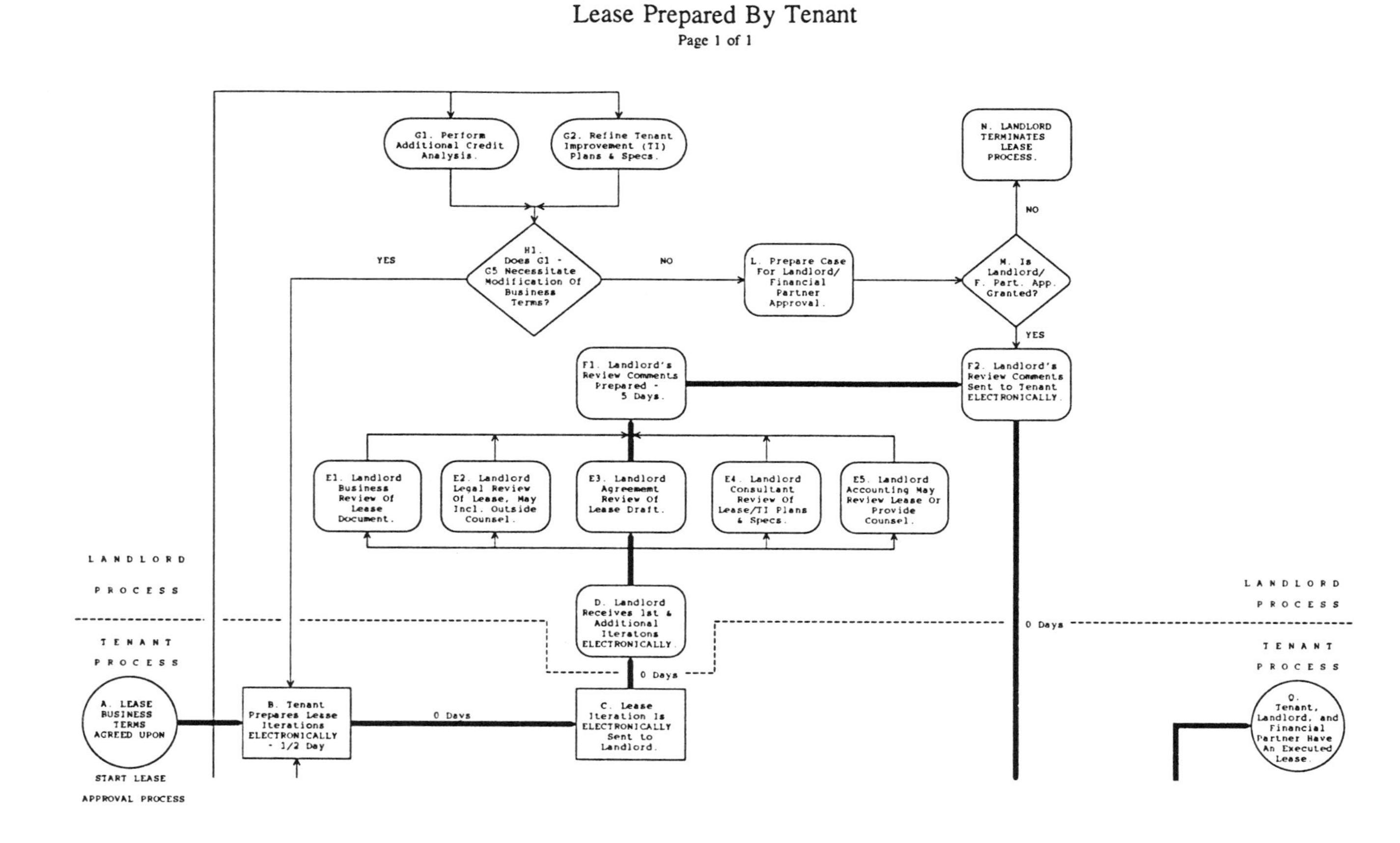

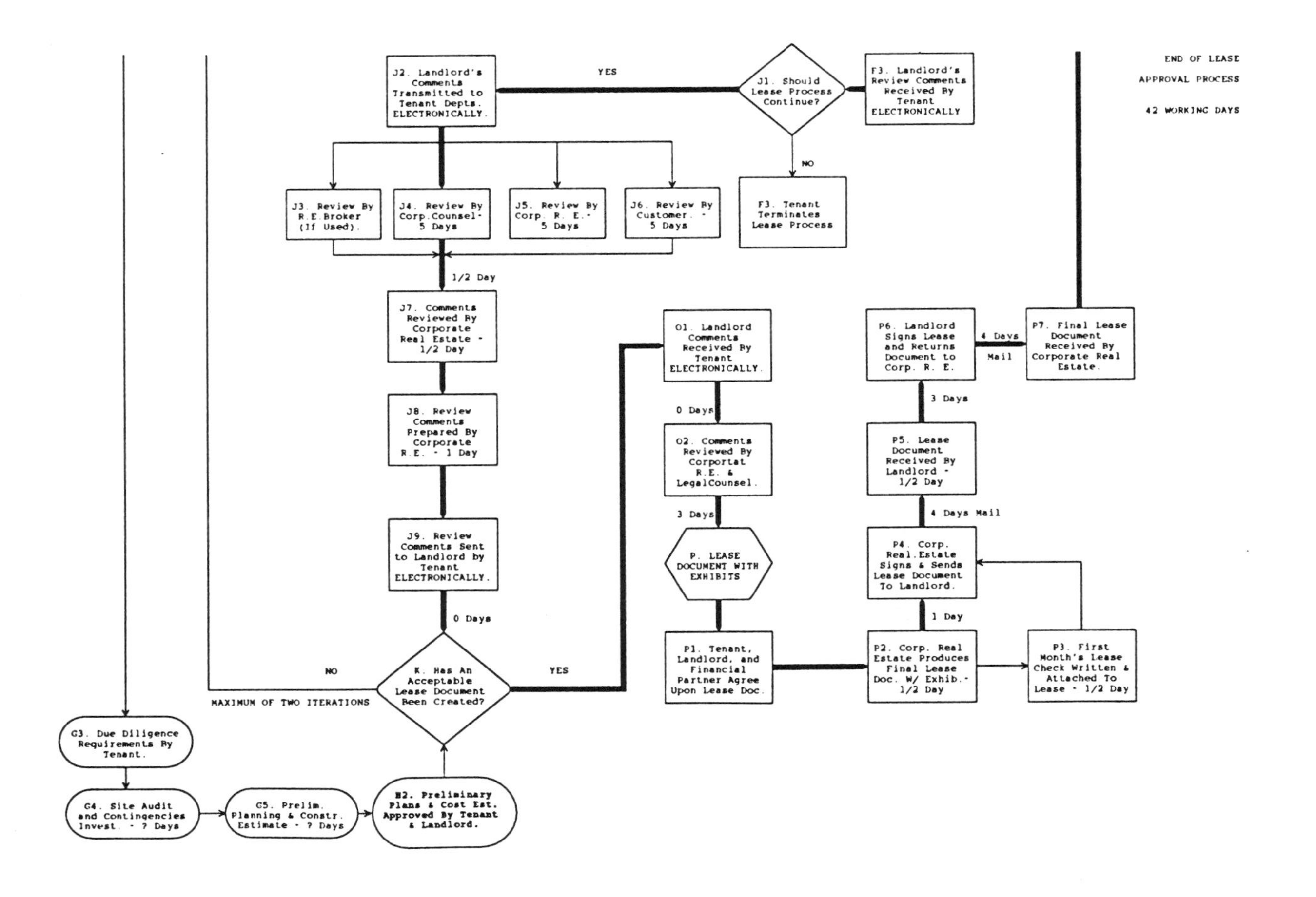
J2. Landlord's Comments Transmitted to Tenant Depts. ELECTRONICALLY.
YES
J1. Should Lease Process Continue?
F3. Landlord's Review Comments Received By Tenant ELECTRONICALLY
END OF LEASE
APPROVAL PROCESS
42 WORKING DAYS
NO
J3. Review By R.E.Broker (If Used).
J4. Review By Corp.Counsel- 5 Days
J5. Review By Corp. R. E.- 5 Days
J6. Review By Customer. - 5 Days
F3. Tenant Terminates Lease Process
1/2 Day
J7. Comments Reviewed By Corporate Real Estate - 1/2 Day
O1. Landlord Comments Received By Tenant ELECTRONICALLY.
P6. Landlord Signs Lease and Returns Document to Corp. R. E.
4 Days
Mail
P7. Final Lease Document Received By Corporate Real Estate.
0 Days
3 Days
J8. Review Comments Prepared By Corporate R.E. - 1 Day
O2. Comments Reviewed By Corportal R.E. & LegalCounsel.
P5. Lease Document Received By Landlord - 1/2 Day
3 Days
4 Days Mail
J9. Review Comments Sent to Landlord by Tenant ELECTRONICALLY.
P. LEASE DOCUMENT WITH EXHIBITS
P4. Corp. Real.Estate Signs & Sends Lease Document To Landlord.
0 Days
1 Day
NO
K. Has An Acceptable Lease Document Been Created?
YES
P1. Tenant, Landlord, and Financial Partner Agree Upon Lease Doc.
P2. Corp. Real Estate Produces Final Lease Doc. W/ Exhib.- 1/2 Day
P3. First Month's Lease Check Written & Attached To Lease - 1/2 Day
MAXIMUM OF TWO ITERATIONS
G3. Due Diligence Requirements By Tenant.
G4. Site Audit and Contingencies Invest. - ? Days
G5. Prelim. Planning & Constr. Estimate - ? Days
H2. Preliminary Plans & Cost Est. Approved By Tenant & Landlord.

Eleven

Property Negotiation

§ 11.1 INTRODUCTION

The corporate real estate department becomes involved in various types of property negotiations. Because each piece of real property is unique, the terms for its purchase, sale, or lease can only be estimated. Negotiation is essential for the corporation and the lessor (or buyer, seller, developer, joint venturer, etc.), to reach an agreement. The specific transaction dictates the issues that will be discussed during negotiation. The outcome of any real estate negotiation depends on the corporation's strategic plan and the negotiator's ability to adhere to that plan, while remaining informed, flexible, and cooperative at the bargaining table.

§ 11.2 PROPERTY NEGOTIATION—ELEMENTS FOR SUCCESS

Negotiation begins with identification of the corporation's need to develop, acquire, lease, sublease, or dispose of real property. The corporate real estate executive, who typically represents the firm in negotiations, initiates the process by recommending a particular real estate plan to senior management. Prior to negotiation, a team of in-house specialists should review negotiation strategy, business goals, and real estate issues, and to agree on a model acquisition to satisfy the corporation's needs. This model should outline anticipated price of purchase, costs of building, rental rates, operating expenses, and other values and incentives that the corporation expects to obtain. A list of prospective properties should be developed from this information. After completing this internal review, the real estate executive can negotiate with the parties essential to the desired real estate transaction.

In either leasing or buying, many topics can enter into negotiations, such as the lease or purchase price, the lease options (rent escalation, purchase, sublease, assignment), lease terms (length or lease, occupancy, expiration dates), provisions for security, maintenance, and garbage disposal services, deposits (earnest), and amenities (communication and postal facilities).

Regardless of the issues involved, three factors can affect any negotiator's ability to obtain a successful outcome: (1) flexibility, (2) preparation, and (3) time. The ability to be flexible on points of conflict and to recognize that some points are not negotiable; can greatly improve the negotiator's chances of achieving mutually beneficial solutions on other points. In addition, the quantity and quality of information gathered ahead of time substantially affects the negotiator's ability to bargain intelligibly. Finally, the amount of time available before and during negotiation sessions can be a determining factor in the outcome.

(a) FLEXIBILITY

The complexity of real estate transactions makes it unlikely for the parties involved to reach an immediate agreement on every issue, and accordingly, experience teaches real estate negotiators to enter every real estate transaction with a flexible attitude. Negotiation with a win–win outcome is possible, however, as each side may be able to relinquish or modify certain demands and replace them with points of mutual benefit. Because negotiation is a process of give and take, remaining flexible, openly conveying an attitude of cooperation, and adopting a "satisficing" strategy (i.e., one that satisfies reasonable standards) during each bargaining session encourage successful negotiation.

The more important a proposed transaction is to either party involved, the more important it is to keep the door open to continuing dialogue because there may be many practical options that could satisfy both parties. Negotiators should look for such solutions, be open minded, and be willing to compromise. Flexibility enables each party to discover small, concession-making opportunities that promote further discussion about the larger, more important issues of a proposed transaction. Win–win solutions require that both parties search for creative alternatives that will allow for bargain and compromise.

Negotiation is a cooperative venture between two parties with often fundamentally conflicting goals who openly strive for solutions that will maximize the advantages to both parties. The willingness to negotiate is often one of the first items that the parties agree on. Because the negotiator's goal is to solve problems, not to debate, conveying the ability and desire to bargain cooperatively, as opposed to initiating confrontation, will increase the likelihood of a successful negotiation. Confrontation, on the other hand, typically puts the opponent on the defensive and inhibits constructive dialogue.

Though the ultimate goal of the corporation is to increase profits, stability and earnings per share aggressively seeking a solution to maximize each variable at the cost of the opposing party may be too risky. The company is more likely to achieve their long-term objective by following a "satisficing" strategy. Seeking solutions that satisfy reasonable standards is necessary because it is impossible or impractical to attain the level for each variable that produces the greatest possible satisfaction. Satisficing helps to avoid failed negotiation attempts and significantly increases the chances of maximizing corporate wealth over time.

(b) PREPARATION

Thorough preparation prior to negotiation is essential to a positive outcome. The quantity and quality of information gathered may dictate the number of options available for meeting the opposing party's requirements and, thus, one's own goals and needs more effectively. Information about the market, the number and types of sites or properties available, local real estate terminology, the corporation's needs, the seller's, lessor's or buyer's needs, financial concepts, and other factors that may affect the selection process can empower the negotiator, who can then estimate, in advance, the range of offers and, therefore, establish his or her own counteroffers.

Preparation should include answers to these questions about the opposing negotiator: Who are the negotiating parties trying to satisfy, and to whom are they accountable. What roles are they likely to play in the negotiation, and what are their negotiation styles? And what cultural, corporate, and business traits will affect the negotiation? In turn, information gathering should include seeking similar insights into one's own style, aims, and responsibilities.

Effective negotiators are aware of their party's strengths and weaknesses, as well as the strengths and weaknesses of the opponent's position. Such knowledge is instrumental in helping a negotiator determine the most effective approach to use during the bargaining sessions. In addition, such information enables the negotiator to understand more clearly the actions taken by the opposing party and to maneuver the negotiation proceedings to meet his or her own party's needs.

Each negotiator must assess the current market, considering the cost-effectiveness of the information. Since prevailing market rates and conditions impact every real estate transaction, knowledge of current rates and prices, as well as the availability of comparable properties, is crucial before negotiation commences. Preparation of the Request for Proposal (RFP) is also an important part of the information-gathering process and is discussed later in this chapter.

For an example of the value of information, consider that the negotiation process can falter over the seller's refusal to lower what the buyer, based on market factors, knows to be a high price for a given property. By using current market information as leverage, the buyer may be able to persuade a serious seller to lower the price, and a deal will be struck. Should the seller refuse to bring the price down, despite current market data, the buyer can cease bargaining and commence negotiations for the acquisition of another available comparable property.

Preparation for negotiations should involve the development of a workplan to help organize and manage the process. The following checklist will be helpful in developing a workplan and strategy.

Achieving Acceptable Terms to Both Parties:

- Determine real estate market activity.
  - ____ Is it a seller's or landlord's market?
  - ____ Is it a purchaser's or tenant's market?
  - ____ Is it a normal or balanced market?

- Understand local real estate and business terminology, cap rates, square foot prices, etc.
- Determine your customer's unique dilemmas and those of sellers and landlords.
- Use financial concepts such as market value, most probable purchase price, lease costs, ROI, ROE, investment value, etc.
- Evaluate in advance the range of the seller's or landlord's offers and your and their counteroffers.
- Consider and understand in advance the subjective factors that may affect your customer's selection process.

Negotiating Psychology:

- Know your customer and the seller or landlord.
  - —— Who are you trying to satisfy?
  - —— Who is the seller or landlord trying to satisfy?
  - —— Who are you, your customer, the seller or the landlord accountable to during this process?
  - —— Understand pertinent corporate, cultural and business traits and practices.
- Know the roles being performed by the negotiating parties.
- Know your and your customer's negotiation style.
  - —— Manage the desire to control others.
  - —— Avoid being overly confident, trusting or overly suspicious.
  - —— Avoid being overly manipulative or exploitive.
  - —— Recognize the need to win, succeed and close by both parties.
- Know your opponent's negotiation style.
- Be alert to flashy, steam roller or rigid types of negotiators who may convey:
  - —— "Trust me—I'm honest."
  - —— "Trust me—I only want what's right."
  - —— "Don't trust me. I'm out to get you."
- Consider and carefully plan the physical factors that can affect negotiations.
  - —— The location—your, your customer's, the seller's or landlord's or a neutral place?
  - —— The facility—table and chair types, where to sit, colors, breaks and refreshments, meals, HVAC and other comfort or distress factors?
  - —— Are there time limits to each session and to complete the process?

- Where appropriate, use professionals ("who care but not that much") to represent you in negotiations.
- Insure that during negotiations all parties know:
  - ____ Who is the spokesperson for each side?
  - ____ What are the limits of the spokesperson's authority and flexibility?

The Process Should Meet Corporate Objectives

- Use cooperative bargaining rather than confrontation.
  - ____ Try not to maximize, but find a satisfactory and reasonable solution.
  - ____ The goal is a basic meeting of the minds.
- Control the process based upon your negotiating strategy and model.
  - ____ Use your negotiating model.
  - ____ Determining essential facts are essential to defining business and negotiating issues.
  - ____ Prudent preparation should result in understanding the assumptions.
  - ____ Discover the strengths and weaknesses of both sides.
- Be prepared for reciprocal provisions.

Ensuring You Get What You Thought You Were Getting:

- What are the necessary requirements for your customer? Are they satisfied?
- What conditions does the seller or landlord require to close?
- Where possible, require specific remedies and liquidated damages.

Concluding the Negotiating Process: The Final Agreement and Closing the "Deal"

- Be ready to concede appropriate items or issues within your negotiating model.
- If you are purchasing, consider using a closing attorney whose experience includes closing where the acquisition is located.
  - ____ Require the right to assign the purchase or lease without unreasonable restraint.
  - ____ Do not waive essential contingencies, warranties and representations that must survive the closing.
  - ____ Require an inspection as appropriate.
  - ____ When rights and duties are indisputably clear in the real estate lease or purchase contract, take a firm position.

- ____ Support your leasing or closing attorney while achieving your business objectives.
- ____ Do not be forget that you can stop the lease process or reschedule a closing if *required business* terms and issues have not been achieved.

- Be gracious, civil and professional.
- Do not squeeze the last buck out of the deal. If it is a good deal, close the transaction.

(c) TIME

The time available to complete the real estate transaction will impact the quality of preparation prior to negotiations. If possible, adequate time should be scheduled for the development of the strategic plan and model acquisition, as well as for the development of the RFP, the analysis of responses to the RFP, and the location of a site.

Information gathering prior to the bargaining sessions can be extremely time consuming; an inadequate time frame can greatly limit the number of acceptable sites the firm has to choose from and can result in the acceptance of an offer that may not meet the corporation's needs and objectives. Since the negotiator's power during bargaining can be determined by his or her store of applicable information, it is essential to spend the time necessary to ensure that the corporation is negotiating for the best possible deals. For example, if the corporate real estate executive is not aware of alternative acceptable sites while the other party is, the corporation is at a distinct negotiating disadvantage. On the other hand, the corporate executive who is aware of numerous alternative acceptable sites, pricing, and lease terms, will have the negotiation advantage.

Time constraints at the bargaining table can add to the pressure of bargaining and can affect the outcome of the session.

§ 11.3 NEGOTIATION GOALS

The goals of the strategic and operating plans should guide the negotiator's behavior during the bargaining session. In a negotiation setting, the issues depend on whether the party is developing, purchasing, leasing, or selling the property. Each party wants to maximize its benefits, but the factors that affect each party's ability to do so may vary drastically. Regardless of the strategy chosen, an appropriate range of offers should always be developed prior to negotiation, and each party should attempt to identify the limits, goals, and strategy of the opposing party.

(a) NEGOTIATION STRATEGY

The negotiation strategy enables the negotiator to meet the goals of the company. The ability to adhere to the previously outlined plan during a "heated" negotiation session determines whether or not the negotiator will leave the bargaining table with the deal originally planned by the company. The negotiation strategy and model should control the negotiator's actions. In the emotionally charged atmosphere of the negotiation, there is often a tendency to strive to win at all costs. At this point, it is essential not to lose sight of the company's original objectives.

If the critical factors for satisfying corporate needs were determined prior to negotiation, the negotiator will have leeway to bargain with insignificant items while holding a rigid position on mandatory issues. To salvage an important deal after a heated negotiation session ending in deadlock, the negotiator will likely grant concessions. By agreeing to some points that the corporation considers to be minor but the other party views as important, the negotiator can establish quick rapport can buttress more difficult issues, and can artfully parlay each successive negotiation session into one closer to the attainment of the corporation's goals.

(b) NEEDS OF THE PARTIES

The differing needs of buyers, sellers, lessors, lessees, and various other parties to the real estate transaction (e.g., developer, broker, architect, building inspector) will have a significant impact on negotiations. For example, matters of concern to the buyer during negotiation include price, down payment, financing, required escrows, closing costs, transaction costs, and personal liability. The marketability and location of the property must also be strong considerations. If time limitations are a factor, the seller may need to provide the buyer with warranties and representations concerning important items affecting value. In turn, the buyer will need to verify the information given and may try to negotiate the right to terminate the deal if the information is inadequate or negative. The buyer must assure the seller that the agreed-on terms of the contract will be executed in full and will be binding on both parties.

To ensure that the property will meet expected requirements at the time of the closing, the buyer seeks to maximize agreed-on conditions in the contract. The seller, in contrast, will typically want to avoid or minimize conditions that are included. To get what they are bargaining for, both parties must be prepared to make assurances to each other that will move the proceeding toward a final settlement and closing.

The main objective of any negotiation is a legally enforceable contract at mutually acceptable terms. A legally enforceable contract is merely a written expression of the mutually acceptable terms arrived at by buyer and seller. It is essential that the parties know the limits of their bargaining power. Negotiating long-term leases requires intensive bargaining because each clause may vary the economic returns of the package.

(c) ESTABLISHING AND RECOGNIZING LIMITATIONS—SETTING PRICE RANGES

Prior to negotiation, both parties should establish appropriate limitations (e.g., price per square foot, location, length of base). Understandably, each party aims to maximize benefits from the transaction, but their opposing roles create limitations that affect each party's ability to accomplish these goals. The parties should clearly define their own limitations prior to bargaining and strive to discover each other's limits, goals, and strategy.

After determining its acceptable price range, each party aims to maximize its net present value during negotiation. The highest price that a party is willing to pay is often called the *ceiling price,* and the lowest price a party is willing to accept is the *floor price.* Ceiling and floor prices can be determined by calculating the net present value of an investment (see § 13.6(c)(2)).

From the purchaser's point of view, acquisitions should be executed at or below current market levels, whereas the seller prefers price ranges set at or above the current market level.

To correctly estimate the range of appropriate offers and counteroffers, the negotiator must properly evaluate and categorize the current market conditions to determine if it is a buyer's or a seller's market, and how the market affects negotiations. Proper preparation for negotiation requires that market information be thorough and up to date.

Using sensitivity analysis, the buyer should determine several factors about the acquisition offer prior to negotiations including financing terms, tax planning, and impact on differences in price. Such information helps negotiators set a reasonable range of minimum and maximum offers. It is also beneficial to evaluate of nonprice concessions and estimate their impact on the return–risk relationship. The effect of nonprice concessions on the return–risk relationship should also be estimated.

It is of utmost importance to identify the true limitations of the opposing party. During the negotiation, the seller will attempt to maximize his benefit by insisting that the floor price, or lowest possible selling price, is higher than it actually is. Similarly, the buyer will try to convince the seller that the highest price he or she is willing to pay, or the ceiling price, is lower than it actually is. In some cases, the opponent may present an offer that is outside the acceptable range. If the negotiator suspects that the price is merely a preliminary offer, the appropriate response may be a counteroffer outside the reasonable range to the other extreme. Such an action may initiate a discussion of each party's minimum requirements.

If the apparent ceiling price is below the apparent floor price, both parties may become convinced that a deal is not possible even if it is. Therefore, while the negotiator does not want to reveal his or her true limitations, it may be necessary to hint at the actual range. And it should be a major goal of each negotiator to pinpoint the true bargaining range of the opposing party.

It is important, also, that each party is aware of its own limits, not only in terms of price but in terms of other concessions, as well.

(d) MAKING THE OFFER

There is some debate about which party should make the initial offer. Many professionals believe that the first price should be set by the party initiating negotiations, and others feel it is the buyer's or lessee's responsibility to make the first offer. In some instances, sellers, considering an offer, feel no obligation to present a counteroffer.

In most cases, a property will be offered for sale or lease for a specified price. The buyer or lessee probably benefits by encouraging the seller or lessor to clarify the advantages of the offer rather than by immediately making a counteroffer. This presentation allows the seller to explain the offer to the buyer or lessee and provides an early opportunity for the parties to seek mutual accommodation. In too many cases, the initial offer, which can reveal important underlying issues, is put on the back burner as attention is shifted to other concessions.

§ 11.4 REQUESTS FOR PROPOSALS

Once the real estate requirements and negotiating strategy have been agreed on, a Request for Proposal (RFP) should be written as part of the preparation and information-gathering process. The RFP is a document that details the company's requirements for space, furnishings, and equipment. Based on the company's specifications for a particular real estate requirement, the RFP should include any critical matters that the company will use to analyze and evaluate each response. Typically, the RFP is written by the real estate broker consultant based on the specifications required by the corporate real estate department.

The RFP should state who will occupy the property or space, the kind and amount of property or space needed, and whether it will be leased or purchased. In addition, the RFP should include the amount of space required for growth and when it will be needed, the length of time the space will be needed, the desired location, and any other specific requirements.

In many situations, it may be advisable at the RFP stage to omit the name of the company and identify it only by type (e.g., Fortune 500 company, manufacturing company). This will remove the potential pressures of state and local politics and publicity on the property search.

(a) REQUEST FOR PROPOSAL FOR LEASE

If the party intends to lease or sublease space or property, the RFP should very clearly state what must be included in response to the items on the following checklist:

____ Premise requirements (in usable or rentable sq. ft.)
____ Term of the lease
____ Term commencement date
____ Rent abatement (free rent)
____ Rental commencement date
____ Rental rate
____ Escalation and any other rental adjustment clause(s)
____ Improvement allowance
____ Space planning and design services
____ Improvement contractor
____ Expansion option(s)
____ Renewal option(s)
____ Property management and tenants
____ Operating hours
____ ADA compliance and access
____ Extended or after-hours HVAC
____ Telecommunication and shared tenant services
____ Security
____ Parking conditions
____ Nondisturbance
____ Asbestos test results and a written certification from landlord
____ Amenities (food service, conference room(s), postal services, health club, branch bank, child care, etc.)
____ Other landlord services
____ Surcharges
____ Landlord's broker
____ Agency disclosure
____ Response to RFP due date
____ Exhibits (when applicable)

Exhibit 11.1 shows a sample RFP to lease office space.

EXHIBIT 11.1 Sample Request for Proposal to Lease Office Space

ABC COMPANY

June 18, 1993

ABC Company (Tenant), a Chicago, Il. based division of XYZ Corporation, is soliciting formal responses to this Request For Proposal for the leasing of office space as specified below. Tenant proposes to initially lease 15,000 rentable square feet of office space in the greater Chicago, Il. area to better serve it's internal customers.

A. **PREMISES:**

1. Approximately 15,000 rentable square feet initially with the option to lease approximately 15,000 contiguous rentable square feet within one year of the initial lease date.

2. Approximately 400 to 600 usable square feet of the leased space will comprise a Computer Room. Is there a space within the proposed Building that would uniquely accommodate this use. Please identify proposed locations within your Building/Project.

B. **TERM:**

1. Three (3) years.

C. **TERM COMMENCEMENT DATE:**

1. October 1, 1993 - September 31, 1996.

D. **RENTAL COMMENCEMENT DATE:**

1. Please specify if, due to a period of rental abatement, it is different than the Term Commencement Date.

E. **RENTAL RATE:**

1. Full-service rate with area calculations based on BOMA Whole Floor Rentable method and BOMA Multi-tenant Usable method. Provide Rentable to Usable conversion factor, as appropriate.

F. **ESCALATION AND ANY OTHER RENTAL ADJUSTMENT CLAUSES(S):**

1. Specify and illustrate method(s). Provide your definition of Operating Expenses, or any expenses/costs that are reimbursable by Tenant to Landlord. All reimbursable-type expenses should be budgeted in the Base Year "peg", if a "peg" is proposed under your particular Lease.

G. **TENANT IMPROVEMENTS:**

1. Please furnish Landlord Workletter or unit (if applicable) and dollar allowances and describe the materials quality and construction specifications of Building Standard Tenant Allowances. Distinguish between Base Building items (define) and Tenant Allowance items.

2. Is any such dollar allowance based upon "slab-to-slab" or "below-a-finished ceiling" ? Specify.

H. **TENANT IMPROVEMENTS CONTRACTOR:**

1. Please specify the contractor proposed by the Landlord for the Tenant Improvement Work. If the Landlord does not propose to construct the Work, please specify Landlord's requirements.

2. If Landlord proposes to construct the Improvements, specify all fees associated with, but not limited to, overhead, profit, and supervision. Are such fees provided for in your Work Letter or Construction Allowance?

EXHIBIT 11.1 *(Continued)*

3. Who is responsible for Construction Management?

4. To what extent, if any does the Landlord and /or the Property Manager receive a fee for initial Tenant Improvements Work?

I. **SPACE PLANNING AND DESIGN SERVICES:**

1. Specify services provided by Landlord, at no additional expense to Tenant, and not chargeable against the Construction Allowance.

2. If Tenant were to employ a design firm for space planning and design purposes, including preparation of Construction Documents, is there a credit due Tenant? If so, what is it?

J. **EXPANSION OPTION(S):**

1. Specific options on additional contiguous space will be required. It is expected that a total of 15,000 r.s.f. will be required at the end of the initial lease year per item A1.

2. Specify location and amount of option space, notice requirements, rate determination method, rental commencement date, treatment of lease term, improvement/renovation allowance, responsibility for demolition (if required), and escalation. In the case of improvement/renovation allowance, distinguish between the treatment of same in regard to first and second generation space.

3. Any such additional space shall be added by amendment to the original Lease, and be identical in all respects to an original Lease.

K. **RENEWAL OPTION(S):**

1. Two (2) consecutive five (5) year renewal options.

L. **PROPERTY MANAGEMENT AND TENANTS:**

1. Who provides property management services? Provide a list of Building Tenants with your proposal.

M. **OPERATING HOURS:**

1. Specify normal business hours for the Building - Monday through Friday, Saturday and Sunday.

N. **ACCESS:**

1. Is 24-hour, seven-day per week access to Tenant's Leased Premises provided? Explain procedure.

O. **EXTENDED OR AFTER HOURS HVAC:**

1. Specify hourly charge and method of determination for such extended/after-hours use of HVAC system and building services.

P. **TELECOMMUNICATION AND SHARED SERVICES:**

1. Does your property offer shared Tenant services via a "switch"? Generally describe the services and costs associated with Tenant's use of such service(s).

Q. **SECURITY:**

1. Describe the Security and Life Safety system(s) of the Building/Project.

R. **PARKING:**

1. Indicate maximum number of parking spaces available. If applicable, is assigned Tenant parking available? What is the cost, if any, for Tenant parking. What are the provisions for visitor parking?

EXHIBIT 11.1 *(Continued)*

S. <u>CONFERENCE ROOM(S)</u>:

1. Do you provide conference facilities within the Building/Project? If so, please describe size, accommodation, procedures, and costs (if any) associated with its use.

T. <u>FOOD SERVICE</u>:

1. Describe eating alternatives within the Building, Project and immediately surrounding area.

U. <u>HEALTH CLUB/FITNESS CENTER</u>:

1. Describe facilities available within the proposed Building or Project. What are the arrangements required for the use by Tenant's employees of such facility?

V. <u>POSTAL SERVICES</u>:

1. Describe Postal Service Facilities available within the Building and Project. What are the current delivery/ pick-up times?

W. <u>OTHER LANDLORD SERVICES</u>:

1. Specify all of the Landlord Services that <u>are</u> and <u>are not</u> provided to the Tenant by the Landlord under the proposed Lease (i.e. janitorial, electrical, taxes, etc.). Also, specify in your proposal that the Building/ Floor(s) are free of friable asbestos.

X. <u>SURCHARGES</u>:

1. Will there be any additional charges to the Tenant for the use of facilities of the Building which will not be incorporated into your proposed rent structure? Such as, but not limited to, Move-in, Telecommunications, Freight Elevator, Loading Dock/Facility, After-Hours Building Standard Security, After-Standard Hours Access, etc. If so, please describe such additional charges.

Y. <u>AGENCY DISCLOSURE</u>:

1. Professional Brokerage Company is acting as Agent for the Tenant in this transaction and will be paid a commission by the Landlord of the office space should a transaction between the parties be consummated.

Z. <u>PROPOSAL DUE DATE</u>:

1. The response to this Request For Proposal is due not later than 10:00 AM (CST), July 15, 1993.

2. Please submit six (6) copies of your Proposal to:

   Ms. Sandra K. Broker
   Vice President
   Professional Brokerage Company
   304 East Wacker Drive
   Chicago, IL. 60631

   Telephone No. (312) 555-8067
   FAX No. (312) 555-0449

■

(b) REQUEST FOR PROPOSAL FOR PURCHASE

If the party plans to purchase the property, the RFP should outline everything that the seller needs to know and to include in the response. The RFP should include detailed requirements on the items in the following checklist:

- ____ Proposed property street and city address
- ____ Seller name, address, phone number
- ____ Property developer and/or developer's financial partner
- ____ Total acreage, land, building, improvements, square feet, etc.
- ____ Topo, survey/plot plan
- ____ Subsoil & hazardous material investigation
- ____ Purchase price and earnest money
- ____ Deed type (general warranty, special warranty, grant, or quitclaim)
- ____ Existing easement(s)
- ____ Clear title and existing title insurance
- ____ Photographs required
- ____ Zoning jurisdiction and zoning
- ____ ADA compliance
- ____ Applicable building code(s) and floor area ration (far)
- ____ Site plan agreement or subdivision of property agreement
- ____ Signage restrictions
- ____ Covenants and restrictions
- ____ Roads dedicated to the municipality
- ____ Landscaping and site lighting requirements
- ____ Site drainage and site storm water retention requirements
- ____ Municipal water service and municipal sewer or well water and/or septic system including fire hydrant service to the site
- ____ Electrical service
- ____ Property taxes (last year, this year, and estimated next year)
- ____ Tax advantages (local or business taxes, local or state income taxes, local occupancy or use taxes, state or local development bonds, etc.)
- ____ Air rights
- ____ Mineral rights
- ____ Environmental issues (asbestos, soil or air pollution, radon, etc.)
- ____ Air pollution
- ____ Noise pollution

____ Security (guards, access card (cost), cameras, parking, after-hour access, fire stairs access, keys, police, etc.)
____ Trained labor force available
____ Fire and life safety, fire stations, hospitals, etc.
____ Competition adjacent or nearby
____ Asbestos test results and written certification from seller
____ Local government smoking policy
____ Contingencies
____ Amenities (food service, conference room[s], fitness facilities, bank, postal service, copy center, and public transportation)
____ Parent company approval
____ Seller's broker
____ Agency disclosure by broker
____ Response to RFP due date
____ Exhibits (when applicable)

Whether the intention is to lease or to buy, the RFP outlines various requirements that the firm may not consider negotiable (usable square feet, parking, security, expansion options). If these items are not obtainable, the deal may not be possible. On the other hand, some items (space planning, free rent, general contractor, and amenities) may be negotiable. These items may be omitted or modified, if necessary, without killing the deal. Exhibit 11.2 shows a sample request for a proposal to purchase property.

§ 11.5 NEGOTIATING PSYCHOLOGY

It is often said that the party with a negotiating advantage (e.g., a corporate user seeking to lease space in a buyer's market) has leverage, strength, or power over the other party. Historically though, corporations did not recognize this leverage even when they had it, whereas entrepreneurial developers, with better information about the marketplace and more skilled real estate negotiators, felt that they had power even when they did not (e.g., in a buyer's market). Often, this feeling of negotiating strength had a tremendous impact on the final terms of the transaction.

Negotiations are conducted in a potentially antagonistic, emotionally loaded environment. However, tension need not lead to insurmountable conflict. If the negotiators use their knowledge of human nature, carefully choosing the individuals to bring to the bargaining session, and are aware of physical aspects affecting the negotiations, they can establish an atmosphere conducive to successful bargaining.

EXHIBIT 11.2 Sample Request for Proposal to Purchase Property

ABC COMPANY

June 18, 1993

ABC Company (Purchaser), a Chicago, Il. based division of XYZ Corporation, is soliciting formal responses to this Request For Proposal for the sale and purchase of property as specified below.

Purchaser proposes to construct and operate a 50,000 square foot Regional Warehouse with 100,000 square feet of adjacent outside storage in the greater Chicago, Il. area to better serve it's internal XYZ Corporate customers. This Region Warehouse design shall be based upon a model Regional Warehouse currently under construction in San Francisco, Ca. This model will be used as a guide to provide a consistent design for site adaptation at the selected site in the greater Chicago, Il. area.

Attachment "A" provides the Purchaser's specific site and project requirements and an outline of the model concepts and design criteria which will be incorporated at this facility.

Purchaser identified a Chicago, Il. based Architectural Consultant to provide professional architectural, engineering, and interior design consulting services for all planning and construction documents necessary to enable the Purchaser to bid and construct this project and other similar projects around the U.S. Design and construction documents shall meet Federal, state and local code requirements.

Purchaser has also identified a General Contractor to provide site evaluation, value engineering, planning, estimating, permitting, construction and project close out services for this project and other similar projects around the U.S.

A. **PROPERTY:**

1. Approximately 9.5 acres zoned for the construction and operation of a warehouse with outside storage as required below and as described in Attachment "A".

2. Provide a plot plan of the proposed property showing the major access roads to the property, the proposed property's street address, legal description, existing covenants and restrictions, size in acres and square feet, and current owner's name, address and telephone number.

3. Provide a schedule of completion for all site improvements proposed and in progress, including roads within the warehouse park, landscaping, retail and service facilities.

4. Provide a list of other tenants in the park.

B. **PROPERTY ZONING:**

1. State the governmental agency which has zoning jurisdiction for the property, current zoning of the proposed property and that this zoning permits the Purchaser's intended use of the property.

C. **PURCHASE PRICE:**

1. Provide the per square foot cost, the number of square feet, and the total purchase price of the property exclusive of closing costs, taxes, commissions, title insurance or other fees.

2. Address costs not included in item C.1.

EXHIBIT 11.2 *(Continued)*

D. **PURCHASE OPTION FOR ADDITIONAL PROPERTY:**

1. Purchaser requires a sale and purchase option for approximately one and one-half (1 1/2) adjacent acres to construct approximately 60,000 square feet of additional warehouse space. The option shall be available to the Purchaser for a period of four (4) months after the initial property Closing Date.

2. State the proposed per square foot cost, the proposed number of square feet, and the total purchase price of the property exclusive of closing costs, taxes, commissions, title insurance or other fees.

3. Provide a plot plan of the proposed option property, the proposed property's street address, legal description, size in acres and square feet, and current owner's name, address and telephone number.

E. **PURCHASE CONTINGENCIES:**

1. Purchaser's obligation to purchase and close on the property is contingent upon but not limited to Purchaser being able to obtain:

   a. Written confirmation from governmental authorities of zoning, utilities available to the site, acceptance of covenants and restrictions, acceptance of the rights of way and streets, etc.;
   b. Written plan approval from development and construction permitting authorities;
   c. Written confirmation from an independent testing laboratory that the site does not contain soil pollutants or contaminants, etc.;
   d. Clear title and title insurance for the property; and
   e. Initial and final approval by the Purchaser's parent company.

F. **SALE AND PURCHASE AGREEMENT:**

1. Purchaser will review all responses to this RFP and subject to initial approval by the Purchaser's parent company, Purchaser expects to enter into a Sale and Purchase Agreement with the Seller in September, 1993.

G. **PURCHASE AND CLOSING DATE:**

1. Purchaser recognizes that time is of the essence and will seek to obtain all necessary contingency items including permitting required in item E.1. toward a purchase and closing date of approximately December 15, 1993.

H. **CONSTRUCTION START DATE:**

1. Purchaser recognizes that permitting is critical to the project and expects a construction start date of approximately January 1, 1994.

I. **OCCUPANCY DATE:**

1. Approximately July 1, 1994.

J. **AGENCY DISCLOSURE:**

1. Professional Brokerage Company is acting as Agent for the Purchaser in this transaction and will be paid a commission by the Seller of the property should a transaction between the parties be consummated.

K. **PROPOSAL DUE DATE:**

1. The response to this Request For Proposal is due not later than 10:00 AM (CST), July 15, 1993.

EXHIBIT 11.2 *(Continued)*

2. Please submit six (6) copies of your Proposal to:

Ms. Sandra K. Broker
Vice President
Professional Brokerage Company
304 East Wacker Drive
Chicago, IL. 60631

Telephone No. (312) 555-8067
FAX No. (312) 555-0449

■

EXHIBIT 11.2 *(Continued)*

SAMPLE ATTACHMENT "A"

Note: Where the word "Owner" appears below, it shall mean ABC Company who may also be identified as the "Purchaser" in the **Request For Proposal**.

SITE CONCEPTS

A. **SITE CONSTRAINTS**

1. Identify any site constraints such as rights-of-way, flood plains, easements, set backs, zoning, etc.

B. **SITE DESIGN CONCEPTS**

1. Provide 150,000 square feet of secured, lighted site storage yard lay down area for cable reels, telephone poles, etc.

2. Provide adequate maneuverability for ingress and egress to the receiving and shipping dock areas and within the storage yard area.

3. Provide a stand-alone concrete ramp in the storage yard for cable reel unloading;

4. Provide adequate lighted, paved parking as a minimum for:

   a. Employee Parking 30 Spaces
   b. Visitor Parking 5 Spaces
   c. Truck Parking 2 Spaces

5. Provide future expansion for the warehouse, storage yard and parking.

C. **DISTRIBUTION CENTER SITE PLAN CONCEPTS**

1. From the main ingress/egress road, visitors, employees and truck and van drivers will access parking areas and roadways to the loading docks and storage yard.

2. The Distribution Center shall be located on the site with designated warehouse expansion. A drive to the receiving and shipping docks shall be shown.

3. The Distribution Center should permit a frontal image to the main access street with a lighted monument sign at the main access street/ingress-egress road.

4. A curb-side loading zone shall be provided for the use of vans.

5. The storage yard will be secured by a 6'- 0" high chain link fence with manual sliding gates.

6. There will be no requirement for on-site storage of truck fuel or motor oil.

7. The site may require a designated area for the temporary storage of hazardous waste products.

CIVIL DESIGN CONCEPTS

A. **SITE DRAINAGE:**

1. Address site drainage and water detention requirements.

EXHIBIT 11.2 *(Continued)*

B. **SITE UTILITIES:**

1. Identify size, location and service of existing water, sanitary sewer or septic tank system, electrical, natural gas, telephone, etc.

2. All utilities shall be underground from the site boundary or main access street into the facility.

C. **SITE IMPROVEMENTS:**

1. The functional layout is very similar to the model site plan drawing shown on page __ and modification/changes to the layout will be required as defined below.

2. Asphalt paving shall be provided in the automobile areas.

3. Pavement subject to heavy truck or tractor trailer loads shall have a base with a wearing surface of asphalt.

4. At turn-around areas and at the Receiving & Shipping Loading Dock areas, concrete paving shall be provided over a base designed for heavy truck and tractor trailer loads.

5. In the site storage yard, a granular base will be designed to meet local soil and code requirements for heavy truck or tractor trailers.

6. All curbs and sidewalks will be concrete with gravel base.

7. All exposed subgrade will be scarified to a 6" depth and recompacted.

FLOOR PLAN CONCEPTS

A. **FUNCTIONAL LAYOUT:**

1. The functional layout is very similar to the model floor plan drawing shown on page __ and modification/changes to the layout will be required as defined below:

			AREA SQ. FT.
a)	**Warehouse Area**	33,600	
b)	**Repair and Return**	6,400	
	Sub Total		**40,000**
c)	**Office Area**		
	1) Office(s) 2 x 200 sq. ft.	400	
	2) Open Plan area	2,700	
	3) Conference	500	
	3) Breakroom	200	
	4) Storage	400	
	5) Clerical	200	
	6) Rest Rooms	400	
	Sub Total		**4,800**
	Building Total		**44,800 Square Feet**

EXHIBIT 11.2 *(Continued)*

2. Warehouse area shall include:

   a) "Cross dock" Warehouse design with linear flow -
      1) Overhead Receiving Doors
         (a) Dock High Min. 4 each
         (b) Drive-In Min. 1 each

      2) Overhead Shipping Doors
         (a) Dock High Min. 4 each
         (b) Drive-In Min. 1 each

   b) Provide three pallet high stacking initially in the warehouse;
   c) Use racking in bulk storage to optimize cube;
   d) Utilize automation at Flow Racks for shipping,
   e) Mezzanine in intermediate storage (expansion)
   f) Re-locatable storage components to achieve flexibility;
   g) Battery charging area for electric forklift trucks.

3. **Repair and Return** shall require heating and cooling for the warehouse and mezzanine levels.

4. The Distribution Center Manager's office shall be designed adjacent to a door directly accessing the warehouse and include appropriate windows looking into the warehouse from the Manager's office.

ARCHITECTURAL/STRUCTURAL CONCEPTS

A. **BUILDING STRUCTURE:**

1. The facility shall be based on 40' x 40' bays. The steel columns will support beams with bar joists which will have a minimum of 24' (high bay) clear to the concrete floor. The Chicago, IL. high bay area will include the **Warehouse** and the **Repair and Return** and will be 200' x 200' which is 5 bays by 5 bays. The **Office** area should also be based on a 40' module and may be high or low bay. Skylights, where appropriate, with security bars will be installed to provide natural light in the warehouse area.

2. The building walls will be tilt-up concrete, precast concrete or reinforced concrete block bearing walls with structural pilasters based upon cost and experience to determine the best exterior building wall material for the Chicago, IL. location.

3. An expansion wall will be included in the architectural and building structure design.

4. The warehouse floor will be clear epoxy sealed concrete.

5. The loading docks will be equipped with overhead doors, dock seals, dock levelers and canopies.

6. The Owner shall furnish and the contractor shall assist in the installation of a number of items which includes but are not limited to: open plan furniture, signage, conveyor system, pallet shelving, computer equipment and cabling, security, fire and telephone system, warehouse equipment, trash dumpster, etc.

ARCHITECTURAL FINISHES

A. **EXTERIOR:**

1. Combinations of color and texture in concrete or concrete block will be the predominant finish.

2. Aluminum storefront with insulating glass will be utilized at the public entry (reception/office areas).

3. Roof will be designed to pitch rain water to down spouts located as required within the facility at the inside face of the exterior wall, and shall be designed to meet code and provide insulation as required. An elastomeric or equal roof membrane system is desired.

4. Hollow metal doors and frames will be painted and utilized for the Warehouse exterior entry doors.

EXHIBIT 11.2 *(Continued)*

B. **INTERIOR:**

1. Offices, Conference Room, Clerical and Open Plan Areas will have furring and painted drywall mounted on the exterior walls, metal studs and painted drywall on interior walls, painted metal door frames and stained wood solid core doors, lay-in ceilings, and carpet tile with 4" vinyl cove base.

2. Breakroom walls to have vinyl wall covering with a 4" cove base with carpet tile and a vinyl tile floor at the base cabinet area. Breakroom to have plastic laminate counter top and plastic laminate base cabinets with a two bowl S.S. sink, space for a 19.0 cu. ft. refrigerator, space for a drink machine, a coffee maker and a microwave oven area with plastic laminate wall cabinets below a lay-in ceiling.

3. Conference Room to have a movable, sound attenuating partition which will enable the division of the Conference Room into two equal small conference rooms.

4. Restrooms will meet handicapped requirements and will have a lay-in ceiling. Restroom walls to have vinyl wall covering, a ceramic tile base with ceramic tile floor and a mirror above a plastic laminate counter top over plastic laminate base cabinets. Toilet partitions shall be floor supported plastic laminate.

5. Open plan office systems provided by the Owner will be used for work stations in open areas.

6. **Return and Repair** and Storage will have furring and painted drywall mounted on the exterior walls, metal studs and painted drywall on interior walls, painted metal door frames and stained wood solid core doors, lay-in ceilings, and vinyl tile floor with 4" vinyl cove base.

7. The interior finish in the **Warehouse** will be paint on concrete.

8. Hollow metal doors and frames will be painted and utilized for the Warehouse interior doors.

MECHANICAL DESIGN CONCEPTS

A. **HEATING VENTILATING AND AIR CONDITIONING:**

1. The **Warehouse** areas will be heated and ventilated by multiple gas fired or electric rooftop heating and ventilating units. Multiple relief fans will be provided for summer ventilation. The battery charging area will have a process exhaust.

2. The **Repair and Return** and the **Office** areas will each be served by a separate package rooftop air conditioner with gas heat or electric heat. Exhaust fans will be provided for toilet rooms.

B. **PLUMBING:**

1. A domestic water main and a sanitary sewer main will serve the building. Where public sewer is not available, a septic tank and system will be designed by the civil engineer to serve the facility. Building roof drains will be served by storm sewers. Domestic hot water will be provided to all lavatories by a gas fired or electric water heater.

2. Emergency eye wash/shower will be provided in the Warehouse at the battery charging area.

C. **FIRE PROTECTION:**

1. The entire building will be fully sprinklered. The office areas area will be served by a light hazard wet pipe sprinkler.

2. The warehouse areas are to be served by an ordinary hazard wet pipe sprinkler system. If research and discussions with Factory Mutual reveal that an extra hazard wet pipe system would be required, an in rack sprinkler system and with multiple hose stations may be required.

EXHIBIT 11.2 *(Continued)*

3. A sprinkler main will be brought into the building from an existing water main. If the building is located at the end of the existing water main, there may not be sufficient water pressure without a fire pump. Therefore, if this case occurs, a fire pump may be required to boost the sprinkler system pressure.

ELECTRICAL DESIGN CONCEPTS

A. **SERVICE:**

1. Electricity will be from a pad mounted transformer. Service capacity requirements will be designed for this specific location and is not expected to exceed 800 amperes at 277/480 volts, three-phase, four wire. Entrance will be in an underground duct bank to the main switchboard located in the electrical closet.

2. Telephone service will be underground encased in PVC conduits.

B. **POWER DISTRIBUTION:**

1. The main switchboard will include the metering current transformers and will distribute radially. Space will be provided in the switchboard for the future expansion.

2. Lighting and HVAC equipment will be fed at 277/480 volts, and receptacle panel boards will be fed through dry type transformers at 120/208 volts.

3. A separate feeder (120/208 volts) will be provided for the warehouse conveyor panel.

C. **GROUNDING:**

1. A ground grid will be provided in the green area adjacent to the electrical closet.

2. The main switchboard will be grounded to a ground grid and to the cold water service.

3. The metal conduit system will serve as the equipment grounding conductor. If PVC conduits are used, a separate green ground conductor will be installed with the circuit conductors.

4. A copper grounding strap will be provided at the telephone service and will be connected to the ground grid.

D. **LIGHTING:**

1. The office lighting will be 35 to 40 foot candles with 1/2 x 1/2 x 1/2 chrome plated plastic louvers in a 2 x 4 lay in fixture. This lighting will be supplemented with task lights located in open office furniture.

2. Entry lighting will be recessed incandescent fixtures.

3. Toilet and breakroom lighting will be recessed florescent fixtures.

4. **Repair and Return** (50 foot candles) and **Warehouse** office lighting (70-75 foot candles) will be with strip florescent fixtures.

5. Pallet storage (30 vertical foot candles) and conveyor lighting (20 foot candles) will be with metal halide fixtures.

6. Wall mounted telescoping dock lights will be provided for all dock doors.

7. Emergency lighting will be provided in the corridors, and office area with invertor ballasts located in the florescent fixtures.

8. Exit lighting will be provided by battery powered red on white exit lights.

EXHIBIT 11.2 *(Continued)*

E. **EXTERIOR LIGHTING:**

1. Parking lot lighting will be .150 foot candle with pole mounted metal halide fixtures.

2. Driveway and roadway (.75 foot candles) lighting will be with pole mounted metal halide fixtures.

3. Entry way lighting will be with bollards.

4. Flood lighting will be provided for the sign.

5. Van and semi parking and storage yard lighting will be 1.0 foot candle with pole mounted floodlights.

F. **RECEPTACLES:**

1. Duplex convenience outlets will be provided as required to fit the space.

2. Ground fault receptacles will be provided in toilets.

3. Weatherproof duplex convenience outlets will be provided outdoors at the main entry, truck docks, Exterior Doors, and at the rooftop equipment.

G. **MOVABLE OPEN PLAN FURNITURE WIRING:**

1. Branch circuits for the movable open plan furniture will be provided in boxes located in the furred columns. The final connections will be provided with the open plan furniture.

H. **TELEPHONE:**

1. Telephone outlets will be provided, which will include a box and empty conduit into the accessible ceiling. All telephone wiring will be provided and installed by the Owner, and where applicable will be plenum rated cable.

I. **FIRE ALARM:**

1. The fire alarm system will be a low voltage, zoned, non-coded supervised system with battery back-up.

2. Ceiling mounted smoke detectors will be provided for the room cavities. Duct mounted smoke detectors will be provided for the air handling equipment in accordance with NFPA codes.

3. Manual fire alarm pull stations will be provided at all exits or in the path of egress, in accordance with NFPA codes.

4. Combination horn/flashers will be provided for audible/visual alerting.

5. The fire alarm system will be tied to the local fire department via leased telephone line.

J. **PAGING/SOUND SYSTEM:**

1. A voice paging system will be provided for the complete complex.
    a) Office area - ceiling speakers with will-mounted volume control switches.
    b) Warehouse, conveyors and storage areas - horn type speakers.
    c) Truck parking and storage yard - pole mounted weatherproof horn type speakers.

2. AM/FM tuner will be provided for music source.

3. Provisions will be provided for a future tape deck.

4. Paging will be accessed by the telephone system.

EXHIBIT 11.2 *(Continued)*

K. **SECURITY SYSTEM:**

1. Door access into the building will be by card and card reader. The system shall be a Schlage microprocessor controlled system with the PC located in the office area.

2. The security system will be connected through a modem over leased telephone wire.

3. Door monitoring will also be included with an annunciator located locally at the reception area.

L. **MOTOR CONTROL:**

1. Packaged mechanical equipment will be provided with built-in motor controls.

2. Individual motors will be controlled by combination magnetic motor starters or manual motor starters, as required.

M. **GENERAL:**

1. The electrical system will be designed to allow an expansion of two tiers of (2) bays. This will add approximately 24,400 square feet of warehousing and storage space.

2. If the Owner elects to add 100,000 square feet of **Warehouse** space, the electrical system will be designed to allow for that expansion including the expansion stated in item M.1.

(Insert Floor Plan Here)

(a) UNDERSTANDING HUMAN NATURE

Knowledge of human nature and cultural differences will clarify the opposing party's actions at the bargaining table. Conflict may arise as a result of differing expectations. A better understanding of the opposition can enable a good negotiator to break down barriers that could potentially hinder progress.

Differences in cultural expectations are not uncommon. For example, it is typical for Southerners to begin negotiations with small talk about issues such as family, friends, and the weather. In the North, on the other hand, social interaction is rarely considered part of the bargaining process, and Northerners customarily initiate negotiations with the business issues of concern. Similarly, in face-to-face conversation, a man in the United States typically stands 18 to 20 inches away from another man. When conversing with a woman, however, he generally stands back another 4 inches. The accepted behavior when rejecting offers also varies by region. For example, many Southeasterners reject an unacceptable offer in an indirect manner to minimize the chance of offending the opposing party. In contrast, it is perfectly acceptable in the north central United States, to reject an offer promptly and in an unambiguous manner.

Problems arising from cultural differences, while not uncommon, are avoidable with proper preparation. Seeking advice from local attorneys, brokers, and other professionals can prove helpful in accommodating such cultural differences. And, as always, clearly displaying goodwill and employing a sense of humor often do much to maintain a cooperative atmosphere during negotiations.

(b) WHO SHOULD NEGOTIATE

The individuals present during negotiation can have a profound psychological effect on the proceedings. Not only can the information that each individual brings influence the party's ability to perform, but the image that each presents can also influence the outcome. In some cases, the sheer number of participants at the table can empower (or weaken) the party.

Professionals often play an influential role. Because of the complexity of real estate transactions, no one person is qualified to handle all aspects of the negotiation. Lawyers, brokers, and accountants can each play an important but limited role. Because they are professionals, each individual can add expertise and lend credibility to a party's position; therefore, it is often desirable for professionals to be present during bargaining. It is essential that the role of each individual be clearly defined and that limits be established prior to the commencement of negotiations. During negotiations, all individuals present must understand who the spokesperson is for each side and what the limits are to that person's authority.

(c) NEGOTIATION SITE

There are advantages and disadvantages to every negotiation site. The location of negotiations can determine the atmosphere of bargaining and, in turn, could significantly influence the behavior of the negotiating parties as well as the final outcome. Negotiations can take place at the company's offices, at the opposing party's offices, or at a neutral location. Also, physical factors might influence negotiations.

(1) Home versus Away

It may be beneficial to hold negotiations in the company's offices (home), to meet at the opposing party's offices (away), or to bargain on neutral grounds. The pros and cons to each alternative must be considered before making a decision.

Meeting at home does have advantages, including simply the psychological advantage of being the "home team." Approval of unanticipated problems is more feasible, and other office matters can be handled during negotiation. In addition, traveling time and other related expenses can be spared, and familiar facilities are available throughout bargaining.

Negotiating on the opponent's grounds can be advantageous as well. Without the interruptions and distractions of office activities, the visiting negotiator can devote all attention to negotiations, and the burden of making preparations will be on the opposing party. In addition, it will be possible to withhold information with the justification that the information is not readily available. And, if needed, negotiation standoffs may possibly be taken to and overruled by members of higher management for the opposing party.

Meeting on neutral grounds may have a beneficial psychological effect because in theory, no one party will have the psychological advantage of being the home team. In reality, however, there are several other factors to consider. The biggest disadvantages are inconvenience and expense. The traveling costs and time away from the office can be concerns for both parties. Similarly, the cost of renting space and supplying other necessary accommodations may possibly outweigh the advantages of neutrality.

(2) Physical Factors to Consider

The physical factors of the room itself also play a role. The layout of the room, including the size and seating arrangements, may or may not be conducive to the desired atmosphere of negotiations. Seating arrangement issues to consider include these questions: Who is sitting at the head of the table, what is this individual's role, and how will this seating position affect his or her appearance of authority? Also, are the opposing parties seated on opposite sides of the table? And does such an arrangement encourage an antagonistic atmosphere? Although they may seem insignificant, the color, lighting and other physical amenities of the room can be influential factors. In addition, the time available for each session can promote either ease or tension at the bargaining table. These physical factors should be managed to create the desired level of comfort or distress in the negotiation.

§ 11.6 CONCLUDING NEGOTIATIONS

The negotiator should be aware that, at the closing, the opposing party may not be fully prepared to complete the real estate transaction. It is not unusual for one of the parties to have failed to satisfy all the required conditions. It is not a good idea to waive essential warranties, contingencies, and representations that will be needed after the closing.

The inability to compromise at the closing is a common handicap. Nevertheless, the negotiator should not change the investment strategy or range of acceptable prices and terms. When rights and duties are clearly defined in the lease or purchase contract, the negotiator must take a firm position. Similarly, if the opposing party has not fulfilled an essential condition, the investor should reset the date of closing.

Phone communications will probably be needed to complete even simple real estate transactions. The purchaser also may require the seller to provide an agent to inspect the premises simultaneously with the closing to verify that all specified equipment and personal property are present on the site at the time of the closing. In addition, the seller and buyer should send any tenants written notification of the change in ownership including instructions for the payment of future rents, if appropriate. Utilities need to be changed over as soon as possible, as the buyer should conduct a personal inspection immediately following the closing. Finally, both parties should promptly deposit all checks and cash transferred in the transaction. A good policy is to accept only cashier's or certified checks at closing.

Using an attorney with experience and skills in dealing with such transactions is prudent to ensure a successful legal closing. In addition to being qualified to handle the details of the transaction, the attorney must be qualified to deal with the complexities of a closing in the appropriate jurisdiction. It is strongly recommended that the company hire an attorney who is experienced with real estate closings in that area.

Twelve

Property Management

§ 12.1 INTRODUCTION

A facility's physical appearance often provides prospects, customers, investors, lenders, and employees with their first impression of the company. Accordingly, the management of those facilities becomes a critical consideration. Unfortunately, many companies have not recognized the significance of the contribution corporate real estate managers and the property management function make to the ultimate success or failure of the business.

§ 12.2 THE IMPORTANCE OF PROPERTY MANAGEMENT

(a) CURRENT TRENDS

For almost 20 years now, the positive effects of good property management have received increased attention. This recognition is due largely to the recognition of the significant contribution real estate makes to the ultimate success or failure of a business and recognition of the strategic importance of real estate to a company's financial structure. The popularity of leveraged buyouts has focused attention on the market value of real estate owned by acquired companies (vs. book value) and the ability to finance those acquisitions with those assets.

In addition, with sale-leaseback transactions becoming a common source of obtaining capital for the selling company, the relationship of the value of corporate property and the impact of good management on that value received a lot of recognition. Corporate real estate professionals and trade and professional associations have been reasonably successful in demonstrating the significant relationship of property management and investment performance.

These trends—combined with the current oversupply and imbalance of commercial real estate created by aggressive and, at times, inept and unscrupulous real estate lending practices by savings and loans, commercial banks, and other organizations—have further highlighted the importance of effective property management. Organizations and individuals that have recognized their real estate problems early enough have often been able to overcome many of the threats to their property(ies) and troubled real estate loan portfolio(s). Without exception, decisive, quality property management has contributed significantly to the workout and restructuring process.

Today, corporate property owners are focusing on management operations as they look for ways to reduce operating costs, dispose of excess properties, or hold on to troubled properties by improving their operating income (and reducing their operating losses). The proliferation of published commercial real estate operating data has also made it easier to evaluate property performance. In addition, these data have helped to establish the importance of property management expertise and performance, which are becoming recognized as a cornerstone of every successful corporation's strategy and operations.

(b) THE MULTIPLIER EFFECT

Senior management and corporate real estate executives are learning to take into consideration the "multiplier effect" as it relates to all recurring property expense (and income) items. All too often, undue attention is given to negotiating annual or one-time "high cost" items such as property and casualty insurance, while small recurring cost items are ignored.

While a $3,000 reduction on an insurance premium will result in a one-time saving of $3,000, a seemingly small decrease in expenses (e.g., lowering cleaning costs) for each square foot of retail, office, or industrial space can have a much more significant effect on cash flow and, ultimately, property and business value. For example, a $.03-per-month decrease in monthly maintenance costs for a 300,000-square-foot office building would decrease monthly and annual maintenance costs by $9,000 and $106,000, respectively. All these savings fall to the bottom line, making the business more profitable and, very likely, the property more valuable.

The property value becomes significant in terms of its use as collateral for obtaining financing, and for engineering a sale-leaseback and/or LBOs. In fact, in the preceding example, the $106,000 annual reduction in costs might increase the value of the property by over $1,200,000. In contrast, the $3,000 savings on casualty insurance would increase the building's value by $36,000.

The multiplier effect must also be considered in its application to increases in costs and their related reduction in income and its power to turn a marginally profitable business into a sizable cash drain. For example, a seemingly small increase in cleaning costs for an 150,000-square-foot office park, where such costs have typically totaled 10 percent of the building's expenses, would significantly decrease the cash flow and adversely impact the property's value by hundreds of thousands of dollars.

The greater the size of the property (i.e., in square footage or acres), the greater the impact of the multiplier effect. The importance of the multiplier effect is enhanced even more when the corporate real estate manager applies it to all properties managed as the organization's real estate holdings grow.

§ 12.3 GOALS OF PROPERTY MANAGEMENT

Property management must conform to overall corporate strategy and two major goals. The first one, which is both strategic and operational, is to ensure that customers, employees, and other constituencies are able to shop, visit, or work in a certain type of location and, along with that, a specific type of environment. At minimum, this goal is likely to include that the environment be safe and clean and that any real estate-related problems (e.g., maintenance and repair) are attended to promptly. If the company ignores this goal, it may have difficulty attracting and retaining employees and customers, thereby decreasing revenues and increasing costs.

The second important goal, which is stated in financial terms, includes target performance for property in terms of costs per square foot, costs per employee, costs as a percentage of revenues, costs as a percentage of total expenses and costs in relation to prior period and budgeted costs. In addition, companies managing excess property or property leased to noncorporate entities, should address other financial targets such as target revenue and net income numbers, estimates of real estate values, and even disposition values.

These goals are accomplished by implementing appropriate strategies, which should be defined and stated in a business or management plan developed by the corporate real estate executive and senior management.

§ 12.4 PROPERTY MANAGEMENT ALTERNATIVES

Property management issues should be considered and addressed early in the development of the company's corporate and real estate strategy.

At that time, strategy decisions and the related implementation plans should dictate or, at minimum, indicate which of three basic property management alternatives is preferred or mandated:

1. No property management required.
2. Internal management of corporate property.
3. Outsourcing of property management functions.

In addition, companies that choose to sublease property to other (nonaffiliated) companies, either by strategic decision making or because of economic necessity, can accomplish this using the preceding alternatives.

The right decision regarding these alternatives should be based on a determination of which alternative will best serve the company's overall strategy. This may be different for different types of corporate property and may change many times at various stages throughout a company's life. In addition, each management alternative has its advantages and disadvantages.

In every case, the goal should be to maximize corporate and real estate objectives by using the highest quality and most cost-effective property management resources available.

(a) NO MANAGEMENT REQUIREMENTS

Companies that lease facilities under a "standard" lease agreement should have no property management responsibilities as the burden of those responsibilities should be shifted to the building owner and, if applicable, the owner's property management agent. The lease should address in detail all the rights and responsibilities of both the tenant and the landlord.

The track record, experience, and financial stability of the building owner and agent should be examined carefully. This should include visiting the properties being managed by the owner/manager and speaking with clients, vendors, and others in the real estate community for references (see § 12.4(c)).

(b) MANAGING CORPORATE PROPERTIES

Traditionally, corporations have managed the properties they own and those leased under a net lease. While the actual organization of the real estate department has varied (see Chapter Three), the functions performed by corporate real estate have, at a minimum, included managing the physical asset. Management of the physical asset is the most significant function performed and includes developing and administering a maintenance plan; selecting, training and supervising departmental and property level employees; hiring and monitoring independent contractors; and making capital improvements.

Additional real estate department responsibilities may include preparation of related operating budgets and detailed record keeping, purchase of maintenance and repair supply items, risk management, and compliance with federal, state, and local laws. In many organizations, these additional functions are performed by other departments, including the accounting, insurance, and legal departments.

(c) OUTSOURCING—SELECTING A PROPERTY MANAGEMENT FIRM

During the past decade, there has been significant interest in outsourcing all the property management functions related to corporate owned and net leased properties to independent property management companies. This interest is increasing and includes joint ventures formed by corporations with real estate organizations. Historically, corporations outsourced only specific management functions, such as elevator and other major equipment maintenance and repair, and general cleaning.

There are many advantages to hiring an experienced property management organization. Since professional management firms handle all the routine and time-consuming property-level management activities such as purchasing, maintenance, employee/tenant communications, and staffing and other human resource management issues, corporate management is free to focus on strategic management issues, not to mention other opportunities or problems.

Seasoned professional management firms have the management proficiency (i.e., experience and staff) to manage a property well while decreasing the operating costs and increasing the long-term value of the property. Local outside management organizations are privy to market trends and legislative proposals that could affect the value of the property. In addition, the purchasing skills and buying power of a large management organization often result in significant savings for the corporation.

If outsourcing is chosen as the method of managing corporate property, corporate management will still need to have an adequate understanding of the property management function. This may include at least one knowledgeable in-house person to negotiate and manage the contract—a detailed specification describing the level of service(s) required and benchmarks to measure daily and long-term performance by the vendor and contractors.

Additionally, if a company chooses to outsource, consideration should be given to the impact on the company's employees (e.g., whether employees should be reassigned within the company or hired by the vendor as part of property management contract). Selection of an organization to manage a corporation's real estate may be accomplished by outsourcing all the real estate functions or just the management function (see Chapter Two).

A company's past performance and depth of experience are important considerations when selecting a property management organization. Interviewing a management company's clients, tenants, vendors, and others in the real estate community, and inspecting the properties being managed by the organization can give a good indication of the organization's management experience, level of service, effectiveness, methods, and style.

After reviewing the preceding information for each firm under consideration, the corporation should schedule a personal visit to each management firm to compare services, costs, firm size, structure, and operation. Such comparisons will help ensure that the chosen organization has an appropriate level of resources for successful management of the property.

(d) TRADITIONAL PROPERTY MANAGEMENT

Companies that choose to lease or sublease property to other (nonaffiliated) companies, either by strategic design or because of economic necessity, will need to perform all the tasks required by a traditional property management company—marketing and leasing property, determining rental rates and collecting rents, and additional financial accounting and reporting.

Traditional property management places the company in the owner/manager role, with all the accompanying responsibilities. It is the reverse of leasing space from an owner/manager, where the corporation has minimal or no property management responsibilities (see § 12.4(a)). Accordingly, the company should weigh the traditional management approach carefully before entering the market. Real estate consultants and property management experts can provide valuable information in this regard. Even if a company decides to enter the traditional real estate marketplace, outsourcing the property management function may still be the best decision.

The anticipated revenues, additional related costs, and level of service to be provided should be carefully estimated and documented prior to embarking on a strategy that requires traditional property management. Nevertheless, in recent years, many corporations have found themselves with additional space and have been forced to enter the very competitive marketplace of traditional real estate operators. Accordingly, all the functions of the traditional property manager are addressed in this chapter.

§ 12.5 THE MANAGEMENT FUNCTION

To many newcomers to the real estate industry, property management appears to involve little more than property supervision—collecting rents, maintaining the property, and filling vacancies. Surprisingly, this limited perspective of building management is found, occasionally, within the property management industry itself. In actuality, the importance of the management function in the real estate investment process cannot be overstated.

Real estate property management is a service industry requiring frequent interactions with tenants, on-site service personnel, contractors, government officials, and other professionals; therefore, it is useful for the company to develop a plan for its own operation—ideally, an operations manual that can be updated as needed and an organizational chart depicting management roles and responsibilities. A carefully developed plan and the selection of quality employees to help carry out the management process can maximize both company efficiency and income, giving corporate owners, managers, and tenants a sense of security about the management of their property.

Successful property management must begin with a carefully constructed plan, prepared with or approved by the owner. The plan must ensure that policies on costs and expenses, staffing, maintenance services, and competition with other properties in the market enhance the profitability of the corporation and the property value. Even undeveloped parcels of land adjacent to an industrial park or shopping center require attention to such management-related issues as site hazards, local development trends, taxes, zoning, and legal codes.

If management functions follow an uncharted course, as they have for many corporate properties, it becomes difficult to make necessary modifications in direction when problems arise. The result is a lack of control that can quickly develop, by crisis, into reactive and ineffective management. Adherence to a management plan does not preclude flexibility. Meeting the management demands of the various types of retail, office, and industrial real estate requires an ongoing reevaluation of such decisions on staffing, repairs and maintenance, insurance, and other aspects of property management.

(a) MANAGEMENT ACTIVITIES

While property management has always been an essential component in achieving corporate goals, it was not until fairly recently that senior managers began to recognize its full importance.

To simplify understanding of the broad range of management activities, property management can be broken down into six basic areas of responsibility:

1. *Management of the Physical Asset.* Involves administration of the maintenance plan, hiring and monitoring of independent contractors, tenant construction, and capital improvements.

2. *Intracompany and Tenant Management.* Includes interdepartmental and tenant relations, rent collections, and evictions.
3. *Financial Reporting and Controls.* Includes preparation of the operating budget, detailed recordkeeping, and purchasing/inventory control.
4. *Administration.* Includes employee selection, training, and supervision, development of appropriate insurance programs; operation of the management office; and compliance with federal, state, and local laws.
5. *Communicating Performance.* Refers to the development of communication systems between the owner and manager.
6. *Marketing and Leasing.* Includes market research, marketing strategy, broker selection, lease preparation, leasing techniques, and tenant selection.

The services required by the corporate real estate department will vary depending on corporate strategy, type and size of real estate holdings, remaining term(s) on leased and subleased properties, organization of company and stage of corporate development. In many corporations, the real estate department may primarily have responsibility for managing the physical asset, while others may have responsibility for all six of the functions listed.

(b) MANAGEMENT ORGANIZATION

The purpose of defining a corporation's structure is to demonstrate how the various positions and functions are interrelated. Some corporations may choose to operate with an informal structure—one without titles or specified lines of responsibility and reporting. With few exceptions (e.g., small companies), an informal structure is not recommended for the corporate real estate or property management function (see Chapter Three).

An organization chart should be prepared to visually depict the company's property management structure. This will facilitate company operations by defining what is to be done and by whom. The chart's detail and narrative should be determined in part by the size of the company's real estate holdings, its stage of development, and management preference.

(c) HUMAN RESOURCES

Quality employees supported by a strong training program, compensated competitively, and supervised properly will help a property meet corporate objectives. Employees should receive clear, specific definitions of duties and responsibilities to reduce misunderstandings and to promote good personnel relations. Without a clear understanding of the employer's expectations, employees cannot perform effectively or efficiently. Accordingly, job descriptions should be prepared for all employees.

A job description should specify in writing the areas of responsibility, authority, and duties of a particular position within the company. It should also define the significant relationships of the individual performing the job with others in the organization, the level of service to be provided, how performance will be evaluated, and how often and in what manner this will be accomplished.

(d) OPERATIONS MANUAL

Preparing an operations manual, which standardizes a company's policies and procedures, forces management to address, in detail, every aspect of the management process. An operations manual increases the likelihood that management and employees will make consistent decisions and act in accordance with federal, state, and local laws.

An up-to-date operations manual is an important permanent resource for property management officers and employees and is an integral part of the training process. It should reflect the company's basic operating policies and procedures. An operations manual should be a primary source of information, providing consistent answers to questions that arise and solutions to most problems that occur. An operations manual also enables decisions to be made more quickly and empowers employees at lower levels of the company, thereby freeing management for other responsibilities, such as planning and control.

Because an operations manual covers a large portion of the property management program, it must be amended and updated on a regular basis to keep pace with changing company, property, and industry conditions. One source of recommendations that often goes unrecognized is feedback from on-site staff responsible for implementing company policies and procedures.

§ 12.6 MANAGEMENT PLANNING PROCESS

A formal, written plan stating the financial and nonfinancial goals for a property or group of properties is essential for a successful property management. The planning process for managing real estate is similar to that for any other aspect of business planning.

Planning requires the development of a course of action based on an understanding of the responsibilities and capabilities of the company and of the expectations and goals of management. The planning process should result in a comprehensive plan that covers all areas of concern. Developing a good plan requires the commitment of everyone involved in the property management process, including senior management, corporate real estate managers, the property manager, and on-site employees. The plan must reflect understanding of the current situation, the company's objectives, and how performance will be measured.

(a) THE MANAGEMENT PLAN

To ensure delivery of the agreed-on services, the property manager and senior management together should prepare a business or management plan for each property. The purpose of the management plan is to (1) direct the operation toward realization of corporate objectives for that property, (2) provide a standard by which the manager's progress can be measured, and (3) allow for the implementation of programs that will improve the property's performance and value.

A good management plan is the foundation of a well-managed property. After stating the agreed-on objectives for the property, the management plan should outline and analyze current and expected demographic and economic conditions of the property and surrounding area. The plan should then state a strategy for achieving management goals based on this analysis. Because it documents what is expected and from whom, the plan is an invaluable communication and performance measurement tool for management, on-site employees, senior management, and, in many cases, lending institutions.

The type and amount of information required to prepare an effective management plan will vary by the type and size of the property, management requirements, and management required. It is often useful to first prepare a preliminary plan that covers the areas to be addressed and the information to be gathered. This preliminary plan should undergo revision and fine tuning until the property manager and senior management approve a final version. Even the final plan will be subject to revision, as time passes, to accommodate changes in circumstances, objectives, and goals. While initial preparation of a management plan will be time consuming and tedious, the revision process becomes easier for the management company with each successive plan.

Generally, the management plan should address the following issues:

1. *Objectives*

   Profile of company.

   Degree of senior management (lender) participation in management (e.g., monthly written reports).

   Expected duration of ownership.

   If appropriate, desired mix and timing of returns.

2. *Neighborhood and Regional Description*

   Population growth and area characteristics (economic, social and political).

Occupancy and rental-rate trends.

Significant opportunities and risks (e.g., major competitor moving in or out of the area, number of new residential and commercial properties).

3. *Description of the Property and Maintenance Requirements*

   Detailed physical description.

   Technical equipment considerations (e.g., security system, energy management, HVAC).

   Maintenance and repairs (routine and extraordinary).

   Optimal improvement of the maintenance program.

   Recommendations for capital improvements—rehabilitation, modernization, or conversion.

   Maintenance management system.

4. *Financial Management*

   Structure and details of property financing.

   Accounting and bookkeeping systems.

   Type and frequency of reporting.

   Preparation of operating budget and pro formas.

   Break-even analysis.

   Purchasing procedures and limitations.

   Insurance requirements.

   Tax management.

5. *Administrative Responsibilities*

   Management company organizational structure.

   General personnel requirements and policy.

   Management office hours, staffing, procedures.

6. *Communication and Decision Making*

   Summary of type and frequency of reports.

   Schedule of meetings.

   Situations requiring notice.

   Decisions critical to the property.

   Decision-making authority and relevant factors.

In addition to the preceding information, company's leasing or subleasing space to nonaffiliated entities should address the following issues:

7. *Marketing*

   Why do tenants choose to rent the property and why other tenants choose not to rent?

   What makes the property distinctive and has that helped the marketing efforts or hindered them?

Reasons for initial visits or contact by tenants?

Audience to which marketing efforts have been directed and should be directed?

8. *Tenant Mix*

Existing tenant profile?

How they perceive the property and why?

Desired tenant profile?

9. *Rental Structure and Other Income*

Current rates (e.g., base and formula for escalations)?

Comparison with similar properties in the area and with industry norms?

Optimal rate level?

Concessions (e.g., free rent, construction allowance)?

Frequency of review?

Increase schedule for rented and vacant space?

Other sources of income (e.g., parking, percentage rents, common area maintenance, use of freight elevator, additional HVAC).

10. *Rent Management*

Description of rent management system (e.g., type and frequency of reporting).

Rental and turnover rates and trends.

Rent collection policies.

Lease provisions.

Deposit requirements.

Tenant policies.

(b) SYSTEMS FOR CONTROL

For management to accurately and effectively control the management function, the management plan should include systems for reporting, communicating, and decision-making. This control should be one of the overall objectives of the management plan.

Control is impossible without a plan. And without control, it is difficult to be aware of the need for changes in policies and procedures or for modifications to the current strategy because there are too many variables—expense items, staffing, turnover, and competing properties. The basics of successful property management practices, while specialized, are basically no different from successful business management practices, of which "planning" and "control" are integral parts.

By regularly and frequently documenting operating results, the reporting system provides the information necessary for evaluation and subsequent appropriate modification. If, for example, a plan is developed that projects a 4 percent increase in occupancy costs over the next year, it is crucial for both the manager and accounting to be aware that two months into the period, occupancy costs have already increased 3 percent. Without timely reporting, it is difficult to give accurate credit for a property's success or to identify and rectify the problems causing a property's failure.

(c) OPERATING BUDGET

The operating budget is a critical part of the management plan and the control system. Accordingly, it is important that its preparation reflect both financial and nonfinancial factors. The operating budget portion of a typical management plan should compare the actual operations with budgeted projections for the current month, year-to-date, and the corresponding month from the previous year, if available. This budget should be reviewed monthly by the property manager and, if desired, by accounting and other members of senior management. It should then be revised to show variations between actual and projected numbers and changes in relevant economic conditions.

To help determine rental income and operating expenses, the manager should compare the current operating data with those of other similar properties by contacting other companies or local real estate or financial trade associations, or by purchasing the yearly operating expense reviews offered by national real estate trade associations. Definitions of operating costs may vary among companies, and accordingly, care should be exercised when using such information.

Published operating data is available from Building Owners & Manager Association (BOMA), Washington, DC; Industrial Development Research Corporation (IDRC), Norcross, GA; Institute of Real Estate Management (IREM), Chicago, IL; International Facility Management Association (IFMA), Houston, TX; The Association for Commercial Real Estate (NAIOP), Merrifield, VA; and the Urban Land Institute (ULI), Washington, DC. (Also see § 3.2(b).)

The management plan and the operating budget should be viewed as guidelines, or points of reference, for asking questions about performance and for improving operations. Questions such as "Why are occupancy costs over or under the plan?" and "Why is a particular expense over or under budget?" may lead to additional questions about related items. Both the questions and answers will improve the planning process and operating results. Comparing actual to projected performance will keep management aware of changes in the operations and improve the skills required to develop future plans. In this respect, planning is more of a process than an end in itself—as skills improve, so do the plans.

Exhibit 12.1 shows a sample operating budget for a 250,000-square-foot, build-to-suit building. The building, located in a suburban

EXHIBIT 12.1 ABC Building Income and Operating Budget—1994

ABC BUILDING (ACCOUNT NO. 1456)
INCOME AND OPERATING PLAN
1994

CODE	ACCOUNT	JAN	FEB	MAR	APR	MAY
42260	RENTAL INCOME	163,014.00	163,269.00	171,112.00	169,972.00	170,026.00
	EXPENSES					
42264	Utilities					
	Electric	9,559.00	8,869.00	9,089.00	10,078.00	10,622.00
	Gas/Fuel Oil	4,042.00	4,417.00	4,716.00	2,795.00	1,152.00
	Water	0.00	0.00	2,576.00	0.00	2,767.00
	Total Utilities	13,601.00	13,286.00	16,381.00	12,873.00	14,541.00
42269	Mechanical	13,421.00	30,971.00	18,821.00	14,621.00	15,571.00
42270	Electrical	2,676.00	2,325.00	450.00	450.00	825.00
42274	Fire Protection	3,126.00	573.00	62.00	244.00	231.00
42267	Cleaning	9,154.00	9,154.00	9,154.00	9,154.00	11,920.00
42268	Landscaping	955.00	955.00	985.00	985.00	4,185.00
42273	Security	808.00	808.00	808.00	808.00	808.00
42271	Elevators	872.00	872.00	872.00	898.00	898.00
42269	Snow Removal	1,400.00	1,200.00	0.00	0.00	0.00
42269	Miscellaneous	485.00	799.00	785.00	1,335.00	1,045.00
42924	Management Fee	6,655.00	6,655.00	6,655.00	6,655.00	6,655.00
42280	Taxes/Insurance	0.00	0.00	0.00	0.00	0.00
42265	EWO Work	0.00	0.00	0.00	0.00	0.00
10504	Leasehold Improv	0.00	0.00	0.00	0.00	5,000.00
	Total Expenses	53,153.00	67,598.00	54,973.00	48,023.00	61,679.00
	OPERATING INCOME	109,861.00	95,671.00	116,139.00	121,949.00	108,347.00
42265	SWITCH EXPENSES					
	Maintenance	0.00	6,678.00	0.00	0.00	6,678.00
	XYZ CORP. Payments	(4,913.00)	(4,913.00)	(4,913.00)	(4,913.00)	(4,913.00)
	Total Switch	(4,913.00)	1,765.00	(4,913.00)	(4,913.00)	1,765.00
	NET OPERATING INCOME	114,774.00	93,906.00	121,052.00	126,862.00	106,582.00
	CHECKBOOK BALANCE					
	Account Minimum	5,000.00	5,000.00	5,000.00	5,000.00	5,000.00
	Net Oper Income	114,774.00	93,906.00	121,052.00	126,862.00	106,582.00
	ABC COMPANY A/C	0.00	0.00	0.00	0.00	0.00
	Transfer to ABC CO.	(114,774.00)	(93,906.00)	(121,052.00)	(126,862.00)	(106,582.00)
	Balance Sheet Items	20,027.21	20,027.21	20,027.21	20,027.21	20,027.21
	MONTH END BALANCE	25,027.21	25,027.21	25,027.21	25,027.21	25,027.21

EXHIBIT 12.1 *(Continued)*

AUGUST 5, 1993
PREPARED BY: STEVEN ADAMS

JUN	JUL	AUG	SEP	OCT	NOV	DEC	TOTAL
170,472.00	171,220.00	172,248.00	172,362.00	172,362.00	173,480.00	173,608.00	2,043,145.00
15,359.00	14,323.00	15,215.00	15,878.00	14,744.00	10,207.00	7,978.00	141,921.00
679.00	35.00	35.00	35.00	150.00	2,079.00	4,725.00	24,860.00
0.00	0.00	0.00	3,360.00	0.00	2,887.00	0.00	11,590.00
16,038.00	14,358.00	15,250.00	19,273.00	14,894.00	15,173.00	12,703.00	178,371.00
13,421.00	13,421.00	14,971.00	15,030.00	13,430.00	13,780.00	13,430.00	190,888.00
3,887.00	450.00	2,425.00	450.00	450.00	825.00	450.00	15,663.00
62.00	244.00	4,063.00	62.00	254.00	241.00	62.00	9,224.00
9,154.00	9,154.00	9,154.00	9,154.00	9,154.00	9,154.00	9,154.00	112,614.00
985.00	985.00	985.00	985.00	2,185.00	985.00	985.00	16,160.00
1,372.00	872.00	872.00	872.00	872.00	872.00	872.00	10,644.00
898.00	898.00	898.00	898.00	898.00	898.00	898.00	10,698.00
0.00	0.00	0.00	0.00	0.00	750.00	500.00	3,850.00
1,206.00	1,292.00	806.00	542.00	492.00	806.00	492.00	10,085.00
6,655.00	6,655.00	6,655.00	6,655.00	6,655.00	6,655.00	6,655.00	79,860.00
0.00	0.00	0.00	198,535.00	0.00	0.00	0.00	198,535.00
0.00	0.00	0.00	0.00	0.00	0.00	0.00	0.00
0.00	0.00	0.00	0.00	0.00	0.00	0.00	5,000.00
53,678.00	48,329.00	56,079.00	252,456.00	49,284.00	50,139.00	46,201.00	841,592.00
116,794.00	122,891.00	116,169.00	(80,094.00)	123,078.00	123,341.00	127,407.00	1,201,553.00
0.00	0.00	6,678.00	0.00	0.00	6,678.00	0.00	26,712.00
(4,913.00)	(4,913.00)	(4,913.00)	(4,913.00)	(4,913.00)	(4,913.00)	(4,913.00)	(58,956.00)
(4,913.00)	(4,913.00)	1,765.00	(4,913.00)	(4,913.00)	1,765.00	(4,913.00)	(32,244.00)
121,707.00	127,804.00	114,404.00	(75,181.00)	127,991.00	121,576.00	132,320.00	1,233,797.00
5,000.00	5,000.00	5,000.00	5,000.00	5,000.00	5,000.00	5,000.00	
121,707.00	127,804.00	114,404.00	(75,181.00)	127,991.00	121,576.00	132,320.00	
0.00	0.00	0.00	0.00	0.00	0.00	0.00	
(121,707.00)	(127,804.00)	(114,404.00)	75,181.00	(127,991.00)	(121,576.00)	(132,320.00)	
20,027.21	20,027.21	20,027.21	20,027.21	20,027.21	20,027.21	20,027.21	
25,027.21	25,027.21	25,027.21	25,027.21	25,027.21	25,027.21	25,027.21	

mid-Atlantic city, is managed by the real estate division of the company and is 50% leased to a nonaffiliated tenant. The rental income reflects income from both the affiliated and nonaffiliated tenants.

(d) MANAGEMENT CONTRACT

If a company outsources the management of its properties, a property management contract (also commonly called a management agreement or service level agreement) should be prepared and executed. In addition, if a corporate real estate subsidiary or real estate department manages corporate property preparation, use of a management contract should be considered. A management contract is a legal contract that establishes an agency relationship between the corporate property owner (the "principal") and the property management entity (the "agent"). It should state specifically the rights and responsibilities of both the manager and corporate property owner and should itemize in detail the duties of the manager, as well as the method and frequency of their performance.

Like the management plan, the management contract should be executed between the managing organization and the corporate property owner. In some cases, the management contract provides for the preparation of the management plan. In other cases, the management plan is prepared prior to hiring a management company.

The management contract should include any desired limitations or restrictions (e.g., minimum contract length of six months, corporate property owner approval of all vended service contracts after three competitive bids have been obtained) and a statement that all management duties are to be performed in compliance with federal, state, and local laws (e.g., Americans with Disabilities Act, wage and hour laws, Occupational Safety and Health Act).

Every management contract should be reviewed and approved by corporate counsel to ensure compliance with current federal, state, and local laws, and for compliance with corporate policies, standards, and requirements. In addition, counsel should review the facts and circumstances influencing management of a particular property and discuss and clarify sections that might lead to misunderstandings or possible litigation. The following items are common to most management contracts:

- Identification of the property or properties to be managed.
- Identification of the parties—the corporate property owner and manager and the form of organization of each.
- Duration of contract.
- Commencement and expiration dates.
- Renewal and termination clauses—how, by whom, when, and what type of notice must be given.

- Type and frequency of reports to be issued to owner.
- Authority to enter into vended service contracts, leases, and other agreements, including any restrictions or limitations.
- Specific management duties agent will perform.
- Authority to employ, train, supervise, set salary for, and terminate on-site employees.
- Clarification of whether on-site employees are employees of the corporate property owner or the property manager.
- Banking instructions.
- Specific purchasing authority, including setting limits, authority to pay bills for property expenses, and specification of party responsible for paying the taxes, insurance, and mortgages.
- A detailed list of insurance coverage on the property.
- An indemnity clause holding the agent harmless for liability arising out of management of the property.
- Amount of fees, or formula(s) for their calculation, to be paid to the agent for management, leasing, and other duties (e.g., remodeling, major repairs), as well as frequency and timing of their payment.
- If appropriate, specific authority to collect rents, security deposits, and other income; to deposit monies; and to institute legal actions to collect rents and other income.
- Signatures of both parties.

If a management plan is not prepared, certain information that would be covered in the plan should be added to the management contract. This information includes a statement of the corporate property owner's objectives and first-year operating budget.

A well-drafted management contract should address all areas of primary concern to the manager and the owner to reduce the possibility of misunderstandings, to increase the probability that each party will meet the other's expectations, and to provide a basis for settling any disputes that may arise.

(e) TRANSFER PRICES

There are several ways to allocate the cost of real property and its maintenance and management among corporate business segments (e.g., subsidiaries, divisions, departments, and products). This allocation is commonly known as transfer pricing—artificial prices used when goods or services are transferred from one segment to another within the same company. The transfer price is recorded as either revenue or expense recovery to the real estate department and as a cost, or expense, of the business segment occupying the property and using the services of the real estate department.

The transfer price for real property should be the amount that would be charged to a business segment if the same property or space and related services were purchased from a nonaffiliated party. Without this "market" price, transfer prices can be determined (a) on a cost basis, (b) on a cost-plus-basis, or (c) by estimating market price. Each of these methods has its complications, and regardless of the method chosen, there is likely to be some internal conflict.

The method used for transfer prices should be consistent with the company's organizational structure and policy, which determines whether service departments are cost centers or profit centers.

§ 12.7 MANAGING THE PHYSICAL ASSET

Management of the physical asset is a crucial part of the overall management process as it significantly affects the value of the property. The appearance and condition of the building and grounds help determine the type of customers and employees attracted, the occupancy cost structure, customer satisfaction, and quality-of-life factors for management and employees.

(a) MAINTENANCE ACTIVITIES

Maintenance of the physical asset is an ongoing process. It can be broken down into four main categories:

1. *Custodial Maintenance.* The routine, day-to-day housekeeping activities, including policing the grounds and vacuuming and cleaning the offices, lobby, and other common areas; trash sorting where required; and trash removal.
2. *Corrective Maintenance.* The repair and restoration of items after problems are identified but before major breakdowns occur.
3. *Preventive Maintenance.* Scheduled inspections, service, and repair to maximize equipment life, and the level of services at the property, and reduce equipment breakdowns and service interruptions.
4. *Emergency Maintenance.* Corrective action that must be taken immediately to protect life, health, or property.

A fifth type of maintenance, "deferred maintenance," occurs when needed maintenance is not or cannot be performed until some later date. The reasons for delay include cash limitations, management plan or budget restrictions, or negligence. Deferred maintenance is the antithesis of preventive maintenance. In fact, it is often nonmaintenance. There are times, however, when work is necessarily delayed, such as when parts are not available or timing is not appropriate for repair. Deferred maintenance should be included in the maintenance reporting system, since both management and the owner need to be aware of items that have not been serviced. It is important to ensure that deferred maintenance does not result in health or safety hazards.

The type of maintenance program, staffing, and allocation of monies should be established in the management plan. They should reflect the condition of the building and the company's overall and specific property objectives. Some properties are better suited for a minimal maintenance program (e.g., back-office or start-up manufacturing facility), while others require an extensive maintenance program (e.g., corporate headquarters, showroom space, Class A office building).

To satisfy tenants and maintain the integrity of the physical asset, the maintenance program requires constant support and cooperation from everyone involved in the management process—from the maintenance staff to the building owner. A good program seeks a balance among planned maintenance (custodial and preventive), responsive maintenance (corrective and emergency), and deferred maintenance.

The property manager is responsible for the satisfactory performance of all preventive maintenance functions and should be aware of all maintenance work on the property, as well as the overall conditions, property operations, and work being performed on surrounding properties. The manager's effectiveness depends on the quality of the preventive maintenance program, which in turn depends on the performance of the maintenance staff and maintenance contractors. Therefore, it is important that the property manager follow up on maintenance system reports and information and perform personal inspections of the building and equipment on a regular basis.

(1) Custodial Maintenance

Custodial maintenance encompasses all day-to-day routine maintenance activities. Generally, these tasks are performed at least once a day, although some may be performed more than once a day. Because of its routine nature, custodial maintenance can easily be scheduled, assigned, and controlled.

While custodial maintenance may be performed by full-time on-site employees, some maintenance (custodial, corrective, and preventive) tasks may be contracted out to independent contractors (e.g., cleaning, elevator, and HVAC maintenance and repair).

(2) Corrective Maintenance

Corrective maintenance is performed to repair and restore items after problems have been identified but before major breakdowns or emergencies occur. Even the best-maintained equipment develops operating problems and occasionally breaks down. In fact, all building components are susceptible to breakdown and may need corrective maintenance, regardless of the quality of the preventive maintenance program. While the on-site staff identifies much of the corrective maintenance required, tenant requests for service probably are the most common source for corrective maintenance. Uneven room temperature (too hot or cold), leaky or noisy plumbing, and electrical malfunctions are common problems identified by tenants. Also, certain weather conditions, such as extreme cold or heavy rain, cause broken waterpipes, leaky roofs, and other problems.

All requests for service should be monitored by management to determine the effectiveness of the preventive maintenance program and revise it accordingly. Also, the source of the problem should be identified (e.g., employee or tenant negligence, inadequate maintenance, faulty equipment) and action should be made to eliminate it.

(i) Work Orders, Logs, and Schedules To control the corrective maintenance function (and the deferred and emergency maintenance functions), work order forms, service request forms, and a work order log should be used to document, schedule, and control the maintenance function. Larger facilities may require an automated maintenance system. Without a system to record and analyze information, there will inevitably be additional problems amounting to far more than the administrative time and cost of developing and maintaining a good service and work order system.

The work order form should include the name of employee or tenant requesting work, location of problem, time and date of service request, phone number where individual requesting service can be reached, nature of problem and its priority, time when maintenance or repairs can be performed, amount of time spent on repairs and materials used, cost of labor and materials, billing codes, and initials of staff member taking request and of individual performing work.

(ii) Detail Maintenance Records Detailed records for all commercial space, the building, grounds, and equipment should be kept for all maintenance and repairs performed. These records should provide for quick reference of what work has been performed for each space and user (e.g., department or tenant).

(iii) Maintenance Inventory To service the majority of corrective maintenance requests on a timely basis, each property should maintain an inventory of maintenance supplies, replaceable parts, appliances, tools, and equipment. These maintenance, repair, and operating supplies are often referred to as "MRO supplies."

The inventory is also necessary for custodial, preventive, and emergency maintenance. The size of the inventory is determined by the size and condition of the property and the types of problems encountered. In addition, an inventory control system is essential for a smooth maintenance program.

(3) Preventive Maintenance

Preventive maintenance, performed on a regular basis, keeps the level of services at the property high and reduces equipment breakdowns and service interruptions. It requires that the maintenance staff and on-site manager make regular inspections for the repair and replacement of items before problems occur.

Preventive maintenance is one of the most important components of successful property management, and it requires the commitment of everyone from the property's staff to its owner. An appropriate preventive maintenance program should be developed for both large and small properties, regardless of whether the building staff consists of only a part-time maintenance worker or a larger number of employees supported by a computerized maintenance program.

Careful preventive maintenance eliminates corrective and emergency repairs later. While some managers consider preventive maintenance a poor use of cash, and some companies claim to have no time for it, the truth is that preventive maintenance, by identifying problems in early stages, saves both money and time.

The following four steps are required to develop a good preventive maintenance program:

1. Preparing an inventory of all items that require servicing during the year.
2. Determining the type of service, frequency, and cost efficiency of performing the work required by each item, and who should do the work (in-house or contractor).
3. Scheduling the work throughout the year.
4. Controlling and revising the preventive maintenance program as needed.

The building, major equipment, and grounds should be inspected regularly by the maintenance supervisor to note both the unusual and normal wear and tear. This inspection is, by and large, a quick visual one, and the details of the inspection do not need to be entered on any form. For work that needs to be performed, a work order should be prepared.

Detailed inspection reports can be used as a reference for the daily inspections, and these forms should be completed on a regular basis in accordance with the maintenance plan. In general, these inspection reports should be completed at least once each month. The property manager should inspect the exterior and interior of the property.

Evidence of building settlement, structural damage, leaks, and corrosion should be among the items noted during the building and property inspections. In addition to regular daytime inspections, there should also be inspections at night to test and examine lighting, signage, and security features. Night inspections should also include an evaluation of the property's appearance to customers, visitors and, if applicable, prospective tenants.

(4) Emergency Maintenance

Emergency maintenance is a form of corrective maintenance. Immediate action must be initiated to correct emergency situations that threaten the life and health of employees, customers, and other occupants, as well as the integrity of the property. Situations requiring emergency maintenance can be created by fires, floods, and burglaries, or the malfunctioning of major equipment (e.g., broken elevator, gas or water main leaks).

Preparation for such an emergency should begin well in advance of occupancy, during the site selection, development, and property negotiation stages. Response plans for mechanical, electrical, plumbing, roofing, elevator, security, and snow and other weather-related emergencies should be developed. For services contracted with outside vendors, detailed specifications for emergency response procedures and response times should be included in the contract.

Employees and building personnel should be versed in emergency procedures such as evacuation, and they should receive a list of telephone numbers for the local police, fire department, and utility repair persons, as well as the building's 24-hour emergency number. Because of the dangerous conditions surrounding an emergency situation and the swift response its correction requires, emergency maintenance is the most costly of all maintenance types.

(b) MAINTENANCE STAFF

While overstaffing a property can be very expensive, so can understaffing. Poor building maintenance shows in the appearance of the building and grounds, which may interfere with achieving corporate objectives, which will, in turn, affect net income and property value.

Personnel requirements should ensure that on-site staff can effectively perform routine maintenance responsibilities. The maintenance supervisor is responsible for the operation and maintenance of the physical and mechanical aspects of the property. The maintenance supervisor's duties should be spelled out in detail in a job description. Typical duties are:

- Training and supervising the maintenance crew.
- Establishing and controlling a preventive maintenance program, including costs.

- Conducting regular inspections of maintenance-related items.
- Identifying maintenance problems.
- Assigning and supervising the execution of work orders.
- Maintaining a clean, orderly, well-stocked, and safe maintenance shop.
- Maintaining the parts and supplies inventory.
- Maintaining the tools and equipment inventory.
- Maintaining records and operating manuals for equipment, machinery, and fixtures.
- Completing special assignments for the property manager.

The maintenance supervisor should report directly to the on-site manager, if there is one, or to the property manager. If a property is not large enough to support a maintenance supervisor, the property manager is responsible for these duties, or one supervisor may be hired to cover two or more properties.

(c) CONTRACT SERVICES

Contract services, also known as vended services, are those services performed regularly by an independent contractor for an agreed-on fee. These contracts may cover cleaning services, trash and snow removal, roof inspection and maintenance, pest and rodent extermination, security, plumbing, electrical, elevator and other mechanical, and amenities maintenance. The property manager should approve all service contracts, after having secured and reviewed several service contract bids. A contractor's references should be checked for quality of service, reliability, and consistency.

(1) Service Contract

All service contracts should be in writing and should address the following items:

1. Identification of parties.
2. Service to be performed, where, and how often.
3. Performance standards and measurements.
4. Hourly, weekly, monthly, and yearly costs.
5. Start and expiration dates of contract.
6. Special provisions (e.g., insurance coverage).
7. Termination provisions.
8. Signature of both parties.

Contracts that involve a substantial amount of labor are likely to contain escalation clauses to offset increases in labor costs and/or material costs. Be certain to analyze the method of escalation and base rates. A limit should be put on the amount of increase acceptable during the life of any contract, and the contract should include the right to audit the contractor's books regarding labor and material costs for the job.

A copy of each contractor's appropriate licenses, liability insurance, fidelity bonds, and workers' compensation should be obtained and retained by the company.

The on-site manager is responsible for all work done on the property, whether it is performed by on-site staff or outside contractors, and to see that service contracts are fulfilled up to standard and on time.

(2) Contractor References

One of the best lines of defense against inferior contractors is a policy of obtaining customer references before selecting a contractor for a major job. A contractor's references, including current and former clients, should be checked for the quality, reliability, and consistency of the service. Usually, a contractor will be able to supply a list of references—6 to 20 recent companies for whom the contractor has done satisfactory work. The property manager should randomly select two or three references from the list and ask them about their experiences with the contractor. If there is any doubt or if the reference simply does not seem very definite or well informed about the job, calling one or two more references should provide more information. If the contractor later asks the company to serve as a customer reference, the manager should not hesitate to agree. A contractor who does satisfactory work has earned a good reference. If problems crop up while the contractor is using the company as a reference, the contractor has an extra incentive to keep doing a good job.

(d) SECURITY AND SAFETY

Security and safety are primary concerns of management. Crime and accidents cannot always be prevented, but the risks can be reduced by taking certain precautions.

Security systems may include changes to the physical site (e.g., lighting and fencing), human resources (e.g., security guards), and electronics (e.g., closed-circuit television and access control systems). A good security system significantly reduces the risk of crime, but even the best system cannot guarantee that a crime will not occur.

Correcting and preventing safety hazards should be primary maintenance concerns. The safety of customers, visitors, and employees is an extremely high priority.

Safety programs should comply with the Occupational Safety and Health Act (OSHA), which imposes comprehensive, detailed safety and health standards and record-keeping requirements on employers. The act states that each employer "shall furnish to each of his employees employment and a place of employment which are free from recognized hazards that are causing or are likely to cause death or serious physical harm to his employees." Employees are also required to comply with OSHA standards and "all rules, regulations, and orders issued pursuant to this Act which are applicable to his own actions and conduct." A copy of the act can be obtained from the U.S. Department of Labor.

(e) MAINTENANCE REPORTING AND CONTROL

Regular reporting and control programs should be set up for each property. The type and frequency of each will depend on the size of the property, the structure of the organization, and the company philosophy. Specific reporting requirements should be included in each employee's job description and should be indicated on each report.

In general, monthly reviews and reporting serve as an adequate control, but many situations may warrant weekly reporting. The frequency of review should be indicated on the appropriate forms (property inspections, work orders, and work order log). The monthly report should include work order statistics, maintenance deferred, and notes on anything unusual at the property. For the unusual items or occurrences, an interoffice memo can be prepared or a standard report can be developed to assure that all significant topics are addressed.

(1) Maintenance Goal Setting

The maintenance program should include a set of goals developed by management with the maintenance staff. These goals should be in writing and might address such items as:

1. The amount of money spent per month on a per-square-foot basis. This amount should probably be set for variable expenses, such as supplies and equipment repairs, and should not include employee salaries.
2. The desired percentage of compliance with the custodial maintenance program. This might be set at 90 percent (no more than 10 percent of missed custodial routine procedure will be tolerated by management without investigation).
3. The desired percentage of compliance with the preventive maintenance program. This should be higher than the custodial compliance percentage because, unlike a missed office cleaning that may never be made up, neglected preventive maintenance tasks can be performed on another day. Consequently, this percentage might be as high as 98 to 99 percent.

4. The desired percentage of response within 24 hours to service requests. This might vary, depending on the property, the type of request, and the company's real estate strategy, from as low as 70 percent to a more reasonable 90 to 95 percent satisfaction rate.
5. Emergency on-call coverage and response to emergencies should demand a 100 percent success rate.

(2) Computerization

Technology has improved energy management, security systems, and the entire maintenance management process. Many computerized maintenance management systems are available in the market today, although their application has not been widespread throughout the industry. An appreciation for the efficiency of a computer-based maintenance program is still developing. While the tedious and time-consuming record-keeping tasks of accounting, including rent management and financial reporting, have been computerized for some time, computerized maintenance systems are just beginning to proliferate.

A good computer-based system should be able to generate and update most of the records discussed here from one source, typically the work order. The entire work order can be prepared at a terminal and should be automatically posted to the work order log. On completion of the work, the information added to the work order by the maintenance staff would be entered into the system. A good system would then update the work order log, the unit service record, the inventory of supplies, and the billing system. This process eliminates the need to enter the same information on several different forms.

Another application of a computer-based maintenance system is the initiation and monitoring of the preventive maintenance system. A properly developed system can provide a list of daily, weekly, and monthly tasks, initiate the work orders, and assign the work. As the work is performed and subsequently entered into the system, the system can update all the related records, as described previously, along with the property service record. All items that have not been attended to appear as items outstanding that require attention.

Reports for items not attended to, work order statistics, and other reports can be generated by the system, thereby minimizing tedious staff work. In addition, a computerized system should enable management staff to spend more time planning and maintaining the property and should supply accurate and timely information.

(3) Maintenance Manual

The maintenance manual information gathering described here is likely to expand to the point at which it may be advisable to use separate binders and files for some of the maintenance information. In particular, the volume of forms and operating instructions may become so large that separate binders and files will permit easier handling.

§ 12.8 INTRACOMPANY AND TENANT RELATIONS

One of the primary goals of property management is to ensure that customers, employees, tenants and other constituencies can shop, visit, or work in a safe and clean environment and have their real-estate-related problems attended to promptly. If the business ignores this goal, it may have difficulty attracting and retaining employees and customers. Accordingly, it is essential for the property management staff to cultivate and preserve good relations with all these constituencies.

Management and staff should remember that an individual's initial impression is often a lasting one; therefore, consideration should be given to these impressions and to improving relations with current customers, employees, tenants, and other constituencies. In addition, these people are the best source of referrals for new customers, employees, and tenants.

(a) TRADITIONAL PROPERTY MANAGEMENT REQUIREMENTS

Companies that have set up their property management departments as separate profit centers and those that lease or sublease property to other (nonaffiliated) companies will need to perform additional intracompany and tenant relations tasks. These duties are the same as those required of traditional property management companies.

Since traditional property management places the company in the owner/manager role with responsibilities to nonaffiliated tenants, the following sections describe owner/manager responsibilities relating to occupancy and rent collection.

(1) Occupancy Procedures

The seeds of the manager/tenant relationship are first planted when the tenant takes occupancy. Consequently, everything possible must be done to ensure that the tenant moves into a clean, well-maintained space. A tenant who is not satisfied at move-in will be very difficult to turn around later.

Move-in procedures should include a prior inspection by the manager followed by a walk-through inspection with the new tenant and the preparation of a move-in inspection report. At this time, the property manager should explain the operation of any equipment, answer any questions, and provide the tenant with an information package detailing building hours, parking policies, security, and emergency procedures.

Building keys, office/apartment keys, and I.D. and parking stickers should also be given to the new tenant at this time.

(2) Rent Management

One of the most important aspects of effective property management is the rent management system for recording, collecting, and depositing rents as well as other income.

A good system enables the manager and staff to efficiently record, report, and manage tenant income. A poor system, on the other hand, may increase the amount of work, create tenant conflicts, and reduce total collections.

(3) Rent Roll and Tenant Ledgers

Each property should have a rent roll, that is, a statement of rents and other income due and received during a particular period, a copy of which should always be kept in the manager's office. The rent roll records each tenant's account, usually listing the office, store, or location, name of tenant, outstanding balance, current rent due, date paid, miscellaneous collections (amounts and descriptions), total amount received during current period, and balance due at end of month. Computerized tenant management systems can provide preprinted rent rolls with the space description, tenant's name, and accounting for monthly rent and other changes and amounts paid along with other information.

In addition to the rent roll, a tenant ledger should be prepared for each tenant as a means of maintaining a complete record of transactions between tenant and management. The property manager uses these ledgers to record payment amounts and what they cover, lease abstract information, security deposit amounts, and other important information. All rents should be recorded daily on both the tenant ledgers and the rent roll, either manually or by computer.

(4) Rent Collection and Recording

An effective, consistent rental collection process is fundamental to successful property management operations. Good collections are a function of (a) a good tenant-screening program, (b) organized and accurate record keeping, (c) clearly stated collection policies and procedures, and (d) a firm collection attitude. Since rental income is applied mainly to meet property operating expenses, a delay or decrease in this income greatly jeopardizes management's effectiveness.

Developing and maintaining a strong rent-collection system requires the establishment of sound rent-collection policies. Policy statements are needed for the following:

- Rental due date.
- Date rent is considered delinquent.
- Schedule of late penalties/charges, conforming to state and local laws.
- Form (cash, check, etc.), and place of payment.
- Type, content, number, and schedule of delinquent notices conforming to all applicable laws.
- Handling of partial payments.
- Procedures for eviction.

Tenants should be advised of rent collection policies when initially applying for tenancy and again at occupancy. Rent collection policies should answer most questions about monthly operating routines and set up references for consistent performance.

(5) Property Rules and Regulations Violations

Violations of building rules and regulations should be addressed in a timely fashion. In many cases, it is sufficient to advise the tenant or send a notice outlining the offense and possible penalties should the violation be repeated. For habitual violations and serious offenses, the manager should seek legal counsel.

§ 12.9 FINANCIAL REPORTING AND CONTROLS

Good financial reporting and strong controls are essential to successful property management. Financial reporting is a product of the accounting and bookkeeping systems. To enable management to analyze the performance of the property and employees, reporting should compare actual income and expense items with those that were anticipated.

Computer technology has simplified record keeping and improved reporting accuracy while permitting more timely comparative analyses. Whether computerized or manual, a good reporting system requires certain reports, the type and format of which may be partially dictated by the company's current systems or by the particular system the property manager uses.

(a) COMPONENTS OF REPORTING AND CONTROL SYSTEM

The basic components of an effective reporting and control system include the following items:

- Operating budget.
- Statement of operations.
- Comparative statements.
- Narrative reports.
- Management summary information.
- Other reports.

(1) Operating Budget

The operating budget is a projected summary of all income and expenses for a given period. The budget is developed considering management's objectives for the property, recognized trends (as indicated by surveys, demographic studies, or reports), anticipated changes in economic factors, and detailed information on the property's physical and fiscal condition. A well-planned budget greatly enhances the property manager's ability to recognize market and financial patterns and to correct problems. Reports should allow individuals to monitor and control those items for which they are responsible (also see discussion at § 12.6(c)).

The operating budget should estimate income and expense items on a monthly basis, and usually includes projections for a one-year period. In preparing this budget, management must determine future rental rates and how they have an impact on operating revenues. Management must also forecast increases and changes in expense categories such as payroll, maintenance and repairs, taxes and insurance, marketing and leasing, and general and administrative costs. Seasonal variances in income and expense items (e.g., utilities) and expenses that are not paid on a monthly basis (e.g., real estate taxes, insurance) should be anticipated and accounted for.

(2) Statement of Operations

The statement of operations—also called income statement, profit and loss statement, statement of earnings and summary of operations—is an accounting of all property revenues and expenses during a given reporting period. It enables management to determine the result of a period's operating activities.

Supporting documentation for the statement of operations includes the rent roll, schedule of miscellaneous receipts, and a schedule of cash disbursements.

(3) Comparative Statements

Comparative statements for financial analysis should be prepared monthly addressing every revenue and expense item. The statements should allow management to review both year-to-date and current-reporting-period income and expenses. Comparisons of current-period income and expenses with prior periods and with the same period for the previous year should also be prepared. In addition, revenue and expenses should be reported as percentages of possible gross revenue, by square foot and by employee.

Financial guidelines presented by the operating budget should be continually reassessed and compared with actual operating results so as to monitor budget compliance and control operations. Operating results should be compared with similar buildings under management and industry statistics where available (see § 12.6(c)). In addition, cost figures should be discussed with vendors for comparison purposes (e.g., utility bills, cleaning costs and services).

(4) Narrative Reports

Narrative reports should accompany numerical reports to senior manager and the corporate owner to explain activities for the period. They should provide information about transactions and events found in the financial reports such as employee turnover, vacancies, rentals for the month, evictions, lease renewals, and delinquent tenants. The reports should explain any variances in the comparative statement, major repairs, or deferred maintenance. Suggested improvements should also be included.

(5) Management Summary

Information contained in a management summary report is useful for measuring management effectiveness on a month-by-month comparative basis. It can include monthly results of leasing and occupancy, the amount of lost rents, total rent and miscellaneous receipts, disbursement totals, and net cash flows and balances.

(6) Other Reports

Depending on the scope of the management assignment, as defined in the management contract, the property manager may have additional reporting responsibility. Additional reports might include:

- *Balance Sheet (or Statement of Financial Position).* A reporting of all assets, liabilities, and net worth or equity (the difference between total assets and total liabilities) as of a specific reporting date.
- *Statement of Changes in Owner's Equity.* A reporting of the additional investments by owners, retirement of owners' interests, and similar events to the owner's capital account(s).

- *Statement of Cash Flows.* A reporting of the cash effects of an organization's operations, investing transactions, and financing transactions.

(b) PURCHASING

The development of a strong purchasing and control system should enable management to purchase items at the best prices and inventory them at costs and quantities that are efficient to operations. The purchasing function of the property management process depends on the company's normal purchasing procedures and the size of the management portfolio and the specific property type.

The property manager is responsible for controlling, reviewing, and approving all purchase orders. Orders should be placed from approved supply sources and service firms. If no supply source has been established, the manager should obtain price quotations from differing firms before choosing the best source.

Authorized purchase orders should be obtained for every purchase, except in emergency situations where life or property would be endangered (e.g., flood, fire, electrical outages). The purchase order is a contract between the property and vendor regarding the purchase of supplies, equipment, or services. Prices, specifications, delivery dates, and any special payment arrangements should be agreed on before any purchase is made and should be noted on the order.

Service contracts for items such as elevator service, mechanical equipment maintenance and repair, extermination, and landscaping should be handled in accordance with standard purchasing procedures.

(c) TAXES

The property manager or a member of senior management must be familiar with real estate and personal property taxes. These taxes are based on the "assessed value" of the property, and the determination of that value can be complicated and somewhat subjective. In most cases, a tax specialist should be employed to determine if the value and rates are correct and to identify any avenues that might reduce the tax assessment.

Since taxes must be paid whether or not a bill is received, management needs to be aware of the payment dates and keep a good tax information file. Estimated tax amounts and the timing of their payment should be included in the budget and cash flow statements.

(d) SAFEGUARDING ASSETS

Assets under management should be protected against three types of losses:

1. Losses from casualty.
2. Losses from theft.
3. Losses from conversion of an asset to another form (receivables to cash, inventory to cash).

Casualty losses can be protected by a good internal control system combined with adequate insurance and an ongoing risk management program. Theft and conversion can be protected by a strong system of internal control combined with periodic internal auditing to check for compliance with the system's policies and procedures.

Controlling conversion (by implementing a firm collection policy, efficient inventory procedures, and an effective preventive maintenance program) reduces the time that assets are at risk from casualty or theft. It also improves profitability and return on investment by lowering expenditures for interest, inventory, insurance, handling, storage, obsolescence, and bad debts. Finally, money saved from more efficient collections and reduced spending can be invested elsewhere.

(1) Internal Control

Good internal control maximizes the probability that the corporate real estate and property management objectives will be met and that operations are in compliance with corporate policies and all applicable laws. It is management's responsibility to develop policies and procedures that achieve this control.

Systems of internal control vary for each company because of unique policies and procedures, management philosophy, and organizational size and structure. A system of internal controls encompasses the numerous safeguards ensuring that (a) assets are used properly and protected from misappropriation, (b) transactions are accurately recorded and reported, and (c) operations are in compliance with management policies.

(2) Insurance

The management company and properties under management should be insured against various risks of loss, if such insurance coverage is cost-effective. While the property manager is not expected to be an insurance expert, he or she should be knowledgeable about the types of insurance available.

The manager should be familiar with workers' compensation, fidelity, fire, rent loss, and liability insurance as well as other specific coverages. Such insurance needs can often be combined into a single, cost-effective package rather than being purchased separately.

Being overinsured serves no purpose and being underinsured can ruin the company. Insurance coverage should be reviewed and approved by senior management prior to purchase.

(3) Risk-Management Program

The purpose of a risk-management program is to identify the risks for potential liability involved in owning and managing commercial properties and for each specific property owned or managed. A risk-management program can reduce potential losses that insurance cannot efficiently cover (e.g., insurance coverage for certain risks may not be available, or the cost may be prohibitive). In addition, it can reduce the cost of insurance coverage (e.g., accurate loss exposure data generated by the risk identification program may persuade underwriters to renew insurance coverage at lower prices).

To create a risk-management program, management should appoint someone to be in charge of the program, such as (a) a full-time risk manager, (b) one person to both manage risk and deal with the insurance brokers, or (c) a risk-management consultant (either to conduct periodic audits or provide continuous support). This individual, along with other members of senior management, should become familiar with local landlord liability laws, estimate accurately the stakes involved in an uninsured loss, and purchase sufficient liability insurance when coverage is available.

§ 12.10 ADMINISTRATIVE RESPONSIBILITIES

The property manager performs various administrative duties, including personnel functions from hiring, training, and supervising on-site employees, to the management of the employee payroll, risk management, and management of insurance programs. The manager must abide by laws regarding antidiscrimination, wages and working hours, establish working standards acceptable to Occupational Safety and Health Act guidelines, and see that license and notice requirements, such as OSHA and workers' compensation, are met. With more than one hundred different forms and reports required to manage larger properties effectively, the manager needs a good forms control, review process, and filing system.

(a) OPERATIONS MANUAL

The property manager should develop a formalized standard for property management operations. This can be done by creating an operations manual designed to help standardize the policies and procedures under which the company operates.

An operations manual can be a useful resource for property management employees and should be an integral part of the training process. The manual should reflect the basic policies and methods under which the company operates and should be a primary source of answers to questions that arise in the process of managing properties, thereby enabling employees to make consistent decisions.

A good operations manual consists of three main elements—policies, procedures, and forms—defined as follows:

- A *policy* is a guiding principle that is adopted to influence or determine decisions and actions.
- A *procedure* is an actual step-by-step course of action for implementing a particular policy.
- A *form* is a procedural by-product, a document that is a mechanism for following procedure.

The greatest value of an operations manual is the operational continuity it provides to overcome the effects of personnel turnover and/or management changes. In addition, an operations manual enables employees to perform at their best, clearly understanding their functions and roles within the company.

The manual should offer specific directives to save time and effort in making minor decisions at all levels. Since an operations manual should attempt to cover the complete property management program, it needs to be updated on a regular basis to keep pace with rapidly changing industry conditions.

§ 12.11 COMMUNICATIONS

Good communication among senior managers, property managers and staff, and property users (e.g., customers, visitors, and employees) is an important aspect of successful property management. The communication process should be ongoing, from the moment management creates a management plan based on the agreed upon objectives, to the dissemination of daily, weekly, monthly, and annual financial reports.

The communication system includes both formal and informal components. Formal components can be specified and quantified (e.g., the organizational charts or the financial reports and leasing statistics). The primary vehicle of communication is the reporting system with its various financial and narrative reports. The management contract should specify all reports that are to be included in the reporting system, as well as their frequency.

The informal system occurs regardless of the formal system and encompasses such interactions as that between a customer and a maintenance employee, supervisor and subordinate, or leasing agent and prospective tenant, as well as discussions visitors may have with maintenance workers or employees.

Meetings with the property manager and other members of management should be scheduled at regular intervals to discuss management-related issues such as marketing and leasing programs and problems, major repairs, problems with personnel, and matters of rent collection. The property manager should communicate any serious problems immediately so that they can be addressed in a timely and cost-effective manner.

The importance of open communication cannot be overemphasized. Without mechanisms for formal communication and encouragement of informal communication, the company's organizational structure may become too unyielding to field the host of people-related problems inherent in the property management business. This leads quickly to employee and tenant dissatisfaction, thereby making it difficult to protect the real estate investment, maximize returns, and achieve corporate objectives.

§ 12.12 MARKETING AND LEASING

Corporate owned and occupied properties should have minimal marketing and leasing requirements, while these requirements for properties leased to nonaffiliated tenants may be quite extensive. For the latter, the amount of revenues generated from a property is directly related to the success of the marketing, leasing, management, and control functions.

For example, one manager may have 100 percent of the company's excess space leased with rents 20 percent below the market rate, while another may be skilled at obtaining higher rents and attracting qualified prospective tenants but poor at securing signed leases. The professional property manager must be capable of effectively balancing marketing and leasing efforts.

The prime purpose of the marketing and leasing effort is to attract qualified prospective tenants who will sign leases at market rent (and then pay the rent). Property factors affecting this goal include:

- Location.
- Overall appearance, including building style and size.
- Condition of the property and adjacent grounds.
- Amenities.
- Rental structure.
- Reputation of the property, the company, and staff.
- Competition.

These factors, along with occupancy trends, employment changes, competition, and other market influences, must be considered to determine accurate tenant profiles and appropriate rental rates for the property.

A carefully planned marketing program is necessary to attract new tenants. If not constrained by law, rent and rent increases should be established on the basis of periodic market surveys, which define maximum income possible while maintaining the property's competitiveness in the marketplace. Every marketing decision has an impact on building services and amenities and the number and compensation package of property employees.

(a) MARKET SURVEYS AND PROFILES OF TENANTS

The owner and manager must study the current market conditions pertinent to the property to plan the most effective marketing program. This information will be used to develop a tenant profile that pinpoints the kind of tenants desired, rental rates, and the best means of reaching prospective tenants. A market survey facilitates this study, as it examines the supply and demand for various kinds of properties.

A definition of the property's market area, which could be as small as several city blocks or extend over a 10-mile radius or more, is the first prerequisite to any market survey. Identifying the specific market area is important because inclusion of the buildings from another market will distort the survey's findings.

The survey should compare similar, local properties, and such factors as the property's accessibility to shopping, housing, educational facilities, entertainment, lodging and transportation. Also, it should define area demographics such as size, wealth, and rate of growth. Changes in the market or changes and additions in competing properties (e.g., cosmetic or facility changes), must be noted in annual updates of the survey.

A profile of current tenants at a given property should be made to aid in targeting advertising and marketing programs.

(b) MARKET POSITIONING

Once the survey and profile have been completed and carefully analyzed, the property manager can make recommendations regarding such basic factors as rental rates, amenities, and desired tenants. These recommendations position or reposition the property in the marketplace by determining the number and character of potential tenants.

Based on these recommendations, a complete marketing plan can be developed, addressing rental rates, lease terms and the lease document; marketing budget; and advertising, public relations, promotions, and direct leasing programs.

Thirteen

Capital Budgeting

§ 13.1 INTRODUCTION

To accomplish corporate goals and objectives, management must first carefully plan and organize the activities that will need to be performed during future days, weeks, months, quarters, and years. These operating plans provide targets for evaluating company performance on an ongoing basis. The process of planning these future business activities in a formal manner is called budgeting. Included in this process should be the reasonable sorting out of capital requests from operating divisions and product groups into "go" and "no-go" decisions.

This chapter describes key elements of financial reporting and control procedures that provide companies with a framework for directing and controlling operations and for presenting real estate performance and analysis. This analysis and the accompanying evaluation of real estate continue to receive increasing attention as businesses strive to maximize bottom-line performance and recognize that the efficient allocation of company resources to various capital projects is essential to the company's health.

§ 13.2 ANNUAL OPERATING PLAN

The annual operating plan (AOP), or annual budget, represents the short-term part of the budgeting cycle, normally restricting the operating units to one-year forecasts. Preparation of the AOP begins at the plant, department, or group level, with each operating unit submitting its short-term expected results of operations, or forecast, to the next organizational level where the individual reports are combined into one plan. This consolidated plan is then submitted to corporate headquarters for further analysis and synthesis into an AOP for the corporation.

A group-level AOP should include a letter of transmittal from the group president to the CEO summarizing the financial results to date, measured against the previous year's AOP and the group long-range plan (LRP), and discussing critical issues and key assumptions of the plan under review. It would also contain comments on the following:

- *Net Cash Flow* (after taxes). The group will prepare brief explanations of each business segment, with detailed reports for business segments planning negative net cash flow, explaining the strategy, plan, and management actions required to improve cash flow, discontinue operations, or sell segment.
- *Risks and Opportunities.* The group will identify and describe potential risks and opportunities not included in the plan, quantify the potential in terms of sales and profit impact, and detail the management action required.

- *Forecast Variance.* The group will identify major differences, if any, between current forecast, actual past performance and the most recent previous forecasts. In addition, a forecast variance schedule should be included as an attachment to the letter of transmittal.

Specific AOP contents will describe and analyze the proposed plan of operation under a number of topical headings, all illustrated by narrative and quantitative material. The operational items normally addressed would include:

- Executive summary.
- Sales and profit summary.
- Annual operating plan (AOP).
- Operating results by quarter (sales, PBT, inventories, and receivables).
- Objectives and major management actions.
- Risks and opportunities—short-range, but related to forecasts.
- Staff operating expenses—for purposes of division allocations.
- Staff engineering expenses—for purposes of division allocations.
- Staff marketing expenses—for purposes of division allocations.
- Staff administrative expenses—for purposes of division allocations.
- Net assets employed.
- Cash flow schedule.
- Current-year plan compared with last-year's actual.
- Last-year's actual compared with last-year's forecast.
- Current-year plan compared with long-range plan.
- The projected base and method for overhead allocations.
- Capital authorization and expenditures.

Several of these items are of particular importance to the real estate department, and the department should provide input on the numbers and strategies outlined in the AOP. Some of these items are discussed in greater detail in the following sections.

(a) NET ASSETS EMPLOYED

One of the basic measures of executive performance at the plant, division, operations, or corporate level is the effectiveness with which assets are employed to produce profit. Accordingly, the return on assets ratio (ROA) is one of the most significant yardsticks of performance measurement. ROA can be calculated by dividing net income (or after-tax cash flow) by net assets employed, expressed by the following formula:

$$\text{Return on Assets} = \frac{\text{Net Income}}{\text{Net Assets Employed}}$$

The numerator, net income, comes from the income statement, or statement of operations. (After-tax cash flow comes the statement of cash flows.) To determine the denominator, net assets employed, a schedule of net assets employed should be prepared. A sample schedule of net assets employed is shown in Exhibit 13.1. Note that net assets employed equals the sum of (a) working capital (current assets minus current liabilities), (b) property, plant and equipment, and (c) other assets.

The real estate department affects the schedule by additions to (acquisitions) and deductions from (surplus property dispositions) the asset base (property and plant). The more effective the real estate asset management program, the higher the ROA *ceteris paribus* (all else remaining equal), and the more accolades and rewards for the operating executive.

The net assets employed schedule demonstrates several attributes of AOP preparation and the manner in which the information is collected and presented for short-term evaluation purposes. The schedule emphasizes relative performance. That is, the proposed AOP, divided into three-month intervals, will be evaluated on this and other schedules against the two previous years' actual performance, the last quarter of the current year's forecast, the total current year's forecast, and the current LRP or five-year forecast. Also note that real estate is included at property, plant, and equipment, not current assets. This is indicative of the short-term illiquid nature of real estate. In other words, it is difficult to convert real estate into liquid assets (such as cash or other assets that will soon be converted to cash) that can be used to pay current liabilities.

Real estate is often given minor attention in the AOP preparation as many corporate executives still have the attitude that real estate assets are sort of a necessary and cumbersome burden on the company's real moneymakers—production, marketing, and sales.

(b) CASH FLOW SCHEDULE

Information about cash flows is critical for planning, organizing, and controlling a company and each operating unit. Accordingly, a cash flow schedule, cash budget, or cash flow forecast should be prepared after the annual operating plan (or long-range plan) has been completed.

The information from the cash flow schedule enables management to identify periods (days, weeks, months, quarters, years) in which the company or unit may need additional cash so such funds can be arranged for or, if funds cannot be obtained, so plans can be modified accordingly. It also identifies periods with excess cash that can be invested to earn additional income for the company or used to support units needing additional cash to fund operations. In addition to highlighting cash needs or

EXHIBIT 13.1 Net Assets Employed (in $ Millions)

	9/30/91	9/30/92	9/30/93	1994 Plan				1994 Plan B/(W) Than	
	Actual	Actual	Forecast	12/31/93	3/31/93	6/30/94	9/30/94	1991 Forecast	1994 LRP
Current assets:									
Formula cash (2.2)	$	$	$	$	$	$	$	$	$
Receivables:									
Trade accounts									
Notes									
Other									
Allowance for doubtful account									
Net receivables									
Inventories:									
Finished goods									
Work-in-process									
Raw materials and other									
Gross inventories									
Valuation reserves									
Obsolescence reserves									
Lifo reserves									
Other (specify)									
Net inventories	$	$	$	$	$	$	$	$	$
Other current assets	$	$	$	$	$	$	$	$	$
Total current assets	$	$	$	$	$	$	$	$	$

Current liabilities:									
Trade payables									
Cash advances									
Other accrued liabilities									
Total accounts payable	$	$	$	$	$	$	$	$	$
Other current liabilities:									
Total current liabilities									
Working capital									
Property, plant, and equipment:									
At cost	$	$	$	$	$	$	$	$	$
Less accumulated depreciation									
Net property									
Other noncurrent assets:									
Investments									
Other									
Total other assets	$	$	$	$	$	$	$	$	$
Net assets employed	$	$	$	$	$	$	$	$	$
Average net assets	$	$	$	$	$	$	$	$	$

EXHIBIT 13.2 Cash Flow Schedule

				1994 Plan					1994 Plan B/(W) Than	
	1991 Actual	1992 Actual	1993 Forecast	1st Qtr.	2nd Qtr.	3rd Qtr.	4th Qtr.	Full Year	1993 Forecast	1994 LRP
Cash Receipts	$	$	$	$	$	$	$	$	$	$
Capital gain/(loss)										
Book value of property, plant, and equipment sold										
Total cash from operations	$	$	$	$	$	$	$	$	$	$
Cash used for:										
Working capital requirements:										
Accounts receivable	$	$	$	$	$	$	$	$	$	$
Inventories										
Other current assets*										
Accounts payable										
Other current liabilities										
Total working capital	$	$	$	$	$	$	$	$	$	$
Other assets and liabilities requirements:										
Capital expenditures†	$	$	$	$	$	$	$	$	$	$
Other assets										
Other liabilities										
Total other	$	$	$	$	$	$	$	$	$	$
Total cash used	$	$	$	$	$	$	$	$	$	$

Net cash flow (pretax)	$	$	$	$	$	$	$	$	$	$
Less: taxes @ 48 percent of PBI dividend allocation										
Net cash flow	$	$	$	$	$	$	$	$	$	$
Exclude from presentation:										
Gross property:										
Capital expenditures†	$	$	$	$	$	$	$	$	$	$
Transfers in less: disposition of existing property at cost										
Gross property	$	$	$	$	$	$	$	$	$	$
Accumulated depreciation:										
Depreciation expense	$	$	$	$	$	$	$	$	$	$
Transfers (net) less: accumulated depreciation on disposition of existing assets										
Accumulated depreciation	$	$	$	$	$	$	$	$	$	$

* Include changes in formula cash.

† Include all capitalized leases; exclude project expense.

availability, the cash flow schedule enables management to (a) evaluate performance of an operating unit, (b) analyze opportunities for expansion and new business development, and (c) estimate the value of the company or unit should management decide to sell, spin off, or obtain additional financing.

The cash flow schedule is a period-by-period statement of (a) cash at the start of each period, (b) expected cash inflows (receipts), (c) expected cash outflows (disbursements), and (d) cash at the end of each period. Expected cash inflows are determined from sales budgets, cash and credit sales data, and accounts receivable collection data. In addition, sales of securities or other assets, and loans are sources of cash inflows. Expected cash outflows are determined similarly, from the costs and expenses related to sales, cost of goods sold, and other operating expenses, and the expected timing of these payments. Purchases of property, plant, and equipment and the paying off of loans and other long-term liabilities also generate cash outflows. All these cash inflows and outflows must be determined to prepare an accurate cash flow schedule. Exhibit 13.2 shows a cash flow schedule.

The cash flow schedule can also be prepared directly from the income statement, or statement of operations, by making adjustments to net income for each period. This method of calculating cash flow starts with net income and makes adjustments for (a) all noncash transactions (depreciation, amortization, accounts payable, accounts receivable, bartering), (b) investing activities (proceeds from selling, and payments to purchase property, plant, and equipment), and (c) financing activities (proceeds and payments relating to issuing/purchasing equity and debt securities, and borrowing transactions).

(c) CAPITAL BUDGETING PLAN

Planning, organizing, and controlling property and plant necessitates the preparation of a capital budgeting plan, or capital budget. This plan shows how the aggregate of capital dollars projected as being available for corporate investment will be allocated among various groups and divisions. Exhibit 13.3 illustrates a capital plan summary schedule showing the status of new authorizations and previously approved expenditures.

Note the comparative information included in the schedule; that is, AOP authorizations and expenditures are evaluated against the current LRP as well as previously established corporate AOP guidelines.

The inclusion of specific expenditures for new real estate and facilities in the AOP capital plan will serve as an advance indicator to the real estate department of potential, near-term acquisition projects. Further, if the department has had an advisory role in AOP preparations and review, several additional benefits may result.

EXHIBIT 13.3 Capital Plan Summary

	Authorizations	Expenditures		
		Carry-Over	New	Total
Group A:				
Division A	$	$	$	$
Division B				
•				
•				
Total group A				
Group B:				
Division A				
Division B				
•				
•				
Total group B				
•				
•				
•				
Total operations	$	$	$	$
Operations LRP	$	$	$	$
AOP over/(under) LRP	$	$	$	$
AOP guidelines	$	$	$	$
AOP over/(under) AOP guidelines	$	$	$	$

1. The real estate department may be aware that a proposed disposition by one division of property not yet officially declared surplus may well fit a proposed acquisition program of another division.
2. The real estate department can provide input on the anticipated timing and yield from projected surplus property sales.
3. The real estate department can coordinate efforts with the facilities department, normally responsible for equipment redeployment.
4. The proposed cost of facilities that are scheduled "as required" can be more accurately stated, providing the base for a better understood appropriation request.

§ 13.3 LONG-RANGE PLAN

Just as the AOP signifies by its title the short-term nature of the budgeting cycle, the long-range plan (LRP) denotes an attempt to forecast corporate business prospects over a longer period—usually five years or more. Therefore, the span of interest will widen significantly when corporate, group, and division leadership create a framework within which long-term growth opportunities can be extrapolated from sequential AOPs. But to be truly effective, the LRP must be more than the AOP repeated five times.

The basic objectives of a LRP are as follows:

1. To assess and define the economic and competitive environment that is likely to be faced within the LRP period.
2. To establish goals that are consistent with the company's approved strategic objectives.
3. To identify and define the major actions required to achieve the LRP goals.
4. To determine the timing, scope, resource requirements, and major milestones of each planned action.
5. To prepare reasonable estimates of the probable financial effect of implementing the LRP.
6. To assess the major risks of accomplishing the LRP objectives, to identify key early warning indicators, and to prepare contingency plans for responding to significant changes in the external environment.
7. To evaluate the aggregate resource requirements and the availability of the necessary resources and to reach resource allocation decisions.
8. To arrive at an agreed-on plan for the managing of the business during the LRP period and to establish preliminary estimates of the probable operating results for each of the fiscal years included in the plan.

The LRP presentation process will closely duplicate that of the AOP—with each operating unit submitting its long-range forecast from plant, to division, to group or operation, to a consolidated plan submitted for corporate office review and evaluation. The basic purpose of the LRP presentation is to describe business strategy of each division over a five-year period (or whatever other term is chosen) and to identify the major management actions necessary to implement the strategy.

The major actions may be specifically planned events or milestones such as major new product developments or introductions, capacity expansions, market penetration objectives, critical decision points, and management organization changes.

The presentation format for a LRP will normally address key long-term planning objectives in the following topical sequence:

- Statement of charter.
- Summary of economic and competitive assumptions.
- Strategic plan summary.
- Division goals and major management actions.
- Risks and opportunities.
- Early warning indicators and contingency plans.
- Summary of product line business strategies.
- Product line analysis—history and future trends.
- Research and engineering plan summary.
- New products—market analysis, sales/profits, investment/expense, and timing.
- Major new programs—investment/expense and timing.
- Capacity utilization by major process/facility.
- Capital plan summary.
- LRP summary.
- Four-box chart—sales, profit, assets, and cash flow.
- Four box chart—inventories, receivables, working capital, and non-current assets.
- Division profit and loss statement.
- Summary of changes in sales and profit.
- LRP assumptions—pricing, economics, and performance improvements.
- Operating results by product line—long-range plan.
- Division net assets employed.
- Division cash flow.
- Foreign location after-tax cash flow (in local currency).
- Projected base for allocations.

The items are relatively self-explanatory. The emphasis leans much more toward existing and emerging market analyses than toward past events. For example, the item "Product line analysis—history and future trends," would normally address the following issues:

1. *Market Developments and Forecasts—Industry and General*
   The basis for industry forecasts and growth trends
   Technology developments and trends

Governmental influences
Competitive actions
Import/Export considerations
U.S. market considerations versus world market considerations
The industry capacity/market demand relationships
Market behavior versus general conditions (and major economic indicators).

2. *Marketing Plans—Company-Specific*
Market share targets, changes versus competition
New product development and introduction plans
Product obsolescence and deletion
Pricing strategy
Distribution strategy
Marketing and sales organization
Advertising and promotional strategy.

The LRP's emphasis on the future is important because the real estate department will be involved implementing LRP forecasts as these relate to changing real estate and facilities requirements that are designed to implement forecasted-market developments and company marketing plans (see Capital Budgeting Evaluation § 13.6).

§ 13.4 APPROPRIATION REQUEST

The appropriation request (AR) is the principal vehicle by which the operating division seeks group, operations, and corporate approval for virtually all proposals affecting operating division financial commitments. The AR has a number of primary objectives:

- Management is advised of the full extent of the financial commitment involved in a proposed action.
- The action is consistent with the fundamental business objectives of the company, as stated in the annual operating plan and the long-range plan.
- The expected financial results and/or other considerations justify the commitment.
- The proposed appropriation is the most profitable and/or cost-effective way to accomplish the desired objectives.

Financial policy should state that no capital transaction is to be started prior to the approval of an appropriation request. The levels of management authorized to approve actions should be identified as a part of financial policy. In addition, no operations, group, or division person, regardless of position, should begin to negotiate the acquisition or disposition of any real estate, or sign any documents pertaining thereto, without prior specific authority regarding each property. The right to perform these actions should be retained within the corporate office, with signature authority subject to delegated limitations.

The AR and its financial justification should be prefaced by a summary narrative addressed to succeeding approval levels, with approval signatures required at each designated level of authority (the signature approval of the chief financial executive at each level should be required on every AR). The summary letter will generally include the following:

1. A description of current operations and of how the project relates to the achievement of the divisional objectives and funding plan, as contained in the long-range plan and the annual operating plan.
2. The purpose of the proposed project, including what the facilities, tooling, and so on, are intended to accomplish and how they relate to the operations of the location.
3. The aggregate amount to the request, the amounts previously approved, the future requirements, and the total commitment expected at the completion of the project. The relationship of the requested funds to the previous and future requirements should be stated.
4. The amount of the request (capital plus related expense) as compared with the amount included in the annual operating plan and the long-range plan.

If the project was not included in the AOP or the LRP, a comprehensive statement of the project's forecast impact on planned results should be included.

Financial justification should be presented on a series of exhibits supporting the summary letter, the required detail being determined by project complexities. Note that this chapter is primarily concerned with the philosophy of the AR and LRP process and, more specifically, with real estate department involvement in their preparation, review, and implementation, not with the procedural detail of the AR or LRP.

§ 13.5 TREND AND RATIO ANALYSES

Management should use trend and ratio analyses to compare operating data that cover a number of periods (months, quarters, years). This analysis should be an integral part of AOP and LRP. In addition, this analysis should evaluate operating efficiency and profitability, liquidity, and risk and capital structure.

Trends can be stated in terms of percentage increases or decreases, and charted and graphed to provide a visual presentation of performance and changes during the period covered. Ratios are found by dividing one number into another and, based on company or industry standards, comparing the result with stated or anticipated goals. See examples of ratio analyses in Exhibit 13.4.

A company's AOP, LRP, balance sheet, and income statements supply information needed to perform trend and ratio analysis. Identifying trends and calculating ratios will serve a number of analytic needs such as the following:

1. Comparing current financial performance with prior and expected performance.
2. Providing financial performance data to support the planning, organizing, directing, and controlling functions of the company.
3. Performing credit analysis by commercial loan officers and suppliers' credit managers looking to extend short-term credit or working capital or long-term capital loans to a company.
4. Evaluating specific public (and private) entities by securities analysts or individual investors, comparing performance with other companies in the same industry.

Some of the common financial ratios and other performance measures used to evaluate (a) short-term liquidity, (b) long-term solvency and capital structure, (c) profitability and operating efficiency, and (d) real estate include the following.

§ 13.6 CAPITAL BUDGETING EVALUATION

The implementation of strategic, financial, and operational plans often requires managers to choose between two or more alternative courses of action, with each requiring commitments of significant capital resources. A typical objective of these situations is to achieve the highest return on capital invested or the greatest cost savings. While such decisions are generally made without complete information and require a great deal of business judgment, there will be information that can be reduced to a quantitative basis. This quantitative information can and should be measured, evaluated, and compared on a systematic basis.

Capital budgeting evaluation, also called project evaluation, project selection, capital budgeting, capital expenditure decisions, and investment analysis, is used for a variety of different decision-making situations. These include planning the acquisition or development of property,

EXHIBIT 13.4 Examples of Commonly Used Ratios

Ratio	Use
Short-term liquidity:	
Current ratio = $\frac{\text{Current assets}}{\text{Current liabilities}}$	Measure of ability to pay current obligations
Acid-test ratio = $\frac{\text{Cash + Short-term investments + Current receivables}}{\text{Current liabilities}}$	Measure of short-term liquidity
Accounts receivable turnover = $\frac{\text{Credit sales}}{\text{Average accounts receivable}}$	Measures relative size of receivable balance and effectiveness of credit policies
Days' sales uncollected = $\frac{\text{Days in year}}{\text{Accounts receivable turnover}}$	Measures time it takes to collect receivables
Inventory turnover = $\frac{\text{Cost of goods sold}}{\text{Average inventory}}$	Measures relative size of inventory
Days' sales in inventory = $\frac{\text{Inventory}}{\text{Average day's sales}}$	Measures effectiveness of inventory policies
Long-term solvency and capital structure:	
Debt to equity ratio = $\frac{\text{Total liabilities}}{\text{Total stockholders' equity}}$	Measure of relationship of debt to equity financing
Times interest charges earned = $\frac{\text{Net income before interest and taxes}}{\text{Interest expense}}$	Measure of protection of the return to creditors

EXHIBIT 13.4 *(Continued)*

Ratio	Use
Profitability and operating efficiency:	
$\text{Profit margin} = \dfrac{\text{Net income}}{\text{Net sales}}$	Measures net income produced from sales
$\text{Contribution rate} = \dfrac{\text{Sales price per unit} - \text{variable costs per unit}}{\text{Sales price per unit}}$	Measures percentage by which sales price exceeds variable costs per unit
$\text{Break-even point in dollars} = \dfrac{\text{Fixed costs}}{\text{Contribution rate}}$	Amount of sales at which earnings are zero
$\text{Total asset turnover} = \dfrac{\text{Net sales}}{\text{Average total assets}}$	Measures how efficiently assets are used to produce sales
$\text{Return on assets (ROA)} = \dfrac{\text{Net income}}{\text{Net assets employed}}$	Measure of operating efficiency and management performance
$\text{Return on total assets employed} = \dfrac{\text{Net income}}{\text{Average total assets}}$	Measure of operating efficiency and management performance
$\text{Return on common stockholders' equity} = \dfrac{\text{Net income} - \text{Preferred dividends}}{\text{Average common stockholders' equity}}$	Measure of profitability of common stockholders' investment

$\text{Earnings per share (EPS)} = \dfrac{\text{Net income}}{\text{Weighted average outstanding shares}}$	Measure of past, present and future performance, and basis for comparing investment opportunities
$\text{Price earnings (P/E) ratio} = \dfrac{\text{Market price per common share}}{\text{Earnings per share}}$	Measure of market value of earnings and profitability of alternative investments
$\text{Dividend yield} = \dfrac{\text{Annual dividends declared}}{\text{Market price per share}}$	Measure of current return to investor
Real estate:	
$\text{Loan-to-value} = \dfrac{\text{Mortgage loan funds}}{\text{Property cost}}$	Measure of relationship of debt and equity financing
$\text{Debt-service-coverage} = \dfrac{\text{Net operating income}}{\text{Debt service}}$	Measure of protection of the return to lenders
$\text{Margin of safety} = \text{Net operating income} - \text{Debt service}$	Measure of protection of the return to lenders
$\text{Gross rent multiplier} = \dfrac{\text{Purchase price of property}}{\text{Annual gross rental income}}$	Measure of the purchase price as a multiple of rental income, basis for comparing investment alternatives

plant, and equipment; analyzing leases; and evaluating business expansion alternatives and acquisition and disposition opportunities.

This section introduces some of the approaches used to measure financial dimensions and provide quantitative data on which real estate decisions can be based—payback period, rate-of-return approaches, and present value models.[1] All of the approaches have strengths and weaknesses and, accordingly, most executives use several approaches to track corporate real estate and evaluate proposed projects.

Regardless of the approach used, each requires estimates of (a) cash inflows and outflows of each proposed project, (b) timing of the cash inflows and outflows, and (c) the tax impact of the different alternatives on these cash flows.

A cash flow schedule for each proposed project should be prepared for this purpose (see § 13.2(b)). The proposed project generates cash inflows from (a) the cash received from additional sales, (b) the financing of the project, and (c) the sale of the project in the future. Cash outflows are caused by (a) the cost of the project and the timing of the payments and (b) the additional cash disbursements required to generate the additional sales. The net cash inflow (outflow) is the result of subtracting the cash outflows from the cash inflows.

To determine the net cash inflow, the effects of depreciation and taxes must be calculated. Depreciation accounting allocates the cost of plant and equipment over the time periods during which the assets are used. Although depreciation does not involve a cash outflow, it is a deductible in arriving at (taxable) net income and thereby reduces the amount of cash outflow for income taxes. For example, if depreciation (a noncash expense) is $100,000 during a period, net income before taxes will be $100,000 less than actual cash flow. If the company's incremental federal income tax rate is 34 percent, income taxes will be reduced by $34,000 for that period using the following formula:

$$\text{Tax savings} = \text{Tax rate} \times \text{Depreciation expense}$$

This $34,000 reduction in income taxes increases the project's net cash flow (after tax) by the same amount.

(a) PAYBACK PERIOD

The payback period method is the most popular of all the capital evaluation techniques, and it is the simplest to use and understand. It determines the time that is required for the cumulative net cash inflow from

[1] Portions of the information presented in this section has been adapted from *Real Estate Investment: Strategy, Analysis, Decisions,* Second Edition (New York: John Wiley & Sons, 1989), by Stephen A. Pyhrr, James R. Cooper, Larry E. Wofford, Steven D. Kapplin, and Paul D. Lapides.

a specific project to equal the related capital outlay. Based on the payback period approach, a project is deemed acceptable when there are adequate cash flows to pay back the initial capital outlays in less than a specified number of years or faster than alternative projects. The payback period model is:

Payback period = Cost of project/Annual net cash flow

For example, if a proposed retail outlet requires an initial cash outlay of $100,000 for build-out and fixtures, and is expected to generate $25,000 in annual net cash flow (after taxes), the payback period would be 4 years ($100,000/$25,000).

For projects with cash flows that vary from year to year, the payback period should be determined by preparing a schedule of annual net cash flows to determine when the cumulative annual net cash flows equals the cost of project.

The primary reason that payback is so popular is its simplicity to calculate and understand. A short payback period is preferred because (a) the invested funds are at risk for a shorter period of time and (b) the sooner cash is received, the sooner those funds will be available for other uses.

The payback period also has its weaknesses. It does not consider (a) the actual timing of the net cash flows during the payback period or (b) the amounts and timing of cash that will continue to be received after the payback period. For an example of the latter case, consider the preceding retail example with two locations—one in a trendy area that is undergoing major changes (zoning, access) with little certainty about cash flow after the fourth year, and the second with strong prospects for this cash flow to continue for seven years. While both locations have a four-year payback period, the second location is clearly preferable.

These weaknesses are significant and, accordingly, other capital evaluation techniques should be used in addition to payback period.

(b) RATE-OF-RETURN APPROACH

The rate-of-return approach calculates returns by dividing average annual net income or cash flow by the total estimated cost of the project. The result is the estimated percentage return on invested capital. This number can then be compared with the estimated returns on alternative proposed projects.

The rate-of-return decision approach requires management to perform the following three steps to arrive at a go/no-go decision for a project:

1. Estimate the expected rate of return.
2. Estimate the rate of return required to justify the investment and compensate for the risks involved.

3. Compare the expected and required rates of return to make a go/no-go decision.

If the expected rate of return is greater than or equal to the required rate of return, the project meets the company's financial criteria for a go decision.

(1) Estimating the Expected Rate of Return

The expected rate of return on a project can be estimated in a variety of ways, not one of which, unfortunately, is universally accepted. Four of the more popular "accounting" or rule-of-thumb rate of return measures that can be computed on a before- or after-tax basis follow:

1. $$\text{Rate of return} = \frac{\text{Net income before depreciation and debt service}}{\text{Total capital invested (purchase price)}}$$

2. $$\text{Rate of return} = \frac{\text{Annual cash flow after debt service}}{\text{Cash equity investment}}$$

3. $$\text{Rate of return} = \frac{\text{Annual cash flow } \textit{plus} \text{ Debt principal amortized}}{\text{Cash equity investment}}$$

4. $$\text{Rate of return} = \frac{\text{Annual cash flow } \textit{plus} \text{ Debt principal amortized } \textit{plus} \text{ property appreciation}}{\text{Cash equity investment}}$$

Although most managers use these measures to calculate the rate of return for a one-year period only, it is beneficial to compute them for each year of a projected holding period on a before- and after-tax basis.

(2) Estimating the Required Rate of Return

Estimation of the required rate of return, the *hurdle rate,* against which management measures expected return, is a subjective judgment that management makes on the basis of experience, the available rates of return on alternative investments, inflation expectations, and the riskiness of the property. The required rate of return should include (a) a real return, that is, a return for deferred consumption, (b) an inflation premium, and (c) a risk premium. Together, the "real return" and the "inflation premium" make up what is called a "risk-free" rate of return, representing the return management could expect from investments that are free of risk (Treasury bills) and of equal duration.

Management should, therefore, require that the expected cash flows from a project compensate for deferred consumption, for the expected rate of inflation over the holding period, and for the chance that actual cash flow may not equal expected cash flow.

(c) PRESENT-VALUE MODEL

Real estate and other capital investments should be made when management expects the investment to generate sufficient cash flows to provide a return *of* the capital invested (the initial cash outlay) and a satisfactory return *on* the investment. Fundamental to understanding return on the investment is the concept of present value. The concept of present value is based on the idea that the right to receive some amount (often stated as $1) in the future (one year) is worth less than that same amount received today. The amount of the difference will depend on how much can be earned on the funds if they are invested (in Treasury bills or corporate bonds). For example, if a 10 percent annual rate of return can be earned, the right to receive $1 in one year has a present value of $0.909091. This can be calculated using net present value financial tables or by using a financial calculator. To confirm this present value calculation, $0.909091 invested today at 10 percent will earn $0.0909091 in one year ($0.909091 multiplied by 10 percent), and when the amount earned is added to the amount invested, the total equals $1.00 ($0.0909091 + $0.909091 = $1.0000001).

Present-value models are more sophisticated evaluation techniques as they incorporate many of the variables that are not included in the payback period and rate-of-return methods. Many of these models have been adapted for computer software programs and desktop calculators to make the models easier for corporate real estate executives and students to use.

(1) Discounted-Cash-Flow Model

The present-value model, also called the discounted-cash-flow (DCF) valuation model, emphasizes (a) defining income flows as after-tax cash flows, (b) placing cash flow in specific time periods, (c) accounting for each type of cash flow to reflect exposure to income taxes, and (d) relying on compound interest discounts. The discount rate is the required rate of return (see § 13.6(b)(2)).

With the aid of financial tables or calculators, each year's net after-tax cash flow is "discounted" by applying a present-value factor derived from formulas based on the time value of money. The present value of each cash flow is computed, and all present values are added to get the total present value of the income stream generated by the project during specified holding period.

The present-value decision rule is the same as that for the rate-of-return methods: if the investment value is equal to or greater than the cost, the investment is acceptable; otherwise, the investment is rejected or modified.

The following is the basic after-tax present value model:

$$PV_E = \frac{CF_1}{(1+R)^1} + \frac{CF_2}{(1+R)^2} + \ldots + \frac{CF_n}{(1+R)^n} + \frac{SP}{(1+R)^n}$$

$$PV_P = PV_E + PV_M$$

where

PV_P = present (investment) value of project
PV_E = present value of equity returns
$CF_1, CF_2, \ldots, CF_n$ = equity cash flow; annual after-tax cash flow over the holding period (n)
SP = after-tax cash flow from sale of project (reversion cash flow)
PV_M = amount of debt borrowed to finance project
R = required rate of return on investment
n = holding period of investment

The after-tax cash flow received in each period ($CF_1, CF_2, \ldots, CF_n$ is discounted back to the point of initial investment at the required (internal) rate of return on equity (cash). The series of discounted cash flows is then totaled to measure the present value of the equity returns (PV_E). The present value of the project (PV_P) is then computed as the present value of the equity returns (PV_E) plus the amount of debt borrowed to finance the project (PV_M). If the present value of the project (PV_P) *is equal to or greater than* the total project investment costs (C, $C = PV_E + PV_M$), the project is acceptable using the decision rule. If PV_P is less, the project should be rejected or modified either to raise the present value of the property or to lower the total project investment costs.

(2) Net-Present-Value Model

The net present value (NPV) of a project is determined by estimating the cash flows inflows from the project, discounting them at a rate that represents an acceptable return, and then subtracting the initial cost of the project from the sum of the present values.

The preceding basic present-value model (§ 13.6(c)(1)) can be used to find the net present value of any series of cash flows by subtracting the total project cost from the present value of the project (NPV $= PV_P - C$).

The decision rule when using the net present value calculation is that as long as the net present value is zero or greater, the project is considered acceptable.

(3) Internal-Rate-of-Return Model

Many financial managers and analysts consider the internal-rate-of-return (IRR) model, or some modified version of it, the proper yardstick for comparing returns between real estate and other investment opportunities, such as bonds, stocks, and annuities.

The internal rate of return is the rate, expressed as an annual percentage, at which the present value of the net cash flows equals the present value of the equity investment. The IRR formula is simply the present-value formula solved for the unique value of the discount rate that results in an NPV of zero.

IRR can be calculated on a before- or after-tax cash flow basis on either total capital or equity capital invested. Most managers prefer an after-tax model, in which IRR is computed on the amount of equity investment, because it explicitly considers the time value of money and management's ability to use financial leverage to increase the return, and then shelter a portion of the return from income taxes.

The decision rule for investing is the same as the basic rule stated earlier: Accept projects that have IRRs equal to or greater than management's minimum required IRR (IRR $\geq R$, where R is management's minimum required IRR on equity). Projects should be rejected or modified if IRR is less than R.

(d) RISK ANALYSIS MODELS

Internal-rate-of-return and present-value models are said to be *deterministic* in nature, in that a specific value for each input variable is entered into the model to calculate the desired output. In contrast, a risk analysis model is said to be *probabilistic;* that is, the values of many of the input variables are uncertain and must be defined as ranges with associated probability distributions, rather than as single-point estimates. A risk analysis model thus generates a range of possible returns rather than a single value and ideally will also compute the probability or chances of receiving different rates of return, depending on how the uncertain future unfolds.

Without the knowledge of how to deal explicitly with risk in decision making, managers typically concentrate on a few key assumptions about the future, examine a few rules of thumb, mull over the situation, and then make a decision. Although some of the risk consideration may be explicit, the mathematics of risk are often left largely to judgment, hunch, instinct, and intuition.

In contrast, financial theory has attempted to make risk analysis more explicit and to suggest some improved procedures. Three common methods of analyzing risk are as follows:

1. The payback decision rule, which focuses on how long it takes management to recover the initial cash investment (see § 13.6(a))
2. The risk-adjusted discount rate, which attempts to account for risk by adding some premium to the required rate of return demanded (see § 13.6(b)(2))
3. Conservative forecasts, which deal with risk by reducing forecasted returns to some more conservative level.

These methods, however, have been subjected to increasing criticism. Although they are simple and familiar, they contain assumptions that are not only unclear but may be erroneous and could lead to decisions at odds with the company's objectives and goals. In addition, these procedures ignore much information that could be valuable for sharpening the decision process.

(1) Sensitivity Analysis

Additional property or project risk information can be calculated using the techniques of ratio and sensitivity analysis. Ratios can be used to measure the level and trends of risk by comparing various output data from a cash flow analysis. Popular ratio measures of risk include the debt coverage ratio and the break-even point (see § 13.5). Sensitivity analysis measures risk in capital budgeting evaluation models by assigning different values to the input variables that are considered to be uncertain, and then measuring their relative impact on the rate of return or other important output variables. Using sensitivity analysis techniques, if the data indicates a level of risk that is not commensurate with the expected level of return, the project is rejected or modified.

(2) Portfolio Analysis

Risk analysis in real estate can be divided into two categories: individual-project risk and portfolio risk. Analysis of individual-project risk examines a single project and implicitly assumes that the risk associated with it can be considered independently of the risk in other investments. Analysis of portfolio risk, conversely, notes the interrelations of various investment projects. For example, the overall risk profile of a portfolio of diversified real estate projects (geographic location, type and size of project) with different cyclical characteristics (ownership characteristics and financial structure) may be significantly less than the mean of the individual-project risks because the contracyclical return patterns of some of the projects in the portfolio have a stabilizing effect.

(e) INVESTMENT VALUE APPROACH

The most common technique for measuring returns for traditional real estate investment analysis is the investment value approach. Investment value is the present value of expected future net returns capitalized at the rate of return required to induce the investment in the first place. Use of the investment value approach requires estimates of the investment value and investment cost for each project being considered. According to the decision rule, projects are accepted only if the investment value is equal to or greater than the investment cost.

The basic model for computing the investment value of a real estate project is the general appraisal capitalization model, as follows:

$$V = I/R$$

where

V = investment value (present worth of future rights to income)

I = net operating income before depreciation and debt service (rental income less operating expenses)

R = capitalization rate (required rate of return on total capital to induce investment)

The capitalization rate (R) is determined in the same manner used to estimate the required rate of return used in the Rate-of-Return Approach (see § 13.6(b)(2)).

Assumptions underlying this model are limiting and include (a) all cash outflows occur at one time, (b) income is a "stabilized amount," and (c) capital is recaptured from income. Accordingly, while this model provides for a quick and easy formula to estimate investment value, it is really only appropriate for the preliminary evaluation of a project.

Fourteen

Valuation of Corporate Real Estate

§ 14.1 INTRODUCTION

Corporate real estate executives need to understand the principles of real estate valuation because companies use appraisals for many reasons. The most common reasons are:

- To determine the fair market value of the fixed asset(s) for financial reporting purposes.

- To assist in evaluating the price of an acquisition.
- To provide benchwork information before establishing the asking price for surplus property.
- To establish fair market value for donation and tax purposes.

Corporate policies may require one or more appraisals in each of these real estate transactions or activities. Since associated appraisal fees can be a major expense, the real estate executive should have enough expertise to identify exactly what type and level of appraisal is needed. Once the appraisal has been completed, the executive must be able to analyze and utilize the information it contains.

A corporate real estate department may have a real estate appraiser on staff to do a preliminary evaluation of the asset, but typically will hire the services of an independent fee appraiser to do the formal appraisal. Using an external consultant presents less potential for the inadvertent introduction of bias into the valuation. A corporate real estate staff is better used to identify appraisal needs, to secure qualified outside appraisers, and to review outside appraisals when they are submitted.

Reviewing the adequacy of appraisal reports and relating the appraisal information to corporate problems is an important task of the corporate real estate executive staff. It requires knowledge of the nature and content of an appraisal as well as the demographic and economic variables that affect value.

Value concepts and value definitions are presented and discussed in the next section. The major variables that influence the market value of several property types as well as the three valuation methods employed by appraisers are also discussed later in this chapter. Each of these topics answers the following types of questions:

- What is the primary purpose of a particular appraisal, and what information is necessary to achieve that purpose?
- Has the appraiser used acceptable and professionally recognized procedures?
- Has the appraiser adequately addressed the important issues in arriving at a final value estimate?
- Based on the analyses and comments in the report, does the appraiser demonstrate a sensitivity to the market and true value components of the property?

§ 14.2 VALUE CONCEPTS—DEFINITIONS

The appraiser can estimate several different types of value that are directly applicable to a corporate asset decision. The definitions of some of the major concepts follow. Interrelationships between and among these value concepts are also discussed.

(a) MARKET VALUE

Market value is the focus of most real property appraisal assignments. The current economic definition of *market value* taken from *The Dictionary of Real Estate Terminology*[1] follows:

> The most probable price in cash, terms equivalent to cash, or in other precisely revealed terms, for which the appraised property will sell in a competitive market under all conditions requisite to fair sale, with the buyer and seller each acting prudently, knowledgeably, and for self-interest, and assuming that neither is under undue duress.

Fundamental assumptions and conditions presumed in this definition are:

1. Buyer and seller are motivated by self-interest.
2. Buyer and seller are well informed and are acting prudently.
3. The property is exposed for a reasonable time on the open market.
4. Payment is made in cash, its equivalent, or in specified financing terms.
5. Specified financing, if any, may be the financing actually in place or on terms generally available for the property type in its locale on the effective appraisal date.
6. The effect, if any, on the amount of market value of atypical financing, services, or fees shall be clearly and precisely revealed in the appraisal report.

Within the main body of the definition, market conditions are competitive so that participants on the supply and demand sides of the market can interact freely and form their agreement in the transaction. Since freedom from undue pressure and influence on either party to the transaction often is not met in actual market conditions, it is necessary to investigate the conditions of sale for each comparable property sale utilized in the direct sales comparison approach and the gross rent multiplier approach. The appraiser should verify all comparable data and reject any unverified or atypical comparable.

[1] The Appraisal Institute, *The Dictionary of Real Estate Appraisal* (Chicago, IL: The Appraisal Institute, 1984), pp. 194–195.

Forced sales are not considered good evidence of market value under this stipulation.[2]

Six items modify and extend the definition of market value. These items clarify that definition and identify certain conditions that must exist to meet its parameters.

1. Rational or prudent buyers and sellers act in their own self-interest in the transactions. They normally use their best negotiating skills and strive to make the best deal they can. The give and take of the negotiating process results in typical or normal market outcomes regarding price, terms, and conditions of sale.
2. Informed buyers and sellers are aware of the available alternatives. Most negotiations are based on reasonable or normal market information rather than absolute or perfect knowledge, and this, too, results in normal market outcomes.
3. Quick sales are not considered evidence of a reasonable turnover period in the market. They may result from some form of undue influence or a lack of market information. Protracted or long listing periods are also not considered evidence of a reasonable turnover period in the market. Some sellers may receive a higher price if they hold out for an unwary or desperate buyer, but this is not a normal circumstance. The appraiser must ascertain the normal or typical turnover period, at the time of the appraisal, for the type of property being appraised.
4. Payment is presumed to be consistent with the standards of behavior in the market. This is almost always interpreted as cash to the seller or its cash equivalent. Financing at normal market rates without any special consideration is usually considered the same as cash, since it provides equivalent cash to the seller. This definitional condition sets up the need for the appraiser to undertake some form of cash equivalency adjustment if there is any type of atypical financing terms. Any such adjustment needs to be explained by the appraiser if it is performed. The explanation should involve answering the questions, "Why is it required?" and "What is its magnitude?"
5. "Specified financing" means atypical financing terms have been used, and a cash equivalency adjustment is usually necessary. Changes in market financing conditions also have to be monitored. Changes in the contract interest rate and changes in the discount points affect the feasibility of acquiring or disposing of

[2] Parts of the discussion in this paragraph and the next paragraph were adapted with much modification from Byrl Boyce and William N. Kinnard, *Appraising Real Property* (Lexington, MA: Lexington Books, 1984), pp. 6–7.

property because they increase transaction costs, thereby affecting market demand. So, the appraiser must adjust for these changes from one market situation to another.

6. As the financial characteristics of the market change, "atypical" financing in the form of below-market-rate loans, seller financing options (i.e., purchase money mortgages subordinated to first loans, land contracts, wraparound loans) and/or the shifting of discount points to the seller can occur. Cash equivalency adjustments may also have to be used to make these loans equivalent to cash.

Market value is an opinion by a qualified appraiser. The appraiser's judgment of the value of a property needs to be supported by citing the market conditions under which the appraisal was performed and plan explaining the data and techniques used. It is a "normative" statement—an unbiased, knowledgeable, and market-supported estimate of what the property should be worth in the open market.

(b) INVESTMENT VALUE

Investment value is:

> The value of an investment to a particular investor, based on his or her investment requirements; as distinguished from market value, which is impersonal and detached.[3]

Alternatively, the investment value of a property is its worth to:

> a particular investor, based on the investor's standards of investment acceptability rather than on objective market standards. An example would be an investor who is willing to accept a lower rate of return on an income property than the going rate on the market. For this reason, the investment value to that investor would be greater than the market value.[4]

(c) USE VALUE

Unlike market value and investment value, *use value* has a less precise definition in the appraisal literature. Use value is "the value of property that is designed to fit the particular requirements or needs of a specific owner or user. In nonresidential real estate, it is the contribution the

[3] The Appraisal Institute, *The Dictionary of Real Estate Appraisal,* (Chicago, The Appraisal Institute, 1984), p. 167.

[4] Boyce and Kinnard, p. 8.

real estate makes to the value of the business."[5] Alternatively, use value is "the value of a particular property for a specific use."[6]

Use value is associated with the concepts of a *limited market property* and a *special use property.* A limited market property is defined as "a property that has relatively few buyers at a particular time."[7] A special use property is defined as a property that has "limited conversion potential."[8] These concepts are imprecise, however, because they are not mutually exclusive. A large manufacturing plant can be, and very often is, both a limited market property and a special purpose property.

The imprecision is evident in the following statement linking limited market and special use properties:

> Many limited-market properties include structures with unique physical designs, special construction materials, or layouts that restrict their utility to the use for which they were originally built. These properties had limited conversion potential, and consequently, are often called special purpose or special design properties. Examples of such properties include houses of worship, museums, schools, public buildings and clubhouses.[9]

Appraisers are aware that use value can differ from market value and that a building can have both a use value and a market value. "An older factory that is still used by the original firm may have considerable use value to that firm, but only a nominal market value for another use."[10]

The first important point to remember is that a decision to divest or to acquire property may require knowledge of both of these values. Acquiring a property with a low market value and a high use value is ideal. But acquiring a property with both a low use value and a low market value is probably inappropriate, and it is obviously inadvisable to acquire one with a high market value and a low use value. On the other hand, it may be a smart move to divest a property that has a high market value and a low use value. The typical independent fee appraiser can provide an estimate of market value but more than likely will not be able to provide the use value of the property. Specialized background and training may be necessary to estimate the use value of an industrial plant that is a limited market property and/or a special use property.

[5] Ibid. p. 10.

[6] The Appraisal Institute, *The Dictionary of Real Estate Appraisal,* (Chicago, IL: The Appraisal Institute, 1984), p. 318.

[7] The Appraisal Institute, *The Appraisal of Real Estate* (Chicago, IL: The Appraisal Institute, 1992), p. 22.

[8] Ibid. p. 23.

[9] Ibid. p. 23.

[10] Ibid. p. 22.

(d) LIQUIDATION PRICE (VALUE)

A single, universally accepted definition of *liquidation value* does not exist. One definition that the appraisal literature provides is:

> The price that an owner is compelled to accept when a property must be sold without reasonable market exposure.[11]

In this instance, "without reasonable market exposure" usually refers to a shorter than normal exposure time.

Another source adds the forced sale issue to the definition by stating that liquidation value is:

> The amount for which a property is likely to sell at forced sale. A residence on which the mortgage has been foreclosed or property being sold for unpaid property taxes would most probably not sell at its market value, because the requisite market conditions for a fair sale will likely not be met [see earlier definition of market value].[12]

A more general definition of liquidation value that we would like to offer is:

> Liquidation value is a percentage of the current market value of the property. The reduced or discounted value is acceptable to the seller because of an immediate need (real or perceived) for cash or its equivalent.

This definition takes the elements and the factors mentioned in the previous definitions into consideration, but goes beyond them. The two previous definitions have limited application. For example, a property could have been on the market for a reasonable time period at a list price considered close to its anticipated or estimated market value, but it has not sold because market conditions have changed since the listing. The seller now needs cash. The list price could be dropped a modest amount, reflecting the decline in current market value from that of the previous market period. Or, it could be reduced a much greater amount, to its liquidation value, to assure a quick sale after the list price reduction. Notice that the property did have reasonable market exposure and that there was no precision (an expected fixed percentage or rate of change) in the relationship between the property's current market value and its current liquidation value. Moreover, this same property could have been offered for sale voluntarily to obtain a quick sale, not at an auction or forced sale.

[11] The Appraisal Institute, *The Dictionary of Real Estate Appraisal*, p. 186.

[12] Boyce and Kinnard, p. 10.

(e) GOING-CONCERN VALUE

The best explanation of the concept of *going-concern value* in the appraisal literature is:

> The value created by a proven property operation. It includes the incremental value associated with the business concern, which is distinct from the value of the real estate only. Going-concern value includes an intangible enhancement of the value of an operating business enterprise which is produced by the assemblage of the land, building, labor, equipment, and marketing operation. This process creates an economically viable business that is expected to continue. Going-concern value refers to the total value of the property, including both real property and intangible personal property attributed to business value.[13]

The acquisition or divestiture of a successful business will be more than the value of the real estate assets. An owner should expect more than the market value of the real estate when selling a "going concern," such as a processing plant, hotel, shopping center, apartment complex. Both the management of the operation and the marketing package are part of the transaction. Conversely, a person may have to pay more than the market value of the real estate assets for a profitable business that includes trade property in the sale.

The appraisal literature does not offer explicit guidelines for estimating going-concern value. Consequently, most independent fee appraisers seldom make this value estimate.

(f) ASSESSED VALUE

The appraisal literature offers the following definition of *assessed value:*

> The value assigned to a property for property tax assessment purposes. In most taxing jurisdictions, it is supposed to be a stipulated percentage of market value. As an indicator

of market value, however, assessed value may be invalid.[14]

(g) INSURABLE VALUE

Insurable value is defined in the appraisal literature as:

> A fire and casualty insurance term that indicates the base used to calculate the dollar amount of insurance that may be or should be carried on

[13] The Appraisal Institute, *The Appraisal of Real Estate,* p. 23–24.

[14] This definition of assessed value was modified from the text in Boyce and Kinnard, p. 9.

the destructible portions of the realty in order to indemnify the owner in the event of loss. Typically, it is calculated in terms of cost new less physical deterioration and insurance exclusions, without reference to obsolescence. For purposes of indemnification, the nonappraisal concepts of actual cash value and replacement value are also used.[15]

(h) BOOK VALUE

Book value is not an appraisal concept; it is not a value estimated by an appraiser. However, it is related to the acquisition price of a property, which had both a market value and an investment value at the time of acquisition. Appraisal literature offers two rather similar definitions:

1. The dollar amount at which real estate and other assets are carried on the books of account of a business or individual. Book value is based on original acquisition cost less accounting depreciation and is used as a basis for calculating income tax profit or loss as well as rate of return on investment.[16]
2. The capital amount at which property is shown on the account books; usually equals the original cost less reserves for depreciation plus additions to capital.[17]

Even though the definitions are found in the appraisal literature, they are accounting, not appraisal, concepts. Any changes in the concept can be identified by consulting the accounting literature.

(i) SALVAGE VALUE

Salvage value is defined in the appraisal literature in the following ways:

- The amount obtainable for all or some parts of a building for removal from the site, usually for use or assembly elsewhere. This could be an issue in setting damages in a condemnation or a residential property under eminent domain. If the building is removable to a nearby site, the condemning authority might well choose to let the condemnee move it or sell it rather than having it demolished. The salvage value could then affect the final determination of damages and of just compensation.[18]

[15] Ibid.

[16] Ibid.

[17] The Appraisal Institute, *The Dictionary of Real Estate Appraisal,* p. 35.

[18] Boyce and Kinnard, p. 10.

- The price expected for a whole property (e.g., a house), or a part of a whole property (e.g., a plumbing fixture), that is removed from the premises, usually for use elsewhere.[19]

Like book value, salvage value is an accounting concept, so users of this term should research the accounting literature for a more precise accounting definition.

(j) SCRAP VALUE

Scrap value is defined in appraisal literature as:

> The estimated price obtainable for materials in a dismantled structure to be sold for scrap. It implies removal from the premises of the basic materials themselves for reclamation of their value (e.g., the copper of the piping), not for continued use of the components as building components elsewhere.[20]

(k) MORTGAGE VALUE OR LOAN VALUE

The terms *mortgage value* and *loan value* are misnomers. A property being considered for a mortgage loan should be, and usually is, evaluated as loan security in terms of its market value. It does not have a different value simply because it is security for a mortgage loan. The amount of loan to grant on the property is an underwriting decision, not a value decision. Appraisers should avoid these terms.[21]

Corporate real estate executives who encounter one of these terms should interpret it simply as the market value of a piece of property used to collateralize a mortgage loan. The lender needs to understand a property's market value since the property would be sold in the market, either voluntarily or involuntarily, if the borrower cannot meet the mortgage debt obligation.

§ 14.3 VALUE CONCEPTS—INTERRELATIONSHIPS

The previous section examined the various value definitions and concepts used by the appraiser. Most of them are applicable to the corporation's needs. The corporate real estate executive must differentiate among various types of value and specify what type of value is needed when instructing a staff member, commissioning an independent fee appraiser or a consultant, or reporting appraisal outcomes.

[19] The Appraisal Institute, *The Dictionary of Real Estate Appraisal*, p. 268.

[20] Boyce and Kinnard, p. 10.

[21] Ibid. p. 9.

This section expands the discussion of the definitions even further by examining interrelationships that exist between the value concepts. Some value concepts are very specific and exclusive while others are broad and include other closely related value terms. Nuances that make distinctions in exact meaning often clarify an issue or make a decision much easier.

(a) MARKET VALUE, MOST PROBABLE SALES PRICE, AND SALES PRICE

Sales price is defined as:

> The amount actually paid, or to be paid, for a property in a particular transaction. It differs from market value in that it is an accomplished or historic fact, whereas market value is and remains an estimate. . . . Market price involves no assumption of prudent conduct by the parties, of absence of undue stimulus or of any other condition basic to the market value concept.[22]

As noted in the definition, the sales price is a historical fact—a statement of what is; whereas market value is a statement of what should be. Sales price may be greater than, less than, or possibly equal to market value in any given transaction.

Sales price as a concept does not involve the strict conditions established for market value. The buyer and seller in the transaction do not have to be motivated by self-interest. They do not have to be well informed. They do not have to act rationally, free from pressure, or at arm's length. Finally, the financial terms of sale are what they are. There is no requirement for typical market practice.

"Most probable sales price" is usually considered virtually synonymous with market value. It represents the transaction or sales price that is most likely to occur, given the available data on market conditions and market sales. It becomes the benchmark showing what a comparable property actually sold for at arm's length in a market operating with "normal" conditions. The appraiser uses that benchmark to estimate the market value of a subject property (a property being appraised).

(b) MARKET VALUE AND INVESTMENT VALUE

Investment value should not be confused with the market value of an investment (or income) property, which is its value to a typical investor. The value of the same property may vary with the investor. For example, a property producing an income stream of $100,000 annually in a market

[22] Ibid. p. 7.

where typical investors require 15 percent overall return may have a market value of $667,000. But an investor willing to settle for a 14 percent return could pay as much as $715,000 for the property. Another investor requiring a 16 percent return would pay no more than $625,000. Both the $715,000 and $625,000 figures are investment values.

(c) MARKET VALUE AND CONSTRUCTION COST

Building construction costs do not create value. Use of the building and the location of the use are the productive elements of a property that cause value to accrue. The improvements and construction costs can be duplicated at a given comparable site and location. However, under appropriate conditions, construction costs are a part of a value-estimating technique known as the *cost approach.* In appraisal, construction cost refers to the outlay for both direct and indirect costs of construction. The direct costs generally include construction labor, materials, equipment, temporary utilities, and construction management and supervision. Indirect costs generally include overhead expenses, advertising and marketing costs, and interest expenses associated with the construction loan.

Construction costs, combined with the acquisition price or cost of the land, do not equate to market value even if the structure is just completed, not yet occupied, and is totally free of any physical deterioration. If the structure is in the wrong location, the market would probably price the property at less than the construction cost. If the structure utilizes the wrong design or floor plan, buyers in the market would discount the price by at least the amount required to correct the design flaw (if it can be corrected at all), and probably more. So, after reality is imposed on the seller, the eventual sales price would be considerably less than the construction cost. The first example is a case of external obsolescence, the second example is a case of functional obsolescence. These issues will be explored when the cost approach to valuation is presented.

The sales price of the property can also be greater than the full or total cost of construction (direct plus indirect costs, or hard plus soft costs) if the completed building is in great demand by its ultimate user who will pay the premium to get early occupancy or to avoid the headaches of supervising a construction project. A needy user might be able to get a site and have the improvements constructed in two years for one million dollars. That same user could get a newly constructed property today for one million plus a negotiated premium.

So, sales price can be greater than, less than, or equal to the total cost of construction. And market value can also be greater than, less than, or equal to the total cost of construction.

This discussion should alert the corporate real estate executive to the logical flaw in the statement: "You couldn't rebuild this structure for less than $400,000, and I can show you the cost figures. So it has to be worth at least that plus the value of the land!"

(d) MARKET VALUE AND LIQUIDATION VALUE

There is no magic or even a logical calculation that would enable an analyst to accurately forecast a liquidation value based on an analysis of past conditions or even a projection of future conditions. First, the current liquidation value of a property is related to current market conditions. Current liquidation value should not be related to historic market value or future market value (i.e., anticipated sales price). This conceptual relationship between liquidation and market values does not cross over market periods.

However, as market conditions change, both market value and liquidation value change. Depending on the current position of the real estate cycle, current liquidation value can be greater than past market value during a recovery and less than past market value in a downturn. For this reason, the use of comparable property sales from a past period representing different market conditions is virtually useless in estimating current liquidation value.

Second, liquidation value can apply to both performing and nonperforming properties. An owner may need to convert a highly profitable investment property into cash. To assure a quick sale, the property would have to be offered at some discount from its investment value or market value. The discount from market value may have to be greater for a nonperforming asset than it would be for a performing asset.

§ 14.4 MARKET INFLUENCES ON VALUE OF PROPERTY TYPES

Directly or indirectly, each of the value concepts identified and discussed in the previous section is affected by market influences acting on the demand side and the supply side of the market. This section identifies the major variables that affect each type of market and provides a primer for the real estate executive to use when reviewing and judging an appraisal report.

(a) INDUSTRIAL PROPERTY

The market for industrial property is affected by the level of current and future employment in those SIC categories that utilize industrial type buildings.[23]

[23] The Standard Industrial Classification code (SIC code) is not discussed in this text. The authors assume that the reader is familiar with this concept in at least general terms. If by chance you are not familiar with the concept, you can obtain sufficient knowledge from Neil Carn, Joseph Rabianski, Ronald Racster, and Maury Seldin, *Real Estate Market Analysis: Applications and Techniques*, (Englewood Cliffs, NJ: Prentice-Hall, Inc., 1988).

These industrial SIC codes include manufacturing (both durable and nondurable) and wholesale trade. However, there is a strong correlation between the type of industry and the type of industrial space needed. For example, industries that use typical space found in an industrial or business park will not demand specialized industrial facilities required by heavy industry. So, if employment growth is occurring in steel production, nonferrous metal production, stone and clay products, or chemical production, there will be very little direct effect on vacancy in the typical industrial park. On the other hand, if there is anticipated employment growth in electrical and electronic machinery, instruments, or optical goods, there will be a strong and direct effect on the demand for space in the typical industrial park.

The first things to check in an industrial park appraisal are the employment forecasts in the manufacturing and wholesale trade SIC codes. Employment growth should be forecasted for the next five years or so, and this employment growth should be segmented by type of industry and type of industrial space user. Then, the existing and proposed supply of space should be matched to this demand. The characteristics and competitive ability of the subject property should be identified to comprehend how marketable it is compared with other available industrial space.

After the employment analysis has been completed, an analysis of recent sales transaction and lease negotiations should be undertaken to make reasonable judgments and forecasts. Some significant items to include in the appraisal report are:

- Recent trends in sales price and sales price per square foot compared with recent changes in the level of employment and the composition of that employment in the SIC codes.
- Recent trends in effective rental rates per square foot. This is the rate actually paid after all forms of rent abatement and concessions, tenant improvement allowances, move-in expenses, and so on, are factored into the deal. These effective rental rates should be considered in relation to recent changes in the level of employment and the composition of that employment in the SIC codes.
- The amount of new industrial space being developed.
- Effective rent levels by type of industrial space. An analysis of rent levels along with future employment growth and new industrial construction is needed to form a judgment about the level of effective rents in the near term.
- Vacancy levels by type of industrial space. This analysis should be used in conjunction with future employment growth and new

industrial construction to judge the level of vacancies in the near term.

After examining the manufacturing and the wholesaling SIC codes (the principal employment sectors using industrial space), the appraiser should look at employment in other SIC categories that may have part of their employment in industrial space. Particularly, some business services and retail trades use industrial parks or business parks to house part of their operations.

The real estate executive should expect the appraisal to consider important market factors. For industrial property, the appraisal report should analyze employment levels and forecasts as well as employment composition among SIC codes. It should also list the type of existing industrial space and the type of new industrial space that will enter the market and economic data such as sales price and sales price per square foot, effective rent levels, and vacancy levels in the market.

(b) OFFICE PROPERTY

The market for office space is most strongly affected by the level of current and future employment in those SIC categories that utilize office buildings—finance, insurance, and real estate (FIRE), business services, and government. However, every SIC code has some portion of its employees working in offices. For example, printing and publishing services, a two-digit, nondurable manufacturing SIC, has a relatively high percentage of its employees (approximately 40%) working in office space. So, in an office market analysis, it is important to estimate the amount of office use in each of the one- or two-digit SIC codes.

After completion of the employment analysis, an analysis of recent sales transactions and lease negotiations should be undertaken to make reasonable judgments and forecasts. Relationships that should be checked and presented in the appraisal report are:

- Recent trends in sales price and sales price per square foot compared with recent changes in the level of employment and the composition of that employment in the SIC codes.
- Recent trends in effective rental rates per square foot. This is the rate actually paid after all forms of rent abatement and concessions, tenant improvement allowances, move-in expenses, and so on are factored into the deal. These effective rental rates should be considered in relation to recent changes in the level of employment and the composition of that employment in the SIC codes.
- The amount of new office space being developed should be listed and analyzed.

- Effective rent levels should be analyzed by type of office space. This information, along with future employment growth and new office construction, helps the analyst to judge the level of effective rents in the near term.
- Vacancy levels should be analyzed by type of office building and space and used in conjunction with future employment growth and new office space construction to judge the level of vacancies in the near term.

After noting the level of employment, its distribution across the SIC codes, and the percentage of that employment found in offices, the next major variable to consider is the amount of office space used per office worker. Both current utilization factors and future changes should be included. The amount of space per office worker is typically presented as a single figure and applied to office workers in all SIC codes. However, this square footage per office worker does in fact differ among the SIC codes, it changes over time, and it is different across geographic areas within a metropolitan area as well as across regions of the United States.

These two variables—employees in office space and the amount of square footage per office employee—provide a first approximation of the demand for office space. Depending on the market in which the subject property is located, other variables can enter the analysis.

The office workers can be located in attached office space as well as detached or speculative office space. The percentage of office workers in detached office space differs by SIC code. The FIRE SIC code has approximately 100 percent of its office workers in detached office space. Manufacturing very often has corporate office space attached to the production plant. So, the same growth in office employment in two office markets can lead to two different office space demand levels. The demand for detached office space will be higher in the community experiencing growth in FIRE employment than in the market experiencing growth in manufacturing employment.

Since office space is not a homogeneous product, the allocation of that space across various physical categories of office space is also important. The points of concern here are the structural type of office space—high-rise, midrise, single story; the site characteristics—whether it is freestanding or part of an integrated office park; and its qualitative structural characteristics—Class A, Class B, or Class C space.

In addition to the physical factors, the locational characteristics of the property should also be considered: Proximity to an interstate highway and public transportation, proximity to complementary uses such as restaurants, and proximity to other office space users are important aspects of the analysis. These locational features are also part of the Class A, Class B, and Class C office space definitions.

The real estate executive should expect the appraisal to consider important office market factors and to analyze employment levels and forecasts and their composition among SIC codes. The report should also include the type of existing office space and the type of new office space entering the market along with sales price and sales price per square foot, office space per employee, effective rent levels, and vacancy levels in the market.

(c) RETAIL PROPERTY

In appraisals, retail market analysis focuses on a forecast of purchasing power followed by a forecast of retail sales for a particular retail establishment or shopping center. The procedure is commonly known as "residual analysis" or by its older name "the vacuum technique," and is summarized by the following steps.

1. A geographic market area is identified in which the subject property directly competes with other retail establishments and from which it draws most of its customers.
2. The amount of purchasing power available for retail expenditures in the market area is estimated, usually by finding the gross income of available customers and multiplying per capita income by population, or mean household income by the number of households.
3. The amount of purchasing power directed toward all retail goods and services is estimated by multiplying purchasing power by the percentage of income spent in retail establishments. Based on 1991 data, this percentage is approximately 41 percent. The latter percentage figure is usually found by analyzing expenditures in the Consumer Price Index.
4. The amount of square feet of occupied retail space is identified in the market area and is multiplied by the median sales per square foot of retail space. This calculation should be done for specific retail establishments, such as supermarkets, drug stores, and clothing stores, instead of using a single number to represent sales.
5. The amount of retail-oriented purchasing power is compared with the amount of current retail sales in the market area to determine if the market contains excess retail space or unmet consumer demand for retail goods and services.

Based on the degree requested in the appraisal report, the retail market analysis can be expanded by adding retail trade area analysis. However, the following procedure is performed by a market analyst who is not found in the typical appraisal report. Retail trade area analysis is summarized in the following steps.

1. The subject property's retail trade area is delineated. It is a subset of the market area and contains that geographic space from which the subject property is expected to draw most of its customers.
2. The purchasing power in the retail trade area is estimated and allocated to the purchase of retail goods and services sold by supermarkets, drug stores, clothing stores, etc. located in the subject property. This generates an estimate of sales for the retail establishment[s].
3. The estimated retail sales figures for each establishment located in the subject property are divided by median sales per square foot to obtain an estimate of "justifiable or warranted square footage."

For a proposed shopping center, this analysis generates data on the amount of anticipated sales and the amount of retail space that the consumers in the retail trade area will absorb. For an existing shopping center, this analysis can be used to evaluate existing performance against a trade area benchmark.

When the trade area's retail sales for the product have been forecast, the expected level of sales per square foot of retail area must then be found. There are several secondary data sources for this information, and often primary data (sales data from local stores or from a chain store operation collected specifically for this type of analysis) are available. The sales-per-square foot figure can then be divided into the forecast of retail sales, resulting in an estimate of the total amount of retail space to service demand for this retail product in the trade area.

The final step of allocating amounts of retail space to specific retail locations or outlets may also involve several alternative techniques. Gravity models, vacuum techniques, microanalytical models, or other methods are used to allocate space. A principal consideration is the ability of the individual retail outlet to compete with competitive retail outlets in the same trade area. To develop this information, the appraiser must collect primary data that identify characteristics of competitive and complimentary uses and locations.

Based on this retail analysis, the appraiser can perform a relatively accurate forecast of retail sales for the subject property, reflecting its competitive capability and physical limitations (such as amount of floor space or parking). The valuation is completed using the income approach as the principal approach, where net sales figures are capitalized to produce a value indication.

Not all valuations of retail space will employ this methodology, but the corporate real estate executive should expect the opinion of value for retail space to be supported by some form of analysis that identifies trade area characteristics and retail sales estimates for the trade area, and analyzes the subject property's ability to capture a share of the market.

§ 14.5 VALUATION METHODS AND TECHNIQUES

The corporate real estate executive and his or her staff do not need to be trained as appraisers, but they need to understand the various valuation techniques used by appraisers. This section presents basic information about appraisal approaches.

(a) INCOME CAPITALIZATION

The appraiser will use one of three techniques to value an income-earning real estate asset. Two of these techniques—discounted cash flow and direct capitalization—are income capitalization techniques. The third technique, the gross rent multiplier (GRM) or gross income multiplier (GIM), is technically a sales comparison technique and will be discussed later in this chapter.

These income capitalization techniques are applied to office buildings, retail shopping centers, hotels/motels, industrial and business parks, and apartment complexes. They are less useful, and possibly not even applicable, to the valuation of industrial plants, although they are used to value speculative industrial space such as warehouses or space in business parks.

Each income capitalization technique starts with the historic revenues and expenses of the subject property that are obtained from the owner of the property, the property manager, or the accountant. The appraiser analyzes these data to determine and adjust for any omissions or any unnecessary expenses included in the financial statement. Very often, the financial record of the property will contain items not essential to operate the property. Typically, these are expenses for mortgage payments, income tax payments, depreciation, improvement expenditures, and miscellaneous expenditures. These items are one-time or nonrecurring outlays for legal fees or expenditures for items and services not related to operating the property.

The appraiser also checks the magnitude of the revenues and appropriate expenses and compares them with market norms. Market norms can be obtained from data from comparable properties or from adequate secondary sources. For example, expense data for several types of properties can be obtained from publications by the Institute of Real Estate Management (IREM). Trade organizations, such as the Building Owners and Managers Association (BOMA) for office buildings, are also a potential source. The entire procedure is known as "reconstructing the operating statement for the subject property."

From this information, the appraiser constructs a revenue and operating expense statement for the first year of operation. From this start, the appraiser can use either the direct capitalization or the discounted cash flow technique.

Each of these techniques will be discussed in the following subsections. The discounted cash flow technique (DCF) is discussed first because it is considered the state of the art in income capitalization valuation. Direct capitalization is presented because it can be used to verify the results of the DCF technique, and because some appraisers still rely on it.

(1) Discounted Cash Flow Analysis

To use the discounted cash flow (DCF) model, the appraiser starts with the reconstructed revenue and operating expense statement and then investigates the following market variables: effective rents, common area charges, vacancies, capitalization rates (initial period and terminal period), and the appropriate discount rate. The appraiser also determines the appropriate time period for the analysis. This time period can differ depending on the type of property and its prevalent lease term in the market. For example, an office building may be using 5-year leases, so an 11-year period may be chosen to include at least two lease renewal periods. For a shopping center using 3-year lease terms, the time period of the analysis can be 7 years. For hotels/motels and apartment complexes that use short lease terms (daily to yearly) the time period can be as short as 4 or 5 years.

Exhibit 14.1 is a hypothetical example of the structure of the DCF technique. It is stated as simply as possible since the principal objective here is to identify the basic technique and its use. The explanation of the DCF methodology preceding Exhibit 14.1 demonstrates how the figures in the exhibit were derived.

The appraiser will do the following things within the structure of the DCF technique, but may perform these tasks in a different order.

(i) Estimate Current Market Rent and Rent Revenue Starting with the reconstructed income obtained from the property's financial records, the current effective market rental rate will be determined and multiplied by the space available for rent. This would be rentable square footage in an office building, gross leasable square footage in a shopping center, rentable units in the hotel and the apartment. A figure of $12.25 per square foot times 100,000 square feet is recorded under potential gross income for the initial year.

(ii) Estimate Future Period Market Rent and Rent Revenue Starting with the market rent for the initial year, the appraiser establishes the appropriate time period for the analysis, say seven years in this situation. The appraiser estimates the change in market rent revenue into the future. A thorough analysis of existing leases is needed to check for rent escalation clauses, percentage lease rates, the term of the lease and any renewal options and/or concessions. Using this information and judgment about the potential market, the appraiser extends this line item into the future. Some appraisers will enter distinct dollar amounts for each year, representing their judgment about the specific market and lease factors for that year. Other appraisers will establish a compound rate of change that serves as a proxy for the specific market and lease factors. Each approach is acceptable, but the user of the appraisal should receive some explanation of what is being done and why. For the sake of simplicity and ease of using spreadsheet software, a 2.75 percent rate of growth is used.

(iii) Estimating Common Area Maintenance (CAM) Charges and Other Income for the Initial Period and Future Periods Based on the current leases for the subject property and evidence obtained from the market, the CAM receipts on a year-by-year basis are estimated. In the example provided in Exhibit 14.1, CAM receipts are established at $1.80 in years 1 through 4, and $2.25 for years 5 through 8.

(iv) Estimating Vacancies and Credit and Collection Losses for the Initial Period and Future Periods Based on current market experience and making a judgment about the relationship between demand for space and its supply, the appraiser shows vacancies at 12 percent for years 1 through 4 and 8 percent for years 5 through 8. Credit and collection losses are estimated at 1 percent for the holding period.

(v) Estimating Total Operating Expenses for the Initial Period and Future Periods Operating expenses are initially established by reconstructing the expense data for the past three years or so obtained from the owner or his representative. Then the appraiser establishes a trend in these expenditures into the future. In Exhibit 14.1, the variable, fixed, and reserve categories of total operating expenses are judged to increase by 2.25 percent, 2.21 percent, and 2.5 percent respectively.

(vi) Establishing Net Operating Income for the Initial Period and Future Periods The net operating income (NOI), is effective gross income (EGI), less total operating expenses (TOEs).

(vii) Estimating the Future Sales Price and the Net Proceeds from the Sale When the array of NOIs for the seven-year period is generated, the appraiser will call the seventh year the terminal year and use the NOI figure for that year to estimate the future sales price. The first priority in establishing a future sales price is the selection of an appropriate capitalization rate for this end year.

In most instances, the appraiser will research the specific property market to obtain a current period capitalization rate. If data for that

EXHIBIT 14.1 Example of a Discounted Cash Flow Model

Square Footage of Rentable Space	100000
Effective Rent Rate	12.25
Growth in Rent Revenue	1.0275
Common Area & Maintenance Receipts—yrs. 1–4	1.8
Common Area & Maintenance Receipts—yrs. 5–8	2.25
Other Income 0.12 per sq. ft.	0.12
Growth in Other Income	1.01
Vacancy Losses—yrs. 1–4	0.12
Vacancy Losses—yrs. 5–8	0.08
Credit and Collection Losses	0.01
Growth of Variable Operating Expenses	1.0225
Growth of Fixed Operating Expenses	1.021
Growth of Reserves	1.025
Property Management Fee	0.05
Leasing Fee	0.05
INITIAL PERIOD CAPITALIZATION RATE	0.1
TERMINAL CAPITALIZATION RATE	0.105
DISCOUNT RATE	0.1175

	YR. 1	YR. 2	YR. 3	YR. 4	YR. 5	YR. 6	YR. 7	YR. 8
POTENTIAL GROSS INCOME								
Rent Revenue [100,000 sq. ft. @ $12 per sq. ft.]	1225000.00	1258687.00	1293301.00	1328867.00	1365411.00	1402959.00	1441541.00	1481183.00
CAM Revenues [@ $1.80 per sq. ft.]	180000.00	180000.00	180000.00	180000.00	225000.00	225000.00	225000.00	225000.00
Other Income	12000.00	12120.00	12241.20	12363.61	12487.24	12612.12	12738.24	12865.62
PGI	1417000.00	1450807.00	1485542.00	1521230.00	1602898.00	1640571.00	1679279.00	1719049.00
EFFECTIVE GROSS INCOME								
Vacancy Losses	170040.00	174096.90	178265.10	182547.60	128231.80	131245.70	134342.30	137523.90
Credit and Collection Losses	14170.00	14508.07	14855.42	15212.30	16028.98	16405.71	16792.79	17190.49
EGI	1232790.00	1262202.00	1292422.00	1323470.00	1458637.00	1492920.00	1528144.00	1564334.00

TOTAL OPERATING EXPENSES								
Variable Expenses:								
Property Management Fee [@5% of EGI]	61639.50	63110.12	64621.10	66173.54	72931.87	74646.02	76407.21	78216.74
Leasing Fees [@5% of Rent Rev.]	61250.00	62934.37	64665.07	66443.35	68270.55	70147.99	72077.06	74059.18
Subtotal for FEES	122889.50	126044.50	129286.10	132616.80	141202.40	144794.00	148484.20	152275.90
Utilities	52000.00							
Maintenance and Repair	56000.00							
Supplies and Materials	21000.00							
Other Variable Expenses	5000.00							
Subtotal for Other Variable Expenses	134000.00	137015.00	140097.80	143250.00	146473.10	149768.80	153138.60	156584.20
Fixed Expenses:								
Real Property Taxes	68000.00							
Insurance	15000.00							
Subtotal for Fixed Expenses	83000.00	84743.00	86522.60	88339.57	90194.70	92088.79	94022.66	95997.13
Reserves for Replacement	24000.00	24600.00	25215.00	25845.37	26491.50	27153.79	27832.64	28528.45
TOES	363889.50	372402.50	381121.60	390051.80	404361.80	413805.40	423478.10	433385.70
NET OPERATING INCOME[NOI]	868900.50	889800.00	911300.40	933418.90	1054275.00	1079115.00	1104666.00	1130949.00
FUTURE SALES PRICE							10770943.00	
NET PROCEEDS FROM THE SALE [6% COMMISSION RATE]							10124686.00	
MARKET VALUE ESTIMATE								
Cashflows:	868900.50	889800.00	911300.40	933418.90	1054275.00	1079115.00	11229353.00	
Present Value of the Cashflows	9060309.00							

procedure isn't available, the capitalization rate will be established by using the market loan-to-value ratio, the effective return to the lender for the mortgage loan, the expected rate of return to the typical investor in the market for this type of property, the rate of equity increase through mortgage reduction, and the estimated appreciation or depreciation of current sales price in the market. Then, this initial capitalization rate is increased by an add-on factor, typically between 0.5 to 1.5 percent. If the initial capitalization rate is 10 percent, the terminal capitalization rate may be 10.5 to 11.5 percent. One reason for adding to the current period capitalization rate is that there is more uncertainty about the future than there is about the present. This uncertainty translates into a higher risk, which translates to a higher rate. However, if current market interest rates are high and current capitalization rates are also high, the appropriate rate will probably be lower than it is today. This would argue for a reduction of the terminal capitalization rate.

In any event, the appraiser should offer the reasoning for his or her determination of the terminal capitalization rate, and users of the appraisal should see if it makes financial sense.

Once the terminal capitalization rate has been established, it is used to capitalize the NOI in the seventh year into an estimate of a sales price. The seventh year NOI is capitalized into a value indicator by dividing NOI in the seventh year by the terminal capitalization rate. This future sales price is established as a receipt for the end of the sixth year.

The final data for the DCF are the costs of selling the property. These costs are subtracted from the future sales price to obtain the Net Proceeds From the Sale, (NPS). The estimate of future selling costs is most typically established by using the current period brokerage commission rate and applying it to the future transaction.

(viii) Establishing the Estimate of Value All the pieces but one are now in place, and the estimate of value for the property can be made. The pieces that are in place are the NOIs for the first six years and the net proceeds from the sale for a sale that is assumed to occur at the end of the sixth year. The missing piece is the discounting interest rate, which is generally established as a weighted cost of capital concept. In this case, the weighted cost of capital is typically determined by using the current effective return to the lender and the expected return to the typical investor for this class of property in the current market.

This discount rate is applied to the NOI stream and the NPS to get the value estimate for the property.

Exhibit 14.1 shows the figures developed in the preceding example and the calculations necessary to convert the income and expense data to a capitalized value for the property.

(2) Direct Capitalization

The process of direct capitalization can be explained using the figures for the initial year in the discounted cash flow analysis. In the context of the direct capitalization technique, the data in that column should represent the best judgment of the appraiser about the future of the property. So, technically, the data for revenues and expenses should change from those shown in year 1 of Exhibit 14.1, and thereby the figure for NOI should also change.

Appraisers using direct capitalization but not the DCF technique would determine the initial period NOI by applying their judgment to the historical income and operating expense figures and current market evidence. In this case, the expectation that market rents will increase by more than operating expenses could lead the appraiser to conclude that initial period NOI is more appropriately $900,000 than $868,901.

This figure is divided by the current period capitalization rate that the appraiser estimates from either the property market in which the subject property would trade, or from data derived from the mortgage and financial markets as well as the return desired by the typical investor in the property market. In Exhibit 14.1, this capitalization rate is set at 10 percent. To generate an estimate of value, $900,000 is divided by 0.1 to obtain a value estimate of $9,000,000.

(b) SALES COMPARISON APPROACH

The sales comparison technique uses confirmed sales prices of comparable properties to estimate the value of a property being appraised. It is one of the most common and intuitive techniques appraisers employ, since sales prices are generally public information and comparison of one similar property to another appears relatively easy on the surface. But the approach is not without pitfalls.

The sales comparison approach is often used as the primary approach for properties that are actively traded on the market but for which income and expense data are not generally available. These properties include smaller residential and commercial properties and all types of owner-occupied properties. If income and expense data are available, and if these data can be verified as being normal for the market, then the income capitalization approach should be used as the primary approach. In such cases, the sales comparison approach would still be used as a benchmark to validate the conclusions of the primary approach. In any event, the corporate user of appraisals will surely encounter the sales comparison approach and must be ready to evaluate its execution.

The basic procedure in this approach is to take the confirmed sales price of a comparable property, adjust that price for the value of the differences between the comparable and the subject property, and use the adjusted price of the comparable as an indication of the value of the subject. It sounds deceivingly simple. It is deceiving; it is not so simple. The first basic problem is to find comparable properties that have recently sold in the same market as the subject property. Complex properties, such as industrial, office, or retail uses, may have few, if any, comparables close by, so identification and selection of comparables can be a difficult and confusing issue, particularly for those uninitiated to the appraisal process. Then, if comparables sales can be found, the next major problem is to identify the differences between a comparable and the subject and account for the value of that difference in the sales price. This second step is necessary to properly adjust the sales price of the comparable.

To better demonstrate how the sales comparison approach is executed, Exhibit 14.2 identifies the steps an appraiser normally takes to perform a valuation using this method.

The corporate user needs to deal with several issues when examining an appraisal that uses the sales comparison approach. Selection of appropriate comparable properties that have recently sold is the first issue that arises. When an appraiser is estimating value for an industrial property or other type of property where the architectural and site features are relatively unique to the specific use, properties with similar design and use (the basic criteria for a comparable) are obviously difficult to

EXHIBIT 14.2 Basic Steps of the Sales Comparison Approach

Selection of Comparable Properties

Identification of characteristics for comparable properties
Compilation of recent sales data for comparable properties
Selection of best comparables from available data
Verification of comparable data

Analysis of Comparable Properties

Exposition of differences among comparables on comparison grid
Identification of critical differences between comparables and the subject property

Development of Adjustment Values

Identification of characteristics requiring an adjustment to sales price
Quantification of the magnitude of the adjustment

Adjusting the Sales Price

Description/ranking of the adjustment
Determining the direction of the adjustment

Use of the Adjusted Sales Price to Estimate Value

Review value indicators
Select the best value indicator
Reconcile variance of value indicators
Provide support for the opinion of value

come by. The appraiser may have to use comparables with a nonrecent date of sale, with sales data that are difficult to verify, with many physical dissimilarities to the subject, or with other problems. The appraiser needs some latitude in identifying and selecting comparables in such instances, but should carefully explain in the appraisal report why the comparables were chosen, what the critical differences are, and how these were taken into consideration when making the adjustments. In no case should the corporate executive reviewing the appraisal accept obviously unsuitable comparables, such as use of a warehouse or retail establishment as a comparable for a small manufacturing use.

The next major issue that arises in the sales comparison approach is the method used to adjust the sale price of a comparable property so it can be used as a value indicator of the subject. Once differences between comparables and the subject have been adequately established, the sale price must be adjusted and should, in theory, reflect the amount the difference contributes to the value of the property, not simply the cost to construct or demolish that feature. For example, suppose a small warehouse property used as a comparable has two loading docks, whereas the subject property is a warehouse with one loading dock. The cost to construct a loading dock to the subject property is $50,000, but as a result of constructing it, net revenues in the warehouse operation will increase by $20,000 annually. Using a capitalization rate of 15 percent, this would add a value of about $133,000 to the property, attributable to the second loading dock. The $133,000 value added by the dock should be used as the adjustment figure on the comparable sales price, not the $50,000 cost to construct it. In assessing the accuracy and relevance of appraisal information, the corporate user must consider both the method used to develop an adjustment figure and whether or not a particular difference in structural design or site characteristic merits an adjustment.

A frequent weakness in appraisal reports presenting the sales comparison approach is providing inadequate support for the opinion of value presented. Ideally, to show the foundation for the value conclusion, the appraiser should cite the quality of the comparables, the accuracy of the data, the applicability of the procedure to the assignment, and problems encountered in employing the methodology. If this information is not clearly present in the report, the user of the appraisal should request a statement from the appraiser that indicates which comparables were relied on, which data had to be assumed or manufactured to complete the analysis, how the adjusted sales prices of comparables were reconciled, and how these key elements logically led to the value conclusion.

(c) COST APPROACH

The cost approach is used in nearly every appraisal as a secondary approach or, in cases where it fits the appraisal objectives, as a primary approach. It is a particularly good benchmark to compare outcomes of other appraisal approaches because the cost approach is applicable to nearly every property. Whenever a property is developed, the land cost and construction cost of the property are critical inputs to its initial value. These cost elements, along with the value of the use at the particular site location (reflected in the site value), are present in every property, so the cost approach methodology has virtual universal application. The corporate appraisal user will need to understand and appreciate the information provided by the cost approach any time the appraisal is reviewed.

Like the sales comparison approach, the cost approach appears on the surface to be a simple method of calculating a value. But it, too, is deceiving. Exhibit 14.3 presents a simplified diagram of the steps involved in this approach.

The cost approach appears familiar to most corporate executives and management personnel because it is an accounting approach, and managers typically have a business background that has required daily use of

EXHIBIT 14.3 Steps in the Cost Approach

Determine Applicability of the Cost Approach

- Relate to appraisal objectives and type of value sought
- Relate to type of property

Estimate Site Value Separately from Improvements

- Based on highest and best use of land as vacant
- Establish/execute methodology for site valuation

Develop Cost to Construct Improvement

- Establish replacement versus reproduction cost
- Select construction cost methodology
- Select construction cost database
- Estimate cost to construct improvements

Perform Depreciation Analysis

- Physically inspect property
- Itemize type and level of depreciation
  - Physical deterioration
  - Functional obsolescence
  - External obsolescence
- Calculate amount of accrued depreciation

Develop Opinion of Value from Cost Approach

	Cost to Construct Improvements
Less:	Accrued Depreciation
Equals:	Depreciated Cost of the Improvements
Add:	Site Value Estimate
Equals:	Value Estimate from Cost Approach

accounting information. Because of this familiarity with some terms and concepts used in the cost approach, corporate managers often expect a book value as the outcome of the appraisal instead of a market value or investment value. One of the first things the corporate appraisal user needs to learn is how best to use the cost approach.

The cost approach is used as a primary approach when the objective is to obtain an insurable value, a value for tax purposes such as establishing a basis for depreciation expense deductions, any accounting value that may be used for legal or reporting purposes, and, critically, when a market value estimate is needed for a nonmarket property. A nonmarket property is one that is not traded on the open market, such as a single-purpose property with unique locational or design features, or a property where there are no comparables or one in a market where there has been no activity for several years. This description fits several types of industrial properties designed to the unique specifications of a manufacturing process or a corporate entity, so there may be several types of nonmarket properties commonly held by corporations. For these properties, as well as for properties for which income and expense data and/or sales comparison data are not available, an appraiser will commonly use the cost approach as the primary approach. If it is not used as the primary approach, it will almost always be used as a secondary approach.

When the cost approach is employed, the appraiser must first separate the property into a site component and an improvements component. The accounting techniques of estimating construction costs apply only to the improvements or building component. In estimating construction costs, a first order of business is to establish if it is appropriate to use a reproduction cost—the cost of producing an exact replica of the existing improvements with original specifications, including obsolete components; or if it is better to use a replacement cost—the cost of constructing improvements functionally equivalent to existing improvements but specified with modern design and materials. If a structure has unique design features, or if it contains design or materials that are no longer available in the market, the replacement cost will be typically used by an appraiser for estimating construction costs. However, replacement cost results in misspecification of improvements as they actually exist on the property as well as an inaccurate estimate of the original construction costs.

A second issue in estimating the cost to construct improvements new is the methodology used to estimate costs. Complex structures will usually require the most detailed and potentially accurate method available, called the quantity-survey method or the general contractor's cost estimating approach. However, with the availability of modern computer cost-estimating methods and data, many appraisers can appropriately use the unit-in-place or segregated cost approach. The comparative-unit method, in which the finished cost of construction is usually reduced to a cost per square foot of floor area, is usable as a comparative figure, but it should not be used to estimate construction costs of complex buildings. The larger issue of construction cost estimating for appraisals is the source, timeliness, and quality of construction cost data. By the time manuals are printed, much of the data are obsolete and require updating. The updating problem is largely overcome with computerized databases, but the quality of the computerized data still needs to be checked.

Depreciation is the next issue in the cost approach. Rather than using the formulas available for estimating depreciation for tax purposes, the appraiser is professionally obligated to estimate the actual dimunition of the economic life of the asset. To do this, the appraiser physically inspects the premises and identifies structural elements that are wearing out or in need of maintenance or repair (physical deterioration) as well as those elements with a design that no longer functions properly (functional obsolescence). Both physical deterioration and functional obsolescence need to be classified into curable and incurable categories to accurately estimate the amount of depreciation. Curable depreciation includes items that can be fixed at a cost less than or equivalent to their contribution to value of the asset, while incurable depreciation will cost more fix than it contributes to value. The relative amount and importance of curable and incurable components may lead to a conclusion that the structure is no longer economically usable or needs to be demolished, resulting in an improvements value that amounts only to its salvage value less demolition costs.

A final element of depreciation is external obsolescence. This results from changes in the off-site environment or in market conditions that diminish the value of the property at its existing location. This depreciation is incurable—there is nothing the property owner can do to correct the problem. When all types of depreciation have been assessed, the aggregate amount is called accumulated depreciation. This amount is subtracted from the cost to construct the improvements new to find the depreciated value of the improvements (see Exhibit 14.3).

In reviewing appraisals of corporate property, the corporate real estate staff can expect many variations in estimating construction costs and in estimating depreciation. But the appraisals should explain the methodologies and assumptions used so the reviewer can clearly see how the value estimate was developed. The company should not expect the appraiser to arrive at the exact figures used by the company to show actual construction costs and tax depreciation to derive book value.

(d) THE ISSUE OF HIGHEST AND BEST USE

Highest and best use is one of the most misunderstood and misused concepts in appraisal. Many laypeople think of it as a socially and individually acceptable use of property that will offend no one (at least no like-thinking person), will provide the individual with an acceptable use of the property, and can be touted as proper use to gain public acceptance in such required approvals as zoning. Others may think of it as any use of real property that will bestow great profits or benefits on the property owner. Both ends of the spectrum are rooted in wishful thinking. The terms "highest" and "best" may not be the best descriptors, but the idea is fundamental to the practice of appraisal. It is an economic concept that supposedly identifies the most appropriate economic use of the land, under current market circumstances, on which to base a value estimate.

A highest and best use (HBU) analysis is supposed to be performed in every valuation. The HBU conclusion about a subject property is the basis for selection of comparables as well as for identifying the use basis for the value estimate. If a subject property has an existing office use but its HBU is for retail commercial, the comparable used must have the same HBU characteristics. If the comparable's HBU were industrial, the sale price would not reflect the commercial potential present at the subject property, so its sale price could not be used to estimate the value of the subject. To come up with an opinion of value for a property, the appraiser must first conclude which type of use the property can economically support, and consequently which market the property is being traded in and how values in that particular market are established. Without a highest and best use conclusion, the appraiser's opinion of value would amount to nothing more than a wild guess.

Highest and best use reflects the appraiser's studied opinion of the highest return *currently available in the market* that the owner can reasonably expect to achieve from the property. To draw this conclusion, the appraiser first identifies, on the basis of his or her knowledge of the market and property operations, which uses (and what scale of those uses) have the greatest probability of producing positive economic returns. Once these potential uses are identified, they are tested and the less profitable uses are eliminated on the basis of four tests:

1. *Test of Physical Possibility.* Will the site and location adequately accommodate the use in a manner that permits it to operate as a competitive use in the market?
2. *Test of Legal Permissibility.* Will the use be able to comply with all relevant legal and regulatory requirements?
3. *Test of Financial Feasibility.* Will the market price or capitalized value of benefits over the economic life of the property cover all costs of the property and provide a positive return to the equity owner (i.e., provide a positive residual value to the site)?
4. *Test of Maximal Productivity.* Which use tested provides the highest positive return or residual value? That use is selected as the highest and best use.

The first two tests are generally used to narrow down the list of uses originally identified so that only those uses with greatest potential will be subjected to financial analysis. The test of financial feasibility is the acid test: For a use to be an HBU for a property, it must produce a positive return or residual value. The final test of maximal productivity simply selects the most profitable use from among those tested for financial feasibility and declares it to be the highest and best use.

The analysis is obviously not as simple and straightforward as the previous passages imply, but the basic system for HBU testing and conclusions is clearly described. The system provides assurance that a spurious or irrelevant conclusion about the use of the property, consequently about its value, is not easily drawn. It forces consideration of reasonable alternative uses for the property; it requires an analysis to determine if there is adequate market support for the use at the time the appraisal is performed; and it mandates that economic and financial data be developed that indicate the relative profitability of the potential operations. The system of testing and concluding for highest and best use is obviously not perfect, but it is an adequate measure that forces the making of economic rather than arbitrary conclusions.

If an appraisal for a corporate property has no HBU analysis, or if it draws an HBU conclusion without citing any of the preceding steps as part of the analysis, the appraisal should not be relied on. One fault an appraisal may have is that it simply declares the HBU to be the existing use of the property, without showing any consideration of alternative uses. That conclusion, like any other part of the highest and best use analysis, needs to be supported by citing results of appropriate data used to reach an HBU conclusion.

If the question arises about the cost of performing an adequate highest and best use analysis, the corporate real estate executive needs to consider the question seriously. This analysis is a time-consuming and data-hungry element of an appraisal, so done properly, it will substantially increase the cost of a valuation. But without full consideration of how a property is best used in the market, the opinion of market value is unlikely to be of much use to the company.

Fifteen

Data and Information Administration

§ 15.1 INTRODUCTION

Diversified, divisionalized corporations, particularly companies that combine all their line and staff functions on national and international market levels, have a major logistical problem in creating and maintaining accurate, adequate, and responsive data systems for real property and facilities management.

Our aim in this chapter is twofold: first, to examine the complexities of large-scale corporate real estate management, and second, to present a workable scheme for effectively handling this vital area with an automated real property information system (RPIS). One of the most significant conclusions of a 1987 corporate real estate research study[1] was that many corporate real estate managers in the United States failed to maintain adequate information on their real estate assets. Two out of three respondents did not maintain a real estate property information system.

The system described in this chapter can handle an enormous volume of information. While the RPIS can be scaled down, it is presented in its larger version because fundamental problems in effective management operations remain the same, regardless of company size; only the amount and value of the inventory will change.

Finally, as discussed in Chapter One, the focus of corporate real estate is asset, rather than property, management. The form and function of an information system designed for property management is entirely different from one that will support the corporate asset management function.

[1] Peter R. Veal, a research affiliate with the Laboratory of Architecture and Planning at the Massachusetts Institute of Technology, conducted this study in 1987 for the International Association of Corporate Real Estate Executives (NACORE). The study was entitled *"Managing Corporate Real Estate Assets: A Survey of U.S. Real Estate Executives."*

§ 15.2 REAL PROPERTY INFORMATION SYSTEM OVERVIEW

There are two primary reasons for computerizing the real property information system (RPIS): First, to save time, and second, to deal efficiently with complex and diverse data. For example, a quarterly real property/facilities report for management may require employees to spend two to three weeks in data collection, compilation, and review. Thus, it may be four or five weeks into a new quarter before the report on the previous quarter is available. In addition, the report may lack important information simply because collecting and modifying that data is too difficult or time consuming. The report may also lack uniformity, particularly if the base data are prepared at different operating divisions of the corporation.

A computer-based system can alleviate these problems while providing a broad base of current and comprehensive real property information for other corporate departments such as tax, legal, security, distribution, transportation, executive management, corporate accounting, industrial engineering, and risk management (insurance).

The potential benefits include the following:

- A broad base of logically associated information concerning all real property, which could be made available to any authorized users throughout the corporation.
- Real property information that would be consistent among users.
- The elimination of quarterly and monthly peak/valley data collection periods. Data could be distributed continuously, and the users would always have the most current data available.

The improvements to reports are as follows:

- Faster turnaround time.
- Uniformity of data.
- Availability of data not currently compiled.
- Acquisition and use of information across corporate operations lines with a single request or inquiry.
- Easily compiled and consolidated corporate reports through a shared data file if a corporation maintains two or more divisional headquarters (e.g., one on the East Coast and one on the West Coast); and the immediate availability of information, without regard to the time differentials.
- Ability to interface with other corporate information systems, such as a financial data system.

§ 15.3 THE ROLE OF A CORPORATE REAL PROPERTY INFORMATION SYSTEM

Three critical functions provide the key rationale for structuring the data and information systems:

1. Corporate and facility strategic planning.
2. Reporting for control of strategic plans.
3. Facility and real property administration.

Understanding the source, nature, and degree of the long-term legal and financial commitments involved in real estate decisions is vital, or implementing and realizing corporate and facility strategic plans becomes an exercise in futility. The effectiveness of strategy will be a function of the quality of information with respect to assumptions and constraining conditions. For example, a leased facility will be governed primarily by a leasehold agreement, and the real estate department will need to know the stipulations in this document that affect corporate decision making for leased property, such as the term, manner, and amount of rental payment; the facility leased; and special conditions. The real estate department also will need to know when the lease expires or is to be renewed so that the affected division can be notified sufficiently in advance of termination. Many leases contain a 6- to 12-month advance notice provision with respect to exercising a renewal option. Not fulfilling this requirement could sideline a corporate strategy of retaining a facility to capitalize on the franchise value of the location.

Reporting and control enable performance evaluation as well as provide information for corrective action where appropriate. These reports may be restricted to real property per se or to facilities alone, or to a combination of the two. In any event, the real estate department can use the RPIS to achieve a speed of report assemblage that is usually lacking in manually performed functions; assuming the accuracy of the raw data input, it may also provide a superior level of accuracy. A periodic formalized report might include, for example, a quarterly status report on surplus property that the corporation wishes to dispose of or to swap around among its various manufacturing divisions. Extending the example, management might wish to know about the current status of a particular parcel of surplus property between two quarterly reports. A properly updated RPIS could furnish such information on what effectively becomes a real-time basis.

The administrative requirements of the RPIS primarily support day-to-day activities. The RPIS should be designed for a series of response capabilities, ranging from annual summary reports to the answering of everyday queries about real property. Additionally, the primary mission of administration is to update data files and maintain their integrity. To fulfill the roles of the RPIS, it is necessary to treat both electronic data files and hard copy files as assets. For example, the complete file on a particular property can be maintained within the real estate department, with a summary sheet denoting the location within the file of relevant documents that communicate obligations and rights of the respective parties (of particular importance if real property is leased). If property is owned, the file summary would indicate the location of every legal document affecting ownership, from the sales contract, closing statement, and the deed to boundary surveys, plot plans, building plans and specifications, and photographs. The importance of data administration makes proper stewardship of data, both hard copy documents and electronic data files, imperative.

§ 15.4 METHODS OF ACQUIRING THE CORPORATE REAL PROPERTY INFORMATION SYSTEM

Every real estate manager should complete the following preliminary steps before acquiring a real property information system. First, list the functions that you and your staff fulfill. Next, break those functions down into tasks and database areas and then analyze them. The reason for the analysis is that computerizing bad processes is only going to achieve faster bad processes. In studying the tasks and databases, you may realize that some of them can be eliminated or streamlined.

Once you have restructured the tasks and database requirements, decide which ones are appropriate for the computer, which excels at counting, doing highly repetitious chores, and sorting information very quickly. There are other things computers do not do well, and it is all right to decide against doing a particular task with a computer. The purpose of installing a RPIS is not to force every corporate real estate operation through the computer, but to increase productivity, improve response time, and realize time and cost savings for your company.

The next step is to decide which potential computer tasks and database information areas will have the biggest payoff. Using this priority list, compare your needs with your current computer system hardware (if any) and what the company plans to have in the future, including communication networks and PC/mainframe communication requirements.

Whether the RPIS is developed internally or acquired externally will be a function of:

- Corporate personnel and financial resources.
- Realization of a match between your corporate needs and the capabilities of available systems.
- Time constraints for being up and running.

Computer firms have a number of products on the market that utilize a base format while allowing broad customization capabilities. This approach can give you the best of all worlds with respect to cost, time to implementation, and the matching of your needs and wants with the system capabilities. Before engaging such a firm, however, thoroughly evaluate its experience and stability, since depending on the customization needed by your company, you will in all likelihood require the vendor to provide support and maintenance.

Obtaining and implementing any new system will normally raise the emotional level significantly in an organization. To guarantee the success of the system, it is essential to identify all possible stakeholders and to formulate a system development team that effectively and fairly represents the interests of all members of the stakeholder group. This team will be responsible for all decision making with respect to the acquisition and implementation of the system.

The system development team will:

- Provide consistent focus on the goals and directions approved by the team and by senior management.
- Provide internal resources including professional, technical, and administrative experience and assistance to meet team goals.
- Assist in the development of the Request for Proposal (RFP) specifications and the detailed justification/cost benefit analysis as required.
- Establish cost/schedule targets.

The system development team should include:

- You or a member of your real estate department staff who will serve as Project Leader. The Leader should be extremely interested in the project, have some computer literacy, and have the ability to direct meetings and schedules as well as facilitate team progress.
- A project sponsor from senior management who has approved the need and preliminary justification/cost benefit analysis, and who is aware of the political issues that may affect the implementation phase of the project.
- Interfacing support department representatives whose information, support, help, or future assistance is required for successful use of the system.
- Information Systems (IS) department representative, whose immediate and future software, hardware, and communications knowledge and support will be required.
- Any other company person or a consultant who would provide appropriate and/or required knowledge or insight to ensure a satisfactory RPIS.

§ 15.5 THE SYSTEMS DEVELOPMENT LIFE CYCLE (SDLC)[2]

The systems development life cycle (SDLC) approach has evolved over the years to detail and guide performance of the requisite activities for acquiring and implementing a real property information system. Although originally formulated for building an internal system from the ground up, the process is equally applicable to systems that are purchased from and/or developed by outside vendors. The SDLC approach breaks down the overall process into three basic phases: (1) the definitions phase, (2) the construction phase, (3) the implementation phase.

(a) DEFINITIONS PHASE

The definitions phase involves conducting a feasibility analysis and establishing a requirements definition.

(1) Feasibility Analysis

The feasibility analysis will isolate needs and wants, that is, define *what* the system must be capable of doing, as well as the requisite inputs and outputs, the timing of the outputs, and the users/departments that will have access to the system.

Given these parameters, the analysis will determine if the system is feasible from the standpoint of costs, existing technology, and operational logistics. Based on this information, the development team will investigate possible systems for purchase. If a system that can be customized for organizational needs cannot be found, the team must determine whether sufficient internal resources and capabilities exist to take on the daunting and expensive task of building a system from the ground up, including the development and writing of a detailed *user's manual.* More than likely, however, an existing base system can be customized sufficiently to meet the development team's needs and wants.

(2) Requirements Definition

The requirements definition phase is the single most important phase of the entire SDLC process, for all other aspects of system acquisition and implementation will depend on the data and decisions generated here. It is at this phase that the system structure is designed and specified.

System requirements will often include:

- Consistent information definitions for all users.
- Capability to send and receive electronic mail.

[2] Martin, DeHayes, Hoffer, and Perkins, *Management Information Technology: What Managers Need to Know,* (New York: Macmillan, 1991).

- Consolidation of information at all business unit levels.
- Systemwide information search capabilities.
- Security system to control access to and input of information.
- Rapid implementation.
- Intuitive user interface (i.e., a user-friendly system).
- Data integrity assured by system design.
- User report writing capability.
- User access from all locations.
- Relative ease in enhancing, modifying, and updating systems as requirements change.
- Unlimited storage capacity.

To ensure that requirements are realistic and available, they should be categorized as specific functional areas and broad classes of problem-solving needs (called *applications*) within corporate real estate. The system development team should implement several applications at a time rather than all at once, and should review the general quality of all applications as well as the communication between them. Some of these applications may include:

- *Inventory.* Property *resources* inventory by leased, owned, ground leased, subleased, organizational, locational, and so on.
- *Cost Accounting.* Aggregation and allocation of detailed real estate acquisition, operation, and asset cost information.
- *Reports.* Specific and general, providing strategic and tactical information for long term and daily use.
- *Real Estate/Financial Strategy.* Lease versus build versus buy, present value life-cycle cost, and so on.

The exact nature of all output should be described, as well as the input data that will be required to generate the outputs. This is truly a collective effort, particularly if divisions other than just real estate will have access to the system and require a different output from that required by real estate. An example of a possible system structure chart is shown in Exhibit 15.1.

In investigating RPIS vendors who offer suitable application packages, the system development team will review the general reputation, consistency, cost, and market strength of the firms. Important factors will include:

- *Reputation, Standing.* What does the "street" think of a particular firm? Do people say good things about its honesty, integrity, and fairness? Is the firm well represented and thought of by trade

EXHIBIT 15.1 Sample System Structure Chart

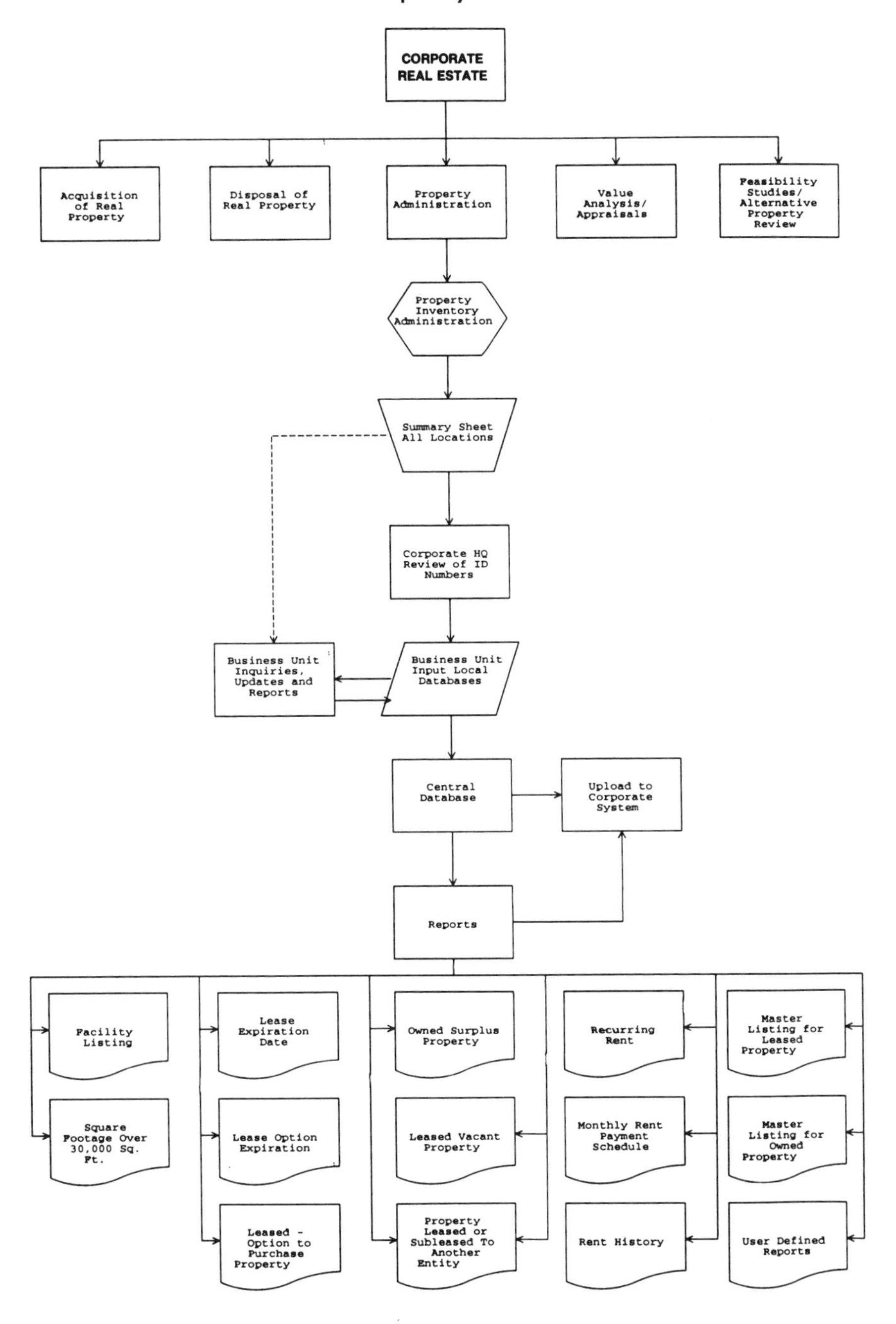

groups and professional societies? Is it adequately represented in the literature? Will any outstanding law suits impact its ability to perform now and in the future?

- *Size of Installed Base.* How many installations of the product does the RPIS vendor have? A large number of installations *may* be a good indicator that the firm will be here tomorrow.
- *Quality of Installed Base.* Do the organizations in the RPIS vendor's customer list resemble your company? Are they "name" organizations or unknowns?
- *Support.* What steps does the vendor take to support its products: Toll-free hotline? Updates? How often? Is there a priority-escalation policy for unsolved problems? How accessible are the support staff and their senior management? How competent?
- *References.* Is the RPIS vendor willing to provide many references from known organizations? Without prodding? When you call the references, are they satisfied with the product? Would they make the same choice again? Are they solving problems similar to those of your company?
- *Consistency, Tenure of Management.* How long has the present top management team been at the helm of the RPIS vendor you are considering? A consistent management team takes the long view and helps to assure the company's stability in business operations. Will management provide a financial statement if the company is a stockholder/public corporation, or the name of its bank as a financial reference if it is a privately held company?

After establishing a "short list" of potential vendors, the system development team should formalize its requirements in a document known as a Request for Proposal (RFP)[3], which will aid in making a final selection. The RFP will define the system, ask the vendor to determine if its current system will satisfy the stated requirements and if not, whether it can be customized to do so. The RFP should ask the vendor to provide full details of implementation, training, documentation, maintenance, and support. Finally, the RFP will request information to evaluate the vendor's experience, reliability, and staying power. The requirements definition must also include a critical path that isolates target dates for completing each phase of the SDLC.

The following general attributes of vendor systems are not application specific (i.e., they affect overall performance and suitability of any

[3] The Computer Applications Council of the International Facility Management Association (IFMA), in June 1989, published *Introduction to Computer Aided Facility Management (CAFM) Applications and (Sample) Request for Proposal, Computer Aided Facility Management (CAFM) System Specifications,* for facility management information systems including a real property information database system.

computer application). These characteristics may include but are not limited to:

- *Industry Standard Hardware.* Unmodified, industry standard hardware will provide the following benefits for your company:
  - It will be able to take advantage of advances in hardware without disrupting applications.
  - It will be able to run programs from one vendor along with those of another, making maximum use of computer resources.
  - It will not risk becoming a user of an "orphaned" hardware product from a vendor that either goes out of business or is unable to keep up with the industry in terms of continuing price/performance.
- *Bundled or Unbundled Software.* Is the software available unbundled (without hardware)?
- *Price.* What is the cost of the Real Property Information System, fully configured with all the required hardware, options, modifications, and software features?
- *Single, Integral Industry Standard Database Management System (DBMS).* Information should be entered into a system *only* once. Individual users should be able to download desired portions of the database onto PCs for their own analysis, but the master database should be integral.
- *Standard Reports.* "Canned" standard reports should be available for all application packages, allowing immediate successful use of a decision support system base. Quantity and variety are especially important.
- *Color Business Graphics.* Canned standard graphics allow rapid start-up use.
- *Industry Standard Query Language.* Special or one-time information needs require an ad hoc query capability. SQL (the language, not any particular program product) already is the standard.
- *Report Writer.* Since it may be necessary to generate reports that are unavailable from the canned report menu, a report writer should be included, with user-friendly report writer language.
- *Unloading Ease to PC or Mainframe.* It should be possible to download portions of the database to other personal or mainframe terminal computers for analysis. The ease with which this can be done and the formats available are evaluation criteria.
- *Interface Ease to Other Databases, Systems.* The ease with which a product can engage in transaction processing with other databases in an organization is important.

- *Documentation Quality.* Documentation should be absolutely comprehensive, easy to use, well indexed, illustrated, highlighted, logically organized, absolutely current, and error free.
- *Documentation Quantity.* Are all aspects of the RPIS package documented in detail, including such esoteric but critical functions as backup, error recovery, database administration?
- *Training.* Computer base training is a good way of dealing with many training issues. Is it inexpensive, always available, consistent, and designed to bring new hires "up to speed" quickly?
- *Procedures.* Procedures are the most important single factor in the success of a RPIS system. RPIS vendors and products should be examined for the amount and quality of procedures they include, as well as their degree of fit with existing organizational procedures.
- *Unified User Interface.* The many different real estate functions should present themselves to the user in a consistent way, so that learning is easier and so that infrequent, casual users still can experience a high degree of success.
- *Menu-Driven Package.* Screen-form menus are the easiest method of interaction for the naive, frightened, or infrequent user. Although menus are frustrating for experts, the majority of RPIS users do not aspire to become expert users; menu-driven RPIS packages are often the better choice.
- *Major Computer-Aided Design (CAD) System Interfaces.* Does the system interface and share data with the CAD system in use within your organization? How about with the industry market share leading CAD systems (e.g., AutoCAD, Intergraph), which one day *may* be in use within your organization, its subsidiaries, partners, consultants, or affiliates?
- *Ease of Use.* Subjectively, how easy is the system to use? During a "road test" of each prospective RPIS vendor's packages, can your staff accomplish their desired tasks? One user-friendly requirement to consider is that an executable command should take place after no more than three key strokes.
- *Ease of Learning.* How quickly can users become familiar with the "feel" and "flow" of the system?
- *On-Line Help.* Can the real property information system under consideration provide users with help *at any time,* in a consistent fashion (e.g., in response to user's pressing a special "help" key or typing "help")? The "help" supplied should be context-dependent, and consistent with the printed documentation (ideally it should be exactly the same text).

The *Request for Proposal* (RPF) can include all information needed to fully describe what you are seeking to purchase, implement, and use.

You may wish to go beyond basic RPIS demonstrations from the various RPIS vendors by setting up *benchmark tests.* These tests use a prototype project to determine if the answers provided by the tested RPIS vendor systems duplicate previous manual results in a usable format. The Request for Proposal should include an Invitation to Bid, stating your company's formal bid requirements, and a detailed Bid Form to be filled out completely. Following this procedure will ensure that all respondents provide a bid in a consistent "apples to apples" format. The RFP packet should be sent to the vendors that meet your RPIS needs. Exhibit 15.2 provides a sample outline of an RFP Table of Contents.

Once the project team has reviewed the responses to the RFP, has recommended a vendor to senior management, and has received approval to proceed, the implementation of the system can proceed.

(b) CONSTRUCTION PHASE

If existing purchasable systems prove to be inadequate or unacceptable and if your organization has the necessary resources to build its own system using in-house expertise, the construction phase becomes relevant. This phase can be broken down into system design, system building, and system testing.

(1) System Design

Based on the system requirements, the information services (IS) department will usually take the lead in the mechanics of designing the system. This process involves determining development costs, deciding which hardware and software language to use, designing the content and structure of the system's databases, and defining the programs that will comprise the system and how they will be related to each other. In addition to designing the system itself, this phase requires designing how users will interact with the system. For example, will certain files be limited to access by user ID and password, or will the system be unsecured? Although IS will be responsible for the design of the system, the system development team must specify the system's attributes and functions.

Like corporate financial data, which can be received by corporate finance from all business units in a consistent format, the RPIS should be designed to develop a consistent real estate database with policies and procedures that will be helpful in making business decisions.

Development costs could include in-house and/or consultant fees to develop the software, to locate and inventory lease and deed documents and correspondence, to abstract the appropriate information, to input the data into the system, to provide initial and follow-up training, to cover travel if required, and to provide ongoing operation, maintenance, and modification. Business units in some corporations may be charged back a

EXHIBIT 15.2 Sample Outline: Table of Contents

REQUEST FOR PROPOSAL
REAL PROPERTY INFORMATION SYSTEM (RPIS)

SPECIFICATIONS

TABLE OF CONTENTS

share of these costs directly or through their corporate overhead allocation charges.

Experiences of companies implementing these systems have shown that business unit real estate managers with more than 50 properties do not have the time, staff, or priority from their management to locate, abstract, and load all their lease and deed information into the system in a timely and consistent manner. Interruptions and the assignment of different staff at different times to complete the abstracting process do not provide continuity, quality, or consistent information for the system. In such situations, the services of an experienced corporate real estate consulting firm are needed to abstract and load all the leased and owned property records. Once the consultant has abstracted all information and has run copies of all reports, the corporate real estate manager's staff can then review all the data and can maintain and update the database when new properties are purchased or leased, leases are renewed, options are executed, and rent and operating costs change.

Business units with fewer than 50 properties can send copies of their leases, deeds, and correspondence for abstraction and loading into the database. However, it is cost and time prohibitive for business units with more than 100 properties to send the corporate office or the consultant copies of the lease and deed documents. The best way to obtain database information from these business units is to abstract their information on site.

To abstract an average office lease without amendments onto an RPIS Lease Property Abstract/Data Entry Sheet (see Exhibit 15.3) will take approximately 30 minutes. More complex leases will take longer, and if files are incomplete or missing, searching for the information or the file will add substantially to the time per document. Exhibit 15.4 provides a listing of lease definitions used in the abstract/data entry sheets (Exhibit 15.3), and Exhibit 15.5 is an example of the Master Listing Report showing all the information that was abstracted from the lease document file.

To abstract an average owned property's Sale and Purchase Agreement, Closing Statement, Plot Plan, and Deed on to an Owned Property Abstract/Data Entry Sheet (see Exhibit 15.6) will take approximately 15 minutes. Exhibit 15.7 provides a listing of owned property definitions used in the abstract/data entry sheets (Exhibit 15.6), and Exhibit 15.8 is an example of the Master Listing Report showing all the information that was abstracted from the owned property document file.

Business units as a minimum should provide a:

- Person to be responsible for their real estate database of information.
- Computer terminal (PC or mainframe).
- VDT monitor (preferably a color monitor).
- Keyboard.

EXHIBIT 15.3 Leased Property Abstract/Data Entry Sheet

```
REAL ESTATE FILE NO.:                                                                PAGE 1 OF 4

STATE --- [_|_]
LEASED ------------ [A]    GROUND LEASE OR EASEMENT  (G/E) [_]              SUBLEASESOR? (Y/N) [_]
COMPANY NO. [_|_|_]                                                  NEW LEASE/
ACCOUNT NO.---------[_|_|_|_]  DATE SUBMITTED:     DATE OF LAST CHANGE:    EXTENSION        VACANCY
BLDG. NO.--[_|_|_|_]                                                 /RENEWAL:        APPROV.:
PARCEL NO.-----------[_|_]   [_|_|/|_|_|/|_|_]   [_|_|/|_|_|/|_|_]     (L/E/R)  [_]     (Y/N)  [_]
**********************************************************************************************

                                  PROPERTY INFORMATION

LOCATION
NAME:        [_|_|_|_|_|_|_|_|_|_|_|_|_|_|_|_|_|_|_|_|_|_|_|_|_|_|_|_|_|_|_|_|_|_|_|_|_|_|_|_]
LESSEE:
(UNIT/       [_|_|_|_|_|_|_|_|_|_|_|_|_|_|_|_|_|_|_|_|_|_|_|_|_|_|_|_|_|_]
DIVISION)
PROPERTY     [_|_|_|_|_|_|_|_|_|_|_|_|_|_|_|_|_|_|_|_|_|_|_|_|_|_|_|_|_|_]  NUMBER OF FLOORS: [_|_]
ADDRESS:
             [_|_|_|_|_|_|_|_|_|_|_|_|_|_|_|_|_|_|_|_|_|_|_|_|_|_|_|_|_|_]  (COUNTRY DEFAULT IS "USA")

COUNTY:      [_|_|_|_|_|_|_|_|_|_|_|_|_|_|_|_|_|_|_|_|_|_|_|_|_]          COUNTRY:    [U|S|A|_|_|_|_|_|_|_|_|_|_|_]

CITY:        [_|_|_|_|_|_|_|_|_|_|_|_|_|_|_|_|_|_|_|_|_|_|_|_|_]    STATE: [_|_]      ZIP: [_|_|_|_|_|_|_|_|_]

LOCATION MANAGER:  [_|_|_|_|_|_|_|_|_|_|_|_|_|_|_|_|_|_|_|_|_|_|_|_|_|_|_|_|_|_|_|_|_|_|_|_|_|_|_|_]

   AREA CODE: [_|_|_]  TELEPHONE:  [_|_|_| - |_|_|_|_]   EXTENSION:  [_|_|_|_]

LESSOR:      [_|_|_|_|_|_|_|_|_|_|_|_|_|_|_|_|_|_|_|_|_|_|_|_|_|_|_|_|_|_]
(LANDLORD)
             [_|_|_|_|_|_|_|_|_|_|_|_|_|_|_|_|_|_|_|_|_|_|_|_|_|_|_|_|_|_]

ADDRESS:     [_|_|_|_|_|_|_|_|_|_|_|_|_|_|_|_|_|_|_|_|_|_|_|_|_|_|_|_|_|_]

             [_|_|_|_|_|_|_|_|_|_|_|_|_|_|_|_|_|_|_|_|_|_|_|_|_|_|_|_|_|_]

             [_|_|_|_|_|_|_|_|_|_|_|_|_|_|_|_|_|_|_|_|_|_|_|_|_|_|_|_|_|_]

CITY:        [_|_|_|_|_|_|_|_|_|_|_|_|_|_|_|_|_|_|_|_|_|_|_|_|_]    STATE: [_|_]      ZIP: [_|_|_|_|_|_|_|_|_]

   AREA CODE: [_|_|_]  TELEPHONE:  [_|_|_| - |_|_|_|_]   EXTENSION:  [_|_|_|_]

TYPE OF FACILITY:      [_|_|_|_|_|_|_|_|_|_|_|_|_|_|_|_|_|_|_|_|_|_|_|_|_|_|_|_|_|_]

LEGAL REVIEW BY:       [_|_|_|_|_|_|_|_|_|_|_|_|_|_|_|_|_|_|_|_|_|_|_|_|_|_]    DATE:  [_|_|/|_|_|/|_|_]

FINANCIAL REVIEW BY:   [_|_|_|_|_|_|_|_|_|_|_|_|_|_|_|_|_|_|_|_|_|_|_|_|_|_]    DATE:  [_|_|/|_|_|/|_|_]

A/R REQUIRED (Y/N) [_];  A/R APPROVED (Y/N) [_];  IL ONLY (Y/N) [_]  IF Y, DATE: [_|_|/|_|_|/|_|_]
PROPERTY
OWNERS REPRESENTATIVE: [_|_|_|_|_|_|_|_|_|_|_|_|_|_|_|_|_|_|_|_|_|_|_|_|_|_|_|_|_|_]

   AREA CODE: [_|_|_]  TELEPHONE:  [_|_|_| - |_|_|_|_]   EXTENSION:  [_|_|_|_]

PROPERTY LEASING AGENT: [_|_|_|_|_|_|_|_|_|_|_|_|_|_|_|_|_|_|_|_|_|_|_|_|_|_|_|_|_|_]
PROPERTY
LEASING AGENT'S REPRESENTATIVE:  [_|_|_|_|_|_|_|_|_|_|_|_|_|_|_|_|_|_|_|_|_|_|_|_|_|_|_|_|_|_]

   AREA CODE: [_|_|_]  TELEPHONE:  [_|_|_| - |_|_|_|_]   EXTENSION:  [_|_|_|_]
```

- Printer (preferably a laser jet).
- Communications hardware and software either through a modem or network.

(2) System Building

Building and testing the system is basically the implementation of the system design—essentially a plan for construction. This phase is primarily the province of the IS department. However, the development team still provides answers to questions and interprets requirements. Its responsibilities are as follows:

- Provide information—verbal and written.
- Provide support and active/ongoing input.
- Participate through team members' comments, help set objective criteria, and provide timely feedback.
- Participate in testing, training, use, modification/evolution.

EXHIBIT 15.3 *(Continued)*

```
REAL ESTATE FILE NO.:                                                                      PAGE 2 OF 4
[_|_|-|A|-|_|_|_|-|_|_|_|_|-|_|_|_|_|-|_|_]
*******************************************************************************************************

RENT PAYMENT        [_|_|_|_|_|_|_|_|_|_|_|_|_|_|_|_|_|_|_|_|_|_|_|_|_|_|_|_|_|_]
PAYABLE TO:
                    [_|_|_|_|_|_|_|_|_|_|_|_|_|_|_|_|_|_|_|_|_|_|_|_|_|_|_|_|_|_]

                    [_|_|_|_|_|_|_|_|_|_|_|_|_|_|_|_|_|_|_|_|_|_|_|_|_|_|_|_|_|_]

RENT PAYMENT        [_|_|_|_|_|_|_|_|_|_|_|_|_|_|_|_|_|_|_|_|_|_|_|_|_|_|_|_|_|_]
ADDRESS:
                    [_|_|_|_|_|_|_|_|_|_|_|_|_|_|_|_|_|_|_|_|_|_|_|_|_|_|_|_|_|_]

                    [_|_|_|_|_|_|_|_|_|_|_|_|_|_|_|_|_|_|_|_|_|_|_|_|_|_|_|_|_|_]

CITY:               [_|_|_|_|_|_|_|_|_|_|_|_|_|_|_|_|_|_|_|_]   STATE: [_|_]   ZIP:  [_|_|_|_|_|_|_|_|_|_]

CORRESPONDENCE      [_|_|_|_|_|_|_|_|_|_|_|_|_|_|_|_|_|_|_|_|_|_|_|_|_|_|_|_|_|_]
NOTIFICATION
ADDRESS:            [_|_|_|_|_|_|_|_|_|_|_|_|_|_|_|_|_|_|_|_|_|_|_|_|_|_|_|_|_|_]

                    [_|_|_|_|_|_|_|_|_|_|_|_|_|_|_|_|_|_|_|_|_|_|_|_|_|_|_|_|_|_]

CITY:               [_|_|_|_|_|_|_|_|_|_|_|_|_|_|_|_|_|_|_|_]   STATE: [_|_]   ZIP:  [_|_|_|_|_|_|_|_|_|_]
*******************************************************************************************************

                                          TERMS OF THE LEASE
EFFECTIVE
DATE:         [_|_|/|_|_|/|_|_]   OCCUPANCY DATE: [_|_|/|_|_|/|_|_]   TERMINATION DATE:   [_|_|/|_|_|/|_|_]

TOTAL TERM:  [_|_]  (YEARS) [_|_|_|_] (MONTHS)  [_|_|_|_] (DAYS)    HOLDOVER:   [_|_|_|_|_|_|_|_|_|_|_|_]

OPTIONS ? (Y/N) [_]; IF YES: NUMBER OF OPTION PERIODS: [_|_]  FOR  [_|_] YEARS EACH OPTION
NOTICE REQUIRED              OPTION FOR                                PURCHASE
(# OF DAYS):    [_|_|_|_];   OTHER SPACE ? (Y/N) [_] IF Y, SEE LEASE;  OPTION ? (Y/N) [_]

OPTION BEGINS:               ENDS:               OPTION EXERCISE NOTIFICATION SENT TO LANDLORD:

     1. [_|_|/|_|_|/|_|_]   [_|_|/|_|_|/|_|_]  (Y/N) ? [_],     IF YES, DATE: [_|_|/|_|_|/|_|_]

     2. [_|_|/|_|_|/|_|_]   [_|_|/|_|_|/|_|_]  (Y/N) ? [_],     IF YES, DATE: [_|_|/|_|_|/|_|_]

     3. [_|_|/|_|_|/|_|_]   [_|_|/|_|_|/|_|_]  (Y/N) ? [_],     IF YES, DATE: [_|_|/|_|_|/|_|_]

     4. [_|_|/|_|_|/|_|_]   [_|_|/|_|_|/|_|_]  (Y/N) ? [_],     IF YES, DATE: [_|_|/|_|_|/|_|_]

OPTION INFORMATION: [_|_|_|_|_|_|_|_|_|_|_|_|_|_|_|_|_|_|_|_|_|_|_|_|_|_|_|_|_|_|_|_|_|_|_|_|_|_|_|_]

                    [_|_|_|_|_|_|_|_|_|_|_|_|_|_|_|_|_|_|_|_|_|_|_|_|_|_|_|_|_|_|_|_|_|_|_|_|_|_|_|_]

                    [_|_|_|_|_|_|_|_|_|_|_|_|_|_|_|_|_|_|_|_|_|_|_|_|_|_|_|_|_|_|_|_|_|_|_|_|_|_|_|_]

                    [_|_|_|_|_|_|_|_|_|_|_|_|_|_|_|_|_|_|_|_|_|_|_|_|_|_|_|_|_|_|_|_|_|_|_|_|_|_|_|_]

                    [_|_|_|_|_|_|_|_|_|_|_|_|_|_|_|_|_|_|_|_|_|_|_|_|_|_|_|_|_|_|_|_|_|_|_|_|_|_|_|_]

                    [_|_|_|_|_|_|_|_|_|_|_|_|_|_|_|_|_|_|_|_|_|_|_|_|_|_|_|_|_|_|_|_|_|_|_|_|_|_|_|_]

                    [_|_|_|_|_|_|_|_|_|_|_|_|_|_|_|_|_|_|_|_|_|_|_|_|_|_|_|_|_|_|_|_|_|_|_|_|_|_|_|_]

                    [_|_|_|_|_|_|_|_|_|_|_|_|_|_|_|_|_|_|_|_|_|_|_|_|_|_|_|_|_|_|_|_|_|_|_|_|_|_|_|_]
```

Planning for system implementation should begin 60 days or more before the scheduled date and may include choosing a name for the system. Software and hardware configurations, screen configurations, reports and report formats, information that has been input, and remote communications are reviewed and adopted during this phase of development.

(3) System Testing

Once the system is built, it will be tested by both the IS department as well as users. IS tests determine whether the system is functionally operational, whereas users determine whether the system conforms with requirements definitions, is user friendly, provides desired access and speed, orients and formats test reports correctly, and can be received at local printers. Test data and test reports for all types of standard and user-defined reports are run, system reliability and communications are tested extensively, and the User's Manual is tested against system

EXHIBIT 15.3 *(Continued)*

```
REAL ESTATE FILE NO.:                                                                    PAGE 3 OF 4
[_|_|-|A|-|_|_|_|-|_|_|_|_|-|_|_|_|_|-|_|_]
**************************************************************************************************

RENT/PENALTY:               [_|_|_|_|_|_|_|_|_|_|_|_|_|_|_|_|_|_|_|_|_|_|_|_|_|_|_|_|_|_|_|_|_|_|_|_|_]
CANCELLATION/PENALTY:       [_|_|_|_|_|_|_|_|_|_|_|_|_|_|_|_|_|_|_|_|_|_|_|_|_|_|_|_|_|_|_|_|_|_|_|_|_|_|_|_|_|_|_|_|_]
DEPOSIT ? (Y/N) [_],   IF YES, AMOUNT $ [_|_|_|_|_|_|.|_|_]     PARKING PER 1000 SQ.FT. [_|_|.|_|_]
UPFIT ALLOWANCE ? (Y/N) [_], IF YES, AMT./U.S.F. $ [_|_|.|_|_]
FLOORS
LEASED: [_|_|_|_|_|_|_|_|_|_|_|_|_|_|_|_|_|_|_|_|_|_|_|_|_]          DATE OF AGREEMENT: [_|_|/|_|_|/|_|_|_|_]
**************************************************************************************************

                                      RENTAL INFORMATION
TOTAL
LEASE COMMITMENT:           $ [_|_|_|_|_|_|_|_|_|_|.|_|_]  RATE PER RENTABLE SQ.FT./YR:  $ [_|_|_|.|_|_]
BASE
RENT PAYMENT PER MO.:       $ [_|_|_|_|_|_|_|_|_|_|.|_|_]  OPERATING EXPENSE PER MO.:   $ [_|_|_|_|_|_|_|.|_|_]
COMMON
AREA MAINT. PER MO.:        $ [_|_|_|_|_|_|.|_|_]         OPTION PERIOD COST:          $ [_|_|_|_|_|_|_|_|_|_|.|_|_]

OPTION PERIOD COST INFO.:   [_|_|_|_|_|_|_|_|_|_|_|_|_|_|_|_|_|_|_|_|_|_|_|_|_|_|_|_|_|_|_|_|_|_|_|_|_|_|_]
TOTAL
AREA (S.F.):  [_|_|_|_|_|_|_|_|_|   OFFICE AREA:    [_|_|_|_|_|_|_|_|_]   WAREHOUSE AREA: [_|_|_|_|_|_|_|_|_]
PRODUCTION
AREA:         [_|_|_|_|_|_|_|_|_]   NET RENTABLE:   [_|_|_|_|_|_|_|_|_]   NET USABLE:     [_|_|_|_|_|_|_|_|_]
COMMON
AREA FACTOR:  .[_|_|_]%             PROPERTY AREA:  [_|_|_|_|_|_|_|_|_|_] SQ. FT. /  [_|_|_|_|_|_|.|_|_|_] ACRES

ADDITIONAL AREA AFFECTED:

   BY OPTION: [_|_|_|_|_|_|_|_|_] SQ. FT.    LAND:  [_|_|_|_|_|_|.|_|_|_| ACRES

ESCALATION CLAUSE ? (Y/N) [_]

ESCALATION TERMS:   [_|_|_|_|_|_|_|_|_|_|_|_|_|_|_|_|_|_|_|_|_|_|_|_|_|_|_|_|_|_|_|_|_|_|_|_|_|_|_|_|_]
                    [_|_|_|_|_|_|_|_|_|_|_|_|_|_|_|_|_|_|_|_|_|_|_|_|_|_|_|_|_|_|_|_|_|_|_|_|_|_|_|_|_]
                    [_|_|_|_|_|_|_|_|_|_|_|_|_|_|_|_|_|_|_|_|_|_|_|_|_|_|_|_|_|_|_|_|_|_|_|_|_|_|_|_|_]
                    [_|_|_|_|_|_|_|_|_|_|_|_|_|_|_|_|_|_|_|_|_|_|_|_|_|_|_|_|_|_|_|_|_|_|_|_|_|_|_|_|_]
                    [_|_|_|_|_|_|_|_|_|_|_|_|_|_|_|_|_|_|_|_|_|_|_|_|_|_|_|_|_|_|_|_|_|_|_|_|_|_|_|_|_]
                    [_|_|_|_|_|_|_|_|_|_|_|_|_|_|_|_|_|_|_|_|_|_|_|_|_|_|_|_|_|_|_|_|_|_|_|_|_|_|_|_|_]
                    [_|_|_|_|_|_|_|_|_|_|_|_|_|_|_|_|_|_|_|_|_|_|_|_|_|_|_|_|_|_|_|_|_|_|_|_|_|_|_|_|_]
                    [_|_|_|_|_|_|_|_|_|_|_|_|_|_|_|_|_|_|_|_|_|_|_|_|_|_|_|_|_|_|_|_|_|_|_|_|_|_|_|_|_]
ESCALATION PERIODS:

      BEGINS                    ENDS        RENT

   1. [_|_|/|_|_|/|_|_]         [_|_|/|_|_|/|_|_]    $ [_|_|_|_|_|_|_|_|_|.|_|_]  PER MONTH
   2. [_|_|/|_|_|/|_|_]         [_|_|/|_|_|/|_|_]    $ [_|_|_|_|_|_|_|_|_|.|_|_]
   3. [_|_|/|_|_|/|_|_]         [_|_|/|_|_|/|_|_]    $ [_|_|_|_|_|_|_|_|_|.|_|_]
   4. |_|_|/|_|_|/|_|_]         [_|_|/|_|_|/|_|_]    $ [_|_|_|_|_|_|_|_|_|.|_|_]
   5. [_|_|/|_|_|/|_|_]         [_|_|/|_|_|/|_|_]    $ [_|_|_|_|_|_|_|_|_|.|_|_]
```

operation before implementing the system. All members of the development team should be kept aware and involved during this process.

During this step, a draft of the proposed implementation schedule should be sent to all members of the development team and to each business unit user along with a listing of hardware/communication requirements at the business unit location, an outline of hardware testing and communications software installation requirements before software/hardware training, and the real estate database to be used during initial training. All this information should be contained in the Real Property Information System User's Manual.

(c) Implementation Phase

The implementation phase will involve a substantial level of commitment from not only the IS department, or the vendor if a purchased system,

EXHIBIT 15.3 *(Continued)*

```
REAL ESTATE FILE NO.:                                                                PAGE 4 OF 4
[_|_|-|A|-|_|_|_|-|_|_|_|_|-|_|_|_|_|-|_|_]
**************************************************************************************************
                              ESCALATION PERIODS (continued)

        BEGINS                     ENDS         RENT

   6.  [_|_|/|_|_|/|_|_]        [_|_|/|_|_|/|_|_]    $ [_|_|_|_|_|_|_|_|.|_|_]  PER MONTH
   7.  [_|_|/|_|_|/|_|_]        [_|_|/|_|_|/|_|_]    $ [_|_|_|_|_|_|_|_|.|_|_]
   8.  [_|_|/|_|_|/|_|_]        [_|_|/|_|_|/|_|_]    $ [_|_|_|_|_|_|_|_|.|_|_]
   9.  [_|_|/|_|_|/|_|_]        [_|_|/|_|_|/|_|_]    $ [_|_|_|_|_|_|_|_|.|_|_]
  10.  [_|_|/|_|_|/|_|_]        [_|_|/|_|_|/|_|_]    $ [_|_|_|_|_|_|_|_|.|_|_]
**************************************************************************************************
                              LESSOR/LESSEE RESPONSIBILITIES

PROPERTY TAXES BY LESSEE ?(Y/N) [_]   PROPERTY TAX I.D. NO. |_|_|_|_|_|_|_|_|_|_|_|_|_|
IF YES:
LAST YEAR   [_|_|/|_|_|/|_|_]   $ [_|_|_|_|_|_|.|_|_]     INSURANCE BY LESSEE ? (Y/N) [_] IF YES, COVERAGE:
THIS YEAR   [_|_|/|_|_|/|_|_]   $ [_|_|_|_|_|_|.|_|_]     [_|_|_|_|_|_|_|_|_|_|_|_|_|_|_|_|_|_|_|_|_|_]
NEXT YEAR   [_|_|/|_|_|/|_|_]   $ [_|_|_|_|_|_|.|_|_]              UTILITIES BY LESSEE ? (Y/N) [_]
SERVICES INCLUDED IN LEASE: [_] [_] [_] [_] [_] [_] [_] [_] [_]   IF YES: [_|_|_|_|_|_|_|_|_|_|_|_|_|_|
SERVICE CODES :                                                   |_|_|_|_|_|_|_|_|_|_|_|_|_|_|_|_|_]

   0 - NO SERVICES INCLUDED     4 - PLUMBING             7 - SIGNAGE
   1 - JANITORIAL               5 - GROUNDS/C.A.M.       8 - LIGHTING
   2 - HVAC                     6 - ROOFING              9 - EXTERIOR
   3 - ELECTRICAL
**************************************************************************************************
                              GENERAL INFORMATION

GENERAL    [_|_|_|_|_|_|_|_|_|_|_|_|_|_|_|_|_|_|_|_|_|_|_|_|_|_|_|_|_|_|_|_|_|_|_|_|_|_|_|_|
COMMENTS:  |_|_|_|_|_|_|_|_|_|_|_|_|_|_|_|_|_|_|_|_|_|_|_|_|_|_|_|_|_|_|_|_|_|_|_|_|_|_|_|_|
           |_|_|_|_|_|_|_|_|_|_|_|_|_|_|_|_|_|_|_|_|_|_|_|_|_|_|_|_|_|_|_|_|_|_|_|_|_|_|_|_|
           |_|_|_|_|_|_|_|_|_|_|_|_|_|_|_|_|_|_|_|_|_|_|_|_|_|_|_|_|_|_|_|_|_|_|_|_|_|_|_|_|
           |_|_|_|_|_|_|_|_|_|_|_|_|_|_|_|_|_|_|_|_|_|_|_|_|_|_|_|_|_|_|_|_|_|_|_|_|_|_|_|_|
           |_|_|_|_|_|_|_|_|_|_|_|_|_|_|_|_|_|_|_|_|_|_|_|_|_|_|_|_|_|_|_|_|_|_|_|_|_|_|_|_|
           |_|_|_|_|_|_|_|_|_|_|_|_|_|_|_|_|_|_|_|_|_|_|_|_|_|_|_|_|_|_|_|_|_|_|_|_|_|_|_|_|
           |_|_|_|_|_|_|_|_|_|_|_|_|_|_|_|_|_|_|_|_|_|_|_|_|_|_|_|_|_|_|_|_|_|_|_|_|_|_|_|_]
DIV.APPROV/DATE:   [_|_|_|_|_|_|_|_|_|_|_|_|_|_|_|_|_|_|_|_|_|_|_|_|_|_|_|_|_|_|_|_],   [_|_|/|_|_|/|_|_];
UNIT APPROV/DATE:  [_|_|_|_|_|_|_|_|_|_|_|_|_|_|_|_|_|_|_|_|_|_|_|_|_|_|_|_|_|_|_|_],   [_|_|/|_|_|/|_|_];
CORP. APPROV/DATE: [_|_|_|_|_|_|_|_|_|_|_|_|_|_|_|_|_|_|_|_|_|_|_|_|_|_|_|_|_|_|_|_],   [_|_|/|_|_|/|_|_].
**************************************************************************************************
```

but also the development team and users. This phase can be broken down into three parts: (1) installation; (2) operation, maintenance, and support; and (3) documentation.

The implementation phase of the real property information system should involve assigning a project manager, setting milestones, and reviewing the scope of the work, cost, and schedule weekly.

As soon as possible, the RPIS vendor should provide detailed information that will:

- Verify the system purchased meets the requirements of the RFP specifications.
- Verify the system purchased provides the performance required.
- Identify enhancements.
- Identify procedure changes.
- Enable training to begin.

EXHIBIT 15.4 Leased Property System Definitions

The following are commonly used leased property definitions used to describe real estate phrases within a Real Property Information System program and are used for the enclosed input sheets for leased properties (see Exhibits 15.3 and 15.5).

RE FILE NO: Real Estate ID number for each individual leased location consists of State Letters, Leased, Company Number, Account or Responsibility Number, Building Number and a Parcel Number:

STATE NO (00): 2 letters representing the state or country where the property is located.

LEASED PROPERTY INDICATOR: "A."

COMPANY NO (000): Up to 3 numbers designating which company within the specific business unit holds the lease at each location.

ACCOUNT OR RESPONSIBILITY NO (0000): Up to 4 numbers designating which account or responsibility center has the budget where the lease payment is charged against.

BLDG. NO (0000): Up to 4 numbers that usually represent the specific location structure or lease.

PARCEL NO (00): Up to 2 numbers representing the parcel the building is located upon (i.e., a building or location may include one or more parcels).

LEASE/GROUND LEASE/EASEMENT (L/G/E): Designation of type of lease.

SUBLESSOR (Y/N): Whether or not the business unit is subleasing the property to a subtenant.

DATE SUBMITTED (MMDDYY): The initial date the information was input into the system. This should be automatically done by the software.

DATE OF LAST CHANGE (MMDDYY): The last date the information was revised in the system. This should be automatically done by the software.

NEW LEASE/EXTENSION/RENEWAL (L/E/R): Explains the current transaction input into the system.

VACANCY APPROVAL (Y/N): A "Y" in this box means that the property is not being used, that the Senior Management has approved subleasing of the property and the property is to be placed on the surplus list.

LOCATION NAME: The name that the business unit commonly calls this location or property.

TENANT (LESSEE): The name of the Business Unit/tenant (i.e., the Business Unit/the Company within the Business Unit that occupies the space).

PROPERTY ADDRESS, CITY, STATE, ZIP, COUNTY, COUNTRY: Street address for the location/leased premises.

TOTAL NUMBER OF FLOORS: Total number of floors occupied per the lease.

LOCATION MANAGER: The name of the Business Unit or Corporation person/facility manager responsible for the day-to-day management of the property.

AREA CODE, TELEPHONE, EXTENSION: The phone number of the Location Manager.

EXHIBIT 15.4 *(Continued)*

LANDLORD (LESSOR): The legal name of the landlord.

ADDRESS, CITY, STATE, ZIP: The street address of the landlord.

AREA CODE, TELEPHONE, EXTENSION: Phone number of the landlord.

TYPE OF FACILITY (Office, Warehouse, etc.): A brief explanation of the intended use for the leased space.

LEGAL REVIEW BY, DATE: If a legal review was made, who within the business unit did the review and the date of completion.

FINANCIAL REVIEW BY, DATE: If a financial review was made, who within the business unit did the review and the date of completion.

A/R REQUIRED (Y/N): Is an Authorization Request for funds required?

A/R APPROVED (Y/N): Has an A/R been approved? If Y, date of approval.

IL ONLY (Y/N): If an Internal Letter rather than an A/R is required.

DATE (MMDDYY): Date the IL was approved.

PROPERTY OWNERS REPRESENTATIVE: The person, broker, or organization who represents the property owner.

AREA CODE, TELEPHONE, EXTENSION: The Property Owner's Representative phone number.

PROPERTY LEASING AGENT: The person, broker, or organization who represents the property owner as its leasing agent.

PROPERTY LEASING AGENT'S REPRESENTATIVE: The person who either works as an employee or agent for the property leasing agent who would be called should the tenant require information or property management services.

AREA CODE, TELEPHONE, EXTENSION: Property Leasing Agent's Representative phone number.

RENT PAYMENT PAYABLE TO: Name of the person or organization to which the rent check is made payable.

RENT PAYMENT ADDRESS, CITY, STATE, ZIP: The name and address of the person or organization who should receive the rent check via mail.

CORRESPONDENCE NOTIFICATION ADDRESS, CITY, STATE, ZIP: The legal address of the lessor where legal notices should be sent (i.e., change of mailing address, contact person, etc.).

LEASE EFFECTIVE DATE (MMDDYY): The date in which the lease becomes effective (also known as the lease commencement date).

OCCUPANCY DATE (MMDDYY): The date in which the tenant (lessee) will or did occupy the leased space.

TERMINATION DATE (MMDDYY): The date the lease expires.

TOTAL TERM: The complete time the tenant occupies the space in years, months, and days.

HOLDOVER (monthly, daily, none): Basis for rent applied for occupying leased space after lease has expired.

OPTIONS (Y/N): Whether or not the tenant has an option to renew the lease.

EXHIBIT 15.4 *(Continued)*

NUMBER OF OPTION PERIODS: Total number of option periods a tenant has to renew the lease.

YEARS EACH OPTION: The number of years of each renewal option.

NOTICE REQUIRED: The number of days prior to the expiration date of the lease the tenant must notify the landlord of its intent to renew.

OPTION FOR OTHER SPACE (Y/N): Whether or not tenant has the option to lease additional space throughout the term of the lease or any renewal.

DATE(S) OPTION(S) BEGINS, ENDS, OPTION NOTIFICATION DATE, DATE OPTION NOTIFICATION LETTER WAS SENT TO THE LANDLORD

OPTION INFORMATION: Brief, general, or specific comments regarding option items that are important to the lease.

RENT/PENALTY: Usually a percentage of the monthly rent charged by the Landlord if the Tenant payment is late.

CANCELLATION/PENALTY: Whether the tenant has the right to cancel the lease during or prior to the term expiration, and if so, what penalties shall be placed upon the tenant.

ESCALATION CLAUSE (Y/N): Y, if the rent/operating expenses, etc. escalates during the initial term or option periods of the lease.

DEPOSIT (Y/N), IF YES AMOUNT: If there is or isn't a security deposit and if so the amount in dollars.

PARKING PER 1000 SQ. FT.: Number of parking spaces per 1,000 square feet of leased space.

UPFIT ALLOWANCE (Y/N), AMOUNT: Y, if monies are allocated for the preparation for leased space and the amount per usable square foot.

IF YES, $ AMOUNT/USABLE SQUARE FOOT

PURCHASE OPTION (Y/N): Whether or not there is an option to purchase the property.

FLOORS LEASED: The actual floor numbers leased (e.g., 16th & 17th Floors).

DATE OF AGREEMENT: Date the lease agreement was signed.

TOTAL LEASE COMMITMENT ($): The total amount due under the contract for the initial term of the lease. This amount is calculated on the base rent plus any planned escalations, if determinable.

RATE PER SQ. FT. PER YEAR ($/RSF): How much the tenant pays per rentable square foot per year. This could be an automatically calculated amount.

BASE RENT PAYMENT PER MONTH ($): The base rent due to be paid by the tenant each month (rsf × $/rsf/12 months).

OPERATING EXPENSE/MONTH ($): Monthly operating charge to the tenant by the landlord for monthly operating expenses (i.e., janitorial, maintenance, taxes, insurance, electrical, water, natural gas, property management fee).

COMMON AREA MAINTENANCE/MONTH ($): Monthly charge for common areas (i.e., site maintenance, snow removal, lawn care, insurance).

TOTAL COMMITMENT ANNUALLY ($)

EXHIBIT 15.4 *(Continued)*

TOTAL ANNUAL COMMITMENT DUE (MMDD): Used only if the tenant makes an annual rental payment.

OPTION PERIOD COST ($): Rent for the option period.

OPTION PERIOD COST INFO.: Brief, general, or specific comments describing anything unique about the option period in the lease.

TOTAL AREA: The total rentable square footage leased by the tenant.

OFFICE, WAREHOUSE, PRODUCTION AREA: The total rentable area broken up to show how the area will be used.

NET RENTABLE, NET USABLE: To show how much of the total square feet will actually be utilized in the different area categories.

COMMON AREA FACTOR: A computed ratio (often the BOMA definition), which is usually expressed in a percentage of usable to rentable sq. feet.

PROPERTY AREA IN SQ. FT. AND/OR ACRES (for Ground Leases):

ADDITIONAL AREA AFFECTED BY OPTION IN SQ. FT. AND ACRES: The total additional space that may be leased by lessee during term.

ESCALATION CLAUSE (Y/N): If yes, go on to escalation terms.

ESCALATION TERMS: Brief, general, or specific comments that describe the terms in the lease which cause increases in the base rental and/or other costs.

ESCALATION PERIODS: Y, if the rent/operating expenses, etc. escalate during the initial term or option periods of the lease.

PROPERTY TAX I.D. NO.: As assigned by the local or state taxing authority.

PROPERTY TAXES BY LESSEE (Y/N): Whether tenant does or doesn't pay property taxes as a separate cost in addition to the base rental, operating expenses, etc.

INSURANCE BY LESSEE (Y/N), COVERAGE ($)

UTILITIES BY LESSEE (Y/N): Are utility costs included or not included in the base rent payment or operating expense payment.

SERVICES INCLUDED IN LEASE: The building or general maintenance services included in the lease as part of the base rent that may include:

NO SERVICES
JANITORIAL
LIGHTING
GROUNDS/CAM
HVAC
PLUMBING SIGNAGE
ROOFING
ELECTRICAL
EXTERIOR

GENERAL COMMENTS: Brief, general, or specific comments describing any unique terms or special information in the lease.

COMPANY OR DIV. APPROVAL/DATE: Signature and date that the transaction was approved at the company or division level.

BUSINESS UNIT APPROVAL/DATE: Signature and date that the transaction was approved at the business unit level.

CORP. APPROVAL/DATE: Signature and date that the transaction was approved at the corporate level.

EXHIBIT 15.5 Leased Property Master Listing Report

MASTER LISTING BY LOCATION
AS OF: 06/18/93

PAGE 1
REAL ESTATE FILE NUMBER: IL-A-601-1000-1000-01

PROPERTY SELECTION			
STAT IL	COMP 100	BISU 01	ACCT 1000
BLDG 1000	PRCL 01		

Lease/Ground lease/Easement: L
New lease/Extension/Renewal: L
Vacancy Approval ....: Y
Sublease ....: Y

Dates:
Submitted 04/07/90
Changed 06/17/93

Location Name ..: TEST PROP. FOR ABC CO. REAL ESTATE
Business Unit...: ABC DIVISION
Property Address: 235 EAST WACKER DRIVE
SUITE 1700
City/State/Zip .: CHICAGO IL 60634-6578
County ....: COOK
Country.........: USA

Landlord ......: RAYSON DEVELOPMENT COMPANY
C/O UNIVERSAL FINANCIAL LIFE
Address ....: 550 SOUTH MADISON AVENUE
SUITE 900
MAIL CODE 907
City/State/Zip.: NEW YORK NY 20246-1234

Location Manager: SANDRA STEPHENS
Phone: (312) 555-5432 ext. 2345

Phone...........: (201) 555-0222 ext. 1234

Legal Review By.......: ROBERT ADAMS 03/15/90
Financial Review By...: KATHERYN SMITH 04/13/90
Auth. Request required: N
Auth. Request approved: N
Internal Letter Only..: Y 10/02/89

Floors.......: 02
Type Facility: CORP. HEADQUARTERS

Owner's Representative: WILLIAMS INVESTMENTS, INC.
Phone......: (312) 555-3209 ext. 4309

Leasing Agent.........: PROFESSIONAL BROKERAGE
Agent's Representative: SANDRA K. BROKER
Phone.......: (312) 555-8067

Rent Payment Payable To: PROFESSIONAL BROKERAGE COMPANY
AS AGENT FOR
RAYSON DEVELOPMENT COMPANY
Rent Payment Address: PROFESSIONAL BROKERAGE COMPANY
P. O. BOX 329856

City/State/ Zip: CHICAGO IL 60634-9856

Correspondence: PROFESSIONAL BROKERAGE COMPANY
Notification: 304 EAST WACKER DRIVE
Address: SUITE 400
City/State/Zip: CHICAGO, IL 60631

Lease Dates: Effective..: 06/18/90
Occupancy..: 06/15/90
Termination: 06/30/95

Total Term: Years : 5
Months: 0
Days..: 12

Holdover: 1.25 TIMES BASE RENT

Options................: Y
No. of Option Periods: 2
Days Notice Required.: 180
For Years Per Option: 5

Option For Other Space: Y (If Yes, See Lease)
Option For Purchase...: Y (If Yes, See Lease)

Option Information:
1. ABC COMPANY HAS THE RIGHT OF FIRST REFUSAL ON 20,000 R.S.F. ON THE 3RD FLOOR, 8,000 R.S.F. ON THE 4TH FLOOR AND 3,000 R.S.F. IN THE BASEMENT.
2. ABC CO. HAS THE OPTION TO PURCHASE THE BUILDING ON 07/01/93. LANDLORD MUST BE NOTIFIED 180 DAYS IN ADVANCE - BY 01/01/93 IF ABC CO. WILL PURCHASE THE BUILDING.

	Option Begins	Ends	Exercise Notification To Landlord: Deadline	Sent
1.	07/01/95	06/30/00	01/01/95	
2.	07/01/00	06/30/05	01/01/00	
3.				
4.				

Rent/Penalty........: 5% OF MO. AMOUNT DUE.
Cancellation/Penalty: NPV OF BALANCE OF RENT @ 10% + 12%.

Deposit.............: Y Amount $ 10,000.00
Parking/1000 Sq. Ft.: 3.21
Upfit Allowance.....: Y Amount $ 345,245.00

Floors Leased....: 17th and 18th.
Date of Agreement: 05/01/90

Total Lease Commitment	$	3,500,000.00
Rate/Rentable Sq.Ft./YR	$	20.00
Base Rent Payment/Month	$	61,885.83
Operating Expense/Month	$	8,956.82
Common Area Maint/Month	$	921.34
Total Monthly Commitment	$	71,763.29
Total Annual Commitment	$	861,159.48
Option Period Cost	$	5,000.00
Option Period Cost Info:	AMOUNT IS CHARGED AGAINST RENT	

Areas: (Sq.Ft.)	
Total.......:	35,000
Office......:	35,000
Warehouse...:	
Production..:	
Net Rentable:	35,000
Net Usable..:	31,500

Annual Commitment Due Date..: $

Common Area: Factor.....: 10.021%
Property Area....: 95,348 Sq. Ft. OR 2.189 Acres
Additional Area Affected By Option....: 31,000 Sq. Ft. - Land: 0.712 Acres

Escalation Clause: Y
Escalation Terms:
1. RENT WILL ESCALATE AT A RATE OF 3% PER YEAR.
2. THE EXPENSE STOP IS $6.30.
3. FOR THE OPTION PERIODS, THE RENT FOR THE 1ST AND 2ND OPTIONS WILL BE MARKET.
4. AT THE END OF THE INITIAL 5 YEAR TERM THE RENT WILL INC. A MIN. OF $1.50/YR.

Periods	Begins	Ends	Rent/Month
1.	07/01/91	06/30/92	$ 60,083.33
2.	07/01/92	06/30/93	$ 61,885.83
3.	07/01/93	06/30/94	$ 63,742.40
4.			
5.			
6.			
7.			
8.			
9.			
10.			

Property Tax I.D. Number: 373-2949-12-04
Property Taxes By Lessee: Y

Last Year:	12/31/92	$ 12,132.34
This Year:	12/31/93	$ 13,238.92
Next Year:	12/31/94	$ 15,000.00

Insurance By Lessee: Y Coverage: $1,000,000/OCCURRENCE
Utilities By Lessee: Y HVAC FOR COMPUTER AND SWITCH RM.

Services Included
1 2 3 4 5 6 7 8 9

0 - No Svcs Incl
1 - Janitorial
2 - HVAC
3 - Electrical
4 - Plumbing
5 - Grounds
6 - Roofing
7 - Signage
8 - Lighting
9 - Exterior

General Comments:
1. ORIGINAL SPACE DESIGN BY: INTERIOR DESIGN OF CHICAGO.
2. BLDG. PLANS LOCATED IN FACILITY DEPT.
3. ENTIRE BUILDING IS BEING UPGRADED FROM THE LOBBY TO THE PENTHOUSE ELEVATOR.
4. THE BUILDING FITNESS CENTER IS AVAIL. AT NO COST TO ABC CO. EMPLOYEES.

	Approval	Date
Division..:	Jane M. Simpson, V.P.	05/03/90
Unit......:	Richard P. Frye, Sr. V.P.	05/04/90
Corporate.:	Samuel R. Wilson, Ex. V.P.	05/05/90

EXHIBIT 15.6 Owned Property Abstract/Data Entry Sheet

```
REAL ESTATE FILE NO:                                                                              PAGE 1 OF 2

STATE ---- [_|_]
OWNED ---------------- [O]
COMPANY NO.---- [_|_|_]
ACCOUNT NO.--------- [_|_|_|_]     DATE SUBMITTED:          LAST DATE OF CHANGE:        SURPLUS
BLDG. NO.-- [_|_|_|_]                                                                     APPROVAL:
PARCEL NO. --------- [_|_]          [_|_|/|_|_|/|_|_]        [_|_|/|_|_|/|_|_]           (Y/N)    [_]
***********************************************************************************************************

                                        PROPERTY INFORMATION
LOCATION
NAME:         [_|_|_|_|_|_|_|_|_|_|_|_|_|_|_|_|_|_|_|_|_|_|_|_|_|_|_|_|_|_|_|_|_|_|_|_|_|_|_|_]
UNIT/
DIVISION:     [_|_|_|_|_|_|_|_|_|_|_|_|_|_|_|_|_|_|_|_|_|_|_|_|_|_|_|_|_|_|_]

PROPERTY      [_|_|_|_|_|_|_|_|_|_|_|_|_|_|_|_|_|_|_|_|_|_|_|_|_|_|_|_|_|_|_]  NUMBER OF FLOORS: [_|_|_]
ADDRESS:
              [_|_|_|_|_|_|_|_|_|_|_|_|_|_|_|_|_|_|_|_|_|_|_|_|_|_|_|_|_|_|_]  (COUNTRY DEFAULT IS 'USA')

COUNTY:       [_|_|_|_|_|_|_|_|_|_|_|_|_|_|_|_|_|_|_|_|_|_|_|_]        COUNTRY: [U|S|A|_|_|_|_|_|_|_|_|_|_|_|_|_]

CITY:         [_|_|_|_|_|_|_|_|_|_|_|_|_|_|_|_|_|_|_|_|_|_|_|_]   STATE: [_|_]     ZIP:   [_|_|_|_|_|_|_|_|_|_|_]

LOCATION MANAGER:  [_|_|_|_|_|_|_|_|_|_|_|_|_|_|_|_|_|_|_|_|_|_|_|_|_|_|_|_|_|_|_|_|_|_|_|_|_|_|_|_|_|_]

     AREA CODE: [_|_|_]   TELEPHONE:  [_|_|_| - |_|_|_|_]   EXTENSION:  [_|_|_|_]

TYPE OF FACILITY:       [_|_|_|_|_|_|_|_|_|_|_|_|_|_|_|_|_|_|_|_|_|_|_|_|_|_|_|_|_|_|_|_|_|_|_|_|_|

LEGAL REVIEW BY:        [_|_|_|_|_|_|_|_|_|_|_|_|_|_|_|_|_|_|_|_|_|_|_|_|_|_|_|_|_|_]     DATE:  [_|_|/|_|_|/|_|_]

FINANCIAL REVIEW BY:    [_|_|_|_|_|_|_|_|_|_|_|_|_|_|_|_|_|_|_|_|_|_|_|_|_|_|_|_|_|_]     DATE:  [_|_|/|_|_|/|_|_]

A/R REQUIRED (Y/N) [_];  A/R APPROVED (Y/N) [_];  IL ONLY (Y/N) [_]   IF Y,   DATE:  [_|_|/|_|_|/|_|_]
TOTAL
ACREAGE:    LAND: [_|_|_|_|_|_|_|_|.|_|_]   BUILDING: [_|_|_|_|_|_|_|_|_|_]SQ.FT.   OTHER: [_|_|_|_|_|_|_|_|_]

                                                  SURVEY/PLOT
TOPO AVAILABLE (Y/N) [_]   DATE: [_|_|/|_|_|/|_|_]   PLAN AVAILABLE (Y/N) [_]   DATE:  [_|_|/|_|_|/|_|_]

APPRAISED VALUE:    $ [_|_|_|_|_|_|_|_|_|_|_|.|_|_]         APPRAISAL DATE:    [_|_|/|_|_|/|_|_]
PICTURES
AVAILABLE (Y/N) [_]  ZONING JURISDICTION: [_|_|_|_|_|_|_|_|_|_|_|_|_|_]    ZONED:  [_|_|_|_|_|_|_|_|_|_|_]

INSURANCE COVERAGE:     [_|_|_|_|_|_|_|_|_|_|_|_|_|_|_|_|_|_|_|_|_|_|_|_|_|_|_|_|_|_|_|_|_|_|_|_|_|_|_|_|_|_|_|_|_|
                        |_|_|_|_|_|_|_|_|_|_|_|_|_|_|_|_|_|_|_|_|_|_|_|_|_|_|_|_|_|_|_|_|_|_|_|_|_|_|_|_|_|_|_|_|_]

PROPERTY TAX I.D. NO.   [_|_|_|_|_|_|_|_|_|_|_|_|_|_|_|_|_]

PROPERTY TAXES :    LAST YEAR [_|_|/|_|_|/|_|_]    $ [_|_|_|_|_|_|_|.|_|_|
                    THIS YEAR [_|_|/|_|_|/|_|_]    $ [_|_|_|_|_|_|_|.|_|_|
                    NEXT YEAR [_|_|/|_|_|/|_|_]    $ [_|_|_|_|_|_|_|.|_|_|
***********************************************************************************************************
                                        MORTGAGE INFORMATION
MORTGAGE                         IN THE
DATED  : [_|_|/|_|_|/|_|_]   AMOUNT OF: $[_|_|_|_|_|_|_|_|_|_|_|.|_|_]  @ [_|_|.|_|_|_]%  FOR [_|_] YRS.  [_|_] MONTHS

PAYOFF DATE: [_|_|/|_|_|/|_|_]       MONTHLY PAYMENT: $[_|_|_|_|_|_|_|_|_|_|_|.|_|_]       [_|_] MONTHS
```

EXHIBIT 15.6 *(Continued)*

PAGE 2 OF 2

REAL ESTATE FILE NO:

[_|_|-|0|-|_|_|_|-|_|_|_|_|-|_|_|_|_|-|_|_]

****

MORTGAGE INFORMATION (continued)

MORTGAGE PAYABLE TO: [_|_|_|_|_|_|_|_|_|_|_|_|_|_|_|_|_|_|_|_|_|_|_|_|_|_|_|_|_|_|_|_|_|_|_|_|_|_|_|_|_|_]
|_|_|_|_|_|_|_|_|_|_|_|_|_|_|_|_|_|_|_|_|_|_|_|_|_|_|_|_|_|_|_|_|_|_|_|_|_|_|_|_|_|_]

MORTGAGE PAYMENT ADDRESS: [_|_|_|_|_|_|_|_|_|_|_|_|_|_|_|_|_|_|_|_|_|_|_|_|_|_|_|_|_|_|_|_|_|_|_|_|_|_|_|_|_|_]
|_|_|_|_|_|_|_|_|_|_|_|_|_|_|_|_|_|_|_|_|_|_|_|_|_|_|_|_|_|_|_|_|_|_|_|_|_|_|_|_|_|_| (COUNTRY DEFAULT IS "USA")
|_|_|_|_|_|_|_|_|_|_|_|_|_|_|_|_|_|_|_|_|_|_|_|_|_|_|_|_|_|_|_|_|_|_|_|_|_|_|_|_|_|_] COUNTRY: [U|S|A|_|_|_|_|_|_]

CITY: [_|_|_|_|_|_|_|_|_|_|_|_|_|_|_|_|_|_|_|_|_|_|_|_|_|_|_|_|_|_] STATE: [_|_] ZIP: [_|_|_|_|_|_|_|_|_|_|_]

****

TITLE INFORMATION

DEED DATED: [_|_|/|_|_|/|_|_] DEED BOOK RECORDED: [_|_|/|_|_|/|_|_] VOLUME: [_|_|_|_|_|_|_|_] PAGE: [_|_|_|_]

TOTAL PURCHASE PRICE: $ [_|_|_|_|_|_|_|_|_|_|_|.|_|_] PURCHASE DATE: [_|_|/|_|_|/|_|_]

BOOK VALUE: LAND: $ [_|_|_|_|_|_|_|_|_|_|_|.|_|_] (INCLUDES PURCHASE PRICE, FEES, SURVEYS, ETC.);

IMPROVEMENTS: $ [_|_|_|_|_|_|_|_|_|_|_|.|_|_] DATE: [_|_|/|_|_|/|_|_]

GENERAL WARRANTY: (Y/N) [_]; SPECIAL WARRANTY: (Y/N) [_]; QUITCLAIM: (Y/N) [_]; GRANT: (Y/N) [_]

TITLE INSURANCE: (Y/N) [_] AMOUNT: $ [_|_|_|_|_|_|_|_|_|_|_|.|_|_]

PURCHASER: [_|_|_|_|_|_|_|_|_|_|_|_|_|_|_|_|_|_|_|_|_|_|_|_|_|_|_|_|_|_|_|_|_|_|_|_|_|_|_|_|_|_|_|_]
|_|_|_|_|_|_|_|_|_|_|_|_|_|_|_|_|_|_|_|_|_|_|_|_|_|_|_|_|_|_|_|_|_|_|_|_|_|_|_|_|_|_|_|_]

SELLER: [_|_|_|_|_|_|_|_|_|_|_|_|_|_|_|_|_|_|_|_|_|_|_|_|_|_|_|_|_|_|_|_|_|_|_|_|_|_|_|_|_|_|_|_]
|_|_|_|_|_|_|_|_|_|_|_|_|_|_|_|_|_|_|_|_|_|_|_|_|_|_|_|_|_|_|_|_|_|_|_|_|_|_|_|_|_|_|_|_]

EASEMENT(S) AT PURCH. (Y/N) [_] IF YES, SEE DEED; EASEMENTS AFTER PURCH. (Y/N) [_] IF YES, SEE FILE.

****

GENERAL INFORMATION

GENERAL COMMENTS: [_|_|_|_|_|_|_|_|_|_|_|_|_|_|_|_|_|_|_|_|_|_|_|_|_|_|_|_|_|_|_|_|_|_|_|_|_|_|_|_|_|_|_|_]
_	_	_	_	_	_	_	_	_	_	_	_	_	_	_	_	_	_	_	_	_	_	_	_	_	_	_	_	_	_	_	_	_	_	_	_	_	_	_	_	_	_	_	_
_	_	_	_	_	_	_	_	_	_	_	_	_	_	_	_	_	_	_	_	_	_	_	_	_	_	_	_	_	_	_	_	_	_	_	_	_	_	_	_	_	_	_	_
_	_	_	_	_	_	_	_	_	_	_	_	_	_	_	_	_	_	_	_	_	_	_	_	_	_	_	_	_	_	_	_	_	_	_	_	_	_	_	_	_	_	_	_
_	_	_	_	_	_	_	_	_	_	_	_	_	_	_	_	_	_	_	_	_	_	_	_	_	_	_	_	_	_	_	_	_	_	_	_	_	_	_	_	_	_	_	_
_	_	_	_	_	_	_	_	_	_	_	_	_	_	_	_	_	_	_	_	_	_	_	_	_	_	_	_	_	_	_	_	_	_	_	_	_	_	_	_	_	_	_	_
_	_	_	_	_	_	_	_	_	_	_	_	_	_	_	_	_	_	_	_	_	_	_	_	_	_	_	_	_	_	_	_	_	_	_	_	_	_	_	_	_	_	_	_
_	_	_	_	_	_	_	_	_	_	_	_	_	_	_	_	_	_	_	_	_	_	_	_	_	_	_	_	_	_	_	_	_	_	_	_	_	_	_	_	_	_	_	_]

DIV.APPROV/DATE: [_|_|_|_|_|_|_|_|_|_|_|_|_|_|_|_|_|_|_|_|_|_|_|_|_|_|_|_|_|_|_|_|_|_|_], [_|_|/|_|_|/|_|_];

UNIT APPROV/DATE: [_|_|_|_|_|_|_|_|_|_|_|_|_|_|_|_|_|_|_|_|_|_|_|_|_|_|_|_|_|_|_|_|_|_|_], |_|_|/|_|_|/|_|_];

CORP. APPROV/DATE: [_|_|_|_|_|_|_|_|_|_|_|_|_|_|_|_|_|_|_|_|_|_|_|_|_|_|_|_|_|_|_|_|_|_|_], [_|_|/|_|_|/|_|_].

****

EXHIBIT 15.7 Owned Property System Definitions

The following are commonly used owned property definitions used to describe real estate phrases within a Real Property Information System program and are used for the enclosed input sheets for owned properties (see Exhibits 15.6 and 15.8).

RE FILE NO: Real Estate ID number for each individual owned location consists of State Letters, Owned, Company Number, Account or Responsibility Number, Building Number, and a Parcel Number:

STATE NO (00): 2 letters representing the state or country where the property is located.

OWNED PROPERTY INDICATOR: "O."

COMPANY NO (000): Up to 3 numbers designating which company within the specific business unit holds the lease at each location.

ACCOUNT OR RESPONSIBILITY NO (0000): Up to 4 numbers designating which account or responsibility center has the budget for the owned property.

BLDG NO (0000): Up to 4 numbers that usually represent the specific property, location, structure, or asset.

PARCEL NO (00): Up to 2 numbers representing the parcel the building is located upon (i.e., a building or location may include one or more parcels).

DATE SUBMITTED (MMDDYY): The initial date the information was input into the system.

LAST DATE OF CHANGE (MMDDYY): The last date the information was revised in the system. This should be automatically done by the system software.

SURPLUS APPROVAL (Y/N): A "Y" in this box means that this property is not being used, that the Senior Management has approved disposal of the property and that the property has been approved as surplus property for disposal.

LOCATION NAME: The name that the business unit commonly calls this location or property.

BUSINESS UNIT: The name of the Business Unit/tenant (i.e., the Business Unit/the Company within the Business Unit which occupies the space).

PROPERTY ADDRESS, CITY, STATE, ZIP, COUNTY, COUNTRY: Street address for the location/owned premises.

NUMBER OF FLOORS: Total number of floors occupied at this owned property.

LOCATION MANAGER: The name of the Business Unit or Corporation person/facility manager responsible for the day-to-day management of the property.

AREA CODE, TELEPHONE, EXTENSION: The phone number of the Location Manager.

TYPE OF FACILITY (Office, Warehouse, etc.): A brief explanation of the intended use for the space.

LEGAL REVIEW BY, DATE (MMDDYY): If a legal review was made, who within the business unit did the review and the date of completion.

FINANCIAL REVIEW BY, DATE (MMDDYY): If a financial review was made, who within the business unit did the review and the date of completion.

EXHIBIT 15.7 *(Continued)*

A/R REQUIRED (Y/N): Is an Authorization Request for funds required?

A/R APPROVED (Y/N): Has an A/R been approved? If Y, date of approval.

IL ONLY (Y/N): If an Internal Letter rather than an A/R is required.

DATE (MMDDYY): Date the IL was approved.

TOTAL ACREAGE, LAND, BUILDING, SQ. FT., OTHER: The total area affected by the purchase contract.

TOPO AVAILABLE (Y/N), DATE (MMDDYY)

SURVEY/PLOT PLAN AVAILABLE (Y/N), DATE (MMDDYY)

APPRAISED VALUE ($): The assessed value of the effected area.

APPRAISAL DATE (MMDDYY): The date of the appraisal.

PICTURES AVAILABLE (Y/N): Whether or not there are pictures of the property or location.

ZONING JURISDICTION: What city or county has authority for zoning.

ZONED: State the zoning of the effected area.

INSURANCE COVERAGE: State what minimum coverage is required by corporation management.

PROPERTY TAX I.D. NO.: As assigned by the local or state taxing authority.

PROPERTY TAXES: These fields list the current, previous, and projected annual taxes.

MORTGAGE DATED: If a mortgage has been taken out against the property and/or facility on the property.

MORTGAGE AMOUNT ($), @ ___.___% INTEREST, FOR ___ YRS. ___ MOS.

MORTGAGE PAYOFF DATE (MMDDYY)

MORTGAGE MONTHLY PAYMENT ($)

MORTGAGE PAYMENT DUE DATE (MMDD)

MORTGAGE PAYMENT PAYABLE TO: Name of the person or organization to whom the mortgage check is made payable.

MORTGAGE PAYMENT ADDRESS, CITY, STATE, ZIP: The name and address of the person or organization who should receive the mortgage check via mail.

CORRESPONDENCE NOTIFICATION ADDRESS, CITY, STATE, ZIP: The legal address of the mortgagor where legal notices should be sent (i.e., change of mailing address, contact person, etc.).

DEED DATED (MMDDYY): The date the deed was signed.

RECORDED (MMDDYY): The date the deed was recorded.

DEED BOOK VOLUME: The volume number in which the deed was recorded.

DEED BOOK PAGE: The page in the deed book where the deed was recorded.

TOTAL PURCHASE PRICE ($): The total amount paid for the property.

PURCHASE DATE (MMDDYY): The date of closing or the date the property was purchased.

EXHIBIT 15.7 *(Continued)*

BOOK VALUE: LAND: Includes purchase price, closing fees, surveys, etc.

BOOK VALUE: IMPROVEMENTS AND DATE (MMDDYY): Total $ Amount of improvements to the property and the date the amount was posted.

GENERAL WARRANTY, SPECIAL WARRANTY, GRANT, QUITCLAIM: To show if any of these agreements are included with the purchase papers.

TITLE INSURANCE (Y/N), AMOUNT ($): If there is or isn't title insurance on the property and if so how much.

PURCHASER: Who (Business Unit/Division) purchased the property?

SELLER: The previous property owner.

EASEMENT(S) AT PURCHASE (Y/N): If Y, see file.

EASEMENTS AFTER PURCHASE (Y/N): If Y, see file.

GENERAL COMMENTS: Brief, general, or specific comments describing anything in the deed or about the property that is of special interest.

COMPANY OR DIV. APPROVAL/DATE: Signature and date that the transaction was approved at the division level.

BUSINESS UNIT APPROVAL/DATE: Signature and date that the transaction was approved at the business unit level.

CORP. APPROVAL/DATE: Signature and date that the transaction was approved at the corporate level.

EXHIBIT 15.8 Owned Property Master Listing Report

```
                MASTER LISTING BY REAL ESTATE FILE NUMBER                  PROPERTY    STAT    IL   COMP  100
                                 AS OF: 06/18/93                           SELECTION   BISU    05   ACCT  1005
PAGE    1                                                                              BLDG  0823   PRCL  02

REAL ESTATE FILE NUMBER: IL-0-702-1005-0823-01

Location Name ..:  TEST PROP. FOR ABC CO. OWNED PROPERTY                   Surplus Approval:      Y
Business U./Div.:  ABC DIVISION                                            Dates:
Property Address:  334 EAST WACKER DRIVE                                   Submitted.......:      05/04/90
                   SUITE 200                                               Changed.........:      06/18/90
City/State/Zip .:  CHICAGO              IL       60634-6578
County/Country .:  COOK                         USA                        Floors:  2

Location Manager:  SANDRA STEPHENS, FACILITY MANAGER
Phone ..........:  (312) 555-5432 ext. 2345

Legal Review By ......:  ROBERT ADAMS                     01/06/90         Land ...:          6.12   Acres
Financial Review By ..:  KATHERYN SMITH                   03/21/90         Building:        42,789   Sq.Ft.
Auth. Request Required:  Y                                                 Other ..:       266,587   Sq. Ft.
Auth. Request Approved:  Y
Internal Letter Only .:  N    If Yes,                     10/15/90
                                                                           Property Tax I.D. No.   373-2949-11-43
Topo Available ...........:  Y                            05/07/90         Property Taxes:
Survey/Plot Plan Available:  Y                            05/10/90         Last Year:  12/31/89 $ 112,345.11
Appraised Value ......... $   12,345,678.90               08/08/87         This Year:  12/31/90 $ 127,853.94
Pictures Available .......:  Y                                             Next Year:  12/31/91 $ 130,000.00
Zoning Jurisdiction ......:  CHICAGO        Zoned:  O-1

Mortgage Dated:  06/02/90    In The Amount Of:    $  6,000,000.00   @  9.70%    For 10 Yrs. 06 Months
Payoff Date:     12/31/00    Monthly Payment:     $     55,555.56   For    126 Months
Mortgage Payable To.....:  FIRST UNITED SAVINGS AND LOAN ASSOCIATION
                           OF GREATER CHICAGO
Mortgage Payment Address:  FIRST UNITED SAVINGS AND LOAN ASSOCIATION
                           4390 NORTH MICHIGAN AVENUE
                           SUITE 120
City/State/Zip..........:  CHICAGO           IL      60634-6578     Country:      USA

Deed Dated:    06/02/90     Deed Recorded:  06/06/90     Book Volume:  65-2375     Page:  4321

Purchase Price:           $    8,065,432.01         06/02/90               Insurance Coverage:   $10,000,000.00
Book Value:    Land:      $    2,665,872.09
       Improvements:      $    5,348,625.90         06/12/90

General Warranty:  Y                                             Purchaser:   ABC COMPANY
Special Warranty:  N
Quitclaim ......:  N
Grant ..........:  N                                             Seller ..:   RAYSON DEVELOPMENT
Title Insurance :  Y       Amount $    8,065,432.01                           COMPANY

General      1. THIS BUILDING HAS BEEN PURCHASED TO          Easement(s) At Purchase ..:  Y  If Yes, See Deed
Comments:       PROVIDE A HEADQUARTERS FOR ABC CO.           Easement(s) After Purchase:  N  If Yes, See File
             2. THE ENTIRE BUILDING WAS RENOVATED IN
                1987 BY RAYSON DEVELOPMENT.                                  Approval                    Date
             3. PARKING FOR ABC MANAGEMENT AND STAFF
                WAS INCLUDED IN THE PURCHASE FOR       Division:   JANE M. SIMPSON, V.P.               10/18/89
                190 SPACES AT 330 EAST WACKER DRIVE.   Bus. Unit:  RICHARD P. FRYE, SR. V.P.           10/18/89
             4. ASBESTOS WAS REMOVED IN 1985.          Corporate:  PHILIP S. MILLER, EXEC. V.P.        10/18/89
```

A person or persons within the systems development team should work with the project manager and RPIS vendor to:

- Administer the training schedule.
- Coordinate warranty work.
- Schedule maintenance.
- Administer updates.
- Administer maintenance agreement(s).
- Provide advanced training when required.
- Meet consulting requirements.
- Provide custom programming.
- Include more memory requirements and additions.
- Establish more terminals.
- Meet networking and communication requirements.
- Acquire enhancements.

- Administer ongoing personnel training.
- Translate existing databases to your RPIS (if applicable).
- Revise, create, and update procedures.
- Maintain security (e.g., user IDs and passwords) backup/data organization.
- Interface systems with other activities: human resources, telecommunications, data management, and so on.

(1) Installation

The two primary functions during the installation phase are imputing all requisite data into the data files and training users. Either existing staff (users) or outside professionals (consultants) can complete the data files. As previously stated, this task is best left for consultants simply because of the staff downtime and the inevitable frustration level associated with novice users, who are unable to perform their normal duties.

A crucial part of installing a new system is training people to use it properly. This process requires adequate planning and a high degree of commitment since the end result of the entire project will be failure if users become frustrated with the system. In many cases individuals may have to change the way they do their job. This tends to arouse emotions and raise stress levels. Consequently, training should be structured to minimize these pressures.

Implementation is the true test of whether or not the system works and meets company requirements. Implementation programs vary depending on the number of leased and owned properties managed by each business unit and the user's expectations and experience. Implementation may include the following four steps:

1. Approximately three to four weeks before implementation and training, make a site visit to meet with the user, his/her staff, his/her manager, and the user's IS representative to review the system, its benefits and implementation requirements regarding system hardware and communications, and initial and follow-up training. Set up a time for a second visit and identify a location (conference room or large work area) where you can go through all the files to identify and abstract lease and deed information. Review their hardware and communications setup and examine their lease and deed records with particular regard to the total number of properties, total number of leased properties, total number of owned properties, and the amount or lack of documentation. This will give you a feel for how much time it may take to complete the abstraction process.

2. Implementation at the business unit location the afternoon before training should include the primary business unit representative, his/her administrative assistant, the business unit's IS support person, your IS representative (if required), and your consultant or the software supplier (if a package system was selected).
   - The system hardware/communications requirements will be discussed, and the software loaded and tested locally by the support person from your IS department, by your consultant, or by the software supplier (if a package system was selected).
   - The system software (if locally resident) will be loaded and tested.
   - The system communications capability (if required) with corporate or other business units will be tested.
3. At the business unit location on the day of initial training, the primary business unit representative, his/her administrative assistant, the business unit's IS support person, your consultant (if part of your training program), and you should be present.
   - The consultant or you will discuss the system hardware/software/communications requirements and how/why the system works.
   - The consultant representative or you will review the following elements of the User's Manual: software capabilities and limitations; how to "log on"; the User ID and Password; System Security; System backup; running of predefined and custom-designed reports; uses of the software including adding, changing, and deleting information; how to "log off"; and system problems. Time should be allotted for answering user questions.
   - During the afternoon training session, the review of the User's Manual will include:
     - An overview of the system.
     - Real estate definitions.
     - The database input sheets.
     - How the user should use the software.
     - An overview of the real estate file number ID system used to track individual properties.
     - An overview of the data fields for owned and leased properties.
     - An overview of the data fields the users will be able to define and the unique information they can track.
     - An overview of predefined reports.

  - Hands-on initial training to add, revise, and delete database information, and run reports.
  - User's responsibilities and control of existing and new database information.
  - Discussion of The *Real Estate Policies and Procedures* found within the User's Manual.
  - The business unit's responsibilities and the system's application to the business unit.
  - The long-term objectives of the system.
  - Again, time should be allowed for discussion, as well as questions and answers.
- During the initial on-site training, the consultant's team will begin their review and abstraction of all leased and owned property information onto abstract/data entry sheets for each property. This will include assigning real estate ID numbers to all properties and identifying which information is missing or incomplete. The time it will take for them to complete their work will be a function of how many total properties are leased or owned by the business unit, how many of these are leased and how many are owned, and how much information is in the file. Past experience has shown that where a business unit has 400 properties with a mix of 2/3 leased and 1/3 owned properties, two people can abstract the available file information in 4½ days, if they work 8 to 10 hours per day.
- After this process has been completed, the consultant's team will take the abstract sheets back to their office and enter the information into your real property information system. Again, past experience has shown that 400 properties in the preceding mix can be entered into the database system by one person in 40 to 50 hours. When all properties have been entered into the system, the consultant should then run copies of all reports, to be ready for review during follow-up training.

4. At the business unit location on the day of follow-up training, the primary business unit representative, his/her administrative assistant, your consultant (if part of your follow-up training program), and you should be present. Your consultant or you should bring the copy of all of the user's standard reports and lead this ½ day session, which could include:
   - An overview of the system.
   - An overview of predefined reports.
   - A detailed review of all the user's real estate file ID numbers and standard reports that have been run by the consultant.

- Hands-on review and follow-up training of all data that have been entered into the system by the consultant including adding, revising, and deleting database information and running reports.
- Answers to user's questions and discussion of future modifications and upgrades.

(2) Operation, Maintenance, and Support

The functional aspects of operation, maintenance, and support are virtually the same whether the system is purchased from a vendor or developed internally. The difference is who is responsible for these areas. These duties generally fall with the developer, so the system, if purchased outside, is the responsibility of the vendor, whereas if it is developed internally, the IS department assumes the role.

Maintenance involves upgrading or altering the system as need be. Support involves having a staff available to assist users with problems and questions. The two tend to go hand in hand because many times a user problem will lead to system maintenance. The most crucial aspect of maintenance, however, is to retain the integrity of the system since any changes that are made will have a ripple effect through the system. Therefore, only maintenance personnel who fully understand such ripple effects should be allowed to make changes.

A meeting to review the implementation of the Real Property Information System might include:

- Evaluation of operating and maintenance (O&M) programs and expenses with business unit assistance to identify cost savings opportunities, and a detailed review of lease operation pass-through and common-area-maintenance expenses.
- Evaluation of the ongoing evolution of the program as software, hardware, and corporate/business unit requirements change or require modifications.
- Discussion of the responsibilities of the business unit representatives. Provide feedback, and respond to future requests for assistance and information.
- An offer to have additional meetings with each business unit representative to learn and understand individual requirements. These meetings are essential to the success of the system for if the users do not buy into the system, it *will not* work.
- Recap of the issues presented—objectives, solutions, benefits, game plan, team, schedule, and implementation and operation of the Corporate Real Estate Management System.

(3) Documentation

One of the most expensive and time-consuming parts of the software construction building and maintenance process is the writing, editing, publishing, and updating of the RPIS User's Manual. If you build you own system, your IS department may or may not have the time, staff, experience, or capability to write, edit, publish, and update all sections of the User's Manual from the viewpoint of a first-time user. You will need to ensure that the User's Manual, whether developed in-house or included with your purchase of an outside system, provides the step-by-step information and definitions for all applications within the software.

The User's Manual and software development documentation provide the blueprint for software maintenance to utilize while updating and revising the system operations. Documentation is a major by-product of the SDLC if it has been properly followed. Without it, the system will quickly degenerate and become unusable.

(d) CRITICAL FACTORS

The SDLC may appear to be a herculean undertaking. However, it is only busy work compared with the time lost, frustration, and wasted resources that will result from attempting to acquire and implement a system on an ad hoc basis. Even if the SDLC is followed from start to finish, however, success is not guaranteed. Some final critical factors to keep in mind are the following:

- Do not underemphasize the importance of accurate requirements definition.
- All stakeholders, internal end external, must communicate freely and honestly.
- All stakeholders must be fully committed to the system; therefore if at all possible, a senior executive should champion the system so as to gain cooperation within all constituencies.
- Understand that the system will involve change and proactively manage this change rather than allow emotions to create crisis.
- Treat the acquisition and development of the system as a process that needs to be continually monitored and improved, rather than as a fixed project.
- Be certain that the system is compatible with existing systems within the organization (i.e., if data from the RPIS is downloaded to the accounting system on a periodic basis and the systems are not compatible, frustration and cost levels to correct the problem increase immensely).

§ 15.6 BASE SYSTEMS WITH FLEXIBLE CUSTOMIZATION CAPABILITY

(a) SOFTWARE PROGRAMS

A number of base system corporate real estate software programs are available for purchase and use for a variety of prices and with a diversity of information which each system can track. One example of such a program is LeaseKIT™. This RPIS software is programmed for a PC-based environment and is available for both a stand-alone PC or a network.[4] The system is flexible enough to provide as much or as little security as desired. Since it was built to be used in a corporate real estate environment, rather than by investment or property management firms, the base system is highly appropriate for use by corporate organizations. In addition, custom tailoring of the program can allow for manipulation based on the company's specific needs. The main menu screen, shown in Exhibit 15.9, provides a view of the program's submenus.

The submenus in this example provide the following options:

- ☐ *A. File Updates.* Allows the user to edit, add, or delete leased or owned property information for each location or separate payment entity within or at a location. Each location requires a unique alpha/numeric real estate ID number code that the user assigns. All functions within this program are keyed to the ID numbers.

  B. Utilities. Allows the user to back up and restore all data files, to index the data files, and to change the real estate ID number. This creates and maintains index files for each location database used in accessing the information input into these submenus.

  C. Reports. Allows the user to generate blank abstracting data entry forms, a Master Listing of Lease Data for *All, Partial,* or *One* location, and Lease Tracking Reports.

  D. View Files. Allows the user to view an alpha/numeric listing of leased and owned properties. This submenu provides the location ID number, location abbreviation, and location name and is used to review and access this information when a hard copy report is not readily available or required.

[4] LeaseKIT™, a PC database software product developed jointly by Edmond P. Rondeau and Applied Software Technology, Inc., Atlanta, Georgia, was designed specifically for the corporate real estate professional who manages leased and owned properties. Robert Kevin Brown also pioneered the development of PC leased corporate real property information systems used by companies such as Royal Insurance, American Express, T.J. Lipton Company, Equifax and Georgia Power Company.

EXHIBIT 15.9 Menu Screen

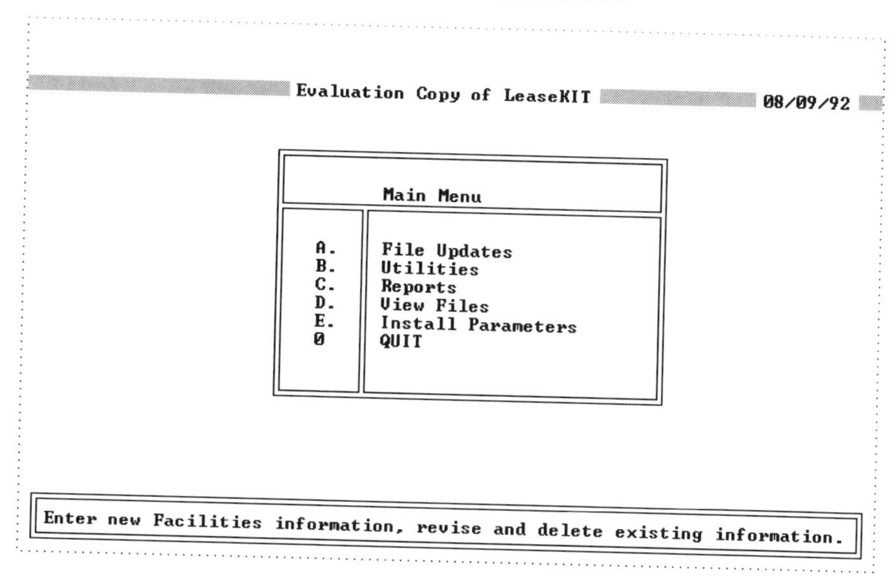

E. Install Parameters. Allows the user to enter the company name that will appear on all reports, enter the title used within the particular organization for the person responsible at that location, enter the organization's "Rent Payable" accounting code (if any), enter up to 10 services describing the Services Included in the majority of the leases, enter up to four names for the signature block(s) to be used in the "Rent Payment" Report, and enter the type of printer that will be used (dot matrix, laser jet, or letter quality with 132-column capability).

(b) REPORTS

Your RPIS should be capable of producing the following reports for use in long-range and day-to-day management of your real property requirements:

- *Facility Listing Report.* This is a "shorthand–address/telephone book" listing of the real estate file number, location name, address, city, state, zip, location manager, area code, and telephone and extension; it is sorted by property that is leased or owned. The report should be able to sort properties either by the real estate file number or by location name.
- *Option Expiration Report.* This lists the real estate file number, location name, current beginning and ending option date, property owner, total area, monthly rate, and yearly rate. The report should

EXHIBIT 15.10 Option Expiration Data by Option Expiration Date—1995

PAGE 1 AS OF: 06/18/93

RECORD SELECTION: STAT X COMP / BISU ACCT / BLDG PRCL

REAL ESTATE FILE NO.	LOCATION OWNER'S REPRESENTATIVE/ LEASE TERMINATION	NOTICE DATE	---OPTION DATES--- BEGINS	ENDS	RATE R/SQFT	TOTAL SQ FT/ NET RENTABLE/ NET USABLE	MONTHLY YEARLY COMMITMENT
IL-A-601-1000-1000-01	CHICAGO, IL RAYSON DEVELOPMENT CO. 06/30/95	01/01/95	07/01/95	06/30/00	20.00	35,000 $ 31,500 $	68,211.49 818,537.88

be able to sort by the real estate file number, the location name, or the option date. You should be able to further select to have the data printed for a range of dates. For example, you may want the report to list properties whose option occurs within the next 60 days, 90 days, and so on, or for a particular year (see Exhibit 15.10).

- *Lease Expiration Report.* This lists the real estate file number, location name, termination date, property owner, total area, monthly rate, and yearly rate. The report should be able to list properties by the real estate file number, the location name, or the termination date. You should be able to further select to have the data printed for a range of dates. For example, you may want the report to list properties whose expiration date occurs within the next 60 days, 90 days, and so on or for a particular year (see Exhibit 15.11).
- *Vacancy/Surplus Report.* This provides reports for all company owned, leased, and subleased properties that are vacant or surplus, including the business unit, location, county, whether owned or leased, cancellation penalities, rent(s), remaining term, options (if any) remaining, rentable square feet, and purchase price of the property (for owned locations). This report should also include vacant land, parking areas, buildings, areas in buildings, floors, or parts of floors that are not being used and would be available to another business unit within the business unit, to other business units, or to a subtenant. The report could be generated by business unit, company, and state, and for all corporate business units including corporate property (see Exhibit 15.12 for leased vacant property and Exhibit 15.13 for owned surplus property).

EXHIBIT 15.11 Lease Expiration Data by Lease Expiration Date—1995

PAGE 1 AS OF: 06/18/93

RECORD SELECTION: STAT X COMP / BISU ACCT / BLDG PRCL

REAL ESTATE FILE NO.	LOCATION OWNER'S REPRESENTATIVE/ LEASE EXPIRATION	NOTICE DATE	---OPTION DATES--- BEGINS	ENDS	RATE R/SQFT	TOTAL SQ FT/ NET RENTABLE/ NET USABLE	MONTHLY YEARLY COMMITMENT
IL-A-601-1000-1000-00	CHICAGO, IL RAYSON DEVELOPMENT CO. 06/30/95	01/01/95	07/01/95	06/30/00	20.00	35,000 $ 31,500 $	68,211.49 818,537.88
IL-A-610-1000-1210-00	Chicago, IL Central Distribution Brokers 09/30/95				1.75	175,000 $ $	25,500.00 306,000.00

EXHIBIT 15.12 ABC Company-Leased Vacant Property

PAGE 1 AS OF: 06/18/93 RECORD SELECTION STAT BISU BLDG X COMP ACCT PRCL

REAL ESTATE FILE NO.	LOCATION TYPE FACILITY CANCELLATION PENALTIES	LEASE EXPIRATION	NET RENTABLE SQUARE FEET	MONTHLY/ YEARLY COMMITMENT
IL-A-624-1000-1000-00	CHICAGO, IL DIVISION HEADQUARTERS NO CANCELLATION CLAUSE	01/01/95	35,000	$ 68,211.49 $ 818,537.88
CA-A-103-1102-1010-00	LOS ANGELES WESTERN DISTRIBUTION CENTER 6 MONTHS RENT & SEE LEASE	05/01/97	165,000	$ 19,166.67 $ 230,000.00

- *Square Footage Listing Report.* This should report all owned and leased property for a default area of over (choose an area appropriate to your search needs) rentable square feet. The default amount can be changed as needed. The report should be sorted by real estate file number or location.
- *Recurring Rent Report.* This should list either the individual/company that the rent is payable to, the real estate file number, the location, the business unit, the state, or a specific location. This report would be generated only for leased or subleased property and should be capable of being generated for a specific month, with that month's totals. Up to four signature block names with comment lines can be included on the report.
- *Rent History Report.* The RPIS should be able to post and save monthly rent payments and sublease income by month and year. At the end of each month and when a change is made, the base monthly rent, operating expenses, and common area maintenance costs should be saved and posted to the real estate management system database. It should also be able to save some, all, or a particular rent history for properties in your business unit and company number.
- *Rent Payment Schedule.* This should provide a one-page summary report for monthly or annual lease payments and sublease income on each leased and subleased property that can be compared with Accounts Payable and Accounts Receivable to ensure the correctness of the amount paid or received, the recipient, and the check address of the landlord or income address of the subtenant (see Exhibit 15.14).

EXHIBIT 15.13 ABC Company-Owned Surplus Property

PAGE 1 AS OF: 06/18/93 RECORD SELECTION STAT BISU BLDG X COMP ACCT PRCL

REAL ESTATE FILE NO.	LOCATION TYPE FACILITY	PURCHASE DATE	ACREAGE	BOOK VALUE LAND & BLDG.	BUILDING(S) GROSS SQ. FT.
NJ-O-534-1034-1023-00	NEWARK, NJ EASTERN REG. DISTRIB. CENTER	07/12/85	23.823	$ 9,682,931.83	125,000
GA-O-214-1021-1237-00	ATLANTA, GA S.E. REGION HEADQUARTERS	11/08/88	5.243	$ 18,919,349.27	189,500

EXHIBIT 15.14 Rent Payment Schedule Report

RECORD SELECTION	STAT	X	COMP
	BISU		ACCT
	BLDG		PRCL

As of 06/18/93

Page 1

REAL ESTATE FILE NO.:	IL-A-601-1000-1000-01
Location Name:	TEST FOR ABC CO. REAL ESTATE
Business Unit:	ABC DIVISION
Property Address:	235 EAST WACKER DRIVE SUITE 1700
City/State/Zip:	CHICAGO IL 60634-6578
Country:	USA
Landlord:	RAYSON DEVELOPMENT COMPANY c/o UNIVERSAL FINANCIAL LIVE
Address:	550 SOUTH MADISON AVENUE SUITE 900 MAIL CODE 907
City/State/Zip:	NEW YORK NY 20246-1234
Phone:	(201) 555-0222 Ext. 1234
Rent Payment Payable To:	PROFESSIONAL BROKERAGE COMPANY AS AGENT FOR RAYSON DEVELOPMENT COMPANY
Address:	PROFESSIONAL BROKERAGE COMPANY P.O. BOX 329856
City/State/Zip:	CHICAGO IL 60634-9856
Lease Effective Date:	06/18/90
Lease Termination Date:	06/30/95
Base Rent Payment/Month:	$ 58,333.33
Operating Expense/Month:	$ 8,956.82
Common Area Maint/Month:	$ 921.34
Total Monthly Payment:	$ 68,211.49
Total Rentable Area:	35,000 Square Feet
Escalation Terms:	1. RENT WILL ESCALATE AT A RATE OF 3% PER SQUARE FEET PER YEAR. 2. OPERATING EXPENSE STOP IS $6.30 PER USABLE SQUARE FEET.
Business Unit Approval:	Jane M. Simpson, Vice President
Date Lease Signed:	05/01/90

- *Master Listing Report.* This report should list *all* the information entered into the database catalogue by the real estate file number or location alphabetically by location name. The report can also be selected to print just one property, a small set of properties, by business unit, company, state, or account number (see Exhibits 15.3, 15.4, and 15.5) for leased property and Exhibits 15.6, 15.7, and 15.8 for owned property).
- *User-Defined Reports—Report Writer.* This allows the creation of reports from database information within the real estate management system. The Report Writer should be able to:
  - Create the format of the report including the report heading, the fields that will print, the column sequence, column heading(s) and the columns that will have totals.
  - Select the database from any subdirectory.
  - Sort the file in the sequence desired.
  - Select the desired records.
  - Create user-defined calculations.
  - Search for specific fields and report only on those specifically requested fields.
  - Preview the report format on the screen.

- Specify that the output be sent to the screen, a specific printer, an ASCII text file or a comma-delimited data file.
- Preserve index, report generation, and printer configuration files for future use.
- Provide Report Writer configuration options.
- Interface with other user database and software configurations (software and hardware).
- Import or export data from any other user mainframe PC, or software system such as unique company software programs, spreadsheets, word processors, facility management database systems, graphics, or any system capable of producing an ASCII file (see Exhibit 15.15).

§ 15.7 THE FILING SYSTEM

Unfortunately, an efficient RPIS still does not allow a corporate real estate department to exist in a paper-free environment. The contractual nature of real estate necessitates retaining originals and copies of legal documents. The filing system should be organized around three central goals: simplicity of structure, ease of access, and completeness of the record inventory. These goals infuse the filing system with the everyday workability that is so necessary to its proper functioning. For example, a number of persons will require routine access into the filing system; simplicity of structure will facilitate their use of the system. Each of informational access will promote the use of the filing system and permit a ready response to queries about specific matters. Completeness of the record inventory is required to fulfill the basic purpose of the record-keeping procedure. In sum, the filing system must be designed for use by a variety of personnel who can retrieve necessary information easily on a "when needed" basis.

EXHIBIT 15.15 User Defined Report—ABC Company All Leased Property in Chicago, IL

PAGE 1 AS OF: 06/18/93

RECORD SELECTION: STAT BISU BLDG — IL — COMP ACCT PRCL

REAL ESTATE FILE NO.	LOCATION NAME	LEASE EXPIRATION	NET RENTABLE SQUARE FEET	NET USABLE SQUARE FEET	MONTHLY/ YEARLY COMMITMENT
IL-A-601-1000-1000-00	CHICAGO DIVISION HEADQUARTERS	01/31/95	35,000	31,500	$ 68,211.49 $ 818,537.88
IL-A-702-1000-1210-00	CHICAGO DISTRIBUTION CENTER	09/30/94	175,000	------	$ 25,500.00 $ 306,000.00
IL-A-329-1000-1000-00	CHICAGO-O'HARE SERVICE OFFICE	06/15/93	23,000	21,754	$ 57,500.00 $ 690,000.00
IL-A-493-1000-1210-00	CHICAGO-DOWNTOWN COMPUTER CTR	11/30/99	43,285	39,752	$ 72,141.77 $ 865,700.00

(a) THE FILE INDEX

The filing system described here organizes each parcel of real property by geography, that is, by the state or country of location. It can also be suborganized by affiliated company, division, or region. Since the physical sites will not change, the redeployment of one property from one operating division to another will not disturb the location of file information within the system. Each category of information pertaining to a parcel of real property will, then, be contained within a master geographic file.

The document numbering system uses a unique identification number for each lease. Further, each property document is assigned a unique number so that paper items affecting each property can be readily identified and located. The automated RPIS uses the same identifiers.

File Code Abbreviations (Alphabetical)

Prefix	Type of Document
A	Leases
B	Correspondence
C	Title matters (reports, abstracts)
D	Agreements of sale (appraisals)
E	Mortgage agreements (releases)
F	Notes and bonds
G	General
H	Railroad easements and R-O-W (Rights of Way)
I	Utility easements and R-O-W (Rights of Way)
J	Agreements (Construction, etc.)
K	Surveys, plot plans, floor plans, photographs, etc.
L	Deeds (Warranty, quit claim, etc.)
M	Corporate purchases
N	Vacation and dedication of public streets and alleys, etc.
O	Company-owned facilities

The system might, for example, identify a lease on a parcel of California property as CA-A-200-001. The coding would tell the searcher that this is a lease agreement and that it is the first one affecting the property. Eleven lease documents affecting the property would be located in the CA-A-200 file. Let's look briefly at how the document numbering system is constructed.

(b) THE DOCUMENT NUMBERING SYSTEM

(1)	(2)	(3)	(4)
CA	A	200	001

Field 1. The CA represents the abbreviation of the particular state in which the property is located.

Field 2. This character represents the type of document or the status of the property involved. "A" stands for a leased facility or leased land, "O" or "C" for an owned property. The "O" file contains only correspondence relating to a property, whereas the "C" file contains the title documents themselves. "H" and "I" are easement files, and generally contain only those easements that have been granted or received since the date of acquisition of the main parcels.

Field 3. This field represents an actual location by geographic area/address. If any facility comprises a complex (and was acquired that way), this number will remain the same for the entire complex and will only change for those acquisitions that follow. A general example of such a change might be:

CA-A-605-001	Lessor Street lease
CA-A-605-002	Lessor Street sublease
CA-A-606-001	Malat Street lease
CA-A-606-002	Malat Street sublease

Even though these buildings are adjacent to each other, they have separate landlords, and they were split for the purposes of subleasing each separately. Field 3 takes the most consideration when assigning numbers, for what may be considered as one complex (Malat-Lessor) by a division may not be considered as such by the corporation. However, as long as the number assigned to each property has been fed into the RPIS, there are various ways of calling up a particular property.

Field 4. This field represents each individual transaction. For instance, there may be two leases or a lease and numerous amendments at one location. They are numbered 001 and 002, with the field in front of those numbers remaining constant. The same would hold true in the example shown for Field 3. The lease at Lessor Street is numbered 001 and the sublease 002. If only a part of what was originally leased in 001 was subleased, the numbers might have read:

001 (main lease, 12,000 square feet)

002 (sublease, 9,000 square feet)

003 (remainder—may or may not be subleased as yet—3,000 square feet)

This type of coding system can be expanded or contracted at will to fit the individual file's circumstances. However, it is necessary to have a formal file system with a code that provides for the logical placement of documents. The central summary location file can be contained in a hard copy file if so desired; this information, however, should be entered on the individual property files on the automated RPIS.

(c) OWNED PROPERTY

If records on owned property are in a functioning depository of relevant information they will be handled in the same manner as records for leased property. The only major difference would probably be one of bulk, since ownership normally involves more legal documents than does leasing (e.g., sales and purchase contract, corporate resolution purchase property, deed, closing statement and documents, title search document and policy).

Again, a file summary will tell the searcher where the documents are located. An efficient file system for a corporate real estate department will interface with those of the legal department and the corporate vault, so summary information will tell the searcher where copies of documents exist, the location of the original in the vault, and the date on which the document was transmitted.

(d) THE VAULT TRANSMITTAL FUNCTION

Original lease documents are transmitted from the real estate department to the corporate vault, with copies distributed to appropriate recipients. The real estate department, as the recipient of original documents for both leased and owned real estate, maintains a complete file of all relevant documents. It serves, therefore, as the contact point for information pertaining to real property. This follows from the underlying logic of the system.

(e) FINAL CONSIDERATIONS

- The basic structure of the RPIS will need to be developed with interface capability for the internal hard copy filing system. For example, the filing code will need to be compatible with the RPIS input and output codes since the internal file will provide the base file data.
- The accumulation of all documents relating to corporate real property will continue, with the goal of creating as complete a database file as possible. Once assembled, this information will be entered into the RPIS.

- The real estate department should also prepare guidelines for the operating divisions for the uniform and logical transmission of file (and subsequent database) information. For example, the department could prepare guidelines for expediting lease executions and transmitting original documents.

§ 15.8 CONCLUSION

To perform its corporate mission, the real estate department must logically compile and organize information. This chapter has presented an operational mode for achieving these objectives.

As stated before, asset management is a universal business activity and because that activity is basic to the financial health of every company, each company should be convinced that doing it well is one key to competing effectively in its industry. The strategic management and administration of a company's real estate resources is a task that is never completed. It is not an easy task, despite its sometimes repetitive and commonplace nature. The corporate real estate function used to be considered humdrum and routine—you bought, sold, leased, and so forth, on an "as needed" basis, giving little thought to whether that unpredictable creature known as the "real estate market" would accommodate such haphazard planning.

Developing a corporate real property information system can be very important to a corporation and may be a major test of senior management, leadership, and communication skills. The purpose and cost of developing and maintaining the system must be carefully assessed and, if implemented, must become an ongoing, regular process for all business unit users. After careful assessment of your corporation's real estate needs and perceived and positive support from senior management and business units, you and your corporation must decide whether to accept or decline this opportunity.

If you accept the challenge, you will, in time, be able to easily and quickly produce strategic planning information and reports such as those shown in Exhibits 15.16, 15.17, and 15.18. For example, major corporations with over 4,000 properties located throughout the United States spent more than two years developing their system with the help of a consultant. The strategic information that became available from this effort provided the corporate management at all levels with up-to-date property, space, and cost data influenced consolidation, location, and real property strategies.[5] Without such an efficient system, your inability to react quickly and easily to information requests will

[5] See, for example, Edmond P. Rondeau, "Contel Finds Great Way to Manage Real Estate," *IFMA Journal*, April 1989.

EXHIBIT 15.16 Sample Inventory Report

ABC Company Real Estate Property Inventory
Loaded in the Real Property Information System as of June 18, 1993

A. **Divisions:**	**Archived* Filter**	**ABC Company**	**Battery**	**Tire**	**Retail**	**Total**
Total Leased	96	35	101	156	879	1,267
Total Subleased	0	15	1	4	21	41
Total Owned	0	2	0	9	2,296	2,307
Total	**96**	**52**	**102**	**169**	**3,196**	**3,615**

B. **Retail Division Western Region:**	**Calif.**	**Wash.**	**Texas**	**Western Region Hq.**	**Total**
Total Leased	118	8	118	1	245
Total Subleased	0	0	0	0	0
Total Owned	153	182	165	0	500
Total	**271**	**190**	**283**	**1**	**745**

C. **Retail Division Central Region:**	**Mo.**	**Minn.**	**Ky.**	**Il.**	**Central Region Hq.**	**Total**
Total Leased	44	41	10	5	1	101
Total Subleased	1	2	0	0	0	3
Total Owned	372	298	84	115	0	869
Total	**427**	**341**	**94**	**120**	**1**	**973**

D. **Retail Division Eastern Region:**	**Penn.**	**Va.**	**Ny.**	**Ga.**	**Ma.**	**Eastern Region Hq.**	**Total**
Total Leased	60	108	76	90	35	0	369
Total Subleased	3	8	3	0	0	0	14
Total Owned	132	188	150	171	84	1	726
Total	**195**	**304**	**229**	**261**	**119**	**1**	**1,109**

E. **Retail Division:**	**Hq.**	**I.S.**	**Office Svcs.**	**Ware. Dist.**	**Credit**	**Total**
Total Leased	1	9	67	9	57	143
Total Subleased	0	13	1	0	1	15
Total Owned	1	2	0	1	87	91
Total	**1**	**24**	**68**	**10**	**145**	**249**

Notes:
*This company has been sold and these properties will be deleted from the Database on June 22, 1993.

EXHIBIT 15.17 Sample Summary Report

ABC Company Office Facilities Summary

As of June 18, 1993

	Divisions:	# Of Leased Offices	Total Leased Office Sq. Ft.	# Of Owned Offices	Total Owned Office Sq. Ft.
1)	ABC Company	27	349,103	2	122,346
2)	Battery	33	720,567	0	74,238
3)	Tire	83	541,672	4	59,534
4)	Retail	101	1,141,169	88	78,415
	GRAND TOTAL	244	2,752,511	94	334,533

remain a frustrating and possibly a costly experience for you and for management.

Today, there is a strong, inescapable trend toward considering corporate real estate as a strategic working asset from which the firm should receive maximum profits. Far from being regarded as a symbol of success, excessive or idle real estate assets are being viewed increasingly as a sign of management inefficiency.

EXHIBIT 15.18 Sample Value Summary Report

ABC Company Leased Office Facilities

SQUARE FOOTAGE AND TOTAL VALUE SUMMARY

As of June 18, 1993

	Divisions:	Total Leased Offices	Total Leased Office Square Footage	Monthly Operating Expenses	Yearly Operating Expense	Annual Lease Commitment
1)	ABC Company	27	349,103	$373,425	$4,481,100	$6,713,486
2)	Battery	33	720,567	$99,911	$1,198,932	$11,216,448
3)	Tire	83	541,672	$57,527	$690,324	$17,624,493
4)	Retail	101	1,141,169	$52,817	$633,804	$12,127,127
5)	Filter*	96	1,069,709	$ ---	$ ---	$407,739
	GRAND TOTAL	340	3,822,220	$583,680	$7,004,160	$48,089,293

Notes:
*These properties will be deleted from the Database on June 22, 1993.

Sixteen

Federal Environmental and Workplace Legislation Affecting Corporate Facilities

§ 16.1 INTRODUCTION

Since the Great Depression of the 1930s, the federal government has made its presence known in real estate markets with a variety of social and economic legislation. Besides addressing the normal health, safety, and welfare objectives, federal legislation has focused on numerous specific measures that significantly affect development projects and real estate market operations. When these laws are combined with local and state measures (many of which supplement and complement federal legislation), the real estate industry often appears to be one of the most regulated economic activities in the nation. Corporations that become involved in facility development encounter all the rules of the real estate industry. Compliance with these rules requires astute examination and understanding not only of the specific regulations, but also of the public objectives the legislation is intended to accomplish.

This chapter summarizes some of the major federal legislation that imposes environmental rules and other workplace requirements on corporate facility planning and development activities. It will also touch on other federal acts that affect real estate market activities. Some of the steps necessary to demonstrate compliance with many of these federal regulations will then be discussed.

§ 16.2 OVERVIEW OF FEDERAL LEGISLATION SINCE THE 1930s

The economic collapse that preceded the Great Depression of the 1930s ushered in an era of heavy federal governmental involvement in economic development, urbanization processes, and social programs. These factors reconfigured the structure of real estate markets. At the time of the Depression, cities were experiencing rapid economic and physical expansion that coincided with revolutionary advances in urban technologies. High-rise building technology, transportation technology, sanitary and medical technologies, and other urban service technologies combined with new production technologies and rural-to-urban population shifts to create a rapidly expanding urban complex upon which the future of the nation rested. It was in this environment that the federal government began involving itself in massive programs of economic recovery and welfare assistance.

(a) OBJECTIVES OF FEDERAL ACTS AFFECTING DEVELOPMENT

While the initial objectives of federal legislation passed in the early 1930s were fairly clear—economic recovery and welfare assistance to those most incapacitated by the economic collapse—these federal actions led to a much more complex governmental role. Subsequent legislation, including extension and expansion of the early economic recovery activities, embraced a multitude of public objectives. Once the economic turnaround from the Great Depression occurred and World War II ended, urban growth and development activities took off again at an even more rapid and complex pace.

Postwar federal actions to address ever more urgent and demanding situations became commonplace. Issues of how to provide and finance public infrastructure needed to rebuild cities (following depression era and wartime disinvestment) and then pave the way for economic development complicated the need for public economy. Expensive federal programs and deficit spending resulted from the rush of programs that followed the Housing Act of 1949. The largest and most expensive highway system—the Interstate Highway program—was undertaken with significant impacts on urban form and urban lifestyles as well as on the economy. Issues of equity arose around who would benefit from and who would pay for governmental involvement and economic expansion. Efficiency of real estate markets in allocating land resources and capital to finance development was questioned, and many new rules were instituted to correct market imperfections.

In the late 1960s and 1970s, environmental concerns and energy shortages began to bring into sharper focus issues of short-term benefits versus long-term consequences of the pace and style of economic and urban development activities being undertaken. All these issues are integrated into a milieu of governmental actions that provide constraints and direction for development activities and real estate market operations.

(b) HISTORIC OVERVIEW OF FEDERAL LEGISLATION

Exhibit 16.1 provides a summary of significant federal legislation affecting development activities and real estate market operations from the depression era up to the adoption of major environmental protection legislation. The legislation is arranged chronologically, by dates of original passage of the legislation, and categorized for convenience in discussing the changes in the nature of federal involvement. It is presented here to provide perspective on the nature of governmental intervention. Environmental and workplace legislation containing many of the current requirements for corporate facilities is listed by date and

EXHIBIT 16.1 Overview of Selected Federal Legislative Actions Affecting Property Development Activities

Economic Recovery and Housing Market Intervention Programs

1932 *Federal Home Loan Bank Act.* Established Federal Home Loan Bank to charter and regulate thrift institutions.

1933 *Home Owners Loan Act.* Established Home Owner's Loan Corporation (HOLC) to buy defaulted home mortgages and provide liquidity to lenders.

1934 *National Housing Act.* Established Federal Housing Administration (FHA) and the FHA mortgage insurance program.

1937 *Housing Act.* Established the public housing program, the basis for the system of federal financial and technical assistance to local governments that became known as the categorical grant system.

1938 *National Mortgage Association of Washington.* Established the Federal National Mortgage Association (Fannie Mae) to purchase FHA mortgages from lenders.

1944 *Servicemen's Readjustment Act.* Established the Veteran's Administration (VA) loan guarantee program.

1968 *Housing and Urban Development Act.* Privatized FNMA and established Government National Mortgage Association (Ginnie Mae) to take over urban assistance functions and issue mortgage-backed securities.

1970 *Emergency Home Finance Act.* Established Federal Home Loan Mortgage Corporation (Freddie Mac) and authorized both FHLMC and FNMA to buy conventional home loans.

Urban Assistance and Urban Infrastructure Programs

1949 *Housing Act.* Established goal of "A decent home and a suitable living environment for every American family" and the urban redevelopment program; beginning of the categorical grant system.

1954 *Housing Act.* Renamed redevelopment to urban renewal and created other categorical grants; established urban planning assistance program.

1956 *Highway Act.* Created Interstate Highway program, largest public works program in history, which facilitated dramatic changes in urban land use and urban form in the United States.

1965 *Housing and Urban Development Act.* Reorganized federal agencies and established Department of Housing and Urban Development and Department of Transportation as cabinet level departments.

1968 *Housing and Urban Development Act.* Reorganized redevelopment and other urban assistance programs and required citizen participation and regional and state reviews for federal funding (along with FNMA and GNMA reforms); began "new federalism."

1972 *General Revenue Sharing Act.* Created formula for local governments to receive federal urban assistance in addition to categorical grants.

1974 *Housing and Community Development Act.* Replaced categorical grants with Community Development Block Grant (CDBG) system, supplementing and gradually replacing general revenue sharing.

EXHIBIT 16.1 *(Continued)*

Real Estate and Mortgage Market Intervention

1968 *Fair Housing Act.* Prohibits discrimination in housing on the basis of race, color, religion, national origin, etc.; later extended to cover age, sex, family size, and other factors.

Consumer Credit Protection Act. Required lenders to disclose effective rate of interest on home loans with inclusion of loan points and fees; called "truth-in-lending."

1974 *Flood Disaster Protection Act.* Prohibits mortgage loans in flood-prone areas without flood insurance.

Real Estate Settlement Procedures Act (RESPA). Requires advance notice of cash needed and standardized settlement formats containing specific closing information for closings on home loans involving funds governed by a federal agency.

Equal Credit Opportunity Act (ECOA). Prohibits discrimination in making home loans.

1975 *Home Mortgage Disclosure Act.* Requires federally regulated lending institutions to report on practices that result in withholding loanable funds from certain areas (redlining) and prohibits overt redlining.

1978 *Community Reinvestment Act.* Requires financial institutions to maintain detailed records for federal audits demonstrating compliance with anti-redlining practices and requires affirmative action programs in areas subject to redlining.

1979 *Housing and Community Development Amendments.* Lifted state and local usury ceilings on home loans for FHA, VA, and ultimately conventional mortgages.

Thrift Institutions Deregulation and Reorganization Programs

1980 *Depository Institutions Deregulation and Monetary Control Act (DIDMCA).* Deregulated federally chartered thrifts and addressed other issues including usury ceilings and truth-in-lending rules.

1982 *Garn–St. Germain Depository Institutions Act.* Preempted state due-on-sale loan restrictions and began the thrift institutions bailout of FDIC/FSLIC assistance while loosening restrictions on consumer loans and other loans.

1989 *Financial Institutions Reform, Recovery and Enforcement Act (FIRREA).* Thrift institutions bailout bill replaced the Federal Home Loan Bank with the Office of Thrift Supervision (OTS), consolidated FDIC and FSLIC, created the Resolution Trust Corporation (RTC), established minimum appraiser qualifications, and required states to adopt appraiser licensing standards for loanable funds controlled by the federal government.

Environmental and Workplace Programs

1947 *Federal Insecticide, Fungicide and Rodenticide Act (FIFRA)*

1969 *National Environmental Protection Act (NEPA)*

1970 *Occupational Safety and Hazard Act (OSHA)*

EXHIBIT 16.1 *(Continued)*

1972	*Clean Air Act (CAA)* *Clean Water Act (CWA)* *Coastal Zone Management Act (CZMA)* *Marine Protection, Research and Sanctuaries Act (MPRSA)*
1973	*Endangered Species Act*
1974	*Safe Drinking Water Act (SDWA)*
1975	*Hazardous Material Transportation Act (HMTA)*
1976	*Resource Conservation and Recovery Act (RCRA)* *Toxic Substances Control Act (TSCA)*
1980	*Comprehensive Environmental Response, Compensation and Liability Act (CERCLA)*
1986	*Asbestos Hazard Emergency Response Act (AHERA)*
1987	*Superfund Amendments and Reauthorization Act (SARA)*
1990	*Pollution Prevention and Recycling Act* *Clean Air Act of 1990 (CAA)* *Americans with Disabilities Act (ADA)*

Note: Current requirements for most of this legislation can be obtained by examining both the original legislation and subsequent amendments.

title only. A more detailed discussion of these legislative provisions is provided in a subsequent section of this chapter.

Exhibit 16.1 contains several eras of federal legislation. Legislation from the depression era focused on revitalization of financial institutions and the housing economy. These acts were intended primarily to generate employment opportunities that would stimulate economic recovery and to provide housing assistance for needy groups most adversely affected by the virtual standstill in the housing economy. They were supplemented by other government actions for economic recovery, such as the establishment of the Federal Home Loan Bank and the Work Programs Administration (WPA).

The postwar era built on the experience of earlier legislation and introduced the categorical grant system of urban assistance with the Urban Redevelopment program. Under the categorical grant system, federal funds were allocated to cities for specific public development activities (open space development, water and sewer programs, etc.) in a given budget year, during which time the local government had to come up with local matching funds to participate in the program. This system fostered a financial dependence of local governments on the federal government for infrastructure development and also resulted in the federal government establishing local priorities for infrastructure development by allocating funding levels during certain years. But the system also required local governments to institute planning and regulatory practices as a means of maintaining their eligibility for federal funding, and this led to reforms of the system of federal urban assistance in 1972 and 1974.

The transition to the new revenue sharing system and the beginning of the era of New Federalism (an intergovernmental partnership format whereby local, regional, state, and federal agencies participate in identifying urban needs for federal funding) actually began with the 1968 Housing Act. At the same time the transition in urban assistance was going on, other federal legislation was passed that focused on environmental issues and more direct intervention into real estate market and mortgage market operations. From this beginning, a great deal of subsequent legislation imposed numerous controls on public and private development activities.

§ 16.3 REQUIREMENTS OF ENVIRONMENTAL AND WORKPLACE LEGISLATION

Most of the current federal requirements for corporate facility development, and property development in general, stem from (a) the environmental concerns that resulted in the National Environmental Protection Act (NEPA, 1969); and (b) the health, safety, and workers' rights concerns that resulted in the Occupational Safety and Hazard Act (OSHA, 1970). From these auspicious beginnings came a host of new regulations and requirements that impacted nearly every public and private development decision. While it is beyond the scope of this book to provide the details of these requirements and the technical procedures needed to comply with them, this section will provide a brief summary of the major provisions involved.

Exhibit 16.2 expands on the environmental and workplace legislation[1] presented in the last part of Exhibit 16.1. Exhibit 16.2 provides information about the enforcement agencies involved, the stated or implied purpose of the legislation, and a summary of the specific provisions of the legislation that must be observed in order to comply.

§ 16.4 MAJOR ISSUES OF COMPLIANCE

Like many current federal and state regulations, environmental and workplace rules do not all date from the recent rush of legislation. For

[1] For an in-depth discussion of federal environmental legislation, see the following: Henry S. Harrison, ed., *National Association of Environmental Risk Auditors Environmental Manual* (New Haven, CT: The H[2] Company, 1990); Steven A. Tasher, Attorney, and the law firm of Donovan, Leisure, Newton and Irvine, *Impact of Environmental Law on Real Estate Transactions* (Rockville, MD: Government Institutes, 1986); Joel S. Moscowitz, *Environmental Liability and Real Property Transactions: Law and Practice* (New York: John Wiley & Sons, 1989); and Marcia L. Russell, "We All Need to Know about the Americans with Disabilities Act," *REEA Journal* (Spring 1992), pp. 11–16.

EXHIBIT 16.2 Requirements of Federal Environmental and Workplace Legislation

Federal Insecticide, Fungicide, and Rodenticide Act (FIFRA, 1947)

Enforcement Agency:	Environmental Protection Agency (EPA) and Food and Drug Administration (FDA).
Purpose:	Controls registration and use of pesticides.
Provisions:	Requires all pesticides and their uses to be tested and registered.
	Establishes maximum concentration or tolerance levels allowable in food or in products transported on federal highways.

National Environmental Protection Act (NEPA, 1969)

Enforcement Agency:	Environmental Protection Agency (EPA).
Purpose:	Establishes environmental protection as a national policy of the federal government.
Provisions:	Requires an Environmental Quality Report to be submitted annually to the President.
	Requires an Environmental Impact Statement (EIS) for any federal action with potential to affect the environment.
	Establishes the Environmental Protection Agency.

Occupational Safety and Hazard Act (OSHA, 1970)

Enforcement Agency:	Occupational Safety and Health Administration (OSHA).
Purpose:	Provides for minimum health and safety standards in the workplace.
Provisions:	Monitors and requires remediation measures in the workplace for: Level of exposure to hazardous materials. Minimum safety procedures. Protective equipment. Medical surveillance. Chemical safety data (to be distributed via Material Safety Data sheets).

Clean Air Act (CAA, 1972, with major amendments in 1990)

Enforcement Agency:	Environmental Protection Agency (EPA) and equivalent state agencies.
Purpose:	Sets standards for discharge of hazardous air pollutants and requires pollution-reducing technologies.
Provisions:	Sets national standards for maximum level of air pollutants, particularly: Carbon monoxide. Inhalable particulates.

EXHIBIT 16.2 *(Continued)*

Nitrogen dioxide.
Ozone.
Sulfur dioxide.
Lead.

Regulates hazardous air pollutants under the National Emission Standards for the Hazardous Air Pollutants Program (NESHAPS), including:

Asbestos.
Bensene (from equipment leaks).
Beryllium.
Inorganic arsenic.
Mercury.
Radionucleides.
Radon −222.
Vinyl chlorides.

Requires states to regulate certain pollutants, including:

Fluoride emissions from aluminum and phosphate plants.
Sulfuric acid mist from sulfuric acid plants.
Reduced sulfur emissions from mills.

Establishes process for states to create air quality control regions.

Clean Water Act (CWA, 1972, with subsequent amendments)

Enforcement Agency:	Environmental Protection Agency (EPA).
Purpose:	Regulates industrial and municipal discharges of certain water pollutants.
Provisions:	Limits discharge of pollutants under the National Pollutant Discharge Elimination System.
	Requires sources discharging effluent and storm water into surface waters to comply with effluent limitations on their permits.

Marine Protection, Research, and Sanctuaries Act (1972)

Enforcement Agency:	Environmental Protection Agency (EPA) and the U.S. Army Corps of Engineers (COE).
Purpose:	Regulates ocean dumping of materials into marine environments to protect coastal waters, estuaries, and the open ocean from toxic contamination.
Provisions:	Prohibits ocean dumping of materials containing: Radiological, chemical, or biological warfare agents. High-level radioactive waste.
	Requires permits of various kinds to dump nondredged materials.
	Permits COE to issue permits for dumping dredged materials but requires EPA to inspect for MPRSA requirements.

EXHIBIT 16.2 *(Continued)*

	Requires research and monitoring of the effects of ocean dumping, including development of alternative disposal methods.
	Permits establishment of marine sanctuaries to preserve critical marine environments for ecological, aesthetic, and recreational purposes or to prevent high-polluting activity such as oil drilling.

Coastal Zone Management Act (CZMA, 1972)

Enforcement Agency:	Department of Commerce.
Purpose:	To effectively manage the use and development of the Coastal Zone, including both land and water resources. To encourage and assist states to exercise their responsibilities in coastal zones through development and implementation of management programs.
Provisions:	Provides for up to 3 grants per state for 2/3 of the annual cost of developing a management program for land and water resources in a coastal zone.
	Provides for establishment of federal guidelines to be followed in development of management programs.

Endangered Species Act (1973)

Enforcement Agency:	Environmental Protection Agency (EPA).
Purpose:	To provide for the conservation of endangered and threatened species of fish, wildlife, and plants and to provide for a program of conservation of the ecosystems upon which these species depend.
Provisions:	Identify endangered and threatened species and publish these in a Federal Register.
	Determine and promulgate appropriate protective legislation.
	Provide for conservation and management programs, including acquiring and managing land containing habitats and providing financial assistance to states to develop and operate such programs.

Safe Drinking Water Act (SDWA, 1974)

Enforcement Agency:	Environmental Protection Agency (EPA).
Purpose:	Regulates maximum pollutant levels acceptable in public water supplies.
Provisions:	Requires testing of public water supplies to ascertain pollutant levels.
	Requires public water suppliers to notify all water users if the water supply exceeds maximum pollutant levels.
	Authorizes EPA to require suppliers to improve water quality according to a strict timetable.

EXHIBIT 16.2 *(Continued)*

	Permits EPA to identify areas with a sole-source aquifer.
	Prohibits any kind of federal assistance to jurisdictions that permit a development posing a threat to a sole-source aquifer.
	Provides for federal assistance in establishing a critical aquifer protection area in states that develop a plan for aquifer protection.

Hazardous Materials Transportation Act (1975)

Enforcement Agency:	Interstate Commerce Commission (ICC).
Purpose:	To control the transportation of hazardous materials.
Provisions:	Establishes criteria for personnel, training, and protective equipment.
	Provides for inspection and registration of facilities and businesses involved in transporting hazardous materials.

Toxic Substances Control Act (TSCA, 1976)

Enforcement Agency:	Environmental Protection Agency (EPA).
Purpose:	Requires premanufacture industry testing of chemicals to protect the environment in a way that does not unduly impede or create economic barriers to technological innovation.
Provisions:	Permits EPA to prohibit or limit the manufacture and distribution of defined chemical substances.
	Bans PCBs (polychlorinated biphenyls) except for existing electrical equipment.
	Regulates existing electrical equipment with disposal restrictions, inspections for leaks, instructions for labeling, and fire protection regulations.

Resource Conservation and Recovery Act (RCRA, 1976, with major amendments in 1984)

Enforcement Agency:	Environmental Protection Agency (EPA).
Purpose:	Authorizes a detailed system of regulating solid and hazardous wastes through production, transportation, treatment, storage, and disposal restrictions, including standards for disposal facilities and landfills.
Provisions:	Requires generators of significant amounts of defined wastes to institute a tracking system that covers production, transportation, treatment, storage, and disposal for EPA to use in assessing liability.
	Requires EPA and states to establish detailed 20-year plans to terminate and deal with defined wastes with recycling and minimal use of landfills.

EXHIBIT 16.2 *(Continued)*

	Requires new standards for underground storage tanks (USTs) for petroleum products or Superfund substances and requires registration except for small tanks (under 1,100 gallons) used for specified limited uses.

Comprehensive Environmental Response, Compensation, and Liability Act (CERCLA, or Superfund Act, 1980)

Enforcement Agency:	Environmental Protection Agency (EPA).
Purpose:	Authorizes EPA to devise a broad program to identify sites contaminated with hazardous substances, clean up or decontaminate the sites, assess liability and damages for the cleanup, establish a system for reporting contaminated sites, and establish a system of funding cleanup costs.
Provisions:	Requires a system of reporting and identifying contaminated sites and evaluating them to determine eligibility as a Superfund site (eligible for funding under the Superfund trust fund).
	Requires EPA to supervise and/or monitor cleanup of contaminated sites.
	Requires a system for assessing liability for cleanup costs of contaminated sites to potentially responsible parties (PRPs), including:
	Present owners and operators of the property.
	Owners and operators of the site at the time of the disposal.
	Parties who generated the waste or arranged to have it transported to the site.
	Persons who transported the waste.
	Persons who accepted the hazardous waste at the site.
	Defines liability as "strict, joint, and several," which means anyone involved with the site with or without knowledge of the problem can be liable, and EPA can assess the entire cost to one party, leaving that party to collect from other contributing parties.
	Sellers must inform buyers of the existence of waste, but buyers must also exercise they have taken reasonable precautions to identify potential problems if a PRP wants to be eligible for a third-party defense in an alleged violation (due diligence requirements).

Superfund Amendment and Reauthorization Act (SARA, 1986)

Enforcement Agency:	Environmental Protection Agency (EPA).
Purpose:	Establishes methods of identifying innocent and nearly innocent parties for liability of cleanup costs of Superfund sites.

EXHIBIT 16.2 *(Continued)*

Provisions:	Defines ways a PRP can avoid liability for a contaminated site as: An act of God. An act of war. An act of omission of a third party. Defines PRPs to potentially include lenders, corporate employees or owners, and others; defines "innocent" landowner as one who: Acquired the property after the hazardous waste had been released. Had no knowledge of the hazardous waste. Had no reason to know of the disposal. Sets standards for innocence on the basis of "no reason to know" as "inquiry into previous ownership and uses of the property consistent with good commercial or customary practice," reaffirming and extending due diligence requirements. Establishes a category for and provides for limited liability for "almost innocent landowners."
Asbestos Hazard Emergency Response Act (AHERA, 1986)	
Enforcement Agency:	Environmental Protection Agency (EPA).
Purpose:	To develop and implement a program of identifying and taking response actions to abate the dangers of asbestos used in the schools and other public facilities.
Provisions:	Requires EPA to identify the extent and danger to human health posed by asbestos in public and commercial buildings and to identify the means to respond to such dangers. Requires EPA to supervise development of asbestos management plans for schools. Authorizes EPA to promulgate regulations describing response actions for dealing with asbestos dangers.
Americans with Disabilities Act (ADA, 1990)	
Enforcement Agency:	Equal Employment Opportunity Commission (EEOC), U.S. Architectural and Transportation Barriers Compliance Board (ATBCB), and other agencies in accordance with their authority.
Purpose:	Mandates a comprehensive set of rules to eliminate discrimination against individuals with disabilities and allow them to enter the economic and social mainstream of society by providing equal opportunities in employment, transportation, access to goods and services offered by both public and private sectors, and communications.

EXHIBIT 16.2 *(Continued)*

Provisions:

Prohibits discrimination in employment and provision of public accommodations for anyone with a defined disability (over 900 disabilities) covering:

Anyone who has a physical or mental impairment substantially limiting a basic life activity.

Anyone with a record of or regarded as having such impairment.

Requires covered employers not to limit, segregate, classify, use standards, use criteria, or use administrative methods in evaluating a job applicant or employee in a way that adversely affects one's employment opportunities on the basis of a disability.

Requires an employer to provide a reasonable accommodation to allow disabled individuals to have equal opportunity to all aspects of employment, including:

Making existing facilities readily accessible to the disabled.
Restructuring jobs.
Offering flexible work schedules.
Providing or modifying equipment.
Modifying training materials or policies.
Providing qualified readers and interpreters.

Prohibits employers from requiring medical examinations before offering employment, and prohibits conditioning an employment offer on successful completion of a medical examination unless required for all entering employees in the same job category.

Prohibits discrimination on the basis of disability in all federal, state, and local government programs, including:

Employment.
Activities and services.
Program accessibility.
Communications.
Transportation.

Requires public entities to take affirmative action to disseminate information to affected persons regarding their rights and protections afforded by ADA.

Prohibits discrimination on the basis of disability that denies a person full and equal enjoyment of goods, services, facilities, or privileges of private entities serving the public (public accommodations), including:

Hotels and motels.
Restaurants.
Retail establishments.

EXHIBIT 16.2 *(Continued)*

Service establishments.
Banks.
Offices of health care providers.
Professional offices such as those of accountants and lawyers.
Schools and social service centers (including homeless shelters).
Recreational facilities.
Museums, galleries, and places of public gathering.

Defines public accommodations to include:

Existing facilities.
Alterations to existing facilities.
New facilities.

Generated corollary legislation to amend the Internal Revenue Code to enable eligible small businesses to obtain a tax credit for certain costs in complying with ADA.

example, many cite the 1947 Federal Insecticide, Fungicide and Rodenticide Act (FIFRA) as one of the points where the federal government became involved with activities associated with facilities development.[2] This act initially required registration and monitoring of the manufacture and use of pesticides and certain other chemicals with potential environmental impacts. Most analysts identify the point of heavy federal involvement in exerting environmental controls as the passage of the 1969 National Environmental Protection Act (NEPA), which contained the requirement for the Environmental Impact Statement (EIS) for federally funded projects. The EIS and its extension to other regulatory procedures is covered in Chapter Eighteen.

There have generally been two principal types of impacts on development decision-making processes. First, environmental and workplace rules now affect on-site project development activities directly by requiring such actions as assessment of potential problems and cleanup or remediation procedures as a condition of obtaining required public approvals to proceed. Second, these rules affect the infrastructure and supporting systems required to service land uses, particularly those provided or controlled by public entities but extending to any facilities affecting the residential environment, the workplace, or public accommodations.

One result of this intervention is to make the development decision-making and planning process much more technical and complex. While

[2] For a brief but revealing discussion of federal environmental and workplace regulations, see Henry S. Harrison, *National Association of Environmental Risk Auditors Environmental Manual* (New Haven, CT: H^2 Company, 1990). Discussion of the 1947 FIFRA legislation is contained on pp. 6.1–6.2.

some of the difficulties of obtaining compliance resolve themselves as education, training, and learning curves advance, the bottom line is that development decisions simply take more time, effort, and money than they did in the past. There are higher perceived (if not actual) risks involved, and there are obvious increases on the capital costs and operating costs of land-based facilities. There is no question that the issues that brought these regulations into place need to be addressed, but there is also little question that development and operating costs have been significantly affected.

The following list identifies some of the specific environmental and workplace concerns from the federal legislation listed in Exhibit 16.2:

- Air pollution.
- Asbestos.
- Facilities for the disabled.
- Hazardous materials.
- Hazardous waste.
- Indoor air.
- Lead.
- PCBs (polychlorinated biphenyls).
- Provisions for workers with disabilities.
- Radon.
- Solid waste.
- USTs (underground storage tanks).
- Video display terminal (VDT) use in the workplace.[3]

(a) ENFORCEMENT OF ENVIRONMENTAL AND WORKPLACE RULES

There are four primary enforcement agencies involved with one or more of the pieces of federal legislation listed in Exhibit 16.2. These are the U.S. Army Corps of Engineers, the Environmental Protection Agency (EPA), the Occupational Safety and Health Administration (OSHA), and the Equal Employment Opportunity Commission (EEOC). Other federal agencies become involved with enforcement of specific requirements, such as the Food and Drug Administration (FDA) in enforcing certain provisions of FIFRA. By and large, however, the major responsibilities for enforcing environmental rules lie with EPA, and workplace rule

[3] A report on the most significant environmental issues in the workplace is contained in International Facility Management Association, *Research Report 6: Environmental Issues in the Workplace—VDT Use, Solid & Hazardous Waste, Air Quality, Water Quality* (Houston, TX: IFMA, 1991).

enforcement rests with OSHA and EEOC. The Corps of Engineers gets involved in numerous environmental activities in conjunction with its responsibilities for maintaining waterways, multipurpose reservoirs, water navigational devices, and its other nonmilitary activities. But the rules each of these agencies are responsible for enforcing are mandated to other federal agencies, so in reality, a corporation could encounter a host of potential federal regulatory agencies.

In addition to federal enforcement, many enforcement activities have been turned over to state agencies where the state has the technical capability and/or supplemental or complementary state laws to enforce. For example, in Georgia the following federal-state enforcement procedures prevail[4]:

- Enforcement of the following types of federal rules have been delegated to Georgia because the state has similar environmental laws to enforce and accepts delegative responsibility.
  - Air emissions.
  - Discharges in surface and ground water.
  - Disposal of hazardous and sanitary wastes.
- Enforcement of the following types of federal rules have been partially delegated to Georgia.
  - Toxic substances.
  - "Right to know" laws (defined in Superfund Amendments and Hazard Communication Standards under OSHA).
- Enforcement of the following types of federal rules have neither been delegated to nor sought by Georgia.
  - Dredge and fill activities along shorelines and clean water rules (enforcement remains with EPA and U.S. Army Corps of Engineers).
  - Surface mining of coal and certain other resources (enforcement remains with EPA and other federal agencies).
  - Enforcement of federal laws not applicable in Georgia.

States will also delegate authority to local governments to enact and enforce environmental rules and other types of regulations. Since state laws are often referenced into local laws, many of the environmental and workplace rules may be initially enforced by local governmental agencies. In facilities planning and development, the corporate real estate manager should be prepared to deal with enforcement agencies at all levels of government.

[4] For a complete discussion of the federal–state enforcement roles in the state of Georgia, see law firm of Sutherland, Asbill and Brennan, *Georgia Environmental Law Handbook*, Christofer Hagy, ed., (Rockville, MD: Government Institutes, 1990).

(b) LANDOWNER LIABILITY AND DUE DILIGENCE RESPONSIBILITIES

Under the common law of nuisance, a landowner is generally liable, if sued, for any damage suffered by another as a result of the owner's use or maintenance of the land. Generally, however, to prove liability, a complainant must demonstrate that the act was intentional or that there was concealment, or have some other basis for showing landowner negligence. In the case of hazardous materials, toxic substances, or many other types of environmental conditions that may be known or unknown to current landowners, these allegations are extremely difficult to prove. Federal regulations and rules being developed for enforcement of certain environmental regulations (particularly under CERCLA and SARA) convert these common-law procedures into a new process. The new enforcement procedures employed by EPA and others to help enforce certain types of alleged environmental law violations shift the burden of proof to the landowner. If dangerous or unhealthy environmental conditions are found, it is assumed the landowner is responsible and must be liable, or must demonstrate that responsibility and liability lie elsewhere.

These enforcement procedures have increased considerably the potential liability of both acquiring industrial and commercial sites for development and of developing, using, and disposing of those sites.[5] Under new rules, the corporate veil of limited liability may no longer protect individuals working for the corporation, especially those with management and/or executive responsibility, from personal liability, if their acts or negligence have created or exacerbated an adverse environmental situation. A further extension of these rules may assign liability to lenders if they acquire title to property through foreclosure, if they actively manage property, or even if they have de facto management responsibility through a management clause in a mortgage contract.

Not only do the new laws and enforcement procedures increase the risk of land ownership and occupancy, but they bring about a need for corporate landowners and land users (and, indeed, any landowner or land user) to exercise a high level of diligence in assessing environmental conditions before, during, and after using a site. The new rules state that the liability among the owners and users of a site (past, present, and future) for adverse environmental conditions will be "strict, joint, several and retroactive."[6]

[5] For a more complete discussion of landowner liabilities involved under federal legislation and enforcement procedures, see Steven A. Tasher, Attorney, and the law firm of Donovan, Leisure, Newton and Irvine, *Impact of Environmental Law on Real Estate Transactions* (Rockville, MD: Government Institutes, 1986).

[6] For an interesting discussion of the impact of environmental rules on corporate land users and the need for standardized environmental assessment procedures, see Emily W. Carmain, "Superfund Clarifications Answer Environmental Liability Questions," *National Real Estate Investor* (August 1992).

Due diligence, in the context of complying with environmental laws to avoid undue liability, means "making all reasonable inquiry according to good commercial and customary practice." A principal means of exercising due diligence for the purpose of limiting landowner liabilities is to undertake an environmental assessment program.

Exhibit 16.3 presents an Environmental Audit Process and accompanying checklists that can be implemented by corporate facility managers. The exhibit shows the three elements of the environmental audit that are needed to attain the innocent landowner/purchaser status:

- Environmental Audit.
- Site Assessment Checklist.
- Site Inspection Checklist.

(c) IMPLICATIONS OF THE AMERICANS WITH DISABILITIES ACT

The ADA has been described as one of the most far-reaching pieces of civil rights legislation ever passed,[7] enabling up to 43 million individuals with disabilities in the United States access to the workplace and to public accommodations. The impact of this legislation on property owners, employers, and others who design, develop, operate, and use real property is as yet unqualified. Obviously, the impact will be substantial, and the time for compliance will take many years, since it affects existing facilities, improvements to existing facilities, and new facilities.

The impact of the legislation will be widespread among employers, workplaces, public facilities and programs, and all forms of public accommodations. One of the more controversial elements is the inclusion of such disabilities as drug abuse and alcoholism among the over 900 disabilities covered. There are a host of other issues involved with compliance, including how the law will be enforced. Public debate and probable modification, additions, and deletions to provisions of the law and to its appropriate enforcement are certain to occupy a prominent position in the concerns of corporate facility managers and other property providers for years to come.

[7] There are several analyses of the ADA available in current literature as well and renditions of the legislation itself. For a straightforward discussion of some of the more pertinent provisions, see Marcia L. Russell, "We All Need to Know about the Americans with Disabilities Act," *REEA Journal* (Spring 1992), pp. 11–16; and James C. Dinegar, "Opening Doors: The Americans With Disabilities Act," *Industrial Development Section* (BOMA International, March/April 1992), pp. 417–420.

EXHIBIT 16.3 Environmental Audit Process

WINDSHIELD AUDIT
Visual site and area inspection and historical use review.

↓

Visual inspection turned up no apparent environmental concerns; History of use is satisfactory.

DEAL KILLER
Obvious visual detection of environmental problems; Substantial cost to remedy problems; Adjacent property problems; No further interest in the site.

PHASE I
ENVIRONMENTAL AUDIT
Records review, compliance evaluation, close visual inspection including sampling suspect asbestos, PCBs, RADON, operations review, adjacent site review, and recommendations.

↓

Records review revealed no problem compliance issues; Evaluation is good; Visual inspection acceptable; Sampling results are favorable; and operation review is acceptable. If there is concern with waste, UST, adjacent property activities, or groundwater contamination, then recommend PHASE II ENVIRONMENTAL AUDIT.

DEAL KILLER
Previous use is unacceptable; There are compliance problems; Analytical testing results are unsatisfactory, previous disposal practices are unacceptable, and current operations are unacceptable.

PHASE II
ENVIRONMENTAL AUDIT
Sampling of additional buildings, materials or equipment, soil sampling, groundwater sampling, waste disposal sampling and recommendation of action with cost estimate.

↓

Sampling indicates no problems or sampling indicates property not source of the problem or result indicates a problem that can be solved at a cost that still makes the deal profitable or affordable.

DEAL KILLER
Major problem in cleanup procedures and cost is revealed through sampling results. Potential liability is unacceptable.

↓

Due diligence completed. Innocent landowner and/or purchaser provision established.

EXHIBIT 16.3 *(Continued)*

You may also find that an *ENVIRONMENTAL AUDIT SITE ASSESSMENT CHECKLIST* may be helpful during the due diligence phase of your site review. The checklist may include the following:

General Information
- Owner
- Contact person
- Location
- Age
- Size of facility
- Site plot plan
- Prior uses of site
- Number of buildings and size
- Building construction type
- Building construction staging

Asbestos
- Location
- Tests, dates, and results
- Condition(s)
- Disposition/disposal costs, contractor and records
- Removal permits

PCB Equipment
- Location
- Size
- Type
- Test results for equipment
- Inspection reports
- Annual reports
- Disposition/disposal costs, contractor and records
- Removal permits

Underground tanks
- Past/present location(s)
- Size
- Age
- Tank construction type(s)
- Permits
- Registration
- Contents
- Testing results and when
- Monitoring results
- Removed when/how/by whom
- Inspection reports
- Closure plans and follow-up testing

Process Operations
- Principal products
- How much/how many
- Processes used
- Chemicals used/how
- Maintenance chemicals
- Time of present operations

Air Emission Sources
- Sources of emission
- Flow/characteristics
- Emission control and points
- Permit(s) and status
- Monitoring requirements
- Notice(s) of violation(s)
- Compliance history
- Regulatory contact(s)/federal/state/local
- Compliance schedules
- Other enforcement actions/citizens groups, etc.

Wastewater Sources
- What are sources
- Flow/characteristics
- How managed/treated/past/present
- Where is discharge
- On-site or off-site treatment and what kind
- Sludge removal process and to where/how
- Permits
- Wetlands issues and permits
- Spill history
- SPCC plan
- Regulatory contracts
- Notice of violation
- Compliance schedules
- Other enforcement actions/citizen groups, lawsuits, etc.

Solid/Hazardous Waste
- Sources of waste
- Quantities and characteristics

EXHIBIT 16.3 *(Continued)*

Treatment, storage, and disposal (past/present)
On-site or off-site disposal (past/present)
Manifests, carriers, and RCRA permits
Corrective action/solid waste management units
State and local solid waste permits
Compliance reports and compliance history
Regulatory contacts
Notices of violations
Compliance schedules
Other enforcement actions/citizens groups, etc.
Federal Superfund actions
Private party Superfund actions

Fuels Management
What is used
Seasonal and how much
Storage facility

Hazardous Communication
Labeling
Training
MSDS

Community Right to Know Compliance
Toxic chemical release reporting
Other state and local regulatory requirements

A *SITE INSPECTION CHECKLIST* may also be used during the due diligence phase of your site review. This checklist may include the following:

Physical Features
Parking areas/paved or unpaved/under roof
Roads
Power lines and transformers
Water retention pond(s)
Public buildings
Dwellings, fences, wells, structures, improvements, etc.
Rights-of-way
Fencing

Adjacent Land Use
Surface water
Vacant land
Terrain
Roads and utilities
Use (housing, commercial, industry, etc.)
Vegetation types
Water retention pond(s)
Fencing

Buildings
Number, location, size
Type of construction
Age and general condition
Flooring materials
Floor drains and to where
Spill evidence and cleanup

Site Utilities
Electricity
Natural gas
Propane gas
Oil
Diesel
Telephone
Storm water sewer and drains
Sanitary sewer
Water
Fire protection

Geological Features
Rock outcrops
Sinkholes
Excavations
Topography/site slope
Soil type and characteristics
Mining activity and type
Quarry or pit and type
Spoil piles
Diversion ditches
Soil stockpiles
Earthquake activity

EXHIBIT 16.3 *(Continued)*

Pits, Ponds, and Lagoons
- Size and location
- Purpose or use and contents
- Material construction
- Above or below grade
- Lined or unlined
- Leaks and general condition
- Fill/drain pipes
- Level

Catch Basins, Manholes, Drains, and Fill Pipes
- Location(s)
- Use
- Appearance (usual or unusual)
- Odors

Waste Evidence
- Discolored or unnatural soil
- Odor(s)
- Ash or blackened area
- Barrels, containers, and/or drums
- Waste materials
- Discolored soil
- Construction and/or demolition debris

Security Features
- Access roads, trails, and paths
- Natural (water, cliffs, and canyons) and vegetation barriers
- Fencing and gates/location, size, and materials
- Boat docking and launching areas

Vegetation
- Type
- Maturity
- Density
- Condition (healthy or stressed)

Water Features
- Ponds, streams, or rivers
- Springs, seeps, wells, or swamps
- Wetlands
- Direction of runoff
- Direction of runon
- Water table
- Underground water
- Surface erosion
- Floodplain location and 100-year floodplain elevation

Disposal Areas
- Age and general condition
- Location
- Size
- Contents
- Debris
- Drums
- Odors
- Sludge, residue, and/or rubble
- Discoloration
- Vegetation
- Monitoring wells
- Cover materials
- Surface contours
- Erosion
- Equipment condition
- Subsurface conditions

Wastewater and/or Process Tanks
- Tank construction and materials
- Age and general condition
- Purpose and contents
- Inside or outside/on, above or below grade
- Lined or unlined
- Leaks
- Connecting piping secure
- Chemical feed and pump system
- Spill evidence
- Monitoring device

Chemical Drum and/or Fuel Storage Areas
- Age and general condition
- Type of construction
- Security and access
- Spill control
- Spill berms
- Spill evidence

Chemical Transfer Points
- Paved or unpaved
- Inside or outside
- Where and what
- Spill evidence

Seventeen

Impact of the Local Community on Corporate Real Estate

§ 17.1 INTRODUCTION

The jurisdiction in which the company locates its facilities can have a great effect on the costs of development as well as the costs of operation. Local regulations combined with other government controls will have a significant effect on how the company uses its site and how buildings and support facilities are placed on that site. In focusing on these issues, this chapter discusses the property tax and special assessments, the various regulatory powers of the local jurisdiction, and locational inducements and incentives.

§ 17.2 REAL PROPERTY TAXATION AND SPECIAL ASSESSMENTS

Real property taxes and special assessments can affect the cost of operating the company's facility whether it is an industrial plant, an office building, or any other land use. The manner in which the company's property tax bill is determined can become an important issue in the company's profit margin and in its locational strategy.

While this analysis concentrates on problems of owning a facility such as an industrial plant, a warehouse, an office building, or a shopping center, a tenant leasing such a facility is also affected by regulatory problems and governmental controls. For example, the effect of the property tax on an industrial property is principally the landowner's concern, but in a net lease or a gross lease with an expense stop, the financial effect of the tax falls on the tenant. In the same vein, the land use restriction imposed by a zoning ordinance directly affects the landowner. But, if the space is leased, the restriction remains in effect and is binding on the tenant using the property.

(a) ASSESSING TAXABLE VALUE OF COMPANY PROPERTY

The value of the company's property for property tax purposes is usually determined in one of two basic ways. If the transaction price produced by a recent sale of the property reasonably represents market value, the price may be used as the assessed value of the property for tax purposes. In the absence of a recent sale, one of the acceptable real property appraisal techniques—the sales comparison approach, the income approach, or the cost approach—may be used to arrive at an assessed value that represents the market value of the property. The three appraisal techniques and the issue of market value were presented in Chapter Fourteen.

Whether the tax assessor or an independent fee appraiser makes the valuation, the market value estimate of the property is the central point of concern. If there is disagreement with the taxing authority, the techniques used to value the property and the nature of the data used in each technique can form the basis for challenging the assessed value. How a challenge can be brought is more fully developed in a later section of this chapter.

The market value and the assessed value of a property are dynamic concepts. They change over time as the economic and physical circumstances in the market change. As an improved property ages, the value of the land usually increases, but the value of the depreciated improvement declines. The relative changes could result in a situation where the market value of the property as improved is declining even though land value is increasing. Also, if the community is experiencing growth in the demand for space (industrial or office), but the supply is increasing faster than the demand, the market value of the older, existing stock of space may decrease as vacancies increase. The assessed value of the property should reflect these changes. These market conditions can also form the basis for challenging the assessed value of the company's property.

Depending on the state and local jurisdiction of the property, the assessed value can be based on fair market value, or on a mandated percentage of fair market value (an equalization rate). For example, assessed value can be set at an equalization rate of 40 percent of market value. In this situation, the assessed value of a property with a market value of $1,000,000 is set at $400,000. A 50 mill or 5 percent tax rate would produce $20,000 in taxes ($400,000 × .05 = $20,000). If the full market value of the property were used, a 20 mill tax rate (50 mills × .40 = 20 mills) would produce the same amount of taxes ($1,000,000 × .02 = $20,000).

The effect of an equalization rate such as this is more psychological than real. One of its effects is to permit a fixed exemption, such as a $5,000 homestead exemption for owner-occupied residences, to be applied to a lower assessed value, enhancing the illusion of reducing taxes on the personal residence. For example, suppose a residence has a market value of $100,000. The $5,000 exemption reduces the assessed value to $95,000, and a 20 mill tax rate would impose $1,900 ($95,000 × .02 = $1,900) in property taxes on the residence. Alternatively, the 40 percent equalization rate would produce an assessed value of $35,000 ($100,000 × .40 = $40,000; $40,000 − $5,000 = $35,000), and the equivalent tax rate of 50 mills for the 40 percent "equalized value" would produce only $1,750 ($35,000 × .05 = $1,750) from the property. This ostensibly amounts to a $150 reduction for the residential property owner (and the voting citizen of the community). However, if the actual market value of $100,000 were used, and the homestead exemption was raised commensurately to $12,500 ($5,000 ÷ .40 = $12,500), the equivalent 20 mill rate for the market value would produce exactly the same $1,750 in property taxes ($100,000 − $12,500 = $87,500; $87,500 × .02 = $1,750). So, if an equalization rate is not used, adjustments can be made to produce exactly the same outcome as if actual market value were used.

(b) DETERMINING THE COMMUNITY TAX BASE

The tax base for the community is simply the total of all of the assessed values for all the taxable properties in the jurisdiction. The magnitude of this number is affected by the extent to which the community grants tax-free status to properties and the extent to which it provides tax abatements and other tax concessions.

In most instances, the property owned by other governmental agencies is accorded tax-free status. So, a state office building in the local community is not subject to taxes. Property belonging to religious organizations is also usually granted tax-free status. However, local jurisdictions may handle this issue differently. For example, many communities grant tax-free status only to the church's immediate and necessary property. The church itself and the property it uses for other essential church activities are tax-free. But if the church owns other property, the tax-free status of that other property is subject to question. For example, a religious organization receives a gift of a small apartment building or even a vacant site. Either of these properties can be taxed since they are not part of the church's necessary properties. The tax status or properties owned and operated by religious organizations may vary from state to state. Numerous court cases have been heard, but since these are primarily contesting local tax policies, they are decided in state courts. Judicial disposition of the issue of tax-free status for properties held by religious organizations varies from state to state.

In an attempt to attract new companies to the community and/or to retain existing firms, local jurisdictions in some states may grant property tax abatements or concessions of some form. For example, a local government may provide an inducement for companies to locate in their community by guaranteeing firms a 5-year tax exemption period of zero property taxes. Alternatively, they may grant a 10-year tax abatement period, with a levy of only 50 percent of the normal tax bill. In essence, these tax abatements, concessions, exemptions, and/or inducements effectively remove part or all of the assessed value of these properties from the community's tax base for the determination of the millage rate during a given period of time. The impact of this type of policy and possible challenges to it are discussed later on in this chapter.

(c) DETERMINING THE PROPERTY TAX RATE

The property tax rate or the millage rate is established by a twofold process. First, the local jurisdiction establishes its expenditure budget for the next fiscal year, say $100,000,000. Second, it divides that budget figure by the applicable tax base, say $1,980,000,000 in assessed value. This generates a property tax rate of 5.05 percent. This is equivalent to 50.51 mills or a millage rate of $50.51 per thousand dollars of assessed value.

If the local community subsequently exempted $250,000,000 of assessed property value from the tax base, the effect would be felt in the tax bill of the remaining taxpayers. Lost revenues of $12,625,000 ($250,000,000 × .0505 = $12,625,000) would have to be made up by taxing nonexempt properties. The remaining $1,730,000,000 tax base ($1,980,000,000 – $250,000,000 = $1,730,000,000) would have to be taxed at a tax rate of 5.78 percent or $57.80 per thousand to produce the $100,000,000 needed to fund the budget ($100,000,000 ÷ $1,730,000,000 = .0578). This amounts to a 14.4 percent increase in taxes for those properties remaining on the nonexempt tax rolls.

(d) IMPACT OF THE TAX BILL ON COMPANY PROPERTY

There is no question that the property tax bill adds to the cost of operation for the industrial plant or the office building. It affects the profit level of the company and the rate of return on equity.

What is not obvious is the opportunity cost to the firm of the local jurisdiction's granting of tax-free status, tax abatements, and tax exemptions. This is part and parcel of the earlier discussion about business climate. A firm relocating to the community or setting up a branch plant receives obvious benefits from exemptions and abatements. But if the company owns an existing plant in the community, it is in effect subsidizing those property tax inducements. Given the numbers in the previous section, the company's millage rate increases from $50.51 to $57.80 per thousand.

The company needs to determine whether it is receiving any benefits as either a business entity or a good citizen of the community that are an adequate trade-off for this added financial burden. If no such benefits are identified, the company could do several things, including:

- Organize the existing companies in the community to curtail or eliminate the property tax abatements and exemptions, and/or limit tax-free status.
- Argue for a 12.6 percent abatement of the property tax bill on the basis of equity, or on the basis of a threat to relocate.
- Argue for an increased level or quality of public services and facilities funded with long-term debt, special assessments, hookup fees, and/or impact fees on incoming users, so the financial burden would be extended to those currently benefiting from the tax abatement.

(e) CHALLENGING THE PROPERTY TAX ASSESSMENT

Before challenging the assessed value of a corporate property, the company should be armed with a thorough appraisal that clearly shows the property's market value. The market value appraisal should be performed by an independent fee appraiser to avoid an accusation from the tax assessor that the appraisal is biased. The independent fee appraiser should be aware of the procedures the tax assessor uses to arrive at market value and establish assessed value. The differences between the assessed value and the market value established by the independent appraiser are often related to these procedures. Using this information properly is the key to a successful challenge.

Assume the assessor's estimate of value is greater than the independent fee appraiser's estimate. These values may differ for several reasons, including:

- The local tax assessor may establish fair market value based on the cost approach while an independent fee appraiser selects the income approach.
- Both the tax assessor and the independent fee appraiser may agree that the cost approach is the most valid technique, but they may disagree on either the value of the land, the cost of new construction, and/or the estimate of accrued depreciation, in total or for any one of its three subparts—physical deterioration, functional obsolescence, and external obsolescence.
- The tax assessor may use recent sales prices, possibly taking the average of them to determine the fair market value of the subject property, but does not make appropriate adjustments for differences in the attributes of the different properties.

The corporate real estate executive should periodically retain the services of an independent fee appraiser to determine the market value of each significant corporate property. The frequency of the assignment will depend on the financial situation of the building, the rapidity of economic change in the market, and frequency of community property reassessments. For example, an industrial plant in a small community in which the assessed value has not changed in 10 years may need an appraisal only once a decade. On the other hand, an office building with a high vacancy rate in a fluctuating market area may need an immediate appraisal because it is losing its share of business to a competing office node and is declining in value at a time when the city is undergoing a property reassessment.

If the difference between the assessed value and the market value established by the independent appraiser is large enough, the corporate real estate executive has probable cause to initiate a review of the assessment. In most communities, this process typically starts with some form of arbitration. If this process is not satisfactory, the dispute can be taken to court. Before committing to court action, however, the corporate real estate executive should calculate the benefits and costs of litigation. The legal fees are up-front expenses. The benefit is the present value of reduction in the tax bill over a reasonable time period, such as 10 to 20 years. Is it worthwhile to litigate a $2,000 difference in the property tax bill if the discount rate is 10 percent and 10 years is a reasonable time period? The dollar value of the benefit is \$12,289 (\$2,000 × 6.144567 = \$12,289; 6.144567 is the present value of an ordinary annuity factor for 10 years at 10%). This figure sets up the point of indifference. If total front-end costs are less than this figure, then a lawsuit makes financial sense.

(f) IMPACT OF THE PROPERTY TAX BILL ON LOCATIONAL STRATEGY

By comparing community factors among the various sites being considered, the analyst is able to identify the impact of the tax bill on the company's locational strategy. In one situation, the company may face a total property tax bill of \$26,000 in the first year for site 1 in community A. Site 2 in community B has a property tax bill of \$23,000. The present difference may be insignificant in the total financial picture underlying any of the locational strategies—on-site expansion, relocation, or branch plant establishment.

Many researchers have concluded that a property tax differential is not a significant location determinant. However, the tax differential could expand over the near term while the other costs and benefits from relocation could balance out so the tax difference is the largest dollar cost between various alternative sites. The \$3,000 difference is also an annual difference. If the cost of capital is 12 percent and the expected period of time this differential would exist is 25 years, the value of the tax difference to the firm is \$23,529. In this situation, the property tax differential could be viewed as significant.

On the other side of the coin, the analyst must realize property taxes pay for public services, and the relative quality of these public services can vary markedly between the two sites. For example, the property tax bill could be the same, but the cost for trash removal at one site is free while it is an additional \$300 per month at the other site. The property tax bill could be the same, but the quality of police protection for the company and the quality of the public schools for the employees' children could be dramatically different.

As part of the location decision, it is not sufficient to merely catalog the millage rates. In and of themselves, they reveal virtually nothing about the community. The true difference is the quality of the public services that the firm receives for its dollar.

§ 17.3 LOCAL REGULATORY MEASURES

The local government plays at least two key roles in providing an environment worth considering as a location for a corporate facility. First, the local government is primarily responsible for providing site-specific facilities and services to all land uses in the community—water, sewer, streets, drainage, police and fire protection, and often other utilities such as electric power or natural gas. In addition, the local government must provide other community facilities and services, such as schools, recreation areas, libraries, cultural facilities, and so forth. The provision of local public facilities and services is the principal function of a local government, and the tax considerations discussed in the previous section of this chapter reflect the relative efficiency of the local government in doing this aspect of its job.

The second key role a local government performs is not as apparent as its service and tax policies. It is the creation of an amenable environment—physically, economically, socially, and politically—in which growth and development can take place. To gauge how well this broader, more pervasive responsibility is performed, it is necessary to examine the local government's planning and regulatory policies. The local jurisdiction that has well-defined growth and development policies as well as procedures for carrying them out is much more capable of reducing the risks of locating facilities in that community. Even if community attitudes and planning policies are unfavorable toward industry and business in general, this type of analysis will reveal those biases and warn the company about problems of trying to locate there. And if the local government has a prodevelopment bias, a strong planning and regulatory program will provide protections for both the community and new business activities seeking a location there.

Most local governments exercise comprehensive measures that influence and regulate land uses in the community in each stage of development. Most of the regulatory controls are based on the police power of government to enact and enforce regulations through legislative action (enactment and amendment) and proper supervision (approvals, plan reviews, permits, inspections, and other administrative procedures, as well as citations or legal actions). The land use control measures most commonly exercised by local government, and the sequence in which these measures are normally encountered by a landowner developing a site, are as follows:

- *Plans and Capital Improvements Budgets.* These set out the system of public facilities and services planned by the local government to establish schedules; determine priorities for funding those improvements; evaluate adequacy of the land infrastructure and community locations for supporting different types of development.
- *Zoning.* The property owner must request a proper zoning designation and other zoning approvals that permit a specific piece of property to be used in the precise manner desired by the property owner; this is the first regulatory approval that governs the basic land use for a site.

- *Subdivision Regulations.* A plat must be prepared, approved, and recorded for any property being subdivided to show streets, building sites, land infrastructure, and other elements; the plat must conform to prior zoning requirements and may be required for industrial as well as residential developments.
- *Mandatory Dedications and Development or Impact Fees.* These require a landowner developing a site to convey title of (dedicate) those areas improved with infrastructure (streets, utility easements, etc.) to the local government for maintenance and/or to make payments to the local government for a pro rata share of the capital improvements cost of providing specific public facilities and services required by the development; these requirements may be imposed separately or in conjunction with subdivision plat approval or building permit approval.
- *Construction Codes.* The property owner must have construction plans reviewed and approved by enforcement officials to show compliance with all relevant requirements of all construction codes (building code, plumbing code, electrical code, gas code, etc.) in order to obtain a building permit.
- *Other Regulations.* Regulatory measures, such as local environmental controls, may be enforced in conjunction with one of the prior regulatory measures, or as a separate regulatory procedure; a Certificate of Occupancy may be required before a completed structure can be put to use, and it could be revoked if the use failed to meet requirements of various fire, safety, sanitary, health, or other occupancy codes (including possible licensing requirements for certain uses).

As evidenced from the above list, local regulations invoke some type of governmental control at every stage of the life cycle of a piece of real property, from the raw land stage to the end of the structure's economic life, when it is ready for demolition. There is also a sequence of approvals that corresponds to the stage of development the property is going through—starting with the zoning or use permission before the property is developed for a use. Cumulatively, these controls set forth minimum developmental and operational requirements and time-consuming, technical procedures that imply both a cost and a protection for the property owner. Through these regulations, the local government helps fulfill its role as a vital partner in the development process of every land use in the community. Sometimes that partnership role is performed in a helpful and beneficial fashion. In other situations, the regulatory policies and procedures may intentionally impose unnecessary costs and unrealistic requirements to discourage particular types of development. Whichever is the case, corporate facilities strategists should be fully aware of how these governmental activities can potentially affect locational decisions.

All the regulatory activities except the planning process and capital improvements program are based on the police power of government, which involves enacting legislation to establish minimum standards, inspection procedures, and penalties for violations. The planning process includes developing policy directives to guide how the land use regulations are devised and administered. Planning is not based on the police power of government; it, along with governmental budget operations, is based on the proprietary and/or spending power of government. An examination of planning policies and the nature of the community's planning program will reveal a great deal about political attitudes as well as the economic and social environment. The nature of planning will be discussed next.

(a) LOCAL LAND USE PLANNING

Comprehensive planning is a government-conducted activity to evaluate and forecast the impact of the various environmental elements of the community. A framework is planned for taking specific public actions in every major sector of public concern, and specific implementation measures are developed to help effectuate the planning measures. The central focus of the comprehensive planning process is land use. There are separate elements of the plan for each of the major contributors to the establishment of a land use pattern. In total, the plan embodies the objectives, programs, and procedures the local government uses to make land use decisions; that is, how they believe individual land uses should be combined to form an overall amenable land use pattern.

The analyst should look for the following items to gain a complete perspective of the community's comprehensive plan:

- *Environmental Elements.* Each of the following elements of the community should be evaluated and forecast to establish the basis for estimating future community needs:
  - The local economy and economic environment,
  - Social and demographic conditions and environment,
  - Physical environmental elements/existing land use.
- *Plans and Programs.* A planning document containing specific plans and programs should be available for each of the following:
  - Housing and the residential environment,
  - Community facilities and services,
  - Transportation,
  - Land use plan,
  - Special area plans (waterfront, CBD, etc.).

- *Implementation Procedures.* The program for executing the comprehensive plan should be examined for:
  - Land use regulatory measures,
  - Capital improvements program and funding measures,
  - Other implementation procedures (annexation, etc.).

The comprehensive plan is usually legally adopted in a resolution by the governing body of the local government, but it does not have the same weight of law as legislatively enacted regulations such as zoning. It is, rather, identified as a general set of goals and objectives the community is trying to achieve through public policies and actions based on some long-term future planning horizon, usually 20 years. The key element of the plan is the Land Use Plan, which shows a proposed arrangement of land uses that could be achieved if other elements fall into place. It is a desirable arrangement of land uses from the public perspective, but it is not a mandated requirement that each individual property be developed in exactly the way shown on the plan. To do so would preempt the legal rights of private property owners. So the plan is used as a guide instead of a requirement.

The plan is future oriented whereas regulatory measures such as zoning deal with current conditions and realities. When a zoning request is submitted, it is evaluated against the Land Use Plan to determine if there is a conflict. If a conflict exists, the zoning applicant needs to demonstrate that the plan should be amended. Otherwise, the zoning request will be denied. But if the applicant can show that current market conditions, physical conditions, and current land uses in the area justify one use of the property while the plan shows another use, it is usually grounds for amending the plan and granting the zoning request. In this circumstance, the future orientation of the plan may not be based on current market realities, and denial of a reasonable use of private property for future public benefit would be an abrogation of private property rights.

Evaluating a community's planning documents benefits a corporation's locational strategy in two ways. First, the company learns the land use goals and objectives of the community as well as the specific expectations embodied in each planning element. Second, the company becomes familiar with the political attitudes in the community as well as the policies, standards, and procedures it will encounter in locating a corporate facility.

(b) NATURE AND PURPOSE OF ZONING

Land is an immobile, indestructible, and relatively scarce economic resource. Zoning is employed to distribute the available supply among competing uses, such as residential, commercial, public, and industrial. Generally, in a zoning ordinance, the land uses most affected by negative externalities receive the greatest protection from the other competing uses.

Zoning accomplishes a multitude of land use objectives, including the following:

- *Implementation of the Community's Comprehensive Plan.* The success of community planning depends on the ability of the planners to effectively utilize zoning and subdivision regulations. Therefore, these police power regulations must accurately reflect the desires and the intent of the general community plan. Zoning ordinances and subdivision regulations may be ruled invalid if they do not parallel the general plan of development. "Zoning is the legal representation of the community's expectations and aspirations for future land use patterns."[1]
- *Separation of Incompatible Land Uses.* A major objective of zoning regulation is the separation of incompatible uses. Incompatible uses occur when the operational characteristics (parking, traffic generation, noise, glare, odor, etc.), generated by a use have a negative impact on the uses surrounding it. From a planning perspective, an area that contains incompatible land uses is considered to have limited utility and limited ability to attract the desired type of activity. The area is utilized at less than its full potential. From an economic perspective, land values are not sustained where incompatible uses exist.
- *Encouragement of Compatible Land Uses.* Communities are generally interested in developing internally compatible industrial areas, that is, in attracting firms that are highly similar in their use of production processes, products, or raw materials needs. Land adjacent or in proximity to an industrial area is usually set aside for related suppliers, subcontractors, and service industries to the main land user.
- *Provision of Space for Unattractive Uses.* Cities typically need space for industries that many citizens consider to be unattractive. Firms such as auto-wrecking yards, rock quarry operations, bulk product distributors, raw material processors, and food processors often fall in this category. Certain zoning districts should provide for such uses if they are needed in the community. Space designated for these uses should be separated from residential land, protected from encroachment by other land uses, and restricted from

[1] William N. Kinnard, Stephen D. Messner, and Byrl N. Boyce, *Industrial Real Estate* (Washington, DC: Society of Industrial Realtors, 1979), p. 100.

encroaching on incompatible uses. "If the community does not plan for these activities, encroachments against more intensively developed property may result. Alternatively, migration of industry to less rigidly controlled areas may occur, accompanied by serious economic loss for the area."[2]

- *Establishment of Site Development Standards.* Development standards in zoning and subdivision regulations generally promote an efficient use of a single parcel of land and a workable density or intensity of uses in the general area. The height and bulk regulations of the zoning ordinance and the minimum planning standards and requirements for land improvements in subdivision regulation help prevent poorly planned and executed development. Because these controls protect other uses from adverse externalities, their presence often encourages industrial development.

(c) MECHANICS OF ZONING

Each zoning ordinance establishes several zones or land use districts—residential districts, retail commercial districts, office districts, industrial districts, and many kinds of mixed use, single-use, or special purpose districts. Each of these districts has two principal elements of controls—use regulations and development standards for permitted uses. Each zoning district permits principal uses anywhere geographically within the district as a matter of right (i.e., no further zoning approval is necessary to establish a permitted principal use). Some other uses, frequently called conditional uses or special exceptions, may also be permitted within the district, but only with special plan approval requirements or with special conditions that must be met in addition to the normal development standards for other uses.

The second major control mechanism in each zoning district is the set of development standards—minimum standards for site development that each permitted use must meet. These standards specify minimum site size and site dimensions, minimum setbacks from lot lines required for structures, maximum height of structures, maximum proportion of lot coverage for buildings (also called open space or yard requirements), and other alternative or supplemental controls such as floor area ratio (the minimum required ratio of floor area in structures for a principal use to the total site area required for that use). These standards, by and large, control density and intensity of use and the bulk and height of structures on a site. Other controls affecting development standards, consequently development costs, are off-street parking and loading requirements and, often, sign controls. These latter two controls may be

[2] Ibid. pp.100–101.

found either with other development standards or in separate sections of the zoning ordinance.

Since many corporate facilities are located in industrial areas, the following discussion of pertinent zoning details will focus on industrial zoning.

(1) Industrial Zoning or Land Use Districts

Although industrial zoning districts are usually classified as either "light" industrial or "heavy" industrial, the difference between light and heavy industries or these types of industrial districts is not always apparent. Generally, light industry includes manufacturing establishments that do not generate smoke, dust, noise, and odor as a result of their production process. Heavy industries are usually considered to be industries that do generate such noxious characteristics and/or that use raw materials (ores, coal, etc.) and bulk transportation. Steel making, oil refining, and auto manufacturing are examples of heavy industry. However, the real distinction between light and heavy industry is based on the presumed offensiveness of the facility's operating characteristics to nearby land uses and to the public. Land use district regulations are able to distinguish between heavy and light industries in extreme cases, but an objective system of classification is lacking for most industries. This is especially true for industries making new products and using automated techniques.[3]

(2) Bulk and Height Restrictions

Bulk and height controls prevent dark canyons that might result from full coverage of industrial sites by multiple-story buildings. They also enhance the visual attractiveness of industrial sites and buildings and ensure pertinent health and safety features, such as the free flow of light and air or access for emergency vehicles and equipment. These controls include specifications on maximum building heights and minimum setback distances as well as direct bulk controls such as maximum lot coverage or floor area ratio. Often overlooked as bulk controls but among the most critical factors are the off-street parking and loading requirements. The amount of on-site parking required, its placement on the site (parking setbacks, etc.), and the on-site vehicle circulation system required to service the parking and loading areas often prove to be the largest site space consumer the facilities planner must face.

[3] William Shenkel, "Industrial Zoning Regulation and the Demand for Space," *Appraisal Journal* (January 1965), p. 59.

(3) Density and Intensity Controls

Zoning density applies primarily to residential uses and usually refers to the number of units per net acre of land zoned for that use. Minimum lot size is the primary density control for low-density uses while floor area ratio is the primary density control for high-rise/high-density uses. Intensity of use refers to the relative degree to which an individual site is fully utilized by activities directly associated with the use, and it refers to any type of use. One of the quickest ways to estimate intensity is to calculate the floor area ratio actually present on the site and the proportion of the site covered by the footprint of buildings, and tabulate the area covered by all other paved surfaces on the site. There are many public concerns about the relative intensity of uses—traffic generation, accelerated runoff, air and water pollution to name a few. Intensity is controlled by the combination of development standards required for a use. Special conditions, such as requirements for vegetative buffers, on-site sedimentation ponds, or special parking or ingress-egress design may be imposed on high-intensity uses as a condition of approval.

Zoning regulation is based on the application of police power by local governments to control land use and the sites land uses occupy. Traditionally, zoning is viewed as way to regulate property in the interest of protecting public health, safety, morals, and convenience. However, political objectives are also present in the zoning process. It is not uncommon to see industrial zoning used protect residential neighborhoods from industrial nuisances.

(d) INDUSTRIAL ZONING PRACTICES

The planning and political logic behind the creation of an industrial zoning district involve the following three elements:

- Inclusive and Exclusive Districts
- Permissive and Prohibitive Use Lists
- Industrial Performance Standards

(1) Inclusive and Exclusive Zoning Districts

As a result of the hierarchy of land uses established by the Supreme Court case upholding zoning (*Euclid v. Ambler,* 1926), the single-family detached residence has been viewed as the most fragile among land uses and the least capable of competing for an adequate site in a competitive market. It has, consequently, been afforded the maximum protection in zoning. Heavy industrial uses are at the opposite end of the scale. In more intensive use districts, such as higher density residential, office, and retail commercial districts, earlier zoning practices (now obsolete) often permitted any use permitted in a less restrictive district plus additional, more intense uses in the subject district. This practice was often referred to as cumulative-use zoning or pyramid zoning.

While this practice has largely been replaced in modern zoning ordinances, there are vestiges of it in many nonresidential zoning districts, particularly industrial zoning districts. Since industrial districts are usually developed and listed as the last districts in the schedule of district regulations, many still permit a host of nonindustrial, often incompatible uses in industrial zones. The inclusive list of permitted uses usually eliminates low-density residential uses, but many types of high-density residential and commercial uses are permitted. Sometimes this practice is viewed as permitting "working class housing" and "supporting commercial facilities" in industrial areas to minimize excessive traffic generation or other problems. The reality is that neither the industrial uses nor the permitted nonindustrial uses can develop and operate in an environment conflicted and uncontrolled by the needs of incompatible uses. If this situation is encountered in a facility location process, the company should seek to have the industrial district amended to exclude incompatible, nonindustrial uses. If a legal amendment is too costly or time consuming, the company should at least obtain assurances that uses imposing developmental or operational constraints on the corporate facility by locating next to it would not be allowed.

The following problems can arise when some form of inclusive-use district is used:

- Unnecessarily high industrial land prices can result from industry competing with other users for a fixed supply of industrial land.
- Functional obsolescence can result from industrial land being improved with a wide variety of commercial and industrial uses. This mixed, incompatible use causes industrial land to be characterized by traffic congestion, on-street truck loading, and inadequate parking.

Inclusive zoning has been defended on the grounds that these nonindustrial uses are temporary land uses awaiting a future increase in the demand for industrial space. One authority has cited the following cogent arguments against this claim:

> The redevelopment of an improved area is too costly to justify land use succession by industry;
>
> Public improvements suitable for residential and commercial use are poorly adapted to industrial use;
>
> Residential and commercial property owned in small, separate parcels is difficult to reassemble for industrial reuse;

> Mixed districts, especially districts dominated by residential improvements, soon become blighted districts which are unsatisfactory for new industry or other improvements.[4]

The creation of Exclusive Zoning Districts involves recognition of the principle that industry requires the same protection from competing uses that is afforded to single-family dwellings. Areas zoned exclusively industrial protect industry from competing land uses by retail, residential, and commercial land users.

(2) Permissive and Prohibitive Use Lists

Some zoning ordinances will explicitly prohibit certain uses from a zoning district by placing a list of "Prohibited Uses" in the use provisions for the zoning district involved. These prohibited lists usually state that "land in an industrial district may be used for any purpose except the following prohibited industries."[5] The list generally identifies activities that are considered to be nuisances, unattractive, or unsafe, and those that are regarded as undesirable per se. Both Shenkel and Kinnard come to the conclusion that prohibitive lists are obsolete.[6] One reason obsolete practices are still followed is that zoning codes are not revised frequently enough to include the newest technological processes and industries. A second criticism is the prohibitive list, as with any laundry list type of regulation, cannot name all uses that could be included. A third argument against prohibitive listings stems from the contention land use compatibility is not dependent on the type of industry, but on its operation. Consequently, an industry, regardless of its classification, could be acceptable if noise, smells, smoke, and other factors were controlled.

The permitted list approach to zoning is essentially similar to the prohibited list method since each identifies the permitted or prohibited activity by name in the ordinance. Shenkel argues that the "questionable classification of industry between light and heavy groups, and in some instances additional intermediate groups, may be avoided by lists of permitted industries. Under this system industry is divided into functional groups, but with one additional reform: permitted industries are identified with each group. In addition, a classification of subdistricts with lists of permitted industries eliminates the broad all-inclusive nature of prohibited lists."[7] Kinnard states that even though this may not be the intent of the zoning authorities, anything not specifically listed as a

[4] Kinnard et al., *Industrial Real Estate*, p. 106.

[5] William Shenkel, "Economic Consequences of Industrial Zoning," *Urban Land Use Policy*, edited by Richard Andrews (New York: The Free Press, 1972), p. 60.

[6] See Kinnard et al., "Industrial Real Estate," and Shenkel, "Economic Consequences."

[7] Shenkel, "Industrial Zoning Regulation," p. 61.

permitted use is therefore prohibited.[8] However, this is usually used only as a legal screen. Any use not explicitly listed as a permitted use will usually be permitted if it is essentially similar to a permitted use listed. A determination of what constitutes an essentially similar use can often be obtained by asking for an interpretation of that point of the ordinance from the Board of Adjustment (called the Board of Appeals in some areas).

The Board of Adjustment is established in each local zoning jurisdiction to rule on interpretations, appeals from administrative determination in enforcement of the ordinance, variances from finite development standards, and special exceptions. The Board is considered to be a quasi-judicial group in that while the members are appointed by the local governing body, their decisions are final—they cannot be overruled by any local officials. An appeal from the board's finding on an interpretation must be made to the courts.

(3) Industrial Performance Standards

Industrial performance standards can be used to judge an industry by the nature of its production operation and the effects of that operation, rather than the type of product being manufactured. Performance standards use a quantitative measurement, taken by standardized methods with standardized instruments, to determine whether the effect of a particular operation and land use is within predetermined acceptable limits. These quantitative measurements replace qualitative terms such as "offensive" and "objectionable" industries or uses.

Performance standards were designed to eliminate the need for lists of prohibited industries. Eleven basic performance criteria have been identified:

1. Noise.
2. Smoke.
3. Odor.
4. Dust and dirt.
5. Noxious gases.
6. Glare and heat.
7. Fire hazards.
8. Industrial wastes.
9. Transportation and traffic.
10. Aesthetics.
11. Psychological effects.[9]

[8] Kinnard et al., *Industrial Real Estate,* p. 103.

[9] Dennis O'Harrow, "Performance Standards in Industrial Zoning," *Urban Land Use Policy,* edited by Richard Andrews (New York: The Free Press, 1972), p. 60.

Although performance standards are more objective measures than prohibited lists, this method of control has the following disadvantages:

1. Zoning authorities do not agree on the industries that should be controlled under these standards.
2. Performance standards are costly to administer and enforce. If they have merit, however, administration and enforcement costs would represent a nominal investment relative to the benefits realized from industrial growth.
3. The list of standards may need to be updated periodically to determine the acceptability of new industrial land use prospects with operations that have not yet been quantified. For example, although the list provides a quantitative measure for noise, the new firm does not create noise; instead, it produces strong ground vibrations or electromagnetic emissions. Performance standards, for all their relative flexibility, also can fail to respond to changing industrial technology. In this sense, they are as limited as any type of zoning regulation.[10]
4. A firm or industry may be preapproved on the basis of performance standards, but after production is underway, the industry may violate the performance standards. This problem could be mitigated by expert advice, competent administration, and reasonable enforcement. Easing of the standards would, of course, depend on the exact nature of the violations.

(e) ECONOMICS OF INDUSTRIAL ZONING

Industrial zoning ordinances can affect the value of industrial land. Zoning is one of the supply determinants for industrial land, and it also affects the pattern of land utilization.

Zoning regulations affect the supply of industrial space by creating oversupplies and undersupplies of industrial land. If an excessive amount of land is zoned for industrial use, this action can create an oversupply and effectively decrease the value of industrial sites. This can be viewed as a positive factor in site acquisition for a plant or operation that has a long anticipated useful life. But if a chronic oversupply of industrial land exists, it will depress values and lead to lower future land values. Market forces, which generate the balance of demand and supply for industrial land, are responsible in the long run for supply imbalances in the market. But poorly devised local industrial zoning policies can flood or starve a local industrial land market, particularly if most of the desirable industrial sites are within a single jurisdiction.

Restricting the amount of industrial zoning can also create a shortage of new industrial space. This situation constrains supply and increases

[10] Ibid.

the price of industrial land. Acquisition costs for industrial land may be expensive, but if the shortage continues, the value of the land may be maintained at a high level and the sale of industrial land could occur quickly. A divestiture at a later date could be profitable.

Excessively zoned industrial space very likely will encourage the absorption of industrial land by nonindustrial users which, in turn, can lead to haphazard and incompatible development. When industry must compete with residential and commercial uses, the result is very often a mixed use land allocation pattern that can contain incompatible industrial uses as well as incompatible nonindustrial uses. If excessive industrial zoning occurs where residential and commercial uses are prohibited, it can lead to a shotgun pattern of industrial development.

Regulations that specify excessive setbacks, unreasonable parking ratios, excessive buffer areas, or similar requirements will probably force new or relocating industrial firms to look elsewhere for a plant site.

(f) IMPACT OF ZONING ON LOCATIONAL STRATEGY

Zoning ordinances affect the location decisions of industrial site users in many ways. The arbitrary classification of light and heavy industry, the adoption of prohibitive lists, and enforcement of inclusive districts result in incompatible uses that lower the utility and value of land. Inconsistencies between zoning objectives and zoning practices are also apparent. Instead of allocating land between the most urgent uses, which is the desired result of most comprehensive plans, land may be allocated on the basis of protecting other land uses from industrial encroachment. To avoid some of these problems, communities must determine and enforce land uses that result in maximum economic and social satisfaction.

(g) OTHER LOCAL REGULATIONS

Zoning is the first in the sequence of public approvals a land owner needs to develop property. It is also the most politically sensitive and controversial of the local land use controls measures because it establishes the right of the property owner to use a site for a particular use. Once a zoning decision has been made, however, additional regulations will apply that affect other aspects of using the property. These subsequent regulations are more technical in nature than zoning, but they will still require public approvals. In addition, they have substantial potential of affecting the cost of development, perhaps even more than zoning.

(1) Subdivision Regulations

When land is subdivided, a larger, individual parcel of land is replatted into several new smaller sites for which individual title is created. Each of the new sites created in the subdivision has to be provided with street access and a full range of land infrastructure so the sites can support the intended type of development. Some of the land in the large parcel being subdivided, usually about 15 to 20 percent, must be used for street right-of-way and to provide for necessary easements that permit utilities and other essential services to be extended to the new sites. The cost of acquiring the land and developing the infrastructure is borne initially by the subdivider. Before the property can be sold or a building permit issued for a building, the title to all rights-of-way, easements, and improved infrastructure facilities must be dedicated to the local government as a condition of plat approval. The development costs must be passed on to the new owners of subdivided sites in the form of higher prices. The local government thus acquires title to these improvements with no capital costs but must then start spending tax money to maintain the infrastructure.

Most subdivisions are for residential use, but there are also many nonresidential subdivisions, particularly for development of industrial and business parks. When a subdivision is planned, the developer must first prepare a preliminary plat and have it approved by the local planning commission. The plat contains a scale drawing of the layout of all sites and supporting infrastructure along with other pertinent information about natural and man-made features in the subdivision. Following the plat approval, construction plans are reviewed and approved administratively and a development permit is issued. The construction work is continuously inspected, and any noncompliance with minimum subdivision standards must be corrected. On completion of the work, a final plat is prepared and submitted to the governing body (elected officials with legislative authority) for approval. The approved final plat must then be signed by the developer and the head of the governing body (mayor or chairman of the commission, etc.). The acts of approving the final plat, signing it, and subsequently recording it in the court of records effectively convey title to all areas dedicated to the local government. So the subdivision plat is both a map showing the exact layout of the subdivision and a legal instrument that conveys title of the infrastructure to the public.

The key elements of control in the subdivision regulations are contained in two sections: Required Improvements and Design Standards. The Required Improvements specify the number and type of infrastructure improvements that must be made along with requirements for dedication or other actions. These regulations are usually clearly mandated and must be complied with, but there is nothing to prevent installing and voluntarily dedicating certain nonrequired improvements. Sidewalks, special street lighting, or recreational facilities often fall in this category. Design Standards are often more controversial. While street improvement standards and utility standards are fairly straightforward, the design for some improvements, such as for drainage facilities, leave a lot of discretion for the approving administrative official, usually the city or county engineer. Because these officials have discretionary authority, both the design and sometimes the cost of installing facilities may have to be negotiated. Often an essential major thoroughfare or main trunk sewer line may run through a subdivision, but it is not required solely for a specific development. Negotiations as to how these excess features will be paid for by the local government is almost always a point of negotiation.

Well-developed and well-enforced subdivision regulations provide substantial assurance to future property owners that their sites have been developed to adequate standards. But poorly devised subdivision standards and a poorly administered subdivision ordinance can add substantial costs or bring substantial problems to the industrial development process.

(2) Construction Codes and Occupancy Codes

Once a site is ready to support a building and a use, a building permit must be obtained to start construction. The building permit is required under the building code, but it cannot be issued until there is compliance with zoning and subdivision regulations. The building permit and the building code also reference in other construction codes, namely the electrical code, the plumbing code, and the gas code. To obtain a building permit, the construction agent or property owner must submit a complete set of construction plans for approval by a building inspector. When construction starts, the work is inspected and approved continuously by field inspectors. If the construction work does not comply with all relevant requirements, the building inspector will not issue a Certificate of Occupancy. The Certificate of Occupancy is required before the building can be occupied and used.

The key controls in the construction codes are the specification of materials, workmanship specifications, and requirements for essential components and design to meet health and safety standards. Since the local government is not involved directly in any part of the construction, the only major point of coordination and negotiation besides the building permit is hookup of essential services to the building, both during construction and for permanent occupancy.

For sites that are already subdivided but have inadequate infrastructure improvements, actions under the construction codes may require these improvements before building construction is complete and the Certificate of Occupancy issued. Several uses, such as individual office buildings or commercial buildings on freestanding sites, commonly must make infrastructure improvements, including dedications or payment of development or impact fees, as a condition of fulfilling their obligations under the building permit.

Occupancy codes include fire codes, safety codes, sanitary codes, health codes, and other regulations that apply after a building is occupied and in operation. Buildings are inspected for compliance periodically or on complaint. If noncompliance is found and not corrected, the Certificate of Occupancy may be revoked, and the use can no longer be legally operated. Some types of occupancy codes require a minimum level of structural soundness and repairs. If these standards are not met, the local government may pursue a condemnation action in court to have the building demolished.

(3) Development Fees and Impact Fees

Various types of development exactions have been required under subdivision regulations, construction codes, and other development regulations for many years. These exactions include such things as required dedications for streets and utility easements, development fees in lieu of required dedications or improvements, development fees for public construction or expansion of public service facilities required by a particular development, and hookup or service fees for a new development to be connected to public service facilities already in place. It has long been recognized that the capital improvements for public services and facilities required by an individual new development impose an extraordinary cost to the local government and current taxpayers in the community. But a standardized and equitable procedure for passing these costs to developers is of current concern.

In recent times, finding new ways to finance the public infrastructure required for growth and development has become a major priority of local governments, particularly since they have been subjected to severe financial constraints and smaller amounts of federal urban assistance funds for basic services. Imposing "impact fees" on new developments is one of the primary means of funding capital improvements from nontax sources.

Like any other exercise of police or planning power, a local government must be authorized by state-enabling legislation to impose impact fees or require any other kind of development exaction. Typically, state-enabling legislation limits the actions the local government can take and imposes procedural restrictions to ensure a legal and equitable system of handling impact fees.

Generally, an impact fee is permitted to be charged when the requirements or demands of a specific new development on the public infrastructure cannot be accommodated within the existing capacity or with planned improvements identified in the community's capital improvements program. The following facilities, identified here from recent Georgia impact fee legislation, are typically identified as being eligible to receive funds from impact fees:

- Water supply, treatment, and distribution facilities.
- Wastewater collection, treatment, and disposal facilities.
- Roads, streets, and bridges, including rights-of-way and traffic signals.
- Storm water drainage facilities.
- Parks and recreation areas and facilities.
- Public safety facilities.

Impact fees may be imposed to cover the costs of constructing capital improvements or facility expansions. Eligible costs include virtually all hard and soft costs, including direct construction costs, land acquisitions costs, professional fees for required construction planning services, reasonable administrative fees charged by the municipality, and projected interest and financing costs. Making interest and financing costs eligible means impact fees can be used for the payment of bonds, notes, or other financial obligations issued by the municipality to finance the costs of identified capital improvements.

Impact fees are usually specifically prohibited from being used to pay for capital improvements or facility expansion to serve existing development or unrelated new development. However, developers can voluntarily pay impact fees for oversized or off-site improvements to service future development or to provide the community with reserve capacity. When such voluntary fees are paid, there is usually a provision for them to be paid back from future impact fee collections.

The authority to identify and assess impact fees can be handled in a number of ways. Administrative officials as well as committees of elected or appointed officials are usually involved. A special advisory committee, such as an impact fee advisory council, is often authorized to oversee the process of administering impact fees.

§ 17.4 LOCATIONAL INDUCEMENTS AND INCENTIVES

Local and state governments frequently offer special incentive and inducement programs to attract industry to their communities. These incentive and inducement programs increase employment opportunities in the community and promote economic development. The programs are designed to reduce operating and production costs of the industries below the levels that would normally occur in the community. The hope is that the cost reduction will persuade the firm to locate in the community. However, in many instances the incentive and inducement programs serve only to keep the local community competitive with other states and communities.

Knowledge of the various incentive and inducement programs may allow the company to acquire space at a preferred geographic location on a preferred site at a lower cost. The corporate real estate executive needs to research the nature and specifics of these programs to analyze such a possibility.

In general, the locational incentives and inducements fall into the following broad categories:

- Financial assistance programs.
- Tax incentive programs.
- Land and space acquisition and provision programs.
- Labor force training programs.
- Special incentives for pollution control.

A discussion of each of these types of programs follows. In addition, some of the inducements involved in enterprise zones will be discussed. An enterprise zone is a geographic area in an urban setting that requires both physical renovation and economic development. If a firm chooses to locate in a designated enterprise zone, the state and local community may offer a special package of the incentives and inducements.

Before discussing details of inducement and incentive programs, it is appropriate to point out the importance of these opportunities to a company involved in a locational and site selection analysis.

(a) SIGNIFICANCE OF LOCATIONAL INDUCEMENTS AND INCENTIVES

The absolute and the relative importance of these locational incentives and inducements have been investigated periodically by different groups of investigators using different survey instruments. One recently published study,[11] using a survey of "corporate real estate executives," revealed that firms actively seek these incentives, and a high percentage of these accept program benefits when they are offered. Exhibit 17.1 shows the percentage of firms surveyed that seek out and accept governmental incentives as part of their locational strategy.

The incentives the real estate executives rated as "very important" are tax abatements, free or low-cost facilities, employee training packages, and below-market-rate loans. Exhibit 17.2 ranks corporate real estate executives' responses, showing the relative importance of each major type of incentive.

However, the survey supports the conventional wisdom that these incentives are not the principal factors in locational and site decisions. Incentives affect the locational strategy as "icing on the cake," or as a "tie

[11] Jack Lyne, "Incentives Are Important, Executives Say, but Business Concerns Drive the Location Process," *Site Selection* (April 1992), pp. 282–294.

EXHIBIT 17.1 The Importance of Locational Incentives by Facility Type, 1992

	Degree of Importance		
Type of Facility	Firm Actively Accepts Incentives (%)	Firm Accepts Incentives (%)	Firm Does Not Accept Incentives (%)
Back office	67	63	0
Manufacturing	59	41	0
Distribution	57	43	0
Office	35	59	6
Headquarters	53	50	17
R&D	27	64	9

Source: Conway Data survey of corporate real estate executives, December 1991–January 1992.

breaker." The research report accompanying the survey provides the following information.

Almost 80 percent of survey respondents said incentives enter into their firms' corporate location strategies "only if we are choosing between two locations which are roughly equal regarding other considerations." Another 18 percent of executives responded that their firms "locate facilities strictly for operational reasons," so incentives don't play a role in location decisions regardless of their magnitude. That left a scant

EXHIBIT 17.2 Top-Rated Location-Assistance Incentives

Incentive	Percentage
Tax abatements	66
Free or low-cost infrastructure for new facility	48
Specially tailored employee-training packages	38
Free or below-market land for facility site	28
Free or below-market building for facility operation	23
Rent-free or below-market leased space	21
Loans at rates significantly below market	10
State or local grants	6
Incentives for setting up operations in a high-unemployment area	3
State or local loans	3

Source: Conway Data survey of corporate real estate executives, December 1991–January 1992.

Note: Percentages indicate how often respondents rated an incentive as "very important" in their firms' location decisions.

3 percent of respondents who said that incentives "could play a major role in our location decision if the incentives offered would provide us with a substantial savings."[12]

(b) FINANCIAL ASSISTANCE PROGRAMS

Financial assistance programs, which can be offered by the state or by the local community, typically fall into the following subcategories:

- Industrial loan guarantee programs.
- Direct industrial loan programs.
- Industrial bond financing.
- Development credit corporations.
- Development corporations.

(1) Industrial Loan Guarantee Programs

An agency or authority is created or currently exists within the state or a local jurisdiction. This agency issues a repayment guarantee to lenders that provide funds to firms for the purchase of land for industrial purposes, the development and construction of new facilities, the expansion of existing facilities, or the purchase of equipment and machinery.

(2) Direct Industrial Loan Programs

An agency or authority is created or currently exists within the state or a local jurisdiction. This agency makes loans to industrial firms to purchase land, construct plants, and purchase equipment and machinery. The source of funds can be state or local government appropriations from property, income and sales taxation, or the sale of government bonds, which may be tax-exempt.

These loans can be made for construction and related activity in any geographic area within the jurisdiction. But, in many instances, these loans are tied to development and construction activity in economically depressed areas, defined as areas of high unemployment. In most instances, these loans are made at a below-market rate of interest, or if not, they are made under favorable terms in order to attract the firm.

(3) Industrial Development Bond (IDB) Financing

State and local governments are authorized to issue two types of bonds—general obligation and revenue bonds. The proceeds from the sale of these

[12] Ibid. p. 286.

bonds can be used to expand and/or renovate an existing plant, to construct new industrial facilities that are leased to the industrial firm, and to acquire equipment and machinery for either the new or existing plant.[13] In the case of the construction of a new plant, the lease payments may be received by the appropriate government (local or state) and are used to discharge the government's financial responsibility under the bond. Ideally, the lease payments are set at a level that will cover the principal, the interest, and the maintenance and repair of the facilities. Since the facility is owned by either the state or the local government, the firm is exempt from the payment of local property taxes.

In the case of a plant expansion or a renovation, a business loan is provided, and the loan repayments discharge the firm's financial obligation. Very often, this loan is made at a below-market rate of interest. Generally, a loan is made to the firm for the purchase of equipment and machinery, and this loan is paid off in a relatively short period of time.

The bonds are attractive to investors because the interest income earned by the bondholders is usually exempt from federal income tax as well as state income tax in most states.

The distinction between the general obligation bond and the revenue bonds is based on the financial backing for the payment of interest and principal on the bonds. General obligation bonds are secured by the taxing power of the government entity that issued the bond. Industrial revenue bonds (IRBs) are only secured by the property that is acquired or constructed with the proceeds of the bond sale and the income that the property produces under the terms of the lease. The financial rating of the bonds is established on the basis of the credit rating of the issuing government entity for the general obligation bond and, for the revenue bond, by the credit rating of the firm leasing the facility.

(4) Development Credit Corporations

Development credit corporations are state chartered financial entities that rely on private funds to facilitate industrial development. They generally raise money to make industrial development loans through the sale of stock or by borrowing funds under the corporate name. In addition, they can also use the retained earnings of the corporation to make these loans.

[13] The tax-exempt industrial revenue bond can also be used to finance other activities which include pollution and waste control facilities; convention and trade show facilities; airports; docks and wharves; mass communication facilities; electric, gas, and water utilities; parking facilities; and residential facilities. Based on the Tax Equity and Fiscal Responsibility Act of 1982, IRBs cannot be used for golf courses, country clubs, massage parlors, racquet clubs, skating rinks, racetracks, and suntan and hot tub facilities. In addition, they cannot be used if more than 25 percent of the bond proceeds are used to finance restaurants, auto sales and service centers, or other recreational facilities.

Stock in these corporations is primarily sold to businesses, private individuals, and local development corporations. In general, stockholders in these development credit corporations neither expect nor do they typically receive more than token dividends.

Borrowed funds are typically obtained from commercial banks, but they also come from insurance companies and other financial institutions. Development corporations usually borrow at interest rates lower than the rate offered to the business that applies directly for the same loan.

The loans made by the development credit corporation typically go to smaller manufacturing, wholesale, and retail firms. The purposes of the loans are similar to those of the IDBs discussed earlier—to expand and/or renovate an existing plant, to construct new industrial facilities, and to acquire equipment and machinery for either the new or existing plant. At times, these funds have also gone for working capital. The loans are usually given for short term conditions of 5 to 10 years.

(5) Development Corporations

Development corporations use a wide variety of names. They are known as industrial development corporations or authorities; community development corporations, foundations, or authorities; and, economic development corporations, foundations, or authorities. Regardless of their name, these development corporations are empowered to perform a wide series of activities beyond the provision of financial aid in the form of loans. In this context, however, the development corporation acts in approximately the same manner as the development credit corporation.

In addition to financing activities, many development corporations have undertaken the following activities:

- Purchasing and modernizing existing plants to sell or lease.
- Constructing speculative building shells and/or plants to sell or lease.
- Acquiring or optioning industrial sites to sell or lease.
- Giving industrial sites to firms as an inducement to locate in the community.
- Undertaking any cooperative efforts or acting as a facilitator in gaining governmental cooperation or otherwise assisting firms seeking locations in the community.

(6) Conclusion

A complete listing of these financial assistance programs in the 50 states and Puerto Rico is published annually by Conway Publications in the October issue of a magazine entitled *Site Selection* (see Exhibit 17.3).

EXHIBIT 17.3 Financial Incentives Offered by States

CHART 1: *Financial Assistance For Industry**

*See Footnotes Following Chart

STATES	State Sponsored Industrial Development Authority	Privately Sponsored Development Credit Corporation	State Authority or Agency Revenue Bond Financing	State Authority or Agency General Obligation Bond Financing	City and/or County Revenue Bond Financing	City and/or County General Obligation Bond Financing	State Loans for Building Construction	State Loans for Equipment, Machinery	City and/or County Loans for Building Construction	City and/or County Loans for Equipment, Machinery	State Loan Guarantees for Building Construction	State Loan Guarantees for Equipment, Machinery	City and/or County Loan Guarantees for Building Construction	City and/or County Loan Guarantees for Equipment, Machinery	State Financing Aid for Existing Plant Expansion	State Matching Funds for City and/or County Industrial Financing Programs	State Incentive for Establishing Industrial Plants in Areas of High Unemployment	City and/or County Incentive for Establishing Industrial Plants in Areas of High Unemployment
ALABAMA	●	●	●		●	●[1]	●	●	●	●					●[2,12]	●	●	●
ALASKA	●	●	●	●	●	●	●[20]	●[20]			●	●			●	●	●	
ARIZONA					●	●	●	●							●[20]		●[22]	●
ARKANSAS	●	●	●	●	●	●	●	●	●	●					●		●	
CALIFORNIA	●	●[5]	●	●		●	●	●	●[1]	●[1]	●	●			●		●	●
COLORADO	●	●[4]			●		●	●	●[1]	●[1]	●	●	●	●	●	●	●	●
CONNECTICUT	●	●	●	●	●	●	●	●	●	●	●	●	●	●	●	●	●	●
DELAWARE	●	●	●		●		●	●	●	●					●	●	●	●
FLORIDA	●	●			●	●[3]	●[20]	●[20]	●	●					●[20]		●[8]	●
GEORGIA		●	●[23]		●												●	●
HAWAII	●		●	●	●	●	●[15]	●[15]							●[15]		●[8]	●[8]
IDAHO		●			●	●			●[1]	●[1]								
ILLINOIS	●	●	●		●		●	●	●	●	●	●			●	●	●	●
INDIANA	●	●	●		●	●	●	●	●	●	●	●	●	●	●	●	●	●
IOWA	●	●	●		●	●	●[18]	●[18]	●	●	●	●			●	●[18]		●
KANSAS			●		●	●			●	●					●		●	●
KENTUCKY	●		●		●		●	●	●[11]	●[11]					●		●	●[8]
LOUISIANA		●[4]	●[2]	●[2]	●	●	●[25]	●[25]	●[26]	●[26]	●[6]	●[6]			●[2]	●[19]	●	●
MAINE	●		●		●		●	●	●	●	●	●			●		●	●
MARYLAND	●	●	●	●	●	●	●	●	●	●	●	●	●	●[31]	●	●[7]	●	●
MASSACHUSETTS		●	●		●				●	●	●	●			●	●	●	●
MICHIGAN	●	●	●		●	●	●	●	●	●					●		●	●[30]
MINNESOTA	●	●	●	●[13]	●	●	●	●	●[9]	●[9]					●	●	●	
MISSISSIPPI	●	●	●	●	●	●	●[15]	●[15]	●	●	●[15]	●[15]			●[2]		●	●
MISSOURI	●	●[4]	●		●	●	●	●	●	●	●	●			●		●	●
MONTANA		●	●	●	●	●	●	●	●[17]	●	●	●	●	●	●			
NEBRASKA	●	●	●		●		●	●	●	●	●	●	●	●	●[2]		●	●
NEVADA	●	●	●	●	●				●	●							●	●
NEW HAMPSHIRE	●	●	●		●[21]	●[21]			●[21]	●[21]	●	●	●[21]	●[21]	●			
NEW JERSEY	●		●		●[10]	●[10]	●	●	●	●	●	●			●		●	●
NEW MEXICO	●	●	●	●	●	●	●	●							●			
NEW YORK	●	●	●	●	●		●	●	●	●	●	●			●		●	●
NORTH CAROLINA					●												●	
NORTH DAKOTA		●	●	●	●	●	●	●				●			●		●	●
OHIO	●	●	●		●	●	●	●	●	●	●	●	●	●	●	●	●	●
OKLAHOMA	●		●		●	●	●	●	●	●		●			●	●	●	●
OREGON	●	●	●	●	●	●	●	●	●	●	●	●	●[11]	●[11]	●	●	●	●
PENNSYLVANIA	●	●	●	●	●	●	●[14]	●	●[14]	●			●	●	●	●	●	●
RHODE ISLAND	●	●	●	●	●		●	●	●	●	●	●			●	●		●
SOUTH CAROLINA	●	●	●		●	●	●	●	●[1]	●[1]					●		●	
SOUTH DAKOTA	●		●	●	●	●	●	●	●[1]	●[1]					●	●		
TENNESSEE					●	●	●	●[27]							●		●	
TEXAS	●		●	●[28]	●	●	●	●	●	●	●	●			●	●	●	●
UTAH	●	●			●	●			●	●							●[22]	
VERMONT	●	●	●		●	●	●	●	●	●	●	●			●	●		
VIRGINIA	●	●	●		●	●	●	●	●[24]	●[24]					●		●	●
WASHINGTON	●	●	●		●			●				●				●	●	
WEST VIRGINIA	●	●	●		●		●	●	●	●	●	●			●	●		
WISCONSIN	●		●		●	●[16]	●	●	●	●					●		●[29]	
WYOMING	●	●	●		●	●	●	●	●	●	●	●			●			
STATE TOTALS	40	38	43	19	49	36	41	42	41	41	25	28	10	10	44	22	40	33
PUERTO RICO	●	●	●	●	●	●	●	●			●	●			●	●	●	●

Source: From *Site Selection,* October 1991, p. 974.

Note: For more specific information about the programs in each state check the footnotes to this table that appear in the original publication.

(c) TAX-INCENTIVE PROGRAMS

The full array of tax-incentive programs is very broad. They include tax exemptions from corporate income, personal income, property, and excise taxes. They also include various forms of tax credits. The exact form and nature of each tax incentive is available from the specific state and local community that offers it. However, some helpful generalizations about tax incentives can be made.

Corporate state income tax exemptions usually involve an agreement that a firm considering an expansion in the state or a relocation to the state will not pay any state corporate income taxes for a predetermined period of time, or will only pay a reduced percentage of those taxes for a somewhat longer period. In addition, corporate taxes paid to the federal government are usually allowed as a deduction against the corporate income subject to state income tax.

Personal income tax exemptions typically refer to exemptions of capital gains made from the sale of qualified industrial or commercial property. These exemptions also apply to the deductibility of interest payments on loans to qualified businesses and persons for the acquisition of qualified types of properties and/or equipment.

State excise taxes payable by the firm can also be exempted or proportionately reduced to the firm that expands on site or relocates to the state. Excise taxes to the federal government can be credited against the state corporate income tax payment.

As previously discussed, real estate or real property taxes can often be exempted for a predetermined period. They may also be proportionately reduced for a somewhat longer period.

Inventory taxes, like real estate taxes, can be exempted for a predetermined period in areas that allow it, and they can be proportionately reduced for a somewhat longer period. Raw material or inputs may also be exempted from state and local sales taxes.

Tax credits can be given for a wide array of approved actions. Money spent to modernize or renovate an industrial plant may be credited against the firm's corporate tax liability in both the state and the federal tax programs. Tax credits may be given for the installation of specialized equipment, such as pollution control equipment or energy-saving equipment and materials. Tax credits may also be given for special approved activities such as research and development and labor force training programs. Tax credits may also be available for relocation to "areas of special need" or "depressed economic areas."

A complete listing of these tax-incentive programs in the 50 states and Puerto Rico is published annually in *Site Selection* (see Exhibit 17.4).

EXHIBIT 17.4 Tax Incentives Offered by States

CHART 2: *Tax Incentives For Industry**

STATES (*See Footnotes Following Chart)	Corporate Income Tax Exemption	Personal Income Tax Exemption	Excise Tax Exemption	Tax Exemption or Moratorium on Land, Capital Improvements	Tax Exemption or Moratorium on Equipment, Machinery	Inventory Tax Exemption on Goods in Transit (Freeport)	Tax Exemption on Manufacturers Inventories	Sales/Use Tax Exemption on New Equipment	Tax Exemption on Raw Materials Used in Manufacturing	Tax Incentive for Creation of Jobs	Tax Incentive for Industrial Investment	Tax Credits for Use of Specified State Products	Tax Stabilization Agreements for Specified Industries	Tax Exemption to Encourage Research and Development	Accelerated Depreciation of Industrial Equipment
ALABAMA	●	●	●	●	●	●	●	●	●	●	●				●
ALASKA		●	●	●				●	●						●[59]
ARIZONA	●	●		●[30]	●	●	●	●	●	●					●
ARKANSAS	●[17]			●[11]	●[11]	●	●[66]	●	●	●	●	●[20]			
CALIFORNIA		●		●	●	●	●	●	●	●	●			●	●[10]
COLORADO	●		●		●	●	●	●[21]	●	●	●				
CONNECTICUT	●[10]			●	●[23]	●	●	●[21]	●	●[12]	●[12]			●[12]	●[1]
DELAWARE	●	●[65]	●[24]	●	●[65]	●[65]	●[65]	●[65]	●	●	●			●	●
FLORIDA	●	●[25]	●[24]	●[31]	●[31]	●	●	●[57]	●	●[26]	●[26]			●[9]	●[18]
GEORGIA						●	●	●	●	●					●
HAWAII	●[21]	●[21]	●[21,66]		●	●	●	●	●[38]	●[21]			●	●	●[59]
IDAHO	●				●	●	●	●	●	●	●			●	●
ILLINOIS	●[45]	●	●[45]	●	●	●	●	●	●	●	●			●	●[59]
INDIANA	●	●		●[36]	●[39]	●[7]	●[7]	●	●	●	●[36]			●	●
IOWA	●[27]	●[53]	●	●[8]	●[4]	●	●	●[29]	●	●				●	●[59]
KANSAS	●[2]	●[2,53]		●[30]	●[30]	●	●[5]	●[19]	●[6]	●	●			●	●[59]
KENTUCKY				●	●[72]	●[72]	●[72]	●	●	●	●				●[59]
LOUISIANA	●[32]	●[53]		●[33]	●	●	●[89]		●[6]	●[13]	●		●	●	●[59]
MAINE	●	●			●	●	●	●	●[34]	●	●			●	●[59]
MARYLAND	●[63]	●	●	●[31]	●	●	●	●	●	●	●			●[37]	●
MASSACHUSETTS	●[22]	●	●[22]	●[28]	●[42]	●	●	●[35]	●	●[43]	●[22]			●[49]	●
MICHIGAN	●	●		●	●	●	●	●	●		●				●[59]
MINNESOTA			●	●[10]	●	●	●	●[40]	●	●			●	●	●[59]
MISSISSIPPI	●	●		●	●	●	●[73]	●	●	●	●			●	●[59]
MISSOURI	●	●	●[24]	●	●[6]	●	●	●	●	●	●			●[85]	●
MONTANA	●	●		●[64]	●[64]	●	●	●	●	●	●	●	●[88]	●	●
NEBRASKA		●		●[67]	●[67]	●	●	●[50]	●	●	●				●[59]
NEVADA	●[25]	●[25]	●[24]			●	●	●[60]		●					
NEW HAMPSHIRE		●[25]			●	●	●	●[41]	●[41]	●					
NEW JERSEY	●[56]			●	●	●	●	●	●	●	●				
NEW MEXICO				●	●	●	●	●	●		●				●[59]
NEW YORK	●[46,47]	●[46]	●[24]	●	●[48]	●[48]	●[48]	●	●	●[46]	●[46]			●[47]	
NORTH CAROLINA						●	●	●	●						●
NORTH DAKOTA	●		●	●[51]	●[48]	●[48]	●[48]	●	●	●				●[37]	
OHIO	●[76]	●[76]		●[21]	●[77]	●	●[78]	●[77]	●[79]	●[80]	●			●[81]	●[59]
OKLAHOMA	●[87]	●		●[8]	●	●		●	●	●	●		●[14]	●	●[59]
OREGON			●[52]	●[51]	●[51]	●[86]	●	●[41]	●		●			●	●
PENNSYLVANIA	●[16]		●[54]	●	●	●[55]	●	●	●	●				●	●
RHODE ISLAND			●	●	●	●	●	●		●	●	●	●	●	●[59]
SOUTH CAROLINA	●			●	●	●	●	●	●	●	●			●	●
SOUTH DAKOTA	●[25]	●[25]	●	●		●	●		●	●	●			●	●
TENNESSEE		●[71]		●[31]	●[70]	●	●	●	●[3]	●[74]	●[15]				
TEXAS	●[25]	●[25]		●[58]	●[58]	●		●[82]	●	●	●				
UTAH					●	●	●	●	●	●					●
VERMONT			●			●	●	●	●				●		●
VIRGINIA				●[31]	●[31]	●[44]	●	●	●	●[21]	●[21]			●[61]	●[59]
WASHINGTON	●[25]	●[25]	●			●	●	●[83]	●	●	●			●[83]	
WEST VIRGINIA	●[68]	●[68]				●		●	●	●	●	●[69]		●[68]	●
WISCONSIN	●[62]	●[75]			●	●	●	●	●	●[84]	●[84]			●	●
WYOMING	●[25]	●[25]	●			●	●		●						
STATE TOTALS	35	32	22	36	41	49	46	47	48	43	36	4	7	31	39
PUERTO RICO	●	●	●	●	●	●	●	●	●	●	●	●	●	●	●

Source: From *Site Selection,* October 1991, p. 976.

Note: For more specific information about the programs in each state check the footnotes to this table that appear in the original publication.

(d) LAND AND SPACE ACQUISITION AND PROVISION PROGRAMS

In addition to financial and tax incentives and inducements to industry, states and local governments as well as local development corporations can offer a whole series of other incentives, including the following:

- Purchase and modernize existing plants to sell or lease.
- Construct speculative building shells and/or plants to sell or lease.
- Acquire or option industrial sites to sell or lease.
- Give industrial sites to firms as an inducement to locate in the community.
- Provide development-related public works or infrastructure such as highways, access to rail and water transport facilities, etc.
- Provide sites or space in government owned and operated industrial and business parks.
- Fund industry-specific research and development activity at local public universities and publicly funded research institutes.
- Conduct feasibility studies to attract or assist new industry and to generate on-site expansion and thereby retain existing firms.
- Operate a "one-stop" permitting program to facilitate the entry of new industrial firms.
- Provide rate concessions on utilities.

A complete listing of these special incentive programs in the 50 states and Puerto Rico is published annually in *Site Selection* (see Exhibit 17.5).

(e) LABOR FORCE TRAINING PROGRAMS

State and local governments can directly establish labor force training programs to prepare workers with the job skills needed by the industries moving to the community. Local governments may also subsidize training programs offered by the firm. The subsidy could take any form of assistance discussed earlier. Very often, these training programs are linked to training that component of the labor force identified as the structurally or "hard-core" unemployed. These are idled workers whose skill level or training does not match the skills required by the industries moving in.

(f) SPECIAL INCENTIVES FOR POLLUTION CONTROL

States and local communities can use various combinations of financing incentives, tax exemptions, tax credits, and administrative assistance to encourage new firms and especially existing firms to control pollution.

EXHIBIT 17.5 Special Incentives Offered by States

CHART 3: *Special Services For Industrial Development**

*See Footnotes Following Chart STATES	State Financed Speculative Building	City and/or County Financed Speculative Building	State Provides Free Land for Industry	Cities and/or Counties Provide Free Land for Industry	State-Owned Industrial Park Sites	City and/or County-Owned Industrial Park Sites	State Funds for City and/or County Development-Related Public Works Projects	State Funds for City and/or County Master Plans	State Funds for City and/or County Recreational Projects	State Funds for Private Recreational Projects	State Program to Promote Research and Development	State Program to Increase Export of Products	University R&D Facilities Available to Industry	State and/or University Conduct Feasibility Studies to Attract or Assist New Industry	State Supported Training of "Hard-Core" Unemployed	State Incentive to Industry to Train "Hard-Core" Unemployed	State Help in Bidding on Federal Procurement Contract	State Science and/or Technology Advisory Council
ALABAMA		•		•[3]	•	•	•	•	•		•	•	•	•	•	•	•	•
ALASKA	•					•	•	•	•	•	•	•	•	•	•	•		•
ARIZONA		•		•		•	•	•	•		•	•	•	•	•	•	•	•
ARKANSAS	•	•		•[3]		•			•		•	•	•	•	•		•	•
CALIFORNIA		•[3]		•[3]		•	•	•	•		•	•	•	•	•	•	•	•
COLORADO		•[3]	•	•[3]		•	•	•	•		•	•	•	•	•	•	•	•
CONNECTICUT					•	•	•	•		•	•	•	•	•	•	•	•[4]	•
DELAWARE	•[1]	•			•[1]	•	•	•[4]	•		•	•	•	•	•	•	•	•
FLORIDA		•		•		•	•[15]	•	•		•	•	•[5]	•	•[23]	•	•	•
GEORGIA		•				•	•		•		•	•	•	•				•
HAWAII					•		•	•	•		•	•	•	•	•	•	•	•
IDAHO						•	•		•	•	•	•	•	•	•	•	•	•
ILLINOIS		•[32]	•	•		•	•	•	•	•	•	•	•	•	•	•	•	•
INDIANA				•[3]		•	•	•		•[16]	•	•	•	•	•	•	•	•
IOWA	•[17]	•		•		•	•	•	•	•	•	•	•	•	•	•	•	•
KANSAS		•[6]		•[3]		•	•	•			•	•	•[7]	•	•	•		•
KENTUCKY		•[11]		•[3]		•	•	•	•	•	•	•	•	•	•		•	•
LOUISIANA	•[2]	•		•[11]		•	•	•	•		•	•	•	•	•	•	•	
MAINE	•	•		•[8]		•	•	•	•	•[9]	•	•	•[5]	•	•	•	•	•
MARYLAND	•	•			•	•	•	•	•	•[10]	•	•	•	•	•	•	•	•
MASSACHUSETTS	•	•				•	•	•	•		•	•	•	•	•	•	•	
MICHIGAN		•		•		•	•				•	•	•	•	•			•
MINNESOTA		•		•		•	•	•	•	•	•	•	•	•	•	•	•	•
MISSISSIPPI		•		•[11]	•	•	•				•	•	•	•	•	•	•	•
MISSOURI	•	•[20]		•	•[25]	•	•		•	•	•	•	•	•	•	•	•	•
MONTANA				•		•	•[12]	•[12]	•		•	•	•	•	•	•	•	•
NEBRASKA		•[6]		•[6]		•	•		•		•	•	•	•	•	•	•	•
NEVADA				•[3]		•				•	•	•	•	•	•	•	•	•
NEW HAMPSHIRE						•	•	•	•	•	•	•	•	•	•	•	•	
NEW JERSEY					•	•	•	•	•		•	•	•	•	•	•	•	•
NEW MEXICO				•[3]		•	•	•	•		•	•	•	•	•	•	•	•
NEW YORK		•			•	•	•	•	•	•	•	•	•	•	•	•	•	•
NORTH CAROLINA	•	•				•	•	•	•		•	•	•	•	•	•	•	•
NORTH DAKOTA	•	•		•		•	•		•		•	•	•	•	•	•	•	•
OHIO		•[3]	•[3]	•[3]		•	•	•	•		•	•	•	•	•	•	•	•
OKLAHOMA		•		•	•	•	•[22]		•	•	•	•	•	•	•		•	•
OREGON	•	•		•		•	•	•	•		•	•	•	•	•	•	•	•
PENNSYLVANIA	•[18]	•		•[19]		•	•	•	•		•	•	•	•	•	•	•	•
RHODE ISLAND					•	•	•	•	•		•	•	•	•	•	•	•	•
SOUTH CAROLINA		•		•[3]	•	•	•	•	•		•	•	•	•	•			•
SOUTH DAKOTA		•		•		•	•	•	•	•	•	•	•	•	•	•	•	•
TENNESSEE		•		•[3]		•	•	•[14]	•[29]		•	•	•	•	•	•	•	•
TEXAS		•[30]				•[28]	•	•	•		•	•	•	•	•	•	•	•
UTAH				•[24]	•[25]	•	•	•	•		•	•	•	•	•	•	•	•
VERMONT	•	•				•	•	•	•			•	•	•	•	•	•	
VIRGINIA	•[27]	•[6]		•[21]		•	•		•		•	•	•	•	•[26]	•	•	•
WASHINGTON					•	•[13]	•	•	•		•	•	•	•	•	•	•	•
WEST VIRGINIA						•	•		•	•	•	•	•	•	•		•	
WISCONSIN						•	•	•	•	•[31]	•	•	•	•	•		•	•
WYOMING						•	•		•			•	•	•	•		•	•
STATE TOTALS	15	34	3	31	14	49	48	37	44	18	48	50	50	50	49	41	45	45
PUERTO RICO	•				•		•	•	•	•	•	•	•	•	•	•	•	•

Source: From *Site Selection,* October 1991, p. 980. Copyright 1991 by Conway Publications. Reproduced with permission.

Note: For more specific information about the programs in each state check the footnotes to this table that appear in the original publication.

A complete listing of these financial assistance programs in the 50 states and Puerto Rico is published annually in *Site Selection* (see Exhibit 17.6).

(g) ENTERPRISE ZONES

Since the demise of the categorical grant system of providing federal urban assistance to local governments in 1974, there has been a concerted effort by all levels of government to find alternative ways of addressing urban redevelopment needs. Federal funding for urban redevelopment programs, begun under the Housing Act of 1949 and renamed Urban Renewal under the Housing Act of 1954, was largely redistributed to other types of urban assistance activities under the Community Development Block Program (CDBG) authorized in the Housing and Community Development Act of 1974. Since CDBGs have become the principal form of federal urban assistance, local governments have tried to find ways to attract private capital investment into areas in need of redevelopment. Public improvements and other incentives provided in redevelopment areas, funded from CDBGs as well as other sources of local governmental funding, can be used in leveraging private investment to accomplish a community's economic, social, and physical redevelopment objectives. The principal mechanism for accomplishing these activities is called the Urban Enterprise Zone.

Urban enterprise zone legislation has been debated at the national level for many years, but no comprehensive federal program has ever been adopted. However, about two-thirds of the states have adopted some form of enterprise zone program, and many local governments are currently involved in such redevelopment activities. A complete listing of the states that have enterprise zones and the incentives offered is published annually in *Site Selection* (see Exhibit 17.7).

The type of incentives provided can include some combination of the following items:

1. Property tax abatements or reductions.
2. Credit for interest paid on loans.
3. Investment tax credits.
4. Tax increment financing.
5. Industrial revenue bond financing.
6. Direct state financing.
7. Infrastructure and public service improvements.
8. Employer income tax credit.

Urban enterprise zones are generally authorized for economically and socially depressed areas where there is a need for housing renovation and

EXHIBIT 17.6 Incentives Offered for Pollution Control

CHART 4: *State Incentives For Pollution Control** — *Other Laws**

*See Footnotes Following Chart

STATES	Real Property Tax Exemption	Personal Property Tax Exemption	Sales/Use Tax Exemption on Purchase of Pollution Control Facilities	Sales/Use Tax Exemption Applicable to Lease of Pollution Control Facilities	Credit Against Corporate Income Tax	Maximum Dollar Limit of Credit	Accelerated Depreciation of Pollution Control Equipment	Exclusion of Pollution Control Investment from Corporate Franchise Tax	Exemption Applicable to Cost of Operating Pollution Control Facility	State Financing Program for Purchase and Installation of Pollution Control Facilities	State Right to Work Law	State Minimum Wage Law	State Fair Employment Practice Code	Statewide Uniform Property Tax Evaluation Law	Statewide Industrial Noise Abatement Law	Worldwide Unitary Tax	Water's Edge Unitary Tax	Plant Closing Law
ALABAMA	●	●	●	●	●	No Limit	●	●		●[1]	●			●				
ALASKA										●[1]		●	●	●		●		
ARIZONA							●			●[1]	●		●	●				
ARKANSAS	●	●									●	●	●	●				
CALIFORNIA	●[4]	●[5]	●[14]				●			●[1,49]		●	●	●		●[41]	●[41]	
COLORADO										●[1]	●		●	●	●		●	
CONNECTICUT	●[4]	●[5]	●	●	●	No Limit	●			●		●	●		●			
DELAWARE	●[4]	●[5]	●[19]	●[19]	●[16]		●			●[6]		●	●		●			
FLORIDA		●[7]						●[12]		●	●		●	●				
GEORGIA	●	●	●	●							●	●	●	●				
HAWAII		●[5]					●		●	●[9]		●	●		●			●[42]
IDAHO			●	●			●	●		●[8]	●	●	●	●			●	
ILLINOIS	●	●	●	●	●		●			●[1]		●	●	●	●		●	
INDIANA	●	●	●	●			●	●[12]		●[1]		●	●	●				
IOWA	●	●	●	●			●			●[1]	●	●	●	●	●			
KANSAS	●[37]	●[37]	●[47]		●	●[38]	●			●[1]	●	●	●	●				
KENTUCKY	●[39]	●[39]	●	●			●[43]	●[40]		●[1]		●	●	●	●			
LOUISIANA	●[2]	●	●	●			●[17]			●[33]	●			●				
MAINE	●	●	●	●	●			●[12]	●	●[11]		●	●		●		●	●
MARYLAND		●	●				●	●[12]		●[13]		●	●	●	●			
MASSACHUSETTS	●	●[5]	●	●	●	No Limit[3]	●[10]	●[45]		●		●	●	●				
MICHIGAN	●	●	●	●	●		●	●[12]		●[1]		●	●	●				
MINNESOTA							●[17]			●[1]		●	●	●	●			
MISSISSIPPI	●[15]	●[15]	●[18]				●			●[1]	●	●	●	●				
MISSOURI			●	●	●					●[1]		●	●	●				●
MONTANA	●[10]	●[10]	●[19]	●[19]			●		●	●[1]		●	●	●			●	
NEBRASKA			●[20]		●		●[43]			●[1]	●	●	●	●			●	
NEVADA	●		●	●						●[1]	●	●	●	●				
NEW HAMPSHIRE	●	●	●[19]	●[19]	●		●					●	●	●	●		●	
NEW JERSEY	●	●	●	●	●					●[1]		●	●	●	●			
NEW MEXICO	●	●[5]			●	No Limit		●				●	●	●	●		●	
NEW YORK	●[22]	●[5]	●[23]	●[23]	●[24]	No Limit[24]	●[25]	●[25]		●[1]		●	●		●			●
NORTH CAROLINA	●	●	●[21]	●[21]	●	No Limit	●	●		●[1]	●	●	●	●				●
NORTH DAKOTA	●	●[5]			●[26]	●[26]	●[17]			●[27]	●	●	●	●	●	●	●[41]	
OHIO	●	●	●	●	●	No Limit	●	●	●	●		●	●	●				
OKLAHOMA							●			●[1]		●	●	●				
OREGON	●	●	●[19]	●[19]	●	●50%	●[28]	●	●	●[1]		●	●	●	●		●	●
PENNSYLVANIA	●	●[5]	●				●	●		●[29]		●	●					
RHODE ISLAND	●[30]	●	●	●	●	●[25]	●			●[31]		●	●					
SOUTH CAROLINA	●[4]	●[4]	●	●					●	●[1]	●	●	●	●				
SOUTH DAKOTA	●	●[5]				●				●[1]	●	●	●	●				
TENNESSEE	●[4]	●[5]	●	●				●			●		●	●	●			●
TEXAS										●	●	●	●					
UTAH			●	●						●[1]	●	●	●	●			●	
VERMONT	●	●	●				●			●[34]		●	●	●	●			
VIRGINIA	●[35]	●[35]	●[36]	●[36]	●[48]	●[48]	●[43]			●[1]	●	●	●	●				
WASHINGTON						●50%						●	●	●				
WEST VIRGINIA		●[44]	●	●	●[45]	No Limit	●[45]	●[46]		●[1]		●	●					
WISCONSIN	●	●	●		●	No Limit	●	●[12]		●[1]		●	●	●				●
WYOMING	●					No Limit				●[1]	●	●	●	●	●			
STATE TOTALS	35	37	36	28	22		33	18	6	44	22	44	48	41	19	3	12	8
PUERTO RICO										●	●	●	●	●	●			

Source: From *Site Selection,* October 1991, p. 982. Copyright 1991 by Conway Publications. Reproduced with permission.

Note: For more specific information about the programs in each state check the footnotes to this table that appear in the original publication.

EXHIBIT 17.7 Enterprise Zone Incentives

	1	2	3	4	5	6	7	8	9	10	11	12	13	14	15
Alabama			•					•	•					•	
Arizona								•							
Arkansas				•	•		•								
California		•		•	•	•	•	•	•			•	•	•	•
Colorado			•	•			•								
Connecticut	•			•	•		•	•			•	•			
Delaware			•		•		•	•							
Florida	•		•	•			•		•	•		•			
Georgia	•														
Hawaii						•									
Illinois	•	•	•	•	•			•	•						•
Indiana	•	•			•	•	•			•		•		•	•
Kansas			•	•	•		•	•		•			•	•	
Kentucky		•		•											•
Louisiana				•	•		•	•				•		•	•
Maine												•	•	•	
Maryland	•				•		•	•		•	•	•		•	
Michigan	•			•	•										
Minnesota	•	•	•	•	•	•	•								
Mississippi				•	•		•								
Missouri	•		•		•		•	•							•
Nevada									•	•			•		•
New Jersey				•	•		•	•				•		•	•
New York			•	•				•							
Ohio	•				•										•
Rhode Island	•	•			•	•							•		
Tennessee	•												•	•	
Texas				•								•		•	•
Utah					•		•	•					•		
Vermont							•	•				•	•	•	
Virginia				•	•										•
West Virginia		•		•											
Wisconsin			•	•	•		•	•						•	•

Source: Conway Data surveys and U.S. Dept. of Urban Development, Office of Community Planning and Development

TAX INCENTIVES
1. Property tax reduction/abatement
2. Credit for interest paid on loans
3. Investment credit for real improvements
4. Sales/sales & use tax credit
5. Employer income tax credit
6. Employee income tax credit
7. Job creation/wage credit
8. Credit for selective hiring

CAPITAL FINANCING
9. IRB/IDB allocation preference
10. Tax increment financing
11. Venture capital funds
12. Direct state funds

MISCELLANEOUS INCENTIVES
13. Infrastructure/public service improvements
14. Program targeting
15. Regulatory relief

Source: From *Site Selection,* October 1991, p. 987. Copyright 1991 by Conway Publications. Reproduced with permission.

development, nonresidential renovation and development, and new jobs and trade to spur economic revitalization. These areas are usually in need of substantial infrastructure improvements as well. The basic redevelopment strategy involves providing privately funded activities with tax breaks, regulatory relief, technical assistance, and other measures if those activities are directed toward achieving identified public redevelopment objectives. The local government, funded through CDBGs or other state and local sources, designates eligible areas and undertakes necessary public actions and public improvements that support private redevelopment.

The principal advantages to private enterprises or firms locating facilities in enterprise zones are tax abatement or tax relief programs, assistance in financing improvements, regulatory relief measures, and benefits from infrastructure improvements provided by local government. Tax abatement and tax relief programs may involve ad valorem taxes on both real estate and inventories. These usually apply for a period of 5 to 25 years, so long as the enterprise continues to maintain its eligibility. A variety of programs providing assistance in financing improvements may apply, including the ones described earlier in this chapter. Regulatory relief measures may apply in some situations. The principal idea behind this aspect of the enterprise zone program is to cut procedural red tape for enterprises locating in the area and to permit strict development standards to be waived in favor of more realistic standards for a redevelopment area.

Enterprise zones will obviously not fulfill locational objectives for many corporate facilities. But well-conceived and well-executed enterprise zone programs can provide numerous benefits for appropriate industries.

Eighteen

Impact of the Corporation and Its Facilities on the Local Community

§ 18.1 INTRODUCTION

This chapter examines the nature and significance of the effect of a corporate facility on the local community into which it relocates, opens a branch plant, or even starts its initial operation. Also, the company can affect the community when it closes a plant or operation. Several specific studies can generate important information about community impact for use in public relations as well as for strategic planning. The following studies are discussed in this chapter:

- The Economic Impact Study.
- The Fiscal Impact Study.
- The Market Value Impact Study.
- The Infrastructure Impact Study.
- The Environmental Impact Study.

Whenever community concerns arise about the relative costs and benefits to the community of having a new corporate facility or operation, information from these studies becomes invaluable as a public relations device. Performed competently and objectively, the studies can provide revealing data about attributes of the community that make it attractive to the company. The possible impact on these attributes by corporate operations and the company's potential to enhance community life should also be identified. The studies should also deal with community problems, both those already present and those that may result from the presence of the corporate facility. How the company plans to address such problems and to participate in community life will reveal a great deal about its ability to become a compatible and respected neighbor. Such information should go a long way in gaining acceptance for the company in the community as well as in identifying the community problems the company may face.

This chapter addresses three basic questions about each study:

1. What information does the study provide?
2. How is the study conducted?
3. Why is the study useful to the company?

Since the purpose of these studies is to show objectively the company's probable impact on the community as well as why it is choosing this community, it is important to gain the confidence of those to whom the information will be provided. Community leaders and citizens alike will be wary if these studies are prepared internally by the company. They will have much better acceptance if they are "outsourced"; that is, prepared by independent outside consultants who can gain the approval of the community by the quality of their work.

§ 18.2 THE ECONOMIC IMPACT STUDY

When a corporate facility is new to the community or if there is simply an expansion or contraction of an existing facility, that activity will impose changes on the local economy. How the local economy will be affected by a new or expanded producer in the area is the central focus of the economic impact study. However, the study should also provide information about how the new corporate facility will fit into and be served by the local economy.

The economic impact study usually centers around, but is not limited to, three principal concerns: employment, income, and retail sales. Other aspects of the local economy will also be examined—such as levels of production of other local producers, relative health and stability of local financial and business institutions, and labor force productivity—but these are either subcategories of the principal topics or are of secondary concern. The principal objective of the study is to get a clear view of the level of benefits the local economy will experience from the presence of the corporate operation. The flip side of that objective is to identify what problems the corporate operation might impose on the local economy and if the local economy is capable of dealing with them. Information from this aspect of the study can be used by the company to determine how it will deal with these problems, if, indeed, any action can be taken. If a problem in the local economy is exposed and the company finds a way it can contribute to a solution, that information can provide a powerful tool for the company to gain local acceptance and assistance in locating in the community.

(a) NATURE OF THE STUDY

The economic impact study generally comprises two major parts. First, the analyst examines the nature of the proposed corporate operation. These data come from the company records and its plans. The key factors in the analysis are the number and type of employees the plant will require and the wage or salary these employees will earn. The analyst then examines certain characteristics of the community where the facility is to be located. The principal objective is to examine the relationship between the change in the community's total employment and a change in the employment in those firms that ship products outside the locale, called export or basic industries.

The next step is to estimate the total number of new jobs generated by the new corporate operation and add these to the employment figures for total employment and basic employment, assuming the new activity will be a basic industry. The total impact of the new operation is the total number of new jobs provided by the plant (direct employment growth) plus the new jobs that will arise in the community to provide goods and services to the new company operation and the employees who spend their paychecks locally (indirect, induced employment growth). Knowledge of this employment change and the salary structure internal to the firm as well as its impact on jobs elsewhere in the community leads to the analysis of the change in community income from the relocation.

The change in income generated by the payroll from new employment can then be allocated among the major retail categories to show the impact of the new operation on retail establishments in the community. In addition, company records can be used to show the direct retail purchases made from local suppliers.

(b) ESTIMATING DIRECT EFFECTS OF THE CORPORATE FACILITY

Data concerning the nature of the new corporate operation, including the number and types of jobs and anticipated wage and salary levels, is usually derived from interviews with company management and information they have on file. The analyst must verify this internal information by investigating both the staffing of other similar plants and operations in the company as well as elsewhere in the industry. Wage and salary figures are also verified by investigating the prevailing wage and salary level in the community.

The following example reveals the nature of this step in the study: An analyst interviews appropriate management personnel at the headquarters office and discovers that the plant will eventually employ 154 production workers, 12 clerical staff, 8 administrative personnel, and 2 key executives. This long-term level of employment will be achieved at the outset of the second year of operation. The nature and number of

EXHIBIT 18.1 Impact of New Plant on Local Income

	Number of Employees	Annual Salary	Income Payment
Operation Phase			
Long-Term			
Plant Managers	2	$80,000	$ 160,000
Dept. Administrators	8	35,000	280,000
Clerical Staff	12	16,000	192,000
Production Workers			
Shipping/Receiving	24	20,000	480,000
Maintenance	10	24,000	240,000
Line Personnel	154	18,000	2,772,000
Janitorial	12	15,000	180,000
Subtotals	222		$4,304,000
Short-Term			
Plant Managers	2	80,000	160,000
Dept. Administrators	6	35,000	210,000
Clerical Staff	8	16,000	128,000
Production Workers			
Shipping/Receiving	16	20,000	320,000
Maintenance	6	24,000	144,000
Line Personnel	77	18,000	1,386,000
Janitorial	8	15,000	120,000
Subtotals	123		$2,468,000
Construction Phase (18 months)			
Craftspersons	10	24,000	240,000
Laborers	12	17,000	204,000
Subtotals	22		$ 444,000
			×1.5
Total Impact of Construction			$ 666,000

these workers as well as their anticipated wages and salaries are displayed in Exhibit 18.1.

In addition to the long-term employment situation, the analyst also notes the short-term employment the plant will provide during the construction phase and the first year of the plant's operation. This data is given on the bottom portion of Exhibit 18.1.

In the majority of situations, the analyst focuses almost exclusively on the long-term scenario. However, if the firm desires more precision and detail, the short-term aspects can be incorporated. This example considers only long-term effects.

The basic conclusion of the study is that the firm will pay out $4,304,000 per year in wages and salaries. This figure is the direct income effect of the new plant.

(c) ESTIMATING THE TOTAL EFFECT OF THE CORPORATE FACILITY

The next step in the analysis is the determination of the indirect, induced income effects. These effects must be added to the direct effects to understand total impact. The first thing the analyst does here is to develop an economic multiplier for the local community and use it to generate the total income effect of the plant's operation. To develop the multiplier, an estimate is made of the number of "basic employees" working in the local economy. The industrial structure of the community reveals the basic and nonbasic employment.

Employees who produce goods or services that are sold outside the local community are defined as "basic employees." In a small community, basic employment can be identified by simply interviewing the major employers. For example, there may be five other firms employing people in the community. Interviews reveal they employ 1,100 people, and that all the output of each is shipped and sold outside the local area. Further investigation reveals that all the other employers in the community serve only the local market. Basic employment in the community is therefore 1,100. Total employment in the community is 2,000.

In this situation, the employment multiplier for the community is 1.82 (2,000/1,100). The new plant will employ 222 with a payroll of $4,304,000. The multiplier is used to generate the total income change in the community from the direct income change generated by the operation of the plant. This can be done in several ways.[1] In the simplest but least accurate estimation procedure, the analyst would make the following multiplication: $4,304,000 × 1.82 = $7,833,280 (say $7,800,000); and, 222 × 1.82 = 404. The total effect of the plant would be 404 new jobs in the community and an increase in annual income of $7,800,000.

The most predictable effect of the increase of $7,800,000 in income is an immediate increase in retail sales. Based on secondary data concerning retail expenditures, the analyst concludes that approximately 40 to 45 percent of this money will be spent for retail goods and

[1] The estimation of the multiplier is a complex subject that cannot be discussed in detail in this book. If more information on the estimation process is desired, the following text can be consulted: Neil G. Carn, Joseph Rabianski, Ronald Racster, and Maury Seldin, *Real Estate Market Analysis: Applications and Techniques* (Englewood Cliffs, NJ; Prentice-Hall, 1988).

services.[2] The analyst then determines what proportion of these expenditures will occur locally. For example, all convenience goods and services purchases, such as grocery purchases, personal care products, prescription drugs, and dry cleaning, will be made locally. But he or she may discover that only 20 percent of the expenditures on shopper's goods and services such as clothing, furniture, appliances, etc., will be made locally.[3] This data is used to translate the increase in income to an increase in local retail sales. This analysis can be performed at various levels of detail, depending on the desires of the firm.

The analyst estimates that convenience goods purchases are 25 percent of income while shopping goods purchases are 15 percent of income for a total of 40 percent. The following calculations are then made:

Convenience goods: $25\% \times 100\% \times \$7{,}800{,}000 = \$1{,}950{,}000$

Shopping goods: $15\% \times 20\% \times \$7{,}800{,}000 = 234{,}000$

Total Increase in Retail Expenditures = $2,184,000

A more detailed and procedurally correct method for calculating the total effect on income is based on the realization that new positions for top management will not be created, but new jobs for clerical workers, production workers, and general service sector workers will be created. In this case, the 10 upper management jobs are subtracted from the total of 222, leaving an adjusted total 212 jobs. This figure is multiplied by 1.82 for a product of 386 jobs, which is an anticipated net gain of 164 jobs over and above the jobs provided by the firm. These jobs will generally command a wage or salary level that is, on the average, less than the average wage paid by the plant (i.e., retail clerks earn less than production line workers). The analyst finds the average wage and salary in the community is $16,250. Given this estimate, the indirect and induced income increase is $2,665,000 (164 × $16,250) and the total income change is $6,969,000 ($4,304,000 + $2,665,000), say $6,950,000. This amount is approximately $900,000 less than the estimate from the simplest procedure described earlier.

[2] Information concerning the proportion of income spent on retail goods and services can be obtained from several sources. The consultant can estimate these percentages by using data from the *Census of Retail Trade;* a publication entitled *Relative Importance of the Components of the Consumer Price Index;* U.S. Department of Labor, Bureau of Labor Statistics, Washington, DC; and/or data obtained from the consumer expenditure reports of private vendors of data such as National Planning Data Corporation, Urban Decision Systems, and National Decision Systems.

[3] This information is typically generated by performing a survey of the retail establishments in the local community and those external retail facilities that serve the local consumers. These primary data are obtained through fieldwork.

(d) USE OF THE STUDY IN SITE SELECTION

The economic impact study can be particularly useful to the firm in situations where there is community resistance to the entrance of the new corporate facility. The economic data concerning job creation and expansion of retail sales can be effective in swaying public attitudes in communities that have high unemployment rates and a deteriorating retail base, and it can be useful in swaying public attitude in communities that are growing but may have a bias against the heavy industry or other uses the company might bring in.

§ 18.3 THE FISCAL IMPACT STUDY

Not only do new, relocated, or expanded facilities have an impact on the local economy, they also have an impact on the tax revenues and public service expenditures of the local government. The fiscal impact study focuses on these two principal concerns to ascertain how the community and other consumers will fare when the new corporate operation commences.

The questions the study attempts to answer are (a) how does the new company operation affect the level of the property tax base and, thereby, the property tax revenues in the community; and (b) what is the significance of the tax impact relative to the facility's demand for public services and, thereby, the cost of providing public services?

(a) NATURE OF THE STUDY

Fiscal impact analysis is defined as "a projection of the direct, current, public costs and revenues associated with residential or nonresidential growth to the local jurisdiction(s) in which this growth is taking place."[4] The nonresidential aspect of growth is of interest here.

There are six different methods to estimate the public cost impact of a plant or office structure on a community, but only three of them are applied to the case of a commercial property.[5] The Proportional Valuation Method is discussed next.

[4] Robert W. Burchell, et al., *The New Practitioner's Guide to Fiscal Impact Analysis* (New Brunswick, NJ: Rutgers, The State University of New Jersey, 1985), p. 3.

[5] The three methods that are exclusively applied to residential growth are the Per Capita Multiplier, the Service Standard, and the Comparable City techniques. The two methods that are exclusively applied to nonresidential or commercial growth are the Proportional Valuation and the Employment Anticipation techniques. A sixth technique known as the Case Study technique can be applied in either case. See Burchell, *The New Practitioner's Guide*, p. 7.

After the public cost impact of the new operation is estimated, the tax revenues generated by the facility will be discussed and compared with total tax revenues in the community.

(b) ESTIMATING THE PUBLIC COST OF THE CORPORATE FACILITY

The process of estimating the public service cost consists of a series of steps shown in a simplified equation. By completing the tasks set out in the following statements, the analyst can obtain an estimate of the public cost associated with the new facility.

- Determine the assessed value of the facility (AVF) where: $AVF = \$1,500,000$.
- Obtain the total assessed value of all properties in the community (TAV) where: $TAV = \$255,000,000$.
- Obtain the distribution of the total real property value among the major categories of property types. If the records are kept as residential, nonresidential, and vacant land, the distribution is among these three categories. Some communities may subdivide these three broad categories into several subcategories, such as single-family and multifamily; retail, office, and industrial; and vacant land. Subtotals for the three general categories of properties are:

$$\text{Residential Properties: } RES = \$178,500,000\ (70\%)$$

$$\text{Vacant Land: } VL = \$30,600,000\ (12\%)$$

$$\text{Commercial Properties: } COM = \$45,900,000\ (18\%)$$

- Obtain the average value of commercial parcels ($AVCOM = \$750,000$) and the average value of all parcels ($AVTOT = \$450,000$) and construct a ratio where:

$$\text{Ratio 1} = AVCOM/AVTOT = 750,000/450,000 = 1.67.$$

- Calculate ratio of the value of the new facility (VNF) to the average value of all commercial parcels ($AVCOM$) where:

$$\text{Ratio 2} = VNF/AVCOM = 1,500,000/750,000 = 2.0.$$

- Obtain the figure for the most recent total expenditures (TE) for public services, where:

$$TE = \$5,185,000.$$

Once this data has been collected, the estimate of the public cost of the new facility (EPCF) can be made by using the following formula:[6]

[6] Burchell, *The New Practitioner's Guide*, pp. 31–32.

$$EPCF = (COM/TAV) \times (AVF/COM) \times \text{Ratio } 1 \times \text{Ratio } 2 \times TE = [AVF/TAV] \times \text{Ratio } 1 \times \text{Ratio } 2 \times TE$$

Substituting in the data obtained for the community yields an estimate for the public cost of the facility of $101,870. This is the public cost associated with locating the new facility.

(c) ESTIMATING THE TAX REVENUE FROM THE CORPORATE FACILITY

The revenue portion of the fiscal impact study may have to consider a wide array of local fiscal resources generated by the facility.[7] It is not merely a study of real property tax revenues, even though these are usually the largest component. The most important revenue sources are the real property tax, the sales tax, local income tax (if it exists), and the development or impact fees and mandatory dedications the community imposes.

Estimating the property tax revenue generated by the new facility is simply a matter of determining its assessed value and multiplying it by the local millage rate. Some communities may have a different millage rate for residential and nonresidential classes of property. If this situation exists, the appropriate nonresidential millage rate is used.

Sales tax revenues are determined by applying the sales tax rate to the additional retail sales generated by payrolls of the new plant. Income tax revenues are determined by applying the marginal local income tax rate for the average income for employees of the plant to total wages and salaries paid by the plant.

Development fees and/or impact fees are front-end dollar contributions for public infrastructure and services directly benefiting the facility (streets, water mains, sewer lines, etc.) or its employees (schools, hospitals, parks, etc.). The value of mandatory dedications (described in Chapter 17) is established by getting an independent fee appraiser to estimate market value of the land being dedicated at its highest and best use as determined by current market conditions.

An estimate of total public revenues generated by the new facility is obtained by adding total tax revenues, by source, to revenues from development fees and the value of mandatory dedications.

(d) RECONCILING PUBLIC COSTS AND TAX REVENUES

The conclusion of the study is a comparison between the total tax revenue generated from all sources and the public service costs imposed by

[7] The full array of these revenue sources is discussed in Burchell, *The New Practitioner's Guide,* pp. 39–49.

the plant on the community. Revenues in excess of costs make the new corporate operation fiscally attractive to the community. Costs in excess of revenues make the firm fiscally unattractive, but in this situation the employment impact (found in the economic impact study) can be used to present a total picture and, thereby, minimize any shortfall in revenue generation.

(e) USE OF THE STUDY IN SITE SELECTION

The fiscal data concerning total tax revenue and public service costs can be particularly effective in swaying public attitudes in communities that have budget problems. If total tax revenues exceed public service costs, the influx of these additional dollars to the public sector budget should be viewed as a strong benefit.

§ 18.4 THE MARKET VALUE IMPACT STUDY

When a corporate facility is located in a new area, it is very often situated at the edge of existing development or in a sparsely developed area where similar uses have not yet been established. Whenever a substantially new use comes into town, or any large facility that has some impact on surrounding development, there is likely to be community concerns about how this new or expanded use will interact with other nearby uses. The most direct way to address this issue is through the preparation of a market value impact study. While nearby landowners may express a variety of concerns—heavy new traffic being introduced into the street system, potential overcrowding of community facilities such as parks and recreation areas, or simply the manner in which the proximity or view of the new facility will be absorbed into the existing urban pattern—the bottom line of most of these concerns is how the new facility will affect the market for the landowners' properties and consequently their property values. The market value impact study focuses on exactly that issue.

Typically, the market value impact study will center on residential property values. Not only is residential property generally considered to be the most vulnerable to adverse off-site influences, a person's place of residence provokes more emotion and political concern than any other aspect of the community. It is appropriate to address this issue as the first and foremost part of the study. Nonresidential property value impacts should not be ignored, however. Competition by nonresidential uses for public facilities and services as well as for the better commercial and industrial locations in the community can be an issue of great concern. If other businesses in the community expect to have to pay a great deal more when they purchase property, or if they expect to be able to profit considerably when existing business properties are traded, it will certainly color their attitude about the new facility being established. Whether the new facility will accelerate or retard growth, causing property values to either increase or decline, will be in the mind of virtually everyone in the community.

(a) NATURE OF THE STUDY

Studies for both new or expanded facilities follow the same two-step basic procedure. First, an analysis of existing market values is performed. A cross section analysis of values is done for different property types—residential properties, business properties, and/or comparable properties—at various distances from the new facility, and conditions that affect property values in the community are noted. Second, the analyst develops a time series analysis for each property type at each location to identify changes and trends in market values. This procedures provides a fairly complete picture of the market value impacts in the community.

(b) IMPACT OF AN EXISTING FACILITY

Quantitative and qualitative aspects of the residential units and neighborhoods adjacent to or in close proximity to the facility are usually the first item examined. For each specific property type identified adjacent to the facility (e.g., single-family detached high-income housing, multifamily moderate income housing) a comparable property type is identified at another location in the community farther away from the new facility. Typically, the analyst identifies a grouping of relatively comparable housing units in either a subdivision or a neighborhood near the facility.[8] These structures and the neighborhood characteristics are inspected. These features represent basic market attractions in the area and can be displayed on a chart. Based on this array of features, comparable housing units in more distant neighborhoods are identified and used as a control group to evaluate changes in market values.

The cross section analysis uses data on recent sales of housing units in the study area (nearby neighborhoods) and in the control area (more distant neighborhoods). Adjustments to the sales prices in comparables

[8] The term "comparable" and the general concept of comparability rely on the elements of comparison defined by the appraisal literature. In brief, a property is comparable to the subject property (the property being studied) if it possesses physical, neighborhood, and locational characteristics that are very similar to the subject property. In addition, the elements of comparability include the investigation of property rights, time of sale (i.e., the market conditions under which the property sold), condition of sale (arm's-length transaction), and financing terms (cash equivalency). See the Appraisal Institute, *The Appraisal of Real Estate,* Tenth Edition (Chicago, IL: The Appraisal Institute, 1992), pp. 373–384.

are made to minimize any differences in the market characteristics between the two areas. Property characteristics as well as neighborhood features are compared. Conclusions from this analysis show the similarities and differences in market forces present in the two areas. This sets the stage for the time series analysis.

The time series component looks at changes in sales prices of individual properties in both the study area and the control area over time. Changes in these prices indicate the trend of property values by property type under normal market conditions in each area. A marked change in a value trend in the study area that is not present in the control area, after adjusting for the differences in market conditions between the two areas, can be attributed to the existing or expanded corporate facility operation, thus revealing the impact of the facility on area property values.

(c) IMPACT OF A PROPOSED FACILITY

To analyze the impact of a proposed new facility, an additional first step is needed. Both the cross section analysis and the time series analysis, as performed for the existing or expanded facility, will follow.

The point of beginning in this analysis is to carefully analyze all the developmental and operation characteristics of the proposed facility. The analyst needs to find a similar facility or facilities already located and operating in an environment with similar characteristics. These become the surrogate areas that are analogous to the actual study area. Then control areas, similar to the surrogate areas but without a land use like that of the proposed facility, are also established. Cross section analyses, to identify market characteristics and conditions, and time series analyses, to identify value trends, are performed in both a surrogate area and a control area, and differences between the two areas are noted. Value trends that occur in surrogate areas but not in control areas can be attributed to the presence of a facility similar to the one being located in the study area. By analogy, then, these same value trends would be expected to occur in the study area when the new corporate facility is put into operation.

(d) USE OF THE STUDY IN SITE SELECTION

The market value study is possibly the most important study in the battle of the "nimby" (not in my back yard) attitude. While it addresses directly the issue of value impact, it will indirectly address a great many other issues as well. In particular, those conditions that cause values to decline are the very conditions people living or doing business near the proposed facility location fear the most—traffic congestion, overburdened public facilities, air and water pollution, noise, glare, vibration, odors, or simply visual unattractiveness. The presence of these problems, or the perception that they are present, would certainly affect attitudes in the market and, consequently, depress property values. If no adverse value impact can be found, then it can be concluded such problems are insignificant in the area. If adverse value trends are detected and the cause identified, the company will have the opportunity to devise a solution to reverse the situation.

§ 18.5 THE INFRASTRUCTURE IMPACT STUDY

The infrastructure impact study is, in a way, complimentary to the fiscal impact study. Whereas the fiscal impact study looks at the effect of the corporate facility and its operation on required public expenditures, the infrastructure impact study examines how the new facility will affect the physical capacities and service levels of those public services and facilities that require the tax money for support. Like the other studies, the focus is on how the company and its local operations will fit into the system of public services in the community. The results of the study can be both a public relations and a strategic planning tool.

(a) NATURE OF THE STUDY

Unlike planning studies, which are future oriented, the infrastructure impact study looks at what is currently present and available to support development. But the study should include consideration of the short-term improvements that are already programmed and funded. Long-term plans for capital improvements to public services and facilities are usually identified in the Comprehensive Plan, but they can hardly be relied on to provide a service capacity and service level for current development. They are frequently worth noting, but they will not help service the new facility coming into town.

(b) ESTIMATING CAPACITIES AND SERVICE LEVELS

The basic procedure for this study is twofold. First, the array of available public services need to be identified and described, and their capacities quantified. In the second step, the analyst evaluates more detailed information about each facility regarding its planned capacity, actual operating capacity, and short-range plans for expansion. The current capacity is compared with the current service level to see if there is an excess or if the facility will operate with any overload. The service requirements of the new corporate operation are then compared with the available capacity in the system to ascertain the impact.

While traffic congestion, overloading of schools, drainage, and flooding problems, and pollution or other negative externalities of the plant are the most prevalent public concerns, there is a long list of potential public service impacts that can arise. Public services and facilities commonly available in an urban community include:

- Streets and traffic control devices.
- Public transportation services.
- Drainage and flood control system.
- Water supply and distribution system.
- Waste treatment and disposal system:
  - Trash and garbage collection and disposal.
  - Waste water treatment/sanitary sewer system.
  - Solid waste disposal system.
  - Toxic waste/hazardous materials disposal system.
- Electric power generation and distribution.
- Other energy service systems.
- Protective services:
  - Fire protection services and facilities.
  - Police protection services and facilities.
- Educational services and facilities:
  - Public school facilities and programs.
  - Technical training/higher education facilities.
- Parks and recreational facilities.
- Public health care services.
- Public libraries and cultural facilities.
- Public sports and entertainment facilities.
- Local public social services.

(c) USE OF THE STUDY IN SITE SELECTION

If there is a question about how a corporate facility is likely to affect the level and quality of public services in the community, the infrastructure impact study should provide an appropriate response. Both as a public relations tool and a strategic planning implement, this study will provide information about capacities, service levels, and long-term implications of required public service improvements. One of its most valuable uses may be to debunk the notion that a single new facility or land use is responsible for an antiquated or overburdened public infrastructure.

§ 18.6 THE ENVIRONMENTAL IMPACT STUDY

The environmental impact study has somewhat different origins from the other analyses in the array of studies corporations use to develop locational strategies. The National Environmental Protection Act of 1969 was the first comprehensive national commitment to environmental protection and was the first of much legislation throughout the 1970s and 1980s that integrated environmental concerns into nearly all public and private development decision-making processes. The basic tool used to implement the environmental standards imposed by this legislation is the Environmental Impact Statement (EIS). In essence, the EIS is a checklist for analyzing the potential environmental impact of any development project. As a result of its comprehensive approach, the EIS exposes environmental problems that are likely to arise and permits the decision makers, public or private, to consider what actions they might take to avoid, ameliorate, or resolve adverse impacts.

The EIS was originally required only for projects undertaken by the federal government. Many states very quickly adopted environmental requirements that pertained not only to governmental action, but to private developments as well. There are in place today forms of required environmental studies and actions that affect development decision making at every level of government, and most large private organizations have adopted some of the environmental procedures to comply with relevant regulations as well as to update their own development strategies. The EIS and its offsrping have become commonplace, but the format and focus of the study have become more varied and specialized.

(a) NATURE OF THE STUDY

An environmental impact study employs a comprehensive approach that identifies all relevant facets of the environment potentially affected by a development project. Each of these are examined to ascertain how the development project will potentially affect it. The manner of an impact is not always readily apparent, so a technical analysis is performed to determine how well the element being examined will measure up to a performance standard before, during, and after the development. For example, suppose an analyst is examining the impact of noise on the environment surrounding a new quarry that uses explosives. The decibel level at the boundaries of the property as well as at a specified distance away from the property is measured. Technicians make simulated measurements (using data from other similar quarry operations at various stages of development) before any quarry development starts, during the construction and development phase of the quarry, and when the quarry begins normal operation. The decibel level and other technical aspects of noise are evaluated against a predetermined standard at each location during each phase of development to determine if the standard has been exceeded, and, if so to what extent. This evaluation will determine if there is any adverse impact from noise, how significant any impact may be, and the spatial domain affected by any adverse impact. Armed with this information, development planners can devise strategies and plans to control or otherwise deal with any potential noise problem.

Specifications for the EIS (translated directly from the National Environment Protection Act of 1969)[9] include the following items:

- Description of present environmental conditions.
- Description of the proposed action or project.
- Description of probable environmental impact.
- Description of unavoidable adverse impacts.
- Alternatives to the proposed action or project.
- Relationship between short-term use of the environment and long-term productivity or consequences.
- Impacts during development phases and over time.
- Irreversible and irretrievable commitment of resources from implementation of the proposed action or project.
- Mitigation measures, if any.
- Growth-inducing impacts.

While there are many formats for an environmental impact study, one of the more complete formats involves listing elements of the environment to be examined and providing the required information for each such element. Exhibit 18.2 provides a listing of environmental elements to be examined for each step of an environmental impact study.

By using a comprehensive checklist procedure, this analysis can address a wide variety of issues. Some of these issues may also be addressed in other studies. The infrastructure impact study, for example, goes into considerably more detail in examining public facilities and services, but it has a more limited scope (service capacities and service levels) and does not interrelate infrastructure problems to other aspects of environmental impact. There are both advantages and disadvantages to using this type of comprehensive approach. The basic advantages are that dual goals can be accomplished because the information will give an environmental overview that aids the decision process while at the same time accomplishing environmental protection objectives. The basic disadvantages are that time, money, and effort can be wasted if issues aren't properly targeted and/or unnecessary analysis and recommendations are performed.

[9] For a thorough discussion of the original legislation and the requirements the legislation imposed on the Environmental Impact Statement, see Robert W. Burchell and David Listokin, *The Environmental Impact Handbook* (New Brunswick, NJ: Center for Urban Policy Research, Rutgers, The State University of New Jersey, 1975), pp. 38–42.

EXHIBIT 18.2 List of Common Environmental Elements Considered in an Environmental Impact Study

- Project Description
  - Purpose and objectives
  - Project status and plans
  - Site and situation
- Environmental Description
  - Physical features
    - Physiographic features
      - Soils
      - Topography
      - Subsurface conditions
      - Drainage and hydrology
      - Climatic conditions
    - Vegetative and ecological features
    - Existing land uses
    - Land infrastructure
      - Water supply
      - Waste water disposal systems
      - Solid waste treatment
      - Drainage
      - Energy resources
      - Transportation
        - Thoroughfare system
        - Mass transit
        - Parking facilities
        - Other transportation infrastructure
      - Air pollution
      - Noise pollution
      - Water pollution
      - Other physical characteristics
  - Socioeconomic conditions
    - Community facilities
      - Schools
      - Medical and health facilities
      - Public safety facilities
      - Recreational and cultural facilities
    - Local economic conditions
      - Employment
      - Industrial and business composition
      - Economic trends and changes
    - Socioeconomic characteristics
      - Population size
      - Population trends and change
      - Ethnic characteristics
      - Age breakdown
      - Education

EXHIBIT 18.2 *(Continued)*

- Occupation
- Income
- Housing characteristics and conditions
- Relevant historic conditions

Aesthetic environment
- Natural features
  - Natural landforms and features
  - Stands and use of natural vegetation
  - Natural ecological communities
  - Water bodies and water resources
  - Wetlands, marshes, and shorelines
- Man-made features
  - Cityscapes, buildings, and structures
  - Historic and distinctive landmarks
  - Recreational and cultural facilities
  - Special viewpoints
  - Other distinctive features

Environmental Effects
- Physical environment
- Socioeconomic environment
- Aesthetic environment

Limitations on the Project
- Physical environment
- Socioeconomic environment
- Aesthetic environment

Project Alternatives
- Purpose and necessity of the project
- Alternative sites and areas of impact
  - Advantages of acceptable alternatives
  - Disadvantages of acceptable alternatives
- Alternative project plans
  - Size and scale of project
  - Design features
- Additional alternatives or modifications

Unavoidable Adverse Environmental Impacts
- Types of impacts
- Mitigative actions
  - By project management
  - By government
  - By others

Impacts over Time
- Construction phase
- Short-term impacts
- Long-term impacts

Irreversible/Irretrievable Commitment of Resources

(b) USE OF THE STUDY IN SITE SELECTION

In preparing a locational strategy for a corporate facility, the corporation can utilize an environmental impact study for three basic purposes. First, an environmental impact study may be necessary for regulatory purposes. If the facility is locating in an environmentally sensitive area, as defined by federal or state law, some form of an impact study is likely to be required. Such studies, however, may be insufficient to comply with requirements of a specific rule or law. For example, if toxic wastes or hazardous materials are involved, much more detailed analysis on the specific problem will be needed. Some of the more detailed requirements imposed by federal legislation are discussed in Chapter 16. But in many local regulatory processes, an environmental impact analysis should be very beneficial. Zoning procedures in many states and many communities as well as other land use regulations often require information or studies that can be obtained only through a well-executed environmental study.

The second principal use of this study is for internal development decision making. As strategies and tactics for development are devised for a particular facility or operation, environmental information is critical to locational, architectural, and operational planning.

Finally, the company can use an environmental impact study as a vital public relations tool. When regulatory obstacles have been overcome in locating a new or expanded corporate facility, community concerns and public disbelief tend to linger on. Social issues and changes in the demographic profile of the community are frequently underlying, if not overt, issues that beget community reaction to major land use and economic changes. By including population and demographic information in the environmental impact study, these issues can be exposed and interrelated with other environmental concerns. Also, by taking the technical concepts used to demonstrate regulatory and technical compliance with standards and translating them into plain English, the company can properly address most of the community issues. The effort may not overcome all the public concern or opposition to a new facility, but it will strongly establish the company's legal right to operate in the community and define the type of neighbor the company is likely to be. If active public resistance remains, this public relations activity will force the opposition to make a case that is as competent—technically and legally—as the company's presentation.

Index